Lecture Notes of the Institute for Computer Sciences, Social Informatics and Telecommunications Engineering 85

Natarajan Meghanathan   Nabendu Chaki
Dhinaharan Nagamalai (Eds.)

Advances in Computer Science and Information Technology

Computer Science and Engineering

Second International Conference, CCSIT 2012
Bangalore, India, January 2-4, 2012
Proceedings, Part II

 Springer

Volume Editors

Natarajan Meghanathan
Jackson State University, Jackson, MS, USA
E-mail: nmeghanathan@jsums.edu

Nabendu Chaki
University of Calcutta, Calcutta, India
E-mail: nabendu@ieee.org

Dhinaharan Nagamalai
Wireilla Net Solutions PTY Ltd., Melbourne, VIC, Australia
E-mail: dhinthia@yahoo.com

ISSN 1867-8211   e-ISSN 1867-822X
ISBN 978-3-642-27307-0   e-ISBN 978-3-642-27308-7
DOI 10.1007/978-3-642-27308-7
Springer Heidelberg Dordrecht London New York

Library of Congress Control Number: 2011943315

CR Subject Classification (1998): H.4, C.2, I.2, H.3, D.2, I.4, H.5

Typesetting: Camera-ready by author, data conversion by Scientific Publishing Services, Chennai, India

Printed on acid-free paper

Springer is part of Springer Science+Business Media (www.springer.com)

Preface

The Second International Conference on Computer Science and Information Technology (CCSIT-2012) was held in Bangalore, India, during January 2–4, 2012. CCSIT attracted many local and international delegates, presenting a balanced mixture of intellect from the East and from the West. The goal of this conference series is to bring together researchers and practitioners from academia and industry to focus on understanding computer science and information technology and to establish new collaborations in these areas. Authors are invited to contribute to the conference by submitting articles that illustrate research results, projects, survey work and industrial experiences describing significant advances in all areas of computer science and information technology.

The CCSIT-2012 Committees rigorously invited submissions for many months from researchers, scientists, engineers, students and practitioners related to the relevant themes and tracks of the conference. This effort guaranteed submissions from an unparalleled number of internationally recognized top-level researchers. All the submissions underwent a strenuous peer-review process which comprised expert reviewers. These reviewers were selected from a talented pool of Technical Committee members and external reviewers on the basis of their expertise. The papers were then reviewed based on their contributions, technical content, originality and clarity. The entire process, which includes the submission, review and acceptance processes, was done electronically. All these efforts undertaken by the Organizing and Technical Committees led to an exciting, rich and high-quality technical conference program, which featured high-impact presentations for all attendees to enjoy, appreciate and expand their expertise in the latest developments in computer network and communications research. In closing, CCSIT-2012 brought together researchers, scientists, engineers, students and practitioners to exchange and share their experiences, new ideas and research results in all aspects of the main workshop themes and tracks, and to discuss the practical challenges encountered and the solutions adopted. We would like to thank the General and Program Chairs, organization staff, the members of the Technical Program Committees and external reviewers for their excellent and tireless work. We sincerely wish that all attendees benefited scientifically from the conference and wish them every success in their research.

It is the humble wish of the conference organizers that the professional dialogue among the researchers, scientists, engineers, students and educators continues beyond the event and that the friendships and collaborations forged will linger and prosper for many years to come.

January 2012

Natarajan Meghanathan
Nabendu Chaki
Dhinaharan Nagamalai

Organization

General Chairs

David C. Wyld   Southeastern Louisiana University, USA
Natarajan Meghanathan   Jackson State University, USA

General Co-chairs

Jae Kwang Lee   Hannam University, South Korea
Michal Wozniak   Wroclaw University of Technology, Poland

Steering Committee

Abdul Kadhir Ozcan   The American University, Cyprus
Brajesh Kumar Kaushik   Indian Institute of Technology - Roorkee, India
Dhinaharan Nagamalai   Wireilla Net Solutions Pty Ltd., Australia
Eric Renault   Institut Telecom-Telecom SudParis, France
John Karamitsos   University of the Aegean, Samos, Greece
Kamalrulnizam Abu Bakar   Universiti Teknologi Malaysia, Malaysia
Khoa N. Le   University of Western Sydney, Australia
Nabendu Chaki   University of Calcutta, India

Program Committee

A.P. Sathish Kumar   PSG Institute of Advanced Studies, India
Abdul Aziz   University of Central Punjab, Pakistan
Abdul Kadir Ozcan   The American University, Cyprus
Andreas Riener Johannes   Kepler University Linz, Austria
Andy Seddon   Asia Pacific Institute of Information
     Technology, Malaysia

Armendariz-Inigo   Universidad Publica de Navarra, Spain
Atilla Elci   Eastern Mediterranean University, Cyprus
B. Srinivasan   Monash University, Australia
Balasubramanian K.   Lefke European University, Cyprus
Boo-Hyung Lee   KongJu National University, South Korea
Brajesh Kumar Kaushik   Indian Institute of Technology, India
Charalampos Z. Patrikakis   National Technical University of Athens,
     Greece
Chih-Lin Hu   National Central University, Taiwan
Chin-Chih Chang   Chung Hua University, Taiwan
Cho Han Jin   Far East University, South Korea
Cynthia Dhinakaran   Hannam University, South Korea

Danda B. Rawat	Old Dominion University, USA
Debasis Giri Haldia	Institute of Technology, India
Dhinaharan Nagamalai	Wireilla Net Solutions Pty Ltd., Australia
Dimitris Kotzinos	Technical Educational Institution of Serres, Greece
Dong Seong Kim	Duke University, USA
Emmanuel	Bouix iKlax Media, France
Eric Renault	Institut Telecom - Telecom SudParis, France
Farhat Anwar	International Islamic University, Malaysia
Firkhan Ali Bin Hamid Ali	Universiti Tun Hussein Onn Malaysia, Malaysia
Ford Lumban Gaol	University of Indonesia
H.V. Ramakrishnan	MGR University, India
Ho Dac Tu	Waseda University, Japan
Hoang, Huu Hanh	Hue University, Vietnam
Hwangjun Song	Pohang University of Science and Technology, South Korea
Jacques Demerjian	Communication & Systems, Homeland Security
Jae Kwang Lee	Hannam University, South Korea
Jan Zizka	SoNet/DI, FBE, Mendel University in Brno, Czech Republic
Jeong-Hyun Park	Electronics Telecommunication Research Institute, Korea
Jivesh Govil	Cisco Systems Inc. - CA, USA
Johann Groschdl	University of Bristol, UK
John Karamitsos	University of the Aegean, Samos, Greece
Johnson Kuruvila	Dalhousie University, Halifax, Canada
Jose Enrique Armendariz-Inigo	Universidad Publica de Navarra, Spain
Jungwook	Song Konkuk University, South Korea
K.P. Thooyamani	Bharath University, India
Kamaljit I. Lakhtaria	Atmiya Institute of Technology and Science, India
Khamish Malhotra	University of Glamorgan, UK
Khoa N. Le	University of Western Sydney, Australia
Krzysztof Walkowiak	Wroclaw University of Technology, Poland
Kshetrimayum	Indian Institute of Technology-Guwahati, India
Lopes Domingos	University of Lisbon, Portugal
Lu Yan	University of Hertfordshire, UK
Luis Veiga	Technical University of Lisbon, Portugal
Marco Roccetti	University of Bologna, Italy
Michael Peterson	University of Hawaii at Hilo, USA
Michal Wozniak	Wroclaw University of Technology, Poland
Mohsen Sharifi	Iran University of Science and Technology, Iran
Muhsin Abbas	University of Babylon, Iraq
Murugan D.	Manonmaniam Sundaranar University, India
N. Krishnan	Manonmaniam Sundaranar University, India

Nabendu Chaki	University of Calcutta, India
Natarajan Meghanathan	Jackson State University, USA
Nicolas Sklavos	Technological Educational Institute of Patras, Greece
Phan Cong Vinh	London South Bank University, UK
Ponpit Wongthongtham	Curtin University of Technology, Australia
Rajendra Akerkar	Technomathematics Research Foundation, India
Rajesh Kumar P.	The Best International, Australia
Ramayah Thurasamy	Universiti Sains Malaysia, Malaysia
Rituparna Chaki	West Bengal University of Technology, India
S. Hariharan	B.S. Abdur Rahman University, India
Sagarmay Dcb	Central Queensland University, Australia
Sajid Hussain	Fisk University, USA
Salah S.	Al-Majeed University of Essex, UK
Sanguthevar Rajasekaran	University of Connecticut, USA
Sarmistha Neogyv	Jadavpur University, India
Sattar B. Sadkhan	University of Babylon, Iraq
Sergio Ilarri	University of Zaragoza, Spain
Serguei A. Mokhov	Concordia University, Canada
Shivan Haran	Arkansas State University, USA
Somitra Sanadhya	IIT-Delhi, India
Sriman Narayana Iyengar	VIT University, India
SunYoung Han	Konkuk University, South Korea
Susana Sargento	University of Aveiro, Portugal
Syed Rahman	University of Hawaii-Hilo, USA
Syed Rizvi	University of Bridgeport, USA
Velmurugan Ayyadurai	Center for Communication Systems, UK
Vishal Sharma	Metanoia Inc., USA
Wei Jie	University of Manchester, UK
Yan Luo	University of Massachusetts Lowell, USA
Yannick Le	Moullec Aalborg University, Denmark
Yao-Nan Lien	National Chengchi University, Taiwan
Yeong Deok Kim	Woosong University, South Korea
Yuh-Shyan Chen	National Taipei University, Taiwan
Yung-Fa Huang	Chaoyang University of Technology, Taiwan

External Reviewers

Amit Choudhary	Maharaja Surajmal Institute, India
Abhishek samanta	Jadavpur University, Kolkata, India
Anjan K.	MSRIT, India
Ankit	BITS, Pilani, India
Aravind P.A.	Amrita School of Engineering India
Ashutosh Dubey	NRI Institute of Science and Technology, Bhopal, India

Ashutosh Gupta	MJP Rohilkhand University, Bareilly, India
Babak Khosravifar	Concordia University, Canada
Balaji Sriramulu	
Balakannan S.P.	Chonbuk National University, Jeonju, Korea
Bhupendra Suman	IIT Roorkee, India
Cauvery Giri	RVCE, India
Chandra Mohan	Bapatla Engineering College, India
Debdatta Kandar	Sikkim Manipal University, India
Doreswamyh Hosahalli	Mangalore University, India
P. Sheik Abdul Khader	B.S. Abdur Rahman University, India
Durga Toshniwal	Indian Institute of Techniology, India
Gopalakrishnan Kaliaperumal	Anna University, India
Govardhan A.	JNTUH College of Engineering, India
Hameem Shanavas	Vivekananda Institute of Technolgy, India
Hari Chavan	National Institute of Technology, Jamshedpur, India
Kaushik Chakraborty	Jadavpur University, India
Kota Sunitha	G. Narayanamma Institute of Technology and Science, Hyderabad, India
Lavanya	Blekinge Institute of Technology, Sweden
Mahalinga V. Mandi	Dr. Ambedkar Institute of Technology, Bangalore, Karnataka, India
Mohammad Mehdi Farhangia	Universiti Teknologi Malaysia (UTM), Malaysia
Murty Ch.A.S.	JNTU, Hyderabad, India
Mydhili Nair	M.S. Ramaiah Institute of Technology, India
Naga Prasad Bandaru	P.V.P. Siddartha Institute of Technology, India
Nagamanjula Prasad	Padmasri Institute of Technology, India
Nagaraj Aitha	I.T. Kamala Institute of Technology and Science, India
Nana Patil	NIT Surat, Gujrat, India
Omar Almomani	Universiti Utara Malaysia, Malaysia
Osman B. Ghazali	Universiti Utara Malaysia, Malaysia
Padmalochan Bera	Indian Institute of Technology, Kharagpur, India
Pappa Rajan	Anna University, India
Parth Lakhiya	
Pradeepini Gera	Jawaharlal Nehru Technological University, India
R.M. Suresh	Mysore University, India
Rabindranath Bera	Sikkim Manipal Institute of Technology, India
Rajashree Biradar	Ballari Institute of Technology and Management, India
Rajesh Kumar Krishnan	Bannari Amman Institute of Technology, India
Ramin Karimi	University Technology Malaysia

Reena Dadhich	Govt. Engineering College Ajmer, India
Reshmi Maulik	University of Calcutta, India
Rituparna Chaki	West Bengal University of Technology, India
S. Bhaskaran	SASTRA University, India
Saleena Ameen	B.S. Abdur Rahman University, India
Salini P.	Pondichery Engineering College, India
Sami Ouali	ENSI, Manouba, Tunisia
Samodar Reddy	India School of Mines, India
Sanjay Singh	Manipal Institute of Technology, India
Sara Najafzadeh	University Technology Malaysia
Sarada Prasad Dakua	IIT-Bombay, India
S.C. Sharma	IIT - Roorkee, India
Seetha Maddala	CBIT, Hyderabad, India
Selvakumar Ramachandran	Blekinge Institute of Technology, Sweden
Shriram Vasudevan	VIT University, India
Soumyabrata Saha	Guru Tegh Bahadur Institute of Technology, India
Srinivasulu Pamidi	V.R. Siddhartha Engineering College Vijayawada, India
Subhabrata Mukherjee	Jadavpur University, India
Subir Sarkar	Jadavpur University, India
Suhaidi B. Hassan	
Sunil Singh	Bharati Vidyapeeth's College of Engineering, India
Suparna DasGupta	
Swarup Mitra	Jadavpur University, Kolkata, India
Tsung Teng Chen	National Taipei University, Taiwan
Valli Kumari Vatsavayi	AU College of Engineering, India
Yedehalli Kumara Swamy	Dayanand Sagar College of Engineering, India

Technically Sponsored by

Software Engineering & Security Community (SESC)
Networks & Communications Community (NCC)
Internet Computing Community (ICC)
Computer Science & Information Technology Community (CSITC)

Organized By

ACADEMY & INDUSTRY RESEARCH COLLABORATION CENTER (AIRCC)
www.airccse.org

Table of Contents – Part II

Advances in Computer Science and Engineering

Qualitative Optimization of Coupling Parasitics and Driver Width in Global VLSI Interconnects

Devendra Kumar Sharma[1], Brajesh Kumar Kaushik[2], and R.K. Sharma[3]

[1] Department of ECE, Meerut Institute of Engineering and Technology, Meerut, UP, India
[2] Dept. of Electronics and Computer Engg, Indian Institute of Technology, Roorkee, India
[3] Department of ECE, National Institute of Technology, Kurukshetra, Haryana, India
d_k_s1970@yahoo.co.in, bkk23fec@iitr.ernet.in,
mail2drrks@gmail.com

Abstract. Analyses of the effects of interconnect wires in deep sub-micron technology is of prime importance in the modern era integrated circuits. The performance parameters such as crosstalk noise and delay are fundamentally dependent on interconnects and driver sizing. The coupling parasitics are the primary source of crosstalk. This paper addresses the optimization of coupling parasitics and driver sizing qualitatively for delay and peak noise. For this study, a pair of distributed *RLC* lines each of 4mm length is considered. These lines are coupled inductively and capacitively. The SPICE waveforms are generated at far end of lines for varying coupling parasitics and width of aggressor driver PMOS while keeping channel width of NMOS half of PMOS. The simulation is carried out at 0.13µm, 1.5 V technology node. Both the cases of simultaneous switching of inputs *i.e* in-phase and out-of-phase are taken into consideration.

Keywords: Delay, Crosstalk noise, Coupling parasitics, Driver width, Optimization.

1   Introduction

During the last two decades, the level of integration has increased mainly due to rapid progress in processing and interconnects technology [1]. The higher performance and improvement in circuit density has been mainly achieved by scaling down the device dimensions. Scaling device dimensions below 0.2µm resulted large consumption of chip area for complex interconnects. Thus, with technology advancement, interconnects have turned out to be more and more important than the transistor resource. According to International Technology Roadmap for Semiconductors (ITRS) [2], the gap between interconnection delay and gate delay will increase to 9:1 at 65nm technology node and on-chip wire length is expected to increase to 2.22 km/cm^2 by the year 2010. Thus, for high speed high density chips, it is mostly the interconnections rather than the device performance that determines the chip performance [3], [4].

N. Meghanathan et al. (Eds.): CCSIT 2012, Part II, LNICST 85, pp. 1–10, 2012.

The use of low resistance material, faster signal rise time, longer wire length and high switching speed leads to significant value of line inductance [5]. Due to the presence of wire parasitics, the *RLC* distributed model or transmission line model is more effective in current technology [6], [7]. In addition to wire parasitics, interwire or coupling parasitics *i.e.* mutual inductance (M) and coupling capacitance (C_C) have significant value in the circuit because of short spacing between interconnects, long wire lengths, high frequency of operation and complex geometry. The value of mutual inductance between two lines depends on the value of inductance of each line, their separation, the strength of current and its rate of change. The coupling capacitance is limited to adjacent neighbors and to adjacent layers in multilayer structure. However, the mutual inductance is not limited to adjacent wires and layers and it exists among all parallel wires. The performance and reliability of the circuit is affected by multiple effects of parasitics. These parasitics result in crosstalk noise, propagation delay and power dissipation which affects the signal integrity and degrade the circuit performance.

The crosstalk is the coupling of energy from one wire to another via coupling parasitics and adversely affects the circuit operating at higher frequencies [8]. Crosstalk induces faults in the circuit which are glitch and delay faults. The crosstalk induced overshoot and undershoot generated at the circuit node can cause false switching and creates a logic error [9]. A crosstalk induced delay occurs when both the aggressor and victim lines are switching simultaneously. Mostly crosstalk induced delay causes chip failure more than crosstalk induced glitch. The propagation delay and crosstalk noise in high frequency chips are dependent on the value of parasitics per unit length of interconnect [10]. Because of severe effects of parasitics, the optimization of parasitics for their effects is an important area of study.

A great deal of research has been done on the analysis of crosstalk noise [11], [12], [13], [14], [15], [16], [17]. The minimization of crosstalk using different techniques *viz.* resizing drivers, shielding interconnects, rerouting signal, bus encoding and repeater insertion has been reported in [18], [19], [20]. Researchers have reported the optimization of interconnect models/circuit using different approaches [21], [22], [23], [24]. Apart from the literature available, research is needed in the area of optimization of coupling parasitics taking into account the severe effects of crosstalk noise and delay. In [25], the optimization of coupling capacitance for delay and peak noise using qualitative approach is reported.

This paper presents a qualitative approach to optimize both mutual inductance and coupling capacitance collectively for delay. This paper also addresses the optimization of driver width qualitatively for crosstalk noise/delay. The optimization of driver width is equally important because it has effects on crosstalk noise and delay. The interconnect designers sometimes increase driver width to reduce propagation delay which may lead to increase in crosstalk level. The SPICE simulations are run and various waveforms are obtained at far end of interconnect lines.

Following this introduction, the paper is organized such that Section 2 describes the simulation setup for coupled lines. The effects of coupling parasitics and driver width are discussed in section 3. The optimization of coupling parasitics and driver width for delay and peak noise for simultaneously switching inputs is carried out in section 4 and simulation results are discussed. Finally, section 5 draws necessary conclusions.

2   Simulation Setup

In this work, two distributed *RLC* lines coupled inductively and capacitively are used for simulation as shown in Fig.1. The distributed model is the most accurate approximation of the actual behavior than the traditional lumped *R*, *L*, *C* model [3]. The length of interconnect is taken as 4mm and each line of coupled interconnects is 2µm wide, 0.68µm thick and separated by 0.24 µm [11]. Twenty distributed lumps of Gamma type are taken for the interconnect length under consideration. The capacitance and inductance values are obtained from the expressions available in [26], [27]. At far end of interconnect lines, CMOS load is replaced by 30fF capacitor. The interconnect parasitics for one meter length are represented by transmission line matrices in Fig. 2.

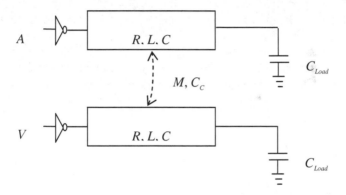

Fig. 1. Model of uniformly distributed coupled interconnect lines

$$R = \begin{bmatrix} 12{,}500 & 0 \\ 0 & 12{,}500 \end{bmatrix} \quad C = \begin{bmatrix} 190p & -64p \\ -64p & 190p \end{bmatrix} \quad L = \begin{bmatrix} 1.722\mu & 1.4\mu \\ 1.4\mu & 1.722\mu \end{bmatrix}$$

Fig. 2. Interconnect Parasitics

The simulations use an IBM 0.13µm technology with copper interconnect process (MOSIS) with a power supply voltage of 1.5V. The threshold voltages are roughly 10% of supply voltage. The transition time of the input ramp is taken as 25ps.

3   Effects of Coupling Parasitics and Driver Width

To capture the effects of coupling parasitics and driver width on peak noise and delay, SPICE simulations are run and various waveforms are generated at far end of lines by taking into consideration both the cases of simultaneous switching of inputs.

Case I: Both inputs are switching in same phase from high to low

Case II: Both inputs are switching in opposite phase *i.e.* aggressor input is switching from high to low and victim input is switching from low to high.

3.1   Effects of Coupling Parasitics

The effects of coupling capacitance and mutual inductance on peak noise and delay have been discussed and SPICE waveforms are shown in [17], [25]. From [17], [25], it is concluded that

(i)   The propagation delay and peak overshoot noise increases with increase in the value of mutual inductance in same phase switching of inputs, however, the propagation delay and peak noise decreases with increasing mutual inductance in case of opposite phase switching of inputs. So, the peak noise and delay have same behavior against changes in mutual inductance in either case of inputs switching.

(ii) In same phase switching of inputs, the delay decreases while peak noise increases with increase in the value of coupling capacitance. In opposite phase switching of inputs, the delay increases while peak noise decreases with increasing coupling capacitance. So, in both the cases of inputs switching, the delay shows opposite behavior than peak noise against variation in coupling capacitance.

3.2   Effects of Driver Width

To observe the effects of driver width on peak noise and delay, the interconnect model under consideration is simulated for both the cases of inputs switching. The aggressor driver PMOS width is varied from 30-120 µm in steps of 10 µm, keeping the corresponding NMOS width half of the PMOS. The width of victim driver is kept fixed. The value of coupling capacitance and mutual inductance is taken as (480 fF, 5.6 nH). The simulation results obtained are shown in Fig. 3 and Fig. 4.

From the simulation results obtained in Fig. 3 and Fig. 4 for Case I of inputs switching, it is observed that the delay decreases while overshoot noise increases with increase in the value of driver width. Similar kind of results are obtained for Case II in which both inputs are switching in opposite phase.

4   Optimization: Observations and Discussions

The optimization of mutual inductance and coupling capacitance is carried out qualitatively for delay. Furthermore, the optimization of driver width is also presented. The basic idea of optimization process is from the fact that in some cases, the parasitic effects *i.e.* crosstalk noise and delay shows opposite behavior with change in the value of parasitics /other parameters.

4.1   Optimization of Coupling Parasitics

The optimization of coupling capacitance for delay and peak noise is reported in [25]. The qualitative optimization of mutual inductance is not feasible because of similar kind of behavior of peak noise and propagation delay. In this paper, the optimization of mutual inductance and coupling capacitance for specified range of values is carried out qualitatively for delay because it shows opposite behavior due to mutual inductance and coupling capacitance as discussed in the previous section. The simulation results are obtained for both the cases of inputs switching under consideration and are shown in Fig. 5 and Fig. 6.

4.1.1   Observations and Discussions

In Case I of inputs switching (Fig. 5), because of opposite tendency of delay due to mutual inductance and coupling capacitance, the curve for delay vs. M and the curve for delay vs. C_C crosses each other. Beyond this crossing point of the curves, if the values of M and C_C are increased, it is clear from the Fig. 5 that delay due to C_C decreases while it increases due to M. However, the behavior of delay is reversed if the values of M and C_C are decreased. Therefore, at crossing point of the curves in Fig. 5, the delay is optimized for some value of coupling capacitance and mutual inductance.

Similarly, in Fig. 6 in which the optimization is carried out qualitatively for Case II of inputs switching, it is observed that the coupling parasitics are optimized for delay at crossing point of the curves. From the results, it is clear that the optimal value of coupling parasitics is somewhere between 250-300fF and 3.8-4.2nH.

4.2   Optimization of Driver Width

The optimization of driver width for specified value of coupling parasitics is carried out qualitatively for both the cases of inputs switching and the results are shown in Fig. 7 and Fig. 8.

4.2.1   Observations and Discussions

From Fig. 7, because of opposite tendency of delay and peak overshoot noise due to change in driver width, the curve for delay and the curve for peak overshoot crosses each other. Beyond the crossing point of these curves, it is observed that delay increases while peak noise decreases with decrease in the value of driver width. These effects are reversed in behavior if driver width is increased. Therefore, the effects *i.e.* delay and overshoot noise for specified value of coupling parasitics are optimized at crossing point of the curves for some value of driver width. Similarly, the effects are optimized for some value of driver width for Case II of inputs switching as shown in Fig. 8. From the results, it is observed that the optimal value of driver width is somewhere between 40-50µm.

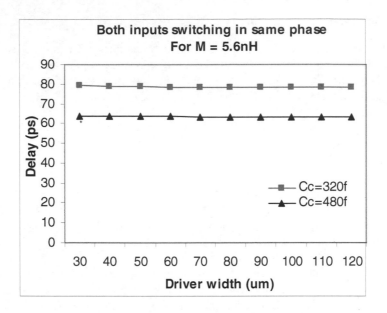

Fig. 3. Effect of driver width on propagation delay

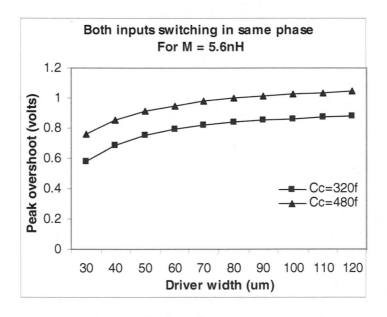

Fig. 4. Effect of driver width on peak overshoot noise

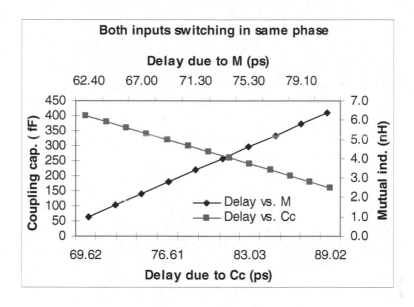

Fig. 5. Optimization of coupling parasitics for propagation delay in Case I

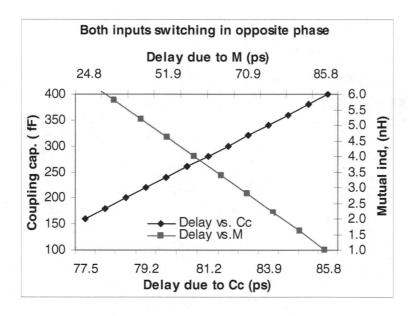

Fig. 6. Optimization of coupling parasitics for propagation delay in Case II

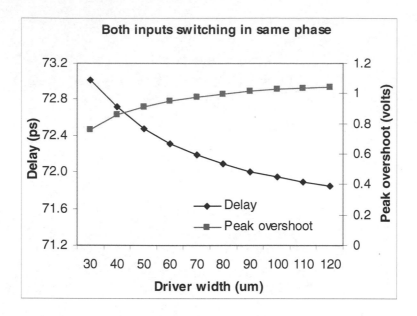

Fig. 7. Optimization of driver width for propagation delay and peak overshoot in Case I

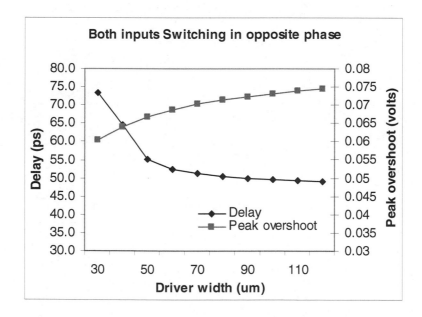

Fig. 8. Optimization of driver width for propagation delay and peak overshoot in Case II

5   Conclusion

A qualitative approach to optimize coupling parasitics and driver width for delay/peak overshoot noise is presented for simultaneously switching inputs. For both the cases of inputs switching, delay shows opposite behavior due to mutual inductance than coupling capacitance. Therefore, an optimum value of coupling parasitics (M and C_C) is observed that suggests the reduction of delay optimally. The optimal value is found to be somewhere between 250 to 300 fF and 3.8 to 4.2 nH. Similarly, on the basis of the effects of driver width observed on delay and peak noise, the optimization of driver width for these effects is carried qualitatively. The optimal value is found to be some where between 40-50 μm.

References

1. Kang, S.M., Leblebici, Y.: CMOS Digital Integrated Circuits-Analysis and Design. TMH, New York (2003)
2. Semiconductors Industry Association: International Technology Roadmap for Semiconductors (2005)
3. Rabaey, J.M.: Digital Integrated Circuits: A Design Perspective. Prentice-Hall, Englewood Cliffs (1996)
4. Bakoglu, H.B.: Circuits, Interconnects and Packaging for VLSI. Addision-Wesley, Reading (1990)
5. Ismail, Y.I., Friedman, E.G.: Figures of Merit to Characterize the Importance of On-Chip Inductance. IEEE Trans. on VLSI Systems 7(4), 442–449 (1999)
6. Kevin, T.T., Friedman, E.G.: Lumped Versus Distributed RC and RLC Interconnect Impedances. In: Proc. 43rd IEEE Midwest Symp. on Circuits and Systems, Lansing MI, pp. 136–139 (2000)
7. Kopcsay, A.G.V., Restle, P.J., Smith, H.H., Katopis, G., Becker, W.D., Coteus, P.W., Surovic, C.W., Rubin, B.J., Dunne Jr., R.P., Gallo, T., Jenkins, K.A., Terman, L.M., Dennard, R.H., Sai-Halasz, G.A., Krauter, B.L., Knebel, D.R.: When are Transmission – Line Effects Important for On-Chip Interconnections. IEEE Trans. on Microwave Theory and Techniques 45(10), 1836–1846 (1997)
8. Sharma, D.K., Kaushik, B.K., Sharma, R.K.: VLSI Interconnects and Their Testing - Prospects and Challenges Ahead. Journal of Engineering, Design and Technology 9(1), 63–84 (2011)
9. Anglada, R., Rubio, A.: An Approach to Crosstalk Effect Analysis and Avoidance in Digital CMOS VLSI Circuits. International Journal of Electronics 65(1), 9–17 (1988)
10. Ismail, Y.I., Friedman, E.G.: Effect of Inductance on Propagation Delay and Repeater Insertion in VLSI Circuits. IEEE Trans. on VLSI Systems 8(2), 195–206 (2000)
11. Kaushik, B.K., Sarkar, S., Agarwal, R.P., Joshi, R.C.: Crosstalk Analysis and Repeater Insertion in Crosstalk Aware Coupled VLSI Interconnects. Microelectronics International 23(3), 55–63 (2006)
12. Elgamel, M.A., Bayoumi, M.A.: Interconnect Noise Analysis and Optimization in Deep Submicron Technology. IEEE Circuits and Systems Magazine. Fourth quarter, 6–17 (2003)

13. Roy, A., Jingye, X., Chowdhury, M.H.: Analysis of the Impacts of Signal Slew and Skew on the Behavior of Coupled RLC Interconnects for Different Switching Patterns. IEEE Trans. on VLSI Systems 18(2) (2010)
14. Chowdhury, M.H., Ismail, Y.I., Kashyap, C.V., Krauter, B.L.: Performance Analysis of Deep Submicron VLSI Circuits in the Presence of Self and Mutual Inductance. Proc. IEEE Int. Symp. Cir, and Syst. 4, 197–200 (2002)
15. Kahng, A.B., Muddu, S., Vidhani, D.: Noise and Delay Uncertainty Studies for Coupled RC Interconnects. In: Proc. IEEE Intl. Conf. on VLSI Design, pp. 431–436 (2004)
16. Roy, A., Noha, M., Chowdhury, M.H.: Effects of Coupling Capacitance and Inductance on Delay Uncertainty and Clock Skew. In: Proc. of IEEE/ACH Design Automation Conf., pp. 184–187 (2007)
17. Sharma, D.K., Kaushik, B.K., Sharma, R.K.: Effect of Mutual Inductance and Coupling Capacitance on Propagation Delay and Peak Overshoot in Dynamically Switching Inputs. In: Proc. IEEE Intl. Conf. on Emerging Trend in Engineering and Technology, pp. 765–769 (2010)
18. Verma, S.K., Kaushik, B.K.: Encoding Schemes for the Reduction of Power Dissipation, Crosstalk and Delay: A Review. International Journal of Recent Trends in Engineering 3(4), 74–79 (2010)
19. Arunachalam, R., Acar, E., Nassif, S.R.: Optimal Shielding/Spacing Metrics for Low Power Design. In: Proc. of the IEEE Computer Society Annual Symposium on VLSI, pp. 167–172 (2003)
20. Zhang, J., Friedman, E.G.: Effect of Shield Insertion on Reducing Crosstalk Noise between Coupled Interconnects. In: Proc. of the IEEE International Symposium on Circuit and Systems, vol. 2, pp. 529–532 (2004)
21. Poltz, J.: Optimizing VLSI Interconnect Model for SPICE Simulation. Int. J. Analog Integrated Circuit Signal Processing 5, 87–94 (1994)
22. Zaabab, A.H., Zhang, Q.J., Nakhla, M.S.: A Neural Network Approach to Circuit Optimization and Statistical Design. IEEE Trans. Microwave Theory Tech. 43, 1349–1358 (1995)
23. Zhang, Q.J., Nakhla, M.S.: Signal Integrity Analysis and Optimization of VLSI Interconnects using Neural Network Models. In: Proc. IEEE Int. Symp. Circuits Syst., London, pp. 459–462 (1994)
24. Veluswami, A., Nakhla, M.S., Zhang, Q.J.: The Application of Neural Networks to EM-Based Simulation and Optimization of Interconnects in High-Speed VLSI Circuits. IEEE Trans. Microwave Theory Tech. 45(5), 712–723 (1997)
25. Sharma, D.K., Kaushik, B.K., Sharma, R.K.: A Qualitative Approach to Optimize Coupling Capacitance for Simultaneously Switching Scenario in Coupled VLSI Interconnects. In: Proc. IEEE Intl. Conf. on Devices and Communications, pp. 1–5 (2011)
26. Delorme, N., Belleville, M., Chilo, J.: Inductance and Capacitance Analytic Formulas for VLSI Interconnects. Electron Lett. 32(11), 996–997 (1996)
27. Lu, Y., Banerjee, K., Celik, M., Dutton, R.W.: A Fast Analytical Technique for Estimating the Bounds of On-Chip Clock Wire Inductance. In: Proc. IEEE Custom Integrated Circuits Conf., pp. 241–244 (2001)

Survey on Optimization Techniques in High Level Synthesis

B. Saravanakumaran[1] and M. Joseph[2]

[1] E.G.S. Pillay Engineering College
Nagore, Nagapattinam - 611002, India
saravanakumaranbalu@yahoo.com
[2] Mother Terasa College of Engineering and Technology
Illuppur, Pudukkottai - 622102, India
mjoseph_mich@yahoo.com

Abstract. This paper provides a detailed survey of optimization techniques available in high level synthesis. This survey contemplates on two parts. The first part deals with the applicability of optimization techniques available in high level language compiler into high level synthesis. The second part address the topics such as Area optimization, Resource optimization, Power optimization and Optimization issues pertaining to the notions value-grouping, value to register assignment, Transfer to wire assignment and wire to FU port assignment.

Keywords: High Level Synthesis, Very Large Scale Integrated Circuits, Functional Units, HDL Compiler.

1 Introduction

High level synthesis is generally used in Integrated Circuit design. The main goal of the HLS is to optimize silicon area, power and time. The use of a Hardware Description Language (HDL) is to understand the optimization techniques at the HDL level of abstraction for the accomplishment of better design, low power and reduced area. The use of a Hardware Description Language is to examine the optimization techniques at the HDL level of abstraction to achieve possible changes in design realization of low power and area reduction. In Very Large Scale Integrated Circuit (VLSI) design, it is required to achieve higher level abstraction. The higher level abstraction of the circuit is a basic requirement due to

- Higher Complexity
- Shrinking device size and
- Shorter time to market

Due to low power requirements in many portable applications such as mobile phones as well as packaging cost consideration, low power design is imperative. To design the chip designer automates on higher levels of abstraction where functionality is easier to understand and tradeoff is more influenced. There are

N. Meghanathan et al. (Eds.): CCSIT 2012, Part II, LNICST 85, pp. 11–21, 2012.

several advantages to automate part of all of the design process and moving automation to higher levels. First, automation assures a much shorter design cycle. Second, it allows for more exploration of different design styles since different designs can be generated and evaluated quickly. Finally, if synthesis algorithms are well understood, design automation tools may-out perform average human designers in meeting most design constraints and requirements.

1.1   High-Level Synthesis

Synthesis is a translation process from a behavioral description into a structural description, similar to the compilation of a high level language program in C or Pascal into an assembly program. Each component in the structural description is in turn defined by its own (low level) behavioral description. Synthesis, sometimes called design refinement, adds an additional level of detail that provides information needed for the next level of synthesis or for manufacturing of the design. High Level Synthesis is also defined as the process of mapping a behavioral description at the algorithmic level to a structural description in terms of functional units, memory elements and interconnections (e.g. multiplexers and buses).The functional units normally implement one or more elementary operations like addition, multiplication, etc. Another important point in high level synthesis is the formal description of the algorithm to be mapped. The study of the HLS leads to the manifestation of shorter design cycle, minimization of errors, exposure to identify the design space and the capability of the design process in self documenting.

1.2   Hardware Description Language

The job of the hardware in modeling, design and documentation of digital systems is wholly governed by the hardware description language. The hierarchical representation of functional and wiring details of the systems receive a complete and compact format only from these languages.

1.3   HDL Compiler

The tool which performs high level synthesis is called Hardware Description Language complier. The main objective is to optimize the code, so that optimized hardware is obtained after synthesis. The optimization factors are different since the aim of synthesis is to generate optimal hardware circuit. They are performance(speed), area and power. As in HLL compiler, optimization techniques are applied onto the intermediate representation but improve the speed, minimize the silicon area and power.

The compiler driven optimization techniques are trying to optimize the logic of the digital system and can be better. The parameters on which the systems optimally can be assessed are testability and design time. The few optimization techniques are Dead code elimination, constant propagation, common sub expression elimination, inline expansion of procedures and loop unrolling. The objective of HDL compiler is to obtain the optimized hardware, which runs faster, occupies the silicon area and consumes less power. Other parameters on which the systems can be accessed are testability and design time.

2   Related Surveys

Youn-Long Lin[8] has examined the latest developments in high level synthesis technology design. This paper provides the detailed survey for basic techniques for various optimization techniques in High level synthesis. Techniques have been proposed in the past few years for various sub tasks of high level synthesis are surveyed. The prime goal of the HLS for testability, low power and reliability were detailed. M.Joseph, Narasimha B.Bhat and K. Chandrasekaran[2] survey paper presents Hardware description language compiler optimization techniques and applicability of high level language compiler optimization techniques to Hardware Description Language Compilers was exhaustively presented. Esther Andres and Maria C.Molina[19] have made an attempt to optimize the area in high level synthesis using combined integer and floating point circuits. Dake Liu and Christer Svensson[20] have investigated the consumption estimation techniques in CMOS VLSI chips. Jason Coog et.al.,[21] have studied the various resource optimization techniques available in high level synthesis.

3   HDL Compiler Optimization Techniques

Program analysis techniques like Data Flow Analysis (DFA), Control Flow Analysis (CFA) and Dependence Analysis (DA) are essential for applying optimization techniques. The major optimization techniques available in HDL compiler are

3.1   Elementary Optimization Techniques

Constant folding: It is an optimization technique, which replaces the runtime computation by compile time computation and is generally done for constants. Eg.:pi=22/7;the value of pi can be replaced by the evaluated value 3.14. This avoids the division operation and the related hardware. Constant folding reduces the number of computations, which in turn reduces the synthesized hardware and thus area and power are reduced.

3.2   Redundancy Elimination

This category of optimization techniques avoids re-computation of the computations which have been done already. In this category of optimization necessitate the Data Flow Analysis.

Common Sub-expression Elimination (CSE): CSE allows no re-computation of an expression which is evaluated already. The common sub expression should not be redefined along the path of its use. This technique can be applied locally or globally. In general the goal of CSE can be defined as follows.

– Identify multiple patterns in the coefficient set.
– Remove these patterns and calculate them only once.

The problem to solve is how to identify the proper patterns for elimination so the optimization impact can be maximal. Our algorithm is based on a combination of an exhaustive search technique with a steepest descent (or greedy) approach in order to select the proper patterns for elimination [17].

Eg.:
a=b+c;
d=e+b+c;

The above expression is an un-optimized expression.

t=b+c;
a=t;
d=e+t;

The above expression is optimized expression.

3.3 Loop Optimization

Strength Reduction: It is an optimization technique, which replaces the costly operator by a cheap operator. Consider the statement; c=2*a this can be replaced by c=a+a. Here the multiplication operator is replaced by addition operator. These optimizations are done inside the loop, so it leads to greater improvement. Strength reduction minimizes the area and power.

3.4 Code Scheduling

This technique discusses about the scheduling of instructions, which will lead to improvement in the speed. Scheduling here refers to ordering or reordering the instructions with respect to clock cycles. The optimization in the scheduling mostly improve the performance i.e. either reduction in the number of cycles needed or reduction in the clock period of particular logic device.

Instruction Scheduling: This optimization technique schedules number of independent instructions in a same cycle. In example, the instructions are scheduled in three cycles in the un-optimized case. The first and second statements are data independent and can be scheduled in a single cycle. The third statement is a data dependant on both first and second. So it should be scheduled after both [15].

a=b+c;
d=e+f;
g=a+d;

The above expression is an un-optimized.

a=b+c; d=e+f;
g=a+b;

The above expression is an optimized.

Loop fusion: This technique allows computations in adjacent loops to be combined into a single loop. If possible two loops can also be integrated together. This reduces the total number of cycles required. This will increase the clock period of that logic.

Resource sharing: The resources like adder, multipliers and other functional units can be shared. This avoids instantiating hardware resources for every operator. The resources can be shared for the operations, which are not scheduled in the same cycle. The resources must be compatible. For example adder is compatible with subtracter and relational operator. When the scheduled operations for a functional unit are completed then those functional units are free and can be shared by other operations. This optimization technique reduces the area and power. The above optimization techniques are already available in High level language compiler. Our present work is to try and apply the programmer level optimization techniques into HDL complier.

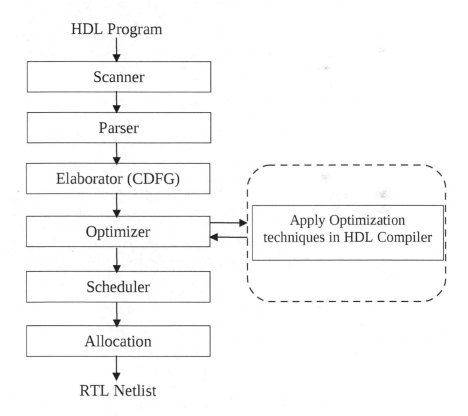

Fig. 1. HDL Compiler Optimization and Proposed Architecture design

3.5   Register Allocation

This is popularly used optimization techniques in HLL compiler for register assignment to the variables. Graph coloring is one such technique used for register allocation. In HDL compiler this problem can be understood in a different perspective. Here storage elements are flip flops and variables can be assigned to them. The assignment of variables to flip flops can be understood as a register allocation problem and accordingly techniques like graph coloring can be applied. The classification is made whether the optimization reduces or increases one of the three metrics: clock period, power consumption and area in the FPGA [14].

4   Recent Developments

Young Long Lin[8] has studied the High level Synthesis. The chief objectives of his investigation are Testability, Power efficiency and Reliability of High Level Synthesis. He has applied Scheduling, Allocation and Binding to achieve the transforming behaviour into structure. By virtue of ASAP (As Soon As Possible) operations are stored into a list according to their scheduling. By virtue of ALAP(As Late As Possible)operations define the latest step into which an operations can be scheduled optimization is realized by minimizing the number of self loops. Along this line Flottes[6] has extensively studied the register allocation. To manifest the testability Potkonjak[7] has proposed a two stage objective function for estimating the area and to reduce the fan-ins and fan-outs of the interconnection wires, capacitance. Rabaey[9] has invoked scheduling, Assignment and allocation techniques. Raghunathan and Jha[11]has applied data path allocation method to the circumstances where low power is prevalent. Musoli and Cortadelia[13] has applied scheduling and resource binding algorithm for reducing the activity of functional units by minimizing the input operations. Martin and Knight[23]attempted an investigation by lowering supply voltage and disabling the clock of idle computers. These findings are highly applicable in Digital Signal Processing design environment, embedded system design environment, Hardware design verification and to solve the software-hardware code design problem.

Hao Li Srinivas Katkori Zhipeng Lin[22] have established that HLS design flow improve the circuit performance once the placement phase is done. They have also established that once the placement is computed estimation of the circuit performance is done by the Xilinx. They proposed a method so that feed back is generated and given to the Automatic design installation. This has provided confidence that the mixture of the HLS tool and physical design that has excellent potential to enhance the performance of modern VLSI design.

Hao Li Srinivas Katkoori, Zhipeng Liu[22], have exposed HLS tool is able to iteratively enhance the system performance with the guidance information obtained from the physical design phase. According to their study estimation shares that the best synthesized design could satisfy the original system design objective. Testing is applied with regard to the predefined number of iterations. This revelation has reduced the running the efficiency.

Jason Coog, Bin Liu and Junjuan XG[21] have examined the coordinated Resource optimization in behavioural synthesis. This study is aimed to reduce resource usage in terms of power, performance and cost. In this study the separating synthesis process in transformed into a sequence of optimization steps.

Esther Andres, Maria C.Molina, Guilerno Botella[19] have proposed HLS algorithms associated with floating point operations. In this paper the authors propose the substitution of the floating point operation by their corresponding fixed point operations. Due to huge area requirement of the floating point operations the authors propose the optimization of the systems through the reuse of the internal modules to perform other operations.

5   Important Optimizations

A major part of the design process for an optimizer is to decide which optimization techniques are most important and which are less important. Typically, a few optimization techniques will provide a very high return in terms of improved execution speed while the remainder provides only marginal improvements. Given that compile-speed and compile space always have limitations, this means the best returns are yielded by focusing on a few, important optimizations.

In general, this investigation requires complicated analysis, some combination of inter procedural analysis, higher level Verilog analysis, or user assertion. While it is desirable to solve the general problem in the long run, in the short run, this information is often available in local cases by a simple analysis of the code. In any case, once the information is available, it is clear that the key global optimizations are constant propagation and dead code elimination. Given a local strategy for code generation that attempts no memory reuse, it should also be evident optimizations focused on recognizing and exploiting memory reuse is important. In particular, users tend to work with the same variables repeatedly in a section of code. Code generators rarely recognize this reuse; they load the locations which they need at the beginning of a unit and store everything changed at the end of a unit.

There are three ways of improving this reuse: 1.Eliminating Common Sub Expressions, 2.Changing variable allocations, 3.Doing good register allocation.

5.1   Area Optimization

Improvement in circuit performance is an important factor in area optimization. For this purpose conventional high level synthesis algorithms employ multi cycle operators to the cycle length. For the execution of one operation operators require several cycles, but at the same time the entire functional unit is not employed in any cycle. Also, the execution of operations in multi cycle operators is infeasible if the results should be available in a smaller number of cycles than the functional unit delay. This obliges to add new functional resources to the data path even if multi-cycle operators are idle when the execution of the operation begins.

Operations are executed in such a manner that functional units are allowed for their internal reuse, which eventually reduces the area of functional units. Since it facilitates the use of multi cycle operators for the calculation of narrower operations faster than the functional units, the possibilities of common hardware sharing get the expansion. At the end of the high level synthesis this technique is employed as an optimization phase. It can also optimize the circuits synthesized by any high level synthesis tool, consequently the area of the circuits synthesized by regular HLS algorithm using multi cycle operators gets reduced by the proposed optimization technique.

5.2   Resource Optimization

One of the most pertinent optimization objective is the abstract reducing resource usage in behavioral sysnthsis. Since it has its influence on power, performance and cost. Functional units, registers and multiplexers are the distinct components of the data path in a typical design. If a behavioral synthesis tool considers all kinds of tools simultaneously then it would optimize the overall resource usage.

Nevertheless the earlier work on behavioral synthesis has its own limitations in terms of the inability to consider all kinds of resources globally and the splitting of the synthesis process into a sequence of optimization steps which is void of a consistent optimization objective. Neilson[12] has examined a behavioral synthesis flow by allowing all types of components in the data path are modeled and optimized consistently. The key idea is to feed to the scheduler the intentions for sharing functional units and to register in favor of the global optimization goal such as total area, so that the scheduler could generate a schedule that makes the sharing intentions feasible.

Performed experiments reveal the fact that minimizing functional unit requirements is scheduling and employing the east number of functional units and registers in binding when compared with our solution promotes a 24 percent reduction on average. Neilson[12] has presented a behavioural synthesis flow, in which all resources in the data path are consistently optimized throughout the whole synthesis flow. This is achieved by guiding the scheduler using sharing intentions in favor of efficient resource usage. Experimental results show significant reduction compared to previous approaches in total area for a set of benchmarks. Our idea can also be used for optimizations of other objectives (e.g., power), by consistent consideration throughout different steps in the behavioral synthesis flow.

5.3   Power Optimization

To address the challenge to reduce power, the semiconductor industry has adopted a multifaceted approach, attacking the problem on four fronts [1]:

- Reducing the chip and package capacitance
- Scaling the supply voltage
- Employing better design techniques
- Using power management strategies

6 Issues in Compiler Driven Optimization Techniques

System Power: When a chip dissipates too much power, it will either become too hot and cease working or will need extra cooling. Besides, there is a special category of applications, viz. portable equipment powered by batteries, for which low power consumption is of primary importance. Here again there are trade-offs: designing for low power may e.g. lead to an increase in the chip area.

Design Time: The design of an integrated circuit is almost never a goal on its own: it is an economical activity. So a chip satisfying the specifications should be available as soon as possible. The design costs are an important factor, especially when only a small number of chips need to be manufactured. Of course, good CAD tools help to shorten the design time considerably as does the use of semicustom design.

Testability: As a significant percentage of the chips fabricated is expected to be defective, all of them have to be tested before used in a product. It is important that a chip is easily testable as testing equipment is expensive. This asks for the minimization of the time spent to test a single chip. Often, increasing the testability of a chip an increase in its area.

7 Optimization Issues

In High Level Synthesis the scheduling and assignment tasks are interrelated. For an optimal design they should be solved simultaneously. Most systems first solve the scheduling problem and then try to find a good assignment given a certain schedule. The assignment problem itself consists of several sub problems.

Operation-to-FU assignment: This is the problem of mapping a computation to functional unit of an appropriate type. Value grouping: This is the problem of partitioning all storage values in such a way that subset does not contain values that are read or written simultaneously. Then each subset can be realized as a register bank. In the case of multiport memories, the conditions for grouping should be adapted accordingly.

Value-to-register assignment: This is the problem of assigning memory location to storage values in the same group. Values with non overlapping life times can share the same location. The life time of a storage value is the time interval starting at the instant that it is created, and ending the moment that it no longer is required.

Transfer-to-wire assignment: A transfer is the actual transport of data from one hardware unit to another. In a bus-based architecture, one has the choice of which bus to write. The choice affects the number of three-state drivers connected to the unit from which the transfer originates and the type of multiplexers connected to the receiving the transfer.

Wire to FU-port assignment: In the case of commutative operations, one can choose one of the two equivalent input ports to feed the data to the functional unit. More in general, the problem exists when a functional unit has ports that are functionally equivalent.

8   Summary

This paper is on the basis of the detailed survey on the optimization techniques available in high level synthesis. This paper exposes the possible application of optimization techniques aimed to transform high level language compiler into high level synthesis. The later part of the paper discusses in detail the notions such as area optimization, resource optimization, power optimization and optimization issues which eventually lead to the concept of value grouping, value to register assignment, transfer to wire assignment and port assignment.

Acknowledgments. We thank to the anonymous reviewers for their numerous insightful and constructive comments.

References

1. Lin, C.-C., Yoon, D.-H.: New Efficient High Level Synthesis Methodology for Low Power Design. In: International Conference on New Trends in Information and Service Science (2009)
2. Joseph, M., Bhat, N.B., Chandra Sekaran, K.: Right inference of Hardware in High-Level Synthesis. In: International Conference on Information Processing, ICIP 2007, Bangalore, India (2007)
3. Zhang, J., Zhang, Z., Zhou, S., et al.: Bit-level optimization for high level synthesis and FGPA-based acceleration. In: Proceedings of FPGA 2010, Monterey, USA (2010)
4. Molina, M.C., Ruiz Sautra, R., Mendias, J.M., Hermida, R.: Area Optimization of multi-cycle operators in high level synthesis. In: Dte Conference Proceedings (2007)
5. McFarland, M.C., Parker, A.C., Campasona, R.: Tutorial on High-Level Synthesis. In: 25th ACM/IEEE Design Automation Conference (1998)
6. Flottes, M.L., Hammad, D., Rouzeyre, B.: High Level Synthesis for easy Testability. In: Proceedings of the European Design and Test Conference, Paris, France, pp. 198–206 (1995)
7. Potkonjak, M., Rabaey, J.: Optimizing Resource Utilization using Transformation. IEEE Trans. Computer Aided Design Integrated Circuits Systems 13(3), 227–292 (1994)
8. Lin, Y.L.: Recent Developments in High-Level Synthesis. ACM Transactions on Design Automation of Electronic Systems 2(1), 2–21 (1997)
9. Rabaey, J., Guerra, L., Mehra, R.: Design guidance in the power dimension. In: International Conference on Acoustics, Speech and Signal Processing, pp. 2837–2840 (1995)
10. Roy, S., Banerjee, P.: An Algorithm for Converting Floating-Point Computations to Fixed-Point in MATLAB based FPGA design. In: Design Automation Conference - DAC 2004, San Diego, California, pp. 484–487 (2004)
11. Raghunathan, A., Jha, N.K.: Behavioral Synthesis for low power. In: Proceedings of the International Conference on Computer Design (ICCD), pp. 318–322 (1994)
12. Neilson, S.G.: Behavioral synthesis of asynchronous circuits. PhD dessertation Technical University of Denmark, Department of Informatics and Mathematics modelling (2005)

13. Musoli, E., Cortadella, J.: Scheduling and Resource binding for low power. In: Proceedings of the Eighth Symposium on System Synthesis, pp. 104–109 (1995)
14. Ozer, E., Nisbet, A., Gregg, D.: Classification of Compiler Optimizations for High Performance. Small Area and Low Power in FPGAs (2003)
15. Joseph, M., Bhat, N.B., Chandra Sekaran, K.: Technology driven High-Level Synthesis. In: International Conference on Advanced Computing and Communication-ADCOM 2007. IEEE, Indian Institute of Technology, Guwahati, India (2007)
16. Taylor, S., Edwards, D., Plana, L.: Automatic compilation of data driven circuits. In: 14th IEEE International Symposium on Asynchronous Circuits and Systems, pp. 3–14. IEEE (2008)
17. Pasko, P., Schaumont, P., Derudder, V., Vernalde, S., Durackova, D.: A New algorithm for Elimination of Common Sub Expressions. IEEE Transactions on Computer Aided Design of Integrated Circuits and Systems 18(1) (1999)
18. Muchnick, S.S.: Advanced Compiler Design Implementations. Harcourt Asia PTE Ltd. (1997)
19. Andres, E., Molina, M.C.: Area Optimization of Combined Integer and Floating Point Circuits in High Level Synthesis. IEEE Transactions on Computer Aided Design of Integrated Circuits and Systems 8(1) (2008)
20. Liu, D., Svensson, C.: Power Consumption Estimation in CMOS VLSI Chips. IEEE Journal of Solid State Circuits 29(6) (1994)
21. Coog, J., Liu, B., Xu, J., et al.: Coordinated Resource Optimization in Behavioural Synthesis 20(2) (2009)
22. Katkoori, H.L., Liu, S.Z.: Feedback driven High Level Synthesis for performance optimization. In: ASICON 2005, 6th International Conference ASIC Proceedings, pp. 961–964 (2006)
23. Martin, R.S., Knight, J.P.: Power-profiler: Optimizing ASICs power consumption at the behavioral level. In: Proceedings of the Design Automation Conference (DAC), San Francisco, CA, p. 4247 (1995)
24. Free Floating-Point Madness, http://www.hmc.edu/chips
25. Electronic Design Interchange Format, http://www.edif.org
26. FPGA, CPLD, and EPP Solutions, http://www.xilinx.com
27. Icarus Verilog Simulation and Synthesis Tool, http://www.icraus.com

An Adaptive Technique Using Advanced Encryption Standard to Implement Hard Disk Security for Personalized Devices

Minal Moharir and A.V. Suresh

R.V. College of Engineering, Bangalore-59
minalmoharir@yahoo.com,
sureshav@rvce.edu.in

Abstract. The main objective of the paper is to develop an efficient and cost effective method for Hard Disk Drive(HDD) Security. The task is implemented using Full Disk Encryption (FDE) with Advanced Encryption Standards(AES) for data security of Personal Computers(PCS) and Laptops . The focus of this work is to authenticate and protect the content of HDD from illegal use. The paper proposes an adaptive methods for protecting a HDD based on Partial Disk Encryption(PDE) which one of the flavor of FDE. The proposed method is labeled as DiskTrust. FDE encrypts entire content or a single volume on your disk. Symmetric key uses same key for encryption as well for decryption. DiskTrust uses these two technology to build cost effective solution for small scale applications. Finally, the applicability of these methodologies for HDD security will be evaluated on a set of data files with different key sizes.

Keywords: Information Security, Integrity, confidentiality, Authentication, Encryption.

1 Introduction

As of January 2011 the internet connected an estimated 941.7 million computers in more than 450 countries on every continent, even Antarctica (Source: Internet Software Consortium's Internet Domain Survey; www.isc.org/index.pl). The internet is not a single network, but a worldwide collection of loosely connected networks that are accessible by individual computer hosts, in a variety of ways, to anyone with a computer and a network connection[1]. Thus, individuals and organizations can reach any point on the internet without regard to national or geographic boundaries or time of day.

However, along with the convenience and easy access to information come risks. Among them are the risks that valuable information will be lost, stolen, changed, or misused. If information is recorded electronically and is available on networked computers, it is more vulnerable than if the same information is printed on paper and locked in a file cabinet. Intruders do not need to enter an office or home; they may not even be in the same country. They can steal or tamper with information without

N. Meghanathan et al. (Eds.): CCSIT 2012, Part II, LNICST 85, pp. 22–31, 2012.

touching a piece of paper or a photocopier. In this way security of stored information is an important issue. The proposed paper consider the security of Hard Disk Drive which is a fundamental element in computing chain.

The paper organized as follows. Related work, gap & problem is described in Section 2. A view of simulation and experimental design is given in section 3. Simulation results are shown in section 4. Finally the conclusions are drawn section 5.

2   Related Work

The related survey is divided into two parts. The first part is survey about full disk encryption. The second part is survey about advanced encryption standards.

Information security is the process of protecting information. It protects its availability, privacy and integrity[2]. More companies store business and individual information on computer than ever before. Much of the information stored is highly confidential and not for public viewing. Without this information, it would often be very hard for a business to operate[3]. Information security systems need to be implemented to protect this information. There are various ways to implement Information security systems. One of the popular technique is full disk encryption. Full Disk Encryption (FDE) is the safest way to protect digital assets[4], the hard drive is a critical element in the computing chain because it is where sensitive data is stored. Full disk encryption increases the security of information stored on a laptop significantly[5]. It helps to keep business critical data absolutely confidential. Moreover, full disk encryption helps to meet several legislative requirements.

Min Liang and Chao wen Chang (2010 IEEE) described a full disk encryption scheme based on XEN virtual machine which is stored in a security flash disk. XEN is used to encrypt (decrypt) all the data in hard disk and manage the whole system.

Li Jun & Yu Huiping (2010 IEEE) introduced the data encryption technologies of encrypting file system (EFS) and traditional full-disk encryption (FDE), and points out the problems of data encryption of EFS and FDE. Combined with the features of trusted platform module (TPM)[6], this paper constructed a trusted full-disk encryption (TFDE)[7] based on TPM.

The second part of survey covers implementation of Encryption Algorithms. Many encryption algorithms are widely available and used in information security. They can be categorized into Symmetric (private) and Asymmetric (public) keys encryption. In Symmetric keys encryption or secret key encryption, only one key is used to encrypt and decrypt data. The key should be distributed before transmission between entities. Keys play an important role. If weak key is used in algorithm then every one may decrypt the data. Strength of Symmetric key encryption depends on the size of key used. For the same algorithm, encryption using longer key is harder to break than the one done using smaller key[8]. The paper uses Symmetric key cryptography to implement disk security. The related work with respect to performance of various encryption algorithm is as follows

Jyothi Yenuguvanilanka Omar Elkeelany (2008 IEEE), This paper addressed the performance of Rijndael AES Encryption algorithm of key length 128 bits. Two hardware models based on HDL and IP core are used to evaluate the performance of the algorithm. The encryption time and also the performance metrics such as size, speed and memory utilization are evaluated, using these models.

Dazhong Wang & Xiaoni Li (2009 IEEE) presented the design, implementation and performance of a FIPS – approved cryptographic algorithm – Advanced Encryption Standard (AES), which can be used to protect electronic data.

El-Sayed Abdoul-Moaty ElBadawy & all (ICES 2010), This paper proposed a new chaos AES algorithm for data security. The algorithm is based on substituting the Rijndael affine transformation S-box by another one based on chaos theory. The new S-box has a low correlation and exhibits a significant performance improvement with an acceptable complexity addition.

S.Anandi Reddy & M.Arul Kumar M.Tech.,(2011 IEEE) In this paper, concurrent structure independent fault detection schemes for designing high performance and reliable architecture of the AES is presented. For high performance applications, instead of using look-up tables alone for the implementation of S-box and inverse S-box and their parity predictions, logic gate implementations based on composite fields are also utilized.

2.1   Research Gap

- The FDE technology discussed in above survey are encrypting the entire contents of Hard disk Drive. However encryption of the entire HDD is expensive in terms of time and cost. The large scale industries needs this much of tough security, as well they can accommodate big cost. For small industries or institution or personal users the data security is needed for partial data, so need some cost effective security scheme.
- The Symmetric Key Cryptography(SKC) is best for the security of personal devices as no need to share the key.
- Rijndael is most robust & better performance algorithm in available SKC

3   Problem Statement

To develop HDD security technique labeled as DiskTrust. DiskTrust technology uses PDE, creates authorized invisible volume on HD & implements SKC with Rijndael to secure the data stored on secured volume.

The technical objectives of the thesis are:

1. Create Hidden partition
2. Check authentication
3. Store/access data from the hidden volume
4. Execute encryption/decryption algorithm while reading /writing data on Hard Disk Drive.

4   AES for Implementation

The standard AES algorithm is as follows:

KeyExpansion: The   keys are derived from the cipher key using Rijndael's key schedule

4.1   Initial Round

- **AddRoundKey:** each byte of the state is combined with the round key using bitwise xor

4.2   Rounds

- SubBytes—a non-linear substitution step where each byte is replaced with another according to a lookup table.
- ShiftRows—a transposition step where each row of the state is shifted cyclically a certain number of steps.
- MixColumns—a mixing operation which operates on the columns of the state, combining the four bytes in each column
- AddRoundKey

4.3   Final Round (no MixColumns)

- SubBytes
- ShiftRows
- AddRoundKey

To improve the performance following modifications are done:
   In order to enhance the security and reliability of AES, we bring in three changes.
In each iterative round, apart from the usual four above mentioned operations, we also include two new operations: The Arithmetic Operator and The Route Cipher.
   We also modify the key schedule so as to increase the number of the AES encryption rounds. For example, for 16 byte key, we generate 336 bit key instead of the usual 176 bit key. By this process, we are able to successfully process 20+1 rounds instead of the previous 10+1 rounds for the 16 byte key. Lets have a look at the modifications and there implications.

4.4   Arithmetic Operation

In this operation, each element of the state is arithmetically added by a number depending on their row number.

   The 1st row is added to 1.
   The 2nd row is added to 2.

The 3rd row is added to 3.
The 4th row is added to 4.

To retain the symmetric nature of AES, during decryption we have inversed the process by subtracting the corresponding same numbers.

The 1st row is added to 1.
The 2nd row is added to 2.
The 3rd row is added to 3.
The 4th row is added to 4.

4.5   Route Cipher

In a route cipher, the plaintext was first written out in a grid of given dimensions, and then read off in a pattern given in the key. For example, using the same plaintext:

W R I O R F E O E
E E S V E L A N J
A D C E D E T C X

4.6   Extending the Key Schedule

We have also extended the key schedule. We have followed the key schedule process but we haven't stopped at the earlier specifications, rather we continued doing so in order to enable more computing iterative rounds, giving the attacker an even tougher code to break. For example, for 16 byte null key, we generate the following 336 bit extended key which facilitates the proper operation of 20+1rounds, i.e. double the number of rounds earlier.

The diskTrust technique implements AES & improved AES with different key size.

5   Simulation and Design

This section describes design and GUI implementation, some of the important results that were found as part of the implementatton.

5.1   Implementation of Hidden Volume

DiskTrust Security user interfaces are shown below in the screenshots. The user interface is basically a frame work application where user can use the application

5.1.1 Main Application Window
The Main application window holds multiple options such as CreateVolume, Mount and Dismount All.

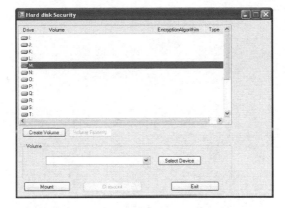

Fig. 1. Screenshot of Main Application Window

This is the first step from methodology which create a hidden volume on the HDD.

5.1.2 Volume Location

Volume Location Window allows the user to select location where the user wants to create the volume.

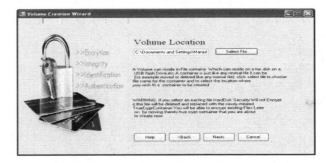

Fig. 2. Screenshot of Volume Location Window

5.2   Volume Password

Volume Password window will allow the user to enter the password and confirm Password.

Password implements user authentication.

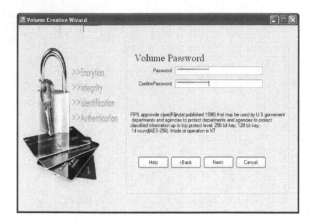

Fig. 3. Screenshot of Volume Password Window

5.3   Encrypt or Decrypt Data Using AES and Imprives AES with Different Key Size While Retrieving from Hidden Volume

For our experiment, we use a laptop PentiumV 2.4 GHz CPU, in which performance data is collected. In the experiments, the laptop encrypts a different file size ranges from 321K byte to 7.139Mega Byte. Several performance metrics are collected:

1- encryption time
2- CPU process time
3- CPU clock cycles and battery power.

The encryption time is considered the time that an encryption algorithm takes to produce a cipher text from a plaintext. Encryption time is used to calculate the of an encryption scheme. It indicates the speed of encryption. The CPU process time is the time that a CPU is committed only to the particular process of calculations. It reflects the load of the CPU. The more CPU time is used in the encryption process, the higher is the load of the CPU. The CPU clock cycles are a metric, reflecting the energy consumption of the CPU while operating on encryption operations. Each cycle of CPU will consume a small amount of energy.

6   Simulation Results

The effect of changing key size of AES on power consumption. The performance comparison point is the changing different key sizes for AES algorithm. In case of AES, We consider the three different key sizes possible. In case of AES it can be seen that higher key size leads to clear change in the battery and time consumption. It can be seen that going from 128 bits key to 192 bits causes increase in power and time consumption about 8% and to 256 bit key causes an increase of 16% . The simulation results with different key sizes are as shown in Table1.

Table 1. Time for Different Key Size

AES Key Size	AES 128	AES 192	AES 256
Time in Milliseconds	287	310	330

The graphical representation of the given data is as follows,

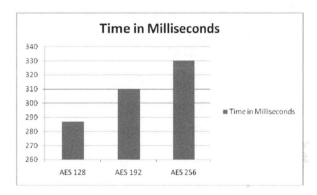

Fig. 4. Time with different key size

The analysis with improved AES is shown in Table3.

Table 2. Time for Different Key Size

Improved AES Key Size	I-AES 128	I-AES 192	I-AES 256
Time in Milliseconds	250	300	330

The graphical representation of the given data is as follows,

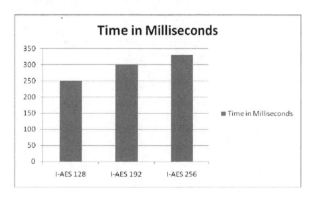

Fig. 5. Time with different key size

7   Conclusion

Proposed DiskTrust model is better suited for disk security of personal devices such PCs/Laptops over existing techniques. Disktrust model is cost effective & userfriendly.

-   DiskTrust stores data on hidden volume so the user's information is in accessible or invisible to the unauthorized user.
-   DiskTrust provides user's authentication.
-   DiskTrust provides confidentiality by encrypting the data stored in invisible & authenticated disk volume.

With Modified Rijndael algorithm, for 128-bits block & 128-bits key encryption time required is 250ms. This gives 023% performance over standard Rijndeal.

References

1. Blömer, J., Krummel, V.: Fault Based Collision Attacks on AES. In: Breveglieri, L., Koren, I., Naccache, D., Seifert, J.-P. (eds.) FDTC 2006. LNCS, vol. 4236, pp. 106–120. Springer, Heidelberg (2006)
2. Blomer, J., Seifert, J.-P.: Fault Based Cryptanalysis of the Advanced Encryption Standard (AES). In: CHESS 2003, pp. 162–181 (2003)
3. Chen, C.-N., Yen, S.-M.: Differential Fault Analysis on AES Key Schedule and Some Countermeasures. In: Safavi-Naini, R., Seberry, J. (eds.) ACISP 2003. LNCS, vol. 2727, pp. 118–129. Springer, Heidelberg (2003)
4. Giraud, C.: DFA on AES. In: Dobbertin, H., Rijmen, V., Sowa, A. (eds.) AES 2005. LNCS, vol. 3373, pp. 27–41. Springer, Heidelberg (2005)
5. Kim, C.H., Quisquater, J.-J.: Faults, Injection Methods, and Fault Attacks. IEEE Design & Test of Computers 24(6), 544–545 (2007)
6. Moradi, A., Shalmani, M.T.M., Salmasizadeh, M.: A Generalized Method of Differential Fault Attack Against AES Cryptosystem. In: Goubin, L., Matsui, M. (eds.) CHES 2006. LNCS, vol. 4249, pp. 91–100. Springer, Heidelberg (2006)
7. Piret, G., Quisquater, J.-J.: A Differential Fault Attack Technique against SPN Structures, with Application to the AES and KHAZAD. In: Walter, C.D., Koç, Ç.K., Paar, C. (eds.) CHES 2003. LNCS, vol. 2779, pp. 77–88. Springer, Heidelberg (2003)
8. FIPS-197, Advanced Encryption Standard (AES), Federal Information Processing Standards Publication 197, November 26 (2001),
   http://csrc.nist.gov/publications/
9. Karri, R., Wu, K., Mishra, P., Kim, Y.: Concurrent Error Detection Schemes for Fault-Based Side-Channel Cryptanalysis of Symmetric Block Ciphers. IEEE Trans. on Computer-Aided Design of Integrated Circuits and Systems 21(12), 1509–1517 (2002)
10. Maistri, P., Vanhauwaert, P., Leveugle, R.: A Novel Double-Data- Rate AES Architecture Resistant against Fault Injection. In: Workshop on Fault Diagnosis and Tolerance in Cryptography, FDTC 2007, pp. 54–61 (August 2007)
11. Monnet, Y., Renaudin, M., Leveugle, R.: Designing Resistant Circuits against Malicious Faults Injection Using Asynchronous Logic. IEEE Trans. on Computers 55(9), 1104–1115 (2006)

12. Wu, K., Karri, R., Kuznetsov, G., Goessel, M.: Low Cost Concurrent Error Detection for the Advanced Encryption Standard. In: International Test Conference, pp. 1242–1248 (2004)
13. Bertoni, G., Breveglieri, L., Koren, I., Maistri, P., Piuri, V.: Error Analysis and Detection Procedures for a Hardware Implementation of the Advanced Encryption Standard. IEEE Trans. on Computers 52(4) (April 2003)
14. Yen, C.H., Wu, B.F.: Simple Error Detection Methods for Hardware Implementation of Advanced Encryption Standard. IEEE Trans. on Computers 55(6), 720–731 (2006)
15. Di Natale, G., Flottes, M.L., Rouzeyre, B.: An On-Line Fault Detection Scheme for SBoxes in Secure Circuits. In: Proc. of 13th IEEE International On-Line Testing Symposium, IOLTS 2007, pp. 57–62 (2007)
16. Mozaffari Kermani, M., Reyhani-Masoleh, A.: Parity-Based Fault Detection Architecture of S-box for Advanced Encryption Standard. In: 21st IEEE Int. Symp. on Defect and Fault-Tolerance in VLSI Systems (DFT 2006), pp. 572–580 (2006)
17. Dusart, P., Letourneux, G., Vivolo, O.: Differential Fault Analysis on A.E.S. In: Zhou, J., Yung, M., Han, Y. (eds.) ACNS 2003. LNCS, vol. 2846, pp. 293–306. Springer, Heidelberg (2003)
18. Bosio, A., Di Natale, G.: LIFTING: a Flexible Open-Source Fault Simulator. In: Proc. of the IEEE Asian Test Symposium, pp. 35–40 (2008)
19. Wolkerstorfer, J., Oswald, E., Lamberger, M.: An ASIC Implementation of the AES SBoxes. In: Preneel, B. (ed.) CT-RSA 2002. LNCS, vol. 2271, pp. 67–78. Springer, Heidelberg (2002)

Design of Fractional Order Digital Differentiator Using Inverse Multiquadric Radial Basis Function

Nitin Kumar* and Tarun Kumar Rawat

Digital Signal Processing Group,
Division of Electronics and Communication Engineering,
Netaji Subhas Institute of Technology,
Dwarka Sector 3 , New Delhi 110075, India
tarundsp@gmail.com, nitinkumar2007@yahoo.co.in

Abstract. In this paper, a fractional order digital differentiator is designed by using Inverse multiquadric radial basis function (RBF). First, the RBF interpolation approach is described. Then, the non-integer delay sample estimation is derived by using RBF approach. Next, the Grünwald-Letnikov derivative and non-integer delay sample delay are applied to obtain the transfer function of the proposed method i.e. fractional order digital differentiator. The design accuracy of the proposed method is better then the conventional methods like examples Time domain least squares method, Fractional sample delay method and Frequency response approximation method.

Keywords: Digital differentiator, fractional derivative, non-integer delay, radial basis function.

1   Introduction

During the past three decades, fractional calculus has received a great deal of attention in many engineering applications and science including fluid flow, automatic control, electrical networks, electromagnetic theory and image processing [1]-[4]. Fractional dimension is used to measure some real-world data such as coastline, clouds dust in the air and network of neurons in the body [5]-[6]. We aim out interests at the digital realization of fractional derivative, which named as digital fractional order differentiator (FOD). Because digital FOD can determine and estimate the more characteristic of a given digital signal than integral order differentiator (IOD), it has been being an especial and useful tool in many increasing application, such as fractional order controls, radar and sonar processing, nonlinear or chaos time series processing and forecasting, geological signal detecting and processing, image processing etc. Fractional sample delay has become an important device in the applications of time adjustment in the digital receiver, antenna array processing, speech coding and synthesis, modelling of musical instrument, and comb-filter design etc [7]-[10].

---

* Corresponding author.

N. Meghanathan et al. (Eds.): CCSIT 2012, Part II, LNICST 85, pp. 32–49, 2012.

The integer order n of derivative $D^n f(x) = (d^n f(x)/dx^n)$ of function is generalized to fractional order $D^v f(x)$, where v is a real number. One of the important research topics in fractional calculus is to implement the fractional operator D^v in continuous and discrete time domain. An excellent survey of this implementation has been presented in [11]. Some techniques have been used already for the rational function approximation of continuous-time case i.e. curve fitting, evaluation and interpolation. These methods include Carlson's method, Roy's method, Chareff's method and Oustaloup's method [12]-[15]. For discrete-time case, there have been several methods presented to design finite-impulse-response (FIR) and infinite-impulse-response (IIR) filters for implementing operator D^v, including fractional differencing formula or Euler method, Tustin method, continued fraction method, least square method and Prony's method [16]-[22].

On the other hand, the radial basis function (RBF) has been widely used in multivariate interpolation, neural network, time series prediction, control of nonlinear systems, mesh-free approximation, and target tracking in voice data [23]-[26]. The early work has been done on the designing of fractional order differentiator using Gaussian radial basis function (RBF) [28]. But in this paper we are using Inverse multiquadric basis function (RBF). The theory and implementation of radial basis function(RBF) is surveyed in the book [27]. A radial basis function is defined as a real valued function $\phi(t)$, whose value depends only on the distance from the origin. The notation $|\cdot|$ denotes the absolute value. Generally the radial basis function are used i.e. Gaussian, Inverse multiquadric, Raised-Cosine.

$$Gaussian : \phi(t) = \exp -t^2/\sigma^2 \tag{1}$$

$$Inverse Multiquadric : \phi(t) = \sigma/\sqrt{t^2 + \sigma^2} \tag{2}$$

$$Raised - Cosine : \phi(t) = 1/2 * \sigma(1 + \cos(\pi * t/\sigma)) \tag{3}$$

where σ is known as the shape parameter, which is used to change the shape of function $\phi(t)$. The purpose of this paper is to use RBF interpolation approach to design the fractional order digital differentiator. The design error can be reduced using RBF interpolation approach by varying the shape parameter of radial basis function.

This paper is organized as follows: In section II, the radial basis interpolation method is described. By using the radial basis function interpolation the values of non-integer delay sample estimation of discrete-time sequence is obtained. In section III, apply the definition of fractional derivative i.e. Grünwald-Letnikov and non-integer delay sample estimation for obtaining the transfer function of fractional order differentiator. And, some numerical examples have given in this paper which show the effectiveness of this design approach. Finally, a conclusion is made.

2   Radial Basis Function

In this section the RBF interpolation method is first described [28]. Then, this interpolation method is applied to solve the non-integer delay sample estimation problem which is used in the design of fractional order differentiator in next section.

Radial Basis Function Interpolation The details of Radial basis function interpolation method can be found in [26]. Now this method is described briefly below: Given a set of N+1 different points $t_0, t_1, t_2, t_3, \cdots, t_N$ and a corresponding set of $N + 1$ real numbers $s_0, s_1, s_2, \cdots, s_N$, the interpolation problem is to find a function $s(t)$ that satisfies the interpolation condition

$$s(t_k) = s_k \qquad k = 0, 1, 2, \cdots, N \tag{4}$$

The RBF interpolation method consists of choosing a function $s(t)$ that has the following term

$$s(t) = \sum_{k=0}^{N} w_k \phi(\|(t - t_k)\|) \tag{5}$$

The above equation can be written in the matrix form as

$$\begin{bmatrix} \phi(\|(t_0 - t_0)\|) & \phi(\|(t_0 - t_1)\|) & \phi(\|(t_0 - t_2)\|) & \cdots & \phi(\|(t_0 - t_N)\|) \\ \phi(\|(t_1 - t_0)\|) & \phi(\|(t_1 - t_1)\|) & \phi(\|(t_1 - t_2)\|) & \cdots & \phi(\|(t_1 - t_N)\|) \\ \phi(\|(t_2 - t_0)\|) & \phi(\|(t_2 - t_1)\|) & \phi(\|(t_2 - t_2)\|) & \cdots & \phi(\|(t_2 - t_N)\|) \\ \vdots & \vdots & \vdots & \ddots & \vdots \\ \phi(\|(t_N - t_0)\|) & \phi(\|(t_N - t_1)\|) & \phi(\|(t_N - t_2)\|) & \cdots & \phi(\|(t_N - t_N)\|) \end{bmatrix} \begin{bmatrix} w_0 \\ w_1 \\ w_2 \\ \vdots \\ w_N \end{bmatrix} = \begin{bmatrix} s_0 \\ s_1 \\ s_2 \\ \vdots \\ s_N \end{bmatrix}$$

Function $s(t)$ represent a sum of $N+1$ radial basis function, each associated with a different center t_k and weighted coefficient is w_k. substituting interpolation condition of (4) into (5), we get the following simultaneous linear equation

$$\phi(\|(t_m - t_k)\|) = \phi_{mk}$$

$$\begin{bmatrix} \phi_{00} & \phi_{01} & \phi_{02} & \cdots & \phi_{0N} \\ \phi_{10} & \phi_{11} & \phi_{12} & \cdots & \phi_{1N} \\ \phi_{20} & \phi_{21} & \phi_{22} & \cdots & \phi_{2N} \\ \vdots & \vdots & \vdots & \ddots & \vdots \\ \phi_{N0} & \phi_{N1} & \phi_{N2} & \cdots & \phi_{NN} \end{bmatrix} \begin{bmatrix} w_0 \\ w_1 \\ w_2 \\ \vdots \\ w_N \end{bmatrix} = \begin{bmatrix} s_0 \\ s_1 \\ s_2 \\ \vdots \\ s_N \end{bmatrix} \tag{6}$$

Let vectors S and W be

$$S = \begin{bmatrix} s_0 & s_1 & s_2 & \cdots & s_N \end{bmatrix}^T \tag{7}$$

$$W = \begin{bmatrix} w_0 & w_1 & w_2 & \cdots & w_N \end{bmatrix}^T \tag{8}$$

Where φ denotes an $(N + 1) \times (N + 1)$ matrix with the element ϕ_{mk}, then (6) can be written as

$$\varphi W = S \tag{9}$$

if $t_0, t_1, t_2, t_3, \cdots, t_N$ are distinct points, then the matrix φ is non-singular matrix. Thus the unknown vector W is given by

$$W = \varphi^{-1}S \tag{10}$$

$s(t)$ is computable for the given t and it can be obtained only if the value of W is known.

2.1 Non-integer Delay Sample Estimation

In the following, we will use the RBF interpolation method to solve the non-integer delay sample estimation problem because the proposed fractional order differentiator design method is based on this estimation method. The problem to be studied is how to estimate the non-integer delay sample $s(n - d)$ from the given integer delay samples $s(n), s(n - 1), s(n - 2), \cdots, s(n - N)$, where N is an integer and d is a real number in the interval $d \in [0, N]$. In this paper we use weighted average approach that is to find the non-integer delay samples is estimated by

$$s(n - d) = \sum_{m=0}^{N} g(m, d)s(n - m) \tag{11}$$

Now, the remaining problem is how to use the RBF interpolation method to determine the weights $g(m, d)$. To solve this problem, let us choose $t_k = n - k$ and $s_k = s(n - k)$, then the RBF interpolation in (5) becomes

$$s(t) = \sum_{k=0}^{N} w_k \phi(|(t - t_k)|)$$

$$s(t) = \sum_{k=0}^{N} w_k \phi(|(t - (n - k))|) \tag{12}$$

Because $t_k = n - k$ and $t_m = n - m$, are chosen we have

$$\phi(|(t_m - t_k)|) = \phi(|k - m|) = \phi_{mk} \tag{13}$$

Using the above expression and $s_k = s(n - k)$, the new simultaneous linear equation in (6) reduces to

$$
\begin{bmatrix}
\phi(0) & \phi(1) & \phi(2) & \cdots & \phi(N) \\
\phi(1) & \phi(0) & \phi(1) & \cdots & \phi(N-1) \\
\phi(2) & \phi(1) & \phi(0) & \cdots & \phi(N-2) \\
\vdots & \vdots & \vdots & \ddots & \vdots \\
\phi(N) & \phi(N-1) & \phi(N-2) & \cdots & \phi(0)
\end{bmatrix}
\begin{bmatrix}
w_0 \\
w_1 \\
w_2 \\
\vdots \\
w_N
\end{bmatrix}
=
\begin{bmatrix}
s(n) \\
s(n-1) \\
s(n-2) \\
\vdots \\
s(n-N)
\end{bmatrix}
\tag{14}
$$

This equation can be shortened as the form of $\varphi W = S$ as described in (9). Clearly, φ is an Symmetric matrix and Toeplitz matrix. Let the inverse of matrix φ be denoted by

$$
\varphi^{-1} = \begin{bmatrix}
\alpha_{00} & \alpha_{01} & \alpha_{02} & \cdots & \alpha_{0N} \\
\alpha_{10} & \alpha_{11} & \alpha_{12} & \cdots & \alpha_{1N} \\
\alpha_{20} & \alpha_{21} & \alpha_{22} & \cdots & \alpha_{2N} \\
\vdots & \vdots & \vdots & \ddots & \vdots \\
\alpha_{N0} & \alpha_{N1} & \alpha_{N2} & \cdots & \alpha_{NN}
\end{bmatrix}
\tag{15}
$$

We know that, $W = \varphi^{-1}S$

$$
\begin{bmatrix}
w_0 \\ w_1 \\ w_2 \\ \vdots \\ w_N
\end{bmatrix} = \varphi^{-1}
\begin{bmatrix}
s(n) \\ s(n-1) \\ s(n-2) \\ \vdots \\ s(n-N)
\end{bmatrix} =
\begin{bmatrix}
\sum_{m=0}^{N} \alpha_{0m}s(n-m) \\
\sum_{m=0}^{N} \alpha_{1m}s(n-m) \\
\sum_{m=0}^{N} \alpha_{2m}s(n-m) \\
\vdots \\
\sum_{m=0}^{N} \alpha_{Nm}s(n-m)
\end{bmatrix}
\tag{16}
$$

Above expression implies that

$$
w_k = \sum_{m=0}^{N} \alpha_{km}s(n-m) \qquad k = 0,1,2,\cdots,N
\tag{17}
$$

substituting (17) into (12)

$$
s(t) = \sum_{k=0}^{N} w_k \phi(|(t-(n-k))|)
$$

$$
s(t) = \sum_{k=0}^{N} \left(\sum_{m=0}^{N} \alpha_{km}s(n-m) \right) \phi(|(t-(n-k))|)
$$

$$
s(t) = \sum_{m=0}^{N} \left(\sum_{k=0}^{N} \alpha_{km}\phi(|(t-(n-k))|) \right) s(n-m)
\tag{18}
$$

Taking $t = n - d$ for the expression in the discrete form

$$
s(n-d) = \sum_{m=0}^{N} \left(\sum_{k=0}^{N} \alpha_{km}\phi(|(k-d)|) \right) s(n-m)
\tag{19}
$$

After comparing the eq.(19) with (11),we get the weights g(m,d)

$$
g(m,d) = \sum_{k=0}^{N} \alpha_{km}\phi(|(k-d)|)
\tag{20}
$$

Finally, given the radial basis function $\phi(t)$ and estimate the non-integer delay sample $s(n - d)$ from the given integer delay samples $s(n), s(n - 1), s(n - 2), \cdots, s(n - N)$ is summarized below:

Step 1) Compute the matrix φ whose matrix elements are given by $\phi_{mk} = \phi(|k - m|)$.

Step 2) Calculate the inverse matrix φ^{-1} with element α_{km}.

Step 3) Use (20) to compute the weights g(m,d).

Step 4) The non-integer delayed sample is estimated by

$$s(n - d) = \sum_{m=0}^{N} g(m, d)s(n - m)$$

In the next section with the help RBF based non-integer delay estimation method to design the fractional order differentiator.

3   Design of Fractional Order Differentiator

In this section fractional derivative will be explained and then apply RBF based non-integer delay sample estimation method to obtain the transfer function of the fractional order differentiator.

3.1   Fractional Derivative

There are several definiton for fractional integral and fractional derivative to obtain the transfer function of the fractional order differentiator such as the Riemann-Liouville, the Grünwald-Letnikov and Caputo definitions [1]-[4]. But in this paper we will use the Grünwald-Letnikov definition which is given by

$$D^v s(t) = \lim_{h \to 0} \sum_{k=0}^{\infty} \frac{(-1)^k C_k^v}{h^v} s(t - kh) \tag{21}$$

Where coefficient C_k^v is given by

$$C_k^v = \frac{\Gamma(v+1)}{\Gamma(k+1)\Gamma(n-k+1)}$$

$$= \begin{cases} 1 & k = 0 \\ \frac{v(v-1)(v-2)\cdots(v-k+1)}{1.2.3\cdots k} & k \geq 1 \end{cases} \tag{22}$$

The above notation $\Gamma(.)$ is gamma function. Based on this definition, the fractional derivative of exponential and sinusoidal signals are given by

$$D^v e^{\alpha t} = \alpha^v e^{\alpha t} \tag{23}$$

$$D^v A \sin(wt + \phi) = Aw^v \cos(wt + \phi) = Aw^v \sin(wt + \phi + \frac{\pi}{2}v) \tag{24}$$

The fourier transform of $D^v s(t)$ is $(jw)^v S(w)$. This means that when a signal $s(t)$ passes through a differentiator with frequency response $(jw)^v$, then the output of the differentiator is the fractional derivative $D^v s(t)$. Thus the ideal frequency response of fractional order differentiator is $(jw)^v$. So we will use the Grünwald-Letnikov derivative method in (21) and RBF-based non-integer delay sample estimation method to design fractional order differentiator.

3.2   Design of Fractional Order Differentiator

Now we will use the RBF interpolation method and Grünwald-Letnikov derivative to design a fractional order digital differentiator that approximates the following frequency domain specification as well as possible:

$$H_d(w) = (jw)^v e^{-jwI} \tag{25}$$

Where I is a prescribed delay value. First, let us define coefficient $a(k)$ below

$$a(k) = (-1)^k C_k^v \tag{26}$$

Eq.(21) can be written as

$$D^v s(t) = \lim_{h \to 0} \sum_{k=0}^{\infty} \frac{(-1)^k C_k^v}{h^v} s(t - kh)$$

$$D^v s(t) = \lim_{h \to 0} \sum_{k=0}^{\infty} \frac{a(k)}{h^v} s(t - kh) \tag{27}$$

Fig.1 show the coefficient response of $a(k)$ for various order. Figure shows that $a(k)$ is rapidly decaying sequence for various order v. Thus after truncation the eq.(27) can be approximated by

$$D^v s(t) \approx \lim_{h \to 0} \sum_{k=0}^{L} \frac{a(k)}{h^v} s(t - kh) \tag{28}$$

Where L is the truncation length. Moreover by removing the limit, the $D^v s(t)$ can be approximated by

$$D^v s(t) \approx \sum_{k=0}^{L} \frac{a(k)}{h^v} s(t - kh) \tag{29}$$

Where h is the smaller and the better approximation in (29). By taking $t = n - I$, the discrete-time derivative signal $D^v s(n - I)$ can be obtained as

$$D^v s(n - I) \approx \sum_{k=0}^{L} \frac{a(k)}{h^v} s(n - I - kh) \tag{30}$$

because $s(n-I-kh)$ are non-integer delay samples of signal $s(n)$, the $s(n-I-kh)$ needs to be estimated by using the formula (11):

$$s(n - I - kh) = \sum_{m=0}^{N} g(m, I + kh)s(n - m) \tag{31}$$

Substitute the value of $s(n - I - kh)$ in eq.(30)

$$D^v s(n - I) \approx \sum_{k=0}^{L} \frac{a(k)}{h^v} \sum_{m=0}^{N} g(m, I + kh)s(n - m)$$

$$D^v s(n - I) = \sum_{m=0}^{N} \left[\frac{1}{h^v} \sum_{k=0}^{L} a(k)g(m, I + kh) \right] s(n - m) \tag{32}$$

Defining the coefficients

$$b(m) = \frac{1}{h^v} \sum_{k=0}^{L} a(k)g(m, I + kh) \tag{33}$$

then eq.(32) can be written as

$$D^v s(n - I) \approx \sum_{m=0}^{N} b(m)s(n - m)$$

$$D^v s(n - I) = b(n) * s(n) \tag{34}$$

Where $*$ denotes the convolution sum operator. Taking the z-transform at both sides of eq.(34), we get

$$Y(z) = \left(\sum_{m=0}^{N} b(m)z^{-m} \right) S(z) \tag{35}$$

$Y(z)$ is the z-transform of $D^v s(n-I)$ using the property of z-transform and $S(z)$ is the z-transform of $s(n)$.

The definition of FIR filter can be defined as

$$B(z) = \sum_{m=0}^{N} b(m)z^{-m} \tag{36}$$

Ideally the frequency response of FIR filter is $(jw)^v e^{-jwI}$ and eq.(36) show the transfer function of fractional order digital differentiator. Now, given the radial basis function $\phi(t)$ with shape parameter σ, integer N, fractional order v, delay I, integer L and small positive number h, the procedure to design fractional order digital differentiator $B(z)$ is summarized below:

Step 1) Compute the matrix φ whose elements are given by $\phi_{mk} = \phi(|k-m|)$.
Step 2) Calculate the inverse matrix φ^{-1} with element α_{nm}.
Step 3) Use (20) to compute the weights

$$g(m, I + kh) = \sum_{n=0}^{N} \alpha_{nm}\phi(|n - I - kh|).$$

Step 4) Compute the coefficient of $a(k)$ by using (26).
Step 5) Use (33) to calculate the coefficients of $b(m)$.
Step 6) The transfer function of the designed fractional order differentiator is given by $B(z) = \sum_{m=0}^{N} b(m)z^{-m}$.

Finally, some remarks are made follows: First, a large integer L needs to be chosen for reducing errors which occur in (28). Second, a smaller positive number h needs to be chosen for reducing the approximation error which occur in (29). Third, if N is large, the designed fractional order digital differentiator is a long FIR filter. To reduce the calculation complexity and implementation complexity the Prony Method in [30] can be used to approximate the long-length FIR filter B(z) by an IIR filter below

$$\bar{B}(z) = \frac{\sum_{n=0}^{N_1} b_1(n)z^{-n}}{1 + \sum_{n=1}^{N_1} b_2(n)z^{-n}} \qquad (37)$$

The coefficient of $b_1(n)$ and $b_2(n)$ can be obtained by putting $B(Z)$ equal to the $\bar{B}(z)$, then we get an expression.

$$\left(\sum_{m=0}^{N} b(m)z^{-m}\right)\left(1 + \sum_{n=1}^{N_1} b_2(n)z^{-n}\right) = \sum_{n=0}^{N_1} b_1(n)z^{-n}$$

$$\left(\sum_{m=0}^{N} b(m)z^{-m}\right) + \left(\sum_{m=0}^{N}\sum_{n=1}^{N_1} b(m)b_2(n)z^{-n}z^{-m}\right) = \sum_{n=0}^{N_1} b_1(n)z^{-n} \qquad (38)$$

Using the convolution operator, this equation reduces to

$$b(n) + \sum_{k=1}^{N_1} b_2(k)b(n-k) = \begin{cases} b_1(n) & 0 \le n \le N_1 \\ 0 & N_1 + 1 \le n \le N \end{cases} \qquad (39)$$

The above first $N_1 + 1$ equalities can be written in matrix form as

$$\begin{bmatrix} b(0) & 0 & 0 & \cdots & 0 \\ b(0) & b(0) & 0 & \cdots & 0 \\ b(2) & b(1) & b(0) & \cdots & 0 \\ \vdots & \vdots & \vdots & \ddots & \vdots \\ b(N_1) & b(N_1 - 1) & b(N_1 - 2) & \cdots & b(0) \end{bmatrix} \begin{bmatrix} 1 \\ b_2(1) \\ b_2(2) \\ \vdots \\ b_2(N_1) \end{bmatrix} = \begin{bmatrix} b_1(0) \\ b_1(1) \\ b_1(2) \\ \vdots \\ b_1(N_1)) \end{bmatrix} \qquad (40)$$

Eq.(39) for $N_1 + 1 \leq n \leq N$ can be written in matrix form as

$$
\begin{bmatrix}
b(N_1) & b(N_1 - 1) & b(N_1 - 2) & \cdots & b(1) \\
b(N_1 + 1) & b(N_1) & b(N_1 - 1) & \cdots & b(2) \\
b(N_1 + 2) & b(N_1 + 1) & b(N_1) & \cdots & b(3) \\
& \vdots & & & \\
b(N - 1) & b(N - 2) & b(N - 3) & \cdots & b(N - N_1)
\end{bmatrix}
\begin{bmatrix}
b_2(1) \\
b_2(2) \\
b_2(3) \\
\vdots \\
b_2(N_1)
\end{bmatrix}
= -
\begin{bmatrix}
b(N_1 + 1) \\
b(N_1 + 2) \\
b(N_1 + 3) \\
\vdots \\
b(N)
\end{bmatrix}
\quad (41)
$$

In the Prony method, we assume that $N > 2N_1 + 1$. Thus from the eq.(41) we can get the coefficient of $b_2(n)$ using least square method. Once the $b_2(n)$ obtained then we can obtained the coefficient of $b_1(n)$ from the eq.(40). Under the condition $N > 2N_1 + 1$, we prefer to choose a large N_1 for reducing the error. The complexity of IIR filter implementation $B(z)$ will be increased as increasing the order N_1. So N_1 must be chosen by considering the trade-off between the error and complexity. In our experience N_1 must be chosen in the interval $[5, 20]$.

4   Design Example

In this subsection we will study about the design error and compare the performance of RBF-based fractional order digital differentiator with conventional methods. To evaluate the performance of the RBF, the least squares error of frequency response is defined by

$$
E = \sqrt{\int_0^{\lambda\pi} |B(e^{jw}) - H_d(w)|^2 dw} \quad (42)
$$

The smaller the error E is, the better performance of the design method has.

Example 1: In this example, we will study the magnitude and phase response for the Gaussian radial basis function $\phi(t)$ in (1). The design parameters are chosen as $N = 60$, $I = 30$, $L = 620$, $h = 0.05$, and $\lambda = 0.9$. Moreover, Fig. 2(a),(b) show the magnitude and phase responses (solid line) for the Gaussian with $\sigma = 2.3$ and order $v = 0.5$. In Fig. 2(a) the dashed line show the ideal magnitude response w^v. Fig. 2(b) show the phase response $90 * [angle B(e^{jw}) + wI]/0.5\pi$. In Fig. 2(b) the dashed line show the ideal phase response $90v$.

Example 2: In this example, we will study the magnitude and phase response for the Inverse multiquadric radial basis function $\phi(t)$ in (2). The design parameters are chosen as $N = 60$, $I = 30$, $L = 620$, $h = 0.05$, and $\lambda = 0.9$. Moreover, Fig. 3(a),(b) show the magnitude and phase responses (solid line) for the Inverse multiquadric with $\sigma = 6.4$ and order $v = 0.5$. In Fig. 3(a) the dashed line show the ideal magnitude response w^v. Fig. 3(b) show the phase response $90 * [angle(B(e^{jw})) + wI]/0.5\pi$. In Fig. 3(b) the dashed line show the ideal phase response $90v$.

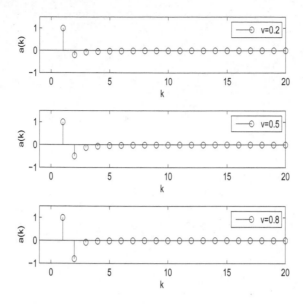

Fig. 1. The coefficient sequence $a(k)$ for various order v

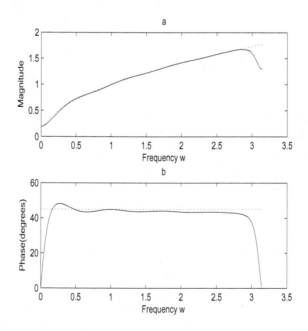

Fig. 2. (a) Magnitude response. (b) Phase response. Solid line show the designed results and dashed line show the ideal response for Gaussian RBF.

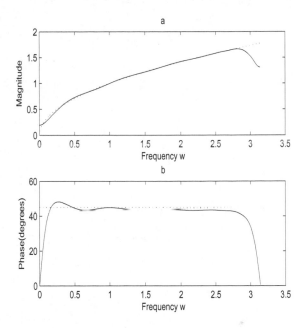

Fig. 3. (a)Magnitude response. (b) Phase response. Solid line show the designed results and dashed line show the ideal response for Inverse multiquadric RBF.

Example 3: In this example, let us compare the proposed method with the conventional time domain least-squares method in [20] whose design procedure is described below:

Step 1) Expand the fractional order Tustin differentiator $[U(z)]^v$ in [20] as the following power series form:

$$[U(z)]^v = \left(2\frac{1 - z^{-1}}{1 + z^{-1}} \right)^v$$

$$[U(z)]^v = 2^v \left[\sum_{k=0}^{\infty} C_k^v (-z^{-1})^k \right] \left[\sum_{k=0}^{\infty} C_k^{-v} z^{-k} \right]$$

$$[U(z)]^v = 2^v \left(1 + \sum_{k=1}^{\infty} u(k) z^{-k} \right)$$

Where filter coefficient $u(k)$ is the convolution sum of $(-1)^k C_k^v$ and C_k^{-v}. After truncating the higher order terms, $[U(z)]^v$ can be approximated by FIR filter

$$\bar{U}(z) = 2^v \left(1 + \sum_{k=1}^{N_c} u(k) z^{-k} \right) \tag{43}$$

Where N_c is the truncation length.

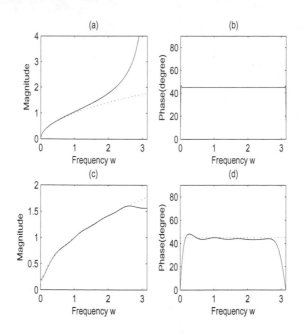

Fig. 4. Solid line show the designed results of fractional order IIR differentiator (a), (b) The results of $\hat{U}(z)$ in conventional method (c), (d) The results of $\bar{B}(z)$ in proposed method. The dashed line is the ideal response.

Step 2) Using the Prony method, the long-length FIR filter $\bar{U}(z)$ can be approximated by IIR filter:

$$\hat{U}(z) = \frac{\sum_{n=0}^{N_2} u_1(n)z^{-n}}{1 + \sum_{n=1}^{N_2} u_2(n)z^{-n}} \tag{44}$$

$$\hat{U}(z) = \bar{U}(z)$$

$$2^v \left[u(n) + \sum_{k=1}^{N_2} u_2(n)u(n-k) \right] = \begin{cases} u_1(n) & 0 \le n \le N_2 \\ 0 & N_2 + 1 \le n \le N \end{cases} \tag{45}$$

Now, one example is used to compare this conventional design method with the proposed design method in (37). The parameters in conventional design are chosen as $N_c = 60$, $N_2 = 10$, $v = 0.5$. Fig. 4(a),(b) show the magnitude and phase response (solid line) of the designed differentiator $\hat{U}(z)$. The dashed line is the ideal response. The maximum pole radius is 0.9719, so IIR filter $\hat{U}(z)$ is stable. From this result the error of phase is very small. But the magnitude error at high frequency band is very large. After $B(e^{jw})$ in (42) is changed to $\hat{U}(e^{jw})$, the error with $\lambda = 0.9$ is 13.6095 for this traditional design. For comparison, the designed result of proposed RBF method are reported below. The design

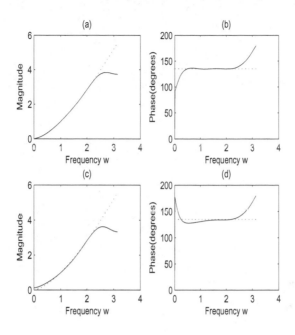

Fig. 5. The designed results (Solid line) of the fractional order FIR differentiator. (a), (b) The results of the method in [21]. (c), (d) The results of the proposed method. The dashed line is the ideal response.

parameter are chosen as $N = 60$, $I = 9$, $L = 620$, $h = 0.05$, $N_1 = 10$, $v = 0.5$ and Inverse Multiquadric RBF with $\sigma = 6.4$. Fig. 4(c),(d) show the magnitude and phase response (solid line) for the designed IIR differentiator $\bar{B}(z)$ in (37). The dashed line is the ideal response. Compared Fig. 4(a), (b) and Fig. 4(c), (d), it can be observed that the proposed RBF method has better magnitude response than conventional method. However, the phase response error of conventional approach is smaller than the proposed method. After $B(e^{jw})$ in (42) is changed to $\bar{B}(e^{jw})$, the error E with $\lambda = 0.9$ is 2.7449 for the proposed RBF design. Thus, the above result show that the proposed method has smaller error than the conventional method.

Example 4: In this example, let us compare the proposed method with the conventional method in [21] where fractional order FIR differentiator has been designed by using frequency response approximation approach.

The transfer function for the frequency response approximation is given as

$$H(e^{jw}) = \sum_{m=0}^{N} a(m) \cos mw + j \sum_{m=0}^{N} b(m) \sin mw, \qquad w \in [-\pi, \pi]$$

$$H(z) = \sum_{m=0}^{N} \frac{a(m)}{2} \left(z^m + z^{-m}\right) + \sum_{m=0}^{N} \frac{b(m)}{2} \left(z^m - z^{-m}\right)$$

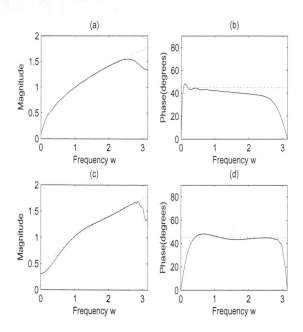

Fig. 6. The designed results (solid line) of the fractional order FIR differentiator. (a), (b) The results of the fractional delay method in [22]. (c), (d) The results of the proposed method. The dashed line is the ideal response.

$$H(z) = a(0) + \sum_{m=1}^{N} \frac{a(m) + b(m)}{2} z^m + \sum_{m=1}^{N} \frac{a(m) - b(m)}{2} z^{-m}$$

When the design parameters are chosen as $N = 10$, $I = 5$ and $v = 1.5$, the FIR filter coefficient $b(m)$ in (33) can be obtained from the data in column 3 of Table 1 of [21]. Fig. 5(a),(b) show the magnitude and phase response (solid line) of this conventional method. The dashed is the ideal response. For comparison under the same implementation complexity, the design parameters of the proposed method are chosen as $N = 10$, $I = 5$, $v = 1.5$, $L = 620$, $h = 0.01$ and Inverse multiquadric RBF with $\sigma = 6.4$. Fig. 5(c),(d) show the magnitude and phase responses (solid line) for the designed FIR differentiator $B(z)$ in (36). The dashed line is the ideal response. Now the error comparison is made. If $\lambda = 0.72$ is chosen, the error E of conventional method in [21] is 0.019 and the error E of proposed method is 0.0198. Thus, the results show that the error is approximately equal to the conventional method in the frequency band $[0, 0.72\pi]$. When $\lambda = 0.9$ is chosen, the error E of the conventional design method is 0.623, and the error E of the proposed RBF design method is 0.565. Thus, the above result show that the proposed method has smaller error than conventional method in the frequency band $[0, 0.9\pi]$.

Example 5: In this example, we will compare the proposed method with the conventional fractional delay method in [22].

$$G(z) = \sum_{k=0}^{N} \alpha(k) z^{-(I_k + f_k)}$$

$$G(z) = \sum_{k=0}^{N} \alpha(k) \left[\sum_{n=0}^{2I_k} \left(\prod_{m=0, m \neq n}^{2I_k} \frac{I_k + f_k - m}{n - m} \right) z^{-n} \right]$$

When the design parameters are chosen as $N = 80$, $I = 20$ and $v = 0.5$, the conventional fractional order FIR differentiator is designed by Lagrange fractional delay method used in Fig. 4 of [22]. Fig. 6(a),(b) show the designed results (solid line) of this method. The dashed line is the ideal response. It can be seen that the phase response does not fit the ideal response well. Moreover, the design parameters of the proposed method are chosen as $N = 80$, $I = 20$, $v = 0.5$, $L = 620$, $h = 0.02$ and the Inverse multiquadric RBF with $\sigma = 6.4$. Fig. 6(c),(d) show the magnitude and phase response (solid line) for the designed fractional order FIR differentiator. The dashed line is the ideal response. If $\lambda = 0.9$ is chosen, the error E of conventional fractional delay method in [22] is 0.2587, and the error E of proposed RBF method is 0.0316. Thus, the above result shows that the proposed method has a smaller error than the conventional method.

5   Conclusion

In this paper, an fractional order digital differentiator has been designed by using Inverse multiquadric radial basis function (RBF). First, the RBF interpolation approach is described. Then, the non-integer delay sample estimation is derived by using RBF approach. Next, the Grünwald-Letnikov derivative and non-integer delay sample delay are applied to obtain the transfer function of the proposed method i.e. fractional order digital differentiator. The design accuracy of the proposed method is better then the conventional methods like examples Time domain least squares method, Fractional sample delay method and Frequency response approximation method. However, only the one-dimensional case is studied here. Thus, it is interesting to extend the proposed method to design a two-dimensional fractional order digital differentiator in the future.

References

[1] K. B. Oldham and J. Spanier: The Fractional Calculus. New York: Academic Press, (1974).
[2] K. S. Miller and R. Ross: An Introduction to the Fractional Calculus and Fractional Differential Equations. New York: Wiley, (1993).
[3] I. Podlubny: Fractional Differential Equations. San Diego, CA: Academic, (1999).
[4] M. D. Ortigueira: Fractional central differences and derivatives. J. Vibration and Control. vol. 14, no. 9-10, pp. 1255–1266, (2008).
[5] M. F. Barnsley: SuperFractals. Cambridge, U.K.: Cambridge Univ. Press, (2006).

[6] H. O. Peitgen, H. Jurgens, and D. Saupe: Chaos and Fractals, New Frontiers of Science. 2nd ed. New York: Springer-Verlag, (2004).

[7] T. I. Laakso, V. Valimaki, M. Karjalainen, and U. K. Laine, Splitting the unit delay: Tool for fractional delay filter design. IEEE Signal Processing Mag. pp. 30–60, Jan. (1996).

[8] S. C. Pei and C. C. Tseng: A Comb Filter Design Using Fractional Sample Delay. IEEE Trans. Circuits Syst. II: Analog Digit. Signal Process. vol. 45, pp. 649–653, Jun. (1998).

[9] T. B. Deng: Symmetric structures for odd-order maximally flat and weighted-least-squares variable fractional-delay filters. IEEE Trans. Circuits Syst. I: Reg. Papers. vol. 54, pp. 2718–2732, Dec. (2007).

[10] J. J. Shyu, S. C. Pei, and Y. D. Huang: Two-dimensional Farrow structure and the design of variable fractional-delay 2-D FIR digital filters. IEEE Trans. Circuits Syst. I: Reg. Papers, vol. 56, pp. 395–404, Feb. (2009).

[11] B. M. Vinagre, I. Podlubny, A. Hernandez, and V. Feliu: Some approximations of fractional order operators used in control theory and applications.: J. Frac. Calculus Appl. Analysis. vol. 4, pp. 47–66, (2001).

[12] G. E. Carlson and C. A. Halijak: Approximation of fractional capacitors $(1/s)^{1/n}$ by a regular Newton process. IRE Trans. Circuit Theory. vol. 11, pp. 210–213, (1964).

[13] S. C. D. Roy: On the realization of a constant-argument immitance of fractional operator. IRE Trans. Circuit Theory. vol. 14, pp. 264–274, (1967).

[14] A. Chareff, H. H. Sun, Y. Y. Tsao, and B. Onaral: Fractal system as represented by singularity function. IEEE Trans. Autom. Contr., vol. 37, pp. 1465–1470, Sep. (1992).

[15] A. Oustaloup, F. Levron, B. Mathieu, and F. M. Nanot, :Frequency- band complex noninteger differentiator: Characterization and synthesis. IEEE Trans. Circuits Syst. I, Fundam. Theory Applicat. vol. 47, pp. 25–39, Jan. (2000).

[16] C. C. Tseng: Design of fractional order digital FIR differentiators. IEEE Signal Process. Lett., vol. 8, pp. 77–79, Mar. (2001).

[17] Y. Q. Chen and K. L. Moore: Discrete schemes for fractional-order differentiators and integrators. IEEE Trans. Circuits Syst. I, Fundam. Theory Applicat., vol. 49, pp. 363–367, (2002).

[18] Y. Q. Chen and B. M. Vinagre: A new IIR-type digital fractional order differentiator. Signal Processing, vol. 83, pp. 2359–2365, (2003).

[19] J. A. T. Machado, A. M. Galhano, A. M. Oliveira, and J. K. Tar: Approximating fractional derivatives through the generalized mean. Communications in Nonlinear Science and Numerical Simulation. vol. 14, pp. 3723–3730, Nov. (2009).

[20] R. S. Barbosa, J. A. T. Machado, and M. F. Silva: Time Domain Design Of Fractional Differintegrators Using Least-Squares. Signal Processing. vol. 86, pp. 2567–2581, (2006).

[21] H. Zhao, G. Qiu, L. Yao, and J. Yu: Design Of Fractional Order Digital FIR differentiators using frequency response approximation. in Proc. 2005 Int. Conf. Communications, Circuits and Systems. May (2005), pp. 1318–1321.

[22] C. C. Tseng: Improved design of digital fractional-order differentiators using fractional sample delay. IEEE Trans. Circuits Syst. I: Reg. Papers. vol. 53, pp. 193–203. Jan. (2006).

[23] A. Neumaier : Introduction to Numerical Analysis. Cambridge, U.K.: Cambridge Univ. Press, (2001).

[24] G. E. Fasshauer. Meshfree Approximation Methods With MATLAB. Singapore: World Scientific, (2007).

[25] J. Madapura and B. Li : Multi-target tracking based on KLD mixture particle filter with radial basis function support. In Proc. ICASSP, Apr. (2008), pp. 725–728.

[26] S. Haykin : Neural Networks and Learning Machines. 3rd ed. New York: Pearson Education, (2009).

[27] M. D. Buhmann : Radial Basis Functions. Theory and Implementations. Cambridge, U.K.: Cambridge Univ. Press, (2003).

[28] Chien-Cheng Tseng and Su-Ling Lee : Design Of Fractional Order Digital Differentiator Using Radial Basis Function : IEEE Trans. Circuits Syst. I: Reg. Papers, pp. 1–11, Jul. (2010).

[29] L.B. Jackson : Digital Filters and Signal Processing. 3rd ed. Boston, MA : Kluwer Academic, (1996).

Cognitive Symmetric Key Cryptographic Algorithm

Y.R.A. Kannan, S. Aravind Prasad, and P. Varalakshmi

Department of Information Technology,
Madras Institute of Technology, Chrompet,
Chennai, 600044
{yra.kannan,raja.avi,varanip}@gmail.com

Abstract. Today, Cryptographic schemes play a major role in storage, retrieval and transfer of data and code in a secured manner. The major factors which determine the efficiency of a cryptographic system are computational speed, level of security provided, cost effectiveness and key size of the algorithm. Choosing the optimal bit size for keys in encryption and decryption algorithm is necessary for the efficient computation of the algorithm and bit size of the key is directly proportional to the complexity of the algorithm and in turn cost of the encryption and decryption algorithm. In this paper, we propose a novel cost-effective small key size symmetric key algorithm which is suitable to all sizes of data and all kinds of data such as audio and video because of its low key size and high computational speed.

Keywords: Key size, Computational speed, Encryption algorithm, Decryption algorithm, Symmetric key algorithm.

1   Introduction

In today's world, data security plays a prominent role in all areas and with latest advancements in the fields of data storage and processing speeds, the focus towards security is even more increased. Basically cryptography is the way of transforming the ordinary data or information into meaningless information in order to maintain the secrecy of its contents. Usually the type of data being dealt with, determines the type of security model to be used for it. Conversion of plain text to cipher text is referred to as Encryption and vice versa is termed as Decryption. Usually the major security goals to be satisfied are *Availability, Confidentiality* and *Integrity*.

The most prominent factor in any cryptographic algorithm is the key size which in turn influences computational speed and level of security provided. As the key size is directly proportional to the complexity of the algorithm, we make use of 4-bit size key which can be used to all sizes of data and all kinds of data such as audio and video because of its low key size and high computational speed.

This paper is organized as follows. The proposed algorithm is given in section 2 and the performance analysis of our algorithm compared with the existing algorithms is done at section 3. Related work is described in section 4. Finally conclusions are drawn in section 5.

N. Meghanathan et al. (Eds.): CCSIT 2012, Part II, LNICST 85, pp. 50–60, 2012.
© Institute for Computer Sciences, Social Informatics and Telecommunications Engineering 2012

2   Proposed Mechanism

In our proposed algorithm, dynamic 4-bit key size and different 4-bit keys are used for different characters in the plain text. Cognitive Symmetric key Cryptographic algorithm (CSCA) can encrypt and decrypt the large data since there will be no increase in key size. Even though any one key is identified in CSCA, other keys cannot be identified because of using different 4-bit keys for different characters rather than choosing only one 4-bit key and adding one to that initial key. Security is also enhanced in CSCA by encrypting secret key by using 4-bit shared key which should be shared securely via Authentication center between the two parties. In order to extract the secret plain text from the cipher text, first the secret key has to be decrypted by using shared key and then the character should be decrypted by using that secret key. In CSCA after decrypting all the characters, plain text will be found.

2.1   Dynamic 4-Bit Secret Key

Choosing the optimal bit size for keys in encryption and decryption algorithm is necessary for the efficient computation of the algorithm. If the bit size of the key is very large, the complexity of the algorithm is increased. This also increases the cost of the encryption and decryption algorithm. In many encryption and decryption algorithms the key size is very large. In [1], the dynamic 4-bit key is used for encryption and decryption for small amount of data. In our proposed algorithm, 4-bit key size is used for encryption as well as decryption. 4-bit Randomizer is used in our algorithm which returns the random value from 10 to 15 i.e. from 1000 to 1111 for encrypting the characters and same key has to be used for decryption since it is a symmetric algorithm. So only 4-bit key size is used throughout the algorithm but different keys are used for characters in the plain text by using 4-bit Randomizer. Hence, our proposed algorithm is used to encrypt and decrypt the large amount of data with small key size in efficient and secured manner.

2.2   4-Bit Shared Key

In order to increase the security 4-bit shared key can be introduced. This key has to be shared between sender and receiver of the data in a secured manner via an Authentication center. The shared key is also 4-bit key. This key is any value between 1000 to 1111 which is chosen by 4-bit Randomizer in Authentication center. This shared key is used to encrypt and decrypt the secret key by using the proposed encryption and decryption algorithm for encrypting and decrypting the keys. Introduction of the 4-bit shared key increases the security and efficiency of our algorithm.

2.3   Encryption Technique

In this technique first the key generated from the 4-bit Randomizer is used to encrypt the first character in the Plain text. Since the 4-bit shared key is constant throughout the encryption and decryption technique consider it as n_1. Then the shared key is used to encrypt the secret key.

CSCA is used to encrypt the data with the 4-bit secret key which is given in Fig 1.

Step1 : 4-bit Randomizer generates a key value that varies between 10 to 15 and considers it as n.

Step2 : Convert the generated value into binary value in 4 bits which is the secret key for encrypting a character.

Step3 : Compute the ASCII value for the character in the plain text and convert ASCII value into binary representation in 8 bits.

Step4 : Perform left circular shift operation for n (the value generated in Step1) times on the binary representation of ASCII value.

Step5 : Divide the result from step 4 by the secret key.

Step6 : Represent the remainder in first four bits and quotient in the last five bits which gives 9-Bit cipher text for the character.

Step7 : Represent the 4-bit key in 8 bits.

Step8 : Perform left circular shift operation for n_1 times on these bits.

Step9 : Divide these bits with the 4-bit shared key.

Step10: Represent the remainder in first four bits and quotient in the last five bits which gives 9-Bit cipher text for the secret key.

Step11: Form 18-Bit cipher text by using 9-Bit cipher text for secret key and 9-Bit cipher text for the character.

Repeat the above steps for encrypting each character in the plain text. If P is the plain text, Ch_1 is the first character, Ch_2 is the second character then C_1 is 9-bit cipher text for Ch_1 encrypted with key K_1 and C_2 is 9-bit cipher text for Ch_2 encrypted with key K_2. EK_1 is 9-bit cipher text for K_1 encrypted with Shared key and EK_2 is 9-bit cipher text for K_2 encrypted with Shared key. The pattern of the resultant Cipher text from this Encryption Technique for Plain Text P will be $EK_1C_1EK_2C_2EK_3C_3EK_4C_4...$

Fig. 1. CSCA for Encryption

2.3.1 Flowchart

The flowchart for Cognitive Symmetric Key Encryption Algorithm for Encryption is given in Fig 2.

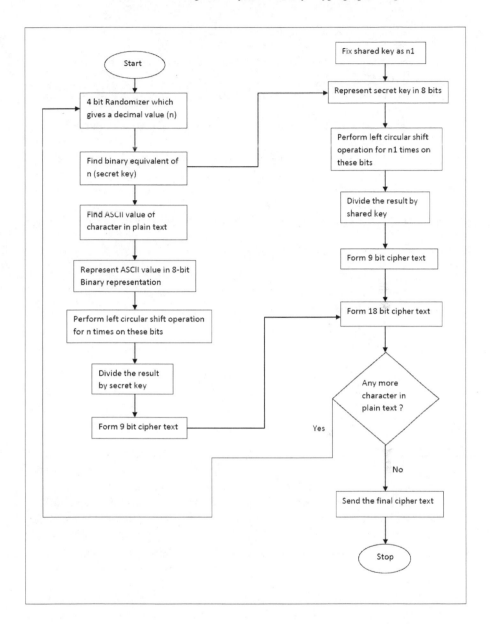

Fig. 2. Encryption Technique in CSCA

2.3.1 Case Study

Let us consider the plain text as "HI". The encryption technique has to be done for each and every character in the plain text individually. First we will consider the character H in plain text HI. Let us consider shared key as 1010 i.e. 10 (n_1).

Step1 : Let say 4-bit Randomizer generates the value 1000.
Step2 : Decimal value of 1000 is 8 and considers it as n.
Step3 : ASCII value for H is 72 and 8-bit binary representation for 72 is
          01001000.
Step4 : Perform left circular shift on 01001000 for n times i.e. 8 times which
          gives the result as 01001000.
Step5 : Divide 01001000 by secret key 1000. Quotient is 01001 and the
          remainder is 0.
Step6 : The 9-Bit cipher text is 000001001.
Step7 : 8-bit representation of secret key is 00001000.
Step8 : Perform the left circular operation on 00001000 for n_1 times i.e. 10 times
          which gives the result as 00100000.
Step9 : Divide 00100000 by shared key 1010. Quotient is 00011 and remainder is
          0010.
Step10: The 9-Bit cipher text is 001000011.
18-Bit Cipher Text for the character H: 001000011000001001.

Let us consider the secret key for I is 1011. Then Final Cipher text for the text "HI" is
001000011000001001010000100100000110.

2.4   Decryption Technique

In this technique first the secret key has to be decrypted from the 9-bit cipher text by
using the shared key then the character has to be decrypted by using the respective
secret key.

Reverse of CSCA is used to decrypt the characters in the plain text from cipher
text.

Step1: Extract 18 bit cipher text from the received bits and extract the quotient and
       remainder from the first 9-bit cipher text for finding the secret key.
Step2: Multiply the quotient with the shared key and add it with the remainder.
Step3: Perform the right circular shift operation for n_1 times on these bits and this
       computes the secret key.
Step4: Compute the decimal value for the secret key and consider it as n_2.
Step5: Extract the quotient and remainder from the next 9-bit cipher text for
       finding the character.
Step6: Multiply the quotient with the secret key and add it with the remainder.
Step7: Perform the right circular shift operation for n_2 times on these bits and
       compute the decimal value.
Step8: Find the secret character based on its ASCII equivalent.
The above steps have to be repeated until all the secret characters in the plain text
are found.

Fig. 3. CSCA for Decryption

2.4.1 Flowchart

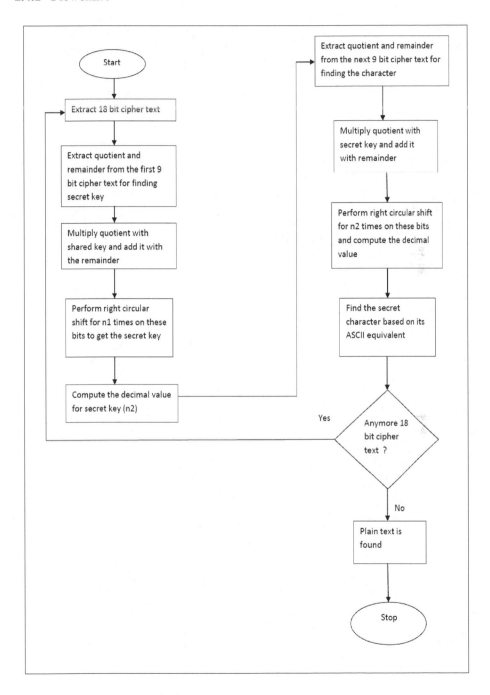

Fig. 4. Decryption Technique in CSCA

2.4.2 Case Study

Let us consider for the decryption of character H. The Cipher text for H is 001000011011100001.

Step1: Quotient and remainder are extracted from first 9 bits as 00011 and 0010.

Step2: Multiply 00011 with shared key 1010 and add it with remainder 0010 and this gives the result as 100000.

Step3: Perform right circular operation on 00100000 for n_1 times i.e. 10 times which gives the secret key as 1000.

Step4: Decimal value for 1000 is 8 and considers it as n_2.

Step5: Quotient and remainder are extracted from next 9 bits as 01001 and 0.

Step6: Multiply 01001 with 1000 and add it with 0 which gives the result as 01001000.

Step7: Perform right circular operation on 00001111 for n_2 times i.e. 8 times which gives the result as 01001000.

Step8: Decimal value for 01001000 is 72 and the corresponding character based on ASCII equivalent "H" is found.

Similarly the character "I" is found by using this decryption technique to get the plain text "HI".

3   Performance Evaluation

In this section, we show performance evaluation of the proposed Cognitive Symmetric Key Cryptographic Algorithm (CSCA) compared to the various existing Algorithms. For our simulations, we made use of Crypto++ tool.

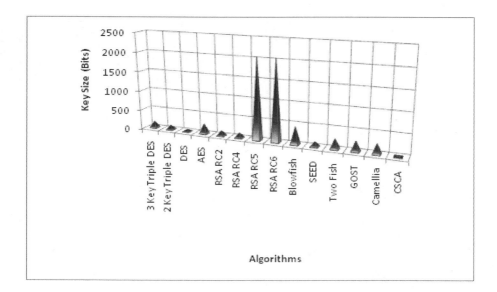

Fig. 5. Key sizes of Algorithms

Fig 5 provides the visual representation of various cryptographic algorithms with different key sizes and clearly depicts the low and effective key size of our proposed algorithm. With larger key sizes, the complexity increases and leads to decrease in cost effectiveness and computational speed of the encryption and decryption processes of the entire message.

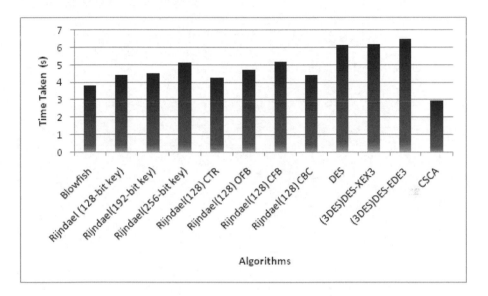

Fig. 6. Time consumption of various Algorithms

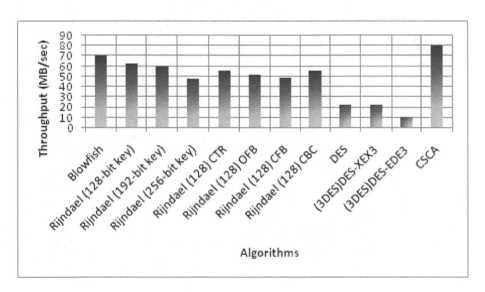

Fig. 7. Throughput for different Algorithms

Fig 6 shows the time consumed by various algorithms. It has to be noted that our algorithm occupies the lowest position among all existing algorithms. Again with the low time consumption, our proposed algorithm performs better than almost all existing algorithms. In the above figure, CTR, OFB, CFB and CBC represent Counter mode, Output Feedback Mode, Cipher Feedback Mode and Chain Block Chaining Mode respectively. Time consumption of operations performed in CSCA is low when compared to other algorithms as shown in Fig 6.

Fig 7 provides the comparison of throughputs of various existing algorithms and with the higher throughput and clearly our algorithm proves to be highly cost-effective and faster when compared to other algorithms.

Table 1. Megabytes processed for various algorithms using Crypto++ tool for Performance evaluation

Algorithm	Megabytes processed	Time consumed	Key size
Blowfish	256	3.79	32 up to 448 bits
Rijndael (128-bit key)	256	4.41	128
Rijndael (192-bit key)	256	4.52	192
Rijndael (256-bit key)	256	5.1	256
Rijndael (128) CTR	256	4.26	128
Rijndael (128) OFB	256	4.71	128
Rijndael (128) CFB	256	5.2	128
Rijndael (128) CBC	256	4.4	128
DES	128	6.123	40/56
CSCA	256	2.97	4

4   Related Work

The two techniques used for cryptography are symmetric and asymmetric cryptographic techniques. Symmetric key encryption is simple, fast and most commonly used. In this technique, same key has to be used for encryption and decryption and so this key has to be shared between the two parties in secured manner. In asymmetric cryptographic technique, two different keys are used for encryption and decryption. Some examples of symmetric key algorithms are DES, RC4, AES, Blowfish, IDEA. According to the symmetric algorithm proposed in [1], 4-bit key size is used for encryption and decryption. In [1], the initial key is chosen as any value from 1000 to 1111 for encrypting and decrypting the first character. For remaining characters in the plain text, the secret key is increased by 1 from the initial value. I.e. If the initial key is 1000 then the keys for the remaining characters will be 1001, 1010, 1011, 1101, 1110, 1111, 10000... Because of increasing the keys, the key size also increases and so error will occur if we encrypt and decrypt the larger amount of data according to the encryption and decryption algorithm proposed in [1]. Also in [1], if any one key is determined then other keys can be easily determined either by adding or subtracting 1 to key which is found.

In [1], ASCII values of the letters in plain text are divided by the secret key and cipher text is generated by using the quotient and remainder of the division. Computational speed is high because of using small key size. But using the algorithm in [1], some letters cannot be encrypted because of using 3 bits in remainder. This problem is solved by using 4 bits in the remainder according to the algorithm proposed in [2]. In these two algorithms, only small data can be encrypted and decrypted because of incrementing keys, key size will be increased and hence error will be occurred while encrypting and decrypting the large data. Also in [1] and [2], if any one key is found then other keys can be easily generated by either adding or subtracting one to the key which is found.

5   Conclusion

Hence our proposed cost-effective small key size Cognitive Symmetric key Cryptographic Algorithm (CSCA) is suitable to all sizes of data and all kinds of data such as audio and video because of its low key size and high computational speed. The bit shifting operations and the independency of keys used from the previous set of keys makes it really challenging and the performance analysis clearly shows the superiority of our algorithm compared to all the existing algorithms in terms of time consumed, throughput and key size which in turn reflects the cost effectiveness and decreased overhead.

References

1. Sarker, M.Z.H., Parvez, M.S.: A Cost Effective Symmetric Key Cryptographic Algorithm for Small Amount of Data. In: 9th International Multitopic Conference, IEEE INMIC (2005)
2. Kumar, R.S., Pradeep, E., Naveen, K., Gunasekaran, R.: A Novel Approach for Enciphering Data of Smaller Bytes. International Journal of Computer Theory and Engineering 2(4) (August 2010)
3. Performance Analysis of Data Encryption Algorithms,
   http://www1.cse.wustl.edu/~jain/
   cse567-6/ftp/encryption_perf/index.html
4. Elminaam, D.S.A., Kader, A.M.A., Hadhoud, M.M.: Performance Evaluation of Symmetric Encryption Algorithms. IJCSNS International Journal of Computer Science and Network Security 8(12) (December 2008)
5. Chan, H., Perrig, A., Song, D.: Random key predistribution schemes for sensor networks. In: IEEE Symposium on Research in Security and Privacy. IEEE Press (2003)
6. Liu, J.K., Au, M.H., Susilo, W.: Self-generated certificate public key cryptography and certificateless signature/encryption scheme in the standard model. In: ACM Symposium on Information, Computer and Communications Security. ACM Press (2007)

7. Malan, D.J., Welsh, M., Smith, M.D.: A public-key infrastructure for key distribution in TinyOS based on elliptic curve cryptography. In: IEEE International Conference on Sensor and Ad Hoc Communications and Networks. IEEE Press (2004)
8. Deng, J., Han, Y.S.: Multipath Key Establishment for Wireless Sensor Networks Using Just-enough Redundancy Transmission. IEEE Transactions on Dependable and Secure Computing (2008)
9. Boris, K., Markus, D.: A Provably Secure And Efficient Countermeasure Against Timing Attacks. In: IEEE Computer Security Foundations Symposium. IEEE Computer Society (2009)
10. Massey, J.L.: Guessing and Entropy. In: IEEE Symposium on Information Theory. IEEE Computer Society (1994)
11. Zhu, S., Xu, S., Setia, S., Jajodia, S.: Establishing Pairwise Keys for Secure Communication in Ad Hoc Networks: A Probabilistic Approach. In: IEEE International Conference on Network Protocols. IEEE Press (2003)
12. MacKinnon, S.J., Taylor, P.D., Meijer, H., Akl, S.J.: An optimal algorithm for assigning cryptographic keys to control access in a hierarchy. IEEE Transactions on Computers (1985)
13. Kumar, K., Begum, J.N., Sumathy, V.: Efficient Region-Based Class Key Agreement Protocols for Ad Hoc Networks using Elliptic Curve Cryptography. In: IEEE International Advance Computing Conference. IEEE Press (2009)

Modeling and Verification of Fiat-Shamir Zero Knowledge Authentication Protocol

Amit K. Maurya, Murari S. Choudhary, P. Ajeyaraj, and Sanjay Singh

Department of Information and Communication Technology
Manipal Institute of Technology, Manipal University, Manipal-576104, India
`sanjay.singh@manipal.edu`

Abstract. Model checking is a multi-purpose, automatic technique for verifying finite-state concurrent systems. Formal verification methods have quite recently become usable by industry. Presently model checking has been widely used in hardware, software validation and security protocol analysis. Fiat-Shamir is one of the many zero-knowledge authentication protocol which is used for security authentication purpose. In this paper, we have proposed a formal model of Fiat-Shamir authentication protocol using Finite State Machine (FSM). Security requirements are represented using Computation Tree Logic (CTL). These security requirements are verified and analyzed using symbolic model checker tool NuSMV. Based on our verification we have identified one of the security flaw of Fiat-Shamir protocol using the NuSMV model checker.

Keywords: Model Checking, Zero Knowledge Authentication Protocol, Fiat-Shamir Protocol, CTL, Finite State Machine (FSM).

1 Introduction

An authentication protocol is a type of cryptographic protocol with the purpose of authenticating entities wishing to communicate securely. In password authentication, the claimant needs to send her secret to the verifier. It leads to a problem of eavesdropping. In addition, a dishonest verifier could reveal the password to others or use it to impersonate the claimant.

In challenge-response entity authentication, the claimant's secret is not sent to the verifier. The claimant applies a function on the challenge sent by the verifier that includes her secret. In some challenge response-methods, the verifier actually knows the claimants secret, which could be misused by the dishonest verifier. In other methods, the verifier can extract some information about the secret from the claimant by choosing a preplanned set of challenges. In zero-knowledge authentication [1][2], the claimant does not reveal anything that might cause danger to the confidentiality of the secret. The claimant proves to the verifier that she knows a secret, without revealing it. The interactions are so designed that they can not lead to revealing or guessing the secret. After exchanging messages, the verifier only knows that the claimant does or does not have the secret, nothing more. The result is a yes or no situation.

N. Meghanathan et al. (Eds.): CCSIT 2012, Part II, LNICST 85, pp. 61–70, 2012.

To the best of our knowledge there is no work on modeling and verification of Fiat-Shamir zero knowledge authentication protocols has been reported in the literature. In this work the Fiat-Shamir Protocol based on the zero-knowledge authentication has been considered for the modeling and verification purpose. Many authentication protocols have been proposed and found to have flaws after the authentication. In order to avoid such problems arising in the design of protocols, several methods have been proposed to analyze them. Among the various methodologies proposed, model checking has been proved to be very useful for this purpose. Model checking [3] [4] is a general purpose, automatic technique for verifying finite-state concurrent systems. This technique provides a way to model a system using state-transition system and all the requirements to be checked is expressed using temporal logic. Given a model and requirements a model checker simulates to verify that whether a requirement is satisfied or not.

The aim of this work is to present a methodology for analyzing cryptographic protocol and to identify the security flaw of Fiat-Shamir authentication protocol using a symbolic model verifier NuSMV.

The rest of this paper is structured as follows. Section 2 gives the overview of the Fiat-Shamir protocol. Section 3 describes model of Fiat-Shamir protocol. In section 4 key properties of the system are verified. Section 5 provide conclusion of the work.

2   Overview of the Fiat-Shamir Protocol

In the Fiat-Shamir protocol [2], a trusted third party chooses two large prime numbers p and q to calculate the value of $n = p \times q$. The value of n is announced to the public. The values of p and q are kept secret. Alice the claimant, chooses a secret number s between 1 and n-1. She calculates v= s mod n. She keeps s as her private key and registers v as her public key with the third party. Verification of Alice by Bob can be done in four steps shown below:

1. Alice, the claimant, chooses a random number r between 0 and n-1. She then calculates the value of $x = r^2 \bmod n$; x is called as witness.
2. Alice sends x to Bob as the witness.
3. Bob the verifier, sends the challenge c to Alice,c is either 0 or 1.
4. Alice calculates the response $y = rs^c$, where r is a random number selected by Alice in the first step. s is her private key and c is the challenge (0 or 1).
5. Alice sends the response to Bob to show that she knows value of her private key, s. She claims to be Alice.
6. Bob calculates $y^2 \bmod n$ and xv^c. If these two values are equal then Alice either knows the value of s (she is honest) or she has calculated the value of y in some other way (dishonest) because we can easily prove that y^2 is the same as xv^c in the modulo n arithmetic as given below

$$y^2 = (rs^c)^2 = r^2 s^{2c} = r^2 (s^2)^c = xv^c$$

These six steps constitute a round; the verification is repeated several times with the value of c equal to 0 or 1. The claimant must pass the test in each round to be verified. If she fails one single round, the process is aborted and she is not authenticated. This entire process is shown in Fig.1.

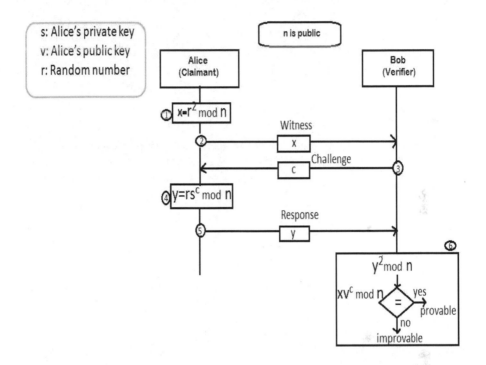

Fig. 1. Fiat-Shamir protocol

3   Model of the Protocol

Our methodology of analysis is based upon model checking, an automatic technique for verifying finite state concurrent systems. In the temporal logic model checking, the concurrent system is modeled as a state transition diagram, whereas properties are expressed in a temporal logic such as Linear Time Temporal Logic (LTL) or CTL [4]. The NuSMV model checker [5][6] following the above approach, adopts a structured input language to describe the model of system and the temporal logic CTL to express desired properties. The model of protocol has a modular structure. Each module is associated to an entity of the system and describes its behavior. The main modules used here are the *Alice*, *Bob* and *Third party* and they are considered to be honest principals. Model of the system is represented by a Kripke structure [4].

3.1   Kripke Structure

Kripke structure is a 4-tuple $M = (Q, I, \Delta, I)$ where:

- Q is a finite set of states.
- $I \subseteq Q$ is the set of initial states.
- $\Delta \subseteq Q \times Q$ is a transition relation which represents a state and its successor states.
- $L: Q \rightarrow 2^{AP}$ is a function which returns the set of atomic proposition that hold true in a state.

Kripke structure is used to represent the static topology and dynamic behavior of a system. Each state relates with a set of atomic propositions.

3.2   Specifying a Protocol as a Finite State Machine

Here the protocol is expressed as a state transition diagram. First an initial state is specified. Then an arc is drawn to another state for each message that can be sent or received at that point. Fig.2 describes the FSM model of Fiat-Shamir protocol.

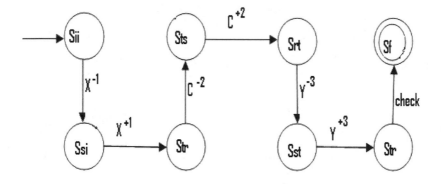

Fig. 2. FSM for Fiat-Shamir protocol

Table 1. Notations Used in the States of FSM

i	idle
s	sending
t	sent
r	received

Table.1 gives the different notations used in the states of FSM.

Table.2 gives the messages that are passing between different states of FSM.

Table.3 shows, what different states are representing and also what will be the state of Bob (verifier) and Alice (claimant) at different input values.

Table.4 gives different states of the FSM and their corresponding labels.

Table 2. Different Messages Exchanged

X^{-1}	First Message X is sent by Alice.
X^{+1}	First Message X is received by Bob.
C^{-1}	Second Message C is sent by Bob.
C^{+1}	Second message C is received by Alice.
Y^{-1}	Third message Y is sent by Alice.
Y^{+1}	Third message Y is received by Bob.
$check$	Event to enter final state.

Table 3. Description of Different States of FSM

S_{ii}	Alice and Bob in Idle State.
S_{si}	Alice is in Sending state and Bob is in Idle state.
S_{tr}	Alice is in Sent state and Bob is in Received state.
S_{ts}	Alice is in Sent state and Bob is in Sending state.
S_{rt}	Alice is in Received state and Sent state.
S_{st}	Alice is in Sending state and Bob is in Sent state.
S_{tr}	Alice is in Sent state and Bob is in Received state.
S_f	Alice and Bob will be in final state.

Table 4. States and their Corresponding Labels

State	State Label
S_{ii}	s, r, n
S_{si}	x, s, r, n
S_{tr}	x, s, r, n
S_{ts}	x, s, r, n
S_{rt}	x, s, r, n, c
S_{st}	x, s, r, n, c, y
S_{tr}	x, s, r, n, c, y
S_f	$value1, value2$

4 Verification and Analysis

4.1 Variables Used

Following are the list of variables maintained by the third party.

- p and q: These are the two prime numbers used for calculating private and public key.
- $nvalue.n$: Here $nvalue.n$ is equal to $p*q$ and is calculated by the third party and announced to the public.

Following are the list of variables maintained by the principal Alice.

- s: A secret key chosen between 1 and n - 1.
- v: Calculated as,
  $(alice.s)^2 \, mod \, (thirdparty.nvalue.n)$. This is the public key. Alice keeps s as her private key and registers v as her public key with the third party.
- r: Random number chosen between 0 and n - 1.
- $i.info.xx$: Temporary variable used by Alice and further assigned to x the witness. $i.info.xx$ is calculated as $(alice.r)^2 \, mod \, (thirdparty.nvalue.n)$
- $challenge : boolean$: The variable and its value is equal to the challenge that is sent by Bob, if he is the honest principal otherwise Alice can guess the value of challenge randomly (0 or 1).
- $i.info.yy\_c1$: Temporary variable calculated as $(alice.r) \times (alice.s) \, mod \, (thirdparty.nvalue.n)$ when the value of challenge is 1. This value will be assigned to y and sent to Bob for further calculation.
- $i.info.yyy\_c0$: Temporary variable calculated as $(alice.r) \, mod \, (thirdparty.nvalue.n)$ when the value of challenge is 0. This value will be assigned to y and sent to Bob for further calculation.

Following are the list of variables maintained by the principal Bob.

- $challenge : boolean$: variable called the challenge is chosen by Bob and the value is either 0 or 1. This challenge will be sent to Alice.
- $value1$: If the value of challenge is 1, the variable calculated as,
  $((alice.r \times alice.s) \, mod \, (thirdparty.nvalue.n))^2 \, mod$
  $(thirdparty.nvalue.n)$
  Otherwise if the value of challenge is 0, the variable is calculated as,
  $(alice.r \, mod \, (thirdparty.nvalue.n))^2 \, mod$
  $(thirdparty.nvalue.n)$.
  this value of $value1$ will be used for comparison with $value2$.
- $value2$: If the value of challenge is 1 then the variable will be calculated as,
  $(((alice.r)^2 mod \, (thirdparty.nvalue.n)) \times v.alice) mod$
  $(thirdparty.nvalue.n)$
  Otherwise, if the value of challenge is 0, the value is calculated as,
  $(alice.r)^2 mod \, (thirdparty.nvalue.n)$
  After calculating $value1$ and $value2$, these values are compared. If these two values are matching then Alice is authenticated.

4.2   Syntax and Semantic of CTL

Security requirements (properties) are expressed with a temporal logic that is Computation Tree Logic (CTL). The BNF of CTL syntax is as follows [4]:

$\Phi ::= \bot \,|\, \top \,|\, (\neg \Phi) \,|\, (\Phi \wedge \Phi) \,|\, (\Phi \vee \Phi) \,|\, (\Phi \rightarrow \Phi) \,|\,$ AX$\Phi \,|\,$ EX$\Phi \,|\,$ AF$\Phi \,|\,$ EF$\Phi \,|\,$ EG$\Phi \,|\,$ A$[\Phi U \Phi] \,|\,$ E$[\Phi U \Phi]$

The first symbol of the pair is either "A" or "E" where "A" represents "all path" and "E" represents "exist a path". "A" and "E" are path operator.

The second symbol of the pair is possibly "X", "F", "G" and "U". "X" represents "next state", "F" represents "some future state", "G" represents "all cases in future", "U" represents "until".

A path operator must accompany with a temporal operator, and vice versa.

4.3 Verification Results

Given the model of the system to analyze, NuSMV the model checker simulates all its possible behaviors in order to verify whether requirement is satisfied. In this model authentication is the major requirement. As specified, in Fiat-Shamir protocol the claimant is authenticated if and only if the values of $y^2 \ mod \ n$ and $xv^c \ mod$ are matching. This is possible when the claimant Alice is honest and she must get the correct challenge from Bob. There is a possibility that a dishonest user can guess the correct value of challenge and can pass the test. This problem can be fixed by repeating this authentication process many times. Claimant is authenticated if and only if she passes all the tests assuming that it is not possible to guess the value of challenge c properly all the time. There are two possible cases under consideration:

- Now we will consider the first case where claimant is considered to be honest. If she is honest user then she must receive the correct value of challenge either 0 or 1. In NuSMV this can be checked using CTL specification, $AF(alice.challenge = bob.challenge- > AF(value1 = value2))$. In simple English it means that in all future states when $alice.challenge$ is equal to $bob.challenge$ then in all the future states $value1$ and $value2$ which are calculated by Bob should be same.
- Considering the second case, where claimant is considered to be a dishonest principal. In this case challenge sent by Bob is not equal to the challenge that is assumed by the Alice. Then the values of $value1$ and $value2$ are going to change because of different interpretation of the value of c by Alice and Bob. This can be verified by the CTL specification $AF(alice.challenge! = bob.challenge- > AF(value1! = value2))$. It means that in all future states when $alice.challenge$ is not equal to $bob.challenge$ then in all the future states $value1$ and $value2$ which are calculated by Bob should not be same.

Though it is said that in the case of dishonest principal when the value of challenge sent by Bob and value of challenge assumed by the Alice are different, protocol is going to give different values for $value1$ and $value2$, it is not the case always. In such situation authentication is going to fail. This is one of the major flaw noticed in the Fiat-Shamir protocol by this work. It is proved by running the second CTL specification $AF(alice.challenge! = bob.challenge- > AF(value1! = value2))$. While running it is noticed that NuSMV gives the result as FALSE. It makes sure that in some cases for different values of c it is not at all possible that $value1$ and $value2$ takes the different values.

```
C:\windows\system32\cmd.exe                                               _ 8
WARNING: single-value variable 'thirdparty.nvalue' has been stored as a constant
-- specification AF (alice.challenge != bob.challenge -> AF value1 != value2)   i
s false
-- as demonstrated by the following execution sequence
Trace Description: CTL Counterexample
Trace Type: Counterexample
-> State: 1.1 <-
  alice.s = 8
  alice.r = 5
  alice.challenge = 1
  alice.state = idle
  bob.challenge = 0
  bob.state = idle
  i.info = yyy_c0
  x = 10
  y = 10
  value1 = 10
  value2 = 10
  status = provable
  i.info.yyy_c0 = 5
  i.info.yy_c1 = 10
  i.info.xx = 10
  v = 4
  thirdparty.nvalue.n = 15
  thirdparty.p = 3
  thirdparty.q = 5
  thirdparty.nvalue = n
-> Input: 1.2 <-
-> State: 1.2 <-
  alice.state = sending_x
  bob.state = wait_for_x
-> Input: 1.3 <-
-> State: 1.3 <-
  bob.state = rcvd_x
-> Input: 1.4 <-
-> State: 1.4 <-
  alice.state = sent_x
-> Input: 1.5 <-
-> State: 1.5 <-
  bob.state = sending_c
-> Input: 1.6 <-
-> State: 1.6 <-
  alice.state = wait_for_c
-> Input: 1.7 <-
-> State: 1.7 <-
  alice.state = rcvd_c
-> Input: 1.8 <-
-> State: 1.8 <-
  bob.state = sent_c
-> Input: 1.9 <-
-> State: 1.9 <-
  alice.state = sending_y
-> Input: 1.10 <-
-> State: 1.10 <-
  bob.state = wait_for_y
-> Input: 1.11 <-
-> State: 1.11 <-
  bob.state = rcvd_y
-> Input: 1.12 <-
-> State: 1.12 <-
  alice.state = sent_y
-> Input: 1.13 <-
-- Loop starts here
-> State: 1.13 <-
  bob.state = checking_value
-> Input: 1.14 <-
-> State: 1.14 <-
-- specification AF (alice.challenge = bob.challenge -> AF value1 = value2)   is
:rue
:\Program Files\NuSMV\2.4.3\bin>
:\Program Files\NuSMV\2.4.3\bin>_
```

Fig. 3. Observation of Protocol's Flaw

The Fig.3 shows the verification output of Fiat-Shamir protocol where the protocol has failed. As we see that the values of challenge of claimant (Alice) and verifier (Bob) are not equal (i.e 1, 0 respectively) but the $value1$ and $value2$ (i.e 10) are still equal, that means if claimant does not have the secret key even though she could pass the test. It also shows that for some values of challenge the protocol passes the test that means Fiat-Shamir protocol could identify that whether claimant has the secret key or not.

```
cm. Administrator: C:\Windows\system32\cmd.exe - n  smv  -int headache_amit_murari.smv          -  □  X
NuSMV > show_traces -t
There is 1 trace currently available.
NuSMV > show_traces -v
<!-- ##################### Trace number: 1 ##################### -->
Trace Description: Simulation Trace
Trace Type: Simulation
-> State: 1.1 <-
      alice.s = 8
      alice.r = 11
      alice.challenge = 0
      alice.state = idle
      bob.challenge = 1
      bob.state = idle
      i.info = yy_c1
      x = 1
      y = 11
      value1 = 1
      value2 = 4
      status = improvable
      i.info.yyy_c0 = 11
      i.info.yy_c1 = 13
      i.info.xx = 1
      v = 4
      thirdparty.nvalue.n = 15
      thirdparty.p = 3
      thirdparty.q = 5
      thirdparty.nvalue = n
-> Input: 1.2 <-
-> State: 1.2 <-
      alice.s = 8
      alice.r = 11
      alice.challenge = 1
      alice.state = sending_x
      bob.challenge = 1
      bob.state = wait_for_x
      i.info = yy_c1
      x = 1
      y = 13
      value1 = 4
      value2 = 4
      status = provable
      i.info.yyy_c0 = 11
      i.info.yy_c1 = 13
      i.info.xx = 1
      v = 4
      thirdparty.nvalue.n = 15
      thirdparty.p = 3
      thirdparty.q = 5
      thirdparty.nvalue = n
-> Input: 1.3 <-
```

Fig. 4. Observation of Protocol

Fig.4 shows one of the observation of the verification where challenge guessed by Alice and challenge sent by Bob are different (0 and 1). *value*1 and *value*2 calculated by Bob are different (1 and 4) and hence the claimant (Alice) is get disqualified.

5   Conclusion

It has been observed that among the various methodologies proposed, model checking has been proved to be very useful to avoid the misconceptions arising in the design of protocols. In this paper we have tried to model check Fiat-Shamir authentication protocol using NuSMV as the symbolic model verifier. We could able to check the initial configuration of the protocol. Also we could find out the limitation of the Fiat-Shamir protocol. This major flaw has been proved using CTL specification over the model.

References

1. Wikipedia: Zero knowledge proof (2011),
   http://en.wikipedia.org/wiki/Zero-knowledge_proof/
2. Forouzan, B.A.: Cryptography & Network Security, 1st edn. McGraw-Hill Press, United Kingdom (2008)
3. Cimatti, A.: Industrial Applications of Model Checking. In: Cassez, F., Jard, C., Rozoy, B., Dermot, M. (eds.) MOVEP 2000. LNCS, vol. 2067, pp. 153–168. Springer, Heidelberg (2001)
4. Huth, M., Ryan, M.: Logic In computer science, 2nd edn. Cambridge University Press, New Delhi (2004)
5. Cavada, R., et al.: Nusmv 2.5 user manual (2010),
   http://nusmv.fbk.eu/NuSMV/userman/v25/nusmv.pdf
6. Cavada, R., et al.: Nusmv 2.5 tutorial (2010),
   http://nusmv.fbk.eu/NuSMV/tutorial/v25/tutorial.pdf

Developing Software Metrics for Analysis and Design Artifacts in Unified Process

Meena Sharma and Rajeev G. Vishwakarma

IET, Devi Ahilya University, Indore, India
SVITS, Rajiv Gandhi Technical University of MP, Indore, India
meena@myself.com, rajeev@mail.com

Abstract. In this paper we have investigated the unified process workflow from analysis and design perspectives of software development life cycle. There are particular well defined roles to perform the life cycle activities. All these activities are streamed up in a typical capability pattern called workflow. When these activities are performed we need some artifacts as inputs. After the activities are done we receive some output artifacts. We have developed software process and software artifact metrics for the major artifacts and process of analysis and design workflow. We have suggested some metrics pertaining to the input and output artifacts. The metrics that we developed are for analysis and design process, software architecture document artifact, and design model artifact. Also we investigated how to quantify the artifact checklist items and make a decision about the quality for different attributes of the process and artifacts, and finally deciding upon the overall quality.

Keywords: analysis & design, software metrics, process metrics, artifact metrics, checklist, CMMI.

1   Introduction

Artifacts based metrics are the software metrics that are developed by us from the work products point of view. The work is based on developing some checklist based metrics for the artifacts developed during the analysis & design (A&D). We have developed metrics using checklist approach to satisfy quality from CMMI [West,2004] perspective also. In unified process the artifacts that are produced; are Software Architecture Document (SAD), Design Model, Analysis Model, Deployment Model and the Data model. In the following section we emphasize on the checklists based metrics for some of these artifacts [Chrissis,2006] [Ahern,2005].

We have developed metrics for A&D Process, Artifact Software Architecture Document, Artifact Design Model, Artifact Deployment Model and Artifact Data Model [Sharma,2009]. Looking in to the space limitation we are describing process metrics for A&D and artifact metrics for Software Architecture Document and Design Model. FI/PI/NI/NA is the abbreviation as described below. We have taken the idea of FI/PI/NI/NA from Capability Maturity Model Integration (CMMI) Artifacts are evaluated on the basis of FI/PI/NI/NA. This is shown in Table 1.

N. Meghanathan et al. (Eds.): CCSIT 2012, Part II, LNICST 85, pp. 71–80, 2012.

Table 1. Explanation of evaluation by the auditor

FI	Fully Implemented in compliance with the documentation
PI	Partially Implemented in compliance with the documentation. One or more noncompliance's noted.
NI	Not Implemented, not even partly in compliance with the documentation. One or more noncompliances noted.
NA	Not Applicable for this project. Approved waivers exist.

2   Unified Process and Process Checklist

The unified process expresses the A&D process in terms of roles, artifacts, activities, and workflow. Roles perform the activities as per the workflow and produce the artifacts. In order to produce artifacts the activities need input artifacts also. The metrics we are developing may be applied to input artifacts or output artifacts. These artifacts are the part of unified software development process. Now we describe the general process checklist items as below for the artifacts. Note that these are process perspective only. All the artifacts must be evaluated against each metrics. First we provide the details pertaining to project as shown in Table 2.

Table 2. Project Details

Project Details Metrics	
1	Project Name: Write the title of the project
2	Project Phase and Iteration: Which phase and iteration the project is running
3	Project Manager: Name of the Project Manager
4	Owner/Author: Owner of the artifact or the author of the artifact
5	Date of Audit: Mention the date of the audit
6	Auditor: Write the name of the auditor
7	Audit Effort (hours): Number of hours taken up to conduct the audit

All the checklist items must be satisfied for the attributes. These checklists are also called as Process Evaluation Checklist (PEC). The objective performing the evaluation using the checklist for different artifacts is to reduce failures in the production of artifacts in unified software development process. We evaluate in the form of a checklist for different categories as shown in Table 3 and Table 4. There are two types of process checklists. There are general and specific checklists. Table 3 shows general process checklist while Table 4 shows the A&D process specific

Table 3. General Checklist Items for Process

General Process Checklist Items	
People & Training	
1	Were non-staff resources (equipment, facilities, and tools) made available for the project's process activities?
2	Was the assigned staff formally trained in how to perform the process activities (including tool training, if needed)?
Document Control	
3	Are artifacts, meeting records, other documentation, etc. produced by this process under the defined configuration management for this project?
Stakeholder Involvement	
4	Do records exist that demonstrate stakeholder participation in all reviews including decision points?
Measuring process effectiveness and efficiency	
5	Have measures demonstrating process execution been collected throughout the project?
Process Evaluation	
6	Have PPQA audits been performed as scheduled?
Working with Management	
7	Do meeting records exist that demonstrate review by project management in accordance with the projects schedule?
Process Improvement	
8	Has a lessons learned document been created for this process and submitted to the process engineering group?
9	Have any process change requests been generated from the execution of this process?

checklist. Checklist approach is one of the important factors to develop the metrics and the quality model in CMMI [Burwick,2008]. Now we present the questionnaire of the checklist metrics for different checklist items in Table 3 for different categories.

Table 4 shows the process specific checklist for analysis and design. This checklist will evaluate the process performed during analysis and design workflow.

This should be noted that the project details, general process checklist items and specific process metrics as shown in Table 2, Table 3 and Table 4 will be applicable to all the artifacts. So these process metrics must be repeated for each and every artifact in the iteration. We will not describe these items again and again for every artifact, but we must make sure that project details, general process metrics and specific process metrics must be followed for every artifact. After describing process metrics we describe artifact metrics in the following sections.

Table 4. A&D Process Specific Checklist Items

Process Specific Checklist Items	
1	Has Candidate Architecture been identified?
2	Has alternate solutions been applied in arriving at the Architecture
3	Have Use Case Realizations been created?
4	Has the Analysis Model been created?
5	Has the Design Model been created?
6	Has the Deployment Model been created?
7	Has the Software Architecture Document been updated with previous information?
8	Has preliminary Use Case Analysis been performed?
9	Have architecturally significant Analysis Classes been described?
10	Has behavior analysis been performed?
11	Has detailed Use Case Analysis been performed? (refinement of analysis classes and use case realizations)
12	Have design elements been identified in the Design Model?
13	Has behavior analysis been reviewed?
14	Has Component Design been performed?
15	Has Use Case Design been performed?
16	Has Subsystem Design been performed to generate Design Subsystem part of the Design Model?
17	Has Class Design been performed to generate Class Design in the Design Model?
18	Have Test Class and Test Packages been designed?
19	Has Database Design been performed? (optional - evidence in Data Model)
20	Has Component Design been Reviewed?
21	Has the architecture been refined?
22	Have the Design Mechanisms been identified and documented in the Software Architecture Document?
23	Have the Design Elements been identified and documented in the Software Architecture Document?
24	Have existing Design Elements been evaluated to be incorporated?
25	Have the Run-Time Architecture been described in the Software Architecture Document?
26	Has the distribution been described in the Software Architecture Document?
27	Has the Architecture been reviewed?

3   Metrics for Software Architecture Document

This artifact is also termed as SAD. It offers a complete and comprehensive architectural overview of the system, using a number of different architectural views to depict different aspects of the system. It provides as a communication medium between the software architect and other team members of the project regarding architecturally significant decisions and documents that have been prepared on the project. The metrics for Software Architecture Document is as follows, shown in Table 5 and Table 6. In Table 5 describes general artifact checklist and Table 6 depicts specific Software Architecture Document metrics. The general artifact checklist will also apply to all the artifacts so it will not be described for rest of the artifacts hereon.

Table 5. General Artifact Checklist- Applicable to All Artifacts

Corrective Action Efficiency	
1	Have corrective actions carried out on previous noncompliance prevented recurrence of the noncompliance? That means we have to evaluate the noncompliance and its remedies done earlier.
Correct Template	
2	Does the layout correspond to the template defined for this type of artifact?
Revision History	
3	Has the artifact revision history been maintained with a description for each of the major changes including the reason for the changes?
Review cycle	
4	Was the audited version of the document managed through the review process as defined in its Project Plan?
Version Numbering	
5	Was the version numbering used in the artifact?
Production Frequency	
6	Was the artifact produced with the defined frequency?
Location	
7	Is the artifact stored in the project library in the location specified in the Software Development Plan?
Configuration Management	
8	If required, has the artifact been placed under configuration management?

The metrics for architecture artifact is described below as shown in Table 6.

Table 6. Software Architecture Document Artifact Specific Checklist

Software Architecture Document Specific Checklist Items	
1	Does the Introduction provide an overview of the entire document?
2	Is the Purpose defined?
3	Is the Scope defined?

Table 6. (*Continued*)

4	Are the definitions of terms, acronyms, and abbreviations defined? Note: This information may be provided by reference to the project's Glossary.
5	Are References been defined?
6	Is the organization of the Software Architecture Document been defined in the overview?
7	Is the Architecture of the system described in the Architectural Representation?
8	Are relevant views (i.e. Use Case, Logical, Process, Deployment, and Implementation) described in the architectural representation?
9	Have Architectural goals been identified?
10	Have Architectural constraints been identified?
11	Have architecturally relevant use cases been described in the Use Case View?
12	Have main use case been detailed with respective Use Case Realizations?
13	Have architecturally significant parts of the Design Model been described in the Logical View?
14	Is the Design Model decomposed in terms of the package hierarchy and layering in the Logical View overview?
15	Have architecturally significant Design Packages been detailed?
16	Have system threads and processes been described in the Process View?
17	Does the Software Architecture Document provide a view of the Deployment Model in the Deployment View section?
18	Does the Software Architecture Document describe the overall structure of the Implementation Model in the Implementation View section?
19	Is an overview of layering provided for the Implementation View?
20	Has the implementation layer been described in the layers section of the Implementation View?
21	Has a view of the Data Model been detailed in the Software Architecture Document? (optional)
22	Have dimensioning characteristics been described?
23	Have performance constraints been described?
24	Is the Software Architecture contributing to all capabilities of the system described (i.e. extensibility, reliability, portability)?

4   Metrics for Design Model

This artifact is an object model that explains the realization of use cases, and serves as an abstraction of the implementation model and the software program code. The design model is used as essential input to activities in implementation and test. It is a comprehensive and composite artifact encompassing all design classes, subsystems, packages, subsystems and collaborations. The metrics for Design Model is described below as shown in Table 7. This is artifact specific metrics whereas for general artifact checklist we can refer to Table 5. This should be noted that the general artifact checklist as shown in Table 5 will be applicable to all the artifacts in the unified software development process. Design model and other models are constructed making use of the unified modeling language that is the analysis and design language in unified software development process. Again, we are making use of the checklists based approach as per CMMI [West,2004].

Table 7. Design Model Specific Checklist Items

Design Model Specific Checklist Items	
1	Does the Design Model have a textual introduction?
2	Have Design Packages been described?
3	Do the Design Packages have brief descriptions?
4	Have the classes contained in the Design Package been defined?
5	Have the relationships inside the package been defined?
6	Have Design Packages contained inside other Design Packages been defined?
7	Have import dependencies with other packages been documented?
8	Have Design Subsystems been defined?
9	Do Design Subsystems include brief descriptions?
10	Are all realized interfaces clearly described?
11	Are all elements contained in the Subsystem defined?
12	Are dependencies with other design element documented?
13	Have Design Classes been defined?
14	Do relevant Design Classes include brief descriptions?
15	Have class responsibilities been defined?
16	Have the relationships of the Design Classes been defined?
17	Have operations of Design Classes been defined?
18	Have attributes of Design Classes been defined?
19	Are requirements associated with Design Classes referenced?
20	Have Interfaces been defined?
21	Do the Interfaces include brief descriptions?
22	Have the Interface operations been described?
23	Have relationships among Design Elements been defined?
24	Have design level Use Case Realizations been defined?
25	Has a textual "Flow of Events" been described for each use case realization?
26	Has an Interaction Diagram been defined for each Use Case Realization?
27	Has a Class Diagram been defined for each Use Case Realization?
28	Have the requirements associated with each Use Case Realization been described?

5   Quantification of Checklist Items and Decision Making

In order to quantify the metrics it is necessary to evaluate each checklist item and award a quantified value based on some scale. We have two process checklists that are general process checklist and process specific checklist. On the artifact side we have general artifact checklist and artifact specific checklist. We know that we have to quantify the attributes of evidence, FI/PI/NI/NA, issue # (category of problem), and comments. After setting the values based on the scale described below we can measure each of our checklist items in all the metrics for process and artifacts. The Table 8 is prepared in such a way that based on the evaluation of the checklist item we can award the weight to each checklist item.

Table 8. Evaluation Scale

Evidence Values	FI/PI/NI/NA Values	Issue # Values	Comments Values
Evidence in the form of template, artifact or guideline	As per Table 1.	Problem ID/Category	Comments by team
Very Strong-4	FI-4	Not Severe-4	Strongly Recommended -4
Strong-3	PI-3	Not Much Severe-3	Recommended-2
Sufficient-2	NI-2	Severe-2	Recommended with Reservations-3
Poor-1	NA-NIL	Very Severe-1	Not Recommended-1

We see that all the values are of the range from 1 to 4. We understand that score of 4 is for the best and score of 1 is the poorest indicator. Let us take an example of Software Architecture Document, and set the scale as follows for the artifact specific checklist as per Table 9. For the sake of convenience we are taking only five checklist items from Table 7.

So there are five checklist items and four attributes for each checklist items. We know that number values that can be awarded to a particular cell are four and the minimum that can be awarded to is one. We have maximum of eighty points of evaluation. In the example we sum up each column and get the values. Finally a grand total is calculated as shown in the last row of the table. This number is the key to evaluation and we can make a decision that how much quality oriented the artifact is. We see that the Software Architecture Document could score 64 out of 80. We can conclude that it is 80 percent quality oriented.

Table 9. Quantifying Checklist Items

Software Architecture Document Specific Checklist Items		Evidence Values	FI/PI/NI/NA Values	Issue # Values	Comments Values
1	Does the introduction provide an overview of the entire document?	4	4	2	4
2	Is the purpose defined?	3	4	1	4
3	Is the scope defined?	4	3	4	3
4	Are the definitions of terms, acronyms, and abbreviations defined? Note: This information may be provided by reference to the project's Glossary.	3	4	4	2
5	Are references been defined?	4	3	2	2
Total		18	18	13	15
Grand Total Out of 80		64			

6   Summary

In this chapter we investigated and understood the unified process workflow metrics from A&D perspective. We gave emphasis on major artifacts involved in these disciplines. There are particular roles to perform the activities. All these activities are streamed up in a workflow. When these activities are performed we need some artifacts as inputs. After the activities are done we receive some output artifacts. We have developed metrics for the major artifacts of these disciplines workflow. We have engineered up some metrics pertaining to the inputs and outputs. The metrics that are developed are for A&D Process Metrics, Analysis Model Artifact, Design Model Artifact, Software Architecture Document Artifact, Deployment Model Artifact and Data Model Artifact. Also we saw how to quantify the artifact checklist items and make a decision about the quality for different attributes.

References

1. Ahern, D.A., Armstrong, J., Clouse, A., Ferguson, J.R., Hayes, W., Nidiffer, K.E.: CMMI® SCAMPI Distilled Appraisals for Process Improvement. Addison-Wesley Professional (2005)
2. Diane, B.: How To Implement the CMMI - Real Process Improvement Using Proven Solutions. BPS Publishing (2008)
3. Haynes, S.R., Skattebo, A.L., Singel, J.A., Cohen, M.A., Himelright, J.L.: Collaborative architecture design and evaluation. In: Proceedings of the 6th Conference on Designing Interactive Systems, University Park, PA, USA, pp. 219–228 (June 2006)
4. Hitz, M., Montazeri, B.: Chidamber and Kemerer's Metrics Suite: A Measurement Theory Perspective. IEEE Transactions on Software Engineering 22(4), 267–271 (1996)
5. Jacobson, I., Booch, G., Rumbaugh, J.: The Unified Software Development Process. Addison-Wesley Professional (1999)
6. Kannengiesser, U., Zhu, L.: An Ontologically-Based Evaluation of Software Design Methods. The Knowledge Engineering Review 24(1), 41–58 (2009)
7. Kazman, R., Bass, L., Abowd, G., Webb, M.: SAAM: A Method for Analyzing the Properties of Software Architectures. In: Proceedings of 16th International Conference on Software Engineering, Sorrento, Italy, pp. 81–90 (May 1994)
8. Kazman, R., Klein, M., Barbacci, M., Longstaff, T., Lipson, H., Carriere, J.: The Architecture Tradeoff Analysis Method. In: Proceedings of Fourth IEEE Conference on Engineering of Complex Computer Systems, Monterey, CA, USA, pp. 68–78 (August 1998)
9. Kruchten, P.B.: The Rational Unified Process: An Introduction. Addison-Wesley Professional (2003)
10. Langer, M.: Analysis and Design of Information Systems. Springer, Heidelberg (2007)
11. Mårtensson, F.: Software Architecture Quality Evaluation Approaches in an Industrial Context. Licentiate Dissertation Series No. 2006:03, School of Engineering Department Of Systems And Software Engineering, Blekinge Institute Of Technology, Sweden (2006)
12. Rational Unified Process®, Base Plug-in, Version 7.0.1, Based on: Base Concepts Plug-in Version: 1.0.1, © Copyright IBM Corp. (2010)
13. Sharma, M., Chandwani, M.: Software Metrics and Object Oriented Business Modeling. In: CSI 2006, 41st Annual National Convention of Computer Society of India, Kolkata, November 23-24, pp. 243–247 (2006)
14. Sharma, M., Chandwani, M.: Quality in Business Modeling using UML. In: Proceedings of 1st International Conference on Digital Information Management IEEE-ICDIM, Bangalore, December 3-5, pp. 294–299 (2006)
15. Sharma, M., Chandwani, M.: Maturing capability in Unified Paradigm. In: Proceedings of the International Conference on Advances in Computing, Communication and Control ACM SIGART, Mumbai, January 23-24, pp. 737–746 (2009)
16. Uttangi, R.V., Rizwan, S.A.: Fast Track to CMMI Implementation: Integrating the CMMI and RUP Process Frameworks. IBM DeveloperWorks Rational Technical Library (2007)
17. Wang, M.H., Lee, C.S.: An Intelligent PPQA Web Services for CMMI Assessment. In: Eighth International Conference on Intelligent Systems Design and Applications, Kaohsiung, Taiwan, vol. 1, pp. 229–234 (November 2008)
18. Michael, W.: Real Process Improvement Using the CMMI. Auerbach Publications (2004)

A Novel Approach for Green Computing through Event-Driven Power Aware Pervasive Computing

Jeeva Susan Jacob[1] and K.G. Preetha[2]

[1] Department of Computer Science,
[2] Department of Information Technology,
Rajagiri School of Engineering & Technology,
Rajagiri Valley, Cochin, India
jeevasj27@gmail.com
preetha_kg@rajagiritech.ac.in

Abstract. Green computing is the term used for eco-friendly computing. It utilizes the computing resources in the most efficient way without raising issues to the environment. The goals of green computing are to reduce the use of hazardous materials, maximize energy efficiency during the product's lifetime, and promote recyclability or biodegradability of defunct products and factory waste. The main purpose of this paper is to use the pervasive computing techniques, the advanced wireless communication strategies and smart hardware for the implementation of green computing. This paper discusses the role of pervasive computing towards achieving green computing by introducing pervasiveness in utilizing computing systems much efficiently in support with environmental well being. And also the paper tries to explore the concept of power aware computing and its implementation using event driven pervasive computing with the support of a handheld device such as a smart phone.

Keywords: Green computing, Event driven computing, Pervasive computing, Power awareness.

1 Introduction

Computing is now an essential part of our day-to-day life. With the advent of advanced gadgets from laptops to smart phones and communication facilities from LANs to portable internet packages, modern technologies have helped us to make computing much easily accessible and simple. The increased number of advanced computing devices adds to utilization of large amount of power around the globe. The large volume of heat thus dissipated add to the global warming in addition to e-waste getting accumulated everywhere.

Researches towards environment-friendly computing methodologies have been going on for about a decade now. Green computing, also known as green IT, aims at developing efficient computing techniques which utilizes energy efficiently, without creating hazardous issues for the environment, and also promotes recycling and reuse of components used to develop such computing devices. In this paper we discuss the

N. Meghanathan et al. (Eds.): CCSIT 2012, Part II, LNICST 85, pp. 81–88, 2012.

concept of pervasive computing and try to reduce the power wastage in green computing by the maximum awareness of power.

The rest of this paper is organized as follows. Section 2 gives a brief introduction to green computing. The current status and issues of present scenario is described in section 3. Section 4 describes the impact of event driven computing on green computing. Section 5 and 6 gives the key features of the new approach. Future enhancement is given in section 7 and a conclusion is given in section 8.

2   Green Computing Techniques: A Brief Idea

Green computing is eco-friendly computing done in support with environmental well-being. It plays an important role in reducing power consumption by the whole lot of computers being used around the globe and improving the energy efficiency during their lifetime [6]. It also replaces the hazardous materials being used in the manufacturing of advanced computing devices with biodegradable and recycled materials to reduce e-waste.

Green computing techniques in both hardware and software components of computing system has to be introduced. These methods should be able to deal with excess power consumption, heat emission, carbon generation and improper utilization of resources available. The green hardware environment is given in the figure1.

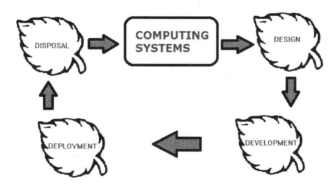

Fig. 1. The figure shows the 4 Ds in the green computing environment

The main phases in the development and usage of hardware components are known as the four D's. These are design, development, deployment and disposal. In the design, the materials to be selected should be having more power efficiency and less carbon emission. Second is the development phase. In this actual development of the design takes place with the power efficient components. Deployment is where we utilize the computing systems developed. The utilization must be made efficient by adopting methods to prevent extra power usage and heat dissipation. Idle time power leakage should also be prevented. The last phase is the disposal phase. Here the non degradable materials should be properly recycled and reused by the use of proper disposal measures.

Green software components can be utilized mainly to reduce idle time power leakage. This is illustrated with describing the following scenario. Suppose we are working on a computing system. We left it for a while for some other work. All this time power is wasted for the idle time of the system. Of course screensavers can save almost 5% of the power wasted. Also hibernation of the system into sleep state, which is enabled in most of the systems nowadays, can save another 10%. But still the external peripherals connected to the system draws power even in this sleep state. This eliminates the 15% we saved. So it is better to use control plugs for external peripherals to avoid this idle time power leakage. Another method to reduce power usage is virtualization. Here multiple applications can be executed in the same system simultaneously. This enables sharing of processing power. By sharing memory and storage using cloud we can reduce number of storage cells and computing time as well. Sharing of display devices during execution can also reduce the power usage. Display unit can be allotted on the basis of order of completion of execution. This reduces the total power usage as well as the total heat dissipation. The various power usages in computing devices are shown in the figure 2.

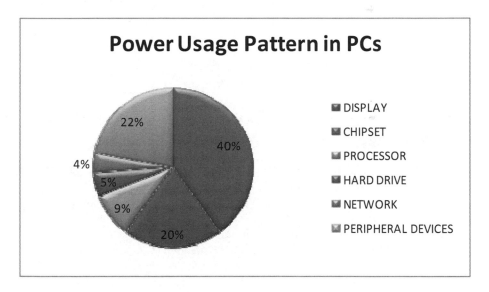

Fig. 2. The figure shows the usage of power in various components

3   Obscurity in Achieving Utmost Power Awareness in Green Computing

Adapting green technologies for conversion into green systems is not an easy process for today's computing systems. Several researches have been going on from the beginning of this millennium to enable green technologies. Scientists from all over the world have been working on eco-friendly projects to implement green computing environments to replace the existing systems. But most of them on implementation could not keep up to the performance improvements towards green computing as they claimed.

Major challenge faced by the researchers in green computing is efficient utilization of power. Most of the power consumed by the computing systems gets converted into heat energy while executing computing processes. This heat energy, generated in large volumes in the long run, could deteriorate the performance of the system and also affect the environment adversely. The computing   systems must be able to do computing tasks in balance with the power required for the execution of those tasks. Idle time power leakage is another major issue in computing environment. Control measures such as hibernation and screensavers are used nowadays. One solution proposed by researchers is event driven pervasive computing. In this once the important events occur, users will be informed at the earliest. So the user can control the usage of unnecessary power. Even if these measures are implemented, still it is difficult to manage the consumption of unnecessary power completely.

Other issues in the green computing are e-waste disposal, heat dissipation and carbon emission. Rather than disposing e-waste by dumping them, we need an efficient mechanism to recycle and reuse it. Excess heat generated by the systems raise the temperature in the environment Measures to cool or remove the excess heat emission should be sought for and implemented. The harmful particles, like carbon, lead and so on, being emitted from these systems adds to the global warming issue of the environment.

The above mentioned issues have been the motivation of developing the new approach to improve the power aware computing.

4   Impact of Event Driven Power Aware Approach in Green Computing

Pervasive computing aims at making our lives much simpler by using advanced tools to manage information by integrating communication technologies in our daily life [4]. Event driven computing has its roots from event driven programming and pervasive computing. It is typically based on Event-Condition-Action (ECA) policy. Here events are anything which happens in the system which can trigger Actions in the behaviour of the system to adapt to the new situation. Conditions are constraints or rules according to which these actions take place and these can be preset. These events and actions can be monitored through our handheld device which gets us alerted if ECA occurs. Also we can send commands through various message services in case of unexpected events or to reset actions for particular events.

Power aware computing includes techniques to distribute power required by processes among themselves before the commencement of execution. But these techniques need constant supervision since each computing processes might be unique with unique power utilization and processing. Also with any small diversion in the execution routine due to some emergency events or happenings the power requirement may change. This is where pervasive computing techniques to handle events could do its magic by keeping an eye on processing all the time.

Introducing this concept into green computing gives rise to a new concept by merging power awareness with event driven computing. This can take care of any emergency power requirement or diverting situations. So finally the users get the control of power distribution and usage in their own computing systems.

5   Event Driven Power Aware Computing (EDPAC): A New Thought

Power awareness computing aims at efficient management of power usage by introducing some constraints to control the power utilized for executing computing processes. This includes techniques like hibernation during idle time, control of the power flowing into the system for each execution processes, cutting off power from inactive components of the systems during computing and so on. Even if these measures are implemented, still it is difficult to monitor the consumption of power completely and continuously for each processing activity.

Applying Event Driven Computing in Power Awareness gives rise to Event Driven Power Aware Computing (EDPAC). Here we merge the properties of power aware computing with event driven computing. This gives us continuous control over power flow to computing procedures without interruption. Merging the pervasiveness of event driven computing in power aware computing can increase its efficiency for achieving greenness in its computing procedures by almost 15 percentages. It gives us the power to manipulate the processing and regulate power flow in our system from any part of the world at any time. Figure 3 shows the comparison of existing power aware computing and our proposed system EDPAC.

6   Salient Features of EDPAC

Event Driven Power Aware Computing (EDPAC) gives the maximum control of power usage in pervasive computing. The new approach enables constant continuous monitoring over our computing system processing from anywhere anytime. With EDPAC we can divert the power usage in right direction. Apart from the normal power control, our system is enriched with the following features.

6.1   Power Flow Regulation

EDPAC gives us the control to regulate the flow of power through different components in computing systems. If only some components are active during a particular computing procedure, power flow through the system can be restricted to these components.

6.2   Efficient Power Utilization

Power consumed by the whole system can be efficiently utilized by implementing EDPAC, which ensures adequate power supply for computing procedures. Hence it improves the performance and thus enables faster yet green computing.

6.3   Reduction in Power Conception and Leakage

By monitoring the total consumption and usage pattern of power for a system we can identify the leakage percentage in power during active and idle time. Thus we can prevent leakage of power through peripheral devices by issuing commands through message services enabled by pervasiveness in our handheld devices.

6.4   Continuous Power Monitoring

With the help of continuous monitoring, we can keep track of power aware events happening and the necessary actions performed in the system. If we need any changes, in the current scenario, to the actions preset with constraint matching, we can issue commands through our handheld device accordingly.

6.5   Power Allocation to Computing Procedures

We can regulate the power allocated to different computing procedures as per the demands of the scenario. For instance, if the procedure to be executed is not an urgent or complex one we can issue commands accordingly to perform them with medium power in a moderate pace.

6.6   Emergency Power Control

For emergency situations, EDPAC empowers us to create and perform new power regulation constraints and actions through message services as soon as the events are triggered. This gives us the power to take control of any worst case situations affecting power utilization.

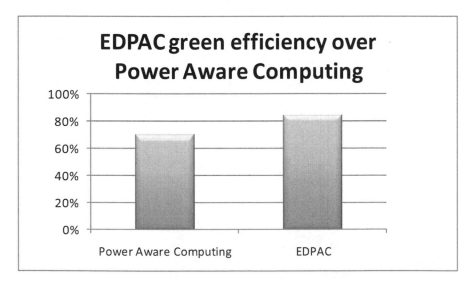

Fig. 3. The figure shows the comparison of efficiency in achieving Green computing between EDPAC and PAC

7   Future Enhancements

In future EDPAC can be extended to control over heat dissipation issues in green computing. Since the primary reason for heat dissipation is inefficient power utilization, implementing EDPAC can reduce much of the impact of the issue. This will aid the users to get aware of the situation and use the computing system in an efficient and eco-friendly manner.

8   Conclusion

In this paper we have listed the advantages of pervasive computing and its role in green computing. With the awareness of this we have developed a power aware computing system EDPAC, which will lead to extended event driven approach in green computing thus creating an environment of power awareness.

References

1. Murugesan, S.: Making IT Green. IT Professional 12(2) (2010)
2. Paradiso, J., Dutta, P., Gellersen, H., Schooler, E.: Smart Energy Systems. IEEE Pervasive Computing 10(1) (2011)
3. Stan, M.R., Skadron, K.: Power-aware computing. Computer 36(12) (2003)
4. Lo, C.-T.D., Qian, K.: Green Computing Methodology for Next Generation Computing Scientists. In: 34th Annual IEEE Computer Software and Applications Conference (2010); Dey, A., Abowd, G., Towards a Better Understanding of Context and Context-Awareness. Presented at Workshop on the What, Who, Where, When and How of Context-Awareness at CHI (2000)
5. Chilamkurti, N., Zeadally, S., Jamalipour, A., Das, S.K.: Enabling Wireless Technologies for Green Pervasive Computing. EURASIP Journal on Wireless Communications and Networking (2009)
6. Reddy, Y.V.: Pervasive Computing: Implications, Opportunities and Challenges for the Society. In: 1st International Symposium on Pervasive Computing and Applications (2006)
7. Bhaskar, P., Ahamed, S.I.: Privacy in Pervasive Computing and Open Issues. In: Second International Conference on Availability, Reliability and Security, ARE 2007 (April 2007)
8. Green Computing Guide, The University of Colorado – Boulder, http://ecenter.colorado.edu/energy/projects/green_computing.html
9. Murphy, R., Sterling, T., Dekate, C.: Advanced Architectures and Execution Models to Support Green Computing. Computing in Science and Engineering 12 (2010)
10. Qian, K., Lo, C.-T.D., Yang, L.: Work in Progress – Bring green computing to CS core curriculum with a portable lab. In: Frontiers in Education Conference (FIE), IEEE (2010)
11. Chang, J.-Y.: Green Technology and Service. In: ICMECG 2008 International Conference on Management of e-Commerce and e-Government (2008)
12. Williams, J., Curtis, L.: Green: The New Computing Coat of Arms? IT Professional 10(1) (2008)
13. Want, R.: How Green is Green? . IEEE Pervasive Computing 8(1) (2009)

14. Wang, D.: Meeting Green Computing Challenges. In: International Symposium on High Density Packaging and Microsystem Integration, HDP 2007 (2007)
15. Zhou, B., Marshall, A., Lee, T.-H.: Wireless Security Issues in Pervasive Computing. In: Fourth International Conference on Genetic and Evolutionary Computing, ICGEC (2010)
16. Kishino, Y., Terada, T., Tsukamoto, M., Nishio, S.: A ubiquitous computing environment composed by cooperation between visual markers and event-driven compact devices. In: International Workshop on Ubiquitous Data Management, UDM 2005 (2005)
17. Dasgupta, S., Bhat, S., Lee, Y.: Event driven service composition for pervasive computing. In: IEEE International Conference on Pervasive Computing and Communications, Percom 2009 (2009)
18. Jimeno, M., Christensen, K., Nordman, B.: A Network Connection Proxy to Enable Hosts to Sleep and Save Energy. In: IEEE International Performance, Computing and Communications Conference, IPCCC 2008 (2008)
19. van Bemmel, J., Dockhorn, P., Widya, I.: Paradigm: Event Driven Computing (white Paper), https://doc.novay.nl/dsweb/Get/Document-55291/
20. Green Computing Guide, The University of Colorado – Boulder, http://ecenter.colorado.edu/energy/projects/green_computing.html

Coloured Petri Net for Modelling and Validation of Dynamic Transmission Range Adjustment Protocol in an Ad-Hoc Network

Lopamudra Mohapatra and Debansu Panda

Computer Science and Engineering Department,
National Institute of Technology Rourkela
lopamudra.cse@gmail.com, debansu89@hotmail.com

Abstract. The IEEE 802.11 standard defines two operational modes for WLANs: infrastructure-based and infrastructure-less or ad-hoc. With constrained resources and limited computational capability, it may not be able for a node to serve more number of neighbours at the same time. The Dynamic Transmission Range Adjustment Protocol provides a mechanism for adjusting transmission range of the ad-hoc nodes to register or de-register a communicating node as its neighbour by dynamically varying the transmission range. Coloured Petri Nets is the modelling tool which provides a framework for design, specification, validation and verification of systems. In this paper, this tool is used to model and validate Dynamic Transmission Range Adjustment Protocol.

Keywords: Coloured Petri Nets, Ad-hoc network, Dynamic Transmission Range Adjustment Protocol, Transmission Range, Neighbouring nodes, Topology Control, Routing.

1   Introduction

In an infrastructure-based wireless network, the nodes communicate through an access point that serves as a bridge to a wired-network infrastructure. However, we can have peer-to-peer communication in an infrastructure-less network.

1.1   Ad-Hoc Network

The IEEE 802.11 defines similar modes of operation for both infrastructure-based and ad-hoc networks. The use of ad-hoc mode has an impact on the protocols implemented, and there is no effect on the physical layers (802.11a and 802.11b).

In the MAC layer, the handling of frames and the carrier-sensing responsibilities are quite the same in the modes. However, due to the absence of access-points in the ad-hoc mode, more of the MAC layer tasks must be taken up by the ad-hoc wireless LAN. Factors like saving the cost of purchase or installation of access-points, less set-up time, etc favour the use of ad-hoc network.

N. Meghanathan et al. (Eds.): CCSIT 2012, Part II, LNICST 85, pp. 89–99, 2012.

1.2   Coloured Petri Nets

To validate dynamic and adaptive routing protocols, Coloured Petri Nets serves as an excellent modelling and validation tool to depict discrete events. It combines standard MLs and Petri Nets. CPN models of a system can be built to represent the various states the system is in and the transitions that cause a change of state. Using CPN tools, simulations are run to investigate the behaviour and verify its properties. Free license for this tool is available.

2   Mobile Ad-Hoc Networks (MANET)

MANET, which communicate using radio frequency has a decentralized architecture. With the advent of MANETs, a new art in the field of network management was discovered which enabled a network to be designed without being heavily dependent of the infrastructure establishment. The Quality of Service (QoS) of the network is likely to be affected unless specialized schemes are developed to handle such dynamic networks. The nodes are the transmitting stations and are limited by a transmission range, so in most cases a direct communication between the source and receiver is not facilitated. To solve this issue, the nodes communicate in a multi-hop fashion to relay packets from the source to the destination. Therefore, the nodes function as both hosts and routers. This enables communication between nodes even when they are not in the transmission range of one another. Due to the decentralized nature of the network, it is not possible for a node to know the entire state of the network. So, the nodes frequently transmit messages to get updated about the network. Moreover, the motion of the nodes results in disruption of the links as they may frequently go out of the transmission range, thereby hampering routing in MANETs.

The MANET network interfaces differ from conventional wired network interfaces based on various scenario-dependent factors like:-

-Relative motion of the neighbours resulting in environmental and distance effects
-Dynamic local noise and interference caused by the nodes itself
-Links established between the nodes are often asymmetric in nature
-Time varying communication channels
-Lower layer wireless protocol behaviours.

2.1   Routing Approaches

Routing in MANETs is a dynamic optimization task aimed at providing an optimal path in terms of some criterion and also satisfying some constraints like limited power, transmission range, etc. Therefore, based on when the routing tables are built MANET routing algorithms are categorised as:-

1) **Proactive algorithms:** where routes to all other nodes are maintained at all times[1].

2) **Reactive algorithms:** which are on-demand routing techniques.

3) **Hybrid algorithms:** which exhibit reactive and proactive behaviour depending on the circumstances. They maintain routes to nearby nodes even if they are not needed and maintain routes to far away nodes only when needed [2].

The typical design goals for routing protocols in MANETs include: minimal control overhead, minimal processing, multihop routing, dynamically changing topology and prevention of occurrence of loops.

2.2   Protocol Stack

The MANET protocol stack is quite similar to the TCP/IP protocol stack except for the network layer. The network layer is divided into two parts- network and ad hoc routing. Since the nodes in a MANET can act as both hosts and routers, the implement an ad-hoc routing protocol to relay packets. The network part uses the IP protocol where the ad-hoc part uses various other protocols specifically designed for ad hoc networks. The lower layers, the datalink and the physical layer implement protocol designed for wireless communication.

3   Coloured Petri Nets (CPN)

Coloured Petri nets (CP-nets or CPNs) is a language used for modelling and validation of systems having concurrency, communication and synchronization as vital aspects [4]. They provide a framework for the design, specification, validation and verification of systems [5]. CP-nets is used to model discrete-event systems.CPN is a combination of Petri nets and Standard ML. Standard ML is a functional programming language that provides primitives for defining data types and for their manipulation, describing how data can be manipulated and for the creation of compact and parameterisable models [4]. A CPN model describes the various states the system is in at different points of time. It also specifies the events (transitions) that cause the system to change its state. By making simulations, the system design can be investigated, the different scenarios it can possibly be explored and the behaviour of the model can be tested therein. Also, it is possible to verify the properties of the system by state-space methods and a simulation-based performance analysis can be generated. The users can interact with the CPN tool by direct manipulation of the graphical representation using user-interaction techniques like the tool palette and marking menus [6].

3.1   Modelling of States

The basic constructs of the CPN model are:

1) **Places:** These are ellipses or circles and indicate the states of the system.

2) **Types:** Each place is associated with a type, also called as a colour-set. These indicate the type of data a place can hold, very similar to that in programming languages.

3) **Transitions:** These are represented by rectangles. The names of transitions are written inside these rectangles. The actions of the system are represented by means of transitions. An action of a CP-net consists of one or more transitions occurring concurrently.

4) **Markings:** They indicate the state of the system. Marking refers to the tokens positioned over the individual places. Tokens refers to the data value(colour) present at the place. The colour-sets are synonymous to the data-types and the colours are synonymous to the data-values.

5) **Initial Marking:** A CP-net has a distinguished marking called the initial marking, which is used to describe the initial state of the system.

6) **Arcs and Arc Expressions:** Arcs are used to connect transitions and places. A transition can be enabled only when the two criteria are satisfied:-

1) All the arc expressions must evaluate to the tokens which are present on the corresponding places connected to the incoming arc.
2) The guard conditions must be satisfied, if any.

Places and transitions are referred to as nodes. Nodes along with the directed arcs constitute the net structure. An arc always connects a place to a transition or a transition to a place. However, two transitions or two places cannot be connected directly by arcs. A number of tokens along with the token colours on the individual places are representative of the state of the system and is called a marking of the CPN model. On the other hand, the tokens on a specific place form the marking of that place [5].

3.2   Construction of Hierarchical Models

The concept of hierarchical CP-nets allows the modeller to construct a large model by an aggregation of a number of small CP-nets called pages. Substitution transitions are used to implement the hierarchy concept. They are replaced by subpages which contain the detailed description of the activity represented by the corresponding substitution transition. The subpages have a number of places marked with an In-tag, Out-tag, or I/O-tag. These places are called port places. They provide an interface through which the subpage communicates with its surroundings. The port places of the subpage must be assigned to the socket places in the main page in-order to specify the relationship between a substitution transition and the subpage. This is referred to as the port-socket assignment [4]. The Hierarchy palette provided by the GUI helps in the construction of hierarchical models. The different steps to construct hierarchical models are described later in the paper. Heirarchy can be implemented as:

Top-Down Approach:- using The Move to Submodule tool

Bottom-Up Approach:- using The Assign Submodule tool.

3.3   Syntax Check and Code Generation

CPN Tools performs syntax and type checking, and simulation code generation. The processes of syntax checking and code generation are incremental in nature. They are parallel performed with editing.When a simulation is run, the following is the simulation feedback shown:

1) Current markings of places are indicated near the individual places.
2) The number of tokens currently present at a place is given by a green circle.
3) The corresponding token values at the places are shown in green boxes.
4) Green auras are present around enabled transitions.
5) Green underlines are shown on the pages with enabled transitions.
6) The step count and time taken is shown in the index for the net under simulation.
[6] The main outcome of the code generation phase is the generation of the simulation code. The simulation code contains the functions for inferring the set of enabled binding elements in a given marking of the CPN model, and for computing the marking reached after an enabled binding element occurs [4].

4   Topology Control in MANETS

The network topology is determined by the links between the nodes that is used by the routing mechanism. MANETs are indeterministic in nature and the topology of the network is dependent on a number of factors like mobility of the nodes, their battery power, the traffic patterns in the network, noise, interference and transmission power of nodes. However, these factors are subject to changes depending on the current state of the network and its present demands.

The network size, referring to the number of nodes in the network and their distribution has an effect on the performance of the network. A sparse network may have numerous network partitions and the entire network may be divided into disconnected portions. Thereby, the connectivity is hampered and it may result in lack of routes for packet transmission. On the other hand, dense networks may have problems like congestion and contention for bandwidth leading to a low packet delivery ratio. More number of collisions are also caused and thereby more energy is expended in overcoming these.

4.1   Dynamic Transmission Range Adjustment Protocol

In a multi-hop ad-hoc network, communication between two nodes may be disrupted if an intermediate node moves out of the fixed transmission range. So the nodes must be capable of dynamic reconfiguration by self-adjusting the variable transmission range. A low transmission range may result in a sparse network and the connectivity among nodes may not be effective. On the contrary, a high transmission range will ensure connectivity but collision and congestion of control packets will increase, which may significantly increase the end-to-end delay. In an operating area, when there are fixed number of nodes distributed uniformly, the optimality in transmission range is essential. Thus, a variable transmission range protocol like the Dynamic Transmission Range Adjustment Protocol (DTRAP) would be highly effective in such a dynamic environment [5].

The Dynamic Transmission Range Adjustment Protocol provides a mechanism for adjusting the transmission range of the ad hoc nodes. The nodes are configured to maintain a threshold number of neighbours based on their available resources. The nodes protect their neighbourhood relationship during data communication by controlling their transmission range. It can register or de-register a node as its neighbour by dynamically varying its transmission range in steps. However, there is a maximum limit of the transmission range. It can register or de-register a node as its neighbour by dynamically varying its transmission range in steps. However, there is a maximum limit of the transmission range beyond which it cannot be increased. If the separating distance between the nodes is less than the maximum transmission range and;

1) if the number of neighbours of a node is less than the threshold value, the node dynamically increases its transmission range in steps until it is ensured of an optimal number of neighbours.

2) if the number of neighbours of a node exceeds the threshold value, the node dynamically decreases its transmission range in steps until it is ensured of an optimal number of neighbour [5].

5   Design and Validation

In the field of multi-hop wireless network, it is almost inevitable for any design to overcome the disturbance in communication process and also a design which allows us to control the packet congestion in a dynamic field, which in turn reduces delay in end-to-end communication. The self adjustable transmission protocol, which forms a part of DTRAP is an efficient protocol with regards to the ad hoc network.

The work is based on two significant phases:

1) Design and modelling the ad hoc network using CPN.
2) Validate the above model for the Dynamic Transmission Range Adjustment Protocol using CPN.

5.1   Installation

The CPN tool software was downloaded from the Aarhus University site which provides license for the use of this tool. On downloading the set up file, it was successfully installed alongwith its component files.

As a start up the help page is referred to get used to the different options and components of of this tool.

5.2   Establishing Link by Finding Neighbours

This forms the core part of our project where in we have taken five static nodes in an ad hoc network. These five nodes share a common message store *MsgStore*. The page *MsgStore* shows the five nodes and their messages being sent to the *MsgStore*.

which portrays the establishing of link of each node with its neighbours. The subpage *AH(3)* demonstrates the neighbour node determination. Here the parameters of the node such as its co-ordinates, battery power, mobility and counter (which keeps a note of its number neighbour, initialized as zero) is broadcast to the *MsgStore*. The appropriate or intended node retrieves the *MSG* from the *MsgStore*.

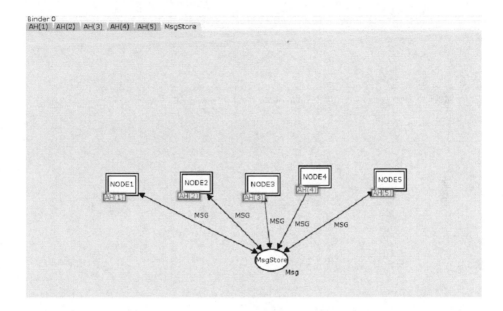

Fig. 1. Model of five nodes communicating

Distance Calculation: *CalculateDistance* transition is fed with the senders and the receivers co-ordinates. On _ring this transition it calculates the distance between them. If the distance is within a specified transmission range then it returns a Boolean yes else no.

```
fun GetDistance(k:INT,l:INT,p:INT,q:INT)=if (((k-p)*(k-
       p)+(1-q)*(1-q))<961) then yes else no;
```

Counter Increment: *IncrememntCounter* is fed with the previous step counter value and the boolean returned by *CalculateDistance*. So initially it is fed with zero. Whenever is the boolean is yes, the counter gets incremented by1.

```
fun Update Cnt(m:BOOL)=if(m=yes) then 1 else 0;
                c+Update Cnt(b);
```

The place CntNei keeps a track of the counter value for each and every node.

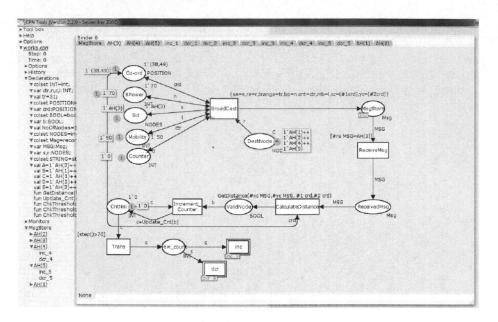

Fig. 2. Extensive view of AH(3)

5.3   Validation of DTRAP Using CPN

TRANS: We use a transition Trans which is fed with updated final counter value. This transition is fired only when the no. of steps is greater than the no. of steps taken so that no token value is left behind at any place. Here we use the control flow concept. We only take the counter value when it has reached to the end of execution leading to no leaving behind of tokens in any of the places in the model. The advantage of using such control flow mechanism is: The place *CountNei* acts as a store and the value stored in this place can be used subsequently in the DTRAP validation.

5.4   Transmission Range Adjustment

The output of the Trans is fed to a place, new count which is the node parameter as specified earlier. This dynamic counter keeps the updated value of the count of number of nodes. This updated c is passed to two substitution transitions:

1)inc
2)dcr

Here we use the hierarchy concept of CPN tools. *inc* and *dcr* are substitution transitions and when fired, they invoke two subpages , *inc* # and *dcr* # respectively.

Subpages are used to replace the substitution transition *inc* in order to increment the transmission range whenever the number of neighbours falls short of the threshold value. The increment is done in steps of 5. The updated transmission range is stored in a place, *newrng*. Subpages are used to replace the substitution transition dcr in order to decrement the transmission range whenever the number of neighbours falls short the threshold value. The increment is done in steps of 5. The updated transmission range is stored in a place, *newrng*.

```
fun ChkThreshold(c:INT)=if(c>=2)then tr-5 else tr+5;
```

The steps to construct a hierarchical model are:-

1) Move a transition or group to a new submodule.
2) Replace a substitution transition with its submodule.
3) Assign a submodule to a substitution transition.
4) Assign a port to a socket.
5) Set port type to input.
6) Set port type to output.
7) Set port type to input/output.
8) Assign a place to a fusion set. [4]

For example; if we take node 3: the no. of neighbours=3. Initial transmission range was 31. So now since 3>2 (as used in the simulation, the threshold no. of nodes are 2), hence new range is 31-5= 26.

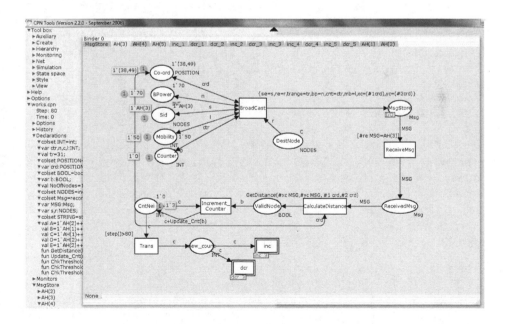

Fig. 3. Counter value of AH(3) after simulation is run

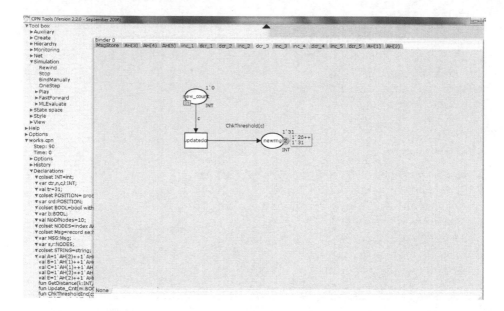

Fig. 4. Transmission range of AH(3) after simulation is run

The Dynamic Transmission Range Adjustment protocol is implemented here using five nodes. The situation of incrementing the transmission range has been successfully achieved. The next task towards the validation of the Dynamic Transmission Range Adjustment protocol is by validation of the decrementing the transmission range for the same, using Coloured Petri Net Tool.

6   Conclusion

Our work is based on ad hoc network which works on static nodes. It can be further extended to mobile nodes. Validation of this protocol ensures that the self adjusting transmission range protocol can be implemented in ad hoc network for bringing optimality in the resource utilization of nodes. It has got variety of application in the field of sensor network as well and also in emergency situations like natural disasters or military conflicts.

References

[1] Basagni, S.: Mobile Ad Hoc Networking. John Willey and Sons Publication (2004)
[2] Hu, Y.-C., Johnson, D.B.: Securing Quality-of-Service Route Discovery in On- Demand Routing for Ad Hoc Networks (1999)
[3] Paul, K., Bandopadhyay, S.: Self Adjusting Transmission Range Control of Mobile Hosts in Ad Hoc Wireless Networks for Stable Communication. In: Banerjee, P., Prasanna, V.K., Sinha, B.P. (eds.) HiPC 1999. LNCS, vol. 1745. Springer, Heidelberg (1999)

[4] Jensen, K., Kristensen, L.M., Wells, L.: Coloured Petrinets and CPN Tools for Modelling and Validation of Concurrent Systems. Int. J. Softw. Tools Technol. Transfer 9, 213–254 (2007); University of Aarhus (1996)

[5] Kristensen, L.M., Christensen, S., Jensen, K.: The Practitioners Guide to Coloured Petri nets. Int. J. STTT 2, 98–132 (1998); University of Aarhus (1998)

[6] Tan, H.X., Seah, W.K.G.: Dynamic Topology Control to Reduce Interference in MANETs, Department of Computer Science, School of Computing, National University of Singapore. In: Proc. of 2nd International Conference on Mobile Computing and Ubiquitous, 2005 Networking (2005)

Security Analysis of Proxy Blind Signature Scheme Based on Factoring and ECDLP

Namita Tiwari and Sahadeo Padhye

Department of Mathematics,
Motilal Nehru National Institute of Technology,
Allahabad-211004, India
{namita.mnnit,sahadeomathrsu}@gmail.com

Abstract. Proxy blind Signature is a digital signature where an original signer delegates his/her signing capability to a proxy signer who performs message signing blindly, on behalf of original signer but he cannot make a linkage between the blind signature and the identity of the message's owner. Recently, Qi et al proposed an improved proxy blind signature scheme based on factoring and elliptic curve discrete log problem (ECDLP). In this paper we show that Qi et al's scheme does not hold the identifiability and unlinkability properties. Moreover, we also point out that their scheme is not secure against universal forgery attack. Furthermore, we propose an improved proxy blind signature scheme to remedy the weaknesses of Qi et al.'s scheme. The security and performance of the improved scheme are also analyzed.

Keywords: Proxy Signature, Blind Signature, Elliptic Curve Discrete-log problem, Integer Factorization.

1 Introduction

A digital signature is an electronic signature that can be used to authenticate the identity of the sender of a message or the signer of a document, and possibly to ensure that the original content of the message or document that has been sent is unchanged. A lot of researches have been contributed to this field using various cryptographic primitives [8]. However, there are many practical environments where digital signatures do not possess specific requirements, and thereby digital signatures appear in several other forms viz. proxy signatures, blind signatures etc. For example, a manager of the company needs to go on a business trip which does not have very good computer network accesses, he expects to receive his e-mail and has instructed his secretary to respond accordingly. Question is, how a manager gives secretary the power, to sign message for her without giving him, her private key? Proxy signature is the solution of this problem. The concept of proxy signature was firstly introduced by Mambo et al [9]. Proxy signature enables a proxy signer to sign messages, on behalf of an original signer.

On the other hand, blind signature also has its own importance for specific situations and purposes. The notion of blind signature was firstly introduced by

N. Meghanathan et al. (Eds.): CCSIT 2012, Part II, LNICST 85, pp. 100–108, 2012.
© Institute for Computer Sciences, Social Informatics and Telecommunications Engineering 2012

David Chaum [2] in 1982. Blind Signature is a signature on a message, signed by another party without having any information about the message. Its name is so, because the message is blind to the signer. Blind signatures are applicable where sender's privacy is important, like: digital cash scheme, electronic voting *etc.*

A proxy blind signature scheme is a digital signature scheme which combines the properties of proxy signature and blind signature schemes. In a proxy blind signature scheme, the proxy signer is allowed to generate a blind signature on behalf of the original signer. This is a typical untraceable scheme which allows a user to withdraw a valid e-coin from a proxy bank and spend the coin anonymously at a shop. It is very important in electronic cash payment system [1,3,4], anonymous proxy electronic voting *etc.* Proxy blind signature must satisfy the security properties of proxy signature and blind signature.

Distinguishability- The proxy blind signature must be distinguishable from the normal signature.

Verifiability- The verifier should be able to verify the proxy signature in a similar way to the verification of the original signature.

Unforgeability- Only the designated proxy signer can create a valid proxy signature, for the original signer (even the original signer can not do it).

Nonrepudiation- Neither the original signer nor the proxy signer can sign in place of the other party. In other words, they cannot deny their signatures against anyone.

Identifiability- Anyone can determine the identity of the corresponding proxy signer from a proxy signature.

Prevention of misuse- It should be confident that proxy key pair should be used only for creating proxy signature, which conforms to delegation information. In case of any misuse of proxy key pair, the responsibility of proxy signer should be determined explicitly.

Unlinkability- After proxy blind signature is created, the proxy signer knows neither the message nor the signature associated with the signature scheme.

Elliptic curve cryptography (ECC) is considered as an important topic in public key cryptography. In 1985, Koblitz [6] and Miller [7], independently proposed it using the group of points on an elliptic curve defined over a finite field. The security of the system is based on ECDLP. The main advantage of ECC is that it provides the same security level with smaller key size [11]. Smaller key means less management time and smaller storage, which supplies convenience to realization by software and hardware. In 2002, by applying Schnorr blind signature, Tan et al. [12] presented two proxy blind signature schemes, which are respectively based on discrete logarithm problem (DLP) and ECDLP.

In 2005, Wang et al. [13] proposed a proxy blind signature scheme based on ECDLP. In 2008, Yang et al. [14] proved that Wang et al.'s scheme did not possess the strong nonrepudiation, strong unforgeability and unllinkability properties and proposed an improved proxy blind signature scheme, to remedy the weaknesses of Wang et al.'s scheme. In 2009, Hu et al [5] presented a security analysis on Yang's proxy blind signature scheme [14], and demonstrated that scheme is insecure. It suffers from the original signer's forgery attack and the universal forgery attack. It didn't possess the strong identifiability property in addition. Furthermore, an improved proxy blind signature scheme based on ECDLP was given to overcome the weaknesses of Yang's scheme.

Recently, Qi et al [10] introduced a proxy blind signature scheme based on factoring and ECDLP, which ensures security properties of both the schemes, namely, the blind signature schemes and the proxy signature schemes. In this paper, we analyze the security of Qi et al's proxy blind signature scheme [10] and demonstrate that this scheme is insecure against universal forgery attack. We also show that it does not satisfy the unlinkability requirement and identifiability property. To overcome the weaknesses of Qi et al's scheme [10], we propose an improved proxy blind signature scheme which satisfies all the security requirements for a proxy blind signature. At the same time, the performance of the new scheme is superior to Qi et al's scheme [10].

The rest of this paper is organized as follows. In section 2, we briefly introduce some preliminary works. Brief review of Qi et al's [10], with security analysis is summarized in section 3. Section 4 includes improved scheme with security and comparative analysis. The last section concludes this paper.

2   Preliminaries

2.1   Background of Elliptic Curve Group

The symbol E/F_p denotes an elliptic curve E over a prime finite field F_p, defined by an equation
$$y^2 = x^3 + ax + b, \ a, b \in F_p, \text{ and}$$
discriminant $\Delta = 4a^3 + 27b^2 \neq 0$.

The points on E/F_p together with an extra point O called the point at infinity form a group $G = \{(x, y) : x, y \in F_p, E(x, y) = 0\} \cup \{O\}$.

Let the order of G be n. G is a cyclic additive group under the point addition "$+$" defined as follows: Let $P, Q \in G$, l be the line containing P and Q (tangent line to E/F_p if $P = Q$), and R, the third point of intersection of l with E/F_p. Let l' be the line connecting R and O. Then $P + Q$ is the point such that l' intersects E/F_p at R and O and $P + Q$.

Scalar multiplication over E/F_p can be computed as follows:
$tP = P + P + \ldots\ldots + P(t \ times)$.

2.2   Complexity Assumption

The following problems assumed to be intractable within polynomial time in the proposed scheme.

Elliptic curve discrete logarithm problem (ECDLP)- For $x \in_R Z_n^*$ and P the generator of G , given $Q = x.P$ compute x.

Integer Factoring Problem (IFP)- For a given composite integer n, compute prime factors p' and q' such that $n = p'q'$.

3 Brief Review of Qi et al's Scheme

In this section, we present a brief review of the scheme [10], with security analysis. Further, we demonstrate that this scheme is insecure against universal forgery attack. We also show that it does not satisfy the unlinkability and identifiability property.

3.1 Scheme Description

Qi et al's Scheme [10] with notations used in [10], is given below.

Delegation Phase- The original signer initializes the scheme by first generating two modulus: a prime p and a composite $n = p'q'$. The signer A next computes public and secret keys of the scheme and sends the public keys to proxy signer B and keeps secret keys secretly. The original signer A generates the following system parameters :

- chooses $e' \in_R Z_n$ such that $gcd(e', n) = 1$,
- selects d such that $e'd \equiv 1 mod\phi(n)$,
- chooses randomly an integer x' from $0 < x' < n$, computes $y' = g^{x'} mod(p)$, then publishes (y', e').
- chooses randomly w, u such that $w, u < n$
computes $M = g^{h(m)^w} \bmod (p)$, $N = g^{h(m)^u} \bmod (p)$,
then $s^* = (x'h(m) + Mh(m)^u + Nh(m)^w)^d \bmod (p)$,
- A large prime number N which is the order of the elliptic curve cryptosystem, where $\#E(GF(p))$ lies between $p + 1 - 2\sqrt{p}$ and $p + 1 + 2\sqrt{p}$,
- chooses randomly k' such that $1 < k' < n$, computes $R' = k'P$, $r' = x(R')$
- computes $s' = k_A r' + k' \bmod n$

A sends the delegation parameter (r', s', R', M, N, s^*) to B.
Proxy signer B checks whether $R' = s'P - r'P_A$ and $g^{s^* e'} = y'^{h(m)} M^N N^M \bmod (p)$. If these equations hold, B computes $\bar{s} = s' + k_B \bmod n$.

Signing Phase- Proxy signer B chooses $1 < k < n$, computes $T = kP$, Then he/she sends (r', s', T) to owner C.
Owner C chooses $1 < a, b < n$, computes
$R = T + bP + (-a - b)P_B + (-a)R' + (-ar')P_A$,
$r = x(R)$, $e = h(r||m) \bmod n$, $e^* = e - a - b$
$U = (-e + b)R + (-e + b)r'P_A - eP_A$ and send e^* to B.
Proxy signer B computes $s'' = e^*\bar{s} + k \bmod n$ and returns s'' to C.
Owner C computes $s = s'' + b \bmod n$. The resulting signature is (m, s, e, U).

Verification Phase- It can be verified by checking whether $e = h(x(sP - eP_B + eP_A + U)||m)$ mod n holds. Here, P_A and P_B are public keys of original and proxy signer respectively.

3.2   Security Analysis of Qi et al's Scheme

We demonstrate here that scheme [10] is insecure.

Universal Forgery Attack- Suppose there is an adversary E, who wants to forge a valid proxy blind signature on any message of his choice (say m'),
E chooses $k', s' \in_R Z_n^*$ and computes
$$R' = (k' + s')P$$
$$r' = x(R') \text{ and } e' = h(r'||m') \text{ mod } n$$
$$U' = k'P + e'P_B - e'P_A, \text{ and outputs the forged proxy blind}$$
signature (m', s', e', U'). Here, P_A and P_B are public keys of original and proxy signer respectively.
Indeed,
$$h[x(s'P - e'P_B + e'P_A + U')||m'] \text{ mod } n$$
$$= h[x(s'P - e'P_B + e'P_A + k'P + e'P_B - e'P_A)||m'] \text{ mod } n$$
$$= h[x(s'P + k'P)||m'] \text{ mod } n$$
$$= h(r'||m') \text{ mod } n$$
$$= e'$$
Therefore, the tuple (m', s', e', U') is a valid proxy blind signature.

Absence of Unlinkability- The proxy signer can save the signing transcripts $(T, e^*, s")$ during generation of the signature. With a proxy blind signature tuple (m, s, e, U), the proxy unlinkability holds, if and only if there is no conjunction between $(T, e^*, s")$ and (m, s, e, U). In the above scheme [10], with (m, s, e, U), proxy signer B can find its corresponding signing transcripts as follows:
B computes $b = (s - s") \text{ mod } n$,
$$a = (e - b - e^*) \text{ mod } n,$$
$$R = T + bP + (-a - b)P_B + (-a)R' + (-ar')P_A,$$
Now B checks
$$U = (-e + b)R + (-e + b)r'P_A - eP_A,$$
If it does, B can link (m, s, e, U) to $(T, e^*, s")$ successfully.

Absence of Identifiability- In Qi et al's scheme, the proxy blind signature is (m, s, e, U) and the verification equation is $e = h(x(sP - eP_B + eP_A + U)||m)$ mod n. The public keys P_A and P_B of original signer and the proxy signer respectively are in the same position. Therefore, it is difficult to distinguish the identity of proxy signer from proxy signature. The scheme does not satisfy identifiability.

4   Improved Scheme

To remedy the weakness of Qi et al's scheme [10], we propose an improvement on [10], and present the security analysis and efficiency comparisons of proposed scheme with [10].

4.1   Scheme Description

Our scheme is described as follows.

System Parameters- System Parameters used in the scheme are as follows.
- p and q are two large primes such that $q/p - 1$.
- An additive group $Z_p = \{0, 1, 2, ..., p - 1\}$.
- $g \in Z_p^*$ having order q.
- P is the generator of elliptic curve group of order n.
- (k_A, P_A): private & pubic key pair of original signer A such that $P_A = k_A P$.
- (k_B, P_B): private & pubic key pair of proxy signer B such that $P_B = k_B P$.
- $H : \{0, 1\}^* \rightarrow Z_n^*$ is a public cryptographically strong hash function.
- $\|$ is the concatenation of strings.
- a message m represents a monetary value which the customer can spent.
- $\phi(.)$ is the phi-Euler function.
- $gcd(a, b)$ is the greatest common divisor of a and b.
- $x(Q)$ is the x coordinate of a point Q on the elliptic curve E..

Proxy Phase- The original signer A generates the following system parameters.
- chooses $e' \in_R Z_p^*$ such that $gcd(e', \phi(p - 1)) = 1$,
- selects d such that $e'd \equiv 1 mod \phi(p - 1)$,
- chooses $x' \in \{2, 3, ...p - 2\}$, computes $y' = g^{x'} mod(p)$, then publishes (y', e').
- chooses $w, u \in \{2, 3, ...p - 2\}$ and computes $M = g^{H(m_w)^w} \bmod (p)$, $N = g^{H(m_w)^u} \bmod (p)$, then $s^* = (x'H(m_w) + MH(m_w)^u + NH(m_w)^w)^d \bmod \phi(p)$,
- chooses $k' \in_R Z_n^*$, computes $R' = k'P$, $r' = x(R')$
- computes $h = H(r'\|m_w)$ and $s' = k_A h + k' \bmod n$.
   A sends the delegation parameter (m_w, s', R', M, N, s^*) to B.

Proxy signer B checks, whether $R' = s'P - hP_A$ and $g^{s^{*e'}} = y'^{H(m_w)} M^N N^M$ mod (p). If these equations hold, B computes $\overline{s} = s' + k_B \bmod n$.

Signing Phase- Proxy signer B chooses $k \in_R Z_n^*$, computes $T = kP$, Then he/she sends (m_w, R', s', T) to owner C.
Owner C chooses $a, b, c \in_R Z_n^*$, computes
$R = aT + bP + c(P_B + R' + hP_A)$,
$r = x(R)$, $e = H(r\|m) \bmod n$, $e^* = a^{-1}(e + c) \bmod n$ and sends e^* to B.
Proxy signer B computes $s'' = e^*\overline{s} + k \bmod n$ and returns s'' to C.
Owner C computes $s = as'' + b \bmod n$. The resulting proxy blind signature is (m_w, m, R', e, s).

Verification Phase- The verifier can verify the validity of the proxy blind signature by checking that $e = H(x(sP - e(P_B + R' + hP_A))\|m) \bmod n$ holds.

4.2   Security Analysis

We analyze the security of our scheme as follows.

Distinguishability- The proposed proxy blind signature (m_w, m, R', e, s) contains the warrant m_w while the normal signature does not, so both are different in the form. Also in the verification equation of proxy blind signature, public keys P_A, P_B and warrant m_w are used. So anyone can distinguish the proxy blind signature from normal signature easily.

Verifiability- The verifier of proxy blind signature, can check whether verification equation $e = H(x(sP - e(P_B + R' + hP_A))||m) \bmod n$ holds or not. We prove this as follows.

$$e= H(r||m) \bmod n$$
$$= H[x(R)||m] \bmod n,$$
$$= H[x(aT + bP + c(P_B + R' + hP_A))||m] \bmod n,$$
$$= H[x(aa^{-1}(e + c)(P_B + R' + hP_A) + akP + bP - e(P_B + R' + hP_A))||m]$$
$$\bmod n,$$
$$= H[x(ae^*(k_B + s')P + akP + bP - e(P_B + R' + hP_A))||m] \bmod n,$$
$$= H[x(a(e^*\bar{s} + k)P + bP - e(P_B + R' + hP_A))||m] \bmod n,$$
$$= H[x((as") + b)P - e(P_B + R' + hP_A))||m] \bmod n,$$
$$= H[x(sP - e(P_B + R' + hP_A))||m] \bmod n.$$

Unforgeability- In our scheme, only the designated proxy signer can create a valid proxy blind signature, since proxy private key $\bar{s} = s' + k_B$ includes the private key k_B of proxy signer and to compute k_B, is equivalent to solve ECDLP. In addition, if anyone wishes to forge secret keys (x', d), then he needs to solve $e'd \equiv 1 \bmod \phi(p - 1)$ and $y' = g^{x'} \bmod(p)$ respectively, for d and x'. But solving both congruences, is as difficult as solving IFP and DLP.

On the other hand, our scheme can withstand the universal forgery attack. Suppose, there is an adversary E, having a valid proxy blind signature (m_w, m, R', e, s) and he attempts to forge a valid proxy blind signature on message m', of his choice as (m_w, m', R', e', s'). Then E does as follows.

- computes $r' = x(R')$, $h = H(r'||m_w) \bmod n$
- selects $k_2 \in_R Z_n^*$, computes $R = k_2 P$
- computes $r = x(R)$, $e' = H(r||m') \bmod n$

then (m_w, m', R', e', s') being a valid proxy blind signature must satisfy the verification equation $e' = H[x(s'P - e'(P_B + R' + hP_A))||m'] \bmod n$.
E needs to solve $s'P - e'(P_B + R' + hP_A) = R$ for s'. But to do so, is as difficult as solving ECDLP.

Nonrepudiation- As in the verification equation, warrant m_w and public keys P_A, P_B are used. Also generation of proxy blind signature needs original and proxy signer's private key k_A, k_B respectively. It is already proved that neither the original signer nor the proxy signer can sign in place of other party. So the original signer can not deny his delegation and proxy signer can not deny having signed the message m on behalf of original signer to other party.

Identifiability- In the proposed scheme, it can be checked who is original signer and who is proxy signer, from warrant m_w. Also seeing from the verification equation, $e' = H[x(s'P - e'(P_B + R' + hP_A))||m']$ mod n, the public keys P_A, P_B are asymmetrical in position. So anyone can distinguish the identity of proxy signer from proxy blind signature.

Prevention of Misuse- Original signer generates the delegation parameter (m_w, s', R', M, N, s^*) and sends it to B. So the values of (m_w, s', R', M, N, s^*), can not be modified or forged. Also it is not possible for proxy signer B to transfer his proxy power to other party D, unless he provides proxy private key $\bar{s}$ to D. In addition, warrant m_w contains the limit of delegated signing capability. So it is not possible to sign the messages that have not been authorized by original signer.

Unlinkability- The proxy signer can save the signing transcripts $(T, e^*, s")$ during generation of the signature. With a proxy blind signature tuple (m_w, m, R', e, s), the proxy unlinkability holds if and only if there is no conjunction between $(T, e^*, s")$ and (m_w, m, R', e, s). In our scheme $(T, e^*, s")$ is associated with signature through following three equations

$R = aT + bP + c(P_B + R' + hP_A)$,
$e^* = a^{-1}(e + c)$ mod n,
$s = as" + b$ mod n.

If anyone knows the value of R, then by checking equation $e = H(x(R)||m)$ mod n, he can link $(T, e^*, s")$ to (m_w, m, R', e, s). But it is infeasible to find four unknowns a, b, c, R using three equations. Hence our scheme achieves unlinkability property.

4.3 Comparative Analysis

While maintaining the security, our scheme is more efficient as compared to Qi et al's [10]. The detailed costs in each phase are compared in the given table, where T_H denotes the once running of hash operation, M_E and A_E denote the once running of multiplication and addition operations on non-singular elliptic curve E.

Computational Cost Comparison:

Scheme	signing phase	verification phase	Total
scheme [10]	$8M_E + 6A_E + 1T_H$	$3M_E + 3A_E + 1T_H$	$11M_E + 9A_E + 2T_H$
Our scheme	$5M_E + 4A_E + 1T_H$	$3M_E + 3A_E + 2T_H$	$8M_E + 7A_E + 3T_H$

From the given table, we notice that the improved scheme has less computational cost than Qi et al's [10], except one more operation of hash function needed in the improved scheme. Even in this way, the improvement is still much more efficient ($3M_E + 2A_E$ - $1T_H$ computation less) than Qi et al's [10].

5   Conclusion

In this paper, We analyzed the security and improvement given in Qi et al's proxy blind signature scheme [10]. We demonstrated that scheme [10] is insecure against universal forgery attack. It also does not satisfy the unlinkability and identifiability property. To remedy the weaknesses of scheme [10], we proposed an improvement on it and proved that the improved scheme is secure, effective and more efficient than Qi et al's scheme [10].

References

1. Brands, S.: Untraceable Off-Line Cash in Wallets with Observers. In: Stinson, D.R. (ed.) CRYPTO 1993. LNCS, vol. 773, pp. 302–318. Springer, Heidelberg (1994)
2. Chaum, D.: Blind signatures for untraceable payments. In: Advances in Cryptology- Crypto 1982, pp. 199–203. Springer, Heidelberg (1983)
3. Chaum, D., Fiat, A., Naor, M.: Untraceable Electronic Cash. In: Goldwasser, S. (ed.) CRYPTO 1988. LNCS, vol. 403, pp. 319–327. Springer, Heidelberg (1990)
4. Chaum, D., den Boer, B., van Heyst, E., Mjoelsnes, S.F., Steenbeek, A.G.: Efficient Offline Electronic Checks. In: Quisquater, J.-J., Vandewalle, J. (eds.) EURO-CRYPT 1989. LNCS, vol. 434, pp. 294–301. Springer, Heidelberg (1990)
5. Hu, L., Zheng, K., Hu, Z., Yang, Y.: A Secure Proxy Blind Signature Scheme Based on ECDLP. In: 2009 International Conference on Multimedia Information Networking and Security. IEEE (2009), doi:10.1109/MINES.2009.220
6. Koblitz, N.: Elliptic curve cryptosystems. Mathenmatics of Computation 48(177), 203–209 (1987)
7. Miller, V.S.: Use of Elliptic Curves in Cryptography. In: Williams, H.C. (ed.) CRYPTO 1985. LNCS, vol. 218, pp. 417–426. Springer, Heidelberg (1986)
8. Menezes, A., Oorschot, P.C.V., Vanstone, S.: Handbook of Applied Cryptography. CRC Press (1996)
9. Mambo, M., Usuda, K., Okamoto, E.: Proxy signatures: Delegation of the power to sign messages. IEICE Transactions Fundamentals E79-A(9), 1338–1353 (1996)
10. Qi, C., Wang, Y.: An Improved Proxy Blind Signature Scheme Based on Factoring and ECDLP. In: Computational Intelligence and Software Engineering, pp. 1–4. IEEE (2009), doi:10.1109/CISE. 2009.5365847
11. SECI. Elliptic Curve Cryptography, Standands for Efficient Cryptography (September 2000), http://www.secg-talklistscerticom.com
12. Tan, Z., Liu, Z., Tang, C.: Digital proxy blind signature schemes based on DLP and ECDLP. MM Research Preprints, No.21, MMRC, AMSS, Academia, Sinica, Beijing, No. 21, 212–217 (2002)
13. Wang, H.Y., Wang, R.C.: A proxy blind signature scheme based on ECDLP. Chinese Journal of Electronics 14(2), 281–284 (2005)
14. Yang, X., Yu, Z.: Security Analysis of a Proxy Blind Signature Scheme Based on ECDLP. In: The 4th International Conference on Wireless Communications, Networking and Mobile Computing (WiCOM 2008), pp. 1–4 (2008)

Dynamic Enterprises Architecture
for One or More Clouds

P. Mangayarkarasi[1] and R. Selvarani[2]

[1] TOCE, Bangalore
[2] CSE, MSRIT, Bangalore
mangaivelu@yahoo.com, selvarani.riic@gmail.com

Abstract. Cloud computing goal is to support the IT organizations to integrate their services globally. It can help enterprises to improve their creation and delivery of IT solutions by providing them to access services in a cost effective and flexible manner. Cloud applications have different compositions, configurations, and deployment requirements. Quantifying the performance of scheduling and allocation policies in a real Cloud environment is extremely challenging due to several reasons like, variety of demands, supply patterns, and system size, heterogeneous and meeting the requirements of users competitively. To simplify this process, we develop a Dynamic Enterprise Architecture- (DEA) through industry collaboration to enable interoperability among various clouds and service providers. The Dynamic Architecture helps the user to utilize the services and integrate their applications from anywhere in the world by on demand, at competitive costs. Resources can be dynamically adjusted pertaining to the demand. It selects the suitable service provider or the coordination of the service provider according to the requirement of the user.

Keywords: Cloud Computing, Cloud Service Provider, Dynamic Enterprise Architecture, Service on Demand, Service Level Agreement.

1   Introduction

Cloud computing[1] is a pay-per-use model for enabling available, convenient, on-demand network access to a shared pool of configurable computing resources like networks, servers, storage, applications and services that can be rapidly provisioned and released with minimal management effort or service provider interaction . These services in industry are referred to as Infrastructure as a Service (IaaS), Platform as a Service (PaaS), and Software as a Service (SaaS). It offers a readily available and scalable computing environment without substantial capital investment and hardware administrative and maintenance cost.

Service Level Agreement (SLA) is a contract between customers and service providers. It is an indenture between the service provider and the customer to describe the commitment of the providers and to specify penalties if their commitments are not met [5]. Service providers are not created equal. Some are excellent in computing power, some are good in security issues and some are good at offering unlimited

N. Meghanathan et al. (Eds.): CCSIT 2012, Part II, LNICST 85, pp. 109–114, 2012.

storage at the lowest cost. Documenting the effective SLAs is always a challengeable task. The main aim of the document is to maintain the agreement level based on their requirements between the user and the provider.

There are different types of users with different types of Applications, different sets of requirements and different sets of environments. Some Applications require high computing power and some Applications need maximum security. From the perspective of the users, their goal is to run their Application efficiently to meet their performance and security requirements within the cost.

Companies with global operations require faster response time to save time by distributing workload requests to multiple clouds in various locations at the same time. This creates the need for establishing a computing atmosphere for dynamically inter connecting and provisioning clouds from multiple domains within and across enterprises. To support maximum optimization the Application or the components of the Application needs to be located in anywhere (independent, location free), or in any type of clouds Such as private cloud, public cloud and hybrid cloud.

Existing systems do not support mechanisms and policies for dynamically coordinating the work among different clouds in order to determine optimal location. Further, the Cloud service providers are unable to predict geographic distribution of consumption of their services by users; it is also difficult to manage the distribution of services when there are changes in application behaviour.

Hence DEA is developed. It is loosely joined and highly interoperable software architecture, for deploying the application in the cloud. DEA supports application deployment to happen automatically, in a particular cloud with a suitable service provider or a coordination of service providers. The organization can leverage storage-as-a-service from one service provider, database-as-a-service from another service provider and even a complete development and deployment platform from a third service provider. DEA also supports distributed computing technology and database distribution for deployment.

2   DEA Framework

Once the organization has decided to integrate their services in cloud computing, the next task is to identify the processes contained in its service strategy and service design. Figure 1, shows the high level architectural view of the application and service mapping system. A user sends a request with their requirements to the DEA, which automatically assigns a service provider or a coordination of service providers based on the application requirements.

The goal of this architecture is to help clients to determine and plan how to manage in-house IT and its relationship to one or many clouds. Service providers use specific technologies, system architectural designs and the best practices in the industry to provide and support the multiple customers. This helps end users to have more agile and flexible service oriented architectures for their applications and services.

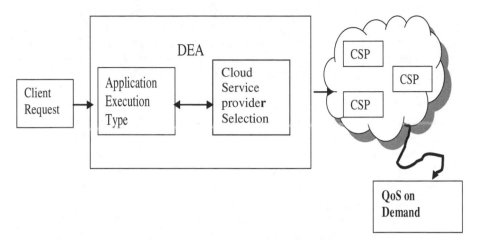

Fig. 1. High Level Architecture

Figure 2 shows the overview of the architecture with its different phases. The first phase of the frame work is to understand the utilities as they relate to the service strategy of an organization. In this phase, prioritization of candidate services to be put into the cloud is identified and analysis of the impact on business, data, applications and security issues is done.

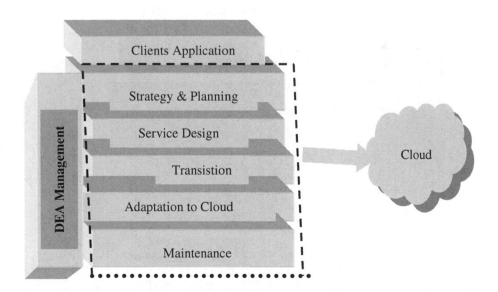

Fig. 2. Dynamic Enterprises Architecture

Once a service is approved, the process moves to the second phase of the framework, the service design phase. This is where the service is chartered, designed, developed, built and is entered into the service catalog for future reference. The decision regarding the type of cloud computing and service providers or the coordination of service providers are decided to support the requirements. The selection process is given in figure 3.

The third phase of the frame work is the validation phase where the SLA is finalized, mutually agreed upon and signed by both parties. Once the SLA has been documented, the service then moves to the transition stage, where the planning will begin to convert the transition from service to production. The transition phase deals with cloud option assessment and transition strategy. It also works with the cloud based system and the service integration plan.

The Adaptation phase relates Enterprises Architecture to functional mappings in the cloud. It also deals with the general project review and support. In the final phase, the maintenance of architecture and updates of transitions are carried out. Monitoring of the architectures viability is done over time and new cloud products and services are assessed. Technology update or insertion plan is created.

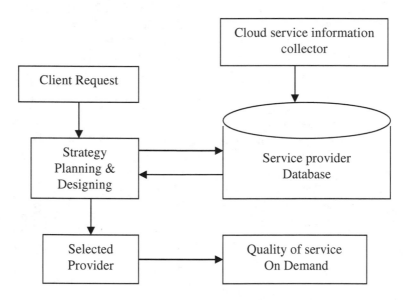

Fig. 3. Applications and Service Providers selections overview

Figure 3 shows the overview of the Strategy planning and designing. System applications are broadly classified in to small, medium and large scale. Applications based on their attributes such as security, integrity, availability and resource requirements, classified as transactional and analytic Applications. Based on their characteristics they are divided into small fragments. Later, these are mapped to the service provider's specific level of performance within the cost target.

The overview also includes a cloud service provider information collector and a repository for storing the metrics of each available cloud service provider. Database, which includes historical data about each service provider with characteristics such as security issues, memory availability, CPU utilization, I/O performance and the cost charged by the service providers, level of performance and also physical properties such as mean time to repair and the percentage of incidents of successful correction in the first attempt. Based on the nature of applications and QoS provided by the Service Provider, the DEA automatically maps the Application into the cloud with suitable CSP to extract the result.

3   DEA Advantages

Two or more independent cloud computing providers can join together to create a federated cloud. The participants of the federated cloud can share their resources on agreement with price. The sharing and paying models will help individual providers to effectively deal with shortage level of resources when spikes in capacity demand occur. In a multi cloud environment, system automated decisions need to address federated decision of determining which cloud to be used for a particular work load.

4   DEA Challenges

There are no standards for integrating all the bits and pieces of IT information on the cloud. The Organization has to monitor how everything works together and supports the business needs. Data ownership, security and reliability, and the coordination to manage the delivery over the clouds are very tough. Organizations still have to define and manage relationships and dependencies among mission, processes, technologies and business initiatives. The architecture requires the user to manage application binaries and dependencies. Images and packages must be created and redeployed in the event of any change to an application, its configuration or its dependencies on clouds. Sometimes, maintenance becomes tedious as nature of applications and their clients needs increase in time or there is the change in API's.

5   Conclusion and Future Work

This paper introduces a new software architecture called DEA - Dynamic Enterprises architecture. Based on the analysis performed on the emerging requirements of the enterprises dynamic architecture is introduced. It is targeted to support the requirements of enterprises and deploy complex Application services for a complete solution in the cloud computing environment. This Architecture supports and manages its in-house IT and its relationship to one or many cloud without manual intervention.

In this paper outline of the Dynamic architecture is discussed at the conceptual level. The detailed architectural design and its implementation techniques are taken for future work.

References

1. Cloud Computing and SOA Convergence in your Enterprise A step-by-step Guide by David S. Linthicum
2. Cloud Computing A Practical Approach by Anthony t Velte Toby J Velte, Ph.D, Robert Elsenpeter, Tata McGraw Hill edn. (2010)
3. Gruman, G.: What cloud computing really means. InfoWorld (January 2009)
4. Chieu, T.C., Mohindra, A., Karve, A.A., Segal, A.: Dynamics Scaling of web Applications in a Virtualized cloud computing Environment. In: Proceedings of the IEEE International Conference e-Business Engineering (ICEBE 2009), Macau, China, pp. 281–286 (October 2009)
5. Tian, L.-Q., Lin, C., Ni, Y.: Evaluation of User Behavior Trust in Cloud Computing. In: Proceedings of the 2010 International Conference on Computer Application and System Modeling, ICCASM 2010 (2010)
6. Armbrust, M., Fox, A., Griffith, R., Joseph, A., Katz, R., Konwinski, A., Lee, G., Patterson, D., Rabkin, A., Stoica, I.: Above the clouds: A berkeley view of cloud computing. EECS Department, University of California, Berkeley, Tech. Rep. UCB/EECS-2009-28 (2009)
7. Gillett, F.E.: Future View: The new technology ecosystems of cloud, cloud services and cloud computing. Forrester Report, 62 (August 2008)
8. Vaquero, L., Rodero-Merino, L., Caceres, J., Lindner, M.: A break in the clouds: towards a cloud definition. ACM SIGCOMM Computer Communication Review 39, 50–55 (2008)
9. Kossmann, D., Kraska, T., Loesing, S.: An Evaluation of Alternative Architectures for Transaction Processing in the Cloud. In: ACM SIGMOD/PODS, Indianapolis, IN (2010)
10. World Wide Web Consortium, Web Services, http://www.w3.org/2002/wsl (accessed April 30, 2009)
11. Shieh, C.-S., Hsu, C.-W., Lai, W.K.: Application-Layer Implementation of service Migration. In: IEEE International Conference on Intelligent Intonation Hiding and Multimedia Signal Processing (2008)
12. Vouk, M.A.: Cloud Computing – Issues, Research, and Implementation. In: Proceedings of the 30th International Conference on Information Technology Interfaces (ITI 2008), p. 31 (2008)
13. Leavitt, N.: Is Cloud Computing Really Ready for Prime Time? IEEE Computer 42(1), 15–20 (2009)
14. Gillett, F.E.: Future View: New Tech Ecosystems of Cloud, Cloud Services, and Cloud Computing. Forrester Research Paper (2008)
15. Storage Networking Industry Association. Cloud Storage Reference Model (June 2009)
16. Layton, J.B.: Cloud Storage Concepts and Challenges [OL] (2010), http://www.linux-mag.com/cache/7617/1.html
17. Krafzig, D., Banke, K., Slama, D.: Enterprise SOA: Serviceoriented architecture best practices, 7th edn. Prentice-Hall, Upper Saddle River (2008)
18. Martin, W.: Service-orientiertes Business: Change von Business/ITAlignment. IT Management (01), 16–19 (2010)
19. Link, M., Ortner, E.: Service-oriented Application System Architecture: business process management meets workflow management. In: AMCIS Proceedings (2009)

Congestion Control in Distributed Networks - A Comparative Study

K. Vinodha[1] and R. Selvarani[2]

[1] Dept of ISE, TOCE, Bangalore
[2] Dept of CSE, MSRIT, Bangalore
{mohan.vinodha,selvarani.riic}@gmail.com

Abstract. Network congestion is characterized by delay and packet loss in the network. Increase in the rate of data transmissions as a result of increase in load, declines the throughput. Controlling congestion in network is an attempt to avoid overloading of any of the link capabilities of the intermediate nodes in the network by incorporating measures as reducing the rate of transmission or window size. This paper describes the comparison of different methods used in communication networks for controlling congestion to ensure effective communication. This study shows that the cross layered architecture with stochastic approach is providing an effective control over congestion and the response of the quality parameters is remarkably good in critical traffic situations.

Keywords: Congestion, Layered architecture, Cross layer, Deterministic model, Stochastic model.

1 Introduction

Congestion is an important issue in networks and significantly affects network performance. Congestion control is the key functionality in any communication networks. Controlling congestion leads to high utilization of network capacity, control congestion inside the network and ensure Quality of service [1]. The congestion control algorithms that are designed for wired networks are not directly applicable to wireless or distributed networks. In wired networks the capacity of each link known and the rate constraint is fixed. The rate constraint refers to the rate at which the source generates traffic, is less compared to the rate of the link. In distributed networks the capacity of each link varies [1]. The factors that judge the capacity of links are signal interference levels and power levels of independent link. One of the major TCP control components is the TCP congestion control; it controls the sender's packet transmission rate based on whether or not the network path is congested. The aim of the congestion control is to keep the buffer at least minimally occupied, to preserve fair resource allocation, and to prevent or avoid collapse of the network.

The idea of this paper is to focus the readers with a sketch of the main issues, challenges and techniques in these areas and also identify the open problem to community. The paper is organized as follows. Section 2 deals with the frame works for

N. Meghanathan et al. (Eds.): CCSIT 2012, Part II, LNICST 85, pp. 115–123, 2012.

congestion control. Section2.1 compares the layered approach and cross layer approach to avoid congestion. Section 2.2 introduces two mathematical models to address congestion control which is a comparative study. The final section 3 presents the concluding remarks, and the perspectives for further research.

2   Frame Works for Congestion Control

In this paper, framework for modeling the behavior of distributed networks to control congestion is discussed. Two frame works for congestion control namely layered architecture and the cross layered architecture of distributed networks are discussed. The discussion proves that the cross layered architecture is more effective in controlling congestion and provide better QoS than the layered approach. The main objective is to formulate the mathematical framework associated with a stochastic analysis to control Congestion in networks since the network exhibits randomness in its behavior. Therefore cross layer architecture with a stochastic model prove to be the effective method to control congestion in distributed networks.

2.1   Layered Approach vs. Cross Layer Approach

Network architecture determines functionality allocation rather than just resource allocation. M. Chiang et.al [2007] show that layered architectures form one of the most fundamental structures of network design. They adopt a modularized and often distributed approach to network coordination. Each module, namely layer, controls a subset of the decision variables, and observes a subset of constant parameters and the variables from other layers. [2]Each layer in the protocol stack hides the complexity of the layer below and provides a service to the layer above. [2]Intuitively, layered architectures enable a scalable, evolvable, and implementable network design, while introducing limitations to efficiency, fairness and potential risks to manage the network.

The conventional layered protocols in distributed networks tend to suffer from the inability to distinguish between losses due to route failures and congestion because of the inflexible structure. To overcome the challenges of dynamic environment, protocols those rely on interactions between different layers are of more important. Sometimes it is necessary to have information from various layers in order to make decision in higher layers of the network. This may result in better decision making when it comes to routing, allocating resources, controlling congestion and scheduling [3] [4]. The cross layer design is a promising technique for performance improvement in distributed networks. Cross layering allows network layer which normally are unable to communicate in the traditional layered network models to share data [16]. The shared data may allow more intelligent decision making terms of congestion control Cross layer approach to congestion control do not require precise prior knowledge of the capacity of every link. In this approach to congestion control the network jointly optimizes both the data and the resource allocation at the underlying layers [6].The performance of TCP and MAC layer protocols of the layered architecture can be evaluated using metrics like throughput, Bandwidth delay product, Packet delivery ratio, and delay and Packet loss.

Throughput can be defined as the rate of successful message delivery over a communication channel [14]. This data may be delivered over a physical or a wireless channel and it is usually measured in bits per second (bit/s or bps), and sometimes in data packets. The table 1 shows the variation of throughput as the number of nodes increases. From the graph throughput vs No of nodes it can be noticed that the throughput decreases as the number of nodes increases in case of layered approach.

Table 1. Throughput Vs. No of nodes (Layered Architecture)

Sl.No	No of nodes	Throughput in pbs
1	20	9000
2	30	8500
3	40	8450
4	50	8000
5	60	7900
6	70	7500

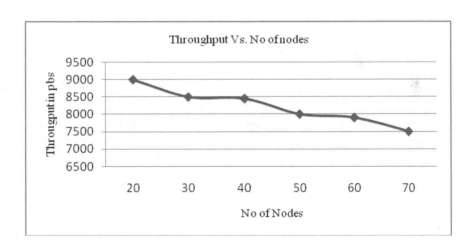

Another parameter is Bandwidth-Delay Product which refers to the product of a data link's capacity (in bits per second) and its end-to-end delay (in seconds). As a result the amount of data measured in bits (or bytes) lost is equivalent to the amount of data that have been transmitted but not yet received at any given instant of time.

Table 2. Bandwidth delay Product Vs. No of Nodes (Layered Architecture)

Sl.No	No of Nodes	Bandwidth delay Product in bits
1	20	2400
2	30	2420
3	40	2430
4	50	2440
5	60	2450

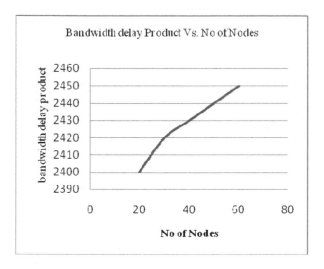

Consider the same set of nodes as layered architecture to study the network parameters like throughput, Bandwidth delay product in cross layer approach. The table 3 shows few sample data for throughput and bandwidth delay product and the number of nodes [14]. The graphs indicate that the variation in throughput as the number of nodes increases is just between 2% to 3% in cross layered approach. The cross layered architecture provides better reliability of data transmission compared to layered approach.

Table 3. Showing Bandwidth delay product, Throughput Vs. No of Nodes (Cross layered Architecture)

Sl.No	No of Nodes	Bandwidth delay product in bits	Throughput in bps
1	20	2400	9000
2	30	2400	9000
3	40	2401	8090
4	50	2401	8089
5	60	2402	8086

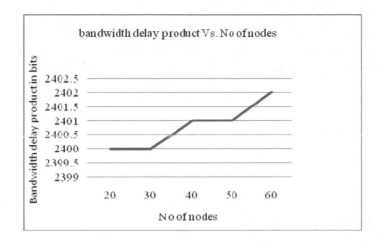

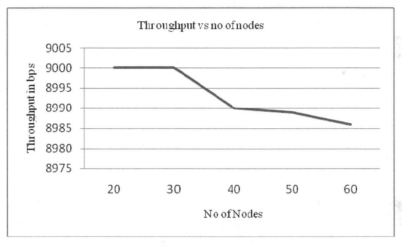

2.2   Deterministic Model to Control Congestion

The growing interest on congestion problems in high speed networks arise from the control of sending rates of traffic sources. Congestion problems result from a mismatch of offered load and available link bandwidth between network nodes. Such problems can cause high packet loss ratio (PLR) and long delays, and even break down the entire network system. High-speed networks must have an applicable flow control scheme not only to guarantee the quality of service (QoS) for the existing links but also to achieve high system utilization. The flow control of high-speed networks is difficult owing to the uncertainties and highly time-varying of different traffic patterns. The flow control checks the availability of bandwidth and buffer space necessary to guarantee the requested QoS. A major problem is the lack of information related to the characteristics of source flow. Devising a mathematical model for source flow is the fundamental issue. However, it has been revealed to be a very difficult task, especially for broadband sources. In order to overcome the above-mentioned difficulties, the flow control scheme with learning capability has been employed in high-speed networks [6]. But the priori-knowledge of network to train the parameters in the controller is hard to achieve for high-speed networks.

The study of Deterministic model show that the outcomes are precisely determined through known relationships among states and events, without any room for random variation. In such models, a given input will always produce the same output. While deterministic models have been shown to very [4] accurately predict the average Row rate [6], [7] such models cannot capture the variance in the rate process which may arise due to different sources of randomness. In real systems, there are two key sources of randomness. First, there can be unresponsive flows that do not react to congestion control. For instance, these could be traffic generated by UDP flows in the Internet or it could be web-mice, which are short flows which terminate before they can react to congestion control. Such unresponsive flows can be modeled as stochastic disturbances rather than deterministic model in the router. Second, the marking decisions at the router are probabilistic which again match with the stochastic nature.

Table 4. Performance Comparison of various communication network models

Sl.No	Network Parameters	Layered architecture	Cross-layered architecture	Deterministic Model	Stochastic Model
1	Throughput	With the increase in the load there is wide variation in throughput between 15% to 20%	As the load increases variation in throughput is between 5% to 8%	With the increase in the load there is wide variation in throughput between 10% to 20%	As the load increases variation in throughput is between 2% to 3%
2	Bandwidth delay Product	Due to increase in the load the buffer capacity exceeds the limit and the excess data placed in the queue so the delay product decreases	It does not change more since due to interaction with all the layers congestion is controlled to some extend	Not much variation in this parameter	optimized performance
3	Packet Loss	More than 25% of the packet are lost	Only 5% of packets are lost	About 10% of packets are lost	2% of packets are lost
4	Packet delivery ratio	75% of packets are delivered Hence 70% of reliability is achieved	95% of packets are delivered Hence 90% of reliability is achieved	85% of packets are delivered Hence 75% of reliability is achieved	95% of packets are delivered Hence 95% of reliability is achieved
5	Delay	Due to highly congested links delay incurred is more than 25% of the packet processing time	Tolerable delay incurred more than 10% of the packet processing time	Moderate delay more than 5% of the packet processing time	Delay is very less compared to other approaches more than 0.5% of the packet processing time.

From the above table it can be analyzed that the primitive layered approach which forms the backbone of all innovative research work in networking does not provide best QoS to the networks. The cross layered approach comparatively provides better Qos the Layered approach. The cross layered architecture with a Stochastic model can control congestion in distributed networks to a greater extend and can provide a good QoS.

2.3   Stochastic Approach to Control Congestion

Stochastic Model is a mathematical modeling phenomenon in the areas of science and technology. [22]It presents contributions on the mathematical methodology, from structural, analytical, and algorithmic to experimental approaches. Stochastic processing networks arise as models to study behavior of distributed computer network systems. Common characteristics of these networks are that they have entities, such as jobs, customers or packets that move along routes wait in buffers, receive processing from various resources, and are subject to the effects of stochastic variability through such quantities as arrival times, processing times, and routing protocols. Stochastic learning and control system is the best to arrive at an efficient distributed network system which will address the problem of congestion in the massive networks system and also provide better QoS as shown in Table 4.

These models are based on independent observations. In this section we discuss some of the applications of stochastic process. The third generation mobile networks are based on IP protocols and provide services to real time applications like multimedia. These applications consist of super imposed on-off sources which lead to bursts of packet streams. [17] To ensure appropriate quality of service they have modeled the networks through approximation by markov modulate rate process. Statistical analysis of high speed communication networks in very heavy traffic e.g. LAN had shown that self-similarity and long range dependence of the underlying data as the two important features. The traffic behavior has been modeled as stochastic model associated with fractional Brownian motion, which is strictly appropriate for heavy traffic limits.

The wireless queuing systems consist of long range dependent arrivals and the service rates to these arrivals vary with the changes in the wireless medium.[19]It is found that the changes in wireless medium occur slowly so it is assumed that service rate vary slower than arrival rate. The different possible limit forms that arise for both the arrival and departure process are driven by Brownian motion or fractional Brownian motion. Sometimes the rate control problem that is associated with single server Makovian queuing system may consist of impatient customer under heavy traffic conditions. [20]This paper address the situation by allowing the system manager to dynamically control the arrival or service rate depending on the current state of the system. In the situation where the service is incomplete, the customer quit the queue before congestion occurs. [21]Stochastic Petri nets (SPN) are used to study the interaction of multiple TCP sources that share a common buffer. Tokens associated with SPN represent the buffer occupancy and congestion window size. The continuous-time Markov chain model with SPN provides realistic modeling of workload and system modeling to control congestion.

Our research area is mainly concerned with designing a stochastic model with cross layered architecture to control congestion in communication networks. From the research work discussed earlier it clearly states that network exhibits a random nature at all levels whether it could be at the source or router. Hence we conclude that a stochastic model would be the best feasible model to a study the behavior of distributed network to control congestion and provide better QoS.

3   Conclusions

Congestion plays a crucial role in deciding QoS of the distributed network. Cross layer approach proves to be better solution to control congestion as it allows more intelligent decision making on the randomness flow of traffic to attain better QoS. Stochastic variability in the network has dynamic behavior of the sending rates (particularly at the onset of limit cycles in a deterministic model) under various regimes, including the more realistic conditions of large delays and resource capacities. A stochastic network with cross layered architecture appears to be more appropriate for controlling the congestion due to randomness in the number of users present and the tasks they perform.

References

1. Low, S.H., Paganini, F., Doyle, J.C.: Internet congestion control. IEEE Control Systems Magazine (February 2002)
2. Chiang, M., Low, S.H., Calderbank, R.A., Doyle, J.C.: Layering as optimization decomposition. To appear in Proceedings of IEEE (January 2007); A shorter version appeared in Proc. Conf. Inform. Sciences and Systems (March 2006)
3. Conti, M., Maselli, G., Turi, G., Giordano, S.: Cross-layering in mobile ad hoc network Design. Computer 37, 48–51 (2004)
4. Iannone, L., Kabassanov, K., Fdida, S.: The real gain of cross-layer routing in wireless mesh Networks. In: Int. Symposium on Mobile and Ad Hoc Networking and Computing, pp. 15–22 (May 2006)
5. Li, X., Dimirovski, G.M., Jing, Y., Jing, Y., Zhang, S.: A Q-Learning Model-Independent Flow Controller for High-speed Networks. In: Proceedings of The 42nd IEEE Conference on Decision and Control, Maui, Hawaii, USA (December 2003)
6. Lin, X., Shroff, N.B.: Joint rate control and scheduling in multihop wireless networks. In: Proc. IEEE Conf. Decision and Control, Paradise Island, Bahamas, pp. 1484–1489 (December 2004)
7. Papoulis, A.: Probability, random variables, and stochastic processes, 4th edn. McGraw-Hill, New York (1991)
8. Chen, L., Low, S., Chiang, M., Doyle, J.: Cross-layer congestion control, routing and Scheduling design in ad hoc wireless networks. In: Proceedings of the 25th IEEE International Conference on Computer Communications (INFOCOM 2006), Barcelona, Spain, pp. 1–13 (April 2006)
9. Yi, Y., Chiang, M.: Stochastic network utility maximization. European Transactions on Telecommunications 19(4), 421–442 (2008)

10. Low, S.H., Paganini, F., Doyle, J.C.: Internet congestion control. IEEE Control Syst. Mag. 22(1), 28–43 (2002)
11. Jacobson, V.: Congestion avoidance and control. In: Proc. ACM SIGCOMM (August 1988)
12. Tang, A., Wei, D., Low, S.H., Chiang, M.: Heterogeneous congestion control: Efficiency, Fairness and control. In: Proc. IEEE ICNP (November 2006)
13. Giacomazzi, P.: Quality of service for packet telephony over Mobile Ad Hoc Networks (2006)
14. Premalatha, J., Balasubramanie, P.: Simulation Analysis of QoS parameters by combining MAC and TCP in MANETS. ICGST-CNIR Journal 8(2) (January 2009)
15. He, S., Chen, J., Xu, W., Sun, Y., Thulasiraman, P., Shen, X.: A Stochastic Multiobjective Optimization Framework for Wireless Sensor Networks (2010)
16. Rath, H.K., Sahoo, A.: Cross Layer based Congestion Control in Wireless Network. IEEE Communications Surveys and Tutorials 3, 28–39 (2003)
17. Adan, I.J.B.F., Resing, J.A.C.: A two-level traffic shaper for an on-off source. Performance Evaluation 42, 279–298 (2000)
18. Gong, W.-B., Liu, Y., Misra, V., Towsley, D.: Self-similarity and long range dependence on the Internet: a second look at the evidence, origins and implications. Computer Networks 48, 377–399 (2005)
19. Buche, R., Ghosh, A., Pipiras, V.: Heavy traffic limits in a wireless queuing Model with long range dependence. In: 46th IEEE Conference on Decision and Control, pp. 4447–4452 (2007)
20. Ward, A.R., Glynn, P.W.: A diffusion approximation for a Markovian queue with Reneging. Queuing Syst. 43(1-2), 103–128 (2003)
21. van Foreest, N.D., Haverkort, B.R., Mandjes, M.R.H., Scheinhardt, W.R.W.: Versatile Markovian models for networks with asymmetric TCP sources, Memorandum 1734, Department of Applied Mathematics, Enscheda, the Netherlands (2004), http://www.math.utwente.nl/publications/
22. http://www.businessdictionary.com, http://www.tiffanyandcorings.co.uk

Adaptive Controller and Synchronizer Design for the Qi-Chen Chaotic System

Sundarapandian Vaidyanathan

R & D Centre, Vel Tech Dr. RR & Dr. SR Technical University,
Avadi-Alamathi Road, Avadi, Chennai-600 062, India
sundarvtu@gmail.com
http://www.vel-tech.org/

Abstract. This paper investigates the design problem of adaptive controller and synchronizer for the Qi-Chen chaotic system (2005) with unknown parameters. First, adaptive control laws are derived to stabilize the Qi-Chen chaotic system to its unstable equilibrium at the origin. Then adaptive control laws are also derived to achieve global chaos synchronization of identical Qi-Chen chaotic systems with unknown parameters. The results derived for adaptive stabilization and synchronization for the Qi-Chen chaotic system are established using Lyapunov stability theory. Numerical simulations are presented to demonstrate the effectiveness of the adaptive control and synchronization schemes derived in this paper.

Keywords: Adaptive control, chaos, synchronization, Qi-Chen system.

1 Introduction

Chaotic systems are dynamical systems that possess some special features, such as being extremely sensitive to small variations of initial conditions, having bounded trajectories in the phase space, and so on. The chaos phenomenon was first observed in weather models by Lorenz ([1], 1963). This was followed by a discovery of a large number of chaos phenomena and chaos behaviour in physical, social, economical, biological and electrical systems [2].

The problem of controlling a chaotic system was introduced by Ott *et al.* ([3], 1990). The control of chaotic systems is basically to design state feedback control laws that stabilizes the chaotic systems around the unstable equilibrium points. Active control method is used when the system parameters are known and adaptive control method is used when some or all of the system parameters are unknown ([3]-[5]).

Chaos synchronization is a phenomenon that may occur when two or more chaotic oscillators are coupled or when a chaotic oscillator drives another chaotic oscillator. In most of the chaos synchronization approaches, the *master-slave* or *drive-response* formalism is used. If a particular chaotic system is called the *master* or *drive* system and another chaotic system is called the *slave* or *response* system, then the idea of chaos synchronization is to use the output of the master system to control the slave system so that the output of the slave system tracks the output of the master system asymptotically.

N. Meghanathan et al. (Eds.): CCSIT 2012, Part II, LNICST 85, pp. 124–133, 2012.

Since the pioneering work by Pecora and Carroll ([6], 1990), several approaches have been proposed for chaos synchronization such as the active control method [8], adaptive control method [9], sampled-data control method [10], backstepping method [11], sliding mode control method ([12]-[13]), etc.

This paper investigates the design of adaptive controller and synchronizer for the Qi-Chen chaotic system (Qi, Chen *et al.* [14], 2005). First, we devise adaptive control scheme using state feedback control for the Qi-Chen chaotic system about its unstable equilibrium at the origin. Then we devise adaptive synchronization scheme for identical Qi-Chen chaotic systems. The adaptive control and synchronization results derived in this paper are established using Lyapunov stability theory.

This paper has been organized as follows. In Section 2, we give a system description of the Qi-Chen chaotic system (2005). In Section 3, we derive results for the adaptive control of the Qi-Chen chaotic system with unknown parameters. In Section 4, we derive results for the adaptive synchronization of identical Qi-Chen chaotic systems with unknown parameters. In Section 5, we summarize the main results obtained in this paper.

2   System Description

The Qi-Chen chaotic system ([14], 2005) is described by the dynamics

$$\begin{aligned}
\dot{x}_1 &= a(x_2 - x_1) + x_2 x_3 \\
\dot{x}_2 &= cx_1 - x_2 - x_1 x_3 \\
\dot{x}_3 &= x_1 x_2 - bx_3
\end{aligned} \tag{1}$$

where x_1, x_2, x_3 are the state variables of the system and a, b, c are constant, positive parameters of the system.

The system (1) is *chaotic* when

$$a = 35, \quad b = 8/3 \text{ and } c = 80. \tag{2}$$

Figure 1 describes the state orbits of the Qi-Chen system (1).

When the parameter values are taken as in (2), the Qi-Chen system (1) and the system linearization matrix at the equilibrium point $E_0 = (0, 0, 0, 0)$ is given by

$$A = \begin{bmatrix} -35 & 35 & 0 \\ 80 & -1 & 0 \\ 0 & 0 & -8/3 \end{bmatrix}$$

which has the eigenvalues

$$\lambda_1 = -73.5788, \quad \lambda_2 = -2.6667 \text{ and } \lambda_3 = 37.5788$$

Since λ_3 is a positive eigenvalue of A, it is immediate from Lyapunov stability theory [15] that the system (1)is unstable at the equilibrium point $E_0 = (0, 0, 0)$.

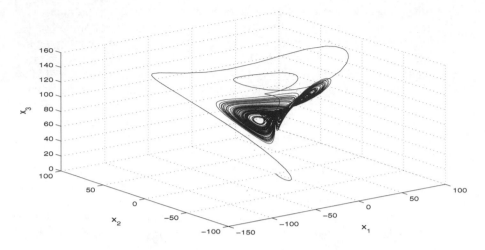

Fig. 1. State Orbits of the Qi-Chen System

3   Adaptive Controller Design of the Qi-Chen Chaotic System

3.1   Main Results

In this section, we discuss the design of adaptive controller for globally stabilizing the Qi-Chen system (2005), when the parameter values are unknown.

Thus, we consider the controlled Qi-Chen system described by the dynamics

$$
\begin{aligned}
\dot{x}_1 &= a(x_2 - x_1) + x_2 x_3 + u_1 \\
\dot{x}_2 &= c x_1 - x_2 - x_1 x_3 + u_2 \\
\dot{x}_3 &= x_1 x_2 - b x_3 + u_3
\end{aligned}
\tag{3}
$$

where u_1, u_2, u_3 are feedback controllers to be designed using the states x_1, x_2, x_3 and estimates $\hat{a}, \hat{b}, \hat{c}$ of the unknown system parameters a, b, c of the system.

Next, we consider the following adaptive control functions

$$
\begin{aligned}
u_1 &= -\hat{a}(x_2 - x_1) - x_2 x_3 - k_1 x_1 \\
u_2 &= -\hat{c} x_1 + x_2 + x_1 x_3 - k_2 x_2 \\
u_3 &= -x_1 x_2 + \hat{b} x_3 - k_3 x_3
\end{aligned}
\tag{4}
$$

where $\hat{a}, \hat{b}$ and $\hat{c}$ are estimates of the system parameters a, b and c, respectively, and $k_i, (i = 1, 2, 3)$ are positive constants.

Substituting the control law (4) into the plant equation (3), we obtain

$$
\begin{aligned}
\dot{x}_1 &= (a - \hat{a})(x_2 - x_1) - k_1 x_1 \\
\dot{x}_2 &= (c - \hat{c}) x_1 - k_2 x_2 \\
\dot{x}_3 &= -(b - \hat{b}) x_3 - k_3 x_3
\end{aligned}
\tag{5}
$$

We define the parameter estimation error as

$$e_a = a - \hat{a}, \quad e_b = b - \hat{b} \text{ and } e_c = c - \hat{c} \tag{6}$$

Using (6), the state dynamics (5) can be simplified as

$$
\begin{aligned}
\dot{x}_1 &= e_a(x_2 - x_1) - k_1 x_1 \\
\dot{x}_2 &= e_c x_1 - k_2 x_2 \\
\dot{x}_3 &= -e_b x_3 - k_3 x_3
\end{aligned}
\tag{7}
$$

We use Lyapunov approach for the derivation of the update law for adjusting the parameter estimates $\hat{a}, \hat{b}$ and $\hat{c}$.

Consider the quadratic Lyapunov function defined by

$$V(x_1, x_2, x_3, e_a, e_b, e_c) = \frac{1}{2}\left(x_1^2 + x_2^2 + x_3^2 + e_a^2 + e_b^2 + e_c^2\right) \tag{8}$$

which is a positive definite function on $\mathbb{R}^6$.

Note that

$$\dot{e}_a = -\dot{\hat{a}}, \quad \dot{e}_b = -\dot{\hat{b}}, \quad \dot{e}_c = -\dot{\hat{c}}. \tag{9}$$

Differentiating V along the trajectories of (5) and using (9), we obtain

$$
\begin{aligned}
\dot{V} = -k_1 x_1^2 - k_2 x_2^2 - k_3 x_3^2 &+ e_a\left[x_1(x_2 - x_1) - \dot{\hat{a}}\right] \\
&+ e_b\left[-x_3^2 - \dot{\hat{b}}\right] + e_c\left[x_1 x_2 - \dot{\hat{c}}\right]
\end{aligned}
\tag{10}
$$

In view of Eq. (10, the estimated parameters are updated by the following law:

$$
\begin{aligned}
\dot{\hat{a}} &= x_1(x_2 - x_1) + k_4 x_1 \\
\dot{\hat{b}} &= -x_3^2 + k_5 x_2 \\
\dot{\hat{c}} &= x_1 x_2 + k_6 x_3
\end{aligned}
\tag{11}
$$

where k_4, k_5 and k_6 are positive constants.

Substituting (11) into (10), we obtain

$$\dot{V} = -k_1 x_1^2 - k_2 x_2^2 - k_3 x_3^2 - k_4 e_a^2 - k_5 e_b^2 - k_6 e_c^2 \tag{12}$$

which is a negative definite function on $\mathbb{R}^6$.

Thus, by Lyapunov stability theory [15], it follows that the plant dynamics (7) is globally exponentially stable and also that the parameter estimate errors e_a, e_b, e_c converge to zero exponentially with time.

Hence, we obtain the following result.

Theorem 1. *The Qi-Chen chaotic system (3) with unknown parameters is globally and exponentially stabilized by the adaptive control law (4), where the update law for the parameters is given by (11) and $k_i, (i = 1, 2, \ldots, 6)$ are positive constants.* □

3.2 Numerical Results

For the numerical simulations, the fourth order Runge-Kutta method with step-size $h = 10^{-6}$ is used to solve the Qi-Chen system (3) with the adaptive control law (4) and the parameter update law (11).

The parameters of the system (3) are selected as $a = 35, b = 8/3$ and $c = 80$.

We also take $k_i = 4$ for $i = 1, 2, \ldots, 6$.

Suppose that the initial values of the estimated parameters are

$$\hat{a}(0) = 5, \quad \hat{b}(0) = 18, \quad \hat{c}(0) = 10$$

Suppose that we take the initial values of the states of (3) as

$$x_1(0) = 20, \quad x_2(0) = 34, \quad x_3(0) = 18$$

When the adaptive control law (4) and the parameter update law (11) are applied, the controlled Qi-Chen system (3) converges to the equilibrium $E_0 = (0, 0, 0)$ exponentially as shown in Figure 2 and the parameter estimates $\hat{a}, \hat{b}, \hat{c}$ converge to the system parameters a, b, c exponentially as shown in Figure 3.

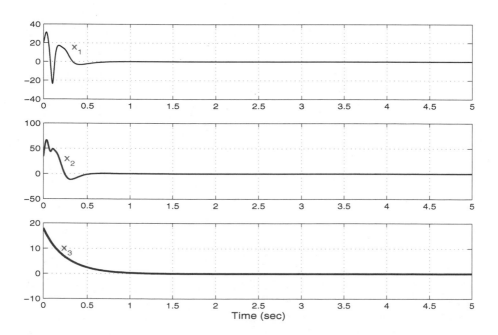

Fig. 2. Time Responses of the Controlled Qi-Chen System

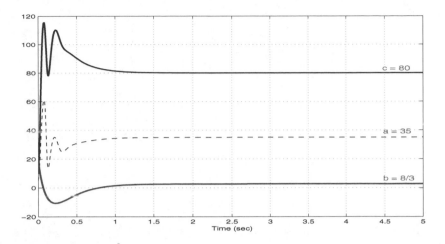

Fig. 3. Parameter Estimates $\hat{a}(t), \hat{b}(t), \hat{c}(t)$

4   Adaptive Synchronizer Design of the Qi-Chen Chaotic System

4.1   Main Results

In this section, we discuss the design of adaptive synchronization of identical Qi-Chen systems (2005) with unknown parameters.

As the master system, we consider the Qi-Chen dynamics described by

$$
\begin{aligned}
\dot{x}_1 &= a(x_2 - x_1) + x_2 x_3 \\
\dot{x}_2 &= c x_1 - x_2 - x_1 x_3 \\
\dot{x}_3 &= x_1 x_2 - b x_3
\end{aligned}
\tag{13}
$$

where x_1, x_2, x_3 are the state variables and a, b, c are unknown system parameters.

As the slave system, we consider the controlled Qi-Chen dynamics described by

$$
\begin{aligned}
\dot{y}_1 &= a(y_2 - y_1) + y_2 y_3 + u_1 \\
\dot{y}_2 &= c y_1 - x_2 - y_1 y_3 + u_2 \\
\dot{y}_3 &= y_1 y_2 - b y_3 + u_3
\end{aligned}
\tag{14}
$$

where y_1, y_2, y_3 are the state variables and u_1, u_2, u_3 are the nonlinear controllers to be designed.

The synchronization error e is defined by

$$
e_i = y_i - x_i, \quad (i = 1, 2, 3)
\tag{15}
$$

Then the error dynamics is obtained as

$$
\begin{aligned}
\dot{e}_1 &= a(e_2 - e_1) + y_2 y_3 - x_2 x_3 + u_1 \\
\dot{e}_2 &= c e_1 - e_2 - y_1 y_3 + x_1 x_3 + u_2 \\
\dot{e}_3 &= -b e_3 + y_1 y_2 - x_1 x_2 + u_3
\end{aligned}
\tag{16}
$$

We define the adaptive synchronizing law

$$
\begin{aligned}
u_1 &= -\hat{a}(e_2 - e_1) - y_2 y_3 + x_2 x_3 - k_1 e_1 \\
u_2 &= -\hat{c} e_1 + e_3 + y_1 y_3 - x_1 x_3 - k_2 e_2 \\
u_3 &= \hat{b} e_3 - y_1 y_2 + x_1 x_2 - k_3 e_3
\end{aligned}
\tag{17}
$$

where $\hat{a}, \hat{b}$ and $\hat{c}$ are estimates of the system parameters a, b and c, respectively, and $k_i, (i = 1, 2, 3)$ are positive constants.

Substituting (17) into (16), we obtain the error dynamics as

$$
\begin{aligned}
\dot{e}_1 &= (a - \hat{a})(e_2 - e_1) - k_1 e_1 \\
\dot{e}_2 &= (c - \hat{c}) e_1 - k_2 e_2 \\
\dot{e}_3 &= -(b - \hat{b}) e_3 - k_3 e_3
\end{aligned}
\tag{18}
$$

We define the parameter estimation error as

$$
e_a = a - \hat{a}, \quad e_b = b - \hat{b} \quad \text{and} \quad e_c = c - \hat{c}
\tag{19}
$$

Substituting (19) into (18), the error dynamics (18) can be simplified as

$$
\begin{aligned}
\dot{e}_1 &= e_a(e_2 - e_1) - k_1 e_1 \\
\dot{e}_2 &= e_c e_1 - k_2 e_2 \\
\dot{e}_3 &= -e_b e_3 - k_3 e_3
\end{aligned}
\tag{20}
$$

We use Lyapunov approach for the derivation of the update law for adjusting the parameter estimates $\hat{a}, \hat{b}$ and $\hat{c}$.

Consider the quadratic Lyapunov function defined by

$$
V(e_1, e_2, e_3, e_a, e_b, e_c) = \frac{1}{2}\left(e_1^2 + e_2^2 + e_3^2 + e_a^2 + e_b^2 + e_c^2\right)
\tag{21}
$$

which is a positive definite function on $\mathbb{R}^6$.

Note that

$$
\dot{e}_a = -\dot{\hat{a}}, \quad \dot{e}_b = -\dot{\hat{b}}, \quad \dot{e}_c = -\dot{\hat{c}}.
\tag{22}
$$

Differentiating V along the trajectories of (20) and using (22), we obtain

$$
\begin{aligned}
\dot{V} = &-k_1 e_1^2 - k_2 e_2^2 - k_3 e_3^2 + e_a \left[e_1(e_2 - e_1) - \dot{\hat{a}}\right] \\
&+ e_b \left[-e_3^2 - \dot{\hat{b}}\right] + e_c \left[e_1 e_2 - \dot{\hat{c}}\right]
\end{aligned}
\tag{23}
$$

In view of Eq. (23), the estimated parameters are updated by the following law:

$$
\begin{aligned}
\dot{\hat{a}} &= e_1(e_2 - e_1) + k_4 e_1 \\
\dot{\hat{b}} &= -e_3^2 + k_5 e_2 \\
\dot{\hat{c}} &= e_1 e_2 + k_6 e_3
\end{aligned}
\tag{24}
$$

where k_4, k_5 and k_6 are positive constants.

Substituting (24) into (23), we obtain

$$\dot{V} = -k_1 x_1^2 - k_2 x_2^2 - k_3 x_3^2 - k_4 e_a^2 - k_5 e_b^2 - k_6 e_c^2 \tag{25}$$

which is a negative definite function on $\mathbb{R}^6$.

Thus, by Lyapunov stability theory [15], it follows that the error dynamics (20) is globally exponentially stable and also that the parameter estimate errors e_a, e_b, e_c converge to zero exponentially with time.

Hence, we obtain the following result.

Theorem 2. *The identical Qi-Chen chaotic systems (13) and (14) with unknown parameters are globally and exponentially synchronized by the adaptive control law (17), where the update law for the parameters is given by (24) and $k_i, (i = 1, 2, \ldots, 6)$ are positive constants.*   ⊔

4.2   Numerical Results

For the numerical simulations, the fourth order Runge-Kutta method with step-size $h = 10^{-6}$ is used to solve the Qi-Chen systems (13) and (14) with the adaptive control law (17) and the parameter update law (24).

The parameters of the system (3) are selected as $a = 35, b = 8/3$ and $c = 80$.

We also take $k_i = 4$ for $i = 1, 2, \ldots, 6$.

Suppose that the initial values of the estimated parameters are

$$\hat{a}(0) = 12, \quad \hat{b}(0) = 6, \quad \hat{c}(0) = 20$$

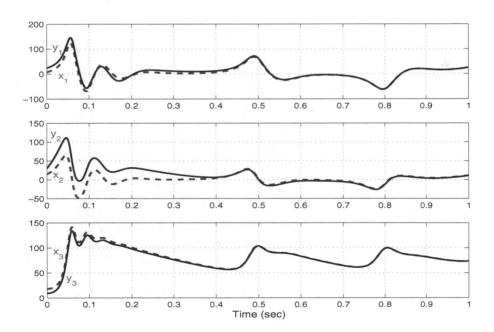

Fig. 4. Time Responses of the Controlled Qi-Chen System

Suppose that the initial values of the master system (13) are taken as

$$x_1(0) = 7, \quad x_2(0) = 15, \quad x_3(0) = 18$$

Suppose that the initial values of the slave system (14) are taken as

$$y_1(0) = 24, \quad y_2(0) = 30, \quad y_3(0) = 9$$

The identical Qi-Chen systems (13) and (14) are synchronized exponentially as shown in Figure 4 and the parameter estimates $\hat{a}, \hat{b}, \hat{c}$ converge to the system parameters a, b, c exponentially as shown in Figure 5.

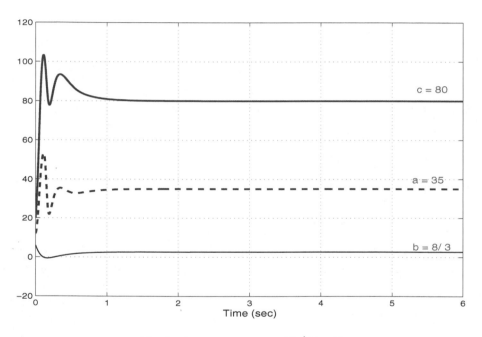

Fig. 5. Parameter Estimates $\hat{a}(t), \hat{b}(t), \hat{c}(t)$

5   Conclusions

In this paper, we derived results for the adaptive controller and synchronizer for the Qi-chen chaotic system (Qi, Chen *et al.* 2005) with unknown parameters. First, we designed adaptive control law to stabilize the Qi-Chen system to its unstable equilibrium point at the origin based on the Lyapunov stability theory. Then we designed adaptive synchronizer for the global chaos synchronization of identical Qi-Chen systems with unknown parameters. Our synchronization results were established using Lyapunov stability theory. Numerical simulations are presented to illustrate the effectiveness of the proposed adaptive controller and synchronizer schemes for the Qi-Chen chaotic system (2005).

References

1. Lorenz, E.N.: Deterministic nonperiodic flow. J. Atmos. Sci. 20(2), 130–141 (1963)
2. Lakshmanan, M., Murali, K.: Nonlinear Oscillators: Controlling and Synchronization. World Scientific, Singapore (1996)
3. Ott, E., Grebogi, C., Yorke, J.A.: Controlling chaos. Phys. Rev. Lett. 64, 1196–1199 (1990)
4. Ge, S.S., Wang, C., Lee, T.H.: Adaptive backstepping control of a class of chaotic systems. Internat. J. Bifur. Chaos 10, 1149–1156 (2000)
5. Sun, M., Tian, L., Jiang, S., Xun, J.: Feedback control and adaptive control of the energy resource chaotic system. Chaos, Solitons & Fractals 32, 168–180 (2007)
6. Pecora, L.M., Carroll, T.L.: Synchronization in chaotic systems. Phys. Rev. Lett. 64, 821–824 (1990)
7. Lu, L., Zhang, C., Guo, Z.A.: Synchronization between two different chaotic systems with nonlinear feedback control. Chinese Physics 16(6), 1603–1607 (2007)
8. Sundarapandian, V.: Hybrid chaos synchronization of hyperchaotic Liu and hyperchaotic Chen systems by active nonlinear control. Internat. J. Computer Sci. Eng. Inform. Tech. 1(2), 1–14 (2011)
9. Liao, T.L., Tsai, S.H.: Adaptive synchronization of chaotic systems and its applications to secure communications. Chaos, Solitons & Fractals 11, 1387–1396 (2000)
10. Yang, T., Chua, L.O.: Control of chaos using sampled-data feedback control. Internat. J. Bifur. Chaos 9, 215–219 (1999)
11. Yu, Y.G., Zhang, S.C.: Adaptive backstepping synchronization of uncertain chaotic systems. Chaos, Solitons & Fractals 27, 1369–1375 (2006)
12. Konishi, K., Hirai, M., Kokame, H.: Sliding mode control for a class of chaotic systems. Phys. Lett. A 245, 511–517 (1998)
13. Sundarapandian, V.: Global chaos synchronization of Pehlivan systems by sliding mode control. Internat. J. Comp. Sci. Eng. 3(5), 2163–2169 (2011)
14. Qi, G., Chen, G., Du, S., Chen, Z., Yuan, Z.: Analysis of a new chaotic system. Physica A 352, 295–308 (2005)
15. Hahn, W.: The Stability of Motion. Springer, New York (1967)

Opinion Mining from Weblogs and Its Relevance for Socio-political Research

Vivek Kumar Singh[1], Mousumi Mukherjee[2], Ghanshyam Kumar Mehta[2], Shekhar Garg[2], and Nisha Tiwari[2]

[1] Department of Computer Science, South Asian University,
New Delhi-110067, India
[2] Department of Computer Science, Banaras Hindu University,
Varanasi-221005, India
{vivek,mou.sonai,ghanshyam4u2000,shekharbhumca08,
nisha.bhumca08}@gmail.com

Abstract. This paper presents our experimental work on mining of opinions from a large number of blog posts and its relevance for socio-political research. The experimental work involves collecting blog data on three interesting topics, transforming the collected blog data into vector space representation, and then performing opinion mining using both a machine learning text classifier and an unsupervised semantic orientation approach. We implemented Naïve Bayes and SO-PMI-IR algorithms for opinion mining. We obtained interesting results, which have been evaluated for correctness and also cross-validated with the outcomes of multiple techniques employed. The paper concludes with a short discussion of the results and relevance of the experimental work.

Keywords: Blogosphere, Computational Sociology, Opinion Mining, Sentiment Analysis, Social Computing.

1 Introduction

The increased penetration of the Internet and the new participative Web 2.0 has facilitated a large number of users to use & interact with web applications. The users are now interacting with web applications and contributing in a variety of forms, such as rating, tagging, writing blogs, social networking and sharing items with friends. This is creating huge amount of user generated information. Weblogs (also termed Blogs) provide an important platform for users to express themselves. The ease of creating blog posts, low barrier to publication, open standards of content generation and the free-form writing style allow large number of people to create their own blogs or post their contributions on community blog sites. People express their opinions, ideas, experiences, thoughts, and wishes in blog posts. The Blogosphere (universe of all blog sites) is now a huge source of user posted data [1]. The tremendous amount of valuable information contained in blogs has attracted the attention of people in academics as well in industry. Over the years, social media platforms such as Blogosphere have become a widely acknowledged platform for commercial exploitation. Companies use it to know the reactions of users on its products; and

N. Meghanathan et al. (Eds.): CCSIT 2012, Part II, LNICST 85, pp. 134–145, 2012.
© Institute for Computer Sciences, Social Informatics and Telecommunications Engineering 2012

advertisers use it to place their advertisement. The high user activity, wide visibility and large amount of user posted data, is attracting people and companies to exploit it in numerous other ways.

The immense potential of the data in Blogosphere has opened new areas of research in and around the blogosphere, with key areas of research including efforts to model the Blogosphere, blog clustering, mining the blog posts, community discovery, searching influential bloggers, filtering spam blogs etc [2]. However, one area that is relatively still unexplored is to use the data on the Blogosphere for socio-political analysis. Blogosphere is a rich and unique treasure house of cross-cultural data that can be used for psychological & socio-political analysis. There are two important motivating factors for this purpose. First, the Internet has reduced the distance between people across the world and allowed them to express themselves and interact with others, irrespective of the geographical, demographic, religious and cultural boundaries. Therefore, we now have opinions on a topic from people across the continents. Secondly, the free form, unedited, first-hand and relatively more emotionally laden expressions of various people on blog sites provide a rich source of original data for cross cultural & sociological analysis. Moreover, one may no longer be required to travel distances to get the cross-cultural perspective on different issues. Blog posts on an issue may be used for an analytical experiment of this kind, which can result in at least a preliminary picture, if not a rigorously validated one. Hence, we get a more original data at a much lower cost.

The unstructured nature of data in blogs, however, presents computational challenges that require sophisticated search and mining techniques. Opinion Mining which has traditionally been an area of exploration by Linguists, is now becoming a mature technique for use with data on the Web. During the last few years there have been interesting works on opinion mining from the user posted data on the Web. Experiments to identify opinions have been performed with product reviews, movie reviews, restaurant reviews, user's posts on social media and about prospects of candidates in elections etc. This paper presents our experimental work on opinion mining on three different collections of Weblogs. We chose the topics of posts taking into account the highly opinionated & emotion laden nature of the prospective posts. The primary aim of the experimental work is to evaluate and demonstrate that the Blogosphere is a platform worth socio-political and cross-cultural psychological research. The rest of the paper is organized as follows. Section 2 describes opinion mining techniques used and the section 3 presents the experimental setup and results. The paper concludes with a short discussion (Section 4) of the relevance of experimental work for socio-political and cross-cultural psychological research.

2   Opinion Mining

The opinion mining problem in its most popular sense can be formally defined as follows: Given a set of documents D, the opinion mining algorithm classifies each document $d \in D$ into one of the two classes, positive or negative. Positive means that d expresses a positive opinion and negative means that d expresses a negative opinion. Most of the experiments performed so far employed one of the following two approaches: (a) using a text classifier (such as Naïve Bayes, SVM or kNN) that takes a machine learning approach to categorize the documents in positive and negative groups; and (b) computing semantic orientation of documents based on aggregated semantic orientation values of selected opinionated POS tags extracted from the document. Some of the past works on opinion mining and sentiment analysis have also attempted to determine the strengths of positive and negative orientations. Few prominent researches works around these themes can be found in [3], [4], [5], [6], [7], [8], [9] & [10].

2.1 Machine Learning Approach

A simple scheme for opinion mining is to use supervised machine learning based text classification approach to classify the documents in two classes (positive and negative). Naïve Bayes and SVM are two widely used machine learning approaches. Naïve Bayes [11] is a probabilistic learning method which computes the probability of a document d being in class c as in eq. 1 below.

$$P\,(c|d) \; \alpha \; P(c)\textstyle\prod_{1\leq k\leq nd} P(t_k|c) \tag{1}$$

where, P (t_k/c) is the conditional probability of a term t_k occurring in a document of class c. $P(t_k/c)$ is thus a measure of how much evidence t_k contributes that c is correct class. $P(c)$ is the prior probability of a document occurring in class c. The goal in text classification is to find the best class for a document. The key idea in this classification is thus to categorize documents based on statistical pattern of occurrence of terms. The selected terms are often called features. Therefore, in order to do topic categorization we may use features like terms having frequency greater than a value. For categorizing documents into two categories of 'positive' and 'negative', a good choice is to use selected terms with specific POS tags such as adjectives (or adjective and adverb combination). The class membership of a document can be computed as in eq. 2

$$c_{map} = arg \max_{c \in C} \widehat{P}(c|d) \; = arg \max_{c \in C} \widehat{P}(c) \prod_{1\leq k\leq n_d} \widehat{P}\,(t_k|c) \tag{2}$$

where, $\overset{.}{P}$ is an estimated value obtained from the training set. In order to reduce the computational complexity resulting from multiplication of large number of probability terms, the eq. 2 can be transformed to eq. 3.

$$C_{map} = arg \max_{c \in C}[\log \widehat{P}(c) + \sum_{1\leq k\leq n_d} \log \widehat{P}(t_k|c)] \tag{3}$$

Each conditional parameter $P(t_k/c)$ is a weight that indicates how good an indicator the term t_k is for class c and the prior log $P(c)$ indicates relative frequency of class c.

2.2 Semantic Orientation Approach

In semantic orientation approach we first extract phrases that conform to a specific pattern [12]. Thereafter, the semantic orientation of extracted phrases is computed using the Pointwise Mutual Information (PMI) measure given in Eq. 4 below,

$$PMI(term_1, term_2) = \log_2\{Pr\,(term_1 \Delta term_2)/Pr(term_1).Pr\,(term_2)\} \tag{4}$$

where, $Pr(term_1 \blacktriangle term_2)$ is the co-occurrence probability of $term_1$ and $term_2$ and $Pr(term_1).Pr(term_2)$ gives the probability that two terms co-occur if they are statistically independent. The ratio between $Pr(term_1 \blacktriangle term_2)$ and $Pr(term_1).Pr(term_2)$ measures the degree of statistical independence between them. The semantic orientation (SO) of a phrase can thus be computed by using the Eq. 5,

$$SO(phrase) = PMI(pharse, "excellent") - PMI(phrase, "poor") \qquad (5)$$

where, PMI (phrase, "excellent") measures the association of the phrase with positive reference word "excellent" and PMI (phrase, "poor") measures the association of phrase with negative reference word "poor". These probabilities are calculated by issuing search query of the form "phrase * excellent" and "phrase * poor" to a search engine. The number of hits obtained is used as a measure of PMI value. The SO value for all the extracted phrases is computed using this scheme. To determine the semantic orientation of the entire document, the SO values of the opinionated phrases in it is aggregated. Every term having SO value greater than a threshold value is assigned a score of '+1' and '-1' otherwise. The SO values of all the extracted subjective terms are then added and if the sum is greater than a threshold value, the document is labeled as 'positive' and 'negative' otherwise. This algorithm is often referred to as SO-PMI-IR.

A variation of this scheme is SO-PMI-LSA [13], which uses Latent Semantic Analysis. In this scheme, the term-document matrix is first reduced using Singular Value Decomposition (SVD) and then $LSA(word_1, word_2)$ is computed by measuring the cosine similarity (described in Eq. 7) of the compressed row vectors corresponding to $word_1$ and $word_2$. Then, the Semantic orientation of a word is computed by Eq. 6,

$$SO(word) = LSA(word, \{positive\ terms\}) - LSA(word, \{negative\ terms\}) \quad (6)$$

where, positive terms refer to words like 'good', 'superior', 'excellent' etc. and negative terms refer to words like 'bad', 'poor', 'inferior' etc. The LSA of a word is computed with term vectors of positive and negative words occurring in the document set. Experimental results have shown that SO-PMI-IR and SO-LSA have approximately the same accuracy on large datasets.

2.3   Mood Analysis

The task of classifying a document by mood involves predicting the most likely state of mind with which the document was written i.e., whether the author was depressed, cheerful, bored, upset etc. The task is similar to opinion mining and has been used for productive purposes viz. filtering results of a search engine by mood, identifying communities and possibly even to assist behavioral scientists in behavioral research and training. Most of the past research on mood analysis used style-related as well as topic-related features in the text for identifying the mood of the author. Usually 'bag of words' or POS tags are extracted along with their frequency counts for subsequent use in mood classification. There has been several interesting works on mood analysis [14], [15], [16]. In an important experiment with mood classification in blog posts Mishne used a Mood PMI-IR based approach. This approach is conceptually similar to SO-PMI-IR scheme. However, instead of using "excellent" and "poor" as reference terms, he used terms corresponding to various moods (such great, annoyed, cheerful, sleepy etc.) for calculating PMI measure.

3   Experimental Setup and Results

We have performed opinion mining, mood analysis and gender analysis on three different blog datasets. We collected blog data on three topics. The collected data was transformed into vector space model representation and bag of words based feature selection was used for opinion mining. We implemented both Naïve Bayes text classifier and SO-PMI-IR algorithms for classifying blogs. To implement SO-PMI-IR, we extracted selected POS tags and computed their SO values. The SO values of terms in a blog were then aggregated using two different schemes to classify the blog as positive and negative. To implement Naïve Bayes, we used a three-fold scheme. One part of the data was used for training and the other two are then classified accordingly. We used both manual opinion labels and opinion labels assigned by SO-PMI-IR for training. The results of both these methods were cross validated.

3.1   Collecting the Blog Data

We obtained a large number of blogs on following three topics: 'Women's Reservation in India', 'Regionalism' and 'Three International Terror Events'. We collected full blogs from Google Blog Search through a Java program. Everyïblog was stored as separate text files. Every blog entry comprised of name of the blog site, permalink of the blog post, author's name, title of the blog post, its text and user comments. In the third dataset we also stored the country (or region) information of the author. In the first dataset we collected blog posts on 'Women's Reservation in India'. We obtained a large number of posts written by male as well as female authors. The second dataset was a collection of blog posts on 'Regionalism'. We did not restrict the data collection to the posts originating from India only; still we obtained a good number of posts in Indian perspective.

The third dataset was a collection of blog posts on three terror events, namely '26/11/08 Mumbai hotel attack in India', 'the March 2009 twin terrorist attacks in Pakistan on Lahore hotel & on Srilankan cricket team', and the '9/11/01 attack on World Trade Centre in USA'. This data was originally collected in a previous experimental work [17]. These events were chosen due to their socio-political relevance, highly discussed nature, and the demographic & social variations of the three different societies in which they occurred. Our goal of analysis for the third dataset was a cross-cultural opinion mining task. It involved observing the variations of opinions and sentiments of bloggers from different demographic & social groups on the events of high social & political concern. The blog data in the third dataset was grouped in three categories, each corresponding to the three demographic areas in which these events took place. These three groups were termed as IND, WAC and USE corresponding to bloggers belonging to India, West Asian Countries and United States & Europe (West) respectively. Table 1 summarizes the scheme of grouping the collected data.

Table 1. Clustering the blog data of the third dataset into different groups

	Event 1	Event 2	Event 3
Blog Data	IND	IND	IND
Blog Data	WAC	WAC	WAC
Blog Data	USE	USE	USE

3.2   Preprocessing the Data

We have used the Vector Space Model to represent each blog post. Every blog post is represented in the form of a term vector. A term vector consists of the distinct terms appearing in a blog post and their relative weights. There are a number of ways to represent the term vectors. Commonly used ones are *tf, tf.idf* and *Boolean presence*. We used tf.idf measure, defined as tf-idf$_{t,d}$ = tf$_{t,d}$ X idf$_t$, where *tf* is the term frequency and *idf* is the inverse document frequency. The vector V(d) derived from the document *d* thus contain one component for each distinct term. Once we have the entire set of posts represented as document vectors, their degree of similarity can also be computed using *cosine similarity* measure as in equation 7 below.

$$\text{Cosine Similarity } (d_1, d_2) = \{ V(d_1).V(d_2) \} / \{ |V(d_1)||V(d_2)| \} \tag{7}$$

The numerator represents the dot product of the vectors V(d$_1$) and V(d$_2$), and the denominator is product of their *Euclidean lengths*. The denominator thus length-normalizes the vectors V(d$_1$) and V(d$_2$) to unit vectors v(d$_1$) = V(d$_1$) / |V(d$_1$)| and v(d$_2$) = V(d$_2$) / |V(d$_2$)| respectively. The Cosine Similarity measure is used for clustering and classification tasks of text documents.

In addition to representing the blog posts as term vectors of tf.idf values, we preserved the original value and position of terms in the blog post for extracting suitable POS tags for opinion mining. We also performed stop word removal from the collected blog but no stemming was done. POS tagging refers to assigning a linguistic category (often termed as POS tag) to every term in the document based on its syntactic and morphological behavior. Common POS categories in English language are: noun, verb, adjective, adverb, pronoun, preposition, conjunction and interjection. We have used Penn Treebank POS Tags [12]. We extracted adjectives from the blog data for opinion mining. The selected adjectives were then used to compute a SO score using PMI value computations with reference words "excellent" and "poor" as in eq. 4 & 5. The opinion label assigned to a post was an aggregate of the SO values of the terms in the post.

3.3   Opinion Mining

We have used both a Naïve Bayes machine learning text classifier and the unsupervised semantic orientation approach for opinion classification. First we implemented the unsupervised semantic orientation approach to assign opinion labels to blog posts in all the three datasets collected. As stated earlier, the SO label of a blog post is computed using an aggregation of SO values of the selected terms in the blog post. We tried two schemes of aggregation. In one scheme we associated '+1' for every term having SO value above a threshold (0.8 in most of the cases) and '-1' for every term having SO value below it. The SO value of a blog post is then computed by obtaining the sum of SO values of all extracted terms of that blog post. If the sum is positive (or greater than a '+ve' reference value say 2 - the one used in our work), the blog post is labeled as positive and negative otherwise. In the other scheme we simply added the SO values of all the extracted terms in a blog post and then divided the sum by the total number of extracted terms of that blog post. For example, if the sum of SO values of n extracted terms is x, then the aggregate SO value of that blog

Table 2. A snapshot of results for a subset of the first data set. The thresholds for two SO aggregation schemes are 0 and 0.70 respectively.

Title of the Blog	Mood	Gender	Aggregate SO Value	Semantic Orientation
Do women need reservation?	happy (70.1 %)	female (74.8 %)	+3	Positive
	upset (29.9 %)	male (25.2 %)	0.76653093	Positive
Reservation for Women: The icing on the cake	happy (54.7 %)	female (52.8 %)	-7	Negative
	upset (45.3 %)	male (47.2 %)	0.73098755	Positive
Reservation to power for Indian women	happy (76.8 %)	female (64.9 %)	+4	Positive
	upset (23.2 %)	male (35.1 %)	0.91197723	Positive
Reservation by custom and tradition is acceptable	happy (50.1 %)	female (65.0 %)	+12	Positive
	upset (49.9 %)	male (35.0 %)	0.9886512	Positive
Women's bill should lead on to real political reform	upset (81.4 %)	male (80.3 %)	-6	Negative
	happy (18.6 %)	female (19.7 %)	0.6081681	Negative

Table 3. A snapshot of results for a subset of the second data set. The thresholds for two SO aggregation schemes are 0 and 0.70 respectively.

Title of the Blog	Mood	Aggregate SO Value	Semantic Orientation
Is Your Region More Important than your Nation?	upset (66.8 %)	1	Positive
	happy (33.2 %)	0.76783	Positive
Is it legitimate to give J&K the status of a special state?	upset (81.2 %)	-2	Negative
	happy (18.8 %)	0.68771	Negative
The whole of India does not belong to all Indians	upset (75.9 %)	-3	Negative
	happy (24.1 %)	0.62420	Negative
Do we need to fear Regionalism?	upset (93.9 %)	+2	Positive
	happy (6.1 %)	0.68932	Negative
A Sense of where you are!	happy (74.1 %)	+10	Positive
	upset (25.9 %)	1.09861	Positive

post is x/n. This aggregate value is then compared with a threshold and the blog post is labeled as positive or negative accordingly. We also performed mood and gender analysis using an online tool uClassify [18]. A snapshot of the opinion label assignments of few blog posts of the first and second datasets is presented in tables 2 and 3. The tables show aggregate SO values using both aggregation schemes and resulting opinion label assignments (columns 4 and 5).

The second implementation for opinion mining used Naïve Bayes text classifier. We used two methods for training. In first method we used the manually assigned opinion labels and in the second scheme we used opinion label assignments generated by the SO-PMI-IR approach as training labels. We employed a three-fold classification scheme. The blog data is divided into three subsets, with one of the three subsets used for training and the remaining two subsets classified using Naïve Bayes run. This is done by taking different parts as the training set. Our implementation of Naïve Bayes used term frequencies and hence is a multinomial Naïve Bayes implementation. A snapshot of the Naïve Bayes run on the first and second datasets is presented in table 4. Table 5 presents a summary of accuracy of the opinion mining results of both the methods (SO-PMI-IR and Naïve Bayes). Table 6 presents the cross-validation of results of opinion label assignments for a sample of 50 blog posts on the first and second datasets using Naïve Bayes and SO-PMI-IR approaches.

Table 4. Classification results of a sample of 50 of blog posts of the first and second datasets. The Naïve Bayes results are on a training data size of 25 and run on 50 blog posts respectively. The SO approach result is on the same 50 blog post data.

50 Blog data subset on	Number of blogs classified as positive		Number of blogs classified as negative		Precision, Recall and F-measure values (NB)
	SO Approach	NB Classifier	SO Approach	NB Classifier	
Women's Reservation in India	36	42	14	08	Precision: 0.5147 Recall: 0.9138 F-measure: 0.8873
Regionalism	38	44	12	06	Precision: 0.5392 Recall: 0.9642 F-measure: 0.8981

Table 5. Classification accuracy of a sample subset of 50 blog posts of the first and the second blog datasets

50 Blog Data subset on	Classification accuracy using first SO aggregation scheme	Classification accuracy using second SO aggregation scheme	Classification accuracy using Naïve Bayes Machine Learning approach
Women's Reservation in India	84%	81%	69%
Regionalism	77%	76%	67%

Table 6. Cross-validation of opinion label assignments of a sample set of 50 blog posts of the first and the second datasets, by both the methods

50 Blog Data subset on	Number of matching opinion label assignments	Number of mismatches in opinion label assignments
Women's Reservation in India	40 (80%)	10 (20%)
Regionalism	42 (84%)	08 (16%)

The third dataset involved data based on three different events and hence was subjected to analysis along two different dimensions: *vertical* and *horizontal*. Vertical analysis involved comparison of the blog posts of IND, WAC and USE groups on one event (say 26/11 Mumbai attack event). This gives an analytical perspective of the reactions of the different demographic groups on a particular event. Horizontal analysis involved comparing the posts of a particular group along three different events. For example comparison of the blog posts of WAC group for all the three events. This would give the variation in opinion, sentiment and mood of a particular group along the three events that happened in three different regions. While vertical analysis could have important inferences about the difference in opinions of IND, WAC and USE groups on a particular event (say 26/11 Mumbai attack); horizontal analysis was expected to have implications about the variations of opinion of the same group about the three different terror events that occurred at different places (for example observing IND group's reaction on 26/11 Mumbai attack, Lahore bombing and 9/11 WTC attack). Table 7 shows the result of mood analysis based on the blog data of the three groups along 9/11 WTC attack event (vertical analysis). Similarly, the horizontal analysis showed varied opinions of the three groups on different events. While IND and USE group's opinions matched to some extent on the 26/11 Mumbai attack and 9/11 WTC attack, there was a slight degree of variation in case of Lahore twin terror attack event. WAC group on the other hand showed quite different opinion on the three different events considered.

Table 7. Mood analysis of the IND, WAC and USE groups on 9/11 WTC event in U.S.A.

Mood	Upset	Happy
IND	85%	15%
WAC	36.6%	63.4%
USE	97.6%	2.4%

3.4   Inferences

The opinion, mood and gender analysis results obtained on the three datasets present an interesting picture. For the first dataset we performed opinion, mood and gender analysis. The blog posts of the first dataset being centered around 'Women's Reservation in India', there were a good number of posts that expressed positive opinion. Moreover, the negative opinion blog posts were largely by male bloggers. The results of mood analysis were however not in perfect congruence with the opinion mining results, with some blog posts classified as positive by both Naïve Bayes and SO-PMI-IR approaches but attributed higher score of 'upset' on mood analysis. This variation in results may be due to the use of different reference words for opinion mining and mood analysis. Also the gender analysis results were not very much accurate for the first dataset, possibly because of the topic of discussion itself.

The second dataset on 'Regionalism' has been subjected to opinion mining and mood analysis. The results of opinion mining by both the techniques produced similar results. Though the accuracy of classification for this dataset was slightly less than that on the first dataset; it has more congruent results on opinion mining and mood analysis. We assumed gender neutrality in the second dataset. Most of the blog posts of this dataset were labeled positive by both the approaches. A cursory look at the contents of the blog show that most of the bloggers express their concern about regionalism but did not use strong negative words (which bloggers did in the posts on Women's reservation).

The vertical and horizontal analysis on the third dataset resulted in one of the most interesting findings. Our focus in this dataset was purely cross-cultural. We wanted to observe how opinions of bloggers vary when they write about three gruesome terror events that took place in three different regions (one being their own country/region). Analysis along vertical dimension show that by and large the IND and USE groups tend to agree on the same set of opinions for a particular event and this was true for all the three events. WAC group's reaction was varied and differed a lot across the three events, namely the 26/11 Mumbai attack event, 9/11 WTC attack event and the twin terror events in Lahore. The findings were also supported by the mood analysis along vertical dimension. While vertical analysis helped in understanding the variation of perceptions and opinions of bloggers from different region on a highly emotion-laden event; horizontal analysis showed opinion variations of the same blogger group across events in different societies. This analysis is more valuable since it uses more original data at almost negligible physical cost.

4   Discussion

The experimental work carried out by us on opinion mining from Weblogs produced interesting results. The results of both the techniques employed were accurate to a good degree. However, it would be worth stating that unsupervised semantic orientation scheme is a better choice for opinion mining (at least for Weblogs). There appears a clear reason for this. The semantic orientation tries to capture the subjectivity in the blog posts by identifying the positive and negative terms, and labeling the blog post accordingly. The Naïve Bayes classifier, however, only uses term occurrence statistics to classify the blog posts into two groups. Since the terms present in the actual data may be quite different from the terms in the training data, it may result in more mis-classifications. This is a more severe problem in case of blog posts as different bloggers tend to use entirely different terms (possibly varied vocabulary). Hence, unsupervised semantic orientation approach may produce better results on opinion labeling of data from social media. However, it is more computationally challenging approach. The experimental work also demonstrates the applicability of opinion mining techniques on the blog data.

It is beyond doubt that the large amount of data in blogosphere is an extremely valuable source for commercial exploitation. What remains however relatively unexplored is to see how good is the huge amount of the data in the Blogosphere for cross-cultural psychological & sociological analysis. Blogosphere being a platform where people across the continent express themselves; we may use it for socio-political and cross-cultural psychological and sociological analysis. In this paper we have demonstrated one such effort using opinion and mood analysis on three different datasets. The preliminary results are interesting and worth further analysis (possibly by a social scientist). This experimental work demonstrates the use of opinion mining techniques for exploiting the blog data for sociologically relevant analysis. Advances in Natural Language Processing, Information Retrieval techniques for mining unstructured data will make this task more relevant and valuable.

References

1. Technorati Blogosphere Statistics (2008),
   http://technorati.com/blogging/state-of-the-blogosphere/
2. Agarwal, N., Liu, H.: Data Mining and Knowledge Discovery in Blogs. Morgan & Claypool Publishers (2010)
3. Turney, P.: Thumbs Up or Thumbs Down? Semantic Orientation Applied to Unsupervised Classification of Reviews. In: 40th Annual Meeting of the Association for Computational Linguistics, ACL 2002, Philadelphia, US, pp. 417–424 (2002)
4. Esuli, A., Sebastiani, F.: Determing the Semantic Orientation of Terms Through Gloss Analysis. In: 14th ACM International Conference on Information and Knowledge Management, CIKM 2005, Bremen, DE, pp. 617–624 (2005)
5. Sebastiani, F.: Machine Learning in Automated Text Categorization. ACM Computing Surveys 34(1), 1–47 (2002)
6. Pang, B., Lee, L., Vaithyanathan, S.: Thumbs up? Sentiment Classification using Machine Learning Techniques. In: Conference on Empirical Methods in Natural Language Processing, Philadelphia, US, pp. 79–86 (2002)
7. Kim., S.M., Hovy, E.: Determining Sentiment of Opinions. In: COLING Conference, Geneva (2004)
8. Durant, K.T., Smith, M.D.: Mining Sentiment Classification from Political Web Logs. In: WEBKDD 2006. ACM Press, New York (2006)
9. Liu, B.: Web Data Mining: Exploring Hyperlinks, Contents and Usage Data. Springer, Heidelberg (2008)

10. Dave, K., Lawerence, S., Pennock, D.: Mining the Peanut Gallery-Opinion Extraction and Semantic Classification of Product Reviews. In: 12th International World Wide Web Conference, pp. 519–528. ACM Press, New York (2003)
11. Manning, C.D., Raghavan, P., Schutze, H.: Introduction to Information Retrieval. Cambridge University Press, New York (2008)
12. Penn Treebank Project, http://www.cis.upenn.edu/~treebank/home.html
13. Turney, P., Littman, M.L.: Unsupervised Learning of Semantic Orientation from a Hundred-Billion-Word corpus. NRC Publications Archive (2002)
14. Mishne, G., Rijke, M.D.: MoodViews: Tools for Blog Mood Analysis. In: AAAI 2006 Spring Symposium on Computational Approaches to Analyzing Weblogs, AAAI-CAAW 2006 (March 2006)
15. Balog, K., Rijke, M.D.: Decomposing Bloggers' Moods. In: 3rd Annual Workshop on the Web Blogging Ecosystem, At WWW 2006 (2006)
16. Mishne, G.: Experiments with Mood Classification in Blog Posts. In: 2005 Stylistic Analysis of Text for Information Access Conference (2005)
17. Singh, V.K.: Mining the Blogosphere for Sociological Inferences. In: Ranka, S., Banerjee, A., Biswas, K.K., Dua, S., Mishra, P., Moona, R., Poon, S.-H., Wang, C.-L., et al. (eds.) IC3 2010. Communications in Computer and Information Science, vol. 94, pp. 547–558. Springer, Heidelberg (2010)
18. Uclassify Mood Analysis Tool, http://www.uclassify.com/browse/prfekt/Mood (retrieved, April 2009)

Generalized Projective Synchronization of Three-Scroll Chaotic Systems via Active Control

Sarasu Pakiriswamy[1] and Sundarapandian Vaidyanathan[2]

[1] Dept. of Computer Science and Engineering,
[2] Research and Development Centre,
Vel Tech Dr. RR & Dr. SR Technical University,
Avadi-Alamathi Road, Avadi, Chennai-600 062, India
{sarasujivat,sundarvtu}@gmail.com
http://www.vel-tech.org/

Abstract. This paper investigates the generalized projective synchronization (GPS) of identical Wang 3-scroll chaotic systems (Wang, 2009) and non-identical Dadras 3-scroll chaotic system (Dadras and Momeni, 2009) and Wang 3-scroll chaotic system. The synchronization results (GPS) derived for the 3-scroll chaotic systems have been derived using active control method and established using Lyapunov stability theory. Since the Lyapunov exponents are not required for these calculations, the active control method is very effective and convenient for achieving the general projective synchronization (GPS) of the 3-scroll chaotic systems addressed in this paper. Numerical simulations are presented to demonstrate the effectiveness of the synchronization results derived in this paper.

Keywords: Active control, chaos, generalized projective synchronization, three-scroll systems, Wang system, Dadras system.

1 Introduction

Chaotic systems are nonlinear dynamical systems, which are highly sensitive to initial conditions. The sensitive nature of chaotic systems is commonly called as the *butterfly effect* [1]. Chaos is an interesting nonlinear phenomenon and has been intensively studied in the last three decades. Chaos theory is applied in many scientific disciplines, viz. Mathematics, Physics, Chemistry, Biology, Engineering, Computer Science, Robotics and Economics.

Chaos synchronization is a phenomenon that may occur when two or more chaotic oscillators are coupled or a chaotic oscillator drives another chaotic oscillator. Because of the butterfly effect which causes the exponential divergence of the trajectories of two identical chaotic systems started with nearly the same initial conditions, synchronizing two chaotic systems is seemingly a very challenging problem.

Chaos theory has wide applications in several fields like physical systems [2], chemical systems [3], ecological systems [4], secure communications ([5]-[7]) etc.

In most of the chaos synchronization approaches, the *master-slave* or *drive-response* formalism is used. If a particular chaotic system is called the *master* or *drive system*

N. Meghanathan et al. (Eds.): CCSIT 2012, Part II, LNICST 85, pp. 146–155, 2012.
© Institute for Computer Sciences, Social Informatics and Telecommunications Engineering 2012

and another chaotic system is called the *slave* or *response system*, then the idea of synchronization is to use the output of the master system to control the slave system so that the output of the slave system tracks the output of the master system asymptotically.

The seminal work by Pecora and Carroll ([8], 1990) is followed by a variety of impressive approaches for chaos synchronization such as the sampled-data feedback synchronization method [9], OGY method [10], time-delay feedback method [11], back-stepping method [12], active control method [13], adaptive control method [14], sliding control method [15], etc.

In generalized projective synchronization [16], the chaotic systems can synchronize up to a constant scaling matrix. Complete synchronization [17], anti-synchronization [18], hybrid synchronization [19], projective synchronization [20] and generalized synchronization [21] are special cases of generalized projective synchronization. The generalized projective synchronization (GPS) has applications in secure communications.

This paper is organized as follows. In Section 2, we provide a description of the 3-scroll chaotic systems studied in this paper. In Section 3, we derive results for the GPS between identical Wang 3-scroll chaotic systems (Wang, [22], 2009). In Section 4, we derive results for the GPS between non-identical Dadras 3-scroll chaotic system (Dadras and Momeni, [23], 2009) and Wang 3-scroll chaotic system (2009). In Section 5, we summarize the main results obtained in this paper.

2   Systems Description

The Wang 3-scroll chaotic system ([22], 2009) is described by the dynamics

$$
\begin{aligned}
\dot{x}_1 &= a(x_1 - x_2) - x_2 x_3 \\
\dot{x}_2 &= -b x_2 + x_1 x_3 \\
\dot{x}_3 &= -c x_3 + d x_1 + x_1 x_2
\end{aligned}
\tag{1}
$$

where x_1, x_2, x_3 are the *state* variables and a, b, c, d are constant, positive parameters of the system.

The system (1) exhibits a 3-scroll chaotic attractor when the system parameter values are chosen as $a = 0.977$, $b = 10$, $c = 4$ and $d = 0.1$.

Figure 1 depicts the state orbits of the Wang 3-scroll system (1).

The Dadras 3-scroll system ([23], 2009) is described by the dynamics

$$
\begin{aligned}
\dot{x}_1 &= x_2 - p x_1 + q x_2 x_3 \\
\dot{x}_2 &= r x_2 - x_1 x_3 + x_3 \\
\dot{x}_3 &= s x_1 x_2 - \epsilon x_3
\end{aligned}
\tag{2}
$$

where x_1, x_2, x_3 are the *state* variables and p, q, r, s, ϵ are constant, positive parameters of the system.

The system (2) exhibits a 3-scroll chaotic attractor when the system parameter values are chosen as $p = 3$, $q = 2.7$, $r = 1.7$, $s = 2$ and $\epsilon = 9$.

Figure 2 depicts the state orbits of the Dadras 3-scroll system (2).

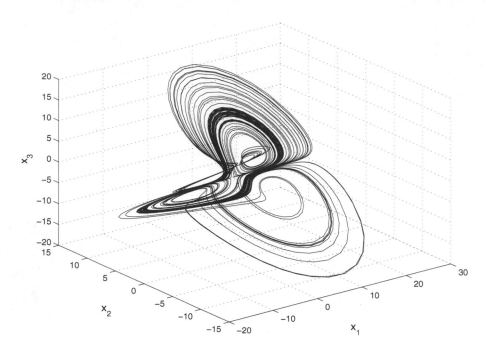

Fig. 1. State Orbits of the Wang 3-Scroll Chaotic System

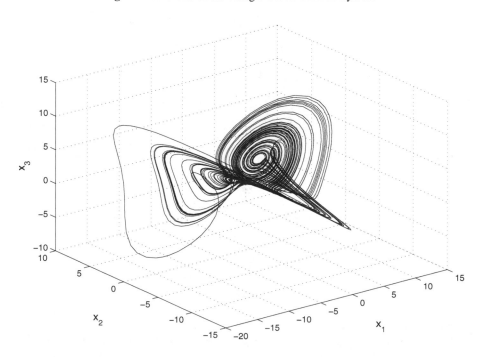

Fig. 2. State Orbits of the Dadras 3-Scroll Chaotic System

3   Generalized Projective Synchronization of Identical Wang 3-Scroll Chaotic Systems

3.1   Main Results

In this section, we discuss the design of active controller for achieving generalized projective synchronization (GPS) of identical Wang 3-scroll chaotic systems ([22], 2009).

Thus, the master system is described by the Wang dynamics

$$\dot{x}_1 = a(x_1 - x_2) - x_2 x_3$$
$$\dot{x}_2 = -bx_2 + x_1 x_3 \qquad (3)$$
$$\dot{x}_3 = -cx_3 + dx_1 + x_1 x_2$$

where x_1, x_2, x_3 are the *state* variables and a, b, c, d are constant, positive parameters of the system.

Also, the slave system is described by the controlled Wang dynamics

$$\dot{y}_1 = a(y_1 - y_2) - y_2 y_3 + u_1$$
$$\dot{y}_2 = -by_2 + y_1 y_3 + u_2 \qquad (4)$$
$$\dot{y}_3 = -cy_3 + dy_1 + y_1 y_2 + u_3$$

where y_1, y_2, y_3 are the *state* variables and u_1, u_2, u_3 are the active controls.

For the GPS of (3) and (4), the synchronization errors are defined as

$$e_1 = y_1 - \alpha_1 x_1$$
$$e_2 = y_2 - \alpha_2 x_2 \qquad (5)$$
$$e_3 = y_3 - \alpha_3 x_3$$

where the scales $\alpha_1, \alpha_2, \alpha_3$ are real numbers.

A simple calculation yields the error dynamics

$$\dot{e}_1 = a(y_1 - y_2) - y_2 y_3 - \alpha_1[a(x_1 - x_2) - x_2 x_3] + u_1$$
$$\dot{e}_2 = -by_2 + y_1 y_3 - \alpha_2[-bx_2 + x_1 x_3] + u_2 \qquad (6)$$
$$\dot{e}_3 = -cy_3 + dy_1 + y_1 y_2 - \alpha_3[-cx_3 + dx_1 + x_1 x_2] + u_3$$

We consider the active nonlinear controller defined by

$$u_1 = -a(y_1 - y_2) + y_2 y_3 + \alpha_1[a(x_1 - x_2) - x_2 x_3] - k_1 e_1$$
$$u_2 = by_2 - y_1 y_3 + \alpha_2[-bx_2 + x_1 x_3] - k_2 e_2 \qquad (7)$$
$$u_3 = cy_3 - dy_1 - y_1 y_2 + \alpha_3[-cx_3 + dx_1 + x_1 x_2] - k_3 e_3$$

where the gains k_1, k_2, k_3 are positive constants.

Substitution of (7) into (6) yields the closed-loop error dynamics

$$\dot{e}_1 = -k_1 e_1$$
$$\dot{e}_2 = -k_2 e_2 \qquad (8)$$
$$\dot{e}_3 = -k_3 e_3$$

We consider the quadratic Lyapunov function defined by

$$V(e) = \frac{1}{2} e^T e = \frac{1}{2} \left(e_1^2 + e_2^2 + e_3^2\right) \tag{9}$$

which is positive definite on $\mathbb{R}^3$.

Differentiating (9) along the trajectories of the system (8), we get

$$\dot{V}(e) = -k_1 e_1^2 - k_2 e_2^2 - k_3 e_3^2 \tag{10}$$

which is a negative definite function on $\mathbb{R}^3$, since k_1, k_2, k_3 are positive constants.

Thus, by Lyapunov stability theory [24], the error dynamics (8) is globally exponentially stable. Hence, we obtain the following result.

Theorem 1. *The active feedback controller (7) achieves global chaos generalized projective synchronization (GPS) between the identical Wang 3-scroll chaotic systems (3) and (4).*   ∎

3.2 Numerical Results

For the numerical simulations, the fourth order Runge-Kutta method is used to solve the two systems of differential equations (3) and (4) with the active controller (7).

The parameters of the identical Wang 3-scroll chaotic systems are chosen as

$$a = 0.977, \quad b = 10, \quad c = 4, \quad d = 0.1$$

The initial values for the master system (3) are taken as

$$x_1(0) = 15, \quad x_2(0) = 28, \quad x_3(0) = 7$$

The initial values for the slave system (4) are taken as

$$y_1(0) = 29, \quad y_2(0) = 10, \quad y_3(0) = 14$$

The GPS scales α_i are taken as

$$\alpha_1 = -2.5, \quad \alpha_2 = 6.3, \quad \alpha_3 = -0.7$$

We take the state feedback gains as $k_1 = 4$, $k_2 = 4$, and $k_3 = 4$.

Figure 3 shows the time response of the error states e_1, e_2, e_3 of the error dynamical system (6) when the active nonlinear controller (7) is deployed. From this figure, it is clear that all the error states decay to zero exponentially in 1.5 sec and thus, generalized projective synchronization is achieved between the identical Wang 3-scroll systems (3) and (4).

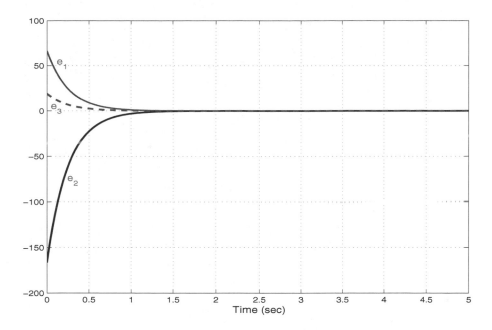

Fig. 3. Time Responses of the Error States of (6)

4 Generalized Projective Synchronization of Non-identical Dadras and Wang 3-Scroll Chaotic Systems

4.1 Main Results

In this section, we derive results for the generalized projective synchronization (GPS) of non-identical 3-scroll chaotic systems, *viz.* Dadras 3-scroll system ([23], 2009) and Wang 3-scroll system ([22], 2009).

Thus, the master system is described by the Dadras dynamics

$$\dot{x}_1 = x_2 - px_1 + qx_2x_3$$
$$\dot{x}_2 = rx_2 - x_1x_3 + x_3 \qquad\qquad (11)$$
$$\dot{x}_3 = sx_1x_2 - \epsilon x_3$$

where x_1, x_2, x_3 are the *state* variables and p, q, r, s, ϵ are constant, positive parameters of the system.

Also, the slave system is described by the controlled Wang dynamics

$$\dot{y}_1 = a(y_1 - y_2) - y_2y_3 + u_1$$
$$\dot{y}_2 = -by_2 + y_1y_3 + u_2 \qquad\qquad (12)$$
$$\dot{y}_3 = -cy_3 + dy_1 + y_1y_2 + u_3$$

where y_1, y_2, y_3 are the *state* variables, a, b, c, d are constant, positive parameters of the system and u_1, u_2, u_3 are the active controls.

For the GPS of (11) and (12), the synchronization errors are defined as

$$
\begin{aligned}
e_1 &= y_1 - \alpha_1 x_1 \\
e_2 &= y_2 - \alpha_2 x_2 \\
e_3 &= y_3 - \alpha_3 x_3
\end{aligned}
\tag{13}
$$

where the scales $\alpha_1, \alpha_2, \alpha_3$ are real numbers.

A simple calculation yields the error dynamics

$$
\begin{aligned}
\dot{e}_1 &= a(y_1 - y_2) - y_2 y_3 - \alpha_1 \left[x_2 - p x_1 + q x_2 x_3\right] + u_1 \\
\dot{e}_2 &= -b y_2 + y_1 y_3 - \alpha_2 \left[r x_2 - x_1 x_3 + x_3\right] + u_2 \\
\dot{e}_3 &= -c y_3 + d y_1 + y_1 y_2 - \alpha_3 \left[s x_1 x_2 - \epsilon x_3\right] + u_3
\end{aligned}
\tag{14}
$$

We consider the active nonlinear controller defined by

$$
\begin{aligned}
u_1 &= -a(y_1 - y_2) + y_2 y_3 + \alpha_1 \left[x_2 - p x_1 + q x_2 x_3\right] - k_1 e_1 \\
u_2 &= b y_2 - y_1 y_3 + \alpha_2 \left[r x_2 - x_1 x_3 + x_3\right] - k_2 e_2 \\
u_3 &= c y_3 - d y_1 - y_1 y_2 + \alpha_3 \left[s x_1 x_2 - \epsilon x_3\right] - k_3 e_3
\end{aligned}
\tag{15}
$$

where the gains k_1, k_2, k_3, k_4 are positive constants.

Substitution of (15) into (14) yields the closed-loop error dynamics

$$
\begin{aligned}
\dot{e}_1 &= -k_1 e_1 \\
\dot{e}_2 &= -k_2 e_2 \\
\dot{e}_3 &= -k_3 e_3
\end{aligned}
\tag{16}
$$

We consider the quadratic Lyapunov function defined by

$$
V(e) = \frac{1}{2} e^T e = \frac{1}{2} \left(e_1^2 + e_2^2 + e_3^2\right)
\tag{17}
$$

which is positive definite on $\mathbb{R}^3$.

Differentiating (17) along the trajectories of the system (16), we get

$$
\dot{V}(e) = -k_1 e_1^2 - k_2 e_2^2 - k_3 e_3^2
\tag{18}
$$

which is a negative definite function on $\mathbb{R}^3$, since k_1, k_2, k_3 are positive constants.

Thus, by Lyapunov stability theory [24], the error dynamics (16) is globally exponentially stable. Hence, we obtain the following result.

Theorem 2. *The active feedback controller (15) achieves global chaos generalized projective synchronization (GPS) between the non-identical Dadras 3-scroll chaotic system (11) and the Wang 3-scroll chaotic system (12).*   ∎

4.2   Numerical Results

For the numerical simulations, the fourth order Runge-Kutta method is used to solve the two systems of differential equations (11) and (12) with the active controller (15).

The parameters of the Dadras 3-scroll chaotic system (11) are taken as

$$p = 3, \quad q = 2.7, \quad r = 1.7, \quad s = 2, \quad \epsilon = 9$$

The parameters of the Wang 3-scroll chaotic system (12) are taken as

$$a = 0.977, \quad b = 10, \quad c = 4, \quad d = 0.1$$

The initial values for the master system (11) are taken as

$$x_1(0) = 3, \quad x_2(0) = 10, \quad x_3(0) = 28$$

The initial values for the slave system (12) are taken as

$$y_1(0) = 24, \quad y_2(0) = 6, \quad y_3(0) = 15$$

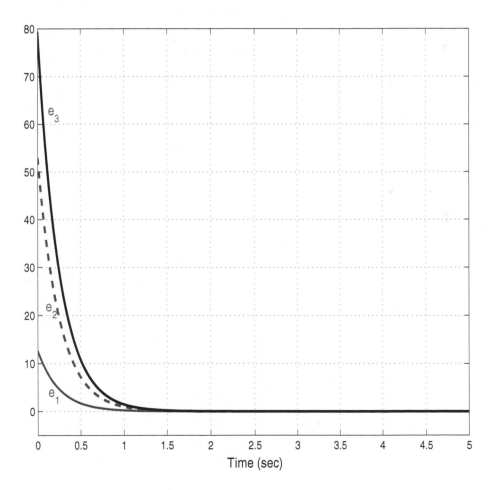

Fig. 4. Time Responses of the Error States of (14)

The GPS scales α_i are taken as

$$\alpha_1 = 3.8, \quad \alpha_2 = -4.7, \quad \alpha_3 = -2.3$$

We take the state feedback gains as $k_1 = 4$, $k_2 = 4$ and $k_3 = 4$.

Figure 4 shows the time response of the error states e_1, e_2, e_3 of the error dynamical system (14) when the active nonlinear controller (15) is deployed.

From this figure, it is clear that all the error states decay to zero exponentially in 1.7 sec and thus, generalized projective synchronization is achieved between the non-identical Dadras 3-scroll system (11) and Wang 3-scroll system (12).

5 Conclusions

In this paper, we derived active control laws for achieving generalized projective synchronization (GPS) of the following 3-scroll chaotic systems:

(A) Identical Wang 3-scroll systems (2009)
(B) Non-identical Dadras 3-scroll system (2009) and Wang 3-scroll system (2009).

The synchronization results (GPS) derived in this paper for the chaotic Wang and Dadras 3-scroll chaotic systems [(A) and (B)] have been proved using Lyapunov stability theory. Since Lyapunov exponents are not required for these calculations, the proposed active control method is very effective and suitable for achieving GPS of the 3-scroll chaotic systems addressed in this paper. Numerical simulations are shown to demonstrate the effectiveness of the synchronization results (GPS) derived in this paper.

References

1. Alligood, K.T., Sauer, T., Yorke, J.A.: An Introduction to Dynamical Systems. Springer, New York (1997)
2. Lakshmanan, M., Murali, K.: Chaos in Nonlinear Oscillators: Controlling and Synchronization. World Scientific, Singapore (1996)
3. Han, S.K., Kerrer, C., Kuramoto, Y.: Dephasing and bursting in coupled neural oscillators. Phys. Rev. Lett. 75, 3190–3193 (1995)
4. Blasius, B., Huppert, A., Stone, L.: Complex dynamics and phase synchronization in spatially extended ecological system. Nature 399, 354–359 (1999)
5. Kwok, H.S., Wallace, K., Tang, S., Man, K.F.: Online secure communication system using chaotic map. Internat. J. Bifurcat. Chaos 14, 285–292 (2004)
6. Kocarev, L., Parlitz, U.: General approach for chaos synchronization with applications to communications. Phys. Rev. Lett. 74, 5028–5030 (1995)
7. Murali, K., Lakshmanan, M.: Secure communication using a compound signal using sampled-data feedback. Applied Math. Mech. 11, 1309–1315 (2003)
8. Pecora, L.M., Carroll, T.L.: Synchronization in chaotic systems. Phys. Rev. Lett. 64, 821–824 (1990)
9. Yang, T., Chua, L.O.: Control of chaos using sampled-data feedback control. Internat. J. Bifurcat. Chaos 9, 215–219 (1999)

10. Ott, E., Grebogi, C., Yorke, J.A.: Controlling chaos. Phys. Rev. Lett. 64, 1196–1199 (1990)
11. Park, J.H., Kwon, O.M.: A novel criterion for delayed feedback control of time-delay chaotic systems. Chaos, Solit. Fract. 17, 709–716 (2003)
12. Yu, Y.G., Zhang, S.C.: Adaptive backstepping synchronization of uncertain chaotic systems. Chaos, Solit. Fract. 27, 1369–1375 (2006)
13. Sundarapandian, V.: Global chaos synchronization of Liu-Su-Liu and Li chaotic systems by active nonlinear control. CIIT International Journal of Digital Signal Processing 3(4), 171–175 (2011)
14. Chen, S.H., Lü, J.: Synchronization of an uncertain unified system via adaptive control. Chaos, Solitons and Fractals 14, 643–647 (2002)
15. Konishi, K., Hirai, M., Kokame, H.: Sliding mode control for a class of chaotic systems. Phys. Lett. A 245, 511–517 (1998)
16. Zhou, P., Kuang, F., Cheng, Y.M.: Generalized projective synchronization for fractional order chaotic systems. Chinese Journal of Physics 48(1), 49–56 (2010)
17. Sundarapandian, V.: Global chaos synchronization of Shimizu-Morioka and Liu-Chen chaotic systems by active nonlinear control. Internat. J. Advances in Science and Technology 2(4), 11–20 (2011)
18. Sundarapandian, V.: Anti-synchronization of Lorenz and T chaotic systems by active nonlinear control. Internat. J. Computer Information Systems 2(4), 6–10 (2011)
19. Sundarapandian, V.: Hybrid synchronization of hyperchaotic Rössler and hyperchaotic Lorenz systems by active control. Internat. J. Advances in Science and Technology 2(4), 1–10 (2011)
20. Mainieri, R., Rehacek, J.: Projective synchronization in three-dimensioned chaotic systems. Phys. Rev. Lett. 82, 3042–3045 (1999)
21. Wang, Y.W., Guan, Z.H.: Generalized synchronization of continuous chaotic systems. Chaos, Solit. Fract. 27, 97–101 (2006)
22. Wang, L.: 3-scroll and 4-scroll chaotic attractors generated from a new 3-D quadratic autonomous system. Nonlinear Dynamics 56, 453–462 (2009)
23. Dadras, S., Momeni, H.R.: A novel three-dimensional autonomous chaotic system generating two, three and four-scroll attractors. Physics Letters A 373, 3637–3642 (2009)
24. Hahn, W.: The Stability of Motion. Springer, New York (1967)

Switching Algorithms in Peer to Peer Networks - Review

M. Padmavathi[1] and R.M. Suresh[2]

[1] R.M.D. Engineering College, Kavaraipetai
[2] R.M.K. Engineering College, Kavaraipetai
mpadmavathi1979@gmail.com, rmsuresh@hotmail.com

Abstract. The peer-to-peer (P2P) network is heavily used for content distribution and is popularly used for internet file sharing. In a peer to peer network the average time to download a given file becomes a key metric for performance measure. The common approach of analyzing the average download time based on average service capacity is fundamentally flawed, and shown that the spatial heterogeneity of service capacities of different source peers and temporal fluctuations in service capacity of a single source peer have significant impact on increasing the average download time in P2P networks. This paper gives a comparative study of various downloading algorithms to effectively remove these negative factors thereby reducing the average download duration of a file.

Keywords: P2P networks, average download time, average service capacity.

1   Introduction

PEER-TO-PEER (P2P) file-sharing applications are becoming increasingly popular for content distribution and it accounts for more than 80% of the internet's bandwidth usage. The early model for content distribution was a centralized one, in which users have to compete for limited resources in terms of bottleneck bandwidth or processing power of a single server which resulted in poor performance to all users. From a single user's perspective, the duration of the download time for that individual user is the most often used performance metric.

P2P technology tries to solve the issue of scalability by making the system distributed. The aggregated output or the service capacity of a peer to peer network generally increases as the number of peers involved in uploading the same file increases in the network [1,2]. With this increasing service capacity, theoretical studies have shown that users of a P2P network enjoy much faster downloads [1][2]. The performance measurement study shows that, the per-user performance in a P2P network may be even worse than that of centralized network architecture as shown in [3]. In reality, even downloading files of less than 10 MB in size may take from 5 minutes to several hours and bigger files with size greater than 100 Mb taking hours to weeks. Further, even when all users try to download the same file, each of them may have different downloading times, depending on the available capacity

N. Meghanathan et al. (Eds.): CCSIT 2012, Part II, LNICST 85, pp. 156–166, 2012.

fluctuation, the path it chooses to download the file, etc. Thus in an ideal scenario, the downloading peer for a given bandwidth will be constrained by the limitation of the access link. In practical scenarios however there are other factors (Peer selection algorithms, free riders to name a few) which prevent a peer from fully utilizing the available bandwidth. Literature study has shown there is still scope for improvement in P2P systems. Using the average service capacity to find the performance of the network has been extensively used in literature [1] [2].

1.1   Restrictions of Average Service Capacity

Consider a P2P network, a peer downloading a file of size F from N possible source peers and C_i the average end-to-end available capacity between the downloading peer and the ith source peer (i =1,2,...N). The actual value of C_i is unknown till the downloading peer actually connects to the source peer i. The average service capacity of the network, $\vec{C}$, is given by $\sum_{i=1}^{N} Ci / N$ .The average download time T , for a file of size F would be

$$T = F\!\!\Big/\!\!\vec{C} \tag{1}$$

In practical scenarios it is found that the actual average download time is far different from the computed average download time shown in equation (1) for each user in the network.

1.2   Impact of Fluctuations in Service Capacity

Fluctuations in service capacity can be attributed to

- The spatial heterogeneity in the available service capacities of different end-to-end paths and
- The temporal correlations in the service capacity of a given source peer.

This paper considers the impact of heterogeneity. Suppose that there are two source peers with service capacities of C_1 =200 kbps and C_2 =50 kbps, respectively, and there is only one downloading peer in the network. Because the downloading peer does not know the service capacity of each source peer prior to its connection, the best choice that the downloading peer can make to minimize the risk is to choose the source peers with equal probability. For this scenario, the average capacity that the downloading peer expects from the network would be (200+50) / 2= 125 kbps. If the file size F is 1 MB, the predicted average download time is 64 seconds from (1). However, the actual average download time is 1/2(1 MB/200 kbps) + 1/2(1 MB/50 Mbps) = 66.7 seconds. It is seen that spatial heterogeneity has an impact in the average download time and actually increases the average download time. If the average service capacity is known before the downloading peer makes the connection, an obvious solution to the problem of minimizing the average download time is to find the peer with the maximum average capacity, i.e., to choose peer j with the average capacity Cj as the average download time Ti over source peer i would be given by F / C_i. Consider again the previous two-source peer example with C_1 =100 kbps and C_2=150 kbps, As the goal is to minimize the download time, an obvious choice would be to choose source peer 2 as its average capacity is higher. Now, let us assume that the service capacity of source peer 2 is not a constant, but is given by a stochastic process C_2 (t) taking values 50 or 250 kbps with equal probability, thus giving $E\{C_2(t)\} = C_2 = 150$ kbps. If the process $C_2(t)$ is strongly correlated over time such that the service capacity for a file is likely to be the same throughout the session duration, it takes on average (1 MB/50 kbps ÷ 1 MB/250 kbps)/2 = 96 seconds, while it takes only 80 seconds to download the file from source peer 1. Thus it is evident that the average download time is increased due to heterogeneity and temporal correlations of service capacity.

The rest of the paper is organized as follows. Section 2, discusses about factors of average download time. Section 3, characterizes average download time based on these factors namely spatial heterogeneity and temporal correlations. Section 4 discusses about various switching algorithms that are in existence to remove the two negative factors. Section 5 concludes the limitations of each algorithm.

2   Factors of Average Download Time

This section describes briefly the characteristics of the service capacity that a single user receives from the network from the user's perspective. Specifically, the system considers the heterogeneity of service capacities over different network paths and the stochastic fluctuation of the capacity over time for a given source peer.

2.1   Heterogeneity of Service Capacity

In a P2P network, the service capacities from different source peers are different. There are many reasons for this heterogeneity. On each peer side, physical connection speeds at different peers vary over a wide range [11] . On the network side, peers are geographically located over a large area and each logical connection consists of multiple hops.

2.2   Correlations in Service Capacity

While the long-term average of the service capacity is mainly governed by topological parameters, the actual service capacity during a typical session is never constant, but always fluctuates over time [12],[13]. There are many factors causing this fluctuation. First, the number of connection a source peer allows is changing over time, which creates a fluctuation in the service capacity for each user. Second, some user applications running on a source peer such as online games may throttle the central processing unit and impact the amount of capacity it can offer. Third, temporary congestion at any link in the network can also reduce the service capacity of all users utilizing that link. The short-term variations in the capacity are mainly due to the window size fluctuation in TCP, while the long-term variations are due to network congestion, changes in workload or the number of connecting users at the source peer, etc. The long-term fluctuation typically lasts over a longer time scale, say, few minutes up to several hours.

3   Characterizing Average Download Time

The formal definition of the download time is given as

Definition 1: Let C(t) denote the time-varying service capacity of a given link (path) at time t $(t = 1 \cdot 2 \cdot \triangleright \triangleright)$ over the duration of a download. Following the definition in [14], the download time T for a file of size F is defined as

$$T = \min \{ s > 0 \mid \sum_{t=1}^{S} C(t) \geq F \} \qquad (2)$$

The random variable T is the first hitting time of the process C(t) to reach level F. If $\P C\ (t) \cdot t \in \mathbb{N} \Diamond$ are independent and identically distributed $(i \triangleright i \triangleright d \triangleright)$, then by assuming an equality in (2), Wald's equation [10] gives that

$$F = E \{ \sum_{t=1}^{T} C(t) \} = E\{C(t)\}E\{T\} \qquad (3)$$

The expected download time, measured in slots, then becomes E $\{T\} = F/\mathbb{E}\P C(t) \Diamond$. Note that (3) also holds C (t) is constant (over t). It can be noted that whenever the service capacity is i.i.d. over time or constant, a direct relationship can be established between the average service capacity and the average download time.

3.1   Impact of Heterogeneity in Service Capacity

The impact of heterogeneous service capacities of different source peers is considered in this section. To decouple the effect of correlations from that of heterogeneity Wald's equation holds true for *each source peer* and this allows the average capacities to be different for various source peers.

Let N be the number of source peers in the network and Ci(t) be the service capacity of source peer at time slot . The paper assumes that Ci (t) is either constant or i.i.d. over t such that (3) holds. Let Ci= E $\{$ $C_i(t)\}$ be the average capacity of source peer . Then, the average service capacity the network offers to a user becomes

$$A (\vec{C}) = \frac{1}{N} \sum_{i=1}^{N} Ci \qquad (4)$$

where $\vec{C} = C1, C_2, \ldots C_N$ is the arithmetic mean A($\vec{C}$) of the sequence . Thus, one may expect that the average download time, E{T} of a file of size F would be

$$E\{T\} = \frac{F}{A(\vec{C})} \qquad (5)$$

Since the user can choose one of N source peers with equal probability, the actual average download time in this case becomes

$$E\{T\} = \frac{1}{N} \sum_{i=1}^{N} \frac{F}{Ci} = \frac{F}{H(\vec{C})} \qquad (6)$$

Where $H(\vec{C})$ is harmonic mean of $C_1, C_2, .. C_N$ defined by

$$H(\vec{C}) = [\frac{1}{N} \sum_{i=1}^{N} \frac{1}{Ci}].$$ $A(\vec{C}) \geq H(\vec{C})$, because, it follows that (6) $\geq$ (5). It is

seen that the actual average download time in a heterogeneous network is always greater than that given by "the average capacity of the network" as in (5).

3.2   Impact of Correlations in Service Capacity

Consider a fixed network path between a downloading peer and its corresponding source peer for a file of size F. Let C(t) be a stationary random process denoting the available capacity over that source at time t and assumes that C(t) is positively correlated over time. Then, as before, the download time of a file (or the first hitting time of the process C(t) to reach a level F) can be defined as T_{cor}, where the subscript "cor" is a correlated stochastic process, if the system is able to remove the correlations from C(t). Let C'(t) be the resulting process and T_{ind} be the stopping time for the process to reach level F , where the subscript "ind" now means that is independent over time. Then, again from Wald's equation,

$$E\{T_{ind}\} = \frac{F}{E\{C'(t)\}} = \frac{F}{E\{C(t)\}} \qquad (7)$$

If C(t) is 100% correlated over time then the download time T_{cor} becomes $T_{cor} = F / C$. Hence, Jensen's inequality shows that

$$E\{T_{cor}\} = FE\{\frac{1}{C}\} \quad \frac{F}{E\{C\}} = E\{T_{ind}\} \qquad (8)$$

i.e., the average first hitting time of an 100% correlated process is always larger than that of an i.i.d. counterpart.

Theorem 1: Suppose that C(t) , $t \geq 1$ is associated. Then, $E(T_{cor}) \geq E(T_{ind})$.

Theorem 1 states that the average download time of a file from a source peer with correlated service capacity is always larger than that of an i.i.d. counterpart. From previous discussions, in general the average download time, E(T) , should be calculated using   E (F/C(t)) rather than the commonly used F / E [C(t)]. The relationship between the average download time and the degree of correlation in the available bandwidth is given by a stationary 1st autoregressive process (AR1) as

$$C(t+1) = \ . \ C(t) + \varepsilon \ (t) + \alpha \tag{9}$$

Equation (9) shows that, the average download time increases as the degree of correlation increases, for different ρ and $\mathcal{E}(t)$.

4   Methods to Minimize File Download Duration

Intuitively, if a downloader relies on a single source peer for its entire download it results in a long download in case of slow source peer. Since the service capacity of each source peer is different and fluctuates over time, utilizing different source peers either simultaneously or sequentially within one download session would be a good idea to diversify the risk. This section briefly describes all the methods that are used to download a file form P2P networks. The methods to download a file are (i) Byte based algorithms; (ii) Time based algorithms. (iii) Choke based algorithm.

The proposed analysis assumes the following properties [4]:

  i.   The service capacity of a source is constant within one time slot.
 ii.   Each downloader selects its source independently.
iii.   Each downloader makes a blind choice, i.e., the sources are randomly chosen uniformly over all available sources.

4.1   Byte-Based Algorithms

Peer-to-peer research has predominately focused on byte based switching algorithms to alleviate the amount of time clients remain with underperforming nodes [1][2][3].

Parallel Downloading

Parallel downloading is one of the most noticeable way to reduce the download time [5],[7]. In parallel download, a file of size F is divided into k chunks of equal size and the single file is allowed to download in parallel with k simultaneous connections yielding a download duration of $\max\{t_1, t_2, \ldots , t_k\}$ (where t_k represents the time chunk k took to download during time t). If parallel downloading is used to download a file of size F from the network with only two source peers of service capacities C_1, C_2 respectively, the download time is given by

$$T_P = \max \ \{ \ \frac{F}{2C1}, \frac{F}{2C2} \ \} = \frac{F}{2C1} \tag{10}$$

From (1) the predicted download time is given by

$$E\{T\} = \frac{F}{A(\bar{C})} = \frac{2F}{C1+C2} \tag{11}$$

Thus, even in the network with one user, parallel downloading may not reduce the download time as the performance of parallel download depends upon the distribution of the underlying service capacities and could be much worse than the ideal case. By making the chunk-size proportional to the service capacity of each source peer, parallel downloading can yield the optimal download time. But such scheme requires global information of the network.

Limitations : This method exposes the entire download session to the slowest server.

Random Chunk-Based Switching

In the random chunk-based switching scheme[4], the file is divided into many small chunks and a user downloads chunks sequentially one at a time. When a peer completes downloading a chunk from the current source peer, the next source peer is selected randomly to download the next chunk. In this way, if the downloader is currently stuck with a bad source peer, it will stay there for only the amount of time required for finishing one chunk. The download time for one chunk is independent of that of the previous chunk. Intuitively, switching source peers based on chunk can reduce the correlation in service capacity between chunks and hence reduce the average download time. Suppose if there is no temporal correlation in service capacity and a file of size F is divided into m chunks of equal size, and let T_j be the download time for chunk . Then, the total download time is given by $T_{Chunk} = \sum_{j=1}^{m} t_j$. Since each chunk randomly chooses one of source peers the expected download time will be given by

$$E\{T_{Chunk}\} = \sum_{j=1}^{m} \frac{1}{N} \sum_{i=1}^{m} \frac{F/m}{C_i} = \frac{F}{H(\vec{C})} \qquad (12)$$

The result in (10) is identical to the download time given in (6) where a user downloads the entire file from an initially randomly chosen source peer.

Limitations: In the chunk-based switching, there is possibilities of getting stuck with a source peer of very low service capacity, so that downloading a fixed amount of bytes from the source peer may still take a long time. This long wait can be avoided by making the size of each chunk very small, but this would cause too much overhead associated with switching to many source peers and integrating those many chunks into a single file. This shows that the chunk-based switching is still subject to the curse of bad spatial heterogeneity .

Random Permanent Connection

In permanent connection, the source selection function does not change in time t . When the list of available source peers is given, the downloader will choose one of them randomly with equal probability and will stay with that source peer *permanently* *[4]* until the download completes.

Limitations: Since the downloader randomly chooses a source peer at each time slot, it is possible for the downloaded to get stuck with bad source peer for that fixed time slot t.

4.2   Time- Based Algorithms

Time-based algorithms allow clients to select a new server based on expiration of a timer rather than using chunks, parallel, or permanent algorithms. Byte-based algorithms rely on average service capacity as a basis for calculating download duration. But temporal fluctuations in network capacity as well as inconsistencies in using average capacity provide for a new model. To accurately reproduce temporal fluctuations, a stochastic model can be used.

Random Periodic Switching

In random periodic switching [9], the downloader randomly chooses a source peer at each time slot t, independently of everything else. In other words, the source selection function U(t) forms an i.i.d. sequence of random variables, each of which is again uniformly distributed over (1,2,...N). Fig. 2 illustrates the operation of the source selection function U(t) for random periodic switching. In this figure, source 1 is selected at time 1, source N is selected at time 2, and so on.

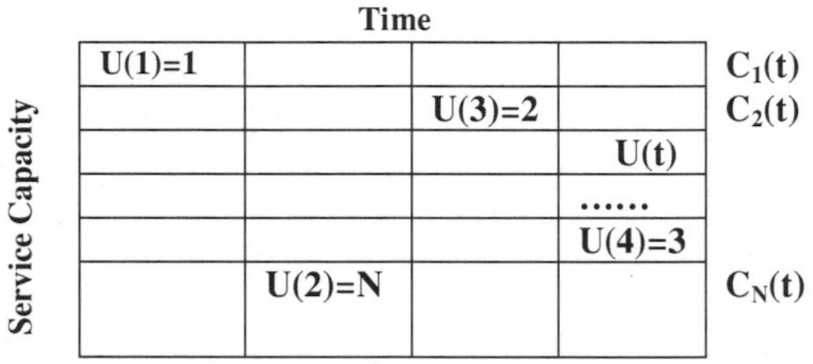

Fig. 1. Source Selection function in random periodic switching

By using random periodic switching, it is always possible to make the capacity process *very lightly correlated*, or almost independent. Fig. 2, shows that the average download time for a lightly correlated process is very close to that given by Wald's equation.(i.e) the time-based switching shows a more accurate representation of download duration in both single client and multi client scenarios.

Limitations: Time-based switching does not address temporal fluctuations during the allotted download time period [10].The initial problem of clients remaining with underperforming servers was not fully addressed in [4].

4.3   Choke-Based Algorithms

Choke based algorithms incorporates a preemptive choke at the client level that enables a client to independently identify a choke threshold that can be used for intelligent departure from poor performing servers. Additionally, the choked-based algorithm increases the accuracy of prediction of the file download duration[10].

Choke Based Switching

Choking algorithm is initialized by performing a global catalog lookup. This initial seeding of the choking algorithm will provide average overlay capacity and is set to 200 Kbps. The chokepoint for current capacity is determined by the choking algorithm (9) with the seeded value and any previous download session capacities. For example, let N be the number of contacted node-servers while C_i is the bandwidth between the client and the node-server for i= 1, 2...N gives

$$CP = \frac{1}{N} \sum_{i=0}^{N} C_i \qquad (13)$$

At the start of every connection, the client will calculate a new chokepoint value using (9). The chokepoint will be evaluated against a margin (θ) to determine if the server has enough capacity where θ = {0.05, 0.1 ... 1}. For example, if the chokepoint is 80Kbps and the server capacity is 50Kbps with a θ = .5, the chokepoint threshold is (80Kbps − (80Kbps*.5)) = 40Kbps. So the server would be accepted [8]. For every degree of heterogeneity (δ), all margin variables θ = {0.2, 0.4 ... 1.0} are simulated. As δ approaches 1, the download duration reduces regardless of θ. The severity of the decrease is controlled by θ. For example when θ = 0.2, there is a decrease in download duration from 95 minutes to 58 minutes. Over the same span, time based switching remains fairly stable at 100 minutes. Experiments involving multiple clients/multiple servers investigation shows that choke based algorithms minimizes the file download duration rapidly compared to time based algorithms.

Table 1. Multi Client results for various switching Algorithms

Clients	Byte Based(min)	Time based (min)	Choke based (min)
100	25440	106	100
200	44160	184	182
300	65760	274	270
400	87360	364	360
500	110880	462	448
600	133920	558	541

The table 1 indicates that as the number of clients increases, the ability of the choke-based algorithm to cope with the congestion increases. The choke threshold margin, θ, is also significant. As the θ increases to 1 (no choke), there is the expected increase in download duration. During the simulations, the smallest values of θ (less that .15 margin) rarely produced the fastest download duration.

5   Conclusions

This paper surveys on minimizing the average download duration of each user in a P2P network. With the devastating usage of network resources by P2P applications in the current Internet, it is highly desirable to improve the network efficiency by reducing each user's download time. In contrast to the commonly-held practice focusing on the notion of average capacity, the spatial heterogeneity and the temporal correlations in the service capacity can significantly increase the average download time of the users in the network, even when the average capacity of the network remains the same. This paper investigated several "byte-based" (file size based) schemes widely researched and used in practice, including chunk-based file transfer, parallel downloading and permanent connections. Investigations reveal that all byte-based schemes are not so effective in reducing the two negative factors that increase the average download time. Time-based switching improves upon byte-based algorithms by alleviating the reliance on average capacity of the overlay for accurate download duration estimation using a stochastic AR model. The investigation revealed time-based switching does not address temporal fluctuations during the allotted download time period. Another major area of concern in time based algorithms is the initial problem of clients remaining with underperforming servers. Choke based algorithm enhances time based algorithms by incorporating a preemptive choke at the client level that enables a client to independently identify a choke threshold that can be used for intelligent departure from poor performing servers. It is shown that in both single client and multi client scenarios that the choke-based algorithm decreases clients download duration.ïAdditionally, the choked-based algorithm increases the accuracy of prediction of the file download duration. Future work will include investigation into client modification of the threshold margin (θ) based upon current network conditions.

References

[1] Yang, X., de Veciana, G.: Service capacity of peer to peer networks. In: Proc. IEEE INFOCOM, pp. 2242–2252 (March 2004)
[2] Qiu, D., Srikant, R.: Modelling and performance analysis of Bittorrent-like peer-to-peer networks. In: Proc. ACM SIGCOMM (August 2004)
[3] Gummadi, K.P., Dunn, R.J., Saroiu, S.: Measurement, modeling, and analysis of a peer-to-peer file sharing workload. In: ACM Symp. Operating Systems Principles, SOSP (2003)
[4] Chiu, Y., Eun, D.: Minimizing file download time in peer to peer networks. IEEE/ACM Transactions on Networking 16(2), 253–266 (2008)
[5] Ng, T., Chu, Y., Rao, S., Sripanidkulchai, K., Zhang, H.: Measurement- based optimization techniques for bandwidth-demanding peer-to-peer systems. In: Proc. IEEE INFOCOM, pp. 2199–2209 (April 2003)
[6] Koo, S.G.M., Rosenberg, C., Xu, D.: Analysis of parallel downloading for large file distribution. In: Proc. IEEE Int. Workshop on Future Trends in Distributed Computing Systems (FTDCS), pp. 128–135 (May 2003)
[7] Ramachandran, K.K., Sikdar, B.: An analytic framework for modeling peer to peer networks. In: Proc. IEEE INFOCOM, pp. 215–269 (March 2005)
[8] Lehrfeld, M.R., Simco, G.: Choke-based Switching Algorithm in Stochastic P2P Networks to Reduce File Download Duration. In: IEEE 2010, pp. 127–130 (2010)
[9] Saroiu, S., Gummadi, K.P., Gribble, S.D.: A measurement study of peer-to-peer file sharing systems. In: ACM Multimedia Computing and Networking, MMCN (2002)

[10] Jain, M., Dovrolis, C.: End-to-end estimation of the available bandwidth variation range. In: Proc. ACM Sigmetrics (June 2005)

[11] Hu, N., Steenkiste, P.: Evaluation and characterization of available bandwidth probing techniques. IEEE J. Sel. Areas Communication 21(6), 879–894 (2003)

[12] Koo, S.G.M., Kannan, K., Lee, C.S.G.: Neighbor-selection strategy in peer-to-peer networks. In: Proceedings of IEEE International Conference on Computer Communications and Networks (ICCCN), Rosemont, IL (October 2004)

[13] Sherwood, R., Braud, R., Bhattacharjee, B.: Slurpie: A cooperative bulk data transfer protocol. In: Infocom, Hong Kong (March 2004)

Proposed Software Development Model for Small Organization and Its Explanation

Vinish Kumar[1] and Sachin Gupta[2]

[1] Department of Computer Science and Information Technology,
Sunder deep College of Engineering & Technology, Ghaziabad,
Affiliated to U.P. Technical University, Lucknow UP, India
vinishkumar_2001@rediffmail.com
[2] Department of Computer Science and Information Technology,
Raj Kumar Goel Institute of Technology, Ghaziabad,
Affiliated to U.P. Technical University, Lucknow, UP, India
imsachingupta@rediffmail.com

Abstract. Software Development is the process to illustrate the overall mechanism involved in the progress of software during different stages of development. To moderate the computational efficiency of earlier and later phases of development often occurred in small scale software developing organization we have proposed a new software development model for small organization. Through this model we can elicit the software requirement and we can also compute the functionality and risk in each and every phase of the software development.

Keywords: Software Model, Elicitation Techniques, Function Point, Software Risk.

1   Introduction

A software development life cycle (SDLC) model is a set of activities, if performed in a manner will produce desired product. A SDLC model specifies about the way these activities are framed to produce quality software.

The various life cycle models are-

1. The Waterfall model
2. Prototype model
3. Iterative model
4. Spiral model
5. Fish model
6. V-model
7. Object oriented modeling.

1.1   The Waterfall Model

This is the most common and classic of life cycle models, which states that the phase are organized in a linear order and phase must be completed before the next phase begins and the output documented in each phase are reviewed to determine that the

N. Meghanathan et al. (Eds.): CCSIT 2012, Part II, LNICST 85, pp. 167–175, 2012.
© Institute for Computer Sciences, Social Informatics and Telecommunications Engineering 2012

project is in the right direction as per the requirement or need. The advantage of this model is that it is a simple model, stage and attributes are well defined and errors can be detected due to verification at each stage. The disadvantage of this model is that it can't incorporate new changes during the project development.

1.2   Prototype Model

In this model a throwaway prototype of the actual product is prepared. The prototype gives the client on actual feel of the system, after interacting with the prototype the client provide feedback to the developer regarding the changed to be needed in the system. Based on the feedback, the prototype is modified to incorporate some of the changes required, and then the client is again given the prototype and the cycle repeat until product completed.

The advantage of this model is that errors can be detected much easier as the system is made side by side, leads to a better system to uses and reduce risk [21].

The disadvantage of this model is that it may increase the complexity of the system as scope of the system may expand beyond original plans, Prototype has to be build on company's cost, The user may strict to the prototype and limit his requirements [25].

1.3   Iterative Model

In this model, the main idea is that software should be developed in increments. In 1st step a simple subset model of the overall problem is designed. The subset designed contains some of the key aspects of the problem. Which are easy to design and forms a useful and usable system? Each increment adds some new functional capability to the existing system and the process continues until the full system is implemented.

The advantage of this model is to generate working software quickly easily during the software life cycle. It accommodates changes easily, easy to test and debug due to smaller iteration and requirements are prioritized.

The disadvantages of this model are that each iteration can have the planning overhead. System structure may suffer as frequent changes are made and cost may increase due to undo work of one stage in other one.

1.4   Spiral Model

Spiral model is competitive of incremental model in which risk analysis has major work. It is most widely used to perform risk analysis at every level of development. It has base line which starts from planning phase, requirements and then terminates with risk analysis every time each subsequent spiral builds on base line spiral.   The advantage of this model is High amount of risk analysis, good for large and mission critical projects.

The disadvantage of this model is that it is complex and can be costly to use, Risk analysis requires highly specifies expertise and does not work well for smaller projects [24].

1.5   Fish Model

This model is totally based on the validation and verification development strategies. It is widely used to avoid the any loss of content mismatch or cause of failure of project/product. It is performed on the basis of verification and validation of product. It is started with initial phase and goes till the completion of project. The disadvantage of this model is that it is time consuming and extra cost for verification & validation [20].

1.6   V-Model

It is similar to waterfall model having sequential path of execution of process. Each phase must be computed before the next phase begins. Testing has move importance in this model as compared to others waterfall model. It has major vision on the testing of deliverables of each phase. We just prepare the test plan for each phase & test the plan objectives at the end of every phase [26].

1.7   Object Oriented Modeling

In order to avoid the different problems associated with quality data; we use the concept based on system dynamics. Now, on this basis an objects oriented approach to the development of software was proposed in late 1960's.This modeling requires the object oriented technique for development of software started with initial analysis phase to the implementation phase.

The advantage of this model is that it is based on problem domain. Hence it is easier to develop and debug the design; it is quick to accept the requirement changes, i.e. backtracking a reporting is much easier in OOM. Its design has higher re-use factor and allow changes easily. Due to above facts, it has reduced development cost and cycle time. The disadvantage of this model is that it has higher cost and cycle time. This paper is organized in various sections as following: The background and related work is explained section two. Section three briefs about block diagram of the proposed model. We have explained the proposed model in section four and at last the paper is concluded in section 5.

2   Background and Related Work

Various models have been developed over the years to manage the structural set of activities involved in developing and maintaining software system [20]. Since the advent of the first software development process model (waterfall model) , a lot of software development process models have been put forward [21], for example prototyping model, iterative model, spiral model[22],agile model[23] ,and so on .

The various models developed so far have come under attack, due to its rigid design and inflexible procedure [24], for example if the problem is well defined and well understood, waterfall model is sufficient .However, when we come up against a poorly defined problem, a popular variation of the prototyping model called Rapid Application Development (RAD) introduce firm time limits and relies heavily on rapid application tool which allow for quick development [25]. Have to go for spiral model [24].Prototyping model helps to understand uncertain requirements but leads to false expectations and poorly designed system.

Software project fails when they do not meet the criteria for success. most of project run over budget or are terminated prematurely and those that reach complication often fall short of meeting user expectations and business performance goals [26].Using various reports on failure of software product, projected by Dan Galorath [27], author in [26] conclude the major factors involved in failure of a project are Requirement Elicitation, Lack of user involvement, Team size, Time Dimensions, Testing Etc.

The successful implementation or failure of a software system is totally dependent on the quality of the requirements. It is influenced by the various techniques employed during the very first phase i.e. requirements elicitation. Requirements elicitation, the most critical part of the software development, prompts errors at this beginning stage propagate through the development process and the hardest to repair later [28].

In the continuation of the above work we have proposed a software development model that will overcome those problems that we have in the previous models.

3   Proposed Software Model for Small Organization

In this paper we have proposed a Software model for small organization, the block diagram of the model is given in the figure (1).There are no   description in the

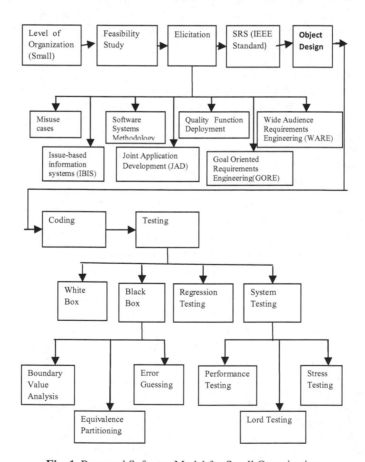

Fig. 1. Proposed Software Model for Small Organization

[21,22,23,24,25,26] about the type of organization where their proposed model works while we have considered the requirement of different types of organizations in our proposed model. The brief description about the organizations will be discussed during the phases of the model.

3.1   Level of Organization

According to Henery Fayal, organization is " A group of people work together i.e. the act of organizing a business or an activity related to business". Every organization has certain goals which they achieve in a specific period of time. There are various factors that play an important role in an organization are Size of organization, Manpower, Cost, Standards followed by the organization. On the basis of these factors the organization can be classified as:-

i). Small organization
ii). Large organization

In this paper we have proposed a model for small organization where the size of the organization is small. The man power is also less and the capital investment is also low, so there main focus is profit maximization along with maintenance of the standards and the product quality. But the organization has the capability to fulfill the functional and structural requirement of the project.

3.2   Feasibility Study

It is performed to decide the worth ability of product .It is based on information assessment, information collection and report writing. It is allowed to perform the feasibility study of any product with in two of three weeks with involvement of project manager, software engineers (who are about to develop the system), technical experts and customers (who will be using the system). Then prepare the FSR (Feasibility study report).It has different fields that incorporate technical, operational, economy, management, legal and time.

3.3   Requirement Elicitation

Elicitation is all about determining the needs of stakeholders. Requirement elicitation is recognized as one of the most critical knowledge intensive activities of the development of software because errors at this beginning stage propagate through the development process and the hardest to repair later. Studies indicate that 70% of the system errors are due to the inadequate system specification [31, 32].

3.4   SRS (IEEE Standard)

The origin of most software system is developed by developer and finally the software is used by the end user. so client does not understand the language of developing process which is used by develops and developers does not understand the need of customer, so to fulfill the communication gap client and developer SRS is made. If the requirement is not understood properly the final product will be of no use, thus a SRS provides a reference for validation of the final product. IEEE (Institute of Electrical and Electronics Engineers) specification provides a standard approach to design SRS [21].

3.5   Object Design

The object design phase refers to the determination of the full definitions of the classes and associations used in the implementation, as well as the interface and algorithms of the methods used to implement operations.

3.6   Coding

Coding implement the design in the best possible manner. Basic criteria to judge a code of program are readability, time complexity, size of code (LOC) and space complexity. These are the objectives should be clear to the programmer. He must know weather to reduce the execution time or to reduce the required memory to save the program etc.It enables different techniques as code inspection, verification, code refraction etc. to avoid bugs.

3.7   Testing

Software testing is used to find out as many errors as possible in the given software. There are two types of software i.e. black box and white box testing [21].

4   Explanation of the Proposed Model

Before the development of any software project, the first step is to understand the requirements of the software. In the literature of software engineering we have standard frameworks like NFR [28] (non- functional requirements), i*[30], KAOS [27], and TROPOS [29]. From these frameworks we can easily find out the functional and non-functional requirements of the software. After capturing the requirements, we have the next step which is the elicitation of the software requirements. There are several techniques to elicit the software requirements like [32], but in this paper we have used the elicitation technique which is the slightly modified version of the algorithm proposed by Mohd. Sadiq et al. [31] and its algorithm is given in algorithm (01).

1. With the help of the following steps elicitate the software requirements
1.1 Draw information about user requirements.
1.2) Test and Train the Users, Clients and Managers.
1.3 Write the description of the user need for the proposed system.
1.4 Now you can apply Wide Audience Requirement Engineering (WARE) because, it helps the requirements engineering process in the international research projects. The different organizations that take part in these kinds of international projects can be divided at least into the following categories: Governmental funding organization, other nonprofit organization, and industrial research centers.

2. In this algorithm we have used AHP technique for prioritization.
  For using AHP algorithm
  The overall performance matrix is created
  Then calculate the Importance Weight (Eigen vector)
3. Find out the risk associated with each requirement.
4. Compare the values of the importance weight of software requirements with step
3 and then rank or Prioritize the requirements.

Proposed Algorithm Using WARE)
(Adopted from [31]
Algorithm (01)

After reviewing several research papers, we conclude that there are no descriptions about the goal oriented requirement engineering (GORE) and Wide Audience Requirement Engineering (WARE) in the previous software development model and there is also no description about the type of the elicitation methods that would be used to elicit the software requirements. Proposed model overcome these problems and gives the detailed information and knowledge about the type of GORE, WARE and also the type of elicitation method to the developers or the software engineer.

Once we have elicit the software requirements, the next step is to prioritize the software requirements, for this purpose we have used the Analytic Hierarchy Process (AHP). The detailed information about the AHP and its applications in software engineering are available in [34].

After prioritizing the software requirements the next step is to document these requirements. For documentation we generally used the IEEE format of the SRS i.e. Software requirements Specification [21]. Once we have finalized the SRS documents the next step is to develop the object design. The last two methods are common in most of the software development models i.e. coding and testing. But in the existing models there are no descriptions about the type of testing. In this paper we have preferred the black box testing [ ], because in this testing we generally work on the functionality of the software, for black box testing, we have several technique, like boundary value analysis, robustness techniques, worst case etc.

Apart from different models, in this model we have also added two extra features. The first feature is the risk estimation and the second feature is to check the functionality of the software. To compute the risk we have applied the risk estimation model proposed by Daya Gupta and Mohd. Sadiq [16] and [9, 11] .To compute the functionality of the software we have used the FFP [13, 14] (Fuzzy Function Point) instead of FP [4, 5, 6, 7, 8, 12, 15] i.e. Function point.

5   Conclusion and Future Work

In this paper we have proposed the software development model for small organization. In this model we have added several new features which are the demand of the software industry. In this model we have included requirement elicitation method. GORE and WARE are two different key concepts that are used to find out the requirements from the stakeholder's point of view. In this model we have also provide the facility to compute the functionality of the software during each phase of the development of the software. Risk estimation is also the added feature of this model. In future we will apply to this model in real life project and will differentiate the functionality of the proposed model with the existing ones.

References

[1] Albrecht, A.J., Gaffney, J.E.: Software Function, Source Lines of Code and development Effort Prediction: A software Science Validation. IEEE Trans. Software Engineering, 639–648 (1983)

[2] Albrecht, A.J.: Measuring Application Development Productivity. In: Proc. IBM Applications Development Symp., Monterey, Calif., pp. 14–17 (1979)

[3] Boehm, B.W.: Software Engineering Economics. Prentice Hall (1981)

[4] Lokan, C.J.: An Emprical Study of the Correlations between Function Point Elements. In: Proc. of 6th International Symposium on Software Metrics (1999)

[5] Ho-Leung, TSOI: To Evaluate the Function Point Analysis: A Case Study. International Journal of the Computer, the Internet and Management 13(1), 31–40 (2005)

[6] International Function Point User Group (IFPUG), Function Point Counting Practices Manual, Release 4.0, IFPUG, Westerville, Ohio (April 1990)

[7] Kemerer, C.F.: An Emprical Validation of Software Cost Estimation Models. Comm. ACM 30(5) (1987)

[8] Low, G.C., Jeffery, D.R.: Function Point in the Estimation and Evaluation of the Software Process. IEEE Trans Software Engineering 16(1) (1990)

[9] Sadiq, M., Rahman, A., Ahmad, S., Asim, M., Ahmad, J.: esrcTool: A Tool to Estimate the Software Risk and Cost. In: IEEE Second International Conference on Computer Research and Development, pp. 886–890, doi:10.1109/ICCRD.2010.29

[10] Sadiq, M., Ahmed, S.: Computation of Function Point of Software on the basis of Average Complexity. In: Proceedings of 2nd International Conference on Advanced Computing and Computing Technologies, ICACCT 2007, Panipat, Haryana, pp. 591–594 (2007)

[11] Sadiq, M., Sunil, Zafar, S., Asim, M., Suman, R.: GUI of esrcTool: A Tool to Estimate the Software Risk and Cost. In: The 2nd IEEE International Conference on Computer and Automation Engineering (ICCAE 2010), Singapore, pp. 673–677 (2010)

[12] Sadiq, M., Ahmed, S.: Relationship between Lines of Code and Function Point and its Application in the Computation of Effort and Duration of a Software using Software Equation. In: International Conference on Emerging Technologies and Applications in Engineering, Technology and Sciences, ICATETS 2008, Rajkot, Gujarat, India (2008)

[13] de Souza Lima Jr., O., Parias, P.P.M., Belchior, A.D.: A Fuzzy Model for Function Point Analysis to Development and Enhancement Project Assessment. CLEI Electronic Journal 5(2) (1999)

[14] Kumar, S., Kumar, V., Gupta, M., Gupta, S.: Function Point Analysis for Small Organization based Projects using Triangular Fuzzy Numbers. In: 2011 3rd International Conference on Conference on Electronics Computer Technology, ICECT 2011 (2011)

[15] Symons, C.R.: Function Point Analysis: Difficulties and Improvements. IEEE Trans. Software Engineering 14(1) (1988)

[16] Gupta, D., Sadiq, M.: Software Risk Assessment and Estimation Model. In: IEEE International Conference on Computer Science and Information Technology, Singapore, pp. 963–967 (2008)

[17] Walston, C.E., Felix, C.P.: A method of program measurement and estimation. IBM System Journal 16 (1977)

[18] Zheng, Y., Wang, B., Zheng, Y., Shi, L.: Estimation of Software Project effort based on functional point. In: Proceeding on 2009 4th International Conference on Computer Science & Education, pp. 941–943. IEEE (2009), 978-1-4244-3521

[19] Zuse, H.: Software Metrics-Methods to Investigate and Evaluate Software Complexity Measures. In: Proc. Second Annual Oregon Workshop on Software Metrics, Portland (1991)

[20] Dieter Rombach, H., Verlage, M.: Directions in Software Process Research. In: Zelkowitz, M.V. (ed.) Advances in Computer, vol. 41, pp. 1–3. Academic Press (1995)

[21] Pressman, R.S.: Software Engineering: A Practitioner's Approach, 6th edn., pp. 77–99. McGraw-Hill, New York (2005)

[22] Boehm, B.W.: TRW Defense Systems Group. A Spiral Model of Software Development and Enhancement

[23] Martin, R.C.: Agile Software Development, Principles, Patterns and Practices. Prentice Hall, NJ (2002)

[24] Boehm, B.: A Sprial Model of Software Development and Enhancement. IEEE Computer 21(5), 61–72 (1988)

[25] Martin, J.: Rapid Application Development. Prentice-Hall Publication (1991)

[26] Kaur, R., Sengupta, J.: Software Process Models and Analysis on Failure of Software Development Projects. IJSER © (2011)

[27] Doerr, J., Kerkow, D., Koenig, T., Olsson, T., Suzuki, T.: Non-Functional Requirements in Industry – Three Case Studies Adopting an Experience-based NFR Method. In: Proceedings of the 2005 13th IEEE International Conference on Requirements Engineering, RE 2005 (2005)

[28] Glinz, M.: On Non-Functional Requirements. In: 15th IEEE International Requirements Engineering Conference, pp. 21–26

[29] Bresciani, P., Perini, A., Giorgini, P., Giunchiglia, F., Mylopoulos, J.: Tropos: An Agent-Oriented Software Development Methodology. Autonomous Agents and Multi-Agent Sytems 8, 203–236 (2004)

[30] Yu, E.S.K.: Towards Modelling and Reasoning Support for Early-Phase Requirements Engineering. In: Proceedings of the 3rd IEEE International Symposium on Requirements Engineering, RE 1997 (1997)

[31] Kumar, S., Kumar, V.: Proposed algorithm using WARE for the elicitation of the software requirements. International Journal of Engineering and Technology

[32] Sadiq, M., Ghafir, S., Shahid, M.: An Approach for Eliciting Software Requirements and its Prioritization using Analytic Hierarchy Process. In: IEEE International Conference on Advances in Recent Technologies in Communication and Computing, Kerala, India (2009)

[33] Sadiq, M., Shahid, M.: Elicitation and Prioritization of Software Requirements. International Journal of Recent Trends in Engineering, Finland

[34] Sadiq, M., Shahid, M., Ahmed, S.: Adding Threat during Software Requirements Elicitation and Prioritization. International Journal of Computer Application

A Comparative Analysis of Reduction Algorithms in Picasso Tool for Cost Based Query Optimizers of Relational Databases

Neeraj Sharma[1] and Yogendra Kumar Jain[2]

[1] Dept. of CSE, Trinity Institute of Tech. and Research,
Kokta By-Pass , Raisen Road, Bhopal - 462 038 (M.P.), India
neeraj.bp183@gmail.com
[2] Dept. of CSE, Samrat Ashok Technological Institute,
Civil Lines, Vidisha-464001 (M.P.), India
ykjain_p@yahoo.co.in

Abstract. Query optimization is a process of selecting an optimal Query Execution Plan from a number of plans available for execution of query which is very critical to the performance of a relational database. Picasso is a Query Optimizer analysis tool developed in the Database lab of Indian Institute of Science [24]. Using Picasso we can visualize the query execution plans and can implement a technique known as Plan Diagram Reduction [15][16][17] which can effectively increase the Query Optimizer performance. In this paper we briefly introduce the query optimization concept and then perform an exhaustive analysis of the reduction algorithms and try to establish some hard fact about their relative performance and reduction efficiency.

Keywords: Query Optimization, Selectivity, Plan Cardinality, Plan Diagrams, Checkpoints, TPCH.

1   Introduction

Structured Query Language (SQL) follows a declarative paradigm which means that the order of execution of instructions has to be determined by the SQL compiler. For this purpose the initial SQL query submitted by user is first converted into its equivalent relational algebra equation and for this expression a canonical query execution tree is generated. From this canonical tree many query execution plans or QEPs [3] can be generated using multiple techniques. Each query execution plan specifies a different order of execution of query with different set of operation. The task of Query optimizer is to search for the best possible query execution plans out of all these query execution plans. Query Optimizer plays a crucial role in determining the efficiency of Database systems. If the choice of query execution plans is not correct then the response time of the query processor will degrade. This increase in response time can be frustrating for the end user especially when the user is querying a large database in the likes of data warehouses or databases for decision support systems. All these requirements make Query Optimization a non trivial task for every commercial database management systems.

N. Meghanathan et al. (Eds.): CCSIT 2012, Part II, LNICST 85, pp. 176–185, 2012.

1.1   Picasso Database Query Optimizer Visualizer

Picasso [24] is a database query optimizer visualizer which generates cubical diagrams showcasing all the query execution plans that can be used for execution of a query in a specified selectivity space.

The diagram in Fig.1 (a) is a basic Picasso Diagram which shows 109 different plans that can be used for execution of query Q8 of TPCH Database. Each plan is represented using a different color. A plan is optimal in the area covered by its color in the plan diagram. The region of the plan diagram covered by a specific plan corresponds to the selectivities of the two base relations for which the plan will be optimal.

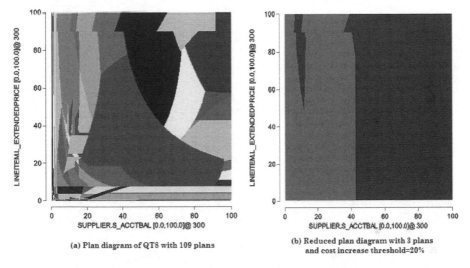

(a) Plan diagram of QT8 with 109 plans

(b) Reduced plan diagram with 3 plans
and cost increase threshold=20%

Fig. 1. Plan Diagram and Reduced Plan Diagram for QT8 of TPCH

In this paper we discuss one of the main diagrams generated by Picasso which is known as the Reduced Plan Diagram. Reduced plan diagram shows a reduced number of query execution plans that can be used for execution of query. This reduced plan diagram can be effectively used for increasing the performance of Query Optimizer. The plan diagram in Fig. 1(a) shows 109 different plans to execute QT8 which are reduced to 3 plans in Fig. 1(b). This reduction will help a lot in increasing the performance of query optimizer by decreasing the searching time for the optimal plan and decreasing the chances of selection of wrong plan.

2   Problems in Query Optimization

Query optimization is a hard problem [4]. The selection for best execution plan is done by using many different techniques of which the prominent ones are using heuristics, some cost formulae, and randomized algorithms or genetic techniques [12]. Most Relational databases use heuristics combined with some cost formulas [22].

It is very time consuming to calculate cost of each and every execution plan to find the most optimal plan and is practically not feasible. Another problem faced by optimizers is the changing selectivity of base relations. The selection of optimal plans is based on the basis of some complex cost functions whose major parameters are the selectivities of base relations. It happens frequently that the estimated selectivities change. These wrong estimates of selectivities will lead to a poor choice of QEP.

2.1   Related Work

System R - A breakthrough work in query optimizers appeared in System R [1]. System R optimizer was the most rudimentary form of query optimizers. The cost function is based on parameters like disk access time and frequency, relation cardinality and number of tuples per page etc. The work on System R optimizer was further elaborated in [2] which discussed how the access path will be selected for execution of basic queries and for complex queries involving JOIN operations.

Eddies - The first ever technique for dynamic query optimization was discussed in [6]. The authors discuss a pure continuous adaptive query processing mechanism named Telegraph which checks for selectivities during "on the fly" time of query. Telegraph overlaps the optimization and execution phases. The initial optimal plan selected for executing a query is based on the cost functions whose parameters are determined from the system catalog. These parameters are subjected to change during run time of query. When such changes in parameters are discovered eddies try to reorder the operators used in the execution plan so as to minimize the execution cost.

Parametric Query Optimization (PQO) - System Rs algorithms were modified to generate multiple optimal plans for query execution and the process was called Parametric Query Optimization or PQO [7]. In PQO multiple candidate QEPs are generated for a query, each of which is optimal for some region of the parameter space. This collection of optimal candidate plans is known as Parametrically Optimal Set of Plans or POSP. Any one plan out of these POSP is used as final QEP during run time depending on the run time values of the parameters.

One significant problem with the PQO technique was that while dealing with piecewise linear functions, the solution proposed is pretty much intrusive. For this the authors of PQO suggests a modified optimization technique for Non Linear cost functions. This is known as AniPQO (Almost Non Intrusive PQO) [8].

Dynamic Optimization – Dynamic query optimization is a modern way for optimizing queries. In [4] a compile time dynamic plan optimization technique is described. Most dynamic optimization techniques use a dynamic programming model which compares cost of two plans and ignores the expensive ones. This requires a total ordering of plans. But authors of [4] suggest a "check plan" operator which maintains a partial ordering of plans.

The main problem of dynamic query optimization as pointed in [5] is the time spent in repeated collection of run time statistics like selectivities and resource availability and the searching of substitute plans. Algorithm described in [5] provides specific points in the query execution plan and the run time statistics are collected and substitute plans are searched only at these points thus minimizing optimization time.

The most practical approach in dynamic query optimization occurs in [9] in which a generalized and practically effective technique for optimization is suggested using CHECK operators. CHECK operators were placed at specific points in a query execution plan and they check the input cardinality. If the cardinality is within the specified range the current query execution plan is retained else the plan is changed during the run time.

CHECKS increase performance but excess of checks increase the execution time. So there is a risk and opportunity tradeoff which makes it important to determine how many CHECKS are to be inserted and where to be inserted. Five different rules for placement of CHECK operators in the Query Execution Plan were suggested by authors.

3   Plan Diagrams Reduction

The biggest motivation for reducing the number of plans arises after observing the skewed distribution of plans in the plan diagrams for different queries. The amount of skewed distribution of plans can be converted into a constant value known as Gini Index [25] which is a standard economic measure of income inequality.

When plan diagrams are generated with Picasso tool the Gini Index values are also generated and surprisingly the Gini Index value of most of the plans diagrams was greater than 0.75 substantiating the skewed distribution of plans over the selectivity space. These high values of Gini Index indicate that a big percentage of plans that cover very small space in the plan diagram need not be considered for execution of query. This is because these plans are highly vulnerable to poor execution times if the selectivities change even by a small order during the execution of query. Thus we can ignore or remove these plans to be considered as a possible candidate for execution of query.

A method used to substitute these plans with other plans which have high plan area coverage is known as *Plan Swallowing* [16][17]. The idea is that these smaller plans can be completely swallowed by their larger sibling plans which will effectively reduce the total number of plan cardinality in the plan diagram. There are two advantages of this approach. Firstly, it will reduce the searching time as the plan cardinality reduces and secondly, it will help us select robust plans which have higher plan space coverage and thus can tolerate higher variations in the plan selectivity. The process of plan swallowing may increase the cost of execution of a query but this increase in cost is controlled by user. This is represented as cost increase threshold (λ). Cost increase threshold (λ) of 10 is also sufficient but as proven in [14], a 20% cost increase (λ) can reduce the number of queries to an anorexic value which can significantly decrease the searching time of optimizers.

3.1   Algorithms Used for Reduction

Picasso uses three different algorithms for reduction. Initially COST GREEDY and AREA GREEDY were introduced in Picasso version 1 of which COST GREEDY proved to be more efficient. In Picasso V2 a new robust plan reduction algorithm SEER (Selectivity Estimate Error Resistance) [18] was introduced which performed plan reduction and gave robust plans which can withstand run time changes in the selectivities.

Cost Greedy - This algorithm operates under the assumption that the Cost Domination Principle holds and therefore only plan swallowing possibilities in the first quadrant are considered with respect to the plan under consideration. Cost Greedy ensure that the replacement plans are within the cost-increase-threshold at all points in the optimality regions of the replaced plans. The complexity of this algorithm is O(mn) where n is the number of plans in the diagram and m is the number of query points.

SEER - (Selectivity Estimate Error Reduction) - Due to wrong selectivity estimates the performance of the replacement plan could be much worse than the replaced plan. This problem naturally leads to the concept of a **robust** replacement – that is, a replacement where the λ-threshold criterion is satisfied at all points in the selectivity space, i.e. the replacement ensures **global safety**. For this we use two implementations of SEER:

Corner Cube-SEER - CC-SEER implements a more conservative test for robust plan replacement applying Abstract-plan-costing operations at the corner hyper-cubes of the selectivity space and is therefore significantly faster than the original SEER. Moreover, its performance is resolution independent unlike SEER, and therefore the performance gap between CC-SEER and SEER increases with higher resolution diagrams. Experimental results [16] indicate that CC-SEER's reduction quality is comparable to that of SEER instead of it being more conservative.

Lite SEER - Lite Seer is a light-weight heuristic-based variant of SEER that makes its replacement decisions solely based on Abstract-plan-costing operations at the corners of the hypercube, and is therefore extremely efficient. Lite SEER is optimal in the sense that it incurs the minimum work (complexity-wise) required by any reduction algorithm. While it does not guarantee global safety, experimental results [16] indicate that in practice, its safety and reduction characteristics are quite close to that of SEER and CC-SEER.

4   Experimental Analyses

Test Bed Environment

The TPC-H database was created using the "dbgen" software supplied with the TPC-H decision support benchmark [23]. A gigabyte-sized (1 GB) database was created on this schema and TPC-H queries templates were used.

An Intel Core i3 CPU M370 running at 2.4 GHz with 2 GB of main memory and 240 GB of hard disk, running 64 bit version of Windows 7 Home Basic operating system, was used in our experiments. The relational engine used is Microsoft SQL Server 2008.

4.1   Comparison of Reduction Algorithms

We performed experimental analysis of the three algorithms and compared their performance and plan reduction efficiency. Analysis is performed in two different parts. In the first part we compare the time taken by the three algorithms for performing the reduction. Then we compare the reduction efficiency of the three algorithms.

Computational Efficiency

Figure 2, 3, and 4 shows the time taken for reduction of plan diagrams by the three algorithms for 2D queries with plot resolution 10 and 3D queries with plot resolution of 10 and 30 respectively.

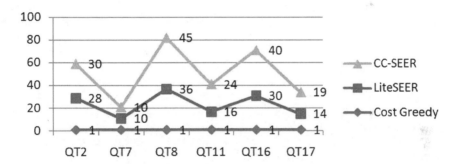

Fig. 2. Reduction time for 2D Queries, plot resolution=30, λ =10 (values in seconds)

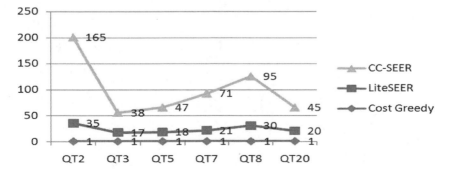

Fig. 3. Reduction time for 3D Queries, plot resolution=10, λ=10 (values in seconds)

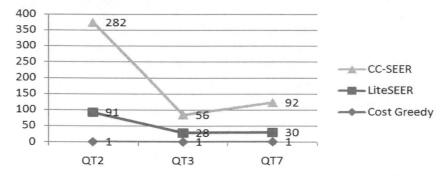

Fig. 4. Reduction time for 3D queries, plot resolution=30, λ=10 (values in seconds)

It is interesting to note that the reduction time taken by Cost Greedy algorithm was almost constant throughout the analysis for any combination of query and plot resolution. This makes Cost Greedy the fastest reduction algorithm. Next is LiteSEER which generates second best timings and then comes CC-SEER with the highest time readings. Conceptually comparison of SEER variants with Cost Greedy is not fair because SEER provides high quality and robust reductions. But when simple plan reductions are required, Cost Greedy proves to be much better than the two SEER algorithms.

Reduction Efficiency

Now we check the reduction efficiency by comparing the number of plans retained after performing reduction by the three algorithms. This analysis is also carried in three parts: Figure 5 shows the number of plans retained for 2D queries with plot resolution of 30 and figure 6 and 7 shows the number of plans retained for 3D queries with plot resolution of 30 and 10 respectively.

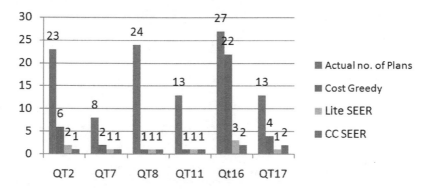

Fig. 5. Plans remaining after reduction of 2D Queries, Plot Resolution=30, λ=10

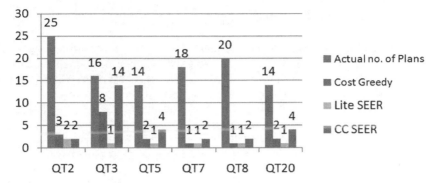

Fig. 6. Plans remaining after reduction of 3D Queries, plot resolution=10, λ=10

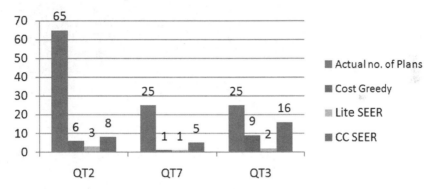

Fig. 7. Plans remaining after reduction of 3D queries, plot resolution=30, λ=10

Values shown in graph are the number of plans retained after reduction was carried. The number of plans before reduction was substantially high. The observation of these three tables and corresponding graphs gives a very interesting insight into the reduction efficiency of three algorithms. The reduction patterns for 2D queries were quite different from the reduction patterns of 3D queries. The following observations were made:

- In Reduction of 2D queries, the final plans retained were different for each algorithm in most of the cases. For example, reduction of QT8, QT11. The plans retained in LiteSEER and CC-SEER were missing from Cost Greedy which proves the quality difference between the three algorithms. Thus the normal assumption about the three algorithms holds true in case of 2D queries and CC-SEER gives robust plans which mostly are missing from the output of Cost Greedy and many times from LiteSEER as well.
- In case of 3D queries the observation was quite opposite. The plans retained in CC-SEER were also present in the list of plans retained in Cost Greedy and LiteSEER. The most extreme observation is that CC-SEER retained some plans which were initially not included in Cost Greedy and LiteSEERs list. This clearly indicates that CC-SEER is not a good choice for reduction of 3D queries because Cost Greedy and LiteSEER already produced the same diagrams in very less time.

5   Conclusion and Future Works

Query optimization is a difficult but a critical process for the database optimizers. Picasso introduces a novice way of plan diagram reduction which decreases the search complexity of query optimizers and also produces robust plans which improves the performance and reliability of query optimizers. Three such algorithms were discussed and the performances were compared. Results proved that Cost Greedy is the best algorithm in terms of execution time but if reliability was desired then Lite SEER and CC-SEER were better. For 2D queries CC-SEER must be used in spite of its long execution time but for 3D queries LiteSEER and Cost Greedy proved better than CC-SEER.

There are many interesting future works to be carried. Cost Greedy and SEER based algorithms are purely compile-time approach and it can be used in conjunction with run-time techniques such as adaptive query processing [13] for addressing selectivity errors in the higher nodes of the plan tree. Another improvisation in the design of these algorithms can be to include the technique of CHECKS suggested in [9] which can further increase the quality of plans produced after reduction. Lastly it would be interesting to use these algorithms on the upcoming TPCE dataset and some other dataset having queries with more than 3 dimensions.

References

1. Astrahan, M.M., et al.: System R: Relational Approach to Database Management. ACM Transactions on Database Systems 1(2) (1976)
2. Selinger, P., Astrahan, M., Chamberlin, D., Lorie, R., Price, T.: Access Path Selection in a Relational Database Management System. In: SIGMOD (1979)
3. Freytag, J.C.: Basic principles of query optimization in relational database management systems. In: Proceedings of IFIP Congress (1989)
4. Cole, L., Graefe, G.: Optimization of dynamic query evaluation plans. In: SIGMOD (1994)
5. Kabra, N., DeWitt, D.: Efficient Mid-Query Re-Optimization of Sub-Optimal Query Execution Plans. In: SIGMOD (1998)
6. Avnur, R., Hellerstein, J.M.: Eddies: Continuously Adaptive Query Optimization. In: SIGMOD (2000)
7. Hulgeri, A., Sudarshan, S.: Parametric Query Optimization for Linear and Piecewise Linear Cost Functions. In: VLDB (2002)
8. Hulgeri, A., Sudarshan, S.: AniPQO: Almost Non-intrusive Parametric Query Optimization, for Nonlinear Cost Functions. In: VLDB (2003)
9. Markl, V., Raman, V., Simmen, D., Loman, G., Pirahesh, H., Cilimdzic, M.: Robust Query Processing through Progressive Optimization. In: SIGMOD (2004)
10. Reddy, N., Haritsa, J.: Analyzing plan diagrams of Database query optimizers. In: VLDB (2005)
11. Aslam, M.: Picasso: Design and implementation of a Query Optimizer Analyzer. Master's Thesis, Dept. of Computer Sci. and Automation, IISc (2006)
12. Kader, R.A., van Keulen, M.: Overview of query optimization in XML Database Systems. University of Twente Publications (2007)

13. Deshpande, A., Ives, Z., Raman, V.: Adaptive Query Processing. In: Foundations and Trends in Databases. Now Publishers (2007)
14. Harish, D., Darera, P., Haritsa, J.: On the Production of Anorexic Plan Diagrams. In: VLDB (2007)
15. Darera, P.: Reduction of query optimizer Plan Diagrams. Master's Thesis, Supercomputer Education & Research Centre, IISc (2007)
16. Harish, D., Darera, P., Haritsa, J.: Robust plans through plan diagram reduction. In: VLDB (2007)
17. Harish, D., Darera, P., Haritsa, J.: Identifying Robust Plans through Plan Diagram Reduction. In: VLDB (2008)
18. Harish, D.: SIGHT and SEER: Efficient Production and Reduction of Query Optimizer Plan Diagrams. Master's Thesis, Dept. of Comp. Sci. and Automation, IISc (July 2008)
19. Dey, A., Bhaumik, S., Harish, D., Haritsa, J.: Efficiently Approximating Query Optimizer Plan Diagrams. In: VLDB (2008)
20. Haritsa, J.: The Picasso Database Query Optimizer Visualizer. In: VLDB (2010)
21. Haritsa, J.: Query optimizer plan diagrams: Production, Reduction and Applications. In: ICDE (2011)
22. Elmasri, R., Navathe, S.B.: Fundamentals of Database Systems, 5th edn. Addison-Wesley (2008)
23. Transaction Processing Council, http://www.tpc.org/tpch
24. Project Picasso, IISC,
    http://dsl.serc.iisc.ernet.in/projects/PICASSO/index.html
25. http://en.wikipedia.org/wiki/Gini_coefficient

Tele-control of Remote Digital Irrigation System Performed through Internet

Akin Cellatoglu[1] and Balasubramanian Karuppanan[2]

[1] Dept. of Comp. Engg.,
[2] Dept. of EE Engg.,
European Univ. of Lefke,
Turkish Republic of Northern Cyprus,
Mersin-10, Turkey
{acellatoglu,kbala}@eul.edu.tr

Abstract. There are two aspects of this project concerning to remote sensing and control related to electronic plantation and irrigation system. First part is dealing with the remote sensing of desired parameters in an unknown location as to decide and establish possibly an appropriate electronic plantation unit. Here, the desired parameters are sensed through appropriate transducers and live data are uploaded into the website automatically. In a remote station, by accessing the website the parameters conveyed are gathered and saved in memory. After collecting the data for a considerable period of time an analysis is made to decide the suitability of the area for establishing a plantation unit. The second part of the project is running an already established irrigation system by monitoring the desired parameters in the remote station and issuing control signals to switch ON or OFF the selected appliances as to maintain the irrigation automatically and efficiently. The methodologies used are presented with an analysis.

Keywords: Telemetry, remote sensing, digital irrigation, tele-control, electronic plantation.

1 Introduction

Deciding to establish an appropriate plantation in an unknown remote area needs a long term investigation of the land in monitoring desirable parameters. An electronic method of area surveillance and monitoring would be helpful for such tasks. The essential parameters to be sensed for establishing an appropriate plantation unit would be water, wind, temperature and few others [1, 2]. Water is the main natural resource of irrigation system which keeps the plants to grow efficiently and without which no plantation unit could be established. The continuous availability of water throughout the period of plantation on cropping has to be ascertained.

2 Telemeter of Essential Parameters for Plantation

In the remote location identified for establishing the plantation unit the appropriate transducers for sensing the parameters are to be installed at chosen points distributed

N. Meghanathan et al. (Eds.): CCSIT 2012, Part II, LNICST 85, pp. 186–195, 2012.

in the identified area of plantation. Transducers installed at chosen locations provide the electrical signals for the parameters under test and the signals are conditioned as in conventional manner and conveyed to the remote end.

2.1   Parameters to Be Sensed

As water is the primary natural resource for the irrigation system the availability of water should be assessed first and confirmed. There can be natural water reservoirs which would collect water flowing as occasional or continuous water streams from rains or from opening of water beds. If there would be hills nearby and if they hold snow during winter they also supply water in summer to the reservoir due to melting. By physical inspection about the deepness of the reservoir and the capacity of the storage in long term the water level accumulated in the reservoir during different days of the year has to sensed and monitored. There are several water level sensors used in practice [3-5]. We use here the capacitive type of transducer where the capacitance changes due to change in dielectric constant resulted due to the level of the water. The capacitance is converted into frequency [6] and frequency is converted into voltage by a frequency discriminator.

During irrigation periods the moisture contents of the soil has to be sensed. Nevertheless, as to assess the natural moisture contents in the absence of plants also would provide information about the selection of plants for that location. Here again we use capacitive type of pickup to get a signal in voltage proportional to moisture content of the soil.

The ambient temperature experienced during different periods of the day, month and year also is an important factor to be monitored. This would help in deciding the type of plants for the plantation. We use Thermistor type of transducer included in Wheatstone bridge to get a voltage signal proportional to temperature. Appropriate linearization [7] is performed by hardware at the transducer level itself.

Natural wind flow within limits helps to make the growth of the plants. Heavy wind will have ill effect on the growth of certain type of plants. Therefore the velocity of wind flow is another desirable parameter needed to be sensed. Several types of wind flow sensors are used in practice such as ultrasonic type. As this type of sensor cannot align itself to the direction of wind we use miniature windmill [8] to sense the wind flow efficiently.

Ambient light available due to solar radiation helps the growth of most plants. This is another desirable parameter to be sensed.   Photo sensor circuit is used to sense the ambient light.

Humidity of the environment influences the growth of most plants. Standard humidity sensor is employed to monitor the humidity [9]. Fire detectors may help in assessing how best the area is immune to catching fire with plantation of certain type of plants. Standard fire detectors [10] are used in this project and kept at selected locations evenly distributed in the field. The frequency of catching fire in summer and also in winter can be monitored.

For assessing the consistency of the fertility of the soil its pH value is monitored [11] throughout the year during different conditions of climate. As manual inspection of the site is only rarely done, the movements of forest animals over the area also are to be monitored. Although sensors could be arranged for sensing moving objects for such requirements, it is desirable to capture the video image of the site and transmitted to the remote location. Frozen still images transmitted would help in assessing several aspects of the site. Heavy fire, animals, hunters and group of birds or grasshoppers which would be bothering the crops are easily captured by video and visualized at the remote end.

If there is a water stream or water channel connecting the site to outside township or village, availability of water flow is sensed by installing flow sensors at selected points in the stream. If water is available throughout the year the crops cultivated could be transported to external places through boating service.

These are the desirable parameters to be sensed. If additional parameters are needed to be studied they can easily be included in the system for sensing and transmission. Appropriate reservations are made in hardware and software for insertion of the extended parameters in future.

2.2   System Design for Telemetry

The sensors are located at chosen locations of the area to be investigated. The signals from the transducers are conveyed to a computer installed in base station setup in the plantation site. The computer in turn arranges to upload the data to website. Once it is uploaded to website it can be monitored in a computer at any remote location and an analysis can be made. In the past, digital control of a model digital factory through web [12] was reported. The features of the project are suitably modified and adopted to the present application yielding enhancement in performance.

Fig.1 shows simplified schematic of the system monitoring remotely the parameters. In the base station of the plantation site one PC, lab top or notebook is needed to be fixed with wireless card attachment accessing the server and the internet. Since the transducers are located at different places, use of cables connecting to computer may not be feasible. Therefore, modular wireless communicating unit such as the popular USB data card is used for computer providing access to internet.

Each transducer has a mini wireless communicator through which the data are continuously transmitted to the base station. The data from all wireless transducers are collected in the receiver extended to PC and saved in memory as a table which is updating its contents continuously. The computer being extended to internet the table is updated periodically in the website. In the remote PC after giving the user name and password the website is open and the table can be visualized. For use in analysis package, the table is periodically transferred and saved in computer hard disc.

Fig.2 shows the simplified schematic of the wireless transducer data communication system. The transducer analogue signal is digitized with an ADC and transmitted as PCM-BPSK signal as to ensure higher probability of detection. All transducer signals are transmitted via the wireless communicating unit except the transmission of video image got through web camera. Video image of web camera is saved in a notebook and directly uploaded to internet through wireless data card. If power supply is not available in the site of exploration then modular power supply unit [13] generating electric power from mini solar panel and mini-windmill are to be included in each transducer sensing and communicating the signal.

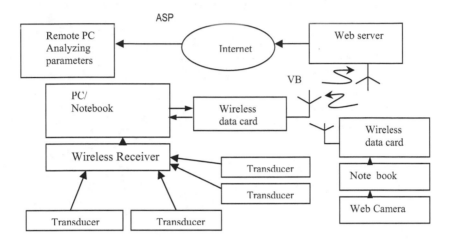

Fig. 1. Telemetering of Plantation Parameters

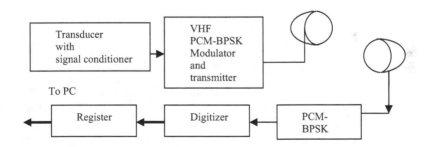

Fig. 2. Wireless Communication of the Transducer Signal

2.2.1 Software Medium and Link

The link to internet from webmail server is made through Visual Basic. As internet is accessible for the system manager as a client stationed at remote location he can view the table as provided by ASP. The server running the VB program gets the data sent from the PC and with the help of ASP put these data into webpage for accessible to remote PC.

2.2.2 Monitoring the Parameters in Remote PC

When the Plantation website is open in the remote manager PC it asks for user name and password as to bring the table of sensed parameters to the screen. Table 1 shows its form of appearance. The current data appearing in the table are saved in reserved memory locations as required for analysis package. There is a test column in which the results of self test made at the transducer end is provided. If it is not OK then corrective measures are to be taken at remote PC.

Table 1. Window Appearing in Website

Name of Sensor	Present Data	Test
Temperature	xxxx	OK
Water Level in lake	xxxx	OK
Water Level in Overhead Tank	xxxx	Error
Present Wind flow	xxxx	OK
Average Wind flow of the day	xxxx	OK
Moisture contets of soil	xxxx	OK
pH value	xxxx	OK
Humidity	xxxx	OK
Fire and smoke	xxxx	OK
Water flow in stream	xxxx	OK
Photo Sensor	xxxx	OK

2.3   An Alternate Design for Telemeter with Wireless Sensor Node

The wireless sensor node is a part of wireless sensor network. The node known as sink node attached with the computer with USB port collects information and transmits to other nodes. This node can be extended to satellite link with the use of appropriate interfaces. By linking the wireless sensor network to a satellite transmission, the data from triangulated radars for regional exploration has been reported recently [14]. This is now extended to the present application for transferring transducer parameters to remote monitoring PC.

The simplified block diagram of the wireless sensor node is shown in Fig.3. A microcontroller is the heart of this node. The microcontroller reads all sensors data and saves them in memory at reserved locations. Through appropriate USART (Universal Synchronous Asynchronous Receiver Transmitter) interface the data are transferred to the STX-2 [15] Satellite Transmission board. It radiates the signal at 2.4GHz. The satellite network receiver gets these data and puts them in the monitoring PC. Therefore the satellite receiver is to be installed in the premises of the PC monitoring the sensed parameters.

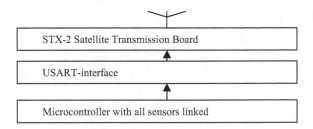

Fig. 3. Simplified Diagram of Satellite Based Sensor Node

2.3.1 Comparison of Wireless Sensor Network and Internet for Transmitting Transducer Data

The wireless sensor network is being used for different applications without access to satellite link. Each node can transmit and receive information as to satisfy the environmental requirements. The processing of information is done at the sink node linked to a computer. It has restricted radio range.

In this application as the remote monitoring PC is situated at a far place, the help of satellite link was necessitated in transferring the transducer parameters. The hardware involvement in using the internet communication and the satellite link are more or less the same. The cost involvement in using internet and satellite link has to be explored. The delay of information is not a critical issue in this application and therefore the performances of both mediums are well acceptable.

3   Digital Irrigation System

In the telemeter system described above the parameters sensed at one place are monitored in computer in a remote location and there is no control activity. The objective of that implementation was to get agricultural parameters for establishing an appropriate plantation system.

In this part we run and maintain automatically a remote irrigation system where the plantation already exists. We use partly the facilities available in the previous project and include remote control activities so as to fulfill the requirements. We observe in a computer the sensed parameters from the irrigation site transferred through internet. After making an analysis control commands are issued through internet to switch ON or OFF selected appliances in the irrigation system.

Regular routine works such as opening the valves periodically to keep watering the plants as per the programmed timings are done locally in the irrigation spot.

3.1   Parameters Sensed for Irrigation

As the main objective of irrigation is to maintain required moisture contents in the soil for entire duration of cropping the moisture sensing becomes essential parameter for this task. The desirable parameters to be sensed are as follows. *i*. moisture contents of the soil *ii*. temperature *iii*. wind flow *iv*. light *v*. water level in the reservoir lake *vi*. water level in the overhead tank. Provisions have been given for including additional parameters in the sensor table.

3.2   System Design

Fig.4 shows the simplified block diagram of the digital irrigation system through internet with duplex communication. The essential parameters sensed by transducers at various locations are transmitted to the computer at irrigation location and then uploaded in the website, all done similar to the previous environment evaluation project. The computer at the irrigation spot is interfaced to a PIC microcontroller which takes care of *i.* controlling the devices as per the command issued by remote PC through website and *ii.* Controlling the regular routine irrigation activities as per its program.

There are two water pumps included in the system. The deep well pump is used to pump the underground water from rigged well to the overhead tank supplying water to irrigation. Natural water reservoir like lake is another source supplying water to the overhead tank. In order for the irrigation to perform smoothly the water level in the overhead tank should be maintained at specified level. When this level drops and if the water level of the reservoir is good enough then that pump is preferred to be switched ON first. If it is not enough then the deep well pump of rigged well is operated to fill the overhead tank. Decisions are made to switch ON a particular pump depending upon the moisture contents, water levels, past history of the switching made on the pumps.

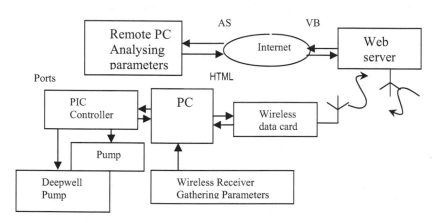

Fig. 4. Remote Control of Digital Irrigation System

When the website is open in the remote PC two windows can be seen in the screen. The first window is like a table shown in Table 1 informing the status of the transducer parameters included in the system. The second window is meant for control action and it appears as shown in Table 2. Only two pumps are included in the system for control and the table shows their present status. Also the present status of irrigation feed whether connected to overhead tank or cut OFF is also indicated . There is another column marked as control column which can be changed by the manager at the remote PC. For instance, in the table the present status of deep well is shown as OFF and the control also is shown as OFF. After making an analysis and decision if the deep well pump has to be switched ON the manager just types 'ON' in this field. This issues necessary command in the PIC at the site to switch ON the deep well pump.

Table 2. A Simple form of Control Table Window Appearing in Website

Control Devices	Present Status	Control
Deepwell pump	OFF	OFF
Overhead tank pump	OFF	ON
Irrigation feed	OFF	ON

The server running the VB program checks for any command issued from the remote manager PC. If a command exists then it formulates the appropriate bytes and sends them to the PC at the irrigation spot for issuing necessary control actions to PIC for switching on the pumps.

3.2.1 PIC Control

The PIC connects the water tap daily to the feed tubes going to all plants for a prefixed time as in the program. The time period is changed by the remote PC after making the analysis of moisture contents of the soil, temperature, water levels in the reservoir and the overhead tank and the ambient light. Therefore, in the PIC monitoring program it checks for the commands issued from the server in response to remote Manager PC. Therefore, while performing the regular daily routines it also actuates the commands issued from the remote PC. The main control actions arising from remote end are switching ON or OFF the two pumps and the irrigation feed tube.

4   Performance Analysis of the Systems

Both the systems described employ internet as the tool for communication. Security concerns, testability, maintainability, limitations and extendibility are the major factors to be analyzed as a means of assessing the performance of the systems.

4.1   Security Concerns

When the website in the remote Manager PC is open it asks for user name and password as to see the respective table as window. As it demands user name and password it ensures security. By making the password issue a complex concern the security aspects could be strengthened.

4.2   Testability

Semi automatic testing is performed by visiting the plantation site and checking the parameters with various sensors and the magnitudes of signals can be verified in the website. Test signals at different levels are inserted and watched in the website for their changes and also the time constant involved are tested. The time constant depends on the communication path between the source and the destination and the bit rate of transmission. The status of sensors and control appliances are checked with other available communication mediums as well. By these cross checks of the data reliability of the remote sensing system and tele-control schemes are ascertained.

4.3   Maintainability

Malfunctioning of any of the devices can provide wrong information about the parameters and the analysis package might produce an error. This is to be avoided by properly maintaining the devices in working conditions. Each transducer is backed up with a standby unit and a local simple testing process is carried periodically as to switch ON the standby unit as active transducer and test the output of both of them. If the outputs do not tally, the error signal is communicated along with the transducer signal to the website for taking corrective measures at the other end. The transducers employed are fool proof ones that it provides self generated error output bit, if any.

4.4   Limitations

The sporadic interruptions occcuring randomly in the internet such as disturbances in the server level or in the satellite communication medium influences the remote data acquisition system. Nevertheless, as the decison is not taken instantly such disturbances do not have any impact on the system performance.

4.5   Extendibility and Inclusion of Several Other Parameters

This system has no limitations in extending additional parameters and control appliances needed for different environment in digital plantation or digital irrigation system. When hardware appliances are brought under remote control it needs revision in the software when it exceeds the reserved number of parameters and control appliances. This is only a minor task and could easily be performed.

5   Discussions and Conclusion

Remote sensing to recover the information about establishing a digital plantation system helps acquiring the information without the manual observation and attention. This being an automatic system unavailing manpower and providing information for long period like a year it is highly preferred in several instants.

As internet usage has become a common means of sharing and exchanging information between users its usage for implementing remote control of a digital irrigation system simplifies its communication process without calling for special communication systems. On the other hand internet is still growing sector with more and more incorporation of additional strategies and overheads and this act would certainly enhance the features of internet based remote sensing and remote control systems.

In place of single channel wireless data transmitter used at each transducer for transmitting information to PC at the base station, one can think to use wireless sensor node and network. In this case it has the advantages of reliability ensured by the wireless sensor network. On the other hand this activity uses only a part of facilities available in the wireless sensor node and utility part is low.

Only three control actions are included in the system reported. It would be easily possible to extend further as many control actions as needed in another environment concerning this application or any other related applications.

References

1. Saygi, B., Yildirim, Y., Cabuko, C., Kara, H., Ramadan, S.S., Esemenl, T.: The effect of dehydration and irrigation on the healing of Achilles tendon: an experimental study. Turkish Journal of Trauma & Emergency Surgery 14(2), 103–109 (2008)
2. Melby, P.: Simplified Irrigation Design. John Wiley and Sons, NewYork (2010)
3. Rangan, S., Sarma, G.R., Mani, V.S.V.: Instrumentation Devices and Systems. Tata McGraw Hill, New Delhi (2003)
4. Balasubramanian, K.: Microprocessor based process control system. J. Instru. Soc. of India 17(2), 151–155 (1987)
5. Bera, S.C., Ray, J.K., Chattopadhyay, S.: A low-cost noncontact capacitance-type level transducer for a conducting liquid. IEEE Transactions on Instrumentation and Measurement 55(3), 778–786 (2006)
6. Balasubramanian, K., Cellatoglu, A.: Precision Pneumatic Pressure Measurement with diaphragm based mechatronic devices. International Journal of Electronics - Taylor and Francis 97(1), 45–62 (2010)
7. Balasubramanian, K.: Improved techniques of transducer linearization. In: Proceedings of the IV National Congress of Electrical Engineers, Izmir, pp. 757–760 (September 1991)
8. Balasubramanian, K., Cellatoglu, A.: Improvements in Home Automation Strategies for Designing Apparatus for Efficient Smart Home. IEEE Trans. on Cons. Electronics 54(4), 1681–1687 (2008)
9. Kim, H., Hong, S.-M., Lee, J.-S., Moon, B.-M., Kim, K.: High sensitivity capacitive humidity sensor with a novel polyimide design fabricated by MEMS technology. In: Proceedings of 4th IEEE Conference on Nano/Micro Engineered and Molecular Systems, pp. 703–706 (2009)
10. Balasubramanian, K., Cellatoglu, A.: Analysis of Remote Control Techniques Employed in Home Automation and Security Systems. IEEE Trans. on Cons. Electronics 55(3), 1401–1407 (2009)
11. Matsuo, J., Hizawa, T., Sawada, K., Takao, H., Ishida, M.: Charge Transfer Type pH Sensor with Super High Sensitivity. In: Proceedings of Solid-State Sensors, Actuators and Microsystems Conference, pp. 1881–1884 (2007)
12. Balasubramanian, K., Cellatoglu, A., Akdemir, T.: Remote Control of Digital Factory through Web. In: Proceedings of the 41st IEEE Southeastern Symposium on System Theory (SSST 2009), Tullahoma, TN, pp. 368–372 (March 2009)
13. Cellatoglu, A., Balasubramanian, K.: Renewable Energy Resources for Residential Applications in Coastal Areas: A Modular Approach. In: Proceedings of the 42nd IEEE South Eastern Symposium on System Theory (SSST 2010), Texas, pp. 340–345 (March 2010)
14. Cellatoglu, A., Sari, M., Rahnama, B., Balasubramanian, K.: Remote Sensing of a Geographical Environment with Portable Radars and Satellite Link. In: Proceedings of ARTCom 2011 Innternational Conference, Bangalore, pp. 128–132 (September 2011)
15. Axonn Corporation, Satellite Transmitter Product STX2, New Orleans (2005)

A Fuzzy Rule Based Expert System
for Effective Heart Disease Diagnosis

E.P. Ephzibah[1] and V. Sundarapandian[2]

[1] School of Information Technology and Engineering,
VIT University, Vellore, TamilNadu, India
ep.ephzibah@vit.ac.in
[2] Research and Development Centre,
Vel Tech Dr. RR & Dr. SR Technical University,
Chennai, Tamil Nadu, India
sundarvtu@gmail.com

Abstract. This is a general method that combines the soft computing techniques like genetic algorithms and fuzzy rule based expert system for effective heart disease diagnosis. It is very important to diagnose the disease in the early stage itself. Prompt and correct diagnosis of the disease by selecting the important and relevant features will help to discard irrelevant and unimportant ones. Genetic algorithms help in feature subset selection. After the subset selection the fuzzy rule based expert system provides the classificatory knowledge. The proposed system generates the rules from the instances and narrows down the limit of the rules using degree of the memberships. The system is designed in Matlab software. The system can be viewed as an alternative method for effective diagnosis of heart disease presence.

Keywords: Fuzzy rule based Expert system, genetic algorithm, heart disease diagnosis.

1   Introduction

One of the leading causes of death in the world is heart disease. Especially in India many people die due to the ignorance of the disease and also due to lack of proper diagnostic methods. It will be of greater value if the disease is diagnosed in its early stage. Prompt and correct diagnosis of the disease will definitely decrease the death rate due to heart failures. There are many tests that are available for the diagnosis of this disease, but in particular they may take more time and also cost more. This paper is proposed to find out the required and relevant tests that should be done on the patients' body to make the diagnosis process faster as well as less expensive. Feature subset selection is a methodology which reduces the features into a subset and subset alone can be considered for further study in the diagnosis process. Classification plays a very important role after selecting the feature subset. The required data is given to the classifier for further classification by dividing the

N. Meghanathan et al. (Eds.): CCSIT 2012, Part II, LNICST 85, pp. 196–203, 2012.
© Institute for Computer Sciences, Social Informatics and Telecommunications Engineering 2012

samples into training and testing samples. Finally the accuracy is checked, which is a measuring agent for the efficiency of the selected features. In this paper a fuzzy expert system is framed with efficient set of rules to determine the presence or absence of heart disease.

2   Related Work

In recent years there were many methods proposed for the generation of fuzzy rules. Hong and Lee (1996) presented a method for inducing fuzzy rules and membership functions from training instances to deal with the Iris data classification problem. Hong and Lee (1999) discussed the effect of merging order on performance of fuzzy rules induction. Hong and Chen (1999) presented a method to construct membership functions and generate fuzzy rules from training instances by finding relevant attributes and membership functions to deal with the Iris data classification problem. A method by Castro et al. (1999) generates fuzzy rules from training data to deal with the Iris data classification problem. A method proposed by Chang and Chen (2001) generates weighted fuzzy rules to deal with the Iris data classification problem. Chen and Chen (2002) presented a method based on genetic algorithms to construct membership functions and fuzzy rules to deal with the Iris data classification problem. Chen and Chang (2005) presented a method to construct membership functions and generate weighted fuzzy rules from training instances. Chen and Tsai (2005) presented a method to generate fuzzy rules from training instances to deal with the Iris data classification problem. Chen and Fang (2005a) presented a method for handling the Iris data classification problem. Chen and Fang (2005b) presented a method to deal with fuzzy classification problems by tuning membership functions for fuzzy classification systems. Chen et al. (2006) presented a method for generating weighted fuzzy rules from training data for dealing with the Iris data classification problem.

The paper is organized in the manner that in section 3 the theory on soft computing has been explained, in section 4 a brief description on genetic algorithms is given , sections 5,6,7 deal with the fuzzy expert system and the sequential steps involved in fuzzy rule generation, section 8 illustrates the heart disease dataset used for our work, section 9 clearly explains the rules that are generated for our work and finally section 10 gives the conclusion.

3   Soft Computing

Soft computing is a methodology that tends to combine the different aspects of fuzzy logic, evolutionary algorithms like genetic algorithms neural networks, and non-linear distributed systems. It is a way to implement hybrid systems that helps to get innovative solutions in the various sectors of intelligent control, modeling and classification.

Soft Computing are Fuzzy Logic, Neural Computing, Evolutionary Computation, Machine Learning and Probabilistic Reasoning and parts of learning theory. Soft computing is a partnership in which each of the partners contributes a distinct methodology for addressing problems in its domain. In this perspective, the principal constituent methodologies in soft computing are complementary rather than competitive. Soft computing may be viewed as a foundation component for the emerging field of conceptual intelligence.

4   Genetic Algorithms

Genetic Algorithm is an optimization technique that yields a solution that fits properly into the objective function. It is a form of generate and test paradigm. It works by creating an initial population of N possible solutions in the form of candidate chromosomes or individuals. The individual chromosomes are the representation of the final solution. The objective function used pay a very important role in measuring the goodness of fit of the individual chromosome. Better the fit, the closer the individual to the target. The evaluation process continues till all the individual chromosomes are evaluated. The termination condition is the stopping criteria. The termination condition depends on any of the following:

    a.   Maximum number of generations,
    b.   Maximum amount of computing time,
    c.   Chromosomes having the fitness value that satisfy the objective function etc…

The genetic operators like the selection, crossover and mutation can influence in finding the optimal and feasible solution to the problem.

In our work we have used the Roulette wheel selection and the values for crossover and mutation are .5 and .08 respectively.

5   Fuzzy Expert System

The general fuzzy inference process proceeds with the following four steps.

1.   **FUZZIFICATION:** Fuzzification is a process of finding the membership value of a scalar in a fuzzy set. This is done by fuzzifying the input values. To obtain the degree of truth for the rules generated, the membership function is applied on the input values.

2.   **FUZZY INFERENCE:** A fuzzy inference engine consists of assessment, correlation, aggregation and reduction. Assessment is the process of gathering initial evidence and determining the truth of the rule antecedent. The amount of evidence of the rule is assessed by combining the individual fuzzy propositions. Correlation matches the truth of the consequent. It takes the form of either scaling or truncating the consequent using the truth. Aggregation updates the current outcome fuzzy set using the correlated consequent fuzzy set. Each rule updates the outcome fuzzy set with its own correlated fuzzy sets. Two methods of aggregation are addition and maximization. This process plays a very important role as heart of the fuzzy inference engine.

3. **DEFUZZIFICATION:** It is a process of reduction that produces a scalar result from the final outcome fuzzy set. There are many methods of defuzzification, but the most commonly used is centroid or center of gravity. This is calculated as the weighted average of the outcome fuzzy set.

6   Rule-Based Fuzzy Expert Systems

One of the most important components in the development of expert system is knowledge acquisition. This could be obtained by questionnaires, interviews and experiences. To find a solution computer programs use well- structured algorithms and some reasoning strategies. For expert systems it may be more useful to employ heuristics: strategies that often lead to the correct solution. Human intelligence is applied to solve conventional rule-based expert systems. Rule based expert systems play a very important role in modern intelligent systems. A rule is a statement that combines or links the input scalar to an output vector.

In the above figure the knowledge base contains all the information, relationships and related data. The inference engine obtains the knowledge from the knowledge base and uses that knowledge for predictions and results. The explanation facility helps in explaining the user how the results are obtained. The purpose of knowledge acquisition facility is to provide the way for capturing, storing all the components of knowledge base. A rule-based system consists of if-then rules with facts. These if-then rules are use to generate conditional statements.

7   Heart Disease Data-Set

In this section the details about the heart disease and its attributes taken for the experiment purpose is described. A database that contains the heart disease data is taken from UCI Machine learning repository. There are 303 samples or instances for 13 attributes like Thal {6—fixed defect,7—reversible defect,3—normal}, Number of major blood vessels colored by fluoroscopy {0,1, 2, 3}, Chest pain type   {1, 2, 3,4}, Exercise induced angina {Yes,No}, Slope of peak exercise ST segment {Medium, High,Low} Oldpeak = ST depression induced by exercise relative to rest , Maximum heart rate achieved , Sex {Female Male},age, resting blood pressure, cholesterol. Out of the mentioned 13 attributes the relevant and best six attributes were found using the genetic algorithms. Genetic algorithm is an optimization technique based on the principles of genetics and natural selection. It uses a population of chromosomes to evolve under specified selection rules and operators like crossover and mutation. In feature selection, Genetic algorithms explore a large search space effectively. The obtained set of selected features include chest pain type, resting blood pressure, exercise induced angina maximum heart rate achieved, old peak and number of major vessels.

8   Fuzzy Rule Generation

In a fuzzy rule-based system the rules can be represented in the following way:

   If   (x is A) and (y is B) … and…. Then (z is Z)

where **x,y** and **z** represent variables (or attributes or features) and **A, B** and **Z** are linguistic variables such as `far', `near', `small'. Ishibuchi *et al* [11] [12] [10] report various results when using GAs to select fuzzy rules in classification. The problem tackled is that of using a set of numerical data to generate if-then rules for pattern classification. There are some steps to be followed for the fuzzy rules to be generated. From the heart disease data set we take a set of input and output attributes and classes. There are around thirteen attributes and we have reduced them into six relevant input attributes and one output attribute, y. Even though there are four classes in the output as 0,1,2,3,4, this work takes them as only two classes as {0,1}. The class 0 represents that the patient has no heart disease and class 1 represents the presence of the heart disease.   We name them as follows:

$$\{ x_1, x_2, x_3, x_4, x_5, \quad x_6\},\{y\}$$

The task of generating the fuzzy rules involves few steps that follow [2]:

Step1: Separate the input space into fuzzy regions:

Find the maximum attribute value and the minimum attribute value of each attribute of the training instances. This shows that the value of the particular attribute is in this interval.   Divide the domain interval of each attribute into 2N+1 region. The following table gives the range of the attributes:

S.No	Attributes	Maximum	Minimum
1	chest pain type	4	1
2	resting blood pressure	200	94
3	maximum heart rate achieved	202	71
4	exercise induced angina	1	0
5	Oldpeak	6.2	0
6	number of major vessels	3	0

Fig. 1. This show the maximum attribute vale and minimum attribute vales

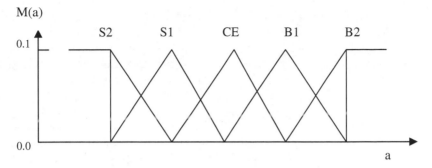

Fig. 2. Division of input spaces into fuzzy regions

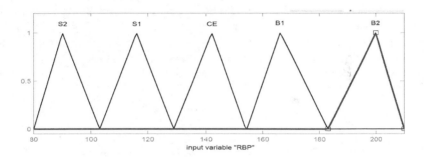

Fig. 3. Fuzzy regions for resting blood pressure attribute

Step2: Develop fuzzy rules from the example set:

The fuzzy rules are generated based on the attribute values of each and every instance.

The selected attributes are named as x_1, x_2, x_3, x_4, x_5, and x_6 for chest pain type, resting blood pressure, maximum heart rate, exercise induced angina, old peak and number of major blood vessels colored by fluoroscopy value respectively. These are some of the rules obtained form the example instances.

Instance 1:
If (x_1 is 1) and (x_2 is high) and (x_3 is medium) and (x_4 is 0) and (x_5,is risk) and (x_6 is 0) then result is 0.

Instance 2:
If (x_1 is 4) and (x_2 is very high) and (x_3 is medium) and (x_4 is 1) and (x_5 is risk) and (x_6 is 3) then result is 1.

Instance 3:
If (x_1 is 4) and (x_2 is low) and (x_3 is medium) and (x_4 is 1) and (x_5 is terrible) and (x_6 is 2) then result is 1.

Instance 4:
If (x_1 is 3) and (x_2 is medium) and (x_3 is medium) and (x_4 is 0) and (x_5 is terrible) and (x_6 is 0) then result is 0.

Instance 5:

If (x_1 is 2) and (x_2 is medium) and (x_3 is medium) and (x_4 is 0) and (x_5 is risk) and (x_6 is 0) then result is 0.

There rules are generated based on the membership values and their region. Like this the rules are generated. Based on the number of instances the number of rules may change.

Step3: Select the best rule based on the degree of the rule:

As there are many rules generated there are more chances of conflicts and redundancy. For example, many rules can have the same IF part but different THEN part. This is where the conflicts occur and to avoid the conflicts the rules are ranked based on their degrees. The degree of a rule is obtained based on the membership values. Sum of all the membership values is obtained and accordingly the rules are selected. If two rules have the same IF part, the rule with higher degree of membership is selected and the other one is discarded. Thus a limited set of definite rules are generated. Finally mapping the input and output values using the generated fuzzy rule base is done to check for any classification.

9 Conclusion

In this paper, we have given a detailed presentation of fuzzy rule-based expert system for effective diagnosis of the heart disease in patients. This expert system will help the doctors to arrive at a conclusion about the heart disease in patients. Our expert system is an enhanced system that accurately classifies the presence of the heart disease. It is shown that the generated fuzzy rule based classification system is capable of diagnosing the heart disease than any other classifiers.

References

1. Chang, C.H., Chen, S.M.: Constructing membership functions and generating weighted fuzzy rules from training data. In: Proceedings of the 2001 Ninth National Conference on Fuzzy Theory and its Applications, Chungli, Taoyuan, Taiwan, Republic of China, pp. 708–713 (2001)
2. Chen, S.M., Chang, C.H.: A new method to construct membership functions and generate weighted fuzzy rules from training instances. Cybernetics and Systems 36(4), 397–414 (2005)
3. Chen, S.M., Chen, Y.C.: Automatically constructing membership functions and generating fuzzy rules using genetic algorithms. Cybernetics and Systems 33(8), 841–862 (2002)
4. Chen, S.M., Fang, Y.D.: A new approach for handling the Iris data classification problem. International Journal of Applied Science and Engineering 3(1), 37–49 (2005a)
5. Chen, S.M., Fang, Y.D.: A new method to deal with fuzzy classification problems by tuning membership functions for fuzzy classification systems. Journal of Chinese Institute of Engineers 28(1), 169–173 (2005b)

6. Chen, S.M., Lin, H.L.: Generating weighted fuzzy rules for handling classification problems. International Journal of Electronic Business Management 3(2), 116–128 (2005a)
7. Chen, S.M., Lin, H.L.: Generating weighted fuzzy rules from training instances using genetic algorithms to handle the Iris data classification problem. Journal of Information Science and Engineering 22(1), 175–188 (2005b)
8. Chen, S.M., Lin, S.Y.: A new method for constructing fuzzy decision trees and generating fuzzy classification rules from training examples. Cybernetics and Systems 31(7), 763–785 (2000)
9. Chen, S.M., Tsai, F.M.: A new method to construct membership functions and generate fuzzy rules from training instances. International Journal of Information and Management Sciences 16(2), 47–72 (2005)
10. Chen, Y.C., Wang, L.H., Chen, S.M.: Generating weighted fuzzy rules from training data for dealing with the Iris data classification problem. International Journal of Applied Science and Engineering 4(1), 41–52 (2006)
11. Fisher, R.: The use of multiple measurements in taxonomic problem. Annals of Eugenics 7, 179–188 (1936); Hong, T.P., Chen, J.B.: Finding relevant attributes and membership functions. Fuzzy Sets and Systems 103(3), 389–404 (1999)
12. Hong, T.P., Lee, C.Y.: Induction of fuzzy rules and membership functions from training examples. Fuzzy Sets and Systems 84(1), 33–47 (1996); Hong, T.P., Lee, C.Y.: Effect of merging order on performance of fuzzy induction. Intelligent Data Analysis 3(2), 39–151 (1999)
13. Ishibuchi, H., Nakashima, T.: Effect of rule weights in fuzzy rulebased classification systems. IEEE Transactions on Fuzzy Systems 9(4), 506–515 (2001)
14. Tsai, F.M., Chen, S.M.: A new method for constructing membership functions and generating fuzzy rules for fuzzy classification systems. In: Proceedings of 2002 Tenth National Conference on Fuzzy Theory and its Application, Hsinchu, Taiwan, Republic of China (2002)
15. Wu, T.P., Chen, S.M.: A new method for constructing membership functions and fuzzy rules from training examples. IEEE Transactions on Systems, Man, and Cybernetics—Part B: Cybernetics 29(1), 25–40 (1999)
16. Zadeh, L.A.: Fuzzy sets. Information and Control 8, 338–353 (1965)
17. Zadeh, L.A.: The concept of a linguistic variable and its application to approximate reasoning, Parts 1, 2, and 3. Information Sciences, 8:199–249, 8:301–357, 9:43–80 (1975)

Moving Object Detection Using Incremental Statistical Mean Technique

Safvan A. Vahora[1], Narendra C. Chauhan[2], and Nilesh B. Prajapati[3]

[1] Information Technology Dept., Vishvakarma Govt. Engg. College, Chandkheda
[2] Information Technology Dept., A. D. Patel Institute of Technology, New V.V. Nagar
[3] Information Technology Dept., Birla Vishvakarma Mahavidyalaya, V.V. Nagar, India
{safvan465,narendracchauhan}@gmail.com,
nilesh.prajapati@bvmengineering.ac.in

Abstract. We propose a new approach for moving object detection. Moving object detection is low-level, important task for any visual surveillance system. The aim of this paper is to, to describe traditional approach of moving object detection techniques such as background subtraction, temporal difference, as well as pros and cons of these techniques. Finally, we propose the statistical mean technique to overcome the problem in traditional techniques. Since, simple statistical mean technique having disadvantages, to defeat those, we propose incremental statistical mean technique. Incremental statistical mean technique have need of computation to perform simultaneously, that requires parallel computation to speed up and reduce the computation complexity.

Keywords: Background subtraction, Incremental statistical mean, Moving object detection, Statistical mean technique, Temporal difference.

1 Introduction

Computer vision system have been developed to simulate most natural systems which have ability to deal with changing environments such as moving objects, objects tracking, changing illumination, changing view point. Video surveillance has received many attentions over the last year and major research topic in computer vision. In video surveillance system detection and tracking of object is lower level vision task to provide higher level event detection. Identifying moving objects is a critical task which requires video segmentation, which is used in many computer vision applications such as video surveillance, traffic monitoring, and remote sensing. [1] There are three major steps in video surveillance analysis are detection of moving objects, tracking of such interested objects from consecutive frames, and third is analysis of these tracked objects to identify the behavior, and identify the desired event.

There are numerous applications those uses video surveillance. Video traffic monitoring is gathering traffic information from various visual sources to redirect the traffic flow. Smart video surveillance system is monitoring scene continuously, to detect a desired event. Gesture recognition is to identify human gesture, fingerprint detection and eyes detection to login into a system. Video indexing can be used for automatically explanation and retrieval of videos in multimedia database.

N. Meghanathan et al. (Eds.): CCSIT 2012, Part II, LNICST 85, pp. 204–210, 2012.
© Institute for Computer Sciences, Social Informatics and Telecommunications Engineering 2012

Moving object detection process of classifying the pixels in video frames into the two classes, foreground pixels are considered as pixels of moving object and background pixels are considered as pixels of stationary background object. In another words, moving object detection handles segmentation of from stationary background object.

Detection of moving object can be complex due to several reasons such as noise in video sequence, sudden illumination changes, shadows and waving tree branches in the wind, rain or snow-fall for outdoor video surveillance, occlusion provide loss of information by projection of 3D world in 2D image [9].

There are various approaches have been proposed by different researchers for moving object detection. Here, we proposed incremental statistical mean technique for moving object detection, that having various advantages over the traditional approaches of moving object detection.

The rest of the paper is organized as follows. In section 2, we give details of traditional background subtraction technique, temporal difference technique of moving object detection. In section 3, we describe statistical mean technique and incremental statistical mean technique that is the modified version of statistical mean technique as described earlier in section 2. Experimental result and conclusion are described in section 4 and section 5.

2   Object Detection Methods

2.1   Background Subtraction

Object detection can be achieved by creating background model and then finding deviations from the model for each and every frame in video. Background subtraction is widely used because of its time complexity less for detecting the foreground object. Background subtraction is particularly a for motion segmentation in static scenes [2].

Background subtraction is most popular choice to detect stationary foreground objects [6],[7], because they work well when the camera is static and illumination change is gradual [8].

In this method, to detect the foreground object, the background subtraction algorithm detects the difference between the current image and the background image or often called reference image or background model. Recent background subtraction algorithms focused on robust background modeling and updating to adapt to   varying illumination condition between night and day, light effects, background structures, background change from whether change and repetitive motion from clutter [3]. For a pixel location (x, y) in the current image I, is identified as foreground pixel along with background image B, if it satisfies the equation 1.

$$| I(x, y) - B(x, y) | > \tau \tag{1}$$

Where τ is a predefined threshold [4]. The background image B is updated by the adaption coefficient η as per the equation 2.

$$B_{i+1} = \eta I_i + (1 - \eta) B_i \tag{2}$$

The core part of this method is to integrate the new upcoming information of a new image into the background image, so that background image becomes more robust. The value of η should not be large, it may create faster new changes in the background image.

The pixels constituting the regions undergoing change are marked for further processing. In general, a connected component algorithm is used to obtain connected regions corresponding to the objects.

Even though the background subtraction technique is well to extract moving object, this background subtraction technique may suffer to dynamic background changes such as the entrance of new background object or sudden illumination change.

2.2   Temporal Differencing

Temporal differencing technique uses the pixel wise difference between two or three frames in frame sequences to extract a moving object. [5] Temporal differencing technique is computationally simple and fast as well as is adaptive to dynamic environment. In temporal difference technique, extraction of moving pixel is simple and fast. It takes difference of the current and previous frames as shown in equation 3

$$| I_i(x, y) - I_{i-1}(x, y) | > \tau \tag{3}$$

where τ is predefined threshold.

Temporal differencing technique is less effective in extracting all information about target object, especially when the target object has uniform texture or target object moves slowly. When a foreground object moves slowly or stops moving in between, temporal difference technique fails in detection a change between consecutive frames and loses the target object information. Temporal difference is most sensitive to the threshold value τ, to determining pixel-wise difference between consecutive frames as well as it may left holes in foreground objects. Temporal difference require special supportive algorithm to detect stopped objects.

3   Statistical Mean Technique

There are so many drawbacks of traditional moving object detection approach, as described above section. To overcome these shortcomings, we propose the next technique is statistical mean technique. Statistical mean technique is based on the computed statistics of each and every frame of video or computed statistics of every k frames by using down sampling to reduce the processing time. In statistical mean technique base, background image is calculated by computing mean of each and every pixel available in video. For n frames and (x, y) is the pixel position of Ith frame, the summation of all frames computed as shown equation 4

$$X(x, y) = \sum_{i=1}^{n} I(x, y) \qquad (4)$$

The summation of each pixel is in X (x, y) of n frames normalized mean model frame N(x, y), is calculated as by dividing each pixel position with n, number of frames as shown in equation 5

$$N(x, y) = X(x, y)/n \qquad (5)$$

Compare this mean model N(x, y) to each and every frame from 1 to n. For every pixel (x, y) of frame I, compare that pixel position with pixel position (x, y) of normalized mean model frame N as shown in equation 6

$$| N(x, y) - I(x, y) | > \tau \qquad (6)$$

where τ is a predefined threshold value. If the current pixel (x, y) of frame I, fall in this category than specify it as foreground object pixel otherwise specify as background pixel.

Although statistical mean technique gives good result, it suffers by the problem of superfluous effects of foreground objects. Whenever, object or more than one objects remains in video for long period of time, for example, an object is presents in half of the number of frames out of total n number of frames. This leads to erroneous mean model, so that the precise result of moving object detection will not be achieved. This erroneous result is created because of the superfluous effect of that object. To overcome the problem of superfluous effect of the object, modified statistical mean technique is used.

In Modified statistical mean technique, initially take k number of frames out of total n frames to calculate mean model N. This mean model N is used for detection of moving object for first frame. As the first frame is processing, simultaneously update mean model N, by taking next frame in derivation of mean model as shown in equation 7. Here, next frame is $I_{(k+1)}$ to update the mean model.

$$N_{new}(x, y) = (N_{old}(x, y) * k + I_{k+1}(x, y))/k + 1 \qquad (7)$$

This updated mean model N_{new} is used to for further processing to find the moving object detection. This process is repeated until it reaches to n, total number of frames.

4   Experimental Results

We tested our method on various sequences of videos acquired on outdoor environments. Figure 1 shows the output of the temporal difference method, by applying the operation as described above, under the outdoor environment. Figure 1 (a) shows the frame sequence 106 to 109 and figure 1 (b) shows frame sequence 107 to 109 of the detected object after applying temporal difference technique as described, in section 2. For example, shown in figure 1, the value of threshold τ is 30.

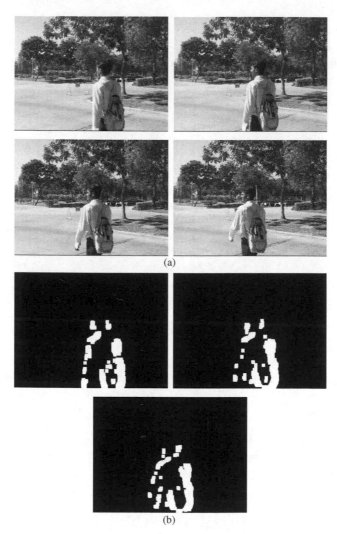

Fig. 1. Temporal Difference for moving object detection, (a) input video frame sequence 106 to 109, (b) Temporal Difference result sequence 107 to 109

As described in section 2, it may leave holes in foreground object detection as shown in result. As stated it requires the support of another algorithm to get accurate output.

Figure 2 shows, the output by applying the incremental statistical method to the video sequence acquired outdoor environment. It provide, detection of moving object accurate, it is able to detect moving object under the dynamic change in the background stationary model. For the example shown in figure 2, the value of threshold τ is 30.

Figure 2 (a) input frame sequence 101 111 121 131 of the video, and 2 (b) shows the output frame sequence 101 111 121 131 that contains moving object detected using the incremental statistical mean method, by using the equation specified in the above section.

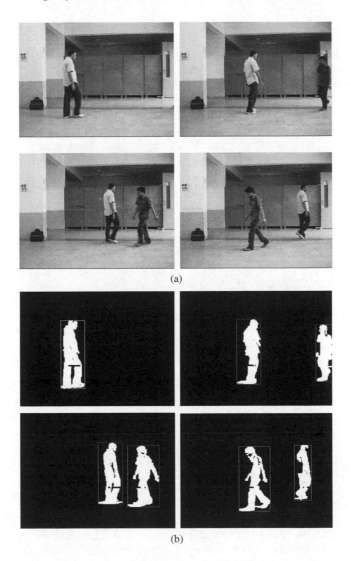

Fig. 2. Incremental statistical mean Technique, (a) Input video frame sequence 101 111 121 131 (c) Moving object detected sequence 101 111 121 131

We have applied this technique on 12 video, indoor as well as the outdoor environment, and gives accurate result for those. Though, incremental statistical mean technique, achieves good result for moving object detection, it have some disadvantages as, it cannot deal with sudden rain or snow fall, in the video. It cannot differentiate the rain drops and moving object from the video frames. This technique requires parallel processing to reduce the time complexity. If the value of threshold is not chosen appropriate, to the environment, it may produce the inaccurate result.

5   Conclusion

Moving object detection is the first and low-level step of any visual surveillance system, after that there are so many steps remaining to perform to complete, any surveillance system. We explain the traditional moving object detection technique, with its pros and cons. As well as, we describe its drawbacks in practically in experimental result.   We propose incremental statistical mean technique that is computationally fast, by allowing the parallel processing. Incremental statistical mean technique, overcome the drawbacks of traditional approach of moving object detection. It provides the good result under the illumination change due to the day and night, stationary background model change, because of this technique is incrementally changes its background model.

References

1. Elhabian, S.Y., El-Sayed, K.M.: Moving object detection in spatial domain using background removal techniques- state of the art. Recent Patents on Computer Science 1, 32–54 (2008)
2. McIvor, A.M.: Background subtraction techniques. In: Proc. of Image and Vision Computing (2000)
3. Kim, I.S., Choi, H.S., Yi, K.M., Choi, J.Y., Kong, S.G.: Intelligent Visual Surveillance - A Survey. International Journal of Control, Automation, and Systems 8(5), 926–939 (2010)
4. Heikkila, J., Silven, O.: A real-time system for monitoring of cyclists and pedestrians. In: Proc. of Second IEEE Workshop on Visual Surveillance, pp. 74–81 (June 1999)
5. Lipton, A.J., Fujiyoshi, H., Patil, R.S.: Moving target classification and tracking from real-time video. In: Proc. of the IEEE Workshop Applications of Computer Vision, pp. 8–14 (1998)
6. Mathew, R., Yu, Z., Zhang, J.: Detecting new stable objects in surveillance video. In: Proc. of MSP 2005, pp. 1–4 (2005)
7. Liao, H.H., Chang, J.Y., Chen, L.G.: A localized Approach to abandoned luggage detection with Foreground –Mask sampling. In: Proc. of AVSS 2008, pp. 132–139 (2008)
8. Alvaro, B., SanMiguel Juan, C., Martínez Jose, M.: Stationary Foreground Detection using Background Subtraction and Temporal Difference in Video Surveillance. In: Proceedings of 2010 IEEE 17th International Conference on Image Processing, September 26-29 (2010)
9. Yilmaz, A., Javed, O., Shah, M.: Object Tracking: A survey. ACM Comput. Surv. 38(4), Article 13 (December 2006)

Classification of Moving Vehicles in Traffic Videos

Elham Dallalzadeh, D.S. Guru, S. Manjunath, and M.G. Suraj

Department of Studies in Computer Science,
University of Mysore, Manasagangothri, Mysore, 570 006, Karnataka, India
elhamdallalzadeh@gmail.com, dsg@compsci.uni-mysore.ac.in,
manju_uom@yahoo.co.in, mgsuraj@yahoo.com

Abstract. In this paper, we propose a model for classification of moving vehicles in traffic videos. We present a corner-based tracking method to track and detect moving vehicles. The detected vehicles are classified into 4 different types of vehicle classes using optimal classifiers. The proposed classification method is based on overlapping the boundary curves of each vehicle while tracking it in sequence of frames to reconstruct a complete boundary shape of it. The reconstructed boundary shape is normalized and a set of efficient shape features are extracted. Vehicles are classified by k-NN rule and the proposed weighted k-NN classifier. Experiments are conducted on 23.02 minutes of moderate traffic videos of roadway scenes taken in an uncontrolled environment during day time. The proposed method has 94.32% classification accuracy which demonstrates the effectiveness of our method. The proposed method has 87.45% of precision with 79% recall rate for classification of moving vehicles.

Keywords: Corner-based tracking, shape reconstruction, shape normalization, shape feature extraction, vehicle classification, k-nearest neighbor, weighted k-nearest neighbor.

1 Introduction

Vision-based traffic video monitoring systems have reduced the cost of traffic monitoring with increased quality. In addition to vehicle counts, a set of traffic parameters such as vehicle labels, lane changes, illegal U-turns, posture, speed and moving direction can be measured. Vision-based traffic video monitoring systems help us in gathering statistical data on traffic activity through monitoring the density of vehicles and also assist us in taking intelligent decisions in any abnormal conditions by analyzing the traffic information. Vehicle classification is one of the key tasks in any vision-based traffic monitoring system. Important data about vehicle classes that use a particular street or highway can be obtained which on the other hand can provide the accurate design of roadways and highways.

Detection and tracking of vehicles are the preliminary steps in the task of vehicle classification. Vehicles are extracted from the scene using motion cues [2], or by background subtraction [3]. The extracted vehicles are tracked in a sequence of

N. Meghanathan et al. (Eds.): CCSIT 2012, Part II, LNICST 85, pp. 211–221, 2012.
© Institute for Computer Sciences, Social Informatics and Telecommunications Engineering 2012

frames using region-based [5], active contour-based [6], model-based [7] and feature-based [3, 8-9] tracking methods. Tracked vehicles have to be classified. However, classification of vehicles in traffic videos imposes challenge due to their high intra class variations. Many types of vehicles belonging to the same class have various size and shape features. Transformation of vehicles, occlusion, shadow, illumination, scale, pose and position of a camera in a scene make the shape of vehicles to be changed while moving. In addition, stereo cameras are rarely used for traffic monitoring [14]. Hence, it would become more complex to recover vehicle parameters such as length, width and height from a single view camera. However, the inherent complexity of stereo algorithms makes them impractical in real-time applications.

The approach proposed in this paper is an integrated approach that combines vehicle extraction, tracking and classification. Moving vehicles are tracked and detected within a video sequence. A complete boundary shape of every vehicle is reconstructed. The boundary shapes of vehicles are normalized and a set of efficient shape features are extracted. Moving vehicles are classified into 4 different categories using optimal classifiers.

The rest of the paper starts by describing an overview of the related works in section 2. A description of our approach for classification of vehicles is presented in section 3. Section 4 details the experimentation carried out on traffic videos along with the results. Finally, conclusions are given in section 5.

2   Related Works

In literature we can find a number of works on classification of vehicles in traffic videos. Sullivan et al. [11] proposed a 3D model matching scheme to classify vehicles into various types like wagon, sedan, hatchback, etc. They developed a simplified version of a model-based tracking approach using orthographic approximations to attain real-time performance. Although, 3D features obtained from stereo cameras might be useful for categorizing different classes of vehicles, the computational time of 3D model approaches are very high and classification of vehicles relies on detailed geometric of various types of traffic vehicles which might not be available all the time. In [12], the virtual loop assignment and direction-based estimation methods are used to identify different types of vehicles. Each type of a vehicle is represented by a 1-D signature chart. A parameterized model was proposed to describe vehicles by Wu et al. [13]. They proposed to consider the vertices and topological structure of vehicles as the key features. However, extracting the topological structures of vehicles requires high quality of frames that is not always achievable in a real traffic monitoring system. Gupte et al. [14] proposed a region-based tracking approach to track vehicles. They classified vehicles based on the establishment of correspondences between regions and vehicles. In their work only two categories, categories of cars and non-cars are considered and occluded vehicles are also misclassified as non-cars. Hsieh et al. [15] proposed a classification method which has a good capability to categorize cars into more specific classes with a new "linearity" feature extraction method. A maximum likelihood estimation based classifier is designed to classify vehicles even in the existence of shadow, occlusion and other noise. To increase the classification accuracy, they integrate the vehicles of the same trajectory from different appearances. In [16], they proposed a method in which vehicles are classified into two groups of vehicles and false vehicles and "Adaboost" is used for such a purpose. Rad and Jamzed [10] proposed speed parameter in addition to the width of the bounding box surrounding the vehicles for classification. They used the fact that usually heavy vehicles run more slowly than the cars. However, this is not always the fact in real-time traffic videos. Vehicle classification based on Eigenvehicle and PCA-SVM was proposed by Zhang et al. [17]. They proposed to normalize the extracted vehicles along the same direction and measured at the same scale. For each vehicle segment, only the most significant eigenvector is chosen to represent the vehicle. They apply One-Class Support Vector Machine to classify vehicles. Chen and Zhang [18] designed an algorithm for vehicle classification at a finer granularity. They proposed an ICA based vehicle classification platform. One-Class Support Vector Machine is then used for classification of vehicles.

From the literature survey, it is clear that vehicle classification based on shape features in traffic videos suffers from high computational time if the extracted features are based on 3D modeling of vehicles or dimensionality reduction of the extracted vehicle features. Besides, the classification methods that are based on template matching of vehicles involve the detailed geometric of various types of traffic vehicles which is impractical to use in real-time traffic videos. In addition, the classification accuracy of detected vehicles depends on the extracted features of vehicles used for classification and the type of a classifier used. Classification accuracy can be obtained with an appropriate combination of the extracted features with a particular classifier. Thus, we still need to further explore methods that can reveal the real, invariant characteristics and shape features of the type of vehicles having no requirement of template matching for classification in real-time traffic videos. The classification system should be robust, efficient and accurate.

In this direction, we propose a shape-based method for classification of moving vehicles in this paper. Moving vehicles are tracked and detected by the method proposed in [3]. We propose to reconstruct a complete boundary shape of every detected vehicle by overlapping all of its boundary curves while it is tracking in a sequence of frames. The reconstructed boundary shape is normalized and for that a set of shape features are extracted. The proposed method has good capability and robustness to categorize vehicles into more specific classes. Vehicles are classified into 4 different categories such as 1- motorcycles and bicycles, 2- cars, 3- heavy vehicles (minibus, bus and truck) and 4- any other (complement class).

3   Proposed Model

This paper presents a vision-based traffic surveillance system to classify detected moving vehicles in a video captured by a stationary camera. Moving vehicles are tracked and detected using the corner-based tracking approach proposed in [3]. The complete boundary shape of every detected vehicle is reconstructed by translating all the boundaries of a vehicle during its tracking to the center of a temporary framework. The reconstructed boundary shape is normalized and the shape features are extracted. k-NN and the proposed weighted k-NN classifiers are then applied to classify vehicles.

3.1   Corner-Based Tracking

We use the approach proposed in [3] to segment, track and detect moving vehicles in traffic videos. To track the extracted moving vehicles, a bounding box is used to initially enclose the corner points of each vehicle of a current frame. The corner points are then labelled based on the label of the candidate corner points located in a mapped bounding box of that of the previous frame. Fig. 1 illustrates the corner-based tracking approach proposed in [3] to track moving vehicles in a traffic video.

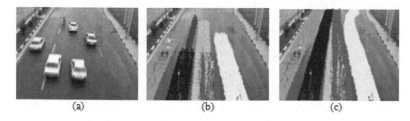

(a)   (b)   (c)

Fig. 1. (a) Main frame. (b) Tracked vehicles in a shot. (c) Vehicles are tracked from the time of appearance to the time of disappearance in the scene.

3.2   Feature Extraction

In this subsection, we outline the proposed approach to extract the shape features of a detected moving vehicle in order to classify it. To extract the shape features of a vehicle, first, we propose to reconstruct a complete boundary shape of a vehicle during the period of its tracking as detailed in section 3.2.1. The reconstructed boundary shape is normalized by sampling the data points. The shape features of the normalized boundary shape are extracted as given in section 3.2.2.

3.2.1 Shape Reconstruction

It is known that a vehicle has many different appearances as it moves along a lane. The factors such as vehicle movement, illumination and shadow might affect the extracted shape of a vehicle while it is moving. Hence, there exists high variation among the extracted boundary curves of vehicles. To extract the robust shape features for a vehicle, we propose to reconstruct the complete boundary shape of a vehicle during the period of its tracking. We propose to overlap all the boundaries of a vehicle while it is tracking in sequence of frames from the time of its appearance to the time of its disappearance in the scene. Thus, for all the frames where a vehicle is tracked, its closed boundary curves are located in the center of a temporary framework such that the centroid of the boundaries, represented in terms of the vector $\vec{V}=(V_{\bar{x}}, V_{\bar{y}})$, coincides with the center of the coordinates of a temporary framework, termed as $\vec{C}=(C_{\bar{x}}, C_{\bar{y}})$. Fig. 2 shows an example of two different traffic vehicles that the closed boundary curves of each vehicle are located to the center of a framework while tracking. Before extracting the shape features, the outline of the reconstructed boundary shape is sampled to a fixed number of points. The sampling process normalizes the sizes of the boundary shapes, smoothes the shapes as well as eliminates the small details along the boundary shapes [4]. In this paper, the boundary shape of a vehicle is normalized using the equal arc-length sampling method [4] as it achieves the best equal space effect. Fig. 3 shows the normalized boundary shapes of the vehicles as reconstructed in Fig. 2.

Fig. 2. (a) A sample car enclosed in a bounding box. (b) The shifted boundary curves of the car to the center of a framework during its tracking. (c) A sample bus circumscribed by a bounding box. (d) The located boundary curves of the bus to the center of a framework while it is tracking.

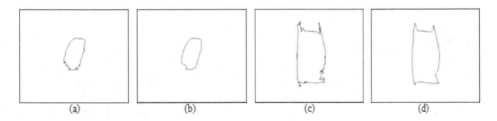

Fig. 3. (a)&(c) The reconstructed boundary shapes of two different vehicles. (b)&(d) Boundary shapes normalization.

3.2.2 Shape Feature Extraction

It is well-known that there exist a number of techniques such as Fourier descriptors, Zernik moments and Boundary moments that can extracts the shape features of vehicles based on boundary. On the other hand, it is also well clear that there are high variations among the boundary shapes of different traffic vehicles belonging to the same class. So, the shape features extracted from such mentioned techniques are not applicable for our application. In this direction, we propose to extract a set of shape features which is robust, efficient and applicable for classification of traffic vehicles. Thus, in this paper the following shape features are extracted.

A number of basic features of a minimum bounding box (MBB) circumscribing the normalized boundary shapes are obtained as follows.

- **Normalized Length**: It is a length of the MBB. The length is as well normalized via NL=L/LF (where, 'LF' is the length of a framework).
- **Normalized Width**: It is a width of the MBB. The obtained width is also normalized with NW=W/WF (where, 'WF' is the width of a framework).
- **Length by Width Ratio**: This ratio is calculated by NL/NW.
- **Width by Length Ratio**: It is the computed ratio of NW/NL.
- **Area**: The area of the MBB i.e., A=NL×NW.
- **Perimeter**: The perimeter of the MBB viz., P=(NL+NW)×2.

Further, the region properties of a vehicle are computed in terms of *Eccentricity*, *Solidity*, *Centroid Size*, *Minimum Distance to Centroid* and *Maximum Distance to Centroid*.

- **Eccentricity**: The eccentricity is the ratio of the distance between the foci of the ellipse of a vehicle and its major axis length.
- **Solidity**: It is a scalar specifying the proportion of the pixels in the convex hull that are also in the region.
- **Centroid Size**: An alternative characterization of the size of a vehicle is defined as the square root of the sum of the squared Euclidean distances between each landmark point and the centroid of a boundary [1].
- **Maximum and Minimum Distance to Centroid**: Maximum distance from the centroid to the boundary points as well as Minimum distance from the centroid to the coordinates of the border [1].

3.3   Vehicle Classification

We use k-Nearest Neighbor approach (k-NN) to classify detected moving vehicles into 4 different categories. To improve the classification accuracy, in this paper we propose weighted k-NN for classification. We propose to estimate the dissimilarity value based on the weighted features. If the features extracted from training and testing sample vehicles are similar, then the dissimilarity values computed among the features can be reduced by weighting. This in turn increases the corresponding classification accuracy. On the other hand, the features with high correlation will have the lesser variation amongst the features. Hence, we propose to assign weights to the extracted shape features in terms of '*global weights*' and '*local weights*'. In this direction, the standard deviation of the entire training sample vehicles belonging to each feature is calculated as '*global weights*'. Moreover, '*local weights*' are obtained by computing the standard deviation of all training sample vehicles belonging to each feature of the same class. Let $[W_1, W_2, W_3, ..., W_Q]$ be a set of 'Q' global weights, $[Fv_1, Fv_2, Fv_3, ..., Fv_Q]$ be a set of 'Q' features of a test vehicle and $[Ft_1^j, Ft_2^j, Ft_3^j, ..., Ft_Q^j]$ be a set of 'Q' features of the jth training sample, then the dissimilarity measure of a testing sample with respect to j^{th} in terms of '*global weights*' is computed as follow.

$$Dis(j) = \sqrt{\sum_{i=1}^{Q} W_i \times \left(Fv_i - Ft_i^j \right)^2}. \tag{1}$$

The value of the dissimilarity measure in terms of *'local weights'* is calculated by Equation 2. For computing the dissimilarity measure, let $[W_1^m, W_2^m, W_3^m, ..., W_Q^m]$ be a set of 'Q' local weights of the mth class of the vehicles, $[Fv_1, Fv_2, Fv_3, ..., Fv_Q]$ be a set of 'Q' features of a test vehicle and $[Ft_1^r, Ft_2^r, Ft_3^r, ..., Ft_Q^r]$ be a set of 'Q' features of the rth training sample in the mth class, then:

$$Dis(r) = \sqrt{\sum_{i=1}^{Q} W_i^m \times \left(Fv_i - Ft_i^r \right)^2}. \tag{2}$$

4   Experimental Results

The traffic videos used in this experiment were captured with a fixed digital camera in RGB color space mounted on a pole or other tall structure, looking down on traffic scenes. The frame rate of the videos is 25 frames per second with resolution of 320×240 pixels. In our system, the experiments are conducted on 23 real traffic videos (34,529 traffic video frames totaling about 23.02 minutes of inner city video) having different complex background, illumination, motion, position of a camera and moving direction.

Extracted vehicles are tracked using the proposed corner-based tracking approach proposed in [3] and vehicles are detected as moving vehicles if the distance of movement from the time of their appearance to the time of their disappearance in the scene is significant. However, some extracted false vehicles are also detected as moving vehicles in our experiment. In this paper, vehicles are classified into 4 categories: 1- motorcycles and bicycles, 2- cars, 3- heavy vehicles (minibus, bus and truck) and 4- any other (compliment class).

From our experimentation, 70,934 vehicles have been tracked in all the frames of the traffic video samples which also include tracking the false detected vehicles. Out of these tracked vehicles in all the frames, 858 vehicles are reconstructed. The reconstructed boundary shape of vehicles are normalized by selecting K=30 as the total number of the candidate points to be sampled along the boundary shapes presented in [4]. The system is trained and evaluated in three sets. In the first set, we consider the reconstructed vehicles belonging to the 40% of the traffic video samples used in this experiment. Similarly, we consider the reconstructed vehicles belonging to the 50% and 60% of the traffic video samples as the second and third sets respectively. The k-NN and weighted k-NN are used under varying parameter for k=1,3,5,7, and 9. From the experimental results, it is observed that the system performs well with k>=9. Furthermore, it is clear that local weights preserve the correlation exist among the values of each feature belonging to the same class and so, local weighted k-NN achieves the highest accuracy in classification. The performance evaluation of the proposed approach for classification of detected vehicles is tabulated in Table 1and shown in Fig. 4 as well. The highest classification accuracy achieved is

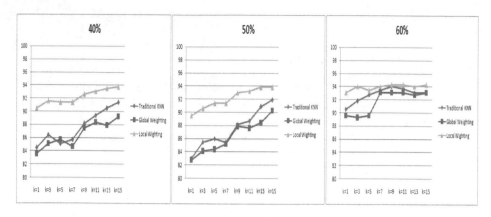

Fig. 4. Classification accuracy under varying parameters and different weighting schemes

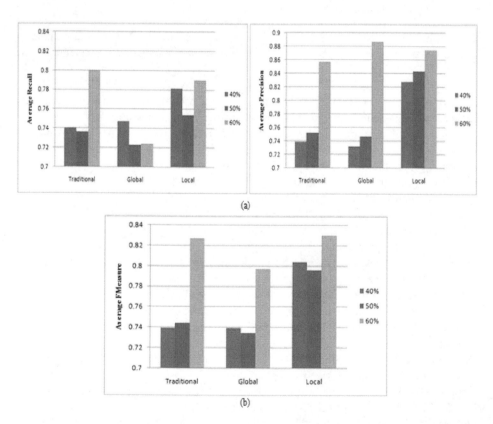

Fig. 5. (a) Average Recall and Precision for k=9 under different weighting schemes. (b) Average FMeasure for k=9 under different weighting schemes.

Table 1. Tabulated values of k-NN classifier under varying parameters and different weighting schemes

	40% of the Traffic Video Samples Total no. of Tested vehicles=463			50% of the Traffic Video Samples Total no. of Tested vehicles=371			60% of the Traffic Video Samples Total no. of Tested vehicles=317		
	Traditional	Global Weighting	Local Weighting	Traditional	Global Weighting	Local Weighting	Traditional	Global Weighting	Local Weighting
k=1	84.45	83.59	90.50	83.02	82.75	89.49	90.54	89.59	93.06
k=3	86.39	85.10	91.58	85.44	84.10	90.57	91.80	89.27	94.01
k=5	85.10	85.75	91.36	85.98	84.37	91.37	92.74	89.59	93.38
k=7	85.75	84.67	91.36	85.44	85.18	91.37	93.38	93.06	94.01
k=9	**88.12**	**87.47**	**92.66**	**88.14**	**87.87**	**93.00**	**94.01**	**93.06**	**94.32**
K=11	89.42	88.34	93.09	88.68	87.60	93.26	93.69	93.06	94.32
K=13	90.50	87.91	93.52	90.84	88.41	93.80	93.06	92.74	94.01
K=15	91.36	89.20	93.74	91.91	90.30	93.80	93.06	93.06	94.32

94.32% using local weighted k-NN with k=9 heuristically. The precision, recall and FMeasure are also computed by considering k=9. The average calculated precision, recall and FMeasure are shown in Fig. 5 respectively. From Fig. 4 and Fig. 5, it can be observed that the traditional k-NN has achieved high performance when the system has been trained by the vehicles belonging to the 60% of the traffic video samples. However, our proposed local weighted k-NN has performed well in case of training the system by using the vehicles belonging to the 40% and 50% of the traffic video samples.

To corroborate the efficacy of the proposed vehicle classification, we have compared the proposed method with the other state of the art techniques on well accepted classifier such as ICA-SVM, PCA-SVM and Eigenvehicle which is given in Table 2. In [18], the pixel values inside the bounding box of each vehicle form a basic feature vector. Independent Component Analysis (ICA) and also a Principle Component Analysis (PCA) are performed on training images to reduce the dimension of the feature space. One-class SVM is used to categorize vehicles into certain classes. The reported performance is on average of 71.12% FMeasure using ICA-SVM. It also gives an average 60.05% FMeasure using PCA-SVM. Zhang et al. [17] proposed two classification algorithms - Eigenvehicle and PCA-SVM to classify vehicles. These two methods exploit the distinguishing power of PCA at different granularities with different learning mechanisms. The performance presents an average 61.70% FMeasure using Eigenvehicle. It provides an average 64.80% FMeasure by PCA-SVM. By using the proposed approach, we accomplish on an average of 82.74% FMeasure using 9-NN after training the system by the reconstructed vehicles belonging to the 60% of the traffic video samples. The performance is also achieved on an average of 83.00% FMeasure using our proposed local weighted 9-NN.

Table 2. Comparative analysis of the proposed method with other state of the art techniques

Title	Method	Number of Frames	Frame Rate (fps)	Number of Training & Testing Vehicles	Average FMeasure in %	Comments
Vehicle Classification from Traffic Surveillance Videos at a Finer Granularity [18]	ICA & SVM	67,635	NA	150 Training Vehicles + 450 Testing Vehicles	71.12%	3 Categories: 1- Passenger Cars (PC) 2- Pickup Tracks (PK) 3- Vans and SUVs
	PCA & SVM				60.05%	
A Pca-Based Vehicle Classification Framework [17]	Eigenvehicle	2,943	5	90 Training Vehicles + 300 Testing Vehicles	61.70%	3 Categories: 1- Passenger Cars (PC) 2- Pickup Tracks (PK) 3- Vans and SUVs
	PCA & SVM				64.80%	
Proposed Method	Shape Features & k-NN	34,529	25	(60% of the Traffic Video Samples) 541 Training Vehicles + 317 Testing Vehicles	82.74%	4 categories: 1-Motorcycles and Bicycles 2- Cars 3- Heavy Vehicles (Minibus, Bus and Truck) 4- Any Other (Complement Class)
	Shape Features & Local Weighted k-NN				83%	

5   Conclusion

In this paper, we propose to overlap the boundary shapes of moving vehicles while tracking to obtain the complete boundary shapes of vehicles. A set of efficient shape features of vehicles are extracted. To increase the classification accuracy, we propose to estimate the dissimilarity measure used in k-NN classifier based on the weight features. Our proposed method is able to detect and classify moving vehicles in an uncontrolled environment having variations in illumination, motion, clutter, position of a camera and moving direction. Our proposed approach is able to deal with different types of deformations on the shape of vehicles even in cases of change in size, direction and viewpoint. Results show the robustness and efficiency of our classification model. In future, we plan to exploit other classification techniques and study the classification accuracy. We will further explore different techniques of fusion of the various classifiers to study the performance.

References

1. da Fontoura Costa, L., Cesar Jr., R.M.: Shape Analysis and Classification. CRC Press LLC, USA (2001)
2. Maurin, B., Masoud, O., Papanikolopoulos, N.: Monitoring Crowded Traffic Scenes. In: 5th Int. Conference on Intelligent Transportation Systems, pp. 19–24 (September 2002)
3. Dallalzadeh, E., Guru, D.S., Manjunath, S., Suraj, M.G.: Corner-Based Tracking of Moving Vehicles in Traffic Videos. In: 5th Indian Int. Conference on Artificial Intelligence, Tumkur (December 2011)
4. Zhang, D., Lu, G.: A Comparative Study on Shape Retrieval Using Fourier Descriptors with Different Shape Signatures. Journal of Visual Communication and Image Representation 14(1), 41–60 (2003)
5. Messclodi, S., Modena, C.M., Zanin, M.: A Computer Vision System for the Detection and Classification of Vehicles at Urban Road Intersections. Pattern Analysis and Applications 8(1), 17–31 (2005)
6. Techmer, A.: Contour-Based Motion Estimation and Object Tracking for Real-Time Applications. In: Int. Conference on Image Processing, pp. 648–651 (October 2001)
7. Ottlik, A., Nagel, H.-H.: Initialization of Model-Based Vehicle Tracking in Video Sequences of Inner-City Intersections. Int. Journal of Computer Vision 80(2), 211–225 (2008)
8. Ticiano, A.C.B., Gabriel, I.S.R., Victor, A.P.B., Marcus, V.L., Daniel, A., George, L.T., Yaeko, Y.: A New Approach to Multiple Vehicle Tracking in Intersections using Harris Corners and Adaptive Background Subtraction. In: Intelligent Vehicles Symposium Eindhoven University of Technology Eindhoven, pp. 548–553 (June 2008)
9. Kim, Z.: Real Time Object Tracking Based on Dynamic Feature Grouping with Background Subtraction. In: Computer Vision and Pattern Recognition, pp. 1–8 (June 2008)
10. Rad, R., Jamzad, M.: Real Time Classification and Tracking of Multiple Vehicles in Highways. Pattern Recognition Letters 26(10), 1597–1607 (2005)
11. Sullivan, G.D., Baker, K.D., Worrall, A.D., Attwood, C.I., Remagnino, P.M.: Model-Based Vehicle Detection and Classification Using Orthographic Approximations. Image and Vision Computing 15(8), 649–654 (1997)
12. Lai, A.H.S., Yang, N.H.C.: Vehicle-Type Identification through Automated Virtual Loop Assignment and Block-Based Direction-Biased Motion Estimation. IEEE Transactions on Intelligent Transportation Systems 1(2), 86–97 (2000)
13. Wu, W., Zhang, Q., Wang, M.: A Method of Vehicle Classification Using Models and Neural Networks. In: Vehicular Technology Conference, vol. 4, pp. 3022–3026 (May 2001)
14. Gupte, S., Masoud, O., Martin, R.F.K., Papanikolopoulos, N.P.: Detection and Classification of Vehicles. IEEE Transactions on Intelligent Transportation Systems 3(1), 37–47 (2002)
15. Hsieh, J.W., Yu, S.H., Chen, Y.S., Hu, W.F.: Automatic Traffic Surveillance System for Vehicle Tracking and Classification. IEEE Transactions on Intelligent Transportation Systems 7(2), 175–188 (2006)
16. Khammari, A., Nashashibi, F., Abramson, Y., Laurgeau, C.: Vehicle Detection Combining Gradient Analysis and AdaBoost Classification. In: 8th Int. Conference on Intelligent Transportation Systems, pp. 66–71 (September 2005)
17. Zhang, C., Chen, X., Chen, W.-B.: A Pca-Based Vehicle Classification Framework. In: 22nd Int. Conference on Data Engineering Workshops, pp. 17–26 (April 2006)
18. Chen, X., Zhang, C.: Vehicle Classification from Traffic Surveillance Videos at a Finer Granularity. In: Cham, T.-J., Cai, J., Dorai, C., Rajan, D., Chua, T.-S., Chia, L.-T. (eds.) MMM 2007. LNCS, vol. 4351, pp. 772–781. Springer, Heidelberg (2006)

Use of Augmented Reality in Serious Game for Training Medical Personnel

Arun Kumar Karthikeyan, Praveen Kumar Mani,
Suresh Kumar Balasubramaniyan, and Praveen Jelish Panneer Selvam

Blekinge Tekniska Högskola,
School of Computing (Sektionen för datavetenskap och kommunikation),
37179-Karlskrona, Sweden
{aruncs08,praveencse88,suresh.draco,
2007praveen.jelish}@gmail.com

Abstract. Serious games are games focused on learning other than pure entertainment. The potential of serious games for training of personnel is considered in many fields. The serious games differ from regular games, by helping the player to learn from the game rather than only entertainment. This paper focuses on the potential of serious game to train medical personnel and the use of augmented reality to enhance the training process. We also prove that the use of augmented reality in the serious games can improve the training of medical personnel and give them real world experience. This paper elaborates the use of serious game for training medical personal and the efficiency of using augmented reality in serious games.

Keywords: Serious games, medical education, augmented reality.

1 Introduction

Serious games differ from ordinary games in the use of learning element in the game, which helps the user to learn a process from the game. Serious games have applications in wide areas such as military, education, government, organization, healthcare, etc. The major purpose of using serious games for training is that it aids in the learning process, the use of augmented reality in the games increases the users real world experience and improve the training. The application of serious games in the field of medical education is wide. Serious games [3] are used in medical field to train and rehabilitate patients. The literature helped us to show the possibility of using serious games for training medical personal.

The main problem in medical training is that they cannot train with live patients. In such cases we can use serious games to train medical personnel. Previously serious games used for training use virtual reality to stimulate the real world experience for the users. Medical training is a very delicate operation and it needs high precision before they can operate on real patients. In this paper we propose using serious games to train medical personnel. Previous researches were done using virtual reality in serious games for training purposes. There has been efforts made to use augmented reality for gaming purpose but it has not been fully achieved.

N. Meghanathan et al. (Eds.): CCSIT 2012, Part II, LNICST 85, pp. 222–230, 2012.

Augmented reality allows the user to see the real world with virtual objects super imposed on each other. Augmented reality enhances the user's perception of the real world [8]. It provides the medical field with potential to display text based medical data graphically combined with real world data. For example consider the case of performing a CPR on a patient in this case augmented reality can be used to project life critical data simultaneously. Using traditional method of gaming in serious games may not be efficient for training in medical field. By using the augmented reality in the games we can simulate the patient virtually and the physician can operate on this virtual patient as in the real world. We propose the use of augmented reality in the serious games to improve the training and give the users a real world experience. The experience of the user is measured using the following aspects such as physical, mental, social and emotional. We finally evaluate the experience gained by the users from the game.

2   Background and Related Work

The application of serious games in the field of medical education is promising. The serious games can be used to train medical personnel in emergency conditions and other delicate things, which cannot be trained in the real world. Augmented reality can be effective when combined with serious games and used for training in emergency situations. Augmented reality integrates virtual information with real environment [1]. The application of games for training people in medical field is in practice for a long time, by using augmented reality in serious games the training process can be made more interactive and help in faster learning [1].

The use of augmented reality in serious games can increase the user's interaction with the game and make the serious game more entertaining. By using I/O controllers such as pinch gloves and 3D glasses the users can be able to feel the virtual objects in the game environment [2]. Stroke causes partial paralyses in some parts of the body; this affects the capability of the people to move around. In such cases the patients should be motivated to undergo therapy. The serious game can be used for rehabilitation of patients affected by stroke. By using this training application of serious game, it can be used for training medical personnel in important medical procedures.

The application of serious game in healthcare education is also the current research going on in the field of medical [4]. Training of medical personnel using live medical subjects is not possible in real world, so to address this problem the serious games can be designed to train them in operations. This paper focuses on using serious games for training medical personnel and the use of augmented reality in the game. The training can be made more interactive and gives the user real world experience of the procedure. Further augmented reality displays the real time medical data which can provide them the essential information during the training in the form of visual projections, such as ECG and Heart Beat sensor data. These data checks the patient's life signs during operation.

In this paper we will focus on the serious game for training medical personnel and how the use of augmented reality in the game will improve the training. Augmented reality creates innovative and interactive interfaces in serious games. Augmented reality makes new ways of interacting with serious games possible [5]. It also improves collaboration and interaction for the game environment.

3   Research Question

Based on the literature review we are able to find the application areas of serious games and how the games can be used to train personals. We formulated the following research questions.

- Can the use of Augmented Reality along with serious games improve the medical training process and user experience?
- How effective is the system (Augmented Reality along with serious games for medical training)?

The effectiveness is measured on a scale of 1 to 5 from the user's feedback about the system.

4   Research Methods

The research is conducted in the following steps to prove our hypothesis

- ❖ Discussing the possibility of using augmented reality in serious games for training medical personnel.
- ❖ Finding a proper metrics to express the effectiveness of the method.
- ❖ Performing an evaluation of our proposed system by using EGM and GSR sensors to record user experience.
- ❖ Using questionnaires to gather user experience data, to complement the result.
- ❖ Discussing the outcome of our experiment.

Research is the systematic way to find solution to the problems. We used both qualitative and quantitative research method to answer our research question.

4.1   Qualitative Methodology

The qualitative method is used for gaining needed background knowledge about serious games and training methods in serious games. Systematic literature review is done to find the possibility of using augmented reality in serious games [1] for training medical personnel. The literature review also gave us idea about the metrics that can be used for measuring the effectiveness of our proposed method. From the literature review we show that augmented reality can be used with serious games for training in medical field. We are also able to identify a metric system for measuring the effectiveness of our system. The qualitative research is done on the data collected from the literature review which is taken from the research databases like ACM, IEEE and Engineering Village.

4.2   Quantitative Methodology

The quantitative research is done by conducting experiment using the augmented reality system with a group of medical personnel and collecting the user experience from them. We would collect the parameters such as physical, mental, social and emotional experience from the medical personnel. Experiment with human subjects and a questionnaire survey are conducted. The experimentation is conducted to evaluate the system and gather user experience data using EMG [11] and GSR sensors.

The sensors are used to measure the user's excitement and arousal. It's hard to intercept what the signal means with just the sensor data, so in order to complement the result we use questionnaires to collect user experience data. The metrics we use for measuring the user experience is formulated from the literature review. The answers for the questionnaire are in the scale of 1 to 10. The result of the experiment is used to plot a learning graph.

4.3   Hypothesis

A null and alternate hypothesis is formulated based on the literature review.

Null hypothesis. The use of augmented reality in serious games for medical training will not affect or improve the training process.

Alternate hypothesis. The use of augmented reality in serious games for medical training improves the learning process and increase user interaction.

4.4   Motivation

The effectiveness of a system can be measured only by testing the system with users and gathering their feedback about the system.

The experimentation is the best method suited for finding the effectiveness of the system.

5   Qualitative Analysis

A systematic literature review is to gain background knowledge about the serious games and augmented reality.

5.1   Literature Review Synthesis

Serious Games for Upper Limb Rehabilitation Following Stroke [2] discusses about using serious games for engaging people in therapy for rehabilitation. The results of their analysis show that people are more engaged in therapy when they do it in the game. This gave us an idea of using serious games for training process of medical personnel. This will make the personnel more engaged in their training process.

A Pervasive Augmented Reality Serious Game [1] discusses about implementing augmented reality for serious games. The paper gave us an idea for using of augmented reality for training process in medical field. The authors have success fully integrated augmented reality system with a car race game. The authors have use AR tool kit [7] for integrating the augmented reality system with the game.

From the synthesis of the above two papers we are able to answer our first research question. The use of augmented reality in serious games is possible and their use will improve the training process.

The metrics system we use for determine the effectiveness is on a scale of 1 to 10. The metrics will be discussed in the questionnaire section. The average for each session for a user is calculated and a learning curve is plotted. The quantitative part deals with proving the effectiveness of the system.

6   Quantitative Analysis

6.1   Context Selection

The experiment context is using augmented reality in serious games for training medical personnel. Attributes of the experiment is how the use of augmented reality in the game affects the leaning process.

6.2   Experimentation Process

The experiment is conducted using Humansim serious game and AR tool kit. The experiment is conducted in sessions of one hour. The users are given two scenarios to work in one hour and their progress and actions are recorded. The user's emotional and mental states during the session are also recorded by using EMG and GSR sensors [11]. After the experiment the actions of the user are reviewed and a report is generated. After the session the user is presented with a questionnaire. The user's answers are recorded and they are compared with the report to find the outcome of the training. The need for using the questionnaire apart from the experiment is to get a feedback from the user to improve the system further.

Table 1. Experiment plan

Session Name	Session Time	Events
Session 1	30 mins	Scenario 1
Session 2	30 mins	Scenario 2
Questionnaire	10 – 20 mins	Answer the questionnaire

6.3   Preparation

Based on the qualitative research we formulated the questions and they are reviewed. The necessary training is given to the participants, to familiarize them with the augmented reality system.

6.4   Execution

The execution of the experiment is done after doing the basic preparations. The participants were made to play the game and their collective user experience in gathered from them using the questionnaire.

6.5   Instrumentation and Serious Game Used

The experiment is conducted using Humansim serious games and augmented reality toolkit. Humansim is a serious game designed by Virtual Heroes Inc for medical training [9]. The AR toolkit is used for building the augmented reality controls for the serious game. The AR toolkit also provides support for the use of controls such as AR glasses and gloves that is used to interact with the game environment [6]. The game is then tested with a group of participants allowing them to train with the game. The player's arousal and excitement levels are measured using the EMG and GSR sensors. The signals are recorded and stored for future reference and analysis.

6.6   Quantitative Questionnaire

The questionnaire is an inexpensive way to collect data from the participants in the experiment. The questionnaire is used to effectively gather data about the overall performance and the game play experience of the users. There are different stages involved in preparing a questionnaire. To make the questionnaire effective every step must be designed carefully [10].

    i. Objective of the survey.

    ii. Determining the Participants group.

    iii. Writing the questionnaire.

    iv. Presenting the questionnaire to the participants.

    v. Interpretation of result.

i. Objective. The objective of this questionnaire is to gather the user experience after playing the game using augmented reality. The questionnaire collects information about the game play experience? How real does the game appear to you? Etc.

ii. Determining participants group. The participants are selected based on their previous medical training.

iii. Writing the questionnaire. The questionnaire is designed in way so that we can capture the quantitative data of game play experience the user had while playing the game. The questionnaire is a written in a closed format where the user can select an option. The options for the question are in the range of 1 to 5.

iv. Presenting the questionnaire. The questionnaire is presented to the users of the system after the experiment session. This is done to capture the user experience after using the system.

v. Interpretation of result. The result collected from the user is then evaluated and a rating is prepared for the each user. From the overall rating from the users, we then evaluate the efficiency of the system for training medical personnel.

The metrics used

The metrics used in the questions is in the scale of 1 to 5.
   There are also some yes or no questions in the questionnaire.
   Each value has a corresponding meaning

1 - Very bad
2 – bad
3 – Satisfactory
4 – good
5 – Very good.

6.6.1   Questionnaire for the Survey. The following is the list of questions that had asked to the medical personnel participated in the experiment.

1. Have you trained previously using augmented reality systems?
2. How would you rate your level of involvement in the game compared to your previous training methods?
3. How well did the training method help you in training process?
4. Rate the quality of the game environment?
5. Breath of learning outcome for serious games using augmented reality and serious games with other methods.
6. How real does the game environment appear to you?
7. How would you rate your overall experience with the learning method using augmented reality?
8. Do you prefer augmented reality system over other training methods?

7   Hypothesis Testing

From the experiment conducted we are able to gather data from the users about their experience with the system.

Null hypothesis. Based on the data from the users we are able to plot a learning curve and show that the use of augmented reality in serious games in medical training improves the learning process. Therefore the null hypothesis is not valid.

Alternate hypothesis. The learning curve below shows that the learning process of the participants increases gradually. We are able to prove that the use of augmented reality in serious games for medical training will improve the learning process and overall user experience. Thus alternate hypothesis is proved.

   The learning curve is slow during the initial trail session but once the user gets familiar with the system the learning curve raises rapidly which shows that the use of augmented reality improves the learning process.

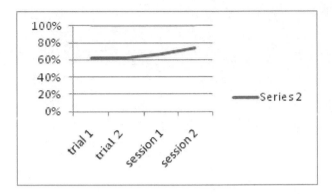

Fig. 1. The learning curve for one participant

8   Recommendations

From the result experiment above we recommend the following:

- The use of augmented reality in serious games will improve the learning process and also allows the user to interact with the game environment freely.

The augmented reality systems are not fully developed for serious games we have to adapt the existing augmented reality systems for serious games.

9   Conclusions

The result of the experiment shows that the use of augmented reality in serious games for training medical personnel will improve the learning process. The users also are excited when they use the system from the EMG and GSR data we collected. The use of augmented reality in games gives the user a real world feeling about the environment as the game elements are superimposed on real world objects. The interaction of the user with the game is improved greatly. We are able to prove our hypothesis from the research that the use of augmented reality in serious games for medical training improves the learning process and user interaction.

9.1   Future Work

Further work is needed to enhance the visual elements of the game to make it more realistic. The current augmented reality system gives the user only two degree of freedom we plan to improve the system to give the users three degrees of freedom.

References

1. Liarokapis, F., Macan, L., Malone, G., Rebolledo-Mendez, G., De Freitas, S.: A Pervasive Augmented Reality Serious Game. In: 2009 Conference in Games and Virtual Worlds for Serious Applications, VS-GAMES 2009, March 23-March 24, pp. 148–155. IEEE Computer Society, Coventry (2009)
2. Burke, J.W., McNeill, M.D.J., Charles, D.K., Morrow, P.J., Crosbie, J.H., McDonough, S.M.: Serious Games for Upper Limb Rehabilitation Following Stroke., University of Ulster, Coleraine, Northern Ireland
3. Serious Games Initiative, http://www.seriousgames.org
4. Tashiro, J., PhD, BSN, RN: What Really Works in Serious Games for Healthcare Education, University of Ontario Institute of Technology
5. Creswell, W.: Research Design - Qualitative, Quantitative and Mixed Method Approaches. Sage Publications (2002)
6. Susi, T., Johannesson, M.: Serious Games-An Overview, Technical Report HS- IKI -TR-07-001, School of Humanities and Informatics, University of Skövde, Sweden
7. ARToolKit,   http://www.ex-ch.com/udk/courses/2010-ws-Digital-Class/AR_Technology_Survey/ARToolKit%20Home%20Page.pdf (accessed: May 26, 2011)
8. Kharrazi, H., Faiola, A., Defazio, J.: Healthcare Game Design: Behavioral Modeling of Serious Gaming Design for Children with Chronic Diseases. Indiana University Purdue University Indianapolis, School of Informatics, 535 W. Michigan St., Indianapolis, Indiana 46202
9. Virtual Heroes, http://www.virtualheroes.com/healthcare.asp
10. Questionnaire, http://www.cc.gatech.edu/classes/cs6751_97_winter/Topics/quest-design
11. Bowker, C.: An Investigation into Neural Interfacing, using an EMG Device in Virtual Reality (2006)

Encouraging the Usage of Neural Network in Video Text Detection Application

Suresh Kumar Balasubramaniyan, Praveen Kumar Mani,
Arun Kumar Karthikeyan, and Ganesh Shankar

Blekinge Tekniska Högskola,
School of Computing (Sektionen för datavetenskap och kommunikation),
37179-Karlskrona, Sweden
{suresh.draco,praveencse88,aruncs08,gshindi}@gmail.com

Abstract. The video text detection is an expert system in which we study how the performance can be enhanced by adding neural network. The implementation of video text detection using algorithm based approach [9] is taken and compared with the neural networks based implementation [11]. A standard protocol [10] for evaluating the video text detection approach is taken and its metrics are used for the comparative study. With this comparison, the evaluation of both the systems for better performance can be done. The conclusions necessary for enhancing the usage of neural network is drawn based on the comparison study. The paper is about encouraging the use of neural network in an expert system (Video Text Detection Application).

Keywords: Neural networks, Expert system, OCR (Optical Character Recognition) and video text detection.

1 Introduction

The expert system [5] is basically a computer program which repeatedly possesses different questions each with a yes or no answer. This process is almost like following through a maze which has many left or right turns. It is done by giving yes or no answer for turning right or left. Usually expert systems start with a small base of information. There are many thousands of expert systems commercially available which exist in applications such as medicine, chemistry and engineering field. The already known limitation of expert system is that its inability to learn new knowledge on its own. But a new knowledge can be added from the outside manually to the knowledge base [6].

The neural network system "video text detection [11]" and an expert system "overlay text detection [9]" are taken to compare the performance of the video text detection. Both systems use different architecture to detect the text from the video. The following paragraphs briefly discuss about existing video text detection methods and how the performance, efficiency etc can be improved.

Text detection is essential to video information retrieval and indexing. Current methods cannot handle diverse contrast or fixed in a complex background. To handle

N. Meghanathan et al. (Eds.): CCSIT 2012, Part II, LNICST 85, pp. 231–240, 2012.

these difficulties, this paper propose a capable text detection approach, which is based on invariant features, such as edge strength, edge density, and horizontal distribution. Text in video is an extremely compact and an accurate clue for video indexing and summarization. Most of the video text detection and extraction techniques have guess on background contrast, text color, and font style. But only few methods can handle multi-language texts well because various languages have various writing style. New results on a different number of video images and comparisons with other methods are reported in detail.

There are many researches going on text detection for document analysis and text based video indexing. Text recognition methods are typically either connected component-based or texture based. In the connected component-based process it can perceive text regions efficiently, however there are numerous difficulties for other graphical objects; this is basically happen because in digital video text is embed in complex backgrounds and the inspection that texts in video images contains distinct texture properties. Through these explanations, text detection can be posed as texture classification problem where the exact problem knowledge is available prior to classification. Video text detection presents a number of challenges since the properties of text can vary. For example, the text in video varies considerably in font size and style; the intensity of text pixels can be higher (normal text) or lower (reverse text) than that of background; and the text can be distorted or blurred due to sensor properties or due to camera or object motion. Other problems, such as lighting and background variation, make the task even more difficult. Previous work on text detection has focused on the detection of graphical text superimposed on a video frame [1, 2, 3, and 4]. Although these methods are able to detect graphical text under certain constraints, it is much harder to achieve good performance for scene text, where those constraints are usually not satisfied.

2   Background and Related Work

In video text detection, there is a problem of text location in digital video as supervised texture classification. To overcome this issue support vector machine (SVM) is used for the texture classifier. The SVM is considered as the expert system application and compared with the neural network based text detection method [12].

To detect texts in an image, SVM shifts the detection window over all locations in the image. This will only detect texts at a single scale, however. To achieve multi-scale detection, SVM incrementally resize the image and run the detection window over each of these resized images. The experiment was performed on 2500 key frames with a size of 320x240 manually selected from 200 Korean news archives and 200 commercials. SVM method detected 94.5 % of the text regions in a set of 1,500 test images with false-detection rate of only 4.2%. Errors occurred primarily because of low resolution. The same experiment is done with neural networks (NNs) [13]. The network has two hidden layers of sizes 50 and 30, respectively and was trained by back propagation algorithm minimizing mean squared error. To avoid the local minima, reported results with NN was obtained by training 10 networks with different initial weights, and selecting the minimal error over all the results.

In contrast to the previous approaches where either neural network or pure expert system is used to Video Text Detection application, we enforce the usage of both neural network and expert system. Our idea is based on the observation that text regions typically are rich of corners and edges and corners and edge points are nearly uniformly distributed in text areas. There are four features we used in this approach: corner density, edge density, the ratio of vertical edge density and horizontal edge density, and center offset ratio of edges [14].

The comparison of the algorithm (HUA) with the other three text detection schemes using our PE protocol on the above mentioned testing data is done. The following criteria's are mainly analyzed; clips, textboxes, missed textboxes, false alarms, detection rate. The first scheme (denoted by QI) for comparison is from "Integrating visual, audio and text analysis for news video" [15], the second one (XI) is from "A video text detection and recognition system" [16], and the third one (XI-2) is an improved version of the second one, in which detection results in consecutive frames are used to enhance the final performance. The evaluation results of the four algorithms are listed in the table [10], algorithm HUA produce better detection results than the other three algorithms.

3   Research Question

At the end of the systematic literature review, we formulated a research question for the comparison study to reveal the usage of neural network and its improvement.

R.Q.1: Which of the system among feed-forward neural network and expert system based on overlay procedure has better performance on video text detection?

We are making a protocol based comparison with the help of metrics proposed by Xian-Sheng Hua [10]. Here we are taking feed-forward neural network based video text detection proposed by Huiping Li and David Doermann [11], and comparing its performance with the algorithm based system proposed by Wonjun Kim and Changick Kim [9].

4   Implementation of Video Text Detection Using Neural Network

This system is proposed by Huiping Li and David Doermann [11]. Here the architecture uses feed-forward neural network for the classification process in the text detection process. The architecture needs the external training from the user by providing the ground-truth of the video text. The neural network is tuned up with the training process and further it performs the detection process without the manual help from the user side.

4.1   Training Process

The architecture uses external tool for generating ground-truth values for the sample set of video frame images. The input is stored in the text file and given to the neural network. The main training sample is split into text and non-text samples. Text sample is given as the sample digital frames images with fixed window values showing the blocks in which the text and the background is defined. The non text samples are given with the blocks of background textures in the same window. The proposed architecture uses a four step algorithm to select the text blocks in the sample window given. After the manual training from the user side, the architecture is trained with the bootstrap method without the user intervention.

4.2   Classification Process in the Neural Network

The text block and the non text block is classified using binary notation with 1 to represent text block and 0 to represent non-text block. It results in the binary frame with 1's and 0's. The parameter that increases the complexity in the detection process is the skew angle. It is the angle between the text box axis and the text direction's vertical axis. It is 90 degree when we are dealing with the straight letters.

5   Implementation of Video Text Detection Using Expert System on Overlay Text

The architecture proposed in this system [9] is an algorithm based approach that determines overlay text from complex background. The explanation to the architecture proposed in this paper is as follows. It is almost intended to determine the subtitles of the video scenes. The following is the procedure or algorithm implemented in this implementation.

5.1   Overlay Text Region Detection

The overlay text will be the opposite texture to the background that is, if the background is dark then overlay text is bright. It is determined that the color of the text changes logarithmically with the color of the overlay. The transition map is found in this way for all frames.

$$d(T_n, T_{n-3}) = \sum_{(x,y) \in T} (T_n(x,y) \otimes T_{n-3}(x,y))$$
$$if(d(T_n, T_{n-3}) < th)TR_n = TR_{n-3}$$
$$\text{otherwise, find new } TR_n$$

Where T_n and T_{n-3} represents the transition map value of nth and $(n-3)^{rd}$ frame respectively. Then if the values of nth frame and $(n-3)^{rd}$ frame are same then overlay value is set to be 0 and 1 if the values are different. Similarly the value of TR in the formula is the detected overlay text regions in the nth and $(n-3)^{rd}$ frame.

5.2   Overlay Text Region Extraction

Gray scale text region is given as input to the color polarity computation and with that the color polarity is determined. The inside region is filled with pixels and the final text is extracted out.

6   Customized Protocol for Performance Evaluation of Video Text Detection Method

In this section we have gathered data for formulating a protocol based on which both the implementation taken for comparison will be evaluated.

The performance metrics are briefly explained in this section. The parameters are taken from the protocol defined by Xian-Sheng Hua [10]. The limitation in this protocol is that they are not categorized, which when categorized can be enhancing the comparison process. In this paper we are customizing this protocol as a category based protocol as follows, (this classification is in context with the process where this parameter can be evaluated in the video text detection procedure).

- Textbox detection
  - Textbox Location.
    - In the given video frame or the image, the text location represents the co-ordinates(x,y) of the textbox
  - Textbox Height.
  - Textbox Width.
- Text property
  - Text String.
  - Text Length.
  - Character Height Variation.
- Detection complexity
  - Skew Angle.
    - It is the angle between the x-axis of the image and the horizontal axis of the text block.
  - Background Complexity.
  - Colour and Texture.
  - String Density.
    - It is width of the string or text box.
  - Contrast.
  - Recognisability Index.
    - It varies from 0 to 3 which vary according to human recognisability.
- Accuracy
  - False Alarm Rate.
  - Detection Rate.
- Processing speed.

7   Research Implementation

The neural network system "video text detection [11]" and an expert system "overlay text detection [9]" are taken to compare the performance of the -video text detection. Both systems use different architecture to detect the text from the video. The parameters used by the system are Textbox Location, Textbox Height, Textbox Width, Text String, Text Length, Character Height Variation, Skew angle, Color and Texture, Background complexity, String density, Contrast and Recognisability Index. These parameters are determined by both the neural network and an expert system, but at the different stage of video text detection architecture.

7.1   Video Text Detection System, a Neural Network System

First the architecture is analyzed to find at which stage the parameters that determine the performance of this system are calculated [11]. In this system the training process is initially conducted to analyze the background of the image with the text. Then the first phase of the architecture is feature extraction. In this phase the text length, character variation, color and texture of the text parameters are determined from this phase. Next phase is classification; here textbox location, textbox height, textbox width, background complexity and contrast color from the background are analyzed. Next phase is skew estimation, here skew angle-the angle which formed between the vertical line and inclination of the text. Finally text block is generated.

7.2   Overlay Text Detection System Based on Automated Testing, an Expert System

Overlay text detection system based on automated testing, an expert system is analyzed as follows. First the architecture is analyzed [9] to find at which stage the parameters that determine the performance of this system are calculated. The system has Overlay Text Region Detection and Overlay Text Extraction. In overlay text region detection phase, the text region that is textbox parameters which covers the text is found. They are Textbox Location, Textbox Height and Textbox Width. Transition map is generated and then candidate region is extracted from the generated map. Then the overlay text region is determined, refined and updated. Then in text extraction phase the Text String, Text Length, Character Height Variation, Skew angle, Color and Texture and Background complexity parameters are determined. Especially in color polarity computation phase the color, texture and background complexity are determined.

7.3   Performance Evaluation

7.3.1   Goal

- To have comparison study on both neural and expert oriented implementation of video text detection application.

- To find in which area which implementation shows high performance. (Efficiency, speed etc)

In the analysis procedure we analyzed the system to determine in which stage of the implementation the parameters described in the protocol can be found. The values of each parameter for both the implementations are obtained separately from [8], [9], [10] and [11]. With the idea from the analysis procedure, we compared the parameters of both implementations as follows,

System 1: Implementation using neural networks [11].
System 2: Implementation using expert system with algorithm based approach [9].

7.3.2 Experiment Explanation

The parameters like recognizability index and skew angle are the properties of the text that explain how difficult the text is to be identified. We are going to compare this parameter with each implementation using the false alarm rate and processing speed. The false alarm rate is the number of failed detection process done by the system and processing speed is the time taken for the process. Now false alarm rate of implementation of system 1 is plotted in 2D graph along with the false alarm rate of system 2. With this the analysis of the performance of each system can be made.

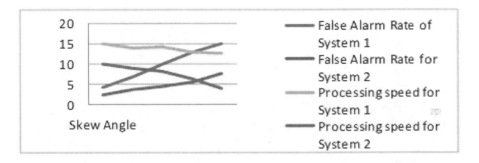

Fig. 1. Evaluation based on Skew Angle

In this analysis the parameters false alarm rate and processing speed (Frames per second) is evaluated by increasing the skew angle (X-axis). The increase in the skew angle means, according to the protocol defined it increases the complexity of the detection process.

Analysis Report. Neural network based implementation shows less in efficiency based on false alarm rate that is higher false alarm rate and expert system based on algorithm based approach shows higher efficiency that is lower false alarm rate. There is a variation at the top of the curve used to denote false alarm rate of system 1, it is because the neural network produces less false alarm rate with the high amount training.

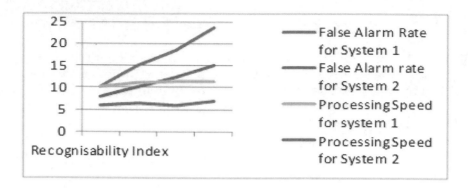

Fig. 2. Evaluation based on Recognisability Index

In this analysis report we are deducing the two performance evaluation criteria False Alarm Rate and Processing Speed with the help of Recognisability Index.

Analysis Report. It is to the report generated with the evaluation using Skew Angle. And also the other complexity detection parameters also produced the same result as the skew angle wherein the neural network based system produces better processing time and higher False Alarm Rate.

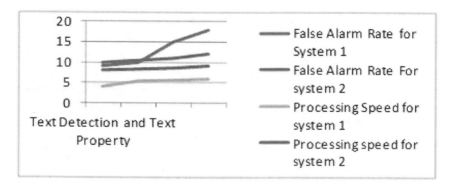

Fig. 3. Evaluation based on Text Detection and text property

Analysis Report. The performance with reference to the text detection parameters and the text property parameters of both the system shows similar variations of skew angle report.

All the above findings are obtained individually from [9] and [11] which are the different implementations of video text detection application.

8   Conclusions and Result of the Research

The performance of neural network in the expert system video based text detection is deduced with comparison to a similar expert system with the same goal but in algorithm based approach. The evaluation resulted to the conclusion that usage of neural network enhances the performance in terms to processing speed considerably.

The neural network makes the classification faster than the algorithm oriented approach. But when taking accuracy as criteria for the performance, usage of neural network drops down. The accuracy decreases in the neural based system with the increase in the complexity involved in the text detection process. But with the proper and required training given to the neural network oriented system, efficiency can also be improved.

To enhance the usage of neural network in expert system, the training process in which the frame is given as sample is to be enhanced with appropriate learning method. In the system we took for comparison the training method involves ground-truth value which does not significantly increase the accuracy as similar to the algorithm based approach.

Finally, to enhance the usage of neural network in expert systems, we should increase the accuracy instead of processing speed. With the good training method added to the neural network based implementation, efficiency factor also can be increased. Because, accuracy is more important than processing speed in terms of efficiency.

References

1. Kim, H.: Efficient Automatic Text Location Method and Content-based Indexing and Structuring of Video Database. Journal of Visual Communication and Image Representation 7, 336–344 (1996)
2. Sato, T., Kanade, T., Hughes, E., Smith, M.: Video OCR for digital news archives. In: Proceedings of IEEE Workshop on Content-Based Access to Image and Video Databases (1998)
3. Lienhart, R., Stuber, F.: Automatic text recognition in digital videos. In: Proceedings of ACM Multimedia, pp. 11–20 (1996)
4. Shim, J., Dorai, C., Bolle, R.: Automatic text extraction from video for content-based annotation and retrieval. In: Proceedings of ICPR, pp. 618–620 (1998)
5. Carretero-Diaz, L.E., Lopez-Sanchez, J.I.: The Importance Of Artificial Intelligence-Expert Systems- In Computer Integrated Manufacturing. In: Proceedings of the International Conference on Engineering and Technology Management, IEMC 1998. Pioneering New Technologies: Management Issues and Challenges in the Third Millennium (Cat. No.98CH36266), pp. 295–301 (1998)
6. McCarthy, J.: Generality in artificial intelligence. Commun. ACM 30(12), 1030–1035 (1987)
7. Carling, A.: Introducing Neural Networks. SIGMA PRESS-Wilmslow, United Kingdom
8. Anderson, M.F., Cohen, M.E., Hudson, D.L.: Combination of a Neural Network Model and a Rule-Based Expert System to Determine Efficacy of Medical Testing Procedures. In: Proceedings of the Annual International Conference of the IEEE Engineering in Medicine and Biology Society, Images of the Twenty-First Century (Cat. No.89CH2770-6), vol. 6, pp. 1991–1992 (1989)
9. Changick, K., Wonjun, K.: A New Approach for Overlay Text Detection and Extraction from Complex Video Scene. IEEE Transactions on Image Processing (February 2009); Sponsored by IEEE signal processing society

10. Zhang, H.-J., Liu, W., Hua, X.-S.: An Automatic Performance Evaluation Protocol for Video Text Detection Algorithms. IEEE Transactions on Circuits and Systems for Video Technology (April 2004)
11. Doermann, D., Li, H.: A video Text Detection System Based on Automated Training. In: Proceedings 15th International Conference on Pattern Recognition (2000)
12. Shin, C.S., Kim, K.I., Park, M.H., Kim, H.J.: Support Vector Machine-Based Text Detection in Digital Video. In: Proceedings of the 2000 IEEE Signal Processing Society Workshop Neural Networks for Signal Processing X, vol. 2, pp. 634–641 (2000)
13. Jeong, K.Y., Jung, K., Kim, E.Y., Kim, H.J.: Neural Network-Based Text Location for News Video Indexing. In: Proc. ICIP 1999, Japan (1999)
14. Hua, X.-S., Chen, X.-R., Wenyin, L., Zhang, H.-J.: Automatic location of text in video frames. In: Proc. ACM Multimedia 2001 Workshops: Multimedia Information Retrieval (MIR 2001), Ottawa, ON, Canada, October 5, pp. 24–27 (2001)
15. Qi, W., et al.: Integrating Visual, Audio and Text Analysis for News Video. In: Proc. Int. Conf. Image Processing (ICIP 2000), Vancouver, BC, Canada (2000)
16. Xi, J., Hua, X.-S., Chen, X.-R., Wenyin, L., Zhang, H.-J.: A Video Text Detection and Recognition System. In: Proc. 2001 IEEE Int. Conf. Multimedia and Expo. (ICME 2001), Tokyo, Japan, August 22-25, pp. 1080–1083 (2001)
17. Ye, J., Huang, L.-L., Hao, X.L.: Neural Network Based Text Detection in Videos Using Local Binary Patterns. In: Chinese Conference on Pattern Recognition, CCPR 2009, November 4-6, pp. 1–5 (2009), doi:10.1109/CCPR.2009.5343973
18. Taylor, G.W., Wolf, C.: Reinforcement Learning for Parameter Control of Text Detection in Images from Video Sequences. In: Proceedings of the International Conference on Information and Communication Technologies: From Theory to Applications, April 19-23, pp. 517–518 (2004), doi:10.1109/ICTTA.2004.1307859
19. Li, M., Wang, C.: An Adaptive Text Detection Approach in Images and Video Frames. In: IEEE International Joint Conference on Neural Networks, IJCNN 2008. IEEE World Congress on Computational Intelligence, June 1-8, pp. 72–77 (2008)
20. Li, H., Doermann, D., Kia, O.: Automatic Text Detection and Tracking in Digital Video. IEEE Transactions on Image Processing 9(1), 147–156 (2000)
21. Li, H., Doermann, D.: A Video Text Detection System Based on Automated Training. In: Proceedings of the 15th International Conference on Pattern Recognition, vol. 2, pp. 223–226 (2000)

A Novel Face Recognition Method Using PCA, LDA and Support Vector Machine

U. Raghavendra[1], P.K. Mahesh[2], and Anjan Gudigar[2]

[1] Manipal Institute of Technology, Manipal, India
raghu_u109@rediffmail.com
[2] Department of Electronics and communication, M.I.T.E., Moodbidri, India
{mahesh24pk,anjangudigar83}@gmail.com

Abstract. Here an efficient and novel approach was considered as a combination of PCA, LDA and support vector machine. This method consists of three steps: I) dimension reduction using PCA, ii) feature extraction using LDA, iii) classification using SVM. Combination of PCA and LDA is used for improving the capability of LDA when new samples of images are available and SVM is used to reduce misclassification caused by not linearly separable classes.

Keywords: Dimension Reduction, Feature Extraction, Classification, Support Vector Machine.

1   Introduction

The face is the primary focus of attention in the society. The ability of human beings to remember and recognize faces is quite robust. Automation   of this process finds practical application in various tasks such as criminal identification, security systems and human-computer interactions [6]. Various attempts to implement this process have been made over the years. In the last years face recognition has become one of the most challenging tasks in the pattern recognition field. The recognition of the face is very important for much application such as video surveillance, retrieval of an identity from a data base for criminal investigation and forensic application.

Appearance based approaches gives the most successful solution since it operate directly on appearance or images of face objects and process the image as two dimensional space. These method extract features to optimally represent faces belongs to a class and separate faces from different classes. Ideally, it is desirable to use only features having high separability power while ignoring the rest. Most effort in the literature has been focused mainly on developing feature extraction methods and employing power full classifiers. The normal approach in feature extraction is representing the data in a higher dimensional space to lower dimensional space. Principal component analysis (PCA), linear discriminant analysis (LDA) [2] and discrete cosine transform (DCT) are three main techniques used for data reduction and feature extraction in the appearance-based approaches. DCT, Eigen-faces and fisher-faces built based on these three techniques, have been proved to be very successful.

DCT remove the some high frequency details and in this way reduce the size of images.LDA algorithm selects features that are most effective for class separability

N. Meghanathan et al. (Eds.): CCSIT 2012, Part II, LNICST 85, pp. 241–249, 2012.
© Institute for Computer Sciences, Social Informatics and Telecommunications Engineering 2012

while PCA selects features important for class representation. A study has demonstrated that PCA might outperform LDA when the number of samples per class is small and in the case of training set with a large number of samples, the LDA still outperform the PCA. Compared to the PCA method, the computation of the LDA is much higher and PCA is less sensitive to different training data sets. Oftenly LDA is not applicable for the face images with high dimensional and therefore we deprive from its advantage to find effective features for class separability.

To resolve this problem we combine the PCA and LDA methods, by applying PCA to pre-processed face images, we get low dimensionality images which are ready for applying LDA. Oftenly intention is to decrease the rate of change of error. We implement a Support vector machines (SVMs) to classify face images based on its computed LDA features.

2   Related Work

As we know dimensionality reduction is a very essential part in real time processing. The most commonly used techniques are PCA and LDA. The following section gives a brief review of these methods.

A. Principal Component Analysis

Let $\{ X1 , X2.......XN \}, X \in \Re_n$ be N samples from L classes $\{W1, W2...WL\}$, and $P(X)$ their mixture distribution [1]. Let us assume the probabilities $P(Wi), i = 1, 2, 3..., L$ are known in advance. Now consider m as a mean vector and Σ is the covariance matrix of samples. Now, find out a subspace by calculating its basis vector which corresponds to maximum variance direction in the space. This sub space is very essential and accurate for presenting original data with minimum error. Consider a linear $n \times p$ transformation matrix, it is possible to map original n dimensional space on to the p dimensional feature subspace where $p < n$. Now we can define a new feature vector $y_i = \Re^n$ as

$$y_i = (\Phi^p_{PCA})^t X_i , i = 1, ..., N \tag{1}$$

And it has proved that in Φ^p_{PCA}, if Eigen vector of covariance matrix corresponds to p largest Eigen values and which are in decreasing order, then a new space is available for data representation.

$$\hat{\Sigma} = (\textstyle\sum_{i=1}^{N}(x_i - \hat{m})(x_i - \hat{m})^t)/(N - 1) \tag{2}$$

Where m in (2) can be estimated by:

$$m_k = m_{k-1} - \eta(X_k - m_{k-1}) \tag{3}$$

Where m_k is estimation of mean value at kth iteration and x_k is the kth input image. PCA is also a very popular method for extracting features for data representation. So the transfer function of the PCA consists of Eigen vectors of covariance matrix [7]. The incremental estimation of the covariance matrix can be done using following equation.

$$\Sigma_k = \Sigma_{k-1} - \eta_k(X_k X_k^t - \Sigma_{k-1}) \tag{4}$$

Where Σ_k the estimation of the covariance matrix at k-th iteration is X_k is the incoming input vector and η_k is the learning rate.

B. Linear Discriminant Analysis

In addition to dimensionality reduction, LDA searches the directions for maximum discrimination of classes [2, 4]. By defining within-class and between-class matrices this goal achieved, A within-class scatter matrix is the scatter of the samples around their respective class means m_i:

$$\Sigma_w = \sum_{i=1}^{L} P(w_i)E[(X - m_i)(X - m_i)^t|w_i] + \sum_{i=1}^{L} P(w_i)\Sigma_l \tag{5}$$

Where Σ_i denotes the covariance matrix of i-th class. The between-class scatter matrix is the scatter of class means m_i around the mixture mean **m**, and is given by:

$$\Sigma_b = \sum_{i=1}^{L} P(w_i)(m_i - m)(m_i - m)^t \tag{6}$$

Regardless of class assignments, Finally,the scatter matrix is the covariance of all samples and is defined by:

$$\Sigma = E[(X - m_i)(X - m_i)^t] = \Sigma_W + \Sigma_b \tag{7}$$

In LDA, the optimum linear transform is composed of $p(\leq n)$ eigenvectors of $\Sigma^{-1}{}_w$ Σ_b corresponding to its p largest Eigen values. Alternatively $\Sigma^{-1}{}_w\Sigma$ can be used for LDA. Simple analysis shows that both $\Sigma^{-1}{}_w\Sigma_b$ and $\Sigma^{-1}{}_w\Sigma$ have the same Eigen vector matrices. In general, Σ_b is not a covariance matrix, because Σ_b is not full rank and, hence we shall use Σ in place of Σ_b. The solution of the generalized Eigen value problem ,$\Sigma\Phi_{LDA}=\Sigma_w\Phi_{LDA} \Lambda$, where Λ is the generalized eigenvalue matrix is equivalent to The computation of the eigenvector matrix Φ_{LDA} of $\Sigma^{-1}{}_w \Sigma$. Under assumption of positive definite matrix Σ_w, there exists a symmetric $\Sigma^{-1/2}{}_w$ such that the problem can be reduced to a symmetric Eigen value problem.

$$\Sigma_W^{-1/2}\Sigma\Sigma_W^{-1/2}\Psi = \Psi\Lambda \tag{8}$$

Where

$$\Psi = \Sigma_W^{1/2}\Phi_{LDA} \tag{9}$$

3   Proposed Methodology

The proposed face recognition method consists of four separate parts:

i) Dimensionality reduction using PCA
ii) Feature extraction for class separability using LDA
iii) Classification using support vector machine.

In the next sections, we describe role of each part.

A. Dimensionality Reduction

In this section we have used cropped input image of size 40×40; as a result the input of this stage is a pre-processed 1600×1 vector. Here these vectors are used to estimate the covariance matrix. The significant eigenvectors of the covariance matrix are computed.

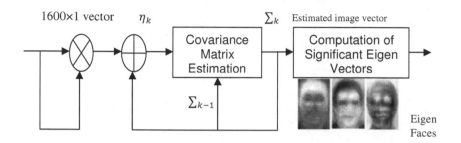

Fig. 1. Dimensionality reduction Block diagram

Computational complexity increased in this step and next step. As number of Eigen-vectors are increased to achieve the accuracy that we need. In this stage, we computed 50 most significant Eigen-vectors and related Eigen-faces. By projection of every input image on these Eigen faces, they will convert to reduce size 50×1 vectors which will be go to LDA feature extraction part. Fig. 1 shows the estimation and computation of both the Eigen-faces. We repeated our experiment with different values of significant Eigen-vectors and choose them equal to 20, 30, and 40 and 50 and compared the performance of the proposed face recognition method.

B. LDA Feature Extraction

Outputs of dimension reduction part are 50×1 vectors which are used to construct within class scatter matrix and covariance matrix. As mentioned in section 2, significant eigenvectors of $\sum^{-1}_w \sum$ can use for separability of classes in addition to dimension reduction. Using 50×1 vectors, $\sum^{-1}_w \sum$ computed and then Eigen vectors related to the greater Eigen values are selected. In our experiment we considered 10 classes, therefore there are 9 major eigenvectors (Fisher faces) associated with non-zero Eigen values which have separability capability. It is clear that extracting all of 9 LDA features increase the discriminatory power of the method. Therefore, this section produces 9×1 vectors. Fig. 2 demonstrates operation of this part, at first covariance and within class scatter matrices are estimated and then significant eigenvector of $\sum^{-1}_w \sum$ are computed (Fisher Faces).

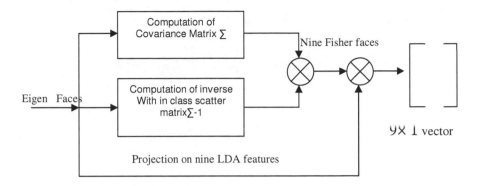

Fig. 2. Generation of Fisher faces

C. Support vector machines (SVMs)

Output of the LDA, which is nothing but nine fisher face is given as the input to the support vector machine as in Fig 3. Then SVM generates support vector for the given nine fisher faces by projecting it to a higher dimension space using Gaussian kernel.

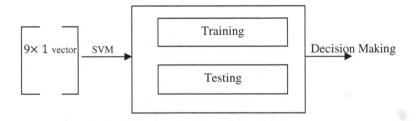

Fig. 3. Classification using Support Vector Machine

For the training process of SVMs, we used the library LIBSVMS [8]. However, in many cases, the data cannot be separated by linear function. A solution is to map the input data into a higher dimensional space as shown in Fig.4. Due to the fact that the training data are used through a dot product, if there was a "kernel function" so that we satisfy K(x_i , x_j) =(ϕ (x_i) , ϕ (x_j)), we can avoid computing ϕ_x explicitly and use the kernel function K(x_i , x_j) .we have used a Gaussian kernel as follows:

$$K(X_i, X_j) = e^{\frac{-||X_i - X_j||^2}{2\sigma^2}} \tag{10}$$

$$f(x) = sgn\left(\sum_{i=1}^{N_s} \alpha_i y_i K(s_i, x) + b\right) \tag{11}$$

Where N_s the number of support is vectors , and s_i are the support vectors.

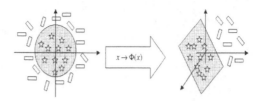

Fig. 4. Mapping of data to a higher dimensional space

Here proper tuning is required for value of σ,either by using Manual tuning or brute force search. An brute force technique could involve stepping through a range of values for σ, perhaps in a gradient ascent optimization, seeking optimal performance of a model with training data. Although this approach is feasible with supervised learning, it is much more difficult to tune σ for unsupervised learning methods. During the testing time the same process has been done and SVM predictor does the classification of the given input data with trained data.

4   Experimental Results

We applied the proposed new face recognition method on ORL face datasets for separation of ten classes. For all experiments, we used Mat lab code running on a PC with Intel dual core CPU and 4096-Mb RAM. Before doing any experiment, we have used cropped   images of size to 40×40.

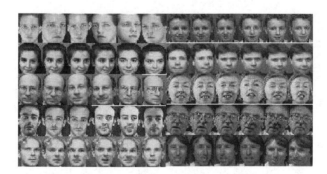

Fig. 5. Pre-Processed Sample Face Images

Our selected database contains gray scale images of 10 subjects in PNG format. In these experiments, we considered 6 images per each subject (total 60 images) containing different illumination and different poses, which 60 images of each used for training and remaining 40 images used for testing the method. Fig. 5 shows some of selected pre-processed subjects in different position and illumination.   Then 50 significant Eigen faces are computed in stage II, where Fig.6 shows those 50 significant Eigen faces.

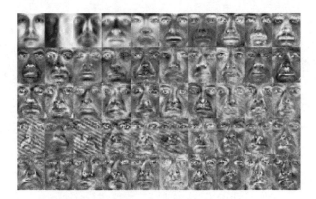

Fig. 6. .50 Most Significant Eigen Faces

As mentioned we repeat the same experiment by extracting 50, 40, 30 and 20 Eigen faces and compared the identification rate of the proposed method, in that cases. In our simulations, we considered 10 subjects. For each selection of Eigen faces we also change the number of selected LDA significant features. We changed number of LDA features from 3 to 9 for each selection of Eigen faces. It means that for example for the case, Eigen faces equal to 50, we repeated the experiment by LDA features equal to 3 to 9 and compared the error rate. Fig. 7 shows 9 estimated fisher faces in the situation that all nine available LDA features are selected. In this case face image projected to nine dimensional spaces.

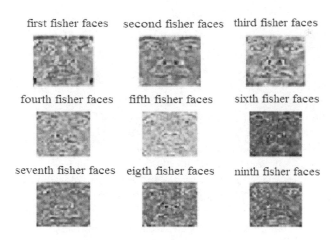

Fig. 7. Computed nine fisher faces

Fig.8 compares average recognition rates by changing the number of PCA and LDA features, it is clear that in the case of PCA features equal to 50 and LDA feature equal to 8 or 9, we get the recognition rate equal to 96.67% (in average two

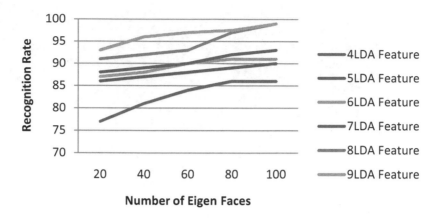

Fig. 8. Comparison of Recognition Rate for Choosing Different Values of Pca and Lda Features

misclassification for 60 test face images). The top line in the Fig. 8 related to the case that all nine LDA feature are computed and as we expected in this case we get the highest recognition rates in comparison with cases that less LDA features are selected. It is also obvious that as number of selected PCA features (Eigen faces) increases (for a fixed number of LDA features) again accuracy of recognition rate improves.

Although choosing 50 PCA features and 8 or 9 LDA features improve the recognition rate in comparison to previous method, but it also increase the computational cost.

5   Conclusion

Here an efficient and novel approach was considered as a combination of PCA, LDA and support vector machine. We can use these algorithms to construct efficient face recognition method with a high recognition rate. Proposed method consists of three parts: i) dimension reduction using PCA that main features that are important for representing face images are extracted ii) feature extraction using LDA that significant features for class separability are selected and iii) svm classifier that classify input face images into one of available classes. Simulation results using ORL face datasets demonstrated the ability of the proposed method for optimal feature extraction and efficient face classification. In our simulations, we chose 10 persons and considered 6 training image and 4 test image for each person (totally 60 training and 40 test face images). Experimental results show a high recognition rate equal to 96.67% (in average two misclassification for 60 face images) which demonstrated an improvement in comparison with previous methods. The new face recognition algorithm can be used in many applications such as security methods.

References

[1] Turk, M., Pentland, A.: Eigen faces for recognition. Journal of Cognitive Neuroscience 3, 72–86 (1991)
[2] Etemad, K., Chellappa, R.: Discriminant Analysis for Recognition of Human Face Images. Journal of Optical Society of America A, 1724–1733 (1997)
[3] Belhumeur, P., Hespanha, J., Kriegman, D.: Eigen faces vs. Fisher-faces: Recognition Using Class Specific Linear Projection. IEEE Transactions on Pattern Analysis and Machine Intelligence 19(7), 711–720, 0162-8828 (1997)
[4] Yan, S., Xu, D., Yang, Q., Zhang, L.: Multi linear Discriminant Analysis for Face Recognition. IEEE Transactions on Image Processing 16(1) (January 2007)
[5] Aizerman, M., Braverman, E., Rozonoer, L.: Theoretical foundations of the potential function method in pattern recognition learning. Automation and Remote Control 25, 821–837 (1964)
[6] Jain, A., Bolle, R., Pankanti, S. (eds.): BIOMETRIC – Personal Identification in Networked Society. Kluwer Academic Publishers, Boston (1999)
[7] Solar, J.R., Navarreto, P.: Eigen space-based face recognition: a comparative study of different approaches. IEEE Tran., Systems Man and Cybernetics- Part C: Applications 35(3) (2005)
[8] Chang, C., Lin, C.: LIBSVM: A Library for Support Vector Machines (2001), http://www.csie.ntu.edu.tw/~cjlin/libsvm

Contextual Strategies for Detecting Spam
in Academic Portals

Balaji Rajendran and Anoop Kumar Pandey

Centre for Development of Advanced Computing,
Electronics City, Bangalore-560100
{balaji,anoop}@cdac.in

Abstract. The emergence of social networking platforms in online space and its
ever increasing user base has opened up a new arena for the spammers to
exploit. Spam, in these kinds of platforms and such other interactive tools like
forums, instant messaging, could be created easily and difficult to stop it from
spreading, which necessitates the development of better detection strategies. In
this paper, we present a contextual strategy for detecting spam in a restricted
domain such as an academic portal. The proposed method uses the relationship
between the concepts of the domain and the concepts of the individual message
fragments to determine the relevancy of the message to the given context and
marks the outliers. The strategy has been tested using a prototype system which
had networking and interactive features for the participants to share
information, and the results indicated that the contextual strategy was fairly
successful in detecting spam.

Keywords: Contextual Strategies, Spam detection, Academic Portal, Socio-
contextual, Information Systems.

1   Introduction

Spamming is the act of spreading unsolicited, unrelated and irrelevant content in the
online world through various utilities such as Email, Discussion forums, Instant
messaging, Social Networking and through interactive information sharing web
applications. The most recognized version of spam is email spam [1-4] and from that
perspective, spam can be classified as Spam without attachment and with attachment
[5]. Spamming remains economically viable because advertisers have no operating
costs beyond the management of their mailing lists, and it is difficult to hold senders
accountable for their mass mailings.

Spam in blogs, also called simply as blog spam or comment spam is a form of
spamdexing, that occurs when unrelated comments to a piece of information is
posted, typically those unrelated ads found in blogs, wikis, guestbooks, and other
publicly accessible online forums. Spammers in the above utilities exploit by
searching for specific widgets or controls, which accept a user's information and
display them, and add links to their sites of interest. This would lead to increased
ranking for those sites, often misleading users and customers [9].

N. Meghanathan et al. (Eds.): CCSIT 2012, Part II, LNICST 85, pp. 250–256, 2012.
© Institute for Computer Sciences, Social Informatics and Telecommunications Engineering 2012

The main problems with spamming are [10]:

- Spammer campaigns result in undeserved higher ranking for dubious pages in search engine results
- Waste the time and effort of real users, by cluttering the information space
- Trick the users and damage the reputation of good systems.

Other negative impacts include involving overwhelming moderators and administrators, to find, obstruct and remove the misleading spam, in order to protect the genuine and legitimate use of systems [11-13]. Previous studies show that comment spam in online discussion forums is prevalent and techniques to counter such type of spam have attracted several researchers' attention [14-18]. Several content-based methods have been proposed to automatically identify spam comments. Content-based methods analyze the text of the post or message (such as checking for the presence of predefined terms or links) in a forum and infer the likelihood of a message being spam or legitimate.

Recently, spammers are also targeting users of social networking services such as Facebook, Orkut etc... Spammers utilize the resource sharing features in the above sites to their advantage, by embedding links to their sites of interest, often pornographic or to sites that sell something. They are also easily able to target a certain demographic segment of users, by exploiting the group or fan page facilities provided by the above sites. Though the above sites may feature a "Repot Spam" or "Report Abuse" facility, the spammers get around it by frequently changing their addresses from one account to another [19].

With the popularity of social networking sites ever increasing, the use of the similar concepts for professional networking [6], and Academic networking [7-8] have become popular. Whatever be the ways of information sharing in whatever domain, the presence of spam is prevalent. However as the domain shrinks or redefines itself within a limited domain, the spam detection methods needs to be redefined for accuracy and for more effectiveness. In this paper we are targeting the practice of spam in academic networking environment, where the prime stakeholders are academicians.

The rest of this paper is organized as follows. Section 2 discusses some of the spam detection techniques primarily in Web 2.0 environments. Section 3 details the Contextual strategies for detecting spam in academic portals. Section 4 discusses the impact of our proposed algorithm and results and section 5 concludes the paper.

2   Related Work

Heymann et al. presented a survey of approaches for fighting spam on social networking portals [12]. Hayati presented an evaluation and analysis of Web 2.0 anti-spam methods [11]. Benevenuto et al. provided a general overview of pollution in video sharing systems such as YouTube [13] with evidence of pollution, types of pollution, effect on the system and control strategies.

Research in blog spam is relatively in its infancy. One of the first articles to talk about blog spam was presented in early 2004 [20] which was limited to existence of spam in blog. In [21] the authors proposed a collaboration spam detection method for detecting link spam inside comments and track back. Authors in [22] proposed an idea to detect blog spam based on vocabulary inside blog post, comment and track back. Methods presented in [23] involve use of supervised machine learning approach to detect spam in Blogs.

A spam detection method was presented in [24] which, employs 40 features to differentiate spam from legitimate profiles in social networking websites. It uses Naïve Bayesian machine learning algorithm to do supervised spam detection task and depend on features that can/cannot be language independent. There is no pressure on user side for differentiation among genuine users and spammers. In [25] authors proposed spam detection method for combating spam in video-sharing websites. Their supervised approach use videos' meta-data information to do the classification task. There is no increase in complexity of user-and-system interaction.

The authors in [26] proposed an idea of tagging system which, can be robust for detection of spam as it counts number of coincident (or common) tags amongst other users and assigns document a relevance ranking number. By looking at the ranking number, one can differentiate among spam and legitimate content. This method is language independent and content based. This domain of spam battle is young and hence the research in strategies is still in its nascent stages. The emergence of Web 2.0 has necessitated the development of sophisticated and unsupervised methods for spam detection.

In [27] Ashish Surekha has developed a heuristics and a solution framework with some key components like ATDC (Average Time Difference between Comments), PCHF (Percentage of Comments with hasSpamHint Flag), CRAV (Comment Repeatability Across Videos), CRR (Comment Repetition and Redundancy) for detecting potential spammers in YouTube.

Our work proposes to develop and use contextual strategies for detecting spam, as explained in the next few sections. These contextual strategies have been used to discover similar knowledge gathering tasks undertaken by users in a Web Information system [28], and also to mine such tasks for providing user assistance [29].

3   Contextual Strategies for Spam Detection

In vertical or domain-specific portals, the main stakeholders and the kind of content that could be found are well known in advance. The restricted audience for these kinds of portals is not going to stop the spammers from their attacks. However the spam detection technique could be improved with the additional knowledge of the subject domain and the users to be more precise, effective and accurate.

In this paper, we consider the special case of academic networking portals, where the main users are academicians viz. students, faculties, researchers etc, whose sole aim is to share knowledge and information about their subjects of interest, information about institutions, courses, events, projects, questionnaires, and such related activities for learning and research. We propose a spam detection technique based on contextual strategies that could be highly effective for academic domains and start by defining the entities involved in it.

3.1   Definitions

Resource: All components of academic networking websites can be treated as resources. Examples may include institutes, faculties, courses, events, projects, web links etc.

Message: Message in this context has been used in a broader sense encompassing all types of information that users share among themselves. Messages could be personal messages addressed to a particular user or could be notifications about a particular event/conference or could be questions asked on a specific topic or could be comments on an academic article or web resource.

Concepts & Relationships: Concept in general, could refer to all the terminologies and vocabulary of a particular domain which is used to describe it. The definition of concepts and relationship between the concepts is typically captured in the form of ontology for a domain. Here for the purpose of the detecting spam in academic domain, we construct a concept tree that captures only two kinds of relationships: is-a and is-in. For instance in the statement, "Java is a Object-oriented language", the concepts 'Java' and 'object-oriented language' are captured using 'is-a' relationship. The is-in relationship is captured as a composition tree. For instance, "Object-oriented Languages" is contained within the concept of "Programming Languages".

Concept Extraction: It is the process of extracting the concepts in a given piece of text, by comparing the main terms with the concept tree.

3.2   Solution Approach

The basic premise of our approach is that a piece of information is going to be of use to a user, only if it captures some interest of that user. In domain-specific scenarios, like an academic environment, the interests of a user get directly mapped to their relevant subject areas. Based on this assumption, we methodize our approach of detecting spam by using the following principles.

- When a message is posted to a user, its relevant concepts are extracted and compared with that of the concepts extracted from the user's profile, interests and navigation history. If the semantics derived from both sides do not match, then that message is a candidate for Spam evaluation.
- When a message is posted in other resources, such as a common forum, the concepts involved in the message are compared against the subject domain and particularly with those concepts related with that resource and if they do not show any similarity then the message is a candidate for Spam evaluation.
- A statistical measure is also considered for detection of spam. If a message gets repeated across several resources within a short span of time, then that message is a candidate for Spam evaluation. Usually spammers would employ spam robots or scripts to do automatic postings.

3.3 Algorithm for Spam Detection

- **Input:** Message M, Concept Model of Resource R where message has been posted M_R.
- **Output:** Spam Hint Y/N.
- **Assumptions: a)** Presence of concept extraction algorithm. **b)** Presence of concept and containment trees. **c)** Resource R has been properly modeled.
- **Algorithm:**

  - Extract concepts from M using concept extraction algorithm and store in an array C_M
  - Extract concepts from M_R and store it an array C_R.
  - Find equivalent concepts corresponding to each concept in C_M and C_R from concept tree and add them to respective arrays.
  - Find the term frequency of occurrence of each concept in C_R and store it as weight-age against each concept.
  - Divide the concept array C_R in 3 parts with respect to the weight-age as highly probable C_{HP}, mid probable C_{MP} and low probable C_{LP} concepts.
  - Analyze M for relevant concepts by computing: $I_H = n(C_M \cap C_{HP})/ n(C_M)$, $I_M = (C_M \cap C_{MP})/ n(C_M)$, $I_L = (C_M \cap C_{LP})/ n(C_M)$
  - Define a Spam filter: $= (I_H < 0.5)$ AND $(I_M < 0.65)$ AND $(I_L < 0.8)$

- **Reason and Consideration:** We have categorized the matching concepts into 3 parts and fixed threshold for different groups (heuristics). They may vary depending on the subject domain, and the environment, with minor deviations.
- We have also defined a Spam filter that could be tweaked to suit different requirements, say a very strict filtering, or medium filtering.

4 Implementation and Results

A prototype of an academic networking website, with interactive features for its users was used for validating our approach. A messaging system and a discussion forum were built within the prototype system. Messaging was used by the participants for communicating among themselves, sharing information and resources. To test our approach, few spam messages were generated and posted to several participants, through scripts, and also to test further, certain spam messages were disguised as system notifications and posted.

Our proposed method was able to successfully detect and classify the spam posted to users in a large number of cases. Even in the case of spam disguised as system notification, the success ratio was fairly good, as the technique was concept based. Also upon activation of our method, logs were analyzed to find 'false' detection in participant messages, and system generated notifications, and though there were instances of false detection, they were very few and far between, and could be attributed to the lesser depth of concepts in concept tree.

In case of discussion forum, participants were split into groups, and each group had a lead, who kick-started the discussion with a lead question, and other participants in the group responded and took the discussions further. As the discussions progressed, 50 different spam messages were generated and put up for testing both manually and through scripts. Our proposed spam detection method was able to successfully discover and label most of the spam put up through scripts. In case of manual posting of spam, a mix of concepts related to the discussions were used, to fool the detection methodology. However even in such cases, the contextual spam detection was able to successfully detect 80% of them, and the technique of weighted concepts helped. The technique failed only, when the spam message was fairly large and contained many concepts relating to the conversation. The detection methodology was also evaluated for "false" detection and in this case of forums, it was considerably nil.

5   Conclusion

We described a method based on contextual strategies to detect spam in academic portals or sites. Application of this method detects the presence of spam more accurately, and effectively. We made the assumption that the resources in the system have been well defined and modeled. We also assumed the existence of ontology in terms of concept tree with simple relationships that defines the domain in which the academic portal operates.

This methodology could be easily extended to other domain-specific vertical portals, though the challenge would be in extending it to a generic and interactive information system.

References

1. Sahami, M., Dumais, S., Heckerman, D., Horvitz, E.: A Bayesian Approach to Filtering Junk E-Mail. In: Learning for Text Categorization: Papers from the 1998 Workshop (1998)
2. Cournane, A., Hunt, R.: An analysis of the tools used for the generation and prevention of spam. Computers & Security 23, 154–166 (2004)
3. Gyongyi, Z., Garcia-Molina, H.: Web spam taxonomy. In: Proceedings of the 1st International Workshop on Adversarial Information Retrieval on the Web, Chiba, Japan (2005)
4. So Young, P., Jeong Tae, K., Shin Gak, K.: Analysis of applicability of traditional spam regulations to VoIP spam. In: The 8th International Conference on Advanced Communication Technology, ICACT 2006, pp. 3–1217 (2006)
5. Nagamalai, D., Dhinakaran, B.C., Lee, J.K.: An in-depth Analysis of Spam and Spammers. International Journal of Security and its Applications 2(2) (April 2008)
6. LinkedIn, http://www.linkedin.com
7. CiteULike, http://www.citeulike.org
8. ArnetMiner, http://www.arnetminer.org
9. Spam in Blogs, http://en.wikipedia.org/wiki/Spam_in_blogs
10. Hayati, P., Potdar, V., Talevski, A., Firoozeh, N., Sarenche, S., Yeganeh, E.A.: Definition of spam 2.0: New spamming boom. In: Digital Ecosystem and Technologies (DEST). IEEE Computer Society, Dubai (2010)

11. Hayati, P., Potdar, V.: Toward spam 2.0: An evaluation of web 2.0 anti-spam meth. In: 7th IEEE International Conference on Industrial Informatics, pp. 875–880. IEEE Computer Society, Cardi (2009)
12. Heymann, P., Koutrika, G., Garcia-Molina, H.: Fighting spam on social web sites: A survey of approaches and future challenges. IEEE Internet Computing 11, 36–45 (2007)
13. Benevenuto, F., Rodrigues, T., Almeida, V.A.F., Almeida, J.M., Goncalves, M.A., Ross, K.W.: Video pollution on the web. First Monday 4 (2010)
14. Bhattarai, A., Rus, V., Dasgupta, D.: Characterizing comment spam in the blogosphere through content analysis. In: IEEE Symposium on Computational Intelligence in Cyber Security (CICS), pp. 37–44. IEEE Computer Society Press, Nashville (2009)
15. Dawei, Y., Davison Brian, D., Zhenzhen, X., Liangjie, H., April, K., Lynne, E.: Detection of harassment on web 2.0. In: CAW2.0 Workshop at WWW 2009 (2009)
16. Dhinakaran, B.C., Nagamalai, D., Lee, J.-K.: Bayesian Approach Based Comment Spam Defending Tool. In: Park, J.H., Chen, H.-H., Atiquzzaman, M., Lee, C., Kim, T.-h., Yeo, S.-S. (eds.) ISA 2009. LNCS, vol. 5576, pp. 578–587. Springer, Heidelberg (2009)
17. Niu, Y., Wang, Y.-M., Chen, H., Ma, M., Hsu, F.: A quantitative study of forum spamming using context-based analysis. In: 14th Annual Network and Distributed System Security Symposium (NDSS), San Diego, CA, pp. 79–92 (2007)
18. Shin, Y., Gupta, M., Myers, S.: Prevalence and mitigation of forum spamming. In: IEEE INFOCOM. IEEE Computer Society (2011)
19. Social Networking Spam,
    http://en.wikipedia.org/wiki/Social_networking_spam
20. McFedries, P.: Technically Speaking: Slicing the Ham from the Spam. IEEE Spectrum 41, 72 (2004)
21. Han, S., Ahn, Y., Moon, S., Jeong, H.: Collaborative blog spam filtering using adaptive percolation search. In: WWW 2006 Workshop on Weblogging Ecosystem: Aggregation, Analysis and Dynamics (2006)
22. Narisawa, K., Yamada, Y., Ikeda, D., Takeda, M.: Detecting blog spam using the vocabulary size of all substrings in their copies. In: WWE 2006 3rd Annual Workshop on the Weblogging Ecosystem, Edinburgh, Scotland (2006)
23. Yu-Ru, L., Hari, S., Yun, C., Junichi, T., Belle, L.T.: Splog detection using self-similarity analysis on blog temporal dynamics. In: Proceedings of the 3rd International Workshop on Adversarial Information Retrieval on the Web. ACM, Banff (2007)
24. Zinman, A., Donath, J.: Is Britney Spears spam. In: Fourth Conference on Email and Anti-Spam Mountain View, California (2007)
25. Benevenuto, F., Rodrigues, T., Almeida, V., Almeida, J., Zhang, C., Ross, K.: Identifying Video Spammers in Online Social Networks. In: AIRWeb 2008, Beijing, China (2008)
26. Georgia, K., Frans Adjie, E., Zolt, G.n, ngyi, Paul, H., Hector, G.-M.: Combating spam in tagging systems. In: Proceedings of the 3rd International Workshop on Adversarial Information Retrieval on the Web, ACM, Banff (2007)
27. Sureka, A.: Mining User Comment Activity for Detecting Forum Spammers in YouTube. In: The Proceedings of 20th WWW Conference, Hyderabad (2011)
28. Rajendran, B.: Socio-Contextual Filters for Discovering Similar Knowledge-Gathering Tasks in Generic Information Systems. In: Yang, C.C., Chen, H., Chau, M., Chang, K., Lang, S.-D., Chen, P.S., Hsieh, R., Zeng, D., Wang, F.-Y., Carley, K.M., Mao, W., Zhan, J. (eds.) ISI Workshops 2008. LNCS, vol. 5075, pp. 384–389. Springer, Heidelberg (2008)
29. Rajendran, B., Iyakutti, K.: Socio-contextual Network Mining for User Assistance in Web-based Knowledge Gathering Tasks. In: Memon, N., Alhajj, R. (eds.) From Sociology to Computing in Social Networks: Theory, Foundations and Applications. Lecture Notes in Social Networks, vol. 1, pp. 81–93. Springer, Wien (2010)

Hybrid Synchronization of Hyperchaotic Chen Systems via Sliding Mode Control

Sundarapandian Vaidyanathan[1] and Sivaperumal Sampath[2]

[1] R & D Centre, Vel Tech Dr. RR & Dr. SR Technical University,
Avadi-Alamathi Road, Avadi, Chennai-600 062, India
sundarvtu@gmail.com
http://www.vel-tech.org/
[2] Institute of Technology, CMJ University,
Shillong, Meghalaya-793 003 India
sivaperumals@gmail.com
http://www.cmjuniversity.edu.in

Abstract. This paper investigates the hybrid synchronization of hyperchaotic Chen systems (Jia, Dai and Hui, 2010) via sliding mode control. The stability results for the sliding mode control based synchronization schemes derived in this paper are established using Lyapunov stability theory. The sliding mode control method is very effective and convenient to achieve global chaos synchronization of the identical hyperchaotic Chen systems because the Lyapunov exponents are not required for these calculations. Numerical simulations are presented to demonstrate the sliding mode control results derived in this paper for the hybrid synchronization of identical hyperchaotic Chen systems.

Keywords: Sliding mode control, hybrid synchronization, hyperchaos, hyperchaotic Chen system.

1 Introduction

Chaotic systems are dynamical systems that are highly sensitive to initial conditions. This sensitivity is popularly known as the *butterfly effect* [1].

In most of the synchronization approaches, the master-slave or drive-response formalism is used. If a particular chaotic system is called the master or drive system and another chaotic system is called the slave or response system, then the idea of synchronization is to use the output of the master system to control the slave system so that the output of the response system tracks the output of the master system asymptotically.

Since the pioneering work by Pecora and Carroll ([2], 1990), chaos synchronization problem has been studied extensively in the literature. Chaos theory has been applied to a variety of fields including physical systems [3], chemical systems [4], ecological systems [5], secure communications ([6]-[8]) etc.

In the last two decades, various control schemes have been developed and successfully applied for the chaos synchronization such as PC method [2], OGY method [9], active control ([10]-[12]), adaptive control ([13]-[15]), time-delay feedback method [16], backstepping design method ([17]-[18]), sampled-data feedback synchronization method ([19]-[20]) etc.

N. Meghanathan et al. (Eds.): CCSIT 2012, Part II, LNICST 85, pp. 257–266, 2012.

So far, many types of synchronization phenomenon have been presented such as complete synchronization [2], generalized synchronization [21], anti-synchronization [22], projective synchronization [23], generalized projective synchronization [24], etc.

Complete synchronization (CS) is characterized by the equality of state variables evolving in time, while anti-synchronization (AS) is characterized by the disappearance of the sum of relevant state variables evolving in time. Projective synchronization (PS) is characterized by the fast that the master and slave systems could be synchronized up to a scaling factor. In generalized projective synchronization (GPS), the responses of the synchronized dynamical states synchronize up to a constant scaling matrix. It is easy to see that the complete synchronization and anti-synchronization are special cases of the generalized projective synchronization where the scaling matrix $\alpha = I$ and $\alpha = -I$, respectively. In hybrid synchronization of two chaotic systems [25], one part of the systems is completely synchronized and the other part is anti-synchronized so that the complete synchronization (CS) and anti-synchronization (AS) co-exist in the systems.

In this paper, we derive new results based on the sliding mode control ([26]-[28]) for the global chaos synchronization of identical hyperchaotic Chen systems ([29], Jia, Dai and Hui, 2010).

The stability results for the sliding mode control based synchronization schemes derived in this paper are established using Lyapunov stability theory [30]. In robust control systems, sliding mode control is often adopted due to its inherent advantages of easy realization, fast response and good transient performance as well as its insensitivity to parameter uncertainties and external disturbances.

This paper has been organized as follows. In Section 2, we describe the problem statement and our methodology using sliding mode control. In Section 3, we discuss the global chaos synchronization of identical hyperchaotic Chen systems ([29], 2010). In Section 4, we summarize the main results obtained in this paper.

2   Problem Statement and Our Methodology Using Sliding Mode Control

In this section, we detail the problem statement for global chaos synchronization of identical chaos systems and our methodology using sliding mode control (SMC) and Lyapunov stability theory.

Consider the chaotic system described by

$$\dot{x} = Ax + f(x) \tag{1}$$

where $x \in \mathbb{R}^n$ is the state of the system, A is the $n \times n$ matrix of the system parameters and $f : \mathbb{R}^n \to \mathbb{R}^n$ is the nonlinear part of the system. We consider the system (1) as the *master* or *drive* system.

As the *slave* or *response* system, we consider the following chaotic system described by the dynamics

$$\dot{y} = Ay + f(y) + u \tag{2}$$

where $y \in \mathbb{R}^n$ is the state of the system and $u \in \mathbb{R}^m$ is the controller of the slave system.

In hybrid synchronization, we define the synchronization error so that the odd states of the systems (1) and (2) are completely synchronized and the even states of the systems (1) and (2) are anti-synchronized.

Thus, we define the *hybrid synchronization error* as

$$
e_i = \begin{cases} y_i - x_i, & \text{if } i \text{ is odd} \\ y_i + x_i, & \text{if } i \text{ is even} \end{cases}
\tag{3}
$$

Then the error dynamics can be expressed in the form

$$
\dot{e} = Ae + \eta(x, y) + u
\tag{4}
$$

The objective of the hybrid synchronization problem is to find a controller u such that

$$
\lim_{t \to \infty} \|e(t)\| = 0 \quad \text{for all } e(0) \in \mathbb{R}^n
\tag{5}
$$

To solve this problem, we first define the control u as

$$
u(t) = -\eta(x, y) + Bv(t)
\tag{6}
$$

where B is a constant gain vector selected such that (A, B) is controllable.

Substituting (6) into (4), the error dynamics simplifies to

$$
\dot{e} = Ae + Bv
\tag{7}
$$

which is a linear time-invariant control system with single input v.

Thus, the original global chaos synchronization problem can be replaced by an equivalent problem of stabilizing the zero solution $e = 0$ of the linear system (7) be a suitable choice of the sliding mode control.

In the sliding mode control, we define the variable

$$
s(e) = Ce = c_1 e_1 + c_2 e_2 + \cdots + c_n e_n
\tag{8}
$$

where $C = \begin{bmatrix} c_1 & c_2 & \cdots & c_n \end{bmatrix}$ is a constant vector to be determined.

In the sliding mode control, we constrain the motion of the system (7) to the sliding manifold defined by

$$
S = \{x \in \mathbb{R}^n \mid s(e) = 0\} = \{x \in \mathbb{R}^n \mid c_1 e_1 + c_2 e_2 + \cdots + c_n e_n = 0\}
$$

which is required to be invariant under the flow of the error dynamics (7).

When in sliding manifold S, the system (7) satisfies the following conditions:

$$
s(e) = 0
\tag{9}
$$

which is the defining equation for the manifold S and

$$
\dot{s}(e) = 0
\tag{10}
$$

which is the necessary condition for the state trajectory $e(t)$ of the system (7) to stay on the sliding manifold S.

Using (7) and (8), the equation (10) can be rewritten as

$$\dot{s}(e) = C\left[Ae + Bv\right] = 0 \tag{11}$$

Solving (11), we obtain the equivalent control law given by

$$v_{eq}(t) = -(CB)^{-1}CAe(t) \tag{12}$$

where C is chosen such that $CB \neq 0$.

Substituting (12) into the error dynamics (7), we get the closed-loop dynamics as

$$\dot{e} = [I - B(CB)^{-1}C]Ae \tag{13}$$

where C is chosen such that the system matrix $[I - B(CB)^{-1}C]A$ is Hurwitz.

Then the controlled system (13) is globally asymptotically stable.

To design the sliding mode controller for the linear time-invariant system (7), we use the constant plus proportional rate reaching law

$$\dot{s} = -q\,\text{sgn}(s) - ks \tag{14}$$

where sgn($\cdot$) denotes the sign function and the gains $q > 0, k > 0$ are determined such that the sliding condition is satisfied and sliding motion will occur.

From equations (11) and (14), we obtain the control $v(t)$ as

$$v(t) = -(CB)^{-1}[C(kI + A)e + q\,\text{sgn}(s)] \tag{15}$$

Theorem 1. *The master system (1) and the slave system (2) are globally and asymptotically synchronized for all initial conditions $x(0), y(0) \in \mathbb{R}^n$ by the feedback control law*

$$u(t) = -\eta(x, y) + Bv(t) \tag{16}$$

where $v(t)$ is defined by (15) and B is a column vector such that (A, B) is controllable. Also, the sliding mode gains k, q are positive.

Proof. First, we note that substituting (16) and (15) into the error dynamics (7), we obtain the closed-loop dynamics as

$$\dot{e} = Ae - B(CB)^{-1}[C(kI + A)e + q\,\text{sgn}(s)] \tag{17}$$

To prove that the error dynamics (17) is globally asymptotically stable, we consider the candidate Lyapunov function defined by the equation

$$V(e) = \frac{1}{2}s^2(e) \tag{18}$$

which is a positive definite function on $\mathbb{R}^n$.

Differentiating V along the trajectories of (17) or the equivalent dynamics (14), we obtain

$$\dot{V}(e) = s(e)\dot{s}(e) = -ks^2 - q\,\text{sgn}(s) \tag{19}$$

which is a negative definite function on $\mathbb{R}^n$.

Thus, by Lyapunov stability theory [30], it is immediate that the error dynamics (17) is globally asymptotically stable for all initial conditions $e(0) \in \mathbb{R}^n$.

This completes the proof.   ∎

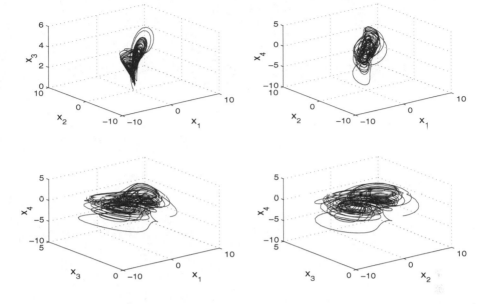

Fig. 1. State Portrait of the Hyperchaotic Chen System

3   Global Chaos Synchronization of Identical Hyperchaotic Chen Systems

3.1   Main Results

In this section, we apply the sliding mode control results obtained in Section 2 for the global chaos synchronization of identical hyperchaotic Chen systems ([29], 2010).

Thus, the master system is described by the hyperchaotic Chen dynamics

$$
\begin{aligned}
\dot{x}_1 &= a(x_2 - x_1) \\
\dot{x}_2 &= 4x_1 - 10x_1x_3 + cx_2 + 4x_4 \\
\dot{x}_3 &= x_2^2 - bx_3 \\
\dot{x}_4 &= -dx_1
\end{aligned}
\tag{20}
$$

where x_1, x_2, x_3, x_4 are the states of the system and a, b, c, d are constant, positive parameters of the system.

The slave system is also described by the controlled hyperchaotic Chen dynamics

$$
\begin{aligned}
\dot{y}_1 &= a(y_2 - y_1) + u_1 \\
\dot{y}_2 &= 4y_1 - 10y_1y_3 + cy_2 + 4y_4 + u_2 \\
\dot{y}_3 &= y_2^2 - by_3 + u_3 \\
\dot{y}_4 &= -dy_1 + u_4
\end{aligned}
\tag{21}
$$

where y_1, y_2, y_3, y_4 are the states of the system and u_1, u_2, u_3, u_4 are the active controllers to be designed.

The systems (20) and (21) are hyperchaotic when

$$a = 35, \quad b = 3, \quad c = 21 \quad \text{and} \quad d = 2$$

The state portrait of the hyperchaotic Chen system (20) is illustrated in Figure 1.
The hybrid synchronization error e is defined by

$$
\begin{aligned}
e_1 &= y_1 - x_1 \\
e_2 &= y_2 + x_2 \\
e_3 &= y_3 - x_3 \\
e_4 &= y_4 + x_4
\end{aligned}
\tag{22}
$$

The error dynamics is easily obtained as

$$
\begin{aligned}
\dot{e}_1 &= a(e_2 - e_1) - 2ax_2 + u_1 \\
\dot{e}_2 &= 4e_1 + ce_2 + 4e_4 + 8x_1 - 10(y_1 y_3 + x_1 x_3) + u_2 \\
\dot{e}_3 &= -be_3 + y_2^2 - x_2^2 + u_3 \\
\dot{e}_4 &= -de_1 - 2dx_1 + u_4
\end{aligned}
\tag{23}
$$

We can write the error dynamics (23) in the matrix notation as

$$\dot{e} = Ae + \eta(x, y) + u \tag{24}$$

where the associated matrices are

$$
A = \begin{bmatrix} -a & a & 0 & 0 \\ 4 & c & 0 & 4 \\ 0 & 0 & -b & 0 \\ -d & 0 & 0 & 0 \end{bmatrix}, \quad
\eta(x, y) = \begin{bmatrix} -2ax_2 \\ 8x_1 - 10(y_1 y_3 + x_1 x_3) \\ y_2^2 - x_2^2 \\ -2dx_1 \end{bmatrix} \quad \text{and} \quad
u = \begin{bmatrix} u_1 \\ u_2 \\ u_3 \\ u_4 \end{bmatrix}
\tag{25}
$$

The sliding mode controller design is carried out as detailed in Section 2.
First, we set u as

$$u = -\eta(x, y) + Bv \tag{26}$$

where B is chosen such that (A, B) is controllable. We take B as

$$
B = \begin{bmatrix} 1 \\ 1 \\ 1 \\ 1 \end{bmatrix}
\tag{27}
$$

In the hyperchaotic case, the parameter values are

$$a = 35, \quad b = 3, \quad c = 21 \quad \text{and} \quad d = 2$$

The sliding mode variable is selected as

$$s = Ce = \begin{bmatrix} -1 & -2 & 0 & 1 \end{bmatrix} e \tag{28}$$

which makes the sliding mode state equation asymptotically stable.

We choose the sliding mode gains as

$$k = 5 \text{ and } q = 0.1$$

We note that a large value of k can cause chattering and an appropriate value of q is chosen to speed up the time taken to reach the sliding manifold as well as to reduce the system chattering.

From equation (15), we can obtain $v(t)$ as

$$v(t) = 10e_1 - 43.5e_2 - 1.5e_4 + 0.05 \operatorname{sgn}(s) \tag{29}$$

Thus, the required sliding mode controller is obtained as

$$u(t) = -\eta(x, y) + Bv(t) \tag{30}$$

where $\eta(x, y)$, B and $v(t)$ are defined in equations (25), (27) and (29).

By Theorem 1, we obtain the following result.

Theorem 2. *The identical hyperchaotic Chen systems (20) and (21) are globally and asymptotically hybrid-synchronized for all initial conditions with the sliding mode controller u defined by (30).* ∎

3.2   Numerical Results

For the numerical simulations, the fourth-order Runge-Kutta method with time-step $h = 10^{-6}$ is used to solve the hyperchaotic Chen systems (20) and (21) with the sliding mode controller u given by (30) using MATLAB.

For the hyperchaotic Chen systems, the parameter values are taken as

$$a = 35, \quad b = 3, \quad c = 21 \text{ and } d = 2$$

The sliding mode gains are chosen as

$$k = 5 \text{ and } q = 0.1$$

The initial values of the master system (20) are taken as

$$x_1(0) = 16, \quad x_2(0) = 19, \quad x_3(0) = 21, \quad x_4(0) = 11$$

and the initial values of the slave system (21) are taken as

$$y_1(0) = 8, \quad y_2(0) = 26, \quad y_3(0) = 36, \quad y_4(0) = 24$$

Figure 2 depicts the hybrid synchronization of the hyperchaotic Chen systems (20) and (21).

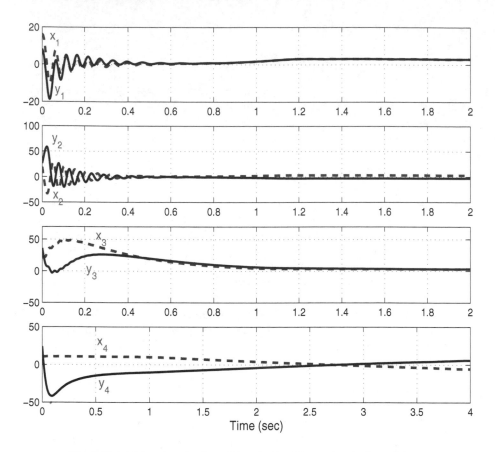

Fig. 2. Hybrid Synchronization of the Identical Hyperchaotic Chen Systems

4   Conclusions

Sliding control method (SMC) is an effective method in control engineering. In robust control systems, sliding mode control is often adopted due to its inherent advantages of easy realization, fast response and good transient performance as well as its insensitivity to parameter uncertainties and external disturbances.In this paper, we have used sliding mode control (SMC) to achieve hybrid chaos synchronization for the identical hyperchaotic Chen systems (Jia, Dai and Hui, 2010). Our synchronization results for the identical hyperchaotic Chen systems have been established using Lyapunov stability theory. Since the Lyapunov exponents are not required for these calculations, the sliding mode control method is very effective and convenient to achieve hybrid chaos synchronization for identical hyperchaotic Chen systems. Numerical simulations are also presented to demonstrate the effectiveness of the synchronization results derived in this paper using sliding mode control.

References

1. Alligood, K.T., Sauer, T., Yorke, J.A.: Chaos: An Introduction to Dynamical Systems. Springer, New York (1997)
2. Pecora, L.M., Carroll, T.L.: Synchronization in chaotic systems. Phys. Rev. Lett. 64, 821–824 (1990)
3. Lakshmanan, M., Murali, K.: Chaos in Nonlinear Oscillators: Controlling and Synchronization. World Scientific, Singapore (1996)
4. Han, S.K., Kerrer, C., Kuramoto, Y.: Dephasing and burstling in coupled neural oscillators. Phys. Rev. Lett. 75, 3190–3193 (1995)
5. Blasius, B., Huppert, A., Stone, L.: Complex dynamics and phase synchronization in spatially extended ecological system. Nature 399, 354–359 (1999)
6. Kwok, H.S., Wallace, K., Tang, S., Man, K.F.: Online secure communication system using chaotic map. Internat. J. Bifurcat. Chaos. 14, 285–292 (2004)
7. Kocarev, L., Parlitz, U.: General approach for chaos synchronization with applications to communications. Phys. Rev. Lett. 74, 5028–5030 (1995)
8. Murali, K., Lakshmanan, M.: Secure communication using a compound signal using sampled-data feedback. Applied Math. Mech. 11, 1309–1315 (2003)
9. Ott, E., Grebogi, C., Yorke, J.A.: Controlling chaos. Phys. Rev. Lett. 64, 1196–1199 (1990)
10. Ho, M.C., Hung, Y.C.: Synchronization of two different chaotic systems using generalized active network. Phys. Lett. A. 301, 421–428 (2002)
11. Huang, L., Feng, R., Wang, M.: Synchronization of chaotic systems via nonlinear control. Phys. Lett. A. 320, 271–275 (2004)
12. Chen, H.K.: Global chaos synchronization of new chaotic systems via nonlinear control. Chaos, Solit. Frac. 23, 1245–1251 (2005)
13. Chen, S.H., Lü, J.: Synchronization of an uncertain unified system via adaptive control. Chaos, Solit. Frac. 14, 643–647 (2002)
14. Lu, J., Han, X., Lü, J.: Adaptive feedback synchronization of a unified chaotic system. Phys. Lett. A. 329, 327–333 (2004)
15. Samuel, B.: Adaptive synchronization between two different chaotic dynamical systems. Adaptive Commun. Nonlinear Sci. Num. Simul. 12, 976–985 (2007)
16. Park, J.H., Kwon, O.M.: A novel criterion for delayed feedback control of time-delay chaotic systems. Chaos, Solit. Fract. 17, 709–716 (2003)
17. Wu, X., Lü, J.: Parameter identification and backstepping control of uncertain Lü system. Chaos, Solit. Fract. 18, 721–729 (2003)
18. Yu, Y.G., Zhang, S.C.: Adaptive backstepping synchronization of uncertain chaotic systems. Chaos, Solit. Fract. 27, 1369–1375 (2006)
19. Yang, T., Chua, L.O.: Control of chaos using sampled-data feedback control. Internat. J. Bifurcat. Chaos. 9, 215–219 (1999)
20. Zhao, J., Lu, J.: Using sampled-data feedback control and linear feedback synchronization in a new hyperchaotic system. Chaos, Solit. Fract. 35, 376–382 (2008)
21. Wang, Y.W., Guan, Z.H.: Generalized synchronization of continuous chaotic systems. Chaos, Solitons & Fractals 27, 97–101 (2006)
22. Sundarapandian, V.: Anti-synchronization of Lorenz and T chaotic systems by active nonlinear control. Internat. J. Computer Information Systems 2(4), 6–10 (2011)
23. Qiang, J.: Projective synchronization of a new hyperchaotic Lorenz system. Physics Letters A 370, 40–45 (2007)
24. Li, R.H., Xu, W., Li, S.: Adaptive generalized projective synchronization in different chaotic systems based on parameter identification. Physics Letters A 367, 199–206 (2007)

25. Sundarapandian, V.: Hybrid synchronization of Cai and Pehlivan systems by active nonlinear control. Internat. J. Computer Information Systems 2(4), 11–15 (2011)
26. Slotine, J.E., Sastry, S.S.: Tracking control of nonlinear systems using sliding surface with application to robotic manipulators. Internat. J. Control 38, 465–492 (1983)
27. Utkin, V.I.: Sliding mode control design principles and applications to electric drives. IEEE Trans. Industrial Electr. 40, 23–36 (1993)
28. Saravanakumar, R., Vinoth Kumar, K., Ray, K.K.: Sliding mode control of induction motor using simulation approach. Internat. J. Control of Computer Science and Network Security 9, 93–104 (2009)
29. Jia, L.X., Dai, H., Hui, M.: A new four-dimensional hyperchaotic Chen system and its generalized synchronization. Chinese Physics B 19, 501–517 (2010)
30. Hahn, W.: The Stability of Motion. Springer, New York (1967)

Design and Implementation of Efficient Viterbi Decoders

K.S. Arunlal and S.A. Hariprasad

R.V. Center for Cognitive Technologies, Bangalore, Karnataka, India
arunlalks1@yahoo.com, harivat2002@yahoo.co.in

Abstract. Viterbi decoders are used for forward error correction, but the algorithm demands more hardware, memory and computational time, hence researchers have come up with other alternatives like fangled viterbi decoder, modified fangled viterbi decoder, but these methods lack error correction capabilities. In this work an innovative method is used to improve error correction capabilities. The results shows it can correct two bit error with less computational time and hardware requirement.

Keywords: Constraint length, hamming distance, path metric, branch metric, Trellis diagram.

1 Introduction

In the present scenarios, data transferring between the systems plays a vital role as the technologies are increasing day-by-day, the number of users is simultaneously increasing. This wide usage leads to major issues in the digital communication systems and results in data corruptions. It's very much essential to have a technique to correct these errors efficiently. One such algorithm used by telecommunication industry is Viterbi algorithm. The major issues in Viterbi decoder is high computational complexity, large memory requirement.

Fangled viterbi decoder is a variant of viterbi decoders which has least computational complexity, delay and memory requirement because it calculates only one path in the trellis diagram which affects error detection capability.

Modified fangled takes it a step further by gaining one bit error correction and detection capability, with increased computational complexity and memory requirement compared with fangled Viterbi decoder but it is lower than Viterbi decoder.

But in reality all parameters such as error correction capability, memory requirement, design complexity and cost are interconnected with each other.

In order to solve these problems, an efficient fangled viterbi algorithm is designed in this paper with 2 bit error correction capability with less hardware complexity and computational time.

The paper is organized as follows. Section 2 describes Viterbi decoding algorithm, section 3 describes fangled viterbi decoding algorithm of convolutional codes, section 4 gives description of modified fangled viterbi algorithm, section 5 describes efficient fangled viterbi decoding algorithm and section 6 concludes this paper with results.

N. Meghanathan et al. (Eds.): CCSIT 2012, Part II, LNICST 85, pp. 267–272, 2012.
© Institute for Computer Sciences, Social Informatics and Telecommunications Engineering 2012

2   Viterbi Decoding Algorithm

The Viterbi decoding algorithm proposed by A. J. Viterbi [1] performs maximum likelihood sequence detection on data which have been convolutionally coded. The decoding uses the trellis diagram to determine the output data sequence path which is the most likely to the input sequences from encoder. The basic units of Viterbi decoder (VD) [2] are branch metric unit (BMU), add compare and select unit (ACS) and survivor memory management unit (SMU) as shown in figure 1.

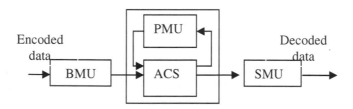

Fig. 1. Viterbi Decoder Block Diagram

Branch metric unit (BMU) compares the received data symbols to the ideal outputs of the encoder from the transmitter and hence calculate the branch metrics. Path metric computation unit (PMU) calculates the path metrics of a stage by adding the branch metrics associated with a received symbol to the path metrics from the previous stage of the trellis. An ACS module adds each incoming branch metric of the state to the corresponding path metric and compares the two results to select a smaller one. Then it will update the path metric storage with selected value. To keep track of information bits associated with the surviving paths, survivor memory management is used.

3   Fangled Viterbi Decoding Algorithm

It's almost similar to Viterbi decoder and it consists following functional units[3].

- Encoder Engine
- Branch metric generator
- Add-Compare-Select unit (ACSU)

The encoder Engine mimics the convolutional encoder and calculates next state and output for the various given states as shown in table 1. The branch metric unit calculates the branch metrics by using hard decision based on hamming distance as it is easy to implement. Hence it takes less hardware, computational time with no error correction capabilities.

Table 1. State and Output table for Viterbi Decoder

Start State	Input Symbol	End State	Output Bit
00	00	00	0
00	11	01	1
01	10	10	0
01	01	01	1
10	11	00	1
10	00	01	0
11	01	10	1
11	10	11	0

The working principle of Fangled Viterbi decoder can be explained with reference to the trellis diagram, for the paths corresponding to input sequence [11 10 10 11 01 01 11]. One bit error is introduced at sixth bit position or third symbol of the original sequence as shown in figure 2. The normal line is for output data bit '0' and dashed line is for '1'the constraint length is taken as (K) =3 encoder, giving rise to four states in Trellis diagram. Dark line is used for correct path and 'X' is for wrong branch like branch 00 on the first frame. The abbreviations which are used in the Trellis diagram are:

- Received erroneous data (RED).
- Original data from encoder (OD).
- Original message to encoder (OM).
- Modified fangled decoder output (OM).
- Fangled decoder output (FO).

As shown in Figure 2 no identifiable path is there for conflicts on third symbol as there is no guarantee that state transition will be from state 2 to state 0 (correct) or state 1 (incorrect) i.e. 10 to 00 (correct) or 11. So in case of an error when selector unit in the ACS finds itself in a dilemma of choosing among equal paths, makes an arbitrary branch selection (here branch 00) leading to serious unreliability of the data thus decoded.

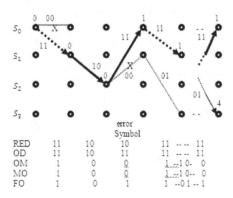

Fig. 2. Trellis diagram of path followed by sequence [11 10 10 11 01 01 11] from K=3, R=1/2, (2, 1, 2) encoder

Advantage of fangled decoder is, for every symbol only one path is stored and two additions and one comparison are done. So for 14 bit received data i.e. 7 symbols only 14 add and 7 comparisons are done [4] and corresponding memory requirement for storing path and state metric, states and survivor as well as decoded data is 88 bits [6].

4   Modified Fangled Viterbi Algorithm

Modified Fangled Viterbi algorithm is a variant of fangled Viterbi algorithm designed to correct one bit errors [5]. Computational complexity and memory requirement is more than fangled but much lower than conventional Viterbi decoder. The main difference is that modified fangled takes both paths in case of a conflict or error and compares them at the end for the choice of optimum path [6]. It fails in case of noisy channel which introduces burst error. The rest of the functional blocks is similar to fangled Viterbi decoder.

If an error occurs in the received data as in third symbol shown in Figure 2, then the branch metric unit of that error frame has two possible states 00 (correct) and 10 with equal metric, leading to a conflict of branch selection between 11 (correct) and 00. In fangled algorithm this conflicting situation is resolved by randomly selecting any path which leads to erroneous decoding of data [4]. But this miscalculation is solved in modified fangled algorithm by selecting both paths and calculating there total path metric from initial state to completion of trellis and storing the error metrics of each path which came as 1 and 4. Both paths are now compared and the minimum path with metric 1 is selected, consequently resolving the issue and giving error free data [1 0 0 1 1]. Note that for error free data both paths will coincide till the end.

Advantage of modified fangled algorithm is its 1 bit error correcting capability giving reliability to the decoder. But it carries the calculation of both the path metrics from the initial stage with and without error, even irrespective of the stage at which the conflict of branch selection or error occurs. Hence leading to 28 adds and 14 compares for 14 bit received data from K=3 encoder. The second path requires additional memory, enhancing memory requirement to 256 bits [6].

5   Efficient Fangled Viterbi Algorithm

Efficient fangled viterbi decoder is an extension of fangled and similar to modified fangled but its decision unit is highly efficient. This removes the redundancies in modified fangled design like extra computations and consequent memory requirement.

The whole design can again be bifurcated into:

- Encoder engine
- Branch metric calculation unit (BMU)
- Decision unit
- Survivor path calculation unit (SMU)

Decision unit works same as ACSU in fangled Viterbi decoder on uncorrupted data but in case of errors, it is more efficient for finding correct path. This work assume that one bit error can cause the path metric to increase by one. When such happens modified fangled used to calculate both path and compare them at the end [6]. Efficient fangled method does so by taking future symbol 11 from received data i.e. the very next two bits after error symbol to compute path metric for choosing correct path.

In Figure 2, one bit error occurred at third symbol i.e. '10' increasing the path metric from 0 to 1. Now fourth symbol i.e. '11' is taken and path metric then calculated increases to 2. This leads to the conclusion that this path is wrong, since correct path metric always increases to one for one bit error and remains the same thereafter. Hence further calculation of this path is terminated. In case of modified fangled both paths coincide.

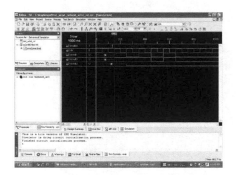 

Fig. 3. Simulation result of Efficient Fangled Viterbi decoder for 1bit error at symbol 2

Fig. 4. Simulation result of Efficient Fangled Viterbi decoder for 2 bit error at symbol 2 & 4

Table 2. Comparison Table for decoding 14 bit input data from (2, 1, 2) encoder of constraint length 3

Parameters	Fangled VD [2]	Modified Fangled VD [2]	Efficient Fangled VD	Efficient Fangled VD	Conventional VD [2]-[3]
Error correction capability (Bits)	0	1	1	2	2
Processing time	150 ns	300 ns	150 ns	150 ns	650 ns
Number of additions required	14	28	16-18	18-22	46
Number of comparisons required	7	14	8-9	9-11	20
Device Utilization (Gate counts)	1019	1194	1542	1758	5242

First and foremost advantage is the reduction of computational complexity to 36-43% of Modified fangled Viterbi decoder for one bit error in 14 bit length data and 64%-78% for 2 bit error in 14 bit data. As for 14 bit data i.e. 7 symbols modified fangled Viterbi decoder takes 28 additions and 14 comparisons while efficient fangled can take either 2 or 4 additions and 1 or 2 comparisons respectively for various error positions as explained earlier. When no error is present this decoder will work as Fangled Viterbi decoder taking only 14 additions and 7 comparisons to decode 14 bit input data.

6   Results and Conclusion

Figure 3 and 4 shows the result of efficient Viterbi decoder obtained for one and two bit errors. The table 2 compares the result obtained for different variants of Viterbi decoders. From the table it is very clear that efficient fangled Viterbi decoder can perform well and also, can correct two bit errors when been compared with other viterbi variants, but with slight increase hardware complexity.

References

1. Viterbi, A.J.: Error bounds for convolutional codes and an asymptotically optimum decoding algorithm. IEEE Trans. Inform. Theory IT-13, 260–269 (1967)
2. Hema, S., Suresh Babu, V., Ramesh, P.: FPGA Implementation of Viterbi Decoder. In: Proceedings of the 6th WSEAS Int. Conf. on Electronics, Hardware, Wireless and Optical Communications, Corfu Island, Greece, February 16-19 (2007)
3. Shivasubramaniam, R., Varadhan, A.: An efficient implementation of IS-95A CDMA Transreceiver through FPGA. DSP Journal 6(1) (September 2006)
4. Ur Rahman, S.U., Kulkarni, S., Sujatha, C.M.: An alternative scheme for Viterbi decoding of convolutional codes. In: NLPPES 2010, Bangalore (2010)
5. Kulkarni, S.: Implementation of convolution- nal Viterbi decoder on FPGA and measuring its performance. MTech thesis in R.V.C.E., Bangalore (2009-2010)
6. Ur Rahman, S.U.: Implementation of fangled Viterbi decoder on FPGA and measuring its performance. MTech thesis in R.V.C.E., Bangalore (2009-2010)

Classification of MRI Brain Images
Using Cosine-Modulated Wavelets

Yogita K. Dubey and Milind M. Mushrif

Dept. of Electronics and Telecommunication Engineering,
Yeshwantrao Chavan College of Engineering, Nagpur-441110, Maharashtra, India
yogeetakdubey@yahoo.co.in, milindmushrif@yahoo.com

Abstract. This paper presents technique for the classification of the MRI images of human brain using cosine modulated wavelet transform. Better discrimination and low design implementation complexity of the cosine-modulated wavelets has been effectively utilized to give better features and more accurate classification results. The proposed technique consists of two stages, namely, feature extraction, and classification. In the first stage, the energy features from MRI images are obtained from sub-band images obtained after decomposition using cosine modulated wavelet transform. In the classification stage, Bays classifier is used to classify the image as normal or abnormal. Average Classification accuracy with a success rate of 100% has been obtained.

Keywords: Brain MRI, Texture classification, cosine-modulated wavelets.

1   Introduction

Brain MRI is commonly used modality for detecting and visualizing brain tumors. It provides detailed information regarding healthy tissue (normal) and pathological process (abnormality). Clinical MRI is based on the hydrogen nucleus. For image formation, a large static magnetic field is used to perturb magnetic moments of proton that exist in the hydrogen nucleus from their equilibrium. Because of this, the protons are oriented randomly. But in existence of a static magnetic field, they line up with the field and the net magnetization of protons tends toward the direction of the field. In the relaxation process an induced electronic signal is recorded. The strength and duration of the signal depend on three quantities:

1. ρ (proton density),
2. Spin-lattice relaxation time: the time which describes how fast the net magnetization takes to relax back to its equilibrium (T1),
3. Spin-spin relaxation time: with this time, magnetization components decrease to zero (T2).

In scanning of a person's body, by using different parameters setting, it is possible to obtain three different images of the same body: T1-weighted, T2-weighted, and ρ-weighted [1].

N. Meghanathan et al. (Eds.): CCSIT 2012, Part II, LNICST 85, pp. 273–281, 2012.

Classification of MR brain images plays a very important role for further processing of MR brain image which is helpful for the diagnosis of diseases. Many techniques for the classification of MR brain images are found in the literature. El-Syed *et al* [2] proposed a hybrid technique for brain MR images classification as tumorous and normal. In this technique discrete wavelet transform coefficients are used as attributes for classification. These attributes are reduced using Principal Component Analysis (PCA) before providing to the classifier. KNN and Feed forward back propagation neural network are used as classifier. They have reported a classification accuracy of 98.6% and 95.7%. Ahmed Kharat *et al* [3] used genetic algorithm and support vector machine to classify the brain tissues into normal, benign or malignant tumor. The performance of the algorithm is evaluated on a series of brain tumor images. Qurat-ul-ain [4] proposed a method for classification and segmentation of brain tumor using texture feature in which texture features are extracted from brain MR image, then Brain images are classified on the bases of these texture feature using ensemble base classifier. Textures provide essential information and cues for the analysis of many image processing problems. One of the major applications of texture analysis is classification, which plays an important role in many applications such as tissue classification in medical imaging. Hsin [5] used a modulated wavelet transform approach for texture segmentation and reported that texture segmentation performance can be improved with this approach. Cosine-modulated wavelet based texture features are used by M. Kokare *et al* [6] for content-based image retrieval with good retrieval efficiency and accuracy. M. M. Mushrif *et al* [7] used cosine modulated wavelet transform based features for texture classification and reported improved classification rates compared to the traditional Gabor wavelet based approach, rotated wavelet filters based approach, DT-CWT approach and the DLBP approach.

In this paper, a technique for the classification MRI brain images using cosine modulated wavelet transform is proposed. The cosine modulated wavelets, introduced by Gopinath and Burrus [8], have the advantages that they occupy adjacent bands in the spectrum that gives better frequency resolution and the analysis/synthesis computations in these wavelet bases can be done very efficiently using combination of two channel unitary filter banks and the discrete cosine transform. The computations of these wavelets have low design and implementation complexity, good filter quality, which yields improved performance in terms of classification accuracy and time.

The paper is organized as follows. First, Section 2 contains details of cosine modulated wavelet transform. Detail description of the classification algorithm is described in Section 3. Section 4 contains the results. Finally, conclusions are presented in Section 5.

2   Cosine Modulated Wavelet Transform

Fig. 1 shows an M-channel filter bank with analysis filters h_i and synthesis filters g_i. Filter bank is said to be *perfect reconstruction* if $y(n) = x(n)$. A perfect reconstruction filter bank is unitary if $g_i(n) = h_i(-n)$.

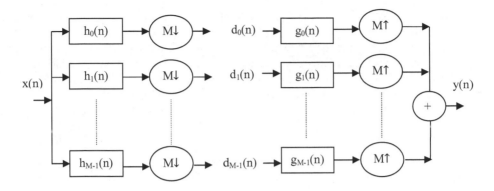

Fig. 1. M Channel Filter bank

Koilpillai and Vaidyanathan [9] reported that unitary (FIR) filter banks are practically important since they can be completely parameterized and efficiently implemented. Moreover, they give rise to orthonormal wavelet bases for $L^2(R)$. A unitary filter bank where the low-pass filter satisfies the additional linear constraints given in Eq. (1) gives rise to wavelet tight frames.

$$\sum_{k=0}^{N-1} h_0(k) = \sqrt{M} .$$ (1)

where $h_0(k)$ is lowpass filter of length N, and the number of channels are M. This filter is the unitary scaling vector, and the remaining filters in the filter bank are the unitary wavelet vectors. The scaling and wavelet vectors determine the scaling function, $\psi_0(t)$, and the $(M-1)$ wavelets, $\psi_i(t)$, are defined by

$$\psi_i(t) = \sqrt{M} \sum_k h_i(k)\psi_0(Mt - k) \quad i \in \{0,1,....M-1\} .$$ (2)

The $(M-1)$ wavelets $\psi_i(t)$ $i \in \{0,1,...M-1\}$ their translates and dilates by powers of M form a wavelet tight frame for $L^2(R)$ as reported by Gopinath and Burrus [8].

For every function $f(t) = L^2(R)$ one has

$$f(t) = \sum_{i=1}^{M-1} \sum_{j,k} \langle f, \psi_{i,j,k}(t) \rangle \psi_{i,j,k}(t) .$$ (3)

Where $\langle \cdot \rangle$ is an inner product and $\psi_{i,j,k} = M^{j/2}\psi_i\left(M^j t - k\right)$.

Modulated filter banks are special class of filter banks where the analysis and synthesis filters are obtained by modulation of prototype filters. Koilpillai and Vaidyanathan [9] had reported that Cosine-modulated FIR filter banks are a special class of unitary FIR filter banks, where analysis filters are all cosine modulates of a low-pass linear phase prototype filter. In an M-channel filter bank, the analysis and the synthesis filters are meant to approximate ideal L^{th} band filters, the pass-bands of which occupy adjacent frequency channels that are π/L apart. If we modulate a real, prototype filter, with pass-band in $\left[-\dfrac{\pi}{2M}, \dfrac{\pi}{2M}\right]$ by $\cos\left((2i+1)\dfrac{\pi}{2M}n + \varepsilon_i\right)$,

where ε_i is an arbitrary phase, the pass-band of the resultant filter occupies the desired bands.. Here we used filter coefficients for $M = 2$ to decompose the texture image in to four channels. The prototype filter h_0 and the analysis filter h_1 are related by

$$h_i(n) = \cos\left(\frac{3\pi}{4}\left(n - \frac{N-1}{2} - \frac{\pi}{4}\right)\right)h_0(n). \qquad (4)$$

where $h_0(n)$ is an even-symmetric prototype filter of length $N = 4m$ for some nonnegative integer m. After obtaining the prototype filter h_0 and the cosine modulated high-pass filter h_1, the wavelet decomposition is performed as explained in Fig. 2.

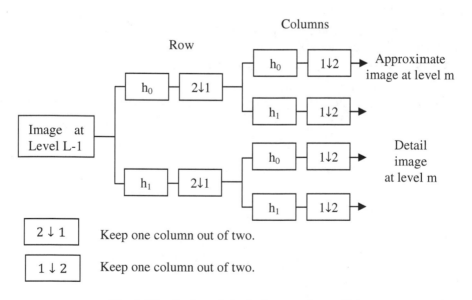

Fig. 2. Filter bank used to calculate wavelet coefficients

Each sub-band image contains the information of a specific scale and orientation. The magnitudes of wavelet coefficients in a particular channel are greater for images with a strong textural content at the frequency and orientation represented by that channel. Therefore, the texture of an image can be represented by a feature vector that contains the average coefficient magnitude, known as averaged energy function. The energy distribution has important discriminatory properties for images and as such can be used as a feature for texture classification. We used energy signature for extraction of texture features as it reflects the distribution of energy along the frequency axis over scale and orientation. The discriminatory properties of the energy distribution in sub-bands result in texture features that have been observed to yield good characterization of textures. The energy feature e_s of the image is given by

$$e_s = \frac{1}{M \times N} \sum_{i=1}^{M} \sum_{j=1}^{N} |x(i, j)| \quad \text{for s} = 1, 2, ..., Q. \tag{5}$$

where x is wavelet decomposed image for any sub-band of dimension $M \times N$. For K-level decomposition of the image, the size of the feature vector is $Q = (3 * K + 1)$. In the proposed work we used 2-level decomposition, so the resulting feature vector is of length 7, given by $f = \{e_1, e_2, ..., e_7\}$.

3   Classification Algorithm

There are two image classes normal and abnormal. We have used Total 20 Brain MRI images for each class. For each image we calculate 7 features by calculating energy feature of each channel of the wavelet decomposition using equation (5). The classification algorithm is a two stage algorithm that involves training and classification (or testing) stages. The block diagram of algorithms is as follows.

Training Phase

Fig. 3a. Block diagram of the proposed algorithm for training phase

Classification Phase

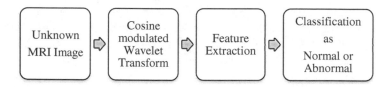

Fig. 3b. Block diagram of the proposed algorithm for classification phase

The algorithm is detailed as follow:

Training Phase

1. Decompose image I, using cosine-modulated wavelet transform.
2. Compute the energy feature of each channel of the wavelet decomposition using equation (5) and obtain a feature vector having Q elements.
3. Repeat steps (1) and (2) for all training images of each class and calculate the cluster center vector fm by taking average over all N samples.

Classification Phase

1. Decompose an unknown brain MR image with the cosine-modulated wavelet transform. Compute the energy feature of each channel of the wavelet decomposition and obtain a feature vector f.
2. Calculate the decision function $D_w = D(f, f_m)$ for the unknown image. Assign unknown image to a class w if $D_w \leq D_j$ for all $j \neq w$ and $w = 1, 2$ (normal or abnormal).

4   Experimental Results

The proposed technique is implemented on a real human brain images. The database consists of total 40 images: 20 normal and 20 abnormal images. These are 1.5 T, axial, T2-weighted images of 300x400 sizes. These images are belonging to 18 persons (12 men and 06 women). Their ages vary between 7 and 80 years. The samples of normal and abnormal images are shown in Fig. 4.

In fig. 4(b), there is altered signal on left fronto- temporo-parietal region intensity appearing heterogeneously hyper intense indicates the possibility of lesion in that image. Out of 40 images, 7 images from each class is randomly selected for training the classifier and the remaining 13 from each class is used for testing the classification accuracy of the proposed technique. Thus there are 7x2= 14 images for training and 13x2=26 images for classification.

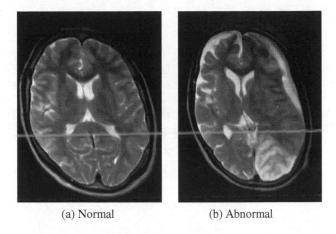

(a) Normal   (b) Abnormal

Fig. 4. Samples of normal and abnormal images in Axial view (T2 Weighted)

The Proposed algorithm is applied to each image of the database. Two levels of wavelet decomposition with Cosine modulated wavelet and Daubechies wavelet of length 4 (db4) is done. After wavelet decomposition 7 sub-bands are generated, for each sub-band energy feature is calculated. Feature vector for all the 14 images of the database is created for training. For similarity matching in classification phase Bays classifier is used. For the query image, classification algorithm computes the feature vector and compares with all features of the feature vector. The similarity between query image and image in the database is calculated by Euclidian distance and query image labeled to its proper class (normal or abnormal) on the basis of minimum distance to the cluster center vector of that class. Cluster vector obtained alter two level of wavelet decomposition for Cosine modulated wavelet and Daubechies wavelet of length 4 (db4) is shown in Table 1. LH1, HL1, HH1 and LH2, HL2, HH2

Table 1. Cluster vector for normal and abnormal images of the database

Wavelets	Image class	Energy feature of 7 sub bands obtained after 2 level wavelet decomposition						
		LH1	HL1	HH1	LL2	LH2	HL2	HH2
Cosine modulated wavelet	NL	0.0053	0.0079	0.0020	0.8234	0.0234	0.0378	0.0103
	ANL	0.0047	0.0064	0.0017	0.7783	0.0214	0.0321	0.0093
Daubechies wavelet (db4)	NL	0.0043	0.0064	0.0043	0.8242	0.0198	0.0036	0.0096
	ANL	0.0039	0.0052	0.0039	0.7789	0.018	0.0308	0.0085

NL: Normal brain MR image, ANL: Abnormal brain MR image.

represent the finest scale wavelet coefficient i.e. detail image at level 1 and level 2 respectively and LL2 coarse level coefficients i.e. approximation image at level 2.

Experimental results with correct classification percentage are presented in Table 2. Very good average classification rate of 100% is achieved using only 7 energy features obtained from a 2-level decomposition of cosine-modulated wavelets against the accuracy of only 92.857 % with wavelet transform using Daubechies wavelet (db4). The classification accuracy of this work shows the advantages of the proposed technique. Cosine modulated wavelet features gives better inter class variability as compared to the Daubechies wavelet features. Better discrimination and low design implementation complexity and good filter quality, of the cosine-modulated wavelets has been effectively utilized to give better features improved performance in terms of classification accuracy and time.

Table 2. Percentage classification accuracy for normal and abnormal MR brain images

	db4 wavelet	*Cosine-modulated wavelets*
Normal image	100	100
Abnormal image	85.714	100
% Average Classification	92.857	100

5   Conclusions

In this paper, we have presented a technique for classification of T2 weighted, MR brain image that uses cosine-modulated wavelet based features. Bays classifier is used to classify brain MRI image as normal or abnormal. The proposed classification algorithm gives very high classification accuracy of 100 % with the available database of MR brain images. The work can be extended to develop the algorithms for localization of tumor in abnormal images as well as for the processing of pathological brain tissues (e.g. necrotic tissue, lesion, edema etc) in MR brain image.

Acknowledgment. The authors would like to thank Dr. Kajal Mitra, Prof & Head, Radiolgy and Diagnostic Imaging department, NKP Salve Institute and Latamangeshkar Hospital, Nagpur, for providing brain MR images and for help in interpretation and validation of results.

References

1. Balfar, M.A., Ramli, A.R., Saripan, M.I., Mashohor, S.: Review of Brain MRI image segmentation Method. Artificial Intelligent Rev. 33, 261–274 (2010)
2. El-Dahshan, E.-S.A., Salem, A.B.M., Younis, T.H.: A Hybrid technique for MRI brain image classification. Studia University, Babes-Bolyai, Informatica, vol. LIV (November 2009)

3. Kharrat, A., Gasmi, K., Messaoud, M.B., Benamarene, N., Abid, M.: A Hybrid approach for automatic classification of Brain MRI using Genetic algorithm and support vector machine. Leonardo Journal of Science (17) (July-December 2010) ISSN 1583-0233
4. Qurat-ul-ain, Latif, G., Kajmi, S.B., Arphan Jafar, M., Mirja, A.M.: Classification and segmentation of Brain tumor using texture features. Recent Advance in Artificial Intelligence. Knowledge Engineering and Databases
5. Hsin, H.C.: Texture segmentation using modulated wavelet transforms. IEEE Transactions on Image Process 9(7), 1299–1302 (2000)
6. Kokre, M., Chatterji, B.N., Biswas, P.K.: Cosine Modulated wavelet based texture features for content- based image retrieval. Pattern Recognition Letters (25), 391–398 (2004)
7. Mushrif, M.M., Dubey, Y.K.: Texture Classification using Cosine modulated wavelets. In: 3rd International Conference on Signal Acquisition and Processing, ICSAP 2011 (2011)
8. Gopinath, R.A., Burrus, C.S.: On cosine-modulated wavelet orthonormal bases. IEEE Transactions on Image Processing 4(2), 162–176 (1995)
9. Koilpillai, R.D., Vaidyanathan, P.P.: Cosine-modulated filter banks satisfying perfect reconstruction. IEEE Transactions on Signal Processing 40(4), 770–783 (1992)

A Novel Approach for Email Login System

Bhavesh Patel, Dipak Patel, Shakti Patel, Rajendra Patel,
Bhavin Tanti, and Nishant Doshi

{bhavesh.patel17,dipak.eng,shakti.infredible,patelraj112,
bhavintanti,doshinikki2004}@gmail.com

Abstract. In real time world password will be compromise by some adversaries is common for different purpose. In ICC 2008 Lei et al. introduced a new user authentication system based on the virtual password system methodology. In virtual password methodology they have used function based on the linear randomization approach, to be secure against identity theft attacks, phishing attacks, keylogging attack and shoulder surfing system. At ICC 2010 Li's given a security attack which compromised the user on the Lei's work. The proposed approach gives modification on Lei's work to prevent the Li's attack with reducing the server overhead. This paper also discussed the problems with current email password recovery system and gives the better approach.

Keywords: Cryptography, Email attack, Security, Virtual password.

1   Introduction

In the client server related security system environment one of the most defensive components is the client or user authentication module which allows the server to grant access and deny to others [1]. In today's world there are many methods available like PIN, secret question, biometrics etc. out of all previously methods the PIN methods used widely due to less complex, less costly etc.

There are certain problem can happen with PIN problem. One of well known is there are static password so they can be stolen means stealing the client identity. Some attacks including phishing [2], malware (record the keystrokes) based attacks [3] and shoulder surfing attacks [4] are also possible. All of these attacks are previously described in [5].

The focus of this paper is the virtual password system which was proposed by Lei et al in [7] [8], secret little functions in [9] and by Li in [6]. The proposed virtual system claimed secure again all the attacks previously given but in [6] proved that with on an average by decoding 2 encrypted messages the virtual password system can be compromised. And the password can be useful to impersonate the user. The initial version of this paper will be at [10] [11].

In email password recovery we use secondary email address to reset the password which was compromised. But the attacker can change the secondary email id after compromising the password. So this paper gives proposed change in this problem.

The rest of the paper is organized as follows. The next section gives background study or literature study which proposed in [7], [8]. In section III we discussed the

N. Meghanathan et al. (Eds.): CCSIT 2012, Part II, LNICST 85, pp. 282–287, 2012.
© Institute for Computer Sciences, Social Informatics and Telecommunications Engineering 2012

how modified system can prevent the attack discussed in [6]. In section IV the system and usability with clients were explained. Related work and future expansion are given in section 5. References are at the end.

2   Background Study

2.1   The Concept of Virtual Password [7]

The idea behind virtual password is to hiding the password by generating fresh password every time or random password every time. The server and user share a virtual password which was composed of two parts. 1) A fixed secret password $X=x_1,x_2,...,x_n$, where each $x_i \in Z$ and Z will be set of all password characters. 2) For each login section server will generate or user will provide with random salt $Y= y_1, y_2,...y_n$, where $y_i \in Z$. Based on this user will enter a virtual password $K= k_1, k_2,...k_n=B(X, Y)$ to clear the authentication the process. So this protocol is common challenge-response method following based on secret key. In section III of [7] and section 3 of [8] Lei considered secret key is the fixed part so in [6] the authors had given a type of attack that possible to impersonate the user. Figure 1,2 and 3 shows the practical example of virtual password.

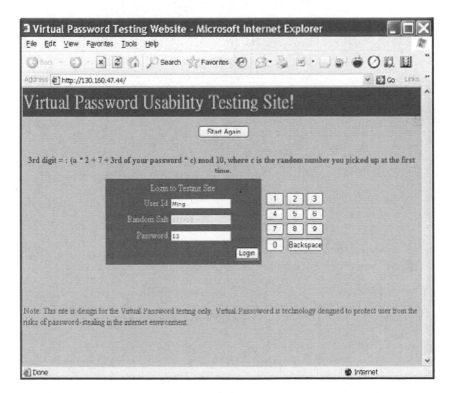

Fig. 1. Login Page[7]

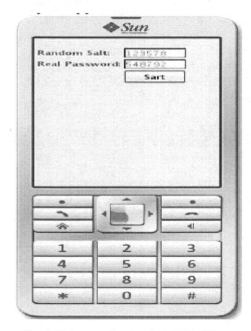

Fig. 2. Helper application for PC [7]

Fig. 3. Helper application for Mobile [7]

2.2   The Virtual Password System [7]

In [7] authors use the randomized linear function which follows the steps as given below. The fixed password is given by $X=x_1,x_2,...x_n$ and a secret integer $a \in Z$. The integer chosen in such a way that $\gcd(a,Z)=1$. We assume the $Z=\{0,1,...,Z-1\}$ i.e. the cardinality of set Z.

1.   The server generates a random salt $Y = y_1, y_2,..., y_n$ and sends it to the user, where $y_i \in Z$.
2.   The user generates a random integer $c \in Z$, calculates $K = k_1,k_2,...,k_n$ as follows:

  - $k_1 = B_1(x_1,a,y_1,c)=(ax_1 +y_1 +x2 +c)\bmod Z;$
  - $k_i = B_i(x_i,a,k_{i-1},y_i,c)=(ak_{i-1} + y_i + x_i + c +x_{i1}) \bmod Z$ for $2 \leq i \leq n$, where $i1=((i +1) \bmod n)+1$. Then, the user sends K to the server.
3. For $c = 0,1,...,Z - 1$, the server calculates K in the same way as in Step 2, and checks if it matches the response received from the user. If no any value of c produces a match, reject the user; otherwise accept him/her.

Lei et al. claimed that using random integer c, the virtual password system is secure against multiple observer login. In [6] authors proved above statement wrong and stated that the secret fixed password can be compromised successfully.

Here in all previous work there were some assumptions required to be made. If we assume that the random salt is provide at login time than at that time user had to calculate the K and this can be detected in phishing or shoulder surfing attack easily. If we assume that user will come with random salt and password K for that and at login time he/she enter both random salt and K and server will verify by decrypting K and compare with random salt provided by user , if both match than user successfully login. The other assumption is server will not records the previous random generated salts so reply attacks can be possible.

2.3 E-Mail System

The current email password recovery system depend upon the secondary email id or secret question and it's answer. But if the password is compromised than attacker can change all the personal setting so it will not be secure to retrieve password. So this paper deals with this problem and suggests solution which can be added as the extensions to the existing email systems.

3 Proposed Work

3.1 Modified Virtual Password System

There are several ways we can defend the attack given by [6]. If we can send the value of c with each transaction than attacker does not know that for which particular c value the particular K value associate. So if we provide wrong c value for K value than server will know that attacker is trying to gain the access so it will deny the login.

Here server will check for message that for which value of c , $c \in Z$ the K is built. So if we assume the sufficiently large value of Z than the processing time of server will be increase in the distributed environment where lots of users are connected to server. So in that case sending c value with K in the encrypted form will save the server time. Another advantage is server will record all previous c values used between user for the same password and after login user can see this values with date and time so reply attack using same c value not possible.

Now if user generates the random number every time than we do not require c value so modified algorithm is as follow.

The randomized linear function will follow the steps as given below. The fixed password is presented by $X = x_1, x_2, ..., x_n$ and a secret integer $a \in Z$. The integer chosen in such a way that gcd(a,Z)=1. We assume the Z={0,1,...,Z-1} i.e. the cardinality of set Z.

1   The user generates a random salt Y = y1 ... yn
     and encrypts using public key of server , where $y_i \in Z$.
2   The user calculates K = k1 ...kn as follows:
     – $k_1 = B_1(x_1,a,y_1)=(ax_1 +y_1 +x_2 +c)\bmod Z$;
     – $k_i = B_i(x_i,a,k_{i-1},y_i)=(ak_{i-1} + y_i + x_i + x_{i+1}) \bmod Z$ for $2 \leq i \leq n$, where i + 1=((i +1) mod n)+1. Then, the user sends K and encrypted random number to the server.
3   The server calculates K by decrypting the random number and in the same way as in Step 2, and checks if the response received from the user is matched with it or not. If no match, reject the user; otherwise accept him/her.

In above steps we are not using random number c. the other way is to add one more step in previously algorithm, send value of c with current time stamp decrypt under public key of server. Server will cross verify the value of c so no need to check all values between 0 to Z-1.

3.2   Email Password System

The problem with current email password reset/recovery system is given in introduction. If we want more security as reasonable cost than we require one more password that will be used to protect the secondary email id. So if the password for email id is compromised than attacker cannot change the secondary email id without as he not has the second password. So in other words we can say that second password only come in picture when user want to change the secondary email id. Suppose that user forgot the second password than to recover user simply make request and password or link to reset password will be send to secondary email id.

Now consider the other scenario, attacker had broken or get the password for some email so now he had access to all that email system for which the hacked email address were used for secondary email id. This attack cannot prevent by the above modified system.

4   System and Usability

4.1   Modified Virtual Password System

In the [7] and [8] the concept of system and usability were discussed. The main aim of this is how quickly user can adapt the system. If we assume the user had mobile phone or laptop or some palmtop devices than user can simple installed the application which is freely available on internet and then enter secret key and random number will be generated by application itself and then application give final key K which user enter at login time. So if we assume that user do not have any of above devices than it's depending on user the ability to do mentally. So the modified system had same problem as previous system.

4.2   Email Password System

In the present email system user has to give one password for doing all the stuff. But in new system user may require to remember both password. We assume that user will enter/select both the password at registration time.

5   Conclusion

This paper try to modify the existing scheme to prevent attack and give the minor change in email password reset system in order to get better security. In future another attack can be possible or we can minimize the overall length as well as can have better scheme for email password reset so the attack which possible in proposed system cannot possible in future system.

References

1. Menezes, A., van Oorschot, P., Vanstone, S.: Handbook of Applied Cryptography. CRC Press (1996)
2. Jakobsson, M., Myers, S. (eds.): Phishing and Countermeasures: Understanding the Increasing Problem of Electronic Identity Theft. John Wiley & Sons, Inc. (January 2007), http://phishing-and-countermeasures.com
3. Aycock, J.: Computer Viruses and Malware. Springer, Heidelberg (2006)
4. Wikipedia, Shoulder surfing (computer security) (2009), http://en.wikipedia.org/wiki/Shouldersurfing (computersecurity)
5. Matsumoto, T., Imai, H.: Human Identification through Insecure Channel. In: Davies, D.W. (ed.) EUROCRYPT 1991. LNCS, vol. 547, pp. 409–421. Springer, Heidelberg (1991)
6. Li, S., Khayam, S.A., Sadeghi, A.-R., Schmitz, R.: Breaking Randomized Linear Generation Functions based Virtual Password System. In: ICC 2010 (2010)
7. Lei, M., Xiao, Y., Vrbsky, S.V., Li, C.-C., Liu, L.: A virtual password scheme to protect passwords. In: Proceedings of IEEE International Conference on Communications (ICC 2008), pp. 1536–1540. IEEE (2008)
8. Lei, M., Xiao, Y., Vrbsky, S.V., Li, C.-C.: Virtual password using random linear functions for on-line services, ATM machines, and pervasive computing. Computer Communications 31(18), 4367–4375 (2008)
9. Xiao, Y., Li, C.-C., Lei, M., Vrbsky, S.V.: Secret little functions and codebook for protecting users from password theft. In: Proceedings of IEEE International Conference on Communications (ICC 2008), pp. 1525–1529. IEEE (2008)
10. Bhavin, T., Doshi, N.: A secure email login system using virtual password. Cryptology ePrint Archive, Report 2010/481.2010 (2010)
11. Tanti, B., Doshi, N.: A secure email login system using virtual password. ArXiv e-prints:1009.5729.2010 (2010)

A Non-revisiting Genetic Algorithm with Adaptive Mutation for Function Optimization

Saroj and Devraj

Deaprtment of Computer Science and Engg.
Guru Jambheshwar University of Science and Technology, Hisar
{ratnoo.saroj,devraj.kamboj}@gmail.com

Abstract. Genetic Algorithm (GA) is a robust and popular stochastic optimization algorithm for large and complex search spaces. The major disadvantages of Genetic Algorithms are premature convergence and revisits to individual solutions in the search space. In other words, Genetic algorithm is a revisiting algorithm that leads to duplicate function evaluations which is a clear waste of time and computational resources. In this paper, a non-revisiting genetic algorithm with adaptive mutation is proposed for the domain of function optimization. In this algorithm whenever a revisit occurs, the underlined search point is replaced with a mutated version of the best/random (chosen probabilistically) individual from the GA population. Moreover, the suggested approach is not using any extra memory resources to avoid revisits. To test the power of the method, the proposed non-revisiting algorithm is evaluated using nine benchmarks functions. The performance of the proposed genetic algorithm is superior as compared to simple genetic algorithm as confirmed by the experimental results.

Keywords: Function optimization, Genetic algorithm, Non-revisiting, Adaptive mutation.

1 Introduction

Developing new optimization techniques is an active area of research and Genetic Algorithm (GA) is a relatively new stochastic optimization algorithm pioneered by Holland [1]. A GA is capable of finding optimal solutions for complex problems in a wide spectrum of applications due to its global nature. A GA is an iterative procedure that maintains a population of structures that are candidate solutions to the specific problem under consideration. In each generation, each individual is evaluated using a fitness function that measures the quality of solution provided by an individual. Further, genetic operators such as reproduction, crossover and mutation are applied to introduce the diversity in the candidate solutions. In fact, a GA mimics the natural principle of survival of the fittest. A fitness proportionate selection and GA operators ensures the better and better fit solutions to emerge in successive generations [2][3][4]. However, GAs are not without limitations. Two of the main problems are-1) premature convergence i.e. many a times a GA converges to some local optimal

N. Meghanathan et al. (Eds.): CCSIT 2012, Part II, LNICST 85, pp. 288–297, 2012.
© Institute for Computer Sciences, Social Informatics and Telecommunications Engineering 2012

solution. 2) Redundant function evaluations. A simple genetic algorithm do not memorizes the search points or solutions to the problem that it visits in its life time and it revisits lots of search points generating duplicate solutions resulting into redundant fitness computations. Here, a revisit to a search position x is defined as a re-evaluation of a function of x which has been evaluated before. The problem of revisit is all the more severe towards the end of a GA run. In many domains, the fitness evaluation is computationally very expensive and lots of time is wasted in revisiting the parts of the search space and duplicate function evaluations.

In this paper, we propose an improved GA with adaptive mutation operator to avoid revisits and redundant fitness evaluations to a large extent. This GA has the elitist approach and retains the best individual in every new population. A look up for revisits is made only in the current population along with the population of previous generation. If any individual produced is found duplicate, it is replaced probabilistically with a mutated version of the best individual or of a random individual. The mutation operator is adaptive in the sense that its power of exploration decreases and power of exploitation increases with the number of generations.

The proposed approach demonstrates that the duplicate removal introduces a powerful diversity preservation mechanism which not only results in better final-population solutions but also avoids premature convergence. The results are presented for nine benchmark functions and illustrate the effectiveness of duplicate removal through adaptive mutation. The results are directly compared to a simple GA which is not removing duplicate solutions generated in its successive generations.

The rest of the paper is organized as below. Section II describes the related work. The proposed non revisiting Genetic algorithm which removes duplicate individuals through adaptive mutation is given in section III. Experimental design and results are enlisted in section IV. Section V concludes the papers and points to the future scope of this work.

2   Related Work

A number of implementations of genetic algorithms in a wide spectrum of applications have been reported in the literature [1][2][3][4][5]. Since the inception of genetic algorithms, several advanced GA approaches came up improving the efficiency and efficacy of the results achieved in the domain of function optimization along with various other domains. Many of these approaches addressed the problem of premature convergence and revisiting behavior of genetic algorithms. One of these advance approaches is devising new GA operators that can be adapted to produce suitable individuals by considering the state of the current population with respect to global optimal solution[6][7][8][9]. Srinivas and Patnaik (1994) employed a self adapted GA that achieved global optima more often than a simple GA for several multimodal functions [8]. In their work, they have suggested use of adaptive probabilities of crossover and mutation to maintain adequate diversity to avoid premature convergence. Another significant contribution came from Herrera and Lozano (2000) who suggested heterogeneous gradual distributed real coded genetic algorithms (RCGAs) for function optimization domain. They devised new fuzzy connective based crossovers with varying degree of exploration and exploitation which proved very effective to avoid premature convergence and achieved one of the best reported results for several benchmark problems of function optimization [9]. Friedrich et al. (2007) have made an important contribution by analyzing the influence of simple diversity mechanisms used in selection procedures on the runtime behaviour [14].

The other important problem with GAs that has been in the recent focus of the GA research community is redundant function evaluations and revisits. Mauldin [10] was among the first ones who enhanced the performance of a genetic algorithm by eliminating duplicate genotypes during a GA run. Mauldin used a uniqueness operator that allowed a new child x to be inserted into the population if x was greater than a Hamming-distance threshold from all existing population genotypes. Davis [4] also showed that a binary coded GA for a comparable number of child evaluations that removes duplicates in the population has superior performance. Eshelman and Schaffer [11] reconfirmed this observation by using selection based innovations and new GA operators that prevented revisits. The problem of duplicate function evaluations has also been addressed by providing GA a short/long term memory i.e. the GA stores all the search points visited and their corresponding fitness into some data structure. In such approaches every time a new search point is produced by GA, before actually computing its fitness, the memory of GA is looked into and if this search point exists, its fitness is not recomputed. If the new solution is not in the memory, its fitness is computed and appended to the memory. Binary search trees, Binary partition tress, heap, hash tables and cache memory have been used to provide the supplement memory to GA. Such strategies have resulted in performance enhancement of GAs by eliminating revisits partially or completely [12][13][14][15]. Recently, Yuen and Chow [16] used a novel binary space partitioning tree to eliminate the duplicate individuals. Saroj et al. used a heap structure to avoid the redundant fitness evaluations in domain of rule mining. Their approach proved to be effective for large datasets. [17]. Though, all these duplicate removal method reduce the run time of a GA, they require huge data structures and a significant amount of time is spent for memory look ups. It is not uncommon for a GA to run for thousands of generations with a population of hundreds of individuals. If we assume a GA with 100 individuals and 5000 generations, we shall need a data structure that can store 250000 problem solutions and that is when we assume half the individuals produced are duplicates. The GA shall require 500000 look ups to avoid redundant fitness computation. GAs is already considered slow as compared to other optimization techniques and these approaches further slow down GA's performance. Clearly this method is successful only in the domains where fitness computations time is significantly larger than the memory look ups time and not suitable at all for domain of function optimization where fitness evaluation is relatively less expensive. Therefore, in this paper, we have adopted a genetic algorithm approach that maintains the diversity through adaptive mutation, avoids revisits to a large extent and that is without any additional memory overheads.

3   Proposed Non-revisiting GA with Adaptive Mutation

Non-revisiting algorithm is the one which do not visit the search points already visited. The improved GA with non-revisiting algorithm and adaptive mutation has to perform some extra steps than a simple GA. These steps are used to found the duplicate individuals. If any duplicate individual is found then it is mutated and reinserted in the current population. The duplicates are looked with respect to current and the previous generation only. There is a special condition that the best individual is preserved and not mutated. The flow chart and algorithm for the proposed GA is given in Fig. 1 and Fig 2 respectively.

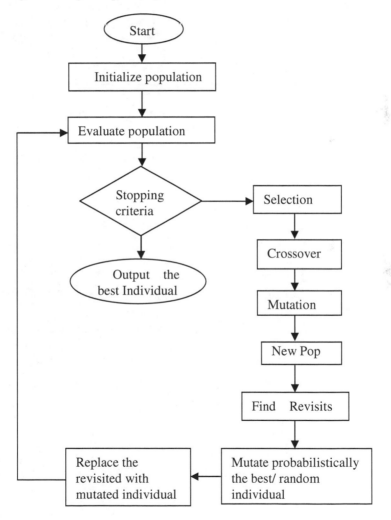

Fig. 1. Step by step procedure for Non-revisiting GA with adaptive mutation

The mutation applied is Gaussian adaptive mutation. The Gaussian function generates a random number around zero mean. The formula for mutation is as follows.

$$mscale = mscale - mshrink * mscale * (current\_generation / total\_generations) \qquad (1)$$

$$x(i) = best\_x \pm (gaussian\_rand * mscale) \qquad (2)$$

The amount of mutation is controlled by the two parameters mscale and mshrink. Here, mscale represents the variance for mutation for the first generation and mshrink represents the amount of shrink in mutation in successive generations. The mutation scale decreases as the number of generation increase. It is clear from the above formulae that such kind of mutation is exploratory during the initial runs and exploitative towards the final runs of the GA. We have kept the mscale as 1.0 and mshrink equals to 0.75.

---

1. Begin
2. Initial condition: Initial population:- old-pop=[], new-pop[], Stopping Flag:-
   SF=0, Best Fit=0, Visiting Flag:- VF[]=0
3. Initialize the population in old-pop
4. Evaluate the fitness of old-pop and calculate the overall best individual up to
   the current generation.
5. If(stopping criteria=yes)
   5.1 SF=1   //set stopping flag
   5.2 Output the best individual
   5.3 Stop
      Else
   5.4 Copy the best individual into new-pop
   5.5 Perform a GA step by applying GA operators i.e. selection, crossover and
      mutation.
   5.6 Maintain the old population and store the newly generated individuals in
      the new pop.
   5.7 For (i=1 to pop-size)
         check revisits within the new-pop and   with respect to old-pop
   5.8 If revisit && not best_individual)
   5.9   VF[i]=1
   5.10 For(i=1 to pop-size)
   5.11 If VF[i]==1
            New-pop[i] =mutated (new-Pop[i])
   5.12 old-pop=new-pop
Go to step 4

Fig. 2. Algorithm for the proposed GA with no-revisit

The proposed non-revisiting GA with adaptive mutation has three key strengths.

1. It automatically assures maintenance of diversity and prevents premature convergence. Most of the individuals in a GA population are guaranteed to be different. By nature of the proposed GA, it is impossible for a population to consist of one kind of individuals only.
2. It might not completely eliminate the revisits. However it doesn't require large data structure to store the individuals to do a look up for duplicates and only uses the previous and current populations which are anyway available.
3. It probabilistically takes the advantage of the best individuals and converges faster without suffering problem of convergence.

4   Experimental Results

We have implemented the proposed non-revisiting GA with adaptive mutation on nine Benchmarks functions in four dimensions and the set of test functions is given below.

4.1   Test Function Set

1. Rastrigin's function   6. Ackley function
2. Sphere function   7. Rotated Griewank's function
3. Generalized Rosenbrock function   8. Rotated Weierstrass's function
4. Generalized Rastrigin function   9. Branin function
5. Griewank's function

All these function are shown in detail in the Appendix I. The first four functions are unimodal functions; the next five are multimodal functions designed with a considerable amount of local minima. The eighth and ninth functions are rotated multimodal functions. The improved GA is implemented in MATLAB. A comparison is made between a simple GA and the proposed GA on the basis of mean and the best fitness over the generations. The best fitness is the minimum score of the population. Both the GA's stop when there is no improvement in the best score over last fifty generations. The population size is kept at 20 for all the functions and, the crossover and mutation rates are equal to 0.6 and 0.01 respectively. The normal mutation rate is kept low as adaptive mutation to remove duplicates is also applied. The best individual or a random individual is mutated with equally likely (probability = 0.5) to replace the revisited points in the new population. We have used real encoding, proportion scaling, remainder stochastic selection, one point crossover and Gaussian mutation. These results are averaged over 20 runs of the GA. A comparison on the basis of mean and best fitness of the final population of the proposed GA and simple GA for nine benchmarks functions is shown Table 1.

Table 1. Best and mean fitness of the final populations of SGA and Non-revisiting GA with adaptive mutation

Benchmarks Function	Best Fitness		Mean Fitness	
	SGA	NRGA	SGA	NRGA
Rastrigin's function	2.561	1.023	21.68	19.81
Sphere function	0.004	0.002	1.474	1.102
Generalized Rastrigins function	2.461	0.024	18.47	15.71
Griewank's function	0.0020	0.0021	1.107	1.062
Generalized Rosenbrock function	2.834	0.091	21.24	19.24
Ackley function	3.324	0.009	22.42	18.96
Rotated Griewank's function	0.009	0.001	1.104	1.014
Rotated Weierstrass's function	3.784	0.092	1.936	1.526
Branin function	3.187	0.335	16.16	14.01

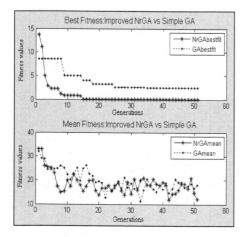

Fig. 3. Performance comparison of NRGA and SGA for Generalized Rastrigin's function

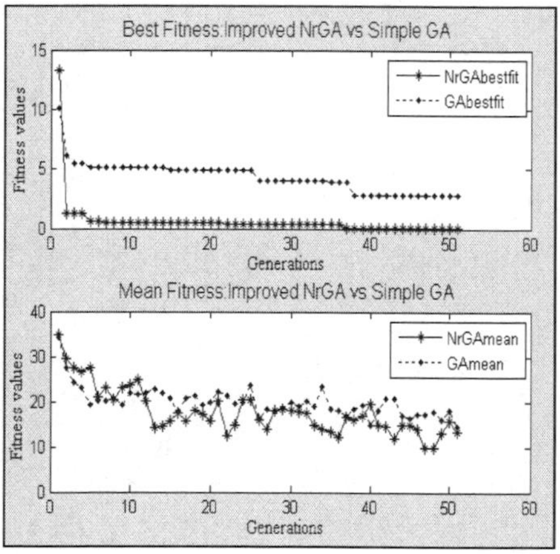

Fig. 4. Performance comparison of NRGA and SGA for Generalized Rosenbrocks's function

Though, our approach performs better for all the nine benchmark functions, Fig. 3 to Fig. 6 show the performance comparison of non-revisiting GA with simple GA for Generalized Rastrigins, Rosenbrock, Ackley and Rotated Griewank functions where NRGA approach dominates significantly. It is quite clear from the results that the performance of the non-revisiting GA with adaptive mutation is better than the simple GA.

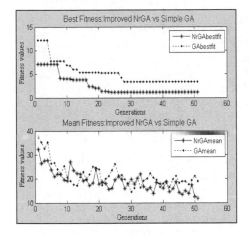

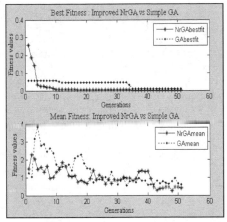

Fig. 5. Performance comparison of NRGA and SGA for Ackley's function

Fig. 6. Performance comparison of NGGA and SGA for Generalized Griewank's

5 Conclusion

In this paper, a novel non-revisiting GA with adaptive mutation is proposed and tested in the domain of function optimization. Though new improved GA may not completely eliminate the revisits and redundant function evaluation, it guarantees enough diversity to avoid the problem of premature convergence. The envisaged approach achieves better accuracy without much overheads of searching time for duplicates individuals and large data structures to serve as the long term memory for a GA as suggested in several earlier approaches [12][13][14][15].

The mechanism of a probabilistic adaptive mutation provides the much required balance between exploration and exploitation along with faster convergence to the optimal. It is exploratory in the initial runs of GA and exploitative towards the final runs of GA. More the number of generations of the GA, smaller will be the change in the new individual that replaces the revisited search point. The experimental results are very encouraging and show that the improved GA is clearly superior to its conventional counterpart. The adaptation of the current approach is underway for the domain of rule mining in the field of knowledge discovery.

References

[1] Holland, J.H.: Adaptation in Natural and Artificial Systems. MI Univ. Michigan Press, Ann Arbor (1975)
[2] Goldberg, D.E.: Genetic Algorithms in Search, Optimization and Machine Learning. Addison-Wesley, New York (1989)
[3] Michalewicz, Z.: Genetic Algorithms + Data Structures = Evolution Programs. Springer, Heidelberg (1999)
[4] Davis, L.: Handbook of Genetic Algorithms. Van Nostrand Reinhold, New York (1991)

[5] De Jong, K.A.: An Analysis of the Behavior of a Class of Genetic Adaptive Systems, PhD Thesis, University of Michigan, Ann Arbor, MI, USA (1975)

[6] Srinivasa, K.G., Venugopal, K.R., Patnaik, L.M.: A Self Adaptive Migration Model Genetic Algorithm for Data Mining Applications. Information Sciences 177, 4295–4313 (2007)

[7] Ono, I., Kita, H., Kobayashi, S.: A Robust Real-Coded Genetic Algorithm using Unimodal Normal Distribution Crossover Augmented by Uniform Crossover: Effects of Self-Adaptation of Crossover Probabilities. In: Proceedings of the Genetic and Evolutionary Computation Conference, vol. 1, pp. 496–503. Morgan Kaufmann, Orlando (1999)

[8] Srinivas, M., Patnaik, L.M.: Adaptive Probabilities of Crossover and Mutation in Genetic Algorithms. IEEE Transactions on Systems, Man and Cybernetics 24, 656–667 (1994)

[9] Herrera, F., Lozano, M.: Gradual Distributed Real-Coded Genetic Algorithms. IEEE Transactions on Evolutionary Computation 4, 43–63 (2000)

[10] Mauldin, M.L.: Maintaining Diversity in Genetic Search. In: Proceeding National Conference on Artificial Intelligence, Austin, pp. 247–250 (1984)

[11] Eshelman, L., Schaffer, J.: Preventing Premature Convergence in Genetic Algorithms by Preventing Incest. In: Proceedings of the Fourth International Conference on Genetic Algorithms. Morgan Kaufmann, San Mateo (1991)

[12] Povinelli, R.J., Feng, X.: Improving Genetic Algorithms Performance by Hashing Fitness Values. In: Proceedings Artificial Neural Network, England, pp. 399–404 (1999)

[13] Kratica, J.: Improving the Performances of Genetic Algorithm by Caching. Computer Artificial Intelligence 18, 271–283 (1999)

[14] Friedrich, T., Hebbinghaus, N., Neumann, F.: Rigorous Analysis of Simple Diversity Mechanisms. In: Proc. Genetic Evolutionary Computation Conference, pp. 1219–1225. ACM Press, London (2007)

[15] Ronald, S.: Duplicate Genotypes in a Genetic Algorithm. In: Proc. IEEE Int. Conf. Evolutionary Computation, Anchorage, Alaska, pp. 793–798 (1998)

[16] Yuen, S.Y., Chow, C.K.: A Non-revisiting Genetic Algorithm. In: Proc. IEEE Congress on Evolutionary Computation, Singapore, pp. 4583–4590 (2007)

[17] Saroj, Kapila, Kumar, D., Kanika: A Genetic Algorithm with Entropy Based Probabilistic Initialization and Memory for Automated Rule Mining. In: Meghanathan, N., Kaushik, B.K., Nagamalai, D. (eds.) CCSIT 2011, Part I. CCIS, vol. 131, pp. 604–613. Springer, Heidelberg (2011)

Appendix I: Benchmarks Function

1. Rastrigin's function: $f1(x) = 10x + \sum_{i=1}^{D}[x^2 - 10\cos(2\pi x) + 10]$
   Where $x \in [-5.12, 5.12]^D$
   Min $f1(x) = f1([0, 0....0]) = 0$

2. Sphere function [14]: $f2(x) = \sum_{i=1}^{D} x^2$
   Where $x \in [-5.12, 5.12]^D$
   Min $f2(x) = f2([0, 0....0]) = 0$

3. Generalized Rosenbrock function: $f3(x) = \sum_{i=1}^{D-1}[100(x_{i+1} - x_i^2)^2 + (x_i - 1)^2]$
   Where $x \in [-5.12, 5.12]^D$
   Min $f3(x) = f3([1, 1....1]) = 0$

4. Generalized Rastrigin function: $f4(x) = \sum_{i=1}^{D}[x^2 - 10\cos(2\pi x) + 10]$
   Where $x \in [-5.12, 5.12]^D$
   Min $f4(x) = f4([0, 0... 0]) = 0$

5. Griewank's function: $f5(x) = \frac{1}{4000}\sum_{i=1}^{D} x^2 - \prod_{i=1}^{D} \cos\frac{xi}{\sqrt{i}} + 1$
   Where $f5(x) \in [-5.12, 5.12]^D$
   Min $f5(x) = f5([0, 0... 0])$

6. Ackley function: $f6(x) = -20 \exp(-0.2\sqrt{\frac{1}{D}\sum_{i=1}^{D} x_i^2}) - \exp(\frac{1}{D}\sum_{i=1}^{D}\cos 2\pi x_i) + 20 + e$
   where $x \in [-5.12, 5.12]^D$
   Min $f6(x) = f6([0, 0... 0]) = 0$

7. Rotated Griewank's function: $f7(x) = \frac{1}{4000}\sum_{i=1}^{D} z^2 - \prod_{i=1}^{D} \cos\frac{zi}{\sqrt{i}} + 1$
   Where $z = xM$, $f7(x) \in [-5.12, 5.12]^D$
   Min $f7(x) = f7([0, 0... 0])$

8. Rotated Weierstrass's function [14]:
   $$f8(x) = \begin{bmatrix} 1 & \cdots & D \\ \vdots & \ddots & \vdots \\ D2 - D & \cdots & D2 \end{bmatrix} \quad //D2 = D^2$$

9. Branin function: $f9(x) = (x_2 - \frac{5}{4\pi 2}x_1^2 + \frac{5}{\pi}x_1 - 6)^2 + 10(1 - \frac{1}{8\pi})\cos x_1 + 10$
   Where $x \in [-5.12, 5.12]$
   Min $f9(x) = f9([-3.142, 12.275]) =$
   $f9([3.142, 2.275])$

xScribble: A Generalized Scheme
for String-Encoding Graphical Data in Multiuser
Graphical Chat

Rahul Anand, Joshy Joseph, P. Dipin Dev, Hegina Alex, and P.C. Rafeeque

Department of Computer Science and Engineering,
Government College of Engineering Kannur,
Kannur, India
rahulanand.fine@gmail.com, rafeeqpc@yahoo.co.in

Abstract. Multiuser graphical chat enables two or more users to communicate user generated graphical data in real time. It is most commonly used in online whiteboards where users can interact simultaneously. In this paper, we introduce xScribble: a generalized scheme for encoding graphical data for real time network communication. The paper discusses how to encode graphical data from various drawing tools into string format flexible enough to be used with any text chat system. The memory efficiency and performance of the xScribble scheme is also analysed.

Keywords: graphical chat, string-encoding, online whiteboard, real-time interaction.

1 Introduction

Usage of graphical aids like diagrams is often necessary to communicate certain concepts in a clear and concise manner. But exchange of graphical data over the Internet is limited by the overhead of available techniques like e-mail or file sharing. This makes Graphical chat an important functionality that is missing in todays instant messaging services. Available closed source online whiteboard applications have implementations apparently dependent on their programming environment [1].

Most of the popular chat clients like Google Talk [2] provide full fledged text chat service together with voice, video chatting and even file sharing. In this scenario, an online whiteboard scheme which can be integrated to the existing system of frequently used clients can be an attractive notion in terms of online communication. Such a scheme has the additional advantage of being able to be used with other available services like video call. This is desirable to the end users in that graphical chat can be quite naturally integrated into their usual choice of chat client. Such a scheme can be implemented by a generalized algorithm which efficiently converts graphical data into a representation compatible with any text chat protocol. Moreover, this scheme realizes graphical chat with minimal additions to the underlying protocol, and optimizes the added memory requirements for communication.

N. Meghanathan et al. (Eds.): CCSIT 2012, Part II, LNICST 85, pp. 298–307, 2012.

In this paper, we describe a scheme for efficiently encoding graphical data into string representation in real time. We call the complete scheme 'xScribble'. The scheme provides a general algorithm to encode graphics into text representation which can be communicated over a text chat protocol.

The rest of the paper is organized as follows. Section 2 discusses related work. Section 3 evaluates the basic features of graphical data from various drawing tools. Section 4 describes encoding and decoding of certain popular class of drawing tools. Section 5 presents the general algorithms used for encoding and decoding graphical data. Section 6 and Section 7 respectively discusses notions for extension of the encoding format to account for other drawing tools, and actual results of implementing the scheme. Section 8 concludes the paper with remarks on its future scope.

2   Related Work

Existing online whiteboard systems use web based technology like Java applet and Adobe Flash [3]. The actual protocol used comes under a closed specification. Scriblink [4] is an online whiteboard with real-time collaboration. The site is built using Java. Groupboard [5] hosts multiple whiteboards with multi-user interaction capability. The underlying technology includes Java applet and Ajax. Twiddla [6] is another browser based whiteboard application intended to support web meetings. It provides inbuilt voice support using Java plug-in. iScribble [7] features an online artist collaboration built in Adobe Flash. openCanvas [8] is a desktop image editing software with additional networking feature. A maximum of 3 users can connect to a running instance of the software using TCP connections.

3   Components of Graphical Data

In this section, we analyse the basic information required to represent and/or reproduce graphical data. The paper discusses the data components associated with two main classes of drawing tools - Free hand tools and Fixed point tools - and other tools which are variations of the above classes. In any drawing environment, deciding where and how to produce the graphical output essentially involves retrieving the coordinates of the user input device. Additional parameters may be supplied to the method - most commonly the selected colour, line style, fill style (for closed figures) etc. We analyse the minimal information required to represent major classes of drawing tools.

3.1   Free-Hand Tools

The sequence of line segments connecting all the mouse coordinates during the free hand drawing can form a smooth curve. A mouse drag is thus represented by a connected sequence of line segments called a polyline [9]. Parameters associated with free hand tools can be the stroke thickness and stroke style.

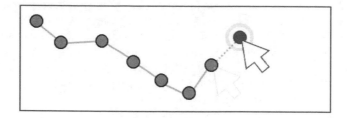

Fig. 1. Free hand drawing starts once the user clicks the mouse inside the drawing area. The point of mouse click is retrieved and stored. As the mouse is dragged from this point, the next mouse coordinate is retrieved. A line segment is drawn from the last stored point to the new point with preferred colour and thickness properties. The new point now becomes the last stored point. The process continues as long as the mouse is dragged. Free hand drawing stops when the mouse release action is detected.

3.2   Fixed-Point Tools

Most common fixed point tools include Rectangle, Oval, and Straight line tool. In these tools, the point of first click of mouse is taken as a fixed point. From here, the user can drag the mouse to decide the dimensions and orientation of the graphic output. When the mouse is released, the final drawing is saved on the drawing board. The user is provided with graphical feedback by painting intermediate shapes during the mouse drag. This gives a sensation of scaling the graphic object by the dragging of the mouse. Anyhow, the final drawing depends only on the point of initial mouse click and the point where the mouse is finally released.

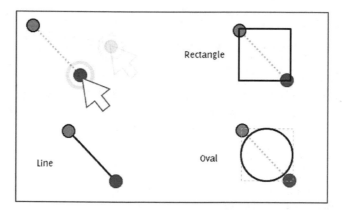

Fig. 2. In Rectangle tool, the points are considered to be forming a diagonal of the rectangle. The required parameters for the drawing method to draw a rectangle are computed from these two points using simple geometry. In Oval tool, the two points again form the diagonal of a rectangle. Here, an ellipse is drawn whose major and minor axes are respectively the width and height of the enclosing rectangle. In Straight line tool, a line segment is drawn between the initial and final points. The closed figures have a parameter determining whether or not they are filled with a selected fill colour.

3.3   Other Tools

This section discusses the component information for three other drawing tools. Most of the drawing tools are variations of the above two categories.

Air Brush. The Air brush tool is similar to a free hand tool in that the user can draw with an air brush by dragging the mouse over the drawing area. But instead of a single stroke, the air brush provides a sensation of spraying the colour over the mouse path within a fixed thickness. The logic behind the Air brush tool is to create a spraying effect at each passing coordinate.

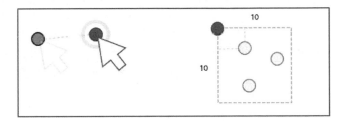

Fig. 3. At each mouse coordinate, a square of dimensions 10 pixel units is assumed adjacent to the mouse coordinate. The algorithm now generate and paint 15 random pixels such that their coordinates fall within this square.

Pseudo code for Air brush

```
Air-brush (x, y, selected-color)
  Repeat 15 times:
    Set rx to an random integer between 0 and 10
    Set ry to an random integer between 0 and 10
    Draw a node of selected-color at (x+rx, y+ry)
```

Flood Fill. The Bucket fill tool uses the flood fill algorithm [10] to fill closed areas in the drawing. It first determines the colour at the pixel where the user clicks. This becomes the target colour. The selected colour is filled in this target pixel. Now the colouring spreads to the top, bottom, left and right pixels of the target pixel. These pixels are painted if their colour is same as the target colour. In case any new pixels are painted, the colouring spreads from them again. Thus, all the pixels in the region formed by the target colour is filled with the selected colour.

Pseudo code for Flood fill

```
Flood-fill (x, y, replacement-color):
  Set Q to the empty queue
  Set node to Node(x,y)
  Set target-color to colour of node
  Add node to the end of Q.
  While Q is not empty:
    Remove first element from Q, let it be n
    If the color of n is equal to target-color
      Set the color of n to replacement-color
      Add the node to the west of n to the end of Q
      Add the node to the east of n to the end of Q
      Add the node to the north of n to the end of Q
      Add the node to the south of n to the end of Q
```

Text Tool. The Text tool writes reads a string of text from the user and paint it on the drawing board at specified coordinates [11]. Clicking the mouse on the drawing board allows the user to input the desired string at this location. The entered string is now painted over the canvas in the required colour.

4   Encoding the Graphical Data

At the heart of xScribble scheme is the technique of encoding the variety of graphical data into individual strings, which can be efficiently decoded at the receiver side. The string should encode the kind of tool used for drawing, its properties and the set of associated mouse coordinates. In order to represent the data in the most optimized format, the scheme uses a comma separated list of decimal integers. Since the data is essentially a text string it can be communicated with HTTP in the web or any other chat protocols like XMPP [12].

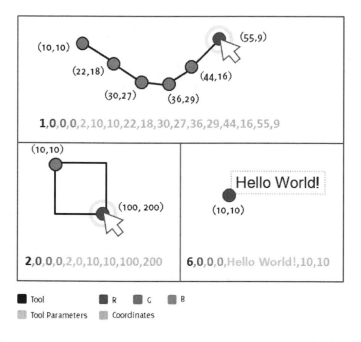

Fig. 4. The integer components in the string are separated by commas. The first component identifies the tool used for creating the graphics. The tool specific parameters follow this. The colour is represented in the form of its Red, Blue, and Green (RGB) components, each which is encoded as integers between 0 and 255 [13]. Other parameters will follow these values. Here colour is only a tool-specific parameter and may be omitted for tools or drawing commands which doesn't require colour information. Finally, the required coordinates which defines the graphic are appended. These integers are processed in pairs as they are alternatively the x and y coordinates of each point. Again, the number of coordinates can vary from a single point to a series of points according to the type of the tool used.

4.1 Free-Hand Tools

Most of the common free hand tools can be represented under a single category and thereby by a single integer in our encoding scheme. As discussed, the parameters for a free hand tool other than colour are line thickness and line style (dotted, dashed, solid) [14]. These class of tools require the entire series of points through which the user has performed the free hand stroke. Thus all the coordinates from the beginning to the the end of drawing are encoded into the string.

4.2 Fixed-Point Tools

The most common fixed point tools in popular drawing applications are Rectangle, Oval and Straight line. Although the technique of producing the graphics differs for each of these tools, they require only a pair of coordinates to represent the position and size of the resulting graphic. These are respectively the fixed point and the final position of the dynamic point where the user stops drawing. The parameters for these tools are also common, which generally include the colour, outline thickness and the fill style for Rectangle and Oval. Although the encoding scheme is structurally similar we should account for the fact that the coordinates are processed in a different way for each of the tools.

4.3 Other Tools

Air Brush. According to the discussed drawing logic of Air brush, a large number of pixels are painted on the canvas as the user draw with the air brush tool in free hand style. Here we may strike a compromise between data size and accuracy of data reproduction by encoding only the coordinates through which the user moves the mouse. At the receiver end, random pixels are generated around each of these path coordinates. Actual test cases show that the random pixels restricted to a small area and in a dense fashion show only negligible differences between the graphic outputs at the two ends.

Flood Fill. Flood fill tool demands only minimal information to produce its graphical output. These information are namely the selected fill colour and the coordinates from where the flood fill procedure is to commence. Major part in producing the graphical output is done by the flood fill algorithm. However the performance of flood fill is critical in the dynamic environment of graphical chat since other graphical data may be added to the canvas before the flood fill is completed.

Text Tool. Text entry tool is a special case in string encoding of graphical data in that this tool uses a character set different from other tools in the encoding. Encoded data of text tool consists of the actual text string entered by the user and the coordinates showing the relative position where the text is to be painted. The character set may even include a wide variety of Unicode symbols if user input in native languages is to be provided.

Drawing Commands. The peculiarity of drawing commands, such as Clear Canvas, is that they do not usually need any graphical information such as colour or any coordinates. When such commands are encoded, basically they only contain the first component integer, which identifies the command itself. Even in an environment where a larger set of commands are used, the same unified encoding scheme can be used.

5   Encoding and Decoding Algorithms

This section provides the actual algorithms for encoding graphical data to text string and for decoding a text string to reproduce original graphics respectively. The algorithms account for the above mentioned categories of drawing tools. The encoding algorithm is not sequentially run for a stream of input data. Rather it spans the entire drawing process from when a user starts drawing on the canvas to when he stops drawing. The encoding algorithm consider drawing in a general context. It may be noted that the ongoing state of drawing is represented by the continuous dragging of the mouse pointer in a classic interface. Most of the other common tools can be accounted for in the algorithm as special cases of existing tools or with minimal additions.

Pseudo code for String encoding

```
if drawing starts:
   Set encode-string to the empty string
   Append current-tool, colour R,G,B values, tool
    parameters, x-coordinate and y-coordinate of current
    tool location to encode-string separated by commas

while drawing:
  if current-tool is a free hand tool
    Append x-coordinate and y-coordinate of current tool
      location to encode-string separated by commas

if drawing ends:
   if current-tool is not bucket-fill or text-input:
     Append x-coordinate and y-coordinate of current tool
       location to encode-string separated by commas
   else if current-tool is text-input:
     Append entered text to encode-string
   Send encode-string to the network
```

Pseudo code for String decoding

```
String-Decode (decode-string)
   Split decode-string at commas and store the elements
    in decode-array

   Set current-tool to the first element of decode-array

   Set R,G,B to the next three elements of decode array
   Set selected-color to Color(R,G,B)

   for each element corresponding to tool parameters:
      Set variables corresponding to the parameter values

   Set x0, y0 to the next two elements in decode array
```

```
if current-tool is a free hand tool:
  while the end of decode-array is not reached:
    Set x1, y1 to the next two elements in decode array
    Call appropriate free hand tool method with
     parameters x0, y0, x1, y1, selected-color
     and tool parameters
    Set x0 = x1, y0 = y1

if current-tool is a fixed point tool:
  Set x1, y1 to the next two elements in decode array
  Call appropriate fixed point tool method with
   parameters x0, y0, x1, y1, selected-color
   and tool parameters

if current-tool is bucket-fill:
  Call Flood-Fill(x0, y0, selected-color)

if current-tool is text-input:
  Set user-text to the last tool parameter
  Call Text-input(x0, y0, user-text, selected-color)
```

6   Implementation Details

xScribble scheme is designed to be implemented in any networking environment which supports sending and receiving text data. While integrating xScribble scheme in existing chat servers there is virtually no property which distinguishes graphical chat data from normal text chat. The encoded graphical data might be prepended with a special header string for this purpose. The application can recognize a graphical chat string when it detects the header string at its beginning.

The design of the encoding format supports efficient compression. For instance, the most commonly occurring character in the encoded string is the comma because it is used as a separator for other components. If Huffman Coding is used for compression, a comma may be represented in a single bit. Also the most frequent character set includes integers from 0 to 9. These characters can also be mapped to bit strings of size not exceeding 3 bits. Thus the size of the encoded data is considerably reduced with the minimal character set [15]. This can be a great advantage when we need to keep track of the drawing board state at a centralized server.

The method of producing the actual graphics on the canvas is implementation specific. The graphical data may be used to construct static graphics or it can be used to create separate graphical objects. Graphical objects, such as in the case of vector image editors like Inkscape [16], allow more flexibility in editing the drawing board. In this case additional information regarding the identifier assigned to the graphical object need to be encoded in the communicated data.

7   Experimental Results

We implemented an integration of the encoding scheme with Google Talk in xScribble instant messaging application [17]. Here the xScribble scheme was implemented with minimal drawing tools using Python over the XMPP protocol

[18]. Users could perform graphical chat using their Google account. The graphical data could be communicated with the same efficiency as in the case of text data. The group chat feature in Google Talk can be utilized to enable any number of users to simultaneously draw on a shared canvas. The size of graphical data was limited only by the inbuilt quota on amount of text data passing through the server. In all the cases, the size of graphics in transit is highly optimized by the encoding scheme.

We have also implemented the xScribble scheme using Java applets at client side and a server running under Tomcat. Text chat functionality was implemented in the server using HTTP messages. The scheme was tested in the Internet at connection speeds of 100 to 200 KBps. The average size of the encoded data from above mentioned drawing tools is 50 to 100 bytes, which is comparable to usual text chat data. The scheme employs an additional overhead at the client ends alone, where an extra processing is done for encoding and decoding purposes. This encoding of graphics in real-time and decoding of received messages could be performed without any noticeable delay. Simultaneous drawing over the network was tested with more than 5 users. This number can be conveniently as high as 20 or more; the scalability of the system (determined by the number of possible simultaneous users) is limited only by the capability of the server. While a basic server can have limitations regarding the maximum number of users using a particular drawing board, integration with fully developed server systems poses no perceivable delay from the side of the string encoding scheme.

8   Conclusion

Our aim in this research was to develop a scheme to efficiently communicate user generated graphics over a multi-user network in real-time. Initial studies found that existing systems have closed and implementation specific communication protocols which cannot be integrated with other server systems. We developed the xScribble scheme which provides a generalized and optimized encoding scheme for graphics. The efficient encoding of graphics to text strings with minimal character set enabled the integration of the scheme into any existing text chat server. Thus the scheme virtually enables graphical chat to be implemented as a feature in all instant messengers. The scheme may be extended further to account for vector graphic objects providing more control over the canvas. Additional exclusive locking features may be included in the encoding when users are allowed to alter the graphic objects on the canvas. We hope our work will contribute to more productive and expressive network communication.

References

1. Oekaki Central, http://www.oekakicentral.com/fp/fp1/index2.php
2. Getting started with Google Talk, http://www.google.com/talk/start.html
3. Paint Chat, http://en.wikipedia.org/wiki/Paint_Chat
4. Scriblink online whiteboard, http://www.scriblink.com/index.jsp?act=about

5. Groupboard, http://www.groupboard.com/products/
6. Twiddla, http://www.twiddla.com/
7. iScribble, http://www.iscribble.net/
8. OpenCanvas image editor, http://en.wikipedia.org/wiki/OpenCanvas
9. Foley, J.D.: Computer graphics: principles and practice, 2nd edn., p. 27. Addison-Wesley Publishing Company, Inc. (1996)
10. Dav Data. A non recursive Flood fill algorithm, http://www.davdata.nl/math/floodfill.html
11. Klawonn, F.: Introduction to Computer Graphics: Using Java 2D and 3D, p. 96. Springer, London (2008)
12. The Extensible Messaging and Presence Protocol (XMPP). RFCs, http://xmpp.org/xmpp-protocols/rfcs/
13. Prez-Quiones, M.A.: Media Computation CS2984-S07 (January 2007), http://happy.cs.vt.edu/~manuel/courses/cs2984/slides/05Colors.html
14. Klawonn, F.: Introduction to Computer Graphics: Using Java 2D and 3D, p. 63. Springer, London (2008)
15. Astrachan, O.L.: From ASCII Coding to Huffman Coding (February 2004), http://www.cs.duke.edu/csed/poop/huff/info/
16. Inkscape vector editor, http://wiki.inkscape.org/wiki/index.php/Inkscape
17. Anand, R., et al.: xScribble instant messaging client for Google Talk, http://code.google.com/p/xscribble/
18. Package xmpp API documentation, http://xmpppy.sourceforge.net/apidocs/index.html

Analysis of IG DV Protocols in MPLS Network for Quality of Video Conference

Swarnalatha Mannar Mannan, Arunkumar Jayaraman,
and Srinivasa Kranthi Kiran Kolachina

M.Sc in Electrical Engineering, Blekinge Institute of Technology, Sweden
{swarnalathamannar,arunbtheespring,skko.kranthi}@gmail.com

Abstract. This paper analyzes the different Interior Gateway (IG) Distance Vector (DV) protocols like Routing Information Protocol (RIP), Interior Gateway Routing Protocol (IGRP) and Enchanced Interior Gateway Protocol (EIGRP) for MultiProtocol Label Switching (MPLS) network in video conference application. In telecommunication networks, delay is one of the major problems which leads the network to discard packets and in turn having a negative impact on a quality. The combination of MPLS prominent execution packet carrying technology along with IG protocol can reduce the packet delay in the network. The simulation results show that Enchanced Interior Gateway Routing Protocol (EIGRP) can be used for achieving better quality.

Keywords: IGP, MPLS, Video Conference, Routing Protocols.

1   Introduction

With increase in usage of computers, the number of users has also increased intensely. As a result, the users' demands of Type of Service (ToS) have also risen. Particularly services like Internet broadcasts; video conferencing etc have become one of the significant services in the users demand. Nevertheless, with increase in usage of internet the traffic has lowered the Quality of Service (QoS). This effect in turn has also affected the services that required guaranteed QoS like video conferencing. Even though Internet Protocols (IP) networks are very expandable and cheap, QoS and the embodiment of traffic engineering are problematic [1].

Multi-Protocol Label Switching (MPLS) is a new technology which provides a solution for effective traffic engineering to manage the growing bandwidth demands. In order to streamline and advance the process of exchanging of IP packets MPLS merges the layer-2 information of bandwidth, latency and utilization of network links with the control protocols used in layer-3 of IP. MPLS uses label switching for effective differentiation and forwarding of packets through pre-calculated routes in the network [2].

This paper analyzes the behavior of different Interior Gateway (IG) protocols which uses Distance Vector (DV) algorithm on MPLS network. It recommends which IG-DV protocol provides a better performance in MPLS network.

N. Meghanathan et al. (Eds.): CCSIT 2012, Part II, LNICST 85, pp. 308–312, 2012.
© Institute for Computer Sciences, Social Informatics and Telecommunications Engineering 2012

The paper is structured as follows: Section II demonstrates with the background. Section III describes with the problem statement and main contribution. Section IV deals with problem solution and conclusion are presented in Section V.

2   Background

MPLS implemented networks enhance the video quality by reducing reasonable amount of packet delay. MPLS utilize the channel capacity efficaciously. It further increases the overall throughput thus results the efficiency of the network [1].

To increase QoS in a network under heavy load condition, a priority technique is applied to handle traffic in real time application such as Voice and Video Streaming [2].

The Fast Self-healing Distance Vector Protocol (FS-DVP) suppresses network failure via exchanging routing information within the network. In case of any network failure, it reroutes the packets to the destination. Thus it effectively handles the link problems and thereby increasing the routing stability [3].

3   Problem Statement and Main Contribution

Demands of real time application are increasing dramatically in MPLS networks like Voice over Internet Protocol (VoIP) and Video. The performance of the MPLS network is measured by the amount of traffic that is being carried by the link and utilization of network bandwidth. The routing techniques lay a way to achieve good performance in video conference application in the MPLS network. Which IG DV protocol gives a better performance for a video conference application in MPLS network? On analyzing the different IG DV protocols like RIP, IGRP, and EIGRP in MPLS network better performing protocol is selected based on the different parameters like throughput and end-end packet delay.

The main contribution of this paper is to implement different IG DV protocols like RIP, IGRP and EIGRP in the MPLS network and analyze the two different parameters like throughput and End to End packet delay for video conferencing application. This research idea is validated with help of network simulation tool called OPNET (Optimized Network Evaluation Tool).

4   Problem Solution

4.1   Modeling

The network model is implemented in OPNET presented in Fig.1. The MPLS network contains Label Switching Router (LSR) and Label Edge Router (LER). LSRs are core devices that switch packets, and LERs are edge devices that are connected with external networks like R1 (Router 1) and R2 (Router 2) and determine the routes. When the server sends a packet to client, the packet reaches LER1 in MPLS network, after the addition of label it is forwarded through LSR1 and LSR2. When the packet leaves each MPLS router, the label of packet is replaced and forwarded to next hop address according to label information which is mentioned in the packet. The same process is done in a client to server communication.

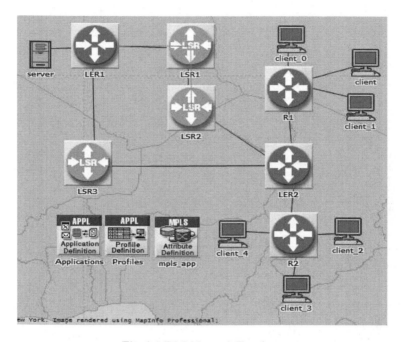

Fig. 1. MPLS Network Topology

4.2   Implementation and Validation

In the designed network, the RIP is activated first and then the simulation is started. The traffic in the network is observed for 40 minutes. Later, the other protocols like IGRP, EIGRP are activated one by one and the traffic in the network is observed for a time period of 40 minutes.

From Fig. 2, it is evident that there is a variation in delay in each scenario. With RIP, end to end packet has a delay of 4.7 seconds for the first 10 minutes of simulation run time and then there is a sudden increase in delay for 8 seconds and thereafter constant. While considering IGRP, end to end packet has a delay of 3.5 seconds for the initial 20 minutes of simulation run time. Consequently, it rises approximately to 7.2 seconds after which it remains constant. While considering the EIGRP, end to end packet delay maintains a constant value of 4.1 seconds after the first 2 minutes till the simulation run time.

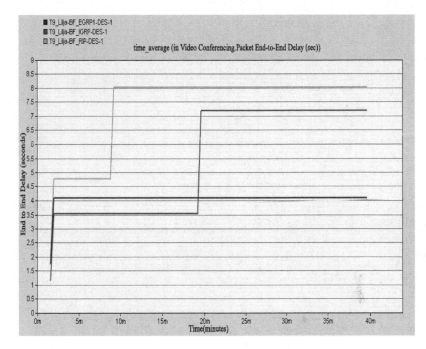

Fig. 2. Packet Delay in the network vs Run time of simulation

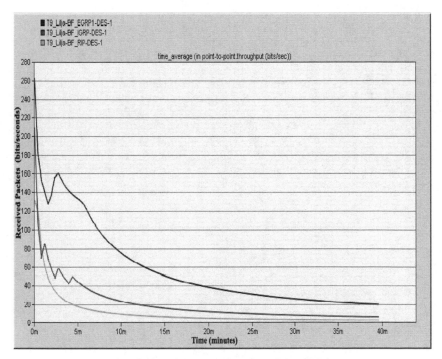

Fig. 3. Throughput vs Run time of simulation

From Fig. 3, it is noticeable that packet throughput is minified when embarking one of the simulations after traffic increased step by step. The packet forwarding is decreased as the traffic increases for RIP, IGRP and EIGRP. It can also be noted from Fig. 3 that EIGRP gives a better packet conduct when compared to the other two protocols namely RIP and IGRP.

5   Conclusion

This paper shows the performance analysis of MPLS network implemented with IG DV protocols such as RIP, IGRP, and EIGRP for video conferencing. From the simulation results it can be seen that EIGRP IG DV protocol provides less packet delay and better throughput than RIP and IGRP.

In Future this work can be extended in implementing the video conferencing application in the wireless networks and other real time applications like Multimedia, VoIP and Video Networks.

Acknowledgments. We would like to thank our Professor Wlodek Kulesza for his motivational support and guidance provided in this project.

References

1. Kim, J.M., Park, I.K., Kim, C.H.: A study on the performance enhancements of video streaming service based on MPLS network. In: Proceedings of 2004 International Symposium on Intelligent Signal Processing and Communication Systems, ISPACS 2004 (IEEE Cat. No.04EX910), November 18-19, pp. 601–603 (2004)
2. Kaarthick, B., Nagarajan, N., Rajeev, S., Angeline, R.: Improving QoS of audio and video packets in MPLS using network processors. In: 2008 16th IEEE International Conference on Networks (ICON), December 12-14, pp. 1–5 (2008)
3. Wang, B., Zhang, J., Guo, Y., Zhou, J.: A study of fast network self-healing mechanism for distance vector routing protocol. In: Proceedings of the 2009 International Conference on Multimedia Information Networking and Security (MINES 2009), November 17-20, pp. 413–416 (2009)

A Comparative Analysis of Watermarking Techniques for Copy Protection of Digital Images

Dolley Shukla[1] and Manisha Sharma[2]

[1] ShriShankaracharya College of Engineering & Technology, Bhilai
dolleyshukla@yahoo.co.in
[2] Bhilai Institute of Technology, Durg
manishasharma1@rediffmail.com

Abstract. Digital watermarking is the process of embedding information into a digital signal, i.e. audio, pictures, video, etc. Embedded marks in the message are generally imperceptible but can be detected or extracted. By imperceptibly hiding information into the video content it is possible to provide copy protection .The embedding takes place by manipulating the content of the digita l data, which means the information is not embedded in the frame around the data. If the signal is copied, then the embedded information is also in the copy. So, Watermarking is an emerging technology that is claimed to have an important application in copy protection. A variety of watermarking techniques have been proposed by researchers for the copy-protection. This paper presents an extensive review of the prevailing literature in watermarking for copy protection.

Keywords: Broadcast monitoring, Copy protection, Digital image watermarking, Video.

1 Introduction

As the digital broadcasting is developing enormous digital multimedia contents are available easily. Digital media have an advantage that can be copied without loss in quality but it is also a disadvantage in the viewpoint of copyright management. Conventional cryptographic schemes permit only valid key holders to access the encrypted data, but once when such data is decrypted there is no way to trick its reproduction & redistribution. Therefore, conventional cryptographic schemes provide little protection against copy protection. A digital watermark is intended to complement cryptographic schemes for copy protection. There are several techniques presented for copy protection and copy right protection by the researchers[1– 3] .This paper concentrates on copy protection techniques.

The procedure of embedding watermark into a multimedia element like image, audio or video is referred to as watermarking [4]. It is possible to extract this embedded data at a later stage, or detected in the multimedia element for diverse purposes including copy protection, access control, and broadcast monitoring .

N. Meghanathan et al. (Eds.): CCSIT 2012, Part II, LNICST 85, pp. 313–318, 2012.

2   Watermark System Design Issues

An array of challenges related to the watermarking technology have arisen. There are a number of other issues, some technical and some non-technical, which have also come to play an important role . An image watermarking procedure needs to satisfy the following requirements [5].

- **Transparency**
The watermarked image should be indistinguishable from the original image even on the highest quality equipment.

- **Robustness**
The ideal watermark must be highly Robust & needs to be flexible to a range of possible attacks by pirates. These attacks may be robustness against compression such as JPEG, scaling and aspect ratio changes, rotation, cropping, row and column removal, addition of noise, filtering, cryptographic and statistical attacks, as well as insertion of other watermarks [6]. The watermark must survive the geometric distortions as well as more arbitrary scaling and cropping which a pirate may use to avoid watermark detection.

- **Economic Costs**
Adding a watermark detector require some degree of redesign. In order to minimize that cost, detector must be implemented in about 30 000 gates. 90 000 gates are often mentioned as a target for the complexity of the watermark detector.

- **False Positives Rate**
A true false positive occurs when a watermark is detected when no watermark has been embedded. An invalid positive occurs in case a watermark has been embedded but the wrong payload is retrieved . An invalid positive occurs in case a watermark has been embedded but the wrong payload is retrieved. False positive probability is 4.7×10^{-23} and is more than sufficient for all practical purposes.

3   Problem Statement

New platform that embeds hard disk drive in the DBR(Digital Broadcast Receiver) system is developed recently [7]. This system can cause a copyright infringement problem if there is no copy protection scheme. Once a scrambled program is descrambled, this stream can be copied several times after saving in the hard disk drive. So there is a need to add copy protection information to the stream. This information must be strongly embedded to the contents. It can only be removed when the contents suffers severe degradation. This is a reason why watermarking method should be used. For copy protection, watermark information must be embedded in the content and detected whether this content is copyrighted or not. Watermarked video data has two kinds of copy control information i.e., 'Copy never', or 'Copy freely'.

When the use users try to copy a stream to another media, after checking this copy control information, the copy process is done when the bit is 'Copy freely'. In the case of 'Copy never', the content cannot be copied anymore.

4   Requirements of Copy Protection System

The main requirements of copy protection system are as follows:

- The copy-protection system may be implemented in four states:
  Copy-Free (CF), Copy-Never (CN), Copy-Once (CO), Copy-No-More (CM).
- Compliant devices (i.e. devices which obey the Content Scrambling System
  (CSS) rules) do not allow copying of Copy-Never (CN) and Copy-No-More
  (CM) content.
- A compliant device should allow copying Copy-Once (CO) content. A legal copy
  of Copy-Once(CO) content should have a Copy-N0-More(CN) state.
- A compliant device should not play Copy-Never (CN) content off recordable
  media.
- The copy protection system should not affect the image quality.
- The copy protection system should not interfere with the content creation process.
- Detection of copy-protection state should be fast.
- The average consumer should not be able to circumvent the copy protection
  system.
- The false-positive rate should be extremely low.
- The copy protection system should be inexpensive to implement.

5   Comparative Analysis of Recent Researches

Watermarking digital media has received a great interest in the research community. In this section we have presented a comparative analysis of literatures provided by researchers in watermarking for copy protection. Most copy watermarking schemes focus on image and video watermarking.

A digital watermark is an imperceptible signal added to cover image , which can possibly be identified at a later stage for copy protection identification, ownership proof, and the like. Contemporary digital watermarking schemes mainly target image and video copy protection. The watermark comprises of information regarding the rules of usage and copying which the content owner desires to enforce. These will commonly be undemanding rules like "this content may not be copied", or "this content may be copied, but no subsequent copies may be made of that copy".

For copy protection several methods are proposed.

Cox et al [8] described the copy-protection system currently under consideration for DVD. This system broadly tries to prevent illicit copies from being made from either the analog or digital I/O channels of DVD recorders. An analog copy-protection system is utilized to protect the NTSC/PAL output channel by preventing copies to Video Hollywood studio (VHS). The digital transmission of content is protected by a robust encryption protocol between two communicating devices. Watermarking is used to encode copy control information retrievable from both digital and analog signals. Hence, such embedded signals avoid the need for metadata to be carried in either the digital or analog domains.

F. G. Depovere, [9] discussed the various issues that play a role in designing a copy-protection system for digital versatile disk (DVD) video as perceived by Millennium, one of the two contenders in the DVD-video copy-protection standardization activity. It has presented the Millennium watermark system, the systems proposed for DVD video copy protection by Philips, Macro-vision and Digimarc. They also address some specific system aspects, such as watermark detector location and copy generation control. The DVD copy protection problem cannot be solved by encryption alone. Digital watermarking is needed to prevent copy-protection being circumvented by noncompliant devices. It describes the Millennium watermark system as proposed for DVD copy protection purposes, and it illustrate how the basic requirements for that application are met.

Ton Kalker [10] discussed that watermarking is an important enabling technology for copy protection or broadcast monitoring of video. A watermarking scheme that meets the requirements for these applications has been introduced. It discusses about the main requirement for watermarking solution for DVD copy protection.

Yeong Kyeong Seong et al [11] suggested a hard disk drive embedded digital satellite receiver with a scene change detector for video indexing. This paper discusses the implementation of a scene change detection algorithm in the compressed domain for low computing power systems. This receiver can store, retrieve and manage the broadcast data by implementing an interface between the conventional digital satellite receiver and digital storage media. In addition this receiver gives users an ability to search the scene change position by implementing a scene change detection algorithm. The detected temporal video segments are stored in the HDD and retrieved when users want. User can obtain more information for efficient video retrieval, using this proposed system.

Yeong et al [12] proposed another watermarking method based on scene segmentation for copy protection in the hard disk drive embedded digital broadcast receivers. In this, initially video sequence is segmented as scenes using the macroblock types of B-picture in the MPEG compressed domain. Second, for each scene, different embedding parameter is determined from the image complexity and motion vector amplitude. For copy protection, copy control watermark information is embedded in the DCT Domain content whether the content is copyrighted or not.

G. Boato et al [13] shows a major limitation of some recently proposed asymmetric watermarking techniques based on linear algebra lies in the strong dependence of the watermark on the original image.

Table 1. Comparative Analysis

S. No.	Author	Application Area	Remarks	Year
1.	I.J.Cox [8]	DVD	1.Improve the protection provided by encryption protocol. 2.Reduce the value of illegal unencrypted copies when they are made by making them unplayable on compliant devices. 3.This paper gives the main requirement for a watermarking solution for DVD copy protection	1999
2.	Ton Kalker [9]	Video or Broadcast Data	1.Differentiate of still Image and Video Watermarking 2. In video,due to the sheer volume of data & interlacing structure, the Quality of the content will reduce & the attack will not remove by consumer.	1999
3.	Ton kalker, Maurice Maes [10]	DVD	1.DVD copy protection problem can not be solved by encryption alone. 2.Correlation method for embedding & detection. 3.Watermark detector should be included in the playback drive. 4.System prevents the Local scrambling or bit inversion attack	2000
4.	Y. K. Seong, Y. H. Choi, J. A. Park, & T. S. Choi[11]	Broadcasting	1.Implemented a Scene change detection algorithm in compressed domain for low computing power system.	
5.	Yeong Kyeong Seong, Yoon-Hee Choi, [12]	Digital Broadcast Receiver	1. Video is segmented into different scenes. 2 .Encoded by using DCT. 3. Uses scene-change detection algorithm.	2004
6.	. Fontanari, F. G. B. De Natale , and G. Boato[13]	Video	1.Scheme is based on Linear Algebra, which is proven to be secure under protection attacks.	2006
7.	Alper Koz,Cigal [14]	Video or Broadcasting	1.Application is emerged as Free-view TV. 2.Image based rendering operation is performed. 3.Frame of multiple views are used. 4.Homography estimation method is proposed.	2010

6   Conclusion

Watermarking for copy protection is a new and emerging area of research. It mainly deals with adding hidden messages or copyright notices in digital video. This paper presents the comparative analysis of various copy protection schemes.

Even though copy protection has received ample attention in the standardization of digital video in the past five years, several issues have not yet been fully resolved. It may be unlikely that a bullet-proof solution will ever be found, but the discussions are converging on what technical mechanisms should be involved and against what these can protect.

References

1. Barni, M., Bartolini, F., Piva, A.: Managing copyright in open networks. IEEE Transactions on Internet Computing 6(3), 18–26 (2002)
2. Liao, M., Lu, C., Yuan, H.: Multipurpose watermarking for image authentication and Protection. IEEE Transactions on Image Processing 10(10), 1579–1592 (2001)

3. Akiyama, T., Motoyoshi, F., Nakanishi, S., Uchida, O.: Hybrid Digital Watermarking for Color Images Based on Wavelet Transform. In: International Conference on Applied Computing, pp. 150–154 (2006)
4. Ganic, A.E., Eskicioglu, A.M.: Robust DWTSVD domain image watermarking: embedding data in all frequencies. In: International Multimedia Conference, pp. 166–174 (2004)
5. Huang, J., Zeng, W., Kang, X.: Improving Robustness of Quantization- Based Image Watermarking via Adaptive Receiver. IEEE Transactions on Multimedia 10(6), 953–959 (2008)
6. Li, X., Xue, X.-Y., Li, W.: An Optimized Multi-bits Blind Watermarking Scheme. In: Qing, S., Gollmann, D., Zhou, J. (eds.) ICICS 2003. LNCS, vol. 2836, pp. 360–369. Springer, Heidelberg (2003)
7. Choi, T.S., Choi, Y.H., Seong, Y.K.: Design and implementation of hard disk drive embedded digital satellite receiver with file management. IEEE Transactions on Consumer Electronics 48(1), 125–130 (2002)
8. Boom, J.A., Cox, I.J., Kalker, T., Miller, M.L., Linnartz, J.-P.M.G., Traw, S., Brendan, C.: Copy protection for DVD video. In: IEEE International Conference on Image Processing, vol. 87(7), pp. 1267–1276 (1999)
9. Depovere, F.G., Haitsma, J., Kalker, T., Linnartz, J.-P.M.G., Maes, M., Talstra, J.: Digital watermarking for DVD video copy protection. IEEE Signal Processing Magazine 17(5), 47–57 (2000)
10. Kalker, T.: System issues in digital image and video watermarking for copy protection. In: IEEE International Conference on Multimedia Computing and Systems, vol. 1, pp. 562–567 (1999)
11. Choi, T.S., Choi, Y.H., Park, J.A., Seong, Y.K.: A hard disk drive embedded digital satellite receiver with scene change detector for video indexing. IEEE Transactions on Consumer Electronics 48(3), 776–782 (2002)
12. Choi, T.-S., Choi, Y.-H., Seong, Y.K.: Scene-Based Watermarking method for Copy-Protection using Image complexity and motion vector amplitude. In: IEEE International Conference on Acoustics, Speech and Signal Processing, vol. 3, pp. 409–412 (2004)
13. Boato, G., Fontanari, C., De Natale, F.G.B.: An Improved Asymmetric Watermarking Scheme Suitable for Copy Protection. IEEE Transactions on Signal Processing 54(7), 2833–2834 (2006)
14. Aydın Alatan, A., Koz, A., Cigla, C.: Watermarking of Free-view Video. IEEE Transactions on Image Processing 19(7), 1779–1785 (2010)

Unique-Minimum Conflict-Free Coloring
for a Chain of Rings

Einollah Pira

The Business Training Center of Tabriz, Iran
pira_ep2006@yahoo.com

Abstract. An optimal algorithm is presented about Conflict-Free Coloring for connected subgraphs of chain of rings. Suppose the length of the chain is $|C|$ and the maximum length of rings is $|R|$. A presented algorithm in [1] for a Chain of rings used $O(log|C|.log|R|)$ colors but this algorithm uses $O(log|C|+log|R|)$ colors. The coloring earned by this algorithm has the unique-min property, that is, the unique color is also minimum.

Keywords: Conflict-Free Coloring, Chain , Chain of Rings.

1 Introduction

A vertex coloring of graph $G=(V,E)$ as an assignment of colors to the vertices such that two adjacent vertices are assigned different colors. A hypergraph $H = (V,E)$ is a generalization of a graph for which hyperedges can be arbitrary-sized non-empty subsets of V. A vertex coloring C of hypergraph H is called conflict-free if in every hyperedge there is a vertex whose color is unique among all other colors in the hyperedge.

A *vertex coloring* of a hypergraph such that the minimum (maximum) color of any vertex of a hyperedge is unique (assigned to only one vertex in this hyperedge) is conflict-free and is called *unique-min (resp. unique-max) (confict-free) coloring*. The problems of computing a unique-min coloring is equivalent to computing a unique-max coloring since we can replace every color i by $c_{max} - i + 1$, where c_{max} is the maximum color among all vertices [1].

In this paper, first i study unique-min (confict-free) coloring in chain and ring, second, present a new algorithm for a chain of rings.

Conflict-free coloring have various applications. For Example in [2] consider the following scenario: vertices represent base stations of a cellular network interconnected through a backbone. Mobile client connect to the network by radio links and the reception range of each agent is a connected subgraph of the base stations graph. Then it may be desirable that in each agent's range there is a base station transmitting in a unique frequency, in order to avoid interference. The problem of minimizing the number of necessary frequencies is equivalent to Connected Subgraphs Conflict-Free Coloring.

N. Meghanathan et al. (Eds.): CCSIT 2012, Part II, LNICST 85, pp. 319–324, 2012.

Related work. The study of conflict-free coloring was initiated in [2] as a geometric problem with applications to cellular networks. Some of the problems proposed in that paper can be defined as hypergraph conflict-free coloring problems. The algorithm that uses O(log^2 n) colors (where n is the number of vertices) is given in [1] about CF-coloring for trees and trees of rings. Some of the problems presented in [2] can be defined as hypergraph conflict-free coloring problems. In [3,4] the conflict-free coloring was studied for grids. In [6] the conflict-free coloring of n points with respect to (closed) disks were studied and were proved a lower bound of $\Omega(\log n)$ colors. In [7] the conflict-free coloring of n points with respect to axis-parallel rectangles were studied. Various other conflict-free coloring problems have been considered in very recent papers [8,12,13,14,15,16,17].

The problem becomes more interesting when the vertices are given online by an adversary. For example, at every given time step i, a new vertex v_i is given and the algorithm must assign v_i a color such that the coloring is a conflict-free coloring of the hypergraph that is induced by the vertices $V_i = \{v_1, v_2,..., v_i\}$. Once v_i is assigned a color, that color cannot be changed in the future. This is an online setting, so the algorithm has no knowledge of how vertices will be given in the future. In [5] there is the online version of conflict-free coloring of a hypergraph. The online version of Connected Subgraphs Conflict-Free Coloring in chains was presented in [8]. Also, in the case of intervals, there are several algorithms [11]. Their randomized algorithm uses $O(\log n \log \log n)$ colors with high probability. Their deterministic algorithm uses $O(\log^2 n)$ colors in the worst case. Recently, randomized algorithms that use $O(\log n)$ colors have been found in [9,10].

2   Preliminaries

The topologies i study during this paper are chain, ring and chain of rings. A graph is a ring when all its vertices V are connected in such a way that they form a cycle of length $/V/$. A chain of rings can be defined recursively in the following manner: it is either a single ring or a ring R attached to a chain of rings C by identifying exactly one vertex of R to one vertex of C. An Example of a chain of rings is displayed in Fig. 1.

Algorithm for unique-minimum conflict-free coloring in a chain: in [2] there exists an algorithm that uses $\lfloor \log n \rfloor + 1$ colors for chains. The algorithm for a chain *{1,2,...,n}* as follows:

step 1: Color vertex $\left\lceil \dfrac{n}{2^1} \right\rceil$ with color 1

step 2: Color vertices $\left\lceil \dfrac{n}{2^2} \right\rceil$, $\left\lceil \dfrac{n}{2^1} + \dfrac{n}{2^2} \right\rceil$ with color 2

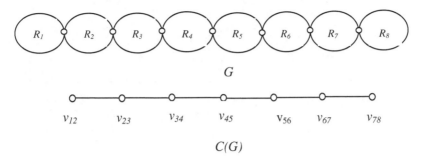

Fig. 1. A chain of rings G and the corresponding chain representation C(G)

step 3: Color vertices $\left\lceil \dfrac{n}{2^3} \right\rceil, \left\lceil \dfrac{n}{2^2} + \dfrac{n}{2^3} \right\rceil, \left\lceil \dfrac{n}{2^1} + \dfrac{n}{2^3} \right\rceil, \left\lceil \dfrac{n}{2^1} + \dfrac{n}{2^2} + \dfrac{n}{2^3} \right\rceil$ with color 3

. . . .

step i: Color verices $\left\lceil \dfrac{n}{2^i} \right\rceil, \quad . \quad . \quad . \quad , \left\lceil \dfrac{n}{2^1} + \dfrac{n}{2^2} + \dfrac{n}{2^3} + ... + \dfrac{n}{2^i} \right\rceil$ with color i

Color i is used only if $\left\lceil \dfrac{n}{2^i} \right\rceil = 1$, so in fact $\lfloor \log n \rfloor + 1$ colors are used by the algorithm.

For example, if $n=8$, the coloring is 32313234. It is clearly to see that the coloring is unique-minimum conflict-free coloring.

The above algorithm with a small change can be used to solve the unique-minimum conflict-free coloring in a ring. Pick an arbitrary vertex v and color it with a color 1 (not to be reused anywhere else in the coloring). The remaining vertices form a chain that color with the algorithm described above. This algorithm colors a ring of n vertices with $\lfloor \log (n-1) \rfloor + 2$ colors. For example, if $n=8$, the coloring is 14342434, where `1' is the first unique color used for v. It is not difficult to see that the coloring is conflict-free: All paths that include v are conflict-free colored, and the remaining graph $G-v$ is a chain of $n-1$ vertices, so paths of $G-v$ are also conflict-free colored.

3   An Algorithm for a Chain of Rings

In order to present my algorithm for a chain of rings, i will use the notion of *chain representation* of a chain of rings. Assume a chain of rings G by names $R_1, R_2,..., R_{|C|}$ is $v_{12}, v_{23},...., v_{(|C|-1)|C|}$. Let me first describe how to construct such a representation C(G) of a chain of rings G: Connect all vertices together that lied in intersection of rings. An Example of a chain of rings and its chain representation is displayed in Fig. 1.

3.1   Analysis of the Algorithm Umccr

Lemma 1. The coloring obtained by Algorithm Umccr is a connected-subgraphs unique-min conflict-free coloring.

Proof. Assume that C is a path in G. There are two cases for C. **Case 1:** C is part of a ring or a ring itself (see Fig. 2). In Fig. 2, if C only contains L_1 (or L_2), C will be colored in a unique-min way because C colored in line 8 from algorithm Umccr. In Fig. 2, if C contains L_1 (or L_2) and vertices u_1, u_2, C will be colored in a unique-min way because the coloring of it start from the max of the colors of the *vertices u_1 ,u_2* (see lines 5,8 from algorithm Umccr). **Case 2:** C lies on a connected subset of rings, say $R_i,..., R_j$; the corresponding vertices of these rings in $C(G)$, say $v_{i(i+1)}...v_{(j-1)j}$. Since these vertices of $C(G)$ in line 2 from algorithm Umccr are colored in a unique-min way, and each ring R_k in C lies between vertices $v_{(k-1)k}, v_{k,(k+1)}$ that colored in line 8 from algorithm Umccr, therefore C has been colored in a unique-min way.

Algorithm Umccr. Unique-Min Coloring for a Chain of Rings

Input: a chain of rings G by names $R_1, R_2,..., R_{|C|}$
Output: a coloring of vertices of G

1: Construct the chain representation $C(G)$ of the chain of rings G.

2: Color chain C(G) with said algorithm in section 2.

3: for i:=1 to $|C|$-1 do
    Color the vertex in intersection of the rings
    R_i, R_{i+1} by color vertex $v_{i(i+1)}$ in chain C(G).
end for
4: for i:=1 to $|C|$ do
5:   set cm:=a max color of the colored vertices of ring R_i .
6:   Delete the colored vertices of ring R_i and connect the neighbors of them.
7:   Let R_i' denote the resulting cycle.
8:   Color cycle R_i' with said algorithm in section 2 by useing colors from $\{cm+1,....,cm+\lfloor \log|R_i'|\rfloor+2\}$.
9: end for

Algorithm Umccr

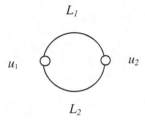

Fig. 2. A ring and the cases for path C: L_1 (or L_2) or L_1 (or L_2) and u_1, u_2

Lemma 2. The Algorithm Umccr uses $O(log|C|+log|R|)$ colors.

Proof. The number of colors for coloring $C(G)$ equal $1+log|C|$. For coloring the rings, in line 5 from algorithm Umccr, the maximum of cm's is $1+log|C|$, therefore the maximum color is used in line 8   are $1+log|C|+2+log|R|$. Thus the Algorithm Umccr uses $O(log|C|+log|R|)$ colors.

4   Conclusions

I have presented an optimal algorithm for coloring a chain of rings such that each connected subgraph has a vertex with a unique minimum color. Also i have proved this algorithm uses $O(log|C|+log|R|)$ colors. An open problem is whether i can achieve a Unique-minimum Conflict-Free Coloring for a tree of rings with $O(log|T|+log|R|)$ colors that $|T|$ is the number of rings.

Acknowledgement. This research has been supported by the business training center of tabriz.

References

1. Georgia, K., Aris, P., Katerina, P.: Conflict-free Coloring for Connected Subgraphs of Trees and Trees of Rings. In: Proc. 11th Panhellenic Conference in Informatics (2007)
2. Even, G., Lotker, Z., Ron, D., Smorodinsky, S.: Conflict-free colorings of simple geometric regions with applications to frequency assignment in cellular networks. SIAM Journal on Computing 33, 94–136; Also in Proceedings of the 43rd Annual IEEE Symposium on Foundations of Computer Science (FOCS) (2002)
3. Bar-Noy, A., Cheilaris, P., Lampis, M., Zachos, S.: Conflict-free coloring graphs and other related problems (2006) (manuscript)
4. Cheilaris, P., Specker, E., Zachos, S.: Neochromatica (2006) (manuscript)
5. Bar-Noy, A., Cheilaris, P., Smorodinsky, S.: Conflict-free coloring for intervals: from offline to online. In: Proceedings of the 18th Annual ACM Symposium on Parallel Algorithms and Architectures (SPAA 2006), Cambridge, Massachusetts, USA, July 30-August 2, pp. 128–137 (2006)

6. Har-Peled, S., Smorodinsky, S.: Conflict-free coloring of points and simple regions in the plane. Discrete and Computational Geometry 34, 47–70 (2005)
7. Pach, J., Toth, G.: Conflict free colorings. In: Discrete and Computational Geometry, The Goodman-Pollack Festschrift, pp. 665–671. Springer, Heidelberg (2003)
8. Alon, N., Smorodinsky, S.: Conflict-free colorings of shallow disks. In: Proceedings of the 22nd Annual Symposium on Computational Geometry (SCG 2006), pp. 41–43. ACM Press, New York (2006)
9. Bar-Noy, A., Cheilaris, P., Smorodinsky, S.: Randomized online conflict-free coloring for hypergraphs (2006) (manuscript)
10. Chen, K.: How to play a coloring game against a color-blind adversary. In: Proceedings of the 22nd Annual ACM Symposium on Computational Geometry (SoCG), pp. 44–51 (2006)
11. Fiat, A., Lev, M., Matousek, J., Mossel, E., Pach, J., Sharir, M., Smorodinsky, S., Wagner, U., Welzl, E.: Online conflict-free coloring for intervals. In: Proceedings of the 16th Annual ACM-SIAM Symposium on Discrete Algorithms (SODA), pp. 545–554 (2005)
12. Ajwani, D., Elbassioni, K., Govindarajan, S., Ray, S.: Conflict-free coloring for rectangle ranges using $O(n^{.382 + \varepsilon})$colors. In: Proc. 19th ACM Symp. on Parallelism in Algorithms and Architectures (SPAA), pp. 181–187 (2007)
13. Bar-Noy, A., Cheilaris, P., Olonetsky, S., Smorodinsky, S.: Online conflict-free coloring for hypergraphs. Combin. Probab. Comput. 19, 493–516 (2010)
14. Chen, K., Kaplan, H., Sharir, M.: Online conflict-free coloring for halfplans, congruent disks, and axis-parallel rectangles. ACM Transactions on Algorithms 5(2), 16:1–16:24 (2009)
15. Lev-Tov, N., Peleg, D.: conflict-free coloring of unit disks. Discrete Appl. Math. 157(7), 1521–1532 (2009)
16. Pach, J., Tardos, G.: Conflict-free colorings of graphs and hypergraphs. Combin. Probab. Comput. 18(5), 819–834 (2009)
17. Smorodinsky, S.: Improved conflict-free colorings of shallow discs (2009) (manuscript)

Enhanced Ad Hoc on Demand Distance Vector Local Repair Trial for MANET

P. Priya Naidu[1] and Meenu Chawla[2]

[1] Department of Computer Science, (M. Tech) MANIT, Bhopal, India
`Priya.cse020@gmail.com`
[2] Department of Computer Science MANIT, Bhopal, India
`chawlam@manit.ac.in`

Abstract. Ad hoc On-demand Distance Vector (AODV) is a routing schema for delivering messages in a connected Mobile Ad hoc Network (MANET). Connectivity between any sources to destination pair in the network exists when they are in radio range of each other. Local Repair is an important issue in routing protocol which is needed for minimizing flooding and performance improvement. Routes can be locally repaired by the node that detects the link break along the end to end path. In this paper, the existing Local Repair Trial method in AODV is extended to achieve broadcasting and minimizing the flooding. The enhanced protocol first creates the group of mobile nodes then broadcasting can be done and if the link breaks then local repair technique can be applied. In the network the numbers of intermediate nodes are increased by using Diameter Perimeter Model. Enhanced AODV-Local Repair Trial (EAODVLRT) protocol is implemented on NS2 network simulator. Simulations are performed to analyze and compare the behavior of proposed protocol (EAODVLRT) for varying parameters such as size of network, node load etc. Proposed protocol has been compared with the existing AODV-LRT in terms of routing load, Data delivery ratio.

Keywords: AODVLRT, MANET, Local Repair ADHOC network and Perimeter routing.

1 Introduction

A wireless network is a rising technology that will allow users to access services and information electronically, irrespective of their geographic position. Wireless communication network is a collection of independent devices connected to each other. Some of the advantages of wireless network are it is easily deployable and flexible in nature as compared to wired networks. A mobile ad hoc network (MANET) (Fig. 1) each device (nodes) is dynamically self organized in network without using any pre-existing infrastructure.

Motivation for current work is that Ad hoc network allows all wireless devices within range of each other without involving any central access point and administration. Increase in number of nodes degrades the performance of large ad hoc

N. Meghanathan et al. (Eds.): CCSIT 2012, Part II, LNICST 85, pp. 325–334, 2012.
© Institute for Computer Sciences, Social Informatics and Telecommunications Engineering 2012

network that makes the design of routing protocols more challenging. There are many simulation study has been done so far for the routing protocols. This paper has been organized as follows: In the following section we briefly review the two protocols AODVLRT (AODV with Local Repair Trials) [1] and AODV [2].

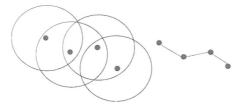

Fig. 1. Mobile Ad-Hoc Network

The main objective of this paper is to enhance AODVLRT (AODV Local Repair Trial) protocol by minimizing flooding using perimeter routing. In the previous implementation [1] throughput increases with the increase of routing overhead but, in this paper a novel method is proposed to reduce the two parameters i.e. controlling overhead and increasing throughput are the major areas of focus. The remainder of this paper is organized as follows. In section 2, a short introduction to AODV, AODVLR (AODV Local Repair), AODVLRT (AODV Local Repair Trial) is presented. In Section 3, we suggest an improvement of AODVLRT by implementing perimeter routing. Section 4 describes the simulation model adopted, and then a detailed simulation is performed to evaluate the performance of the Enhanced AODVLRT (EAODVLRT). Conclusions are presented in section 5.

2   AODV and Route Repair

Ad hoc on demand distance vector routing is an on demand approach of route finding. Routing can be done when source nodes sends the packet for transmission. AODV differs from the other on-demand routing protocols is in a way that it uses a destination sequence number to determine an up-to-date path to the destination but it doesn't broadcast update information in the network. But in this case the entire topology had being change in the network periodically [3].

Major advantage of AODV is that the connection setup delay is much less than other protocol [3]. While the drawback is that the inconsistent routes are also discovered. The periodic beaconing also leads to unnecessary bandwidth consumption.

2.1   Local Repair AODV

AODV is a popular on demand routing protocols for mobile adhoc network. The major drawback which the AODV suffer lots of link failure [4] with the failure of single node the whole route is rejected AODV can basically work in two repair techniques, i.e. source repair and local repair[5, 6]. In the AODV routing protocol is reactive protocol which means route discovery can be done on demand, if the particular node failure can occur then the whole routing can be done again. To avoid this problem local repair technique is being added by AODV and new protocol had being generated called as AODVLRT [1].

2.2   AODV Local Repair Trial (AODVLRT)

AODVLRT [1] enhancement leads to higher throughput and lower latency when compared to AODV. Major difference between AODVLR and AODVLRT is just one trial to find a repair to the route by broadcasting RREQ packet with TTL come from below equation which is taken from [1].

$$TTL = Max (0.5 \times N_H, TTL_{MNR}) + TTL_{LA}$$

Where,

TTL_{MNR}: the last known hop count from the upstream node of the failure to the destination.

TTL_{LA}: constant value

N_H: the number of hops from the upstream node of the failure to the source of the currently undeliverable packet.

3   Improvements to the Standard AODVLRT

Routing can be done from source node to the destination node by flooding the route request packet. It employs destination sequence numbers to identify the most recent path. The destination sequence number is created by the destination that is included along with any route information it sends to the requesting nodes. Destination sequence number gives the choice between two routes; a requesting node is required to select the one with the greatest sequence number. During the process of routing failure, of a node causes the whole route to be rejected. To overcome this, repairing technique can be used. The behavior of AODV in case of link failure as defined in [1, 4]. In EAODVLRT flooding can be minimized by combining the conception of perimeter routing [7].

3.1   System Model

We represent a wireless ad hoc network by a graph G= (V, E) where V is the set of vertices which represents mobile nodes and E subset of V^2 the set of edges between these vertices. An edge exists between two nodes if they are able to communicate to each other, that is two nodes u and v can communicate if they are in communicating radius of each other. If all nodes have the same range R, the set E is defined as:

$$E = \{(u, v) \in V^2 | \ u \neq v \ \& \ d(u, v) \leq R \ R$$

D (u,v) being the Euclidean distance between u and v. we also define neighborhood set N (u) of the vertex u as

$$N(u) = \{v|\ (u,\ v) \in E\}$$

3.2   EAODVLRT Algorithm

- In the algorithm, an AODV-node informs its neighbours about its own existence by constantly sending ``hello messages'' at a defined interval.
- Discovery of neighboring nodes is done by perimeter routing protocol. Through perimeter routing, the sender can only broadcast the RREQ packets to the outer boundary in counter clockwise direction. A RREQ contains the sender's address, the address of the source node and the maximum sequence number received from the node which exists.
- If the source cannot find the destination then that route can be discarded, again new route can be searched by using the local repair techniques.
- Local Repair will increase the routing protocol performance. The major idea is controlling messages from neighbour nodes; this can be done by minimizing flooding.
- In the AODV model, the inquiry about the particular route from source to destination by default is 2 but it can be increased to 7 times in EAODVLRT.
- The receiving node checks whether it has a route to the particular node. If a route exists and the sequence-number for new received route is higher than the existing route then it accepts the new route.
- If the original node does not receive an answer within a time-limit the node can assume that the source nodes are unreachable. Then the request was sent to all neighboring nodes which are easily separated by the sequence numbers. Nodes along the route will keep their routing table updated. Otherwise, the nodes will discard the entries after a particular time.

3.3   Description EAODVLRT Algorithm

In a wireless network, a route is searched from source to destination by broadcasting the route request message by the source node. The broadcasting can be done by using the perimeter routing [7, 8]. Through the perimeter routing the sender can only broadcast the RREQ packet to the outer boundary in counterclockwise direction. When broadcasting is done in perimeter mode, overlapping of links between the neighbor nodes can be avoided by constructing a planer graph using RNG or GG [9, 10]. The major drawback of AODV is that it suffers with a lot of link failures [11]. To overcome this problem local repair technique can be used [4, 12]. In AODV route is searched for two times by default in the previous AODV model but in EAODVLRT protocol it can be maximized to seven times in the particular route. In mobile ad hoc network, the mobility of each nodes can be assumed as random way point mobility model [13, 14] with the static pause time. In Fig. 2 shows the generalized work flow diagram of EAODVLRT which will show the above steps in the diagrammatical form.

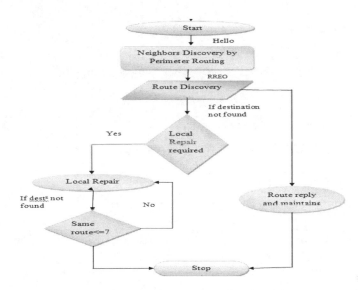

Fig. 2. Generalized work flow diagram of EAODVLRT

3.4   Perimeter Algorithm

The main idea behind perimeter forwarding is to forward the packets using the right hand rule across the faces in the planar graph that intercept the line L_pD (Fig.3). The algorithm used for perimeter forwarding [15, 16] is given below:

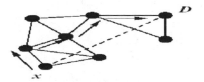

Fig. 3. Perimeter Forwarding

The PERIMETER-INIT-FORWARD [23] algorithm forwards a packet p to a node a_{min}, where,

$(a_{min}$, self) is the first edge encountered countered clockwise from the line L_pD by perimeter routing where p is packet which are send to the destination .

4   Simulation Model and Results

In this section, a series of simulation experiments in NS2 [17] network simulator will be conducted to perform an evaluation analysis on the performance ability of EAODVLRT with the discussed mechanism. We choose ad hoc on demand distance vector (AODV) routing algorithm as the underlying protocol for our base case simulation.

4.1   Simulated Network Scenario and Model

The values of AODVLRT have been taken from base paper [1] which we have
implemented. Table 1 show the simulation parameter used in the evaluation.

Table 1. Simulation Environment

Dimension of simulated area	1500×600m
Simulation Time	300 sec
Mobile Nodes	50
Transferring Mode	Unicast
Pause time	0,50, 100, 150, 200, 250,300 (m/s)
Traffic	CBR
Packet Size	1024 bytes
Routing Protocols	AODV, Enhanced AODVLR
Transport Layer agent type	TCP
Maximum speed	35
Transmission range	250ms
Mobility	Random
Bandwidth	1 megabits/sec

1.1   Performance Metrics

- **Packet Delivery Ratio**

Packet Delivery Ratio = packet received / delivered   packets

- **Average End To End Delay**

Average End to End Delay = Total end to end delay/number of packets received

- **Routing Overhead**

Routing Overhead = Total routing packets / transmitted data packets.

- **Average Throughput**

Average Throughput = Total received packets / simulation time.

1.2   Simulation Results and Technical Analysis

This section presents the simulation results and their analysis for 50 nodes network simulation scenario on a rectangular area $1500*600$ m^2.

Routing message overhead

From Fig (4), it could be noticed that EAODVLRT [5] has lower routing message overhead by on average 42% less that the AODV

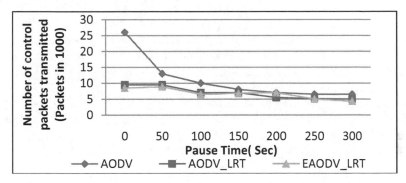

Fig. 4. Routing Overhead Analysis

This result demonstrates the effect of local repair trial using perimeter routing in EAODVLRT on reducing routing message overhead. This is due to the fact that when the node mobility is increased, the frequency of topology changes is also increased.

Throughput

The throughput resulted from AODV, AODVLRT and EAODVLRT has been presented in Fig 5. It can be found that EAODVLRT has higher throughput than AODV routing protocol by an average 1.66% which is a small increase. This result demonstrates that the effect of the modifications in EAODVLRT doesn't appear in

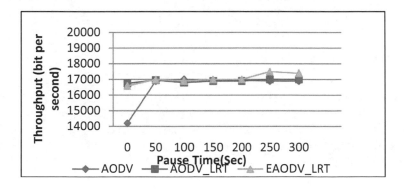

Fig. 5. Throughput Analysis

small sized networks. The number of packets dropped or left wait for a route affect the throughput as the increase in the number of packets dropped or left wait for a route reduce the throughput. The number of packets dropped or left wait for a route reduce the throughput.

Average End to End Delay

Fig (6) presents a graph of average end to end delay of AODV, AODVLRT and EAODVLRT routing protocols. It is clear that EAODVLRT gives average end to end delay higher than the AODV by on average 28% with difference. The result demonstrates the high effect of local repair trial in EAODVLRT on the delay of the small size of networks which resulted from broadcasting RREQ with TTL as in local repairs. The figure shows that when nodes pause time increases, the end-to-end delay of data packets also increases. This is because the paths between sources and required destinations frequently changed and established.

The increase in the number of broken links will led to increase the delay of transferring packets on a route until finding a repair to the route. The number of broken links affected by the route length as longer routes means the higher chances for broken links. In the same time, the number of broken links affected.

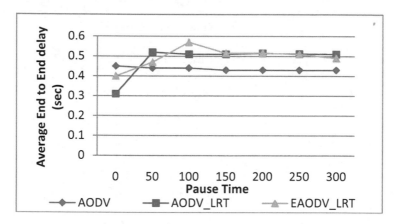

Fig. 6. Average End to End Delay

Packet Delivery Ratio

Fig 7 presents a graph of packet delivery ratio of AODV and EAODVLRT routing protocols. It is clear that EAODVLRT gives average packet delivery ratio 71.98%.If we look at this graph, which is for packet delivery ratio of both the protocols, the packet delivery by EAODVLRT is better than AODV. Results shown above concluded that EAODVLRT has packet delivery ratio which is better as compared to AODV Protocol.

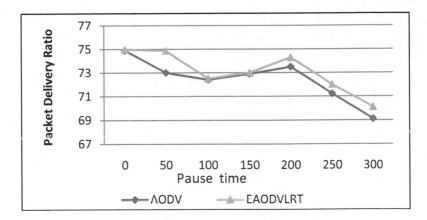

Fig. 7. Packet Delivery Ratio

5   Conclusions

This paper presents a novel approach to minimize routing overheads of AODVLRT. It also analysis enhanced AODVLRT with the existing local repair technique. This approach based on perimeter routing is used to minimize flooding process in EAODVLRT. In this paper we considered the mobile adhoc network routing protocol. Then this work analyzed the issues regarding AODV Local Repair in MANETs while exploring some existing Repair (AODVLRT) technique in literature. This technique consists of three modules. First, broadcasting and can be done by using the perimeter routing. Secondly, flooding is minimized by using local repair method and lastly, number of intermediate nodes from particular source to destination has being increased. This thesis is improved the performance of existing on-demand routing (AODV) protocols by reducing the RREQ overhead during the rout discovery operation. For its implementation and the analysis outcomes NS2 network simulator is used. For analyzing the performance of proposed schema (EAODVLRT) with the existing AODV comparisons had being done. The simulation results show that proposed schema gives the best performance in terms of packet delivery ratio, throughput and number of overhead which is used to compare the performance of these techniques.

References

1. Solimana, M.S.E., Abd El-kaderb, S.M., Eissac, H.S., Barakad, H.A.: New adaptive routing protocol for MANET. Ubiquitous Computing and Communication Journal (2006)
2. Perkins, C.E., Belding-Royer, E., Das, S.: Ad Hoc on-Demand Distance Vector (AODV) Routing. RFC 3561 (2003)
3. Yang, T., Barolli, L., Ikeda, M., Xhafa, F., Durresi, A.: Performance Analysis of OLSR Protocol for Wireless Sensor Networks and Comparison Evaluation with AODV Protocol. IEEE (2009)

4. Azzuhri, S.R., Portmann, M., Tan, W.L.: Evaluation of parameterized route repair in AODV. In: 4th International Conference on Signal Processing and Communication Systems (ICSPCS), December 13-15 (2010)
5. Al-Rodhaan, M.A., Al-Dhelaan, A.: Efficient Route Discovery Algorithm for MANETs. In: Fifth IEEE International Conference on Networking, Architecture and Storage (2010)
6. Youn, J.-S., Lee, J.-H., Sung, D.-H.: Quick Local Repair Scheme using Adaptive Promiscuous Mode in Mobile Ad Hoc Networks. Journal of Networks 1(1) (May 2006)
7. Chang, K.-B., Kim, D.-W., Park, G.-T.: Routing Algorithm Using GPSR and Fuzzy Membership for Wireless Sensor Networks, pp. 1314–1319. Springer, Heidelberg (2006)
8. Karp, B., Kung, H.T.: GPSR: Greedy Perimeter Stateless Routing for Wireless Networks. MobiCom (2000)
9. Toussaint, G.: The Relative Neighborhood Graph of a Finite Planar Set. Pattern Recognition 12(4) (1980)
10. Gabriel, K., Sokal, R.: A New Statistical Approach to Geographic Variation Analysis. Systematic Zoology 18, 259–278 (1969)
11. Jiang, M., Tay, Y.C.: Cluster based routing protocol. IETF Internet Draft, draft-ietf-manet-cbrp-spec-02.txt (1999)
12. Singh, J., Singh, P., Ran, S.: Enhanced Local Repair AODV (ELRAODV). In: International Conference on Advances In Computing, Control, and Telecommunication Technologies. IEEE (2009)
13. Izuan, M., Saad, M., Zukarnain, Z.A.: Performance Analysis of Random-Based Mobility Models in MANET Routing Protocol. European Journal of Scientific Research 32(4), 444–454 (2009) ISSN 1450-216X
14. Chen, C.-W., Weng, C.-C.: Bandwidth-based routing protocols in mobile ad hoc Networks, pp. 240–268. Springer Science+Business Media, LLC (2008)
15. del Mar Alvarez-Rohena, M., Eberz, C.: Implementation and Analysis of GPSR: Greedy Perimeter Stateless Routing for Wireless Networks. IEEE (2010)
16. Karp, B.: Geographic Routing for Wireless Network. Ph.D. Dissertation, Harvard University, Cambridge, MA (October 2000)
17. NS2 manual, http://www.isi.edu/nsnam/ns/doc/ns_doc.pdf
18. Chao, L., Aiqun, H.: Reducing the Message Overhead of AODV by Using Link Availability Prediction. In: Zhang, H., Olariu, S., Cao, J., Johnson, D.B. (eds.) MSN 2007. LNCS, vol. 4864, pp. 113–122. Springer, Heidelberg (2007)
19. Nithyanandan, L., Sivarajesh, G., Dananjayan, P.: Modified GPSR Protocol for Wireless Sensor Networks, IEEE 2(2). (April 2010)
20. Tran, D.A., Raghavendra, H.: Congestion Adaptive Routing in Mobile Ad Hoc Networks. IEEE Transactions on Parallel and Distributed Systems, 1294–1305 (November 2006)
21. Singh, J., Singh, P., Rani, S.: Enhanced Local Repair AODV (ELRAODV). IEEE (2009)

Multi-class SVM for EEG Signal Classification Using Wavelet Based Approximate Entropy

A.S. Muthanantha Murugavel[*] and S. Ramakrishnan

Department of Information Technology,
Dr. Mahalingam College of Engineering and Technology,
Pollachi – 642 003, Tamilnadu, India
{as_ananth2k1,ram_f77}@yahoo.com

Abstract. In this paper, we have proposed a novel wavelet based approximate entropy for feature extraction and a novel Multi-Class Support Vector Machine (MSVM) for the multi-class electroencephalogram (EEG) signals classification with the emphasis on epileptic seizure detection. The aim was to determine an effective classifier and features for this problem. Wavelets have played an important role in biomedical signal processing for its ability to capture localized spatial-frequency information of EEG signals. The MSVM works well for high dimensional, multi-class data streams. Decision making was performed in two stages: feature extraction by computing the wavelet based approximate entropy and classification using the classifiers trained on the extracted features. We have compared the MSVM with Probabilistic Neural Network (PNN) by evaluating with the benchmark EEG dataset. Our experimental results show that the MSVM with wavelet based approximate entropy features gives high classification accuracies than the existing classifier.

Keywords: Electroencephalogram (EEG) signals classification, epileptic seizure detection, Multi-Class Support Vector Machine, Wavelet Transform, Approximate Entropy, Probabilistic Neural Network (PNN).

1 Introduction

The electroencephalogram (EEG) is a complex and aperiodic time series, which is a sum over a very large number of neuronal membrane potentials. Despite rapid advances of neuroimaging techniques, EEG recordings continue to play an important role in both the diagnosis of neurological diseases and understanding the psychophysiological processes. In order to extract relevant information from recordings of brain electrical activity, a variety of computerized-analysis methods have been developed. Most methods are based on the assumption that the EEG is generated by a highly complex linear system, resulting in characteristic signal features like nonstationary or unpredictability [1]. Much research with nonlinear methods revealed that the EEG is generated by a chaotic neural process of low dimension [2]–[4]. As in traditional pattern recognition systems, classification of biomedical

---

[*] Corresponding author.

N. Meghanathan et al. (Eds.): CCSIT 2012, Part II, LNICST 85, pp. 335–344, 2012.
© Institute for Computer Sciences, Social Informatics and Telecommunications Engineering 2012

signals consists of two main modules namely Feature Extraction and Feature Classification. In recent papers, for studying and analyzing the behavior of EEG signals, chaos theory was used [1]–[4]. To quantify the complexity of EEG signals, numbers of entropy estimators are available. This proposed technique uses approximate entropy (ApEn) as the input feature. The general structure of developed EEG signals classification model has two modules (Fig. 1). A significant contribution of our work was the composition of composite features, which were used to train novel classifier. PNN is a type of radial basis network. For the classification and comparison we used the benchmarked datasets (EEG Signals) which includes five classes. The paper is organized as follows. In Section 2, we briefly presented the literature survey that has been performed. In Section 3 we described about the benchmark dataset, our proposed methodology with feature extraction method and classification techniques that are considered. In Section 4, we compared the results of the proposed classifiers using the features with other existing classifier. And Section 5 concludes the paper.

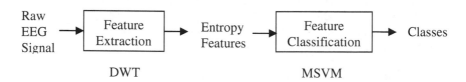

Fig. 1. General Structure of developed EEG- signals classification

2   Literature Survey

Automatic analysis and diagnosis of epilepsy based on EEG recordings is started in the early 1970s. Today, computer-based analysis addresses two major problems: 1) interictal event detection 2) epileptic seizure analysis [1]. Various feature extraction techniques have been used for the classification of EEG signals with the emphasis on seizure detection. Non-linear based feature extraction technique uses Correlation Dimension, Lyapunov Exponent and Standard Deviation for extracting the features of EEG signals [1][2]. Entropy is a term of thermodynamics that is used to describe amount of disorder in a system.Entropy based technique uses Approximate Entropy (ApEn) as the input feature [4] [6]. Wavelet based technique uses Max, Min, Mean and Standard Deviation [2] [7] [8] [9]. Time Frequency based technique, Feature extraction based on Local Variance [3]. The benchmarked dataset that have been used in the existing works was used to compare the proposed method with the existing methods. The EEG signal classification techniques are divided into three broader categories: Conventional classifiers such as Linear Discriminant Analysis [10], Support Vector Machine [8], and Naïve Bayes [1]. Neural Networks such as MLPNN [8], PNN [10], and RBFNN [6], Combinational classifiers such as Boosting, Voting and Stacking [11].

3   Proposed Methodology

3.1   Dataset Description

We have used the publicly available benchmark EEG dataset described in Andrzejak et al. [8]. The complete data set consists of five sets (denoted A–E) each containing 100 single-channel EEG segments. Sets A and B consisted of segments taken from surface EEG recordings that were carried out on five healthy volunteers using a standardised electrode placement scheme. Volunteers were relaxed in an awake-state with eyes open (A) and eyes closed (B), respectively. Sets C, D, and E originated from EEG archive of pre-surgical diagnosis. EEGs from five patients were selected, all of whom had achieved complete seizure control after resection of one of the hippocampal formations, which was therefore correctly diagnosed to be the epileptogenic zone. Segments in set D were recorded from within the epileptogenic zone, and those in set C from the hippocampal formation of the opposite hemisphere of the brain. While sets C and D contained only activity measured during seizure free intervals, set E only contained seizure activity.

3.2   Extraction of Features

Generally feature extraction is transforming the raw input data into set of features. Wavelet Transform (WT) is a spectral estimation technique in which any general function can be expressed as an infinite series of wavelets. Abnormalities in the EEG in serious psychiatric disorders are many times too subtle to be detected using conventional techniques, such as Fourier transform. WT is specific appropriate for analysis of non-stationary signals. It is well suited for locating transient events, which always occur during epileptic seizure. The decomposition of the signal leads to a set of coefficients called wavelet coefficients. The key feature of wavelets is the time-frequency localization.

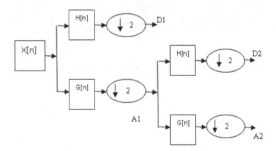

Fig. 2. Wavelet Decomposition of EEG signal into two levels of sub-bands

The decomposition of the signal into the different frequency bands is merely obtained by consecutive high-pass and low-pass filtering of the time domain signal. The procedure of multi-resolution decomposition of a signal x[n] is schematically shown in Fig. 2. Each stage of this scheme consists of two digital filters and two down-samplers by 2. The first filter, h[n] is the discrete mother wavelet, high pass in nature, and the second, g[n] is its mirror version, low-pass in nature. The detail at level j is defined as

$$D_j = \sum_{k \in Z} a_{j,k} \, \psi_{j,k}(t)$$ (1)

The approximation at level J is defined as

$$A_j = \sum_{j > J} D_j$$ (2)

It becomes obvious that

$$A_{j-1} = A_j + D_j$$ (3)

and

$$f(t) = A_j + \sum_{j \leq J} D_j$$ (4)

The down-sampled outputs of first high-pass and low-pass filters provide the detail, D1 and the approximation, A1, respectively.

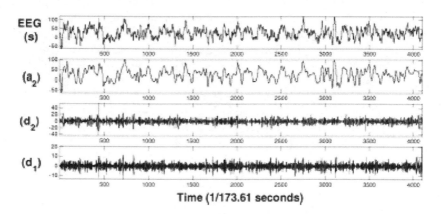

Fig. 3. Level 2 decomposition of the band-limited EEG into three EEG sub bands using fourth-order Daubechies wavelet (s = a2+d2+d1)

Wavelet has several advantages, which can simultaneously possess compact support, orthogonality, symmetry, and short support, and high order approximation. We experimentally found that time-frequency domain feature provides superior performance over time domain feature in the detection of epileptic EEG signals. Usually, tests are performed with different types of wavelets and the one, which gives maximum efficiency, is selected for the particular application. The smoothing feature of the Daubechies wavelet of order 4 (db4) made it more appropriate to detect changes of EEG signals. The EEG sub bands of a2, d2 and d1are shown in fig. 3.

Wavelet based Approximate Entropy (ApEn)

The proposed system makes use of a single feature called ApEn for the epileptic detection. The ApEn is a wavelet-domain feature that is capable of classifying complex systems. The value of the ApEn is determined as shown in the following steps. Table 1 represents the extracted wavelet based Approximate Entropy (ApEn) features for the decomposed sub bands.

Table 1. Wavelet based ApEn values used for Training and testing the classifier

Data Points	Wavelet based ApEn values used for training		Wavelet ApEn values used for testing	
	Intracranial	Normal	Intracranial	Normal
173	1380	1380	920	920
256	932	932	620	620
512	466	466	310	310
1024	233	233	155	155
2048	116	166	77	77

1) Let the data sequence containing N data points be $X = [x(1), x(2), x(3), \ldots , x(N)]$.

2) Let x(i) be a subsequence of X such that $x(i) =[x(i), x(i + 1), x(i + 2), \ldots , x(i + m - 1)]$ for $1 \leq i \leq N - m$, where m represents the number of samples used for the prediction.

3) Let r represent the noise filter level that is defined as

$$r = k \times SD \qquad (5)$$

for k = 0, 0.1, 0.2, 0.3, . . . , 0.9
where SD is the standard deviation of the data sequence X.

4) Let $\{x(j)\}$ represent a set of subsequences obtained from x(j) by varying j from 1 to N. Each sequence x(j) in the set of $\{x(j)\}$ is compared with x(i) and, in this process, two parameters, namely Cim(r) and Cim+1(r) are defined as follows:

$$C_{im}(r) = N-m \qquad (6)$$

where k = 1, if $|x(i) - x(j)| \leq r$ for $1 \leq j \leq N - m$
        0, otherwise

and

$$Cim+1(r) = N-m \qquad (7)$$

with conditions depicted by (A) as shown at the bottom of the page.

5) We define $\Phi m(r)$ and $\Phi m+1(r)$ as follows:

$$\Phi m(r) = N-m \qquad (8)$$

$$\Phi m+1(r) = N-m \qquad (9)$$

Small values of ApEn imply strong regularity in a data sequence and large values imply substantial fluctuations [11].

3.3   Classifiers Used for Classification

Probabilistic Neural Network (PNN)

The PNN was first proposed by Specht [14]. Various multi-class problems can be handled by a single PNN.

$$\phi_{ij}(x) = \frac{1}{(2\pi)^{d/2}\sigma^d} \exp\left[-\frac{(x-x_{ij})^T (x-x_{ij})}{2\sigma^2} \right] \qquad (10)$$

where d denotes the dimension of the pattern vector x,   is the smoothing parameter, and x_{ij} is the neuron vector [8].

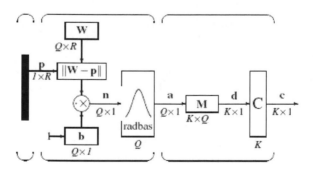

Fig. 4. PNN Architecture, R: number of features, Q: number of training samples, K: number of classes

On receiving a pattern x from the input layer, the neuron x_{ij} of the pattern layer computes its output. The structure of PNN is depicted in Fig. 4.

Multi-class Support Vector Machine (MSVM)

The SVM is basically a binary classifier that can be extended by modifying several of its kind into a multi-class classifier. The general structure of SVM is depicted in Fig. 5. The SVM is a one pass incremental algorithm that does not require the following such as a sliding window on the data stream and monitoring the performance of the classifier as data points are streaming. The principle idea is to assign a binary code word of length N, denoted here

$$t(c) \in \{-1, 0, 1\}^N \tag{11}$$

$$t(c) \in \{0, 1\}^N, t(c) \in \{-1, 1\}^N \tag{12}$$

or even for each class c. The result is the code matrix T represented here

$$T = \begin{pmatrix} t(1) \\ t(2) \\ . \\ . \\ t(N) \end{pmatrix} = \begin{pmatrix} t_{11} t_{12} \cdots t_{1N} \\ t_{21} t_{22} \cdots t_{2N} \\ . \\ . \\ t_{N1} t_{N2} \cdots t_{NN} \end{pmatrix} \tag{13}$$

Now each column defines a separation of the classes in two subsets f¡1; 1g, 0 valued elements are simply ignored. Each column is fed into a separate classifier for learning and recognition. The result is another codeword tL which can be compared with the existing N code words by using Hamming or other distance measures. For dichotomies, a soft margin classifier can be defined. It can be understood as mapping the property $y_n f(\overrightarrow{x_n}) \geq \rho$ with $(\overrightarrow{x_n}, y_n)$ {training set} and some positive constant giving the margin. The function f is also called the embedding. To avoid over fitting some slack variables are also introduced

$$\text{Maximize} \quad \frac{\lambda}{M} \sum_{m=1}^{M} \varepsilon_m + \Omega\{f\} \text{ (the margin)} \tag{14}$$

This margin maximization alone is nothing new, but the notation can be extended to polychotomial problems. The minimal relative difference in distance between f, the correct target t(y) and any other target t(c). The new optimization problem can now be written in the following way.

$$\text{Minimize} \quad \frac{\lambda}{M} \sum_{m=1}^{M} \varepsilon_m + \Omega\{f\} \tag{15}$$

This optimization problem is a multi-class classifier using the distance measure function d and large soft margins.

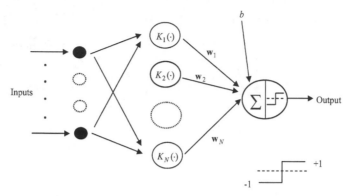

Fig. 5. General Architecture of SVM

4   Results and Discussion

In our work, we employed a discrete wavelet transform for extracting approximate entropy features from the dataset in order to extract temporal information. The wavelet base ApEn possesses good characteristics such as robustness in the characterization of the epileptic patterns and low computational burden. n. ApEn values are computed for selected combinations of m, r, and N. The values of m, r, and N that are used for the experiments are as follows: m = 1, 2, 3; r = 0%–90% of SD of the data sequence in increments of 10%; and N = 4097. Wavelet based ApEn values are computed for both normal and epileptic EEG signals and are fed as inputs to the two neural networks. The potentiality of the wavelet based ApEn to discriminate the two signals, namely, normal and epileptic EEG signals depends on the values of m, r, and N.

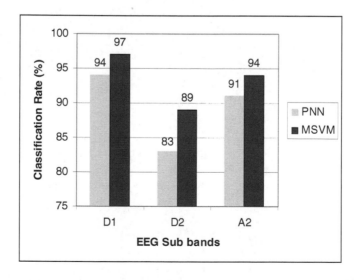

Fig. 6. Comparison of classifiers such as Probabilistic Neural Network and Multi-class Support Vector Machine based on classification rate

For the classification of EEG signals we have used a novel multi-class SVM. Among the available 100 EEG data sets, 50 data sets are used for training and the remaining data sets are used for testing the performance of the neural network and SVM classifiers. Computational cost and the classification time for the proposed MSVM classifier depend on the number of support vectors required for the design of the classifier and the kernel employed. Increase in number of support vectors lead to increase in computational requirements. It is shown that our wavelet based ApEn possesses good characteristics such as robustness in the characterization of the epileptic patterns and low computational burden. The performance in the rate of classification of the two classifiers such as PNN and multi-class SVM have been compared with different sub bands and which is shown in Fig. 6. The Multi-class SVM using wavelet based Approximate Entropy features for the sub-band D1 gives superior performance in terms of classification rate.

5   Conclusion

The MSVM has shown great performance since it measures the predictability of the current amplitude values of a physiological signal based on its previous amplitude values. A robust and computationally low-intensive feature, wavelet based ApEn has been used as the feature for the proposed system. Besides this, the PNN provided encouraging results, which could have originated from the architecture of the PNN. The performance of the other neural network was not as high as the MSVM. The results of the present paper demonstrated that the MSVM with wavelet based Approximate Entropy feature can be used in the classification of the EEG signals by taking the misclassification rates into consideration. In current work, focus was put on normal and epileptic EEG signal classification. In the next stage of research, the results from this preliminary study will be expanded to include a more complete range of datasets.

Acknowledgment. The authors wish to thank Andrzejak et al., 2001 for the benchmark EEG dataset available:(http://www.meb.unibonn.de/epileptologie/science/physik/eegdata.html).

References

1. Adeli, H., Ghosh-Dastidar, S., Dadmehr, N.: A Wavelet-Chaos Methodology for Analysis of EEGs and EEG Subbands to Detect Seizure and Epilepsy. IEEE Transactions on Biomedical Engineering 54(2) (2007)
2. Ghosh-Dastidar, S., Adeli, H., Dadmehr, N.: Mixed-Band Wavelet-Chaos- Neural Network Methodology for Epilepsy and Epileptic Seizure Detection. IEEE Transactions on Biomedical Engineering 54(9) (2007)
3. Ghosh-Dastidar, S., Adeli, H., Dadmehr, N.: Principal Component Analysis-Enhanced Cosine Radial Basis Function Neural Network for Robust Epilepsy and Seizure Detection. IEEE Transactions on Biomedical Engineering 55(2) (2008)

4. Srinivasan, V., Eswaran, C., Sriraam, N.: Approximate Entropy-Based Epileptic EEG Detection Using Artificial Neural Networks. IEEE Transactions on Information Technology in Biomedicine 11(3) (2007)
5. Tzallas, A.T., Tsipouras, M.G., Fotiadis, D.I.: Epileptic Seizure Detection in EEGs Using Time–Frequency Analysis. IEEE Transactions on Information Technology in Biomedicine 13(5) (2009)
6. Jahankhani, P., Kodogiannis, V., Revett, K.: EEG Signal Classification Using Wavelet Feature Extraction and Neural Networks. In: IEEE John Vincent Atanasoff 2006 International Symposium on Modern Computing, JVA 2006 (2006), 0-7695-2643-8/06
7. Muthanantha Murugavel, A.S., Ramakrishnan, S.: Classification of EEG Signals Using Weighted Probabilistic Neural Network and Multiwavelet Transformation. In: Proceedings of the International Conference on Operation Research Applications in Engineering and Management (ICOREM), May 27-29 (2009)
8. Firpi, H., Goodman, E.D., Echauz, J.: Epileptic Seizure Detection Using Genetically Programmed Artificial Features. IEEE Transactions on Biomedical Engineering 54(2) (2007)
9. Güler, I., Übeyli, E.D.: Multiclass Support Vector Machines for EEG-Signals Classification. IEEE Transactions on Information Technology In Biomedicine 11(2) (2007)
10. Garrett, D., Peterson, D.A., Anderson, C.W.: Comparison of Linear, Nonlinear, and Feature Selection Methods for EEG Signal Classification. IEEE Transactions on Neural Systems and Rehabilitation Engineering 11(2) (2003)
11. Hazarika, N., Tsoi, A.C., Sergejew, A.A.: Nonlinear Considerations in EEG Signal Classification. IEEE Transactions on Signal Processing 45(4) (1997)
12. Haselsteiner, E., Pfurtscheller, G.: Using Time-Dependent Neural Networks for EEG Classification. IEEE Transactions on Rehabilitation Engineering 8(4) (2000)
13. Townsend, G., Graimann, B., Pfurtscheller, G.: Continuous EEG Classification During Motor Imagery—Simulation of an Asynchronous BCI. IEEE Transactions on Neural Systems and Rehabilitation Engineering 12(2) (2004)
14. Suffczynski, P., Lopes da Silva, F.H., Parra, J., Velis, D.N., Bouwman, B.M., van Rijn, C.M., van Hese, P., Boon, P., Khosravani, H., Derchansky, M., Carlen, P., Kalitzin, S.: Dynamics of Epileptic Phenomena Determined From Statistics of Ictal Transitions. IEEE Transactions on Biomedical Engineering 53(3) (2006)

Hybrid Intrusion Detection
with Rule Generation

V.V. Korde, N.Z. Tarapore, S.R. Shinde, and M.L. Dhore

Department of Computer Engineering, Vishwakarma Institute of Technology, Pune
{korde.vaibhav,ntarapore}@yahoo.com

Abstract. This paper reports a new experimental hybrid intrusion detection system (HIDS). This hybrid system combines the advantages of
Misuse-based intrusion detection system (IDS) having low false-positive
rate and the ability of anomaly detection system (ADS) to detect novel
unknown attacks. This is done by mining Internet connections records
for anomalies. We have built ADS that can detect attacks not detected
by Misuse-based systems like Snort or Bro systems. Rules are extracted
from detected anomalies and then are added to Misuse-based system's
rule database. Thus Misuse-based intrusion detection system can detect
new attacks. The system is trained and tested using Massachusetts Institute of Technology/ Lincoln Laboratory (MIT/LL) DARPA 1999 dataset
respectively. Our experimental results show a 69 percent detection rate
of the HIDS, compared with 47 percent in using the Snort. This increase
in detection rate is obtained with around 0.08 percent false alarms. This
approach provides a better way to deal with novel attacks using ADS
along with a trustworthy misuse-based Intrusion detection system.

1 Introduction

The widespread use of Internet and computer networks experienced in the past
years has brought, with all its benefits, another kind of threat: those of people
using illicit means to access, invade and attack computers. One can use a firewall
as a preventive measure to maintain the security goals of computer networks.
But, it simply restricts access to the designated points. A computer network
intrusion is a sequence of related actions by a malicious adversary whose goal is
to violate some policy regarding appropriate use of computer network. Since a
preventive approach such as firewall is not enough to provide sufficient security
for computer system, intrusion detection systems (IDSes) are introduced as a
second line of defense.

IDSes can be distinguished by their differing approaches to event analysis.
Misuse-detection is the most widely used approach in commercial IDS technology today. But the problem with these systems is that they cannot detect
novel attacks. Another approach is called anomaly detection. It uses rules or
predefined concepts about "normal" and "abnormal" system activity to distinguish anomalies from normal system behavior and to monitor, report, or block
anomalies as they occur. Anomaly based Intrusion Detection System has the

N. Meghanathan et al. (Eds.): CCSIT 2012, Part II, LNICST 85, pp. 345–354, 2012.

benefit of detecting novel attacks but has high false positive rate. On the other hand, misuse-based systems are rule-based having higher accuracy. Misuse-based Intrusion Detection System fails to detect novel attacks. To overcome these limitations, both Anomaly-based and Misuse-based Intrusion Detection Systems should be combined.

In this paper, a new hybrid intrusion detection system (HIDS) is presented. This system combines the positive features of both intrusion detection models to achieve higher detection accuracy, lower false alarms, and thus a raised level of cyber-trust. Our HIDS is network-based, which should not be confused with the host-based IDS with the same abbreviation by other.

The rest of the paper is organized as follows: Section 2 reviews related works and distinguishes the new approach from previous solutions. Section 3 gives system design internals. We present system implementation details in Section 4. Experimental performance results are reported in Section 5.

2   Related Works and Our Approach

A significant amount of research has been done and various approaches has been used for designing an Intrusion Detection System These approaches attempt to build some kind of a model over the normal data and then check to see how well new data fits into that model [3],[4],[5]. In the past, data mining techniques such as using association rules were suggested to build IDS [7].

Daniel Barbara, et al., [3] described the design and experiences with the ADAM (Audit Data Analysis and Mining) system, which was used as a testbed to study how useful data mining techniques can be in intrusion detection. L. Ertoz, et al [4] introduced the Minnesota Intrusion Detection System (MINDS), which used a suite of data mining techniques to automatically detect attacks against computer networks and systems. H. Mannila and H. Toivonen [14] have compared different approaches to intrusion detection systems to supply a norm for the best-fit system. Snort [9] and Bro [10] are two widely used IDSes that are based on the misuse mode. The MIT/LL IDS (DARPA) evaluation data set and reported IDS performance results were analyzed in [12], [13], [11]. This data set is used to test the effectiveness of proposed HIDS. The concept of frequent episode rules (FERs) was first proposed by Mannila and Toivonen [14]. Tung-Ying Lee, et al [9] made first attempt to study a special episode rule, named serial episode rule with a time lag in an environment of multiple data streams.

In this paper, we propose the HIDS architecture. It is tested for its effectiveness through experiments. The HIDS integrates the flexibility of ADS with the accuracy of misuse-based IDS. ADS is designed by mining FERs [6], [14], over connections from Internet traffic. New rules are generated from anomalies detected by ADS. This new approach automatically enables HIDS to detect similar attacks in the future.

3   System Design Internals

In this section, we introduce the overall system design. Our aim is to combine a misuse based detection system with an Anomaly Detection System. The misuse based system used for this experimentation is Snort.

Snort is an open source network intrusion detection system, capable of performing real-time traffic analysis and packet logging on IP networks. Snort has three primary modes: sniffer, packet logger, and network intrusion detection. One can write one's own rules with Snort to suit the particular needs of one's network. A Snort rule is composed of two major parts: rule headers and rule options. The rule header contains information about what action a rule takes. It also contains criteria for matching a rule against data packets The action part

Action	Protocol	Address	Port	Direction	Address	Port

Fig. 1. Snort rule format

of the rule determines the type of action taken when criteria are met and a rule is exactly matched against packet. Typical actions are generating an alert or log message or invoking another rule. The protocol part is used to apply the rule on packets for a particular protocol only. The address parts define source and destination addresses. Source and destination addresses are determined based on direction field. In case of TCP or UDP protocol, the port field determines the source and destination ports of a packet on which the rule is applied. In case of network layer protocols like IP and ICMP, port numbers have no significance.

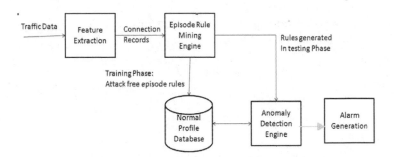

Fig. 2. Anomaly Detection System Architecture

3.1   Anomaly Detection System

Figure 3 explains the Data mining scheme for network anomaly detection. As shown in the figure, there are following major components.

Feature Extraction: Extracts required features from the audit data.

Episode Rule Mining Engine: This component works in two phases: training and testing.

Anomaly Detection Engine: In accordance with normal profile database the anomaly detection engine checks the newly received rules with that of those stored in the database. Depending on the results it triggers the Alarm generation component.

Alarm Generation: This component will generate alarm.

3.2   Episode Rules

An Internet episode is represented by a sequence of connection events. An episode can be generated by legitimate users or malicious attackers. Frequent episodes are mostly resulted from normal users. A rare episode is likely caused by intruders.

Let 'T' be a set of traffic connections and A be a set of attributes defined over 'T'. For example, 'A' consists of timestamp, duration, service, srchost, desthost for TCP connections. Let 'I' be a set of attribute-value pairs defined over 'A'. For example, I = timestamp = 15 sec, duration = 1 sec, service = http, srchost = 192.168.1.1, desthost = 192.168.1.10 for a typical http connection.

1. **Frequent Episode Rules**

   In general, an FER is expressed by the expression:

   $$L_1, L_2, ...L_n \rightarrow R_1, R_2, ...R_m(c, s, window) \tag{1}$$

   where $L_i(1 \leq i \leq n)$ and $R_j(1 \leq j \leq m)$ are ordered itemsets in a traffic record set T. We call $L_1, L_2, ...L_n$ the LHS (left hand side) episode and $R_1, R_2, ...R_m$ the RHS (right hand side) of episode of the rule. Note that all itemsets are sequentially ordered, that is $L_1, L_2, ...L_n, R_1, R_2, ...R_m$ must occur in the ordering as listed. However, other itemsets could be embedded within our episode sequence. We define the support and confidence of rule by the following two expressions:

   $$s = Support(L_1 \cup L_2 \cup .... \cup L_n) \tag{2}$$

   $$c = \frac{Support(L_1 \cup L_2 \cup .... \cup L_n \cup R_1 \cup R_2 \cup .... \cup R_m)}{Support(L_1 \cup L_2 \cup .... \cup L_n)} \tag{3}$$

2. **Axis Attributes**

   Because the FER generation does not take any domain-specific knowledge into consideration, many ineffective FERs are generated. How to eliminate these ineffective rules is a major problem in traffic data mining for effective rule generation. For example, the association rule:

   $$(srcbytes = 200) \rightarrow (destbytes = 300)$$

   is of little interest to the intrusion detection process, since the number of bytes sent by the source (src_bytes) and destination (dst_bytes) is irrelevant to the threat conditions. Lee et al [7] had introduced the concepts of axis attributes to constrain the generation of redundant rules. All Itemsets in an

FER must be built only with axis attributes. Axis attributes are independent of attacks being detected. The choice of axis attributes will reduce the number of FERs generated. According to Lee, axis attributes are selected from essential attributes which are enough to identify a connection. Different combinations of the essential attributes form the axis attributes. The axis attributes can easily be chosen with domain knowledge.

3. **Pruning of Ineffective Episode Rules**
   Keeping all rules generated will enlarge the search space and thus the overhead. The following FER transformation laws will reduce the rule search space significantly.
   - *Transposition of Episode Rules:* Suppose we have two FERs as and . Therefore, the second rule can be induced by the first rule. We only need to keep the first rule. The general rule of thumb is to make the LHS as short as possible. In general, rules with shorter LHSs are more effective than rules with longer LHSs.
   - *Elimination of Redundant Episode Rules:* Many FERs detected from the network traffic have some transitive patterns. Suppose we have two rules A → B and B → C in the rule set. Then, the longer rule A → B, C is implied. Since we reconstruct this rule from two shorter rules, the longer rule A → B, C becomes redundant.

4. **Rule Generation**
   Generating the rules is the most CPU-intensive task. This is because we need to generate all possible combinations of the sequences in a given window size. To generate these episode rules, we first need to find the sequence of the events occurring in the given window size. This is done by querying the database of extracted features to retrieve the event sequence in particular window size. Once the event sequence is retrieved it is fetched to the script for generation of Episode rules. The script generates all Episode rules and also finds the support and confidence for each episode rule.

3.3   MIT/LL DARPA Dataset

We have used MIT/LL's DARPA 1999 dataset for system training and testing purpose. DARPA 1999 dataset is a five week dataset. (Twenty-two hours a day and five days per week). The first and third weeks of the training data do not contain any attacks. The fourth and fifth weeks of data are the "Test Data". These two weeks of testing data consists of network based attacks along with the normal background data.

3.4   System Architecture

Initially the incoming traffic will be fed to Snort to filter out known attacks with existing rules of Snort. Then remaining traffic will be passed to Episode Mining Engine. Episode Mining Engine will generate Frequent Episode Rules (FER). Newly generated FER are compared with those stored in a normal profile database. The anomalous episodes are used to generate rules. Newly generated rules are inserted into Snort's attack rules database.

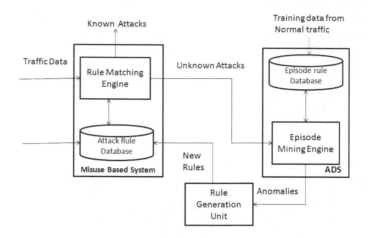

Fig. 3. Proposed System Architecture

4   System Implementation

In this section we first describe some tools used for implementation of the proposed system. Then we give details about stepwise implementation of the proposed system.

The system is implemented and tested on Fedora operating system. Snort 2.9.3 is used for the experimentations. The system is implemented using Java along with Shell script and some Linux based tools. Since the MIT/LL dataset is in the form of TCP dump files, we need to use the tools that can read them as fast as possible and extract the required detail. We have used tcptrace and Tcpdump utilities available on Linux.

4.1   Feature Extraction and Preprocessing

Since we aim at detecting anomalies of network traffic, the content features are not used in this work. The connection features and temporal statistics will be used in HIDS construction. Total features extracted from the connections are enlisted in table 1. The axis attributes described in section III are chosen from these features. Connection level features are used in both FER and rules generation. Temporal statistics are related to connections with the same reference features. They can be used to improve the accuracy of rules generated. Table 2 gives the list of temporal features calculated from connection features extracted.

Table 1. Connection Features Extracted

Feature Name	Description	Feature Name	Description
timestamp	the time when Connection Begins	service	Network Service on destination
duration	duration of the connection	icmp_type	ICMP message type
ip_proto	IP protocol type	src_bytes	Bytes sent by source
src_ip	Source IP address	dst_bytes	Bytes sent by destination
dst_ip	Destination IP address	flags	SYN/FIN Flags in the connection

Table 2. Temporal Features Extracted

Feature Name	Description
src_count	No of connections from same source
dst_count	number of connection to same destination
service_count	Number of connection for same service
avg_duration	Average duration of connection for same service
avg_src_bytes	Average bytes sent by source
avg_dst_bytes	Average bytes sent by Destination

After the features are extracted, we need to calculate relative timestamp, order them and assign a transaction ID for each one of them. The axis attributes chosen for ADS built here are service, IP protocol, and flags. These attributes are enough to classify the instance of a connection. Each such unique possible set of these three values is considered as an Event. These events with unique Event IDs are stored in the EventList database. In the pre-processing phase, every transaction ID is mapped with the Event ID and stored with the relative timestamp in EventOrder database.

4.2 Rule Generation

For generating rules we need to find all the connection records related to the anomalies detected. The table 3 gives mapping between Connection Attributes and Snort Rule Keywords. Let's say we have got an anomaly detected as A $\rightarrow$ B. Where A and B denote events with the following attributes.

$$A(Event\_ID = A, ip\_proto = icmp, icmp\_type = echo\_req, flags = 0)$$
$$B(Event\_ID = B, ip\_proto = icmp, icmp\_type = echo\_req, flags = 0)$$

Here flag=0 means no SYN/FIN flags are observed (obvious for an ICMP connection).Now after searching back in the EventOrder database if we find that these events have occurred many times in a given window size of say 10 sec, it will produce a higher support as well as confidence values for the same. Thus we can conclude to the following Snort rule

alert icmp $EXTERNAL\_NET$ any $<>$ $HOME\_NET$ any (msg: "Anomalous Behaviour"; itype: 8; threshold : type both; count 10 seconds; sid:100001;rev:0)

Table 3. Mapping between connection attributes and Snort rule keywords

Attribute Name	Snort Rule Keyword	Short Description
protocol	protocol	IP protocol type
src_ip	source IP address	Source IP address
dst_ip	destination IP address	destination IP address
service	destination port number	Service type
icmp_type	itype	ICMP message type
src_bytes	Dsize	Packet Payload size
flags	Flags	TCP flags
land	Sameip	Same source and destination Address
src_count	threshold: track by_src, count $< n >$	No. of connection to the same destination
dst_count	threshold: track by_dst, count $< n >$	No. of connection from the same source

5   Experimentation and Results

This section gives brief details about the experiments that were performed on the system built to generate the performance results. The user needs to select a window size (in seconds). The window size will be used by the system as a window size in sliding window implementation of episode rule generation. User needs to specify values of support and confidence for selection of the episode rule into the database.

The system was tested with different values for window size, support and confidence values. Thus a normal profile is created by training the system with week 1 and week 3 dataset. The system was tested by using DARPA 1999's week 4 and week 5 testing dataset. The graph in figure 4.a shows the number

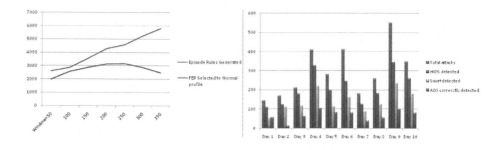

Fig. 4. a)Episode Rule Generation Vs. Window size b)Total Number of Intrusions Detected

of Episode Rules generated for different window sizes. Episode rules here are different from those discussed above in such a way that, rules stated here are unique episode rules among all generated above. Frequent Episode Rules are chosen by applying the criteria of support and confidence to them. From the graph as shown in figure 4.a it is clear that the number of FER that are selectable for normal profile dataset are steady between window sizes 200 and 250. After window size = 250, the total Episode rules becomes higher but comparatively very few FERs are produced. For system testing purpose, DARPA 1999's week 4 and week 5 was used. The detection list is provided by them. The attack results obtained from the detection by the HIDS were compared to that of the attacks in the attack list file. This is shown by the graph as shown in Fig 4.b. The misuse-based Intrusion Detection System: Snort is quite capable of detecting the attacks present in the test dataset. The anomaly detection system has also performed well. There were in total 2959 attacks present in the dataset. The intrusion detection rate (denoted by δ) is formally defined by

$$Detection rate \delta = \frac{detected attacks}{total attacks} \tag{4}$$

Snort could detect 1407 attacks with the help of its own rules. Detection rate

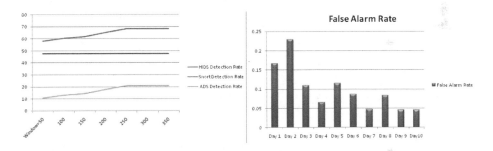

Fig. 5. a)Intrusion Detection Rate of HIDS b)False Alarm Rate per day of testing dataset

for Snort becomes 47.55%. Snort could detect 1667 attacks with only ADS Rule but out of it 1053 were false positives. Thus 614 were correctly detected. Thus detection Rate for Snort with only ADS rules =20.75%. It implies the Total Detection rate = 68.30%. Thus the new hybrid Intrusion Detection System has achieved a detection rate of 68.30% which is better than that of Snort which is 47.55%. The resultant system just had a false alarm of about 0.08%. Note that number of attacks in MIT/LL dataset are much lower than number of normal connections. This affects false alarm rate. The system had false positives of an average of 100 per day. From the figure 5.a, it is clear that the detection rate is almost steady after window =250. The false alarm rate (denoted by η) measures the percentage of false positives among all normal traffic events. A formal definition is given by

$$\eta = \frac{p}{k} * 100 \tag{5}$$

where p is the total number of false positive alarms and k accounts for the total number of connection events.

6   Conclusion

The hybrid intrusion detection system proposed here combines the advantages of low false-positive rate of misuse-based intrusion detection systems and the ability of an anomaly detection system to detect novel unknown attacks. By mining anomalous traffic episodes from Internet connections, an anomaly detection system is built that detects anomalies not detected by misuse-based Snort. Frequent episode rule concept can successfully be applied for detecting the anomalies in the computer network and hence for performing Intrusion detection in the network. The performance of detection rate was increased from 47.55% to 68.30% with the combined rules from Snort and ADS. This increase is just at a cost of average 0.08% false alarm rate.

The ADS is efficient for an offline evaluation since the computational resource requirement is higher. This kind of system can be deployed at network layer along with Snort to locally generate the rules specific to the traffic of the deployed network.

References

1. Qin, M., Hwang, K.: Anomaly Intrusion Detection by Internet Data mining of Traffic Episodes. ACM Transactions on Information and System Security (2004)
2. Yang, J., Chen, X., Xiang, X., Wan, J.: HIDS-DT: An Effective Hybrid Intrusion Detection System Based on Decision Tree. In: International Conference on Communications and Mobile Computing (2010)
3. Barbara, D., Couto, J., Jajodia, S., Popyack, L., Wu, N.: ADAM: Detecting Intrusions by Data Mining. Proceedings of the IEEE (2001)
4. Ertoz, L., et al.: The MINDS-Minnesota Intrusion Detection System. In: Next Generation Data Mining. MIT Press (2004)
5. Lazarevic, A., Ertoz, L., Kumar, V., Ozgur, A., Srivastava, J.: A Comparative Study of Anomaly Detection Schemes in Network Intrusion Detection. In: Proc. Third SIAM Conference Data Mining (2003)
6. Lee, W., et al.: A Framework for Constructing Features and Models for Intrusion Detection Systems. ACM Transactions on Information and System Security (2000)
7. Lee, T.-Y., et al.: Mining Serial Episode Rules with Time Lags over Multiple Data Streams. Springer, Heidelberg (2008)
8. Snort 2.1 Intrusion Detection, 2nd edn. Syngress Publication
9. Roesch, M.: SNORT-Lightweight Intrusion Detection for Networks. In: Proc. USENIX 13th Systems Administration Conf., LISA 1999 (1999)
10. Paxson, V.: Bro: A System for Detecting Network Intrusions in Real Time. In: Proc. Seventh USENIX Security Symposium (January 1998)
11. Lippmann, R., Haines, J.W., Fried, D.J., Korba, J., Das, K.: Analysis and Results of the 1999 DARPA Off-Line Intrusion Detection Evaluation. In: Debar, H., Mé, L., Wu, S.F. (eds.) RAID 2000. LNCS, vol. 1907, pp. 162–182. Springer, Heidelberg (2000)
12. Mahoney, M.V., Chan, P.K.: An Analysis of the 1999 DARPA/Lincoln Laboratory Evaluation Data for Network Anomaly Detection. In: Vigna, G., Krügel, C., Jonsson, E. (eds.) RAID 2003. LNCS, vol. 2820, pp. 220–237. Springer, Heidelberg (2003)
13. McHugh, J.: Testing Intrusion Detection Systems: A Critique of the 1998 and 1999 DARPA Off-line Intrusion Detection System Evaluation as Performed by Lincoln Laboratory. ACM Transactions on Information and System Security (November 2000)
14. Mannila, H., Toivonen, H.: Discovering Generalized Episodes Using Minimal Occurrences. In: Proc. Second International Conference on Knowledge Discovery and Data Mining (August 1996)

Tele-Operation of Web Enabled Wireless Robot for Old Age Surveillance

Yatin Wadhawan and Sajal Gupta

Jaypee Institute of Information Technology, Computer Science Department,
Noida – 201307, Uttar Pradesh, India
{yatinwadhawan07503879,sajalgupta4u}@gmail.com

Abstract. This paper discusses the system design and implementation of web-enabled wireless robotic system for old age surveillance. In societies, surveillance holds valuable importance for aging population. The system presented is meant for surveillance of elder citizens, who might face physical problems and could be potential site of criminal activities. As a solution to this problem, a prototype of a wireless robot mounted with a wireless camera and microphone is developed, which proved to be quiet effective to test various abnormal events occurring with elder ones. The system works using audio-video information that triggers message to remote client if any abnormality is detected. The remote client can receive live feed of the place where elder people are present using media streaming over and the same can also control the motion of the wireless robot over internet. This helps in restraining the felicity of elder citizens.

Keywords: Wireless communication, Web-enabled robot, Video streaming, Old Age surveillance, Embedded system, Image processing, Audio processing.

1   Introduction

Robots are intelligent machines that can be used to serve several purposes. Presently, wirelesses robotic have sufficient effective area of operation and if a system is built in such a manner so as to control these machines over the internet, then they can perform various tasks in the absence of user. There are many global issues which can be eased by the correct usage of the video and audio surveillance, most of which occurs in public places. Usage of surveillance also lies in the home to check the occurrences of abnormal events.

This paper focuses on the design and development of old age surveillance robotic system with the integration of both the video and audio feed for the detection of abnormal events. The prototype is a surveillance robotic system consisting of mounted wireless camera, a microphone and two CC2500 modules for wireless communication. The Wireless camera and the microphone are employed to track the target and send audio and video information to the server where data processing is performed to detect any abnormal behaviour. In case of any abnormality, an SMS is automatically generated by the system and is sent to the remote client. Access is given

N. Meghanathan et al. (Eds.): CCSIT 2012, Part II, LNICST 85, pp. 355–365, 2012.

to the client to control the motion of robotic system through the web and examine the situation in real time.

This paper is the consolidation of various technical domains such as multimedia transfer over the internet, motion detection using image processing and message sending via SMS gateway. These technologies are fused in order to serve the purpose for the design and implementation of wireless tele-operation of web enabled robotic system which is unstructured and dynamic environment.

One of the important parts of this paper is to stream live video from the camera mounted on the robot to the client. The camera should give input wirelessly to the server to send video over network. Bluetooth technology is used to send video from camera to sever. With the recent advances in the field of computing technology, compression, high speed networks and bandwidth have made it easier to provide real-time multimedia services over internet, as explained in [4]. The paper gives an idea about the streaming of a media file over the internet and also discusses the techniques to improve its quality. The Increasing popularity of Motion control of mobile robots, both in scientific research and practical applications have made it an important research field topic these days. An important work in this field [2] that deals with the wireless sensor based remote control motion of mobile robots in an unknown environment with obstacles is using the Bluetooth wireless transmission and Sun SPOT technology. In this paper, CC2500 wireless module is used to send the wireless control signals between the robot and the server which enables user to interact with the real mobile web-based robots, and processes their motion through the Internet via the control interface of their web page. Obstacle avoidance strategy is implemented when the sensors detect an obstacle while making a move towards the target in an unknown environment.

Tracking of human body, modelling and activity analysis in surveillance [5] are one of the tedious tasks of this paper. Tracking refers to identifying the feature points of a human in the video frame and predicting its position in the next frame. The aim of tracking is to find the movement of objects between the two consecutive frame sequences in real time by monitoring of people and analyzing their abnormal activities in both indoor and outdoor environments. Background subtraction algorithm is also used here, in constant background video sequences. It is used to detect the moving regions by subtracting the current image pixels from background image pixels.

Mel Frequency Cepstral Coefficient [7] method is used, for identifying the speaker and differentiating it from one another. In order to increase the area of surveillance, the other concern is audio processing. Suppose there is a gunshot or someone fell down, there will be a screaming which is an abnormal case and to detect this, audio processing is used. There are many such cases when video processing performed does not give you enough information, in such cases audio processing plays an important role. Audio processing processes the audio signals either in analog or digital format in time or frequency domain. It covers diverse fields like Human Hearing, Speech Recognition, High fidelity music etc. The main purpose of the module is to store the sound coming from the remote location and to detect whether it is abnormal or not, using the algorithm used in [7] with several modifications to serve the purpose.

As the problem is concerned, rescue robot [1] is developed in order to meet the demands of this surveillance system using microcontroller, camera, microphone and other basic units. This robot is controlled over internet and it is being compared with other surveillance systems and robots dedicated for such work [8], [9], [10].

Prototype of tele-operated mobile surveillance robot [6] talks about the design and fabrication and find its application in various fields like remote monitoring, urban surveillance and human motion detection etc. In paper [6], it helps to understand that how to proceed and draw framework for the surveillance system in order to meet the requirements.

Internet based robot where robot is controlled over the internet and also sends real time information of remote location to client is implemented in [3]. It explicates the mechanism to drive robot and associated problems which may arise during implementation.

Section 2 explains various systems, section 3 explains about the system design and consolidation of different components in one system. It also includes the comparison with other such systems. In section 4, the video and audio processing algorithms are discussed and in section 5, experimental results are presented. The conclusion is presented in section 6.

2   System Components

The project is the consolidation of various technologies which include wireless communication, multimedia networking, embedded system, abnormal motion detection and abnormal audio detection.

2.1   Robot

Robot comprises camera (Bluetooth enabled), microcontroller, motors, tyres and some set of wires for connection. The basic structure of the robot is taken from the paper [8], [9], [10] and has been modified to suit the purpose. Wireless camera is connected to system via Bluetooth, to send video to the receiver via server over network. Motors are connected with microcontroller, which is connected with the server wirelessly. Wireless modules CC2500, one is connected to microcontroller mounted on robot and another is with server system at remote location which communicates to send control signals. Microphone is attached to the server which takes input from the surrounding for audio processing. Attached to robot, temperature sensors are used to detect if there is any fire event in the house, which is also an abnormal situation.

2.2   Microcontroller and Wireless Communication

Microcontroller is an integrated circuit which is the combination of processor, memory and programmable input/output peripherals. The program for controlling the robot is written in Bascom software and burned in the rewritable memory of microcontroller. The program will guide the robot to move according for the given input control signals.

The input to move robot from one place to another and change its direction is given by client over internet which is transferred to robot via wireless communication module CC2500 attached at both the ends that is robot and server. It works at 2.4 GHz carrier frequency using RS232 UART interface with variable baud rate.

2.3   Media Streaming

Streaming video over the web network is substantial part of this system. To give opportunity to client to see video of the home after logging on webpage, is the motive of this module. Streaming video [4] over a network covers the areas like Video compression, Application-layer quality of Service Control, Streaming servers, Protocols for streaming media etc. Paper [4] helps to understand the way of implementing the media streaming which is an eminent part of the system.

It is important to consider network bandwidth, network traffic and other settings like proxy settings, firewall etc. for achieving successful video streaming. Sender's and receiver's web pages have been developed which are meant for sending and receiving video and control signals for robot over network. They both are connected with server which provides connection, authentication and other facilities. The web pages provide interface where client can login and connect to the server placed at location in concern. After login, client can have overview of the location and can control robot using instruction panel assigned in the web page of receiver.

2.4   Abnormal Motion Detection

The main idea is to detect the abnormality in the video information and trigger a message to the client. Bluetooth enabled camera is mounted on robot which sends real time video to the server which processes it to detect abnormalities. Abnormalities like somebody fell down (especially elder ones since they will be in field of vision of the robot), somebody suddenly running in case of criminal activity or natural calamity or any other abnormality.

Paper [5] explains the basic technique for tracking the motion of human beings. The method is Background subtraction which is used to detect the motion of the target object. After differentiating the motion, abnormality is detected by applying the stated algorithm in section 4.

2.5   Abnormal Audio Detection

Video processing in isolation is not sufficient to detect the abnormality at the remote location. Suppose there is a gunshot or someone scream (especially elder ones), which is an abnormal case and therefore audio processing needs to be implemented to detect it. There are many such cases when video processing is inefficient and audio processing plays a critical role.

This paper implements the algorithm based on Mel frequency [7] for identifying the human and non human activities (like gunshot) and detect the abnormality by using power (intensity) of the sound as one of the parameters. The flow chart for detecting audio abnormality is shown in Figure 1.

If the audio feed is identified as human sound, the system calculate the power of the sound to classify it as screaming or non screaming and send an alert SMS accordingly. Rather if it is perceived as a gunshot then surely it is an abnormal sound case and system triggers an alert message. The algorithm used is stated in section 4.

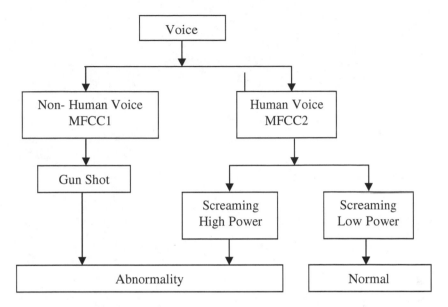

Fig. 1. The flow chart of detecting the abnormality in Audio information collected from the location. Voice is differentiated into non human and human on the basis of MFCC [7] and then power of the sound is computed to check whether it is abnormal or not.

3   System Design and Comparison with Other Systems

3.1   System Design

The Figure 2 presents the design of the developed household surveillance system which detects video and audio abnormal events. Activities at home are observed under surveillance where video feed is provided to server from the wireless camera and audio feed from a microphone. The camera is mounted on robot to stream video to the server and audio information is collected using microphone connected to server. Data processing is performed upon the received audio and video feed at the server and in case of any abnormality being detected; an alert SMS is triggered to the remote client via handset attached to the server using SMS Gateway application.

After getting alert SMS, client makes login on the receiver webpage and ask server to stream video of remote location. Now remote client can have overview of location and can give instructions to the mobile robot to navigate by sending desired control signals through the receiver webpage. These control signals on reaching the server is passed to the mobile robot wirelessly via the CC2500 modules and accordingly the robot is tele-operated over the internet. Robot can also move from one location to another in the house automatically if the blueprint map of the house is customized on receiver page.

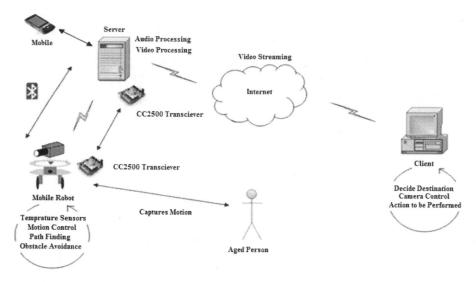

Fig. 2. System Design: Consolidation of various technologies which includes audio and video processing, video streaming, CC2500 transceivers, embedded system, SMS gateway etc.

3.2   Comparative Study

In this section, our robot has been compared to other existing robots of surveillance system. On the basis of parameters like Surveillance use, Tele-presence, Autonomous

Table 1. Comparative study of our system with others implemented so far

Parameters for comparison	Mercury	Xavier	Kaplan Car	Our Robot
Surveillance Use	No	No	No	Yes
Tele-presence	Yes	No	Yes	Yes
Supervisory Control	No	Yes	No	Yes
Autonomous Robot	No	Yes	No	Yes
Web Based Control	Yes	Yes	No	Yes
Direct Control	Yes	No	Yes	No

control, Web based Control etc robot distinction has been established among the candidates. Our robot has one competitive advantage over others as it is being controlled over internet and is also autonomous in nature. Non-availability of direct control is demand of our situation as it doesn't need to be operated by the elderly people.

4   Algorithm Description

4.1   Abnormal Motion Detection

The purpose of this module is to discover abnormalities in video feed and to trigger an alert message to the client present at the distant location. Background subtraction algorithm [5] is used to track the motion of the target. After differentiating the motion, abnormality is detected by applying the stated algorithm.

The first step is to detect foreground images through removal of background images, by applying suitable background subtraction techniques. The background subtraction algorithm should consider the illumination changes, motion changes and geometry of background changes. Second step is motion segmentation, is the process of partitioning of a digital image into different regions or objects and finds the objects and boundaries in the images. It can be used in detection, recognition and tracking purposes, Equation (1) is used for back ground subtraction where Frame_c – Current image, Frame_b – Background image, and T – Threshold value.

$$|Frame\_c - Frame\_b| > T \qquad (1)$$

Last step is to implement motion tracking algorithm like particle filter algorithm to track the human body. Eventually sending the alert message to person concerning on surpassing the set threshold. The value of threshold is calculated by training the system repeatedly. Training is performed by considering all the respective cases and thus by calculating the number of pixels changed for each sample of images and considering their average value.

Pseudocode

```
Program VideoProcessing(Frames)
  Do
    Store frame in a variable of type Bitmap;
    Calculate the width and height of the Frame;
    Apply grey scale;
    Store upcoming frame in another variable of type Bitmap;
    Apply grey scale;
    Apply Background subtraction algorithm on two Frames;
    Store the value returned and display;
    Count number and frequency of changing pixels;
    Train the system;
    Compare with threshold and initiate alert message;
  While Frame! =NULL
```

4.2   Abnormal Audio Detection

This paper implements the algorithm used in paper [7] modified in such a way in order to serve the purpose and it proves to be an immense help. The main purpose of this module is to store the sound from the remote location and detect whether it is abnormal or not. To understand and classify various sound, different feature vectors are used like MFCC coefficients, Power, Frequency (spectrogram) etc. Here we have considered power of sound and its MFCC coefficients to detect abnormality.

The first step is to break the sound signal into frames of 25ms and desired part of the signal is emphasized using Signal Windowing and to implement this Hamming window (2) is used, where N is the number of samples any instant n. The second step is to calculate the FFT of the desired signal using (3) k = 0, 1, . . . ,N− 1, where k corresponds to the frequency f(k) = kfs/N, fs is the sampling frequency in Hertz and w(n) is a time-window.

$$w(n) \; = \; 0.54 - 0.46 \, \cos(2*pi*n/N) \tag{2}$$

$$X(k) \; = \; \sum_{n=0}^{N-1} w(n)x(n)e^{-j2\pi kn/N} \tag{3}$$

For each tone with an actual Frequency, f, measured in Hz, a subjective pitch is measured on the "Mel" scale. The mel-frequency scale is linear frequency spacing below 1000Hz and a logarithmic spacing above 1000Hz. Formula (4) to compute the mels (f Hz).

$$Mel \, (f) \; = \; 2595 * \log 10 (1+f/700) \tag{4}$$

The third step is to calculate the filter bank which acts as a filter for each desired mel frequency component. First, the frequency is scaled logarithmically using the so-called Mel filter bank H (k,m) and then the logarithm is taken, giving equation (5) where m is the number of filter banks and M < N. The Mel filter bank is a collection of triangular filters defined by the centre frequencies fc(m), written as in equation (6).

$$X'(m) \; = \; \ln\{\sum_{n=0}^{N-1} |X(k)|.H(k,m)\} \tag{5}$$

$$\begin{aligned} H(k) \; = \; & \{f(k) - fc(m\text{-}1)\} \; / \; \{fc(m) - fc(m\text{-}1)\} \quad \text{when} \;\; fc(m\text{-}1) <= f(k) < gc(m) \;\; (6) \\ = \; & \{f(k) - fc(m\text{+}1)\} \; / \; \{fc(m) - fc(m\text{+}1)\} \quad \text{when} \;\; fc(m) <= f(k) < gc(m\text{+}1) \\ = \; & 0 \quad \text{when} \; f(k) < fc(m\text{-}1) \quad \text{and} \; f(k) >= fc(m\text{+}1) \end{aligned}$$

In final step, the log mel spectrum has to be converted back to time and the result is called the mel frequency cepstrum coefficients (MFCCs). The MFCCs may be calculated using this equation (7) where n=1,2,...,K. The number of mel cepstrum coefficients, K, is typically chosen as 20.

$$C(n) = \Sigma(\log Sk)[n(k\text{-}1)\pi/2] \tag{7}$$

The VQ (Vector Quantization) [7] approach has been used to match the MFCC of input signal to detect abnormality. Once the sound captured (see Figure 2) from the microphone, if it is non human (gunshot) sound it is taken as abnormality. But if it is human sound, power of the sound is calculated and compared with the threshold (which is maintained by calculating the power of sounds like screaming from various samples).

5   Experimental Results

The robotic system discussed in this paper has been implemented successfully. Webpage for remote client control and server applications for processing of crude audio and video data was developed using the algorithms and approaches described in the paper.

Being capable of detecting all dealt cases of abnormality and communicating the same to the remote client via SMS and also enabling the wireless tele-operation of robot over internet the system performed all the operations to suit the purpose of old age surveillance efficiently. The Figure 3 shows the developed robot prototype.

Fig. 3. Robot prototype consisting of microcontroller, CC2500 module and Bluetooth enabled camera

Fig. 4. Window is showing abnormality detection using algorithm in section 4.1, where warning is incited when a person fell down

Image processing is performed in order to detect the abnormality in video feed using algorithm discussed in section 4.1. Image with the message warning is shown in Figure 4 and testing of same testing when performed with elder person is shown in Figure 5.

Fig. 5. Testing with aged person

6   Conclusion

This system elucidates an efficient method for surveillance and is aimed to be highly beneficial for any person or organization apart from elderly monitoring. This system is the consolidation of different technologies which includes audio-video processing, multimedia networking and embedded systems. This work could be further extended by application of the same in a multi robot environment whereby multiple audio-video feeds are processed at the server to detect the abnormality with precision. Also motion of the multiple robots could be synchronized to have a better coverage of the surveillance area.

References

1. Tang, H., Xie, X., Xiao, J.: Design and Implement of Rescue Robot Control System Based on Wireless Network. In: International Conference on Anti-Counterfeiting Security and Identification in Communication (ASID), pp. 339–342 (2010)
2. Mester, G.: Wireless Sensor-based Control of Mobile Robots Motion. In: 7th International Symposium on Intelligent Systems and Informatics, pp. 197–201 (2009)
3. Han, K., Kim, S., Kim, Y., Lee, S.-E., Kim, J.H.: Implementation of Internet based personal robot with Internet control architecture. In: International Conference on Robotics and Automation, vol. 1, pp. 217–222 (2001)
4. Wu, D., Hou, Y.T., Zhu, W., Zhang, Y.-Q., Peha, J.M.: Streaming Video over theInternet: Approaches and Directions. In: Circuits and Systems for Video Technology, pp. 282–300 (2001)
5. Srinivasan, K., Porkumaran, K., Sainarayanan, G.: Intelligent human body tracking, modelling, and activity analysis of video surveillance system: A survey. Department of Electronics and Instrumentation Engineering, Sri Amakrishna Engineering College, Coimbatore, Tamil Nadu, India ; Journal of Convergence in Engineering, Technology and Science 1 (December 2009)
6. Kayani, S.A., Bhatti, W.h., Jarral, K.K.: On Design and Fabrication of a Prototype Teleoperated Mobile Surveillance Robot. Department of Mechatronics Engineering, College of Electrical and Mechanical Engineering, National University of Sciences and Technology (2009)

7. Hasan, M.D., Jamil, M., Rabbani, G., Rahman, S.: Speaker identification using Mel Frequency cepstral coefficients. In: 3rd International Conference on Electrical & Computer Engineering, Electrical and Electronic Engineering, Bangladesh University of Engineering and Technology (2004)
8. Kaplan, A.E., Keshav, S., Schryer, N.L., Venutolo, J.H.: An Internet Accessible Telepresence: AT&T Bell Laboratories. Murray Hill, N.J. (1997)
9. Goldberg, K., Gentner, S., Sutter, C., Wiegley, J.: The Mercury Project: a feasibility study for Internet robots. IEEE Robotics & Automation Magazine, IEEE; Dept. of Ind. Eng. &Oper. Res., California Univ., Berkeley, CA (2000)
10. Simmons, R., Goodwin, R., Koenig, W., O'Suvillian, J.: Lessons Learned from Xavier. IEEE Robotics & Automation Magazine (2000)

DSP Implementation of Wavelet Transform Based Embedded Block Coder Using Quadtree Partitioning Method

Deepali P. Ladhi and Richa R. Khandelwal

Department of Electronic Engineering
Shri. Ramdeobaba Kamala Nehru Engineering College, Nagpur
dzoting@gmail.com, richareema@rediffmail.com

Abstract. This paper work describes the implementation of embedded block coder for still image compression using only quad-tree partitioning method. This technique is based on Discrete Wavelet Transform. The motivation behind this work is from SPECK (Set Partitioning Embedded bloCK) algorithm. It uses a recursive set-partitioning procedure to sort subsets of wavelet coefficients by maximum magnitude with respect to thresholds that are integer powers of two. The proposed method simplifies the complexity of the embedded wavelet image coding algorithm by combining both sorting pass and refinement pass. In comparison with other methods, this is simpler to be realized on hardware and has higher compression efficiency. This paper work also explains the software and hardware implementation by using TMS320C6713 DSK board. The statistical analysis is done with profile statistic available in Code Composer Studio (CCS) environment. The MATLAB simulation results show that PSNR values are quite improved by lowering threshold values.

Keywords: Image compression, Discrete Wavelet Transform (DWT), Quad-tree Partitioning, TMS320C6713 DSK Board, PSNR, MSE.

1 Introduction

Embedded wavelet image coding techniques are mainly based on the zero-tree coding and zero-block coding. These coding techniques are possible due to the energy clustering feature of sub-bands in both frequency and in space. A set partitioning process to split off the significant coefficients in a hierarchical manner is applicable to these coders. Hence, one symbol can be used to code a large region including zero pixels .This process is called significance mapping. After this, entropy coding can be applied to further increase the image compression ratio. But there is requirement of more number of linked lists and due to which more memory space is required. The realization of zero-tree and zero-block is done iteratively which is not very space-efficient for hardware implementation. But there is generation of two bit-streams by these embedded wavelet image codecs, namely, significance bits and refinement bits. The significance bits are arranged in the order of quad-tree structure while refinement bits do not have such feature. Hence the significance bits have better compression

N. Meghanathan et al. (Eds.): CCSIT 2012, Part II, LNICST 85, pp. 366–375, 2012.
© Institute for Computer Sciences, Social Informatics and Telecommunications Engineering 2012

effect than the refinement bits. This scheme also uses recursive set-partitioning method to sort subsets of wavelet coefficients by maximum magnitude with respect to thresholds that are integer powers of two. The well defined hierarchical structure and energy clustering in frequency as well as in space which are the fundamental characteristics of an image transform get exploited by this coder. We have coded S set in a similar fashion but while coding I set, instead of octave band partitioning used in SPECK algorithm, we have coded it in a simple manner by taking sets of same fixed size. By doing this the code complexity is reduced to a great extent.

This paper is organized as follows: The next section, Section 2 provides the information about literature survey. Section 3 describes the concept of 2-D DWT. Details of our proposed scheme are explained in Section 4. Section 5 explains the details of TMS320C6713 DSK Board. In Section 6, implementation details of embedded block codec is described. Section 7 gives the experimental results obtained using the coding scheme, followed by concluding statements in Section 8.

2   Literature Survey

The transform coefficients are well compressed by using various codec algorithms like Embedded Zero-tree Wavelet (EZW), Set Partitioning In Hierarchical Trees (SPIHT), Set Partitioning in Embedded block (SPECK), and Embedded Block Coding with Optimized Truncation (EBCOT) are the most famous ones. Effective and computationally simple techniques of transform based image coding have been realized using set partitioning and significance testing on hierarchical structures of transformed images. The algorithms of EZW [3] and SPIHT [4] are based on zerotree and its wavelet coefficients can be represented by zero-tree structure. SPIHT also uses spatial orientation tree to increase its coding efficiency. EBCOT [5] provides the highly improved compression rate among all. The concept of EBCOT is also adopted by JPEG2000 compression standard.

SPECK is different from SPIHT and EZW in that it does not use trees which span and exploit the similarity across different sub-bands of wavelets decomposition. It makes use of the sets in the form of blocks of contiguous coefficients within subbands. The main objective is to achieve better energy compaction in frequency as well as in space in hierarchical structures of transformed images which can be achieved effectively using coding methods based on the use of blocks/sets. It is a known fact that the statistics of an image transform vary markedly as one move from one spatial region to another. By grouping transform source samples in the form of blocks and coding those blocks independently, one is able to exploit the statistics of each block in an appropriate manner. The SPECK image coding scheme has all the properties desirable in modern image compression schemes. The proposed scheme has also same properties which are as follows:

- It is completely embedded,
- It employs progressive transmission,
- It has low computational complexity,

- It has low dynamic memory requirements,
- It has fast encoding/decoding,
- It is efficient in a wide range of compression ratios.

3   Discrete Wavelet Transform

Discrete Wavelet Transform (DWT) is being increasingly used for image coding as the DWT can decompose the signals into different subbands with both time and frequency information.   The main features like progressive image transmission, coding of region of interest and further manipulations in compressed image can be achieved.   The separable 2-D wavelet transformation can be implemented by applying a two level decomposition of the 1-D DWT in the horizontal and vertical dimensions respectively. The resulting subband decomposition of this transformation is described in Fig. 1, where *G(n)* and *H(n)* represent the low-pass and high-pass wavelet filters, respectively.[6]

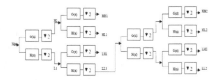

Fig. 1. Two-Level and Two-Dimensional DWT

In the 2-D DWT filter bank structure, in each stage, the row computations precede the column computations. In stage 1, 1-D DWT is computed along the rows of the input array to generate *H1* (high-pass) and *L1* (low-pass) outputs. If the image is of size N x N, then the *H1* and *L1* output arrays are each of size N/2 x N/2. The HH1 and HL1 outputs are obtained by computing the 1-D DWT on the H1 columns. Similarly the LL1 and LH1 outputs are obtained by operating upon the L1 columns. Each of the LL1, LH1, HL1, HH1 arrays are of size N/2 x N/2. The LL1 outputs are again decomposed to obtain the outputs for stage 2 namely, LL2, LH2, HL2, and HH2 which are each of size N/4 x N/4. Out of these the LL2 outputs are sent to stage 3 for further decomposition [5]. Fig. 2 shows pyramidal decomposition takes place after applying two dimensional DWT.

Fig. 2. Original Image and Pyramidal Decomposition after DWT application for level=2

4 Methodology

The proposed scheme follows the popular bitplane coding approach to successive approximation of wavelet coefficients. The coder performs two passes through the set of wavelet coefficients: the significance pass and the refinement pass. The significance pass describes the significance state for each coefficient whether or not the coefficient magnitude is greater than or less than the current significance threshold. Thus, for a given threshold, the significance pass amounts to the coding of a binary valued significance map. On the other hand, the refinement pass produces a successive approximation to those coefficients that are already known to be significant by coding the current coefficient magnitude bitplane for those significant coefficients. After each iteration of the significance and refinement passes, the significance threshold is divided in half, and the process is repeated for the next bitplane.

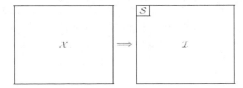

Fig. 3. Partitioning of image X into sets S and I

For coding the binary significance map, we partition sets of coefficients into smaller and smaller sets. Unlike zero-tree set-partitioning algorithms such as SPIHT, this scheme eliminates the cross-scale aggregation of coefficients and focuses the set-partitioning process instead on sets of contiguous coefficients from within a single sub-band. Transformed image X is first divided into two sets S and I In (Fig. 3).where S set is a root set and I set is the remaining portion of X. Specifically, this coder codes the significance map with using only quad-tree partitioning.[2]

In quad-tree partitioning as shown in Fig.(4), the significance state of an entire block of coefficients is tested and coded, the block is subdivided into four sub-blocks of approximately equal size, and the significance coding process is repeated recursively on each of the sub-blocks. The motivation for this so-called quad-tree partitioning of such sets achieves two goals: (1) to quickly identify the areas of high energy (magnitude) in the set S and code them first, and (2) to locate structured groups of coefficients that are below a decreasing sequence of magnitude thresholds, so as to limit the number of bits needed for their representation [1].

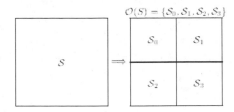

Fig. 4. Partitioning of set S

Next process is to test the set I against the same threshold n. If it is found to be significant, then by taking various subsets inside I ,(each of size 2x2) and process them for passing the significance test. Again the same way significant subsets are quadrisected and pixel information is transferred to output bitstream.

This coder stores sets in implicitly sorted lists. Insignificant sets are placed in a list of insignificant sets (LIS). During the sorting pass, each insignificant set in an LIS is tested for significance against the current threshold. If the set becomes significant, it is split into four subsets according to the quad-tree decomposition structure described above. The four new sets are placed into an LIS, recursively tested for significance, and split again if needed. It maintains multiple LIS lists in order to implicitly process sets according to their size. During the sorting pass, each time a set is split, the resulting subsets move to the next LIS. When a set is reduced in size to a single coefficient, and that coefficient becomes significant, then the singleton set is moved from its LIS to a list of significant pixels (LSP).

The decoder uses the same mechanism as the encoder. It receives significance test results from the coded bitstream and builds up the same list structure during the execution of the algorithm. Hence, it is able to follow the same execution paths for the significance tests of the different sets, and reconstructs the image progressively as the algorithm proceeds.

5   TMS320C6713 DSK

The TMS320C6713 is a fast processor uses velociTI architecture. It is a 32-bit floating processor. Also it is a low-cost standalone development platform to enable users to evaluate and develop applications for the TI C67xx DSP family. It has following key features:

- It operates at 225MHz and sampling rate can be varied from 8 to 96KHz,
- It includes an AIC23 stereo codec which uses sigma delta technology and provides A/D and D/A,
- Synchronous DRAM is of 16 Mbytes,
- Non volatile Flash memory is of 512 Kbytes and its 256 Kbytes are usable in default configuration,
- Four user accessible LEDs and DIP switches,
- Software board configuration through registers implemented in CPLD,
- Configurable boot options,
- Use of daughter card through standard expansion connectors,
- JTAG emulation through on board JTAG emulator with USB host,
- External emulator and interface,
- +5V single power supply.

DSK board provides four connectors for input and output. LINE IN for line input, MIC IN for microphone input, LINE OUT for line output which is multiplexed with HEADPHONE, and HEADPHONE for a headphone output. Code Composer communicates with the DSK through an embedded JTAG emulator with a USB host interface. For further details refer the references from [7]-[9].

6   Implementation

In implementing our scheme on TMS320C6713 DSK Board, we have followed following steps:

- In MATLAB environment, read greyscale image of BARBARA (512x512). To get transformed image, apply dwt2 function using Daubechies filter directly on this image upto sixth level of decomposition. This will result into topmost LL,LH, HL and HH sub-bands, each of size 8x8. The LL subband contains approximate coefficients with more energy compaction and rest of the sub-bands contain detail coefficients with very less energy compaction.

- Now get normalized topmost LL subband (8x8) and use as a input matrix (say, X) to Encoder which is written using 'C' in CCS (Code Composer Studio) environment.

- Now process starts by partitioning X into set S and set I as shown in Fig 3. Set S (2x2) is coded first. LIS (List of Insignificant Sets) is initialised by set S and LSP (List of Significant Pixels) is kept empty.

- Next step is to apply the significance test on root set S First threshold value is calculated using the formula. If a single value in a set is found to be greater than threshold, set S is significant and 't' is displayed in output bitstream. As set S is significant, it is quadrisected i.e., partitioned into four subsets and again each subset is tested against same threshold. This process is continued until singleton set is obtained.

- Now,if coefficient is greater than threshold and it is positive, then 'p' is send to output bitstream and if it is of negative size then 'n' is send otherwise 'z'. Then same way set I is tested for its significance. The significance test is applied on each and every adjacent sets of same fixed size (e.g 2x2 size). If any one found insignificant, they will go to LIS (List of Insignificant Sets) otherwise same quad-tree partitioning is applied on significant sets and rest of the process will be same as applied for coding set 'S'. This way we will get output bit stream, LIS data, LSP data and decoded matrix as shown in Fig. 5 for two sorting passes by lowering threshold value.

- After getting decoder output, apply inverse dwt (idwt2 function) on it for 6 levels to get size of 512x512. Then original image is compared with reconstructed image and MSE along with PSNR are calculated which are coming quite good.

Threshold calculation is done by following formula,

$$n \max = \lfloor \log_2 (\max_{(i,j) \in X} |c_{i,j}|) \rfloor \tag{1}$$

7   Experimental Results

The performance of hardware implementation using TMS320C6713 DSK Board is shown in Fig.6. This coding scheme is applied on 8x8 size image obtained by decomposing 512x512 image for sixth level. The output is in the form of bitstream. This bitstream is then applied as a input to decoder. Reconstructed matrix is not exactly like original matrix as only pixel values in LSP are passed to decoder and values in remaining insignificant sets are replaced by some constant values. The reconstructed 8x8 matrix is again processed in MATLAB. and inverse 2-D DWT (idwt) function is applied for 6 times to achieve image size 512x512.Then error is found by subtracting reconstructed matrix from original matrix.

Fig. 5. Encoder Output for Grey scale BARBARA (8x8) image

MSE (Mean Square Error) and PSNR(Peak Signal to Noise Ratio) values for different grey scale images like Barbara, Fruits, Zelda ,Goldhill (512x512) are also found along with Lena image .The following table shows the numerical results for each test images after completing two passes i.e. decreasing threshold by two (or doing nmax-1). If nmax is lowered , threshold value also decreases which makes other sets /pixels significant in subsequent passes. Due to this LSP gets updated and LIS data gets changed by the removal of significant sets/pixels. Fig 6. shows the original and reconstructed images. The statistical analysis results are shown in Fig.7.

7.1   PSNR and MSE

Peak Signal to Noise Ratio (PSNR) is a measure of distortion. As test images are 8 bpp grey scale images, the PSNR value is calculated from the formula given below,

$$PSNR = 10 \log_{10} \left(\frac{255^2}{MSE} \right) \qquad (2)$$

where MSE (Mean Square Error) is the cumulative squared error between the compressed and the original image. A good PSNR performance is a prerequisite for any modern compression algorithm.

Fig. 6. Original and reconstructed images: Barbara (512x512), Lena (512x512), Goldhill (512x512), Cameraman (256x256)

Table 1. MSE and PSNR values for different images for two sorting passes

Images (512x512)	MSE	PSNR (dB)
LENA	14 4705	36.5260
BARBARA	25.2588	34.1067
FRUITS	1.3684	46.7688
ZELDA	57.9307	30.5017
GOLDHILL	44.4448	31.6526

7.2   Statistical Analysis

Statistical analysis of our scheme is done by using profile statistic available in Code Composer Studio (CCS).The different columns given in Fig .7 are explained as follows:

- Address Range displays the hexadecimal range of the profiled section of code.
- Symbol Name contains the name of the function if the address range is a function.
- cycle.Total: Incl. Total displays the number of cycles that occurred in the entire profiled section of code, including subroutines. This column is included in the data because selecting the "Collect application level profile for set total cycles and code size" automatically selects the cycle□Total event.

- cycle.Total: Excl.Total shows the number of cycles that occurred in the profiled section of code,excluding subroutines.
- cpu.Total: Encl.Total shows the count of the cumulative total of CPU cycles for all functions, ignoring system effects.
- cpu.Total: Excl.Total shows the count of the cumulative total of CPU cycles for all functions, considering system effect.

Fig. 7. Statistical analysis in Code Composer Studio (CCS) environment

8   Conclusion

The proposed scheme is successfully implemented on floating point DSP TMS320C6713. Low cost, very efficient and simple hardware implementation is achieved. The DSP platform of C6713 DSK board provides user friendly development tools. With better optimization technique the total number of cycles for the execution of functions can be further reduced. The Matlab simulation results for different grey scale images for two passes shows that PSNR values increases as well as MSE values decreases as threshold value decreases.

References

1. Pearlman, W.A., Islam, A., Nagaraj, N., Said, A.: Efficient, Low- Complexity Image Coding with a Set-Partitioning Embedded Block Coder. IEEE Trans. Circuits and Systems for Video Technology 14, 1219–1235 (2004)
2. Munteanu, A., Cornelis, J., Van der Auwera, G., Cristea, P.: Wavelet Image Compression – The Quadtree Coding Approach. IEEE Trans. on Information Technology.in Biomedicine 3, 176–185 (1999)
3. Shapiro, M.: Embedded image coding using zerotrees of wavelets coefficients. IEEE Trans. Signal Processing 41, 3445–3462 (1993)
4. Said, A., Pearlman, W.A.: A New Fast and Efficient Image Codec Based on Set Partitioning in Hierarchical Trees. IEEE Trans. Circuits and Systems for Video Technology 6 (June 1996)
5. Taubman, D.: High Performance Scalable Image Compression with EBCOT. IEEE Trans. on Image Processing 9, 1158–1170 (2000)

6. Singh, J., Antoniou, A., Shpak, D.J.: Hardware Implementation of a Wavelet based Image Compression Coder. In: 1998 IEEE Symposium on Advances in Digital Filtering and Signal Processing, pp. 169–173 (June 1998)
7. Chassaing, R.: Digital Signal Processing and Applications with the 6713 and C6416 DSK, ch. 1. Wiley, New York (2005)
8. TMS320C6713 Floating Point Digital Signal Processor, Literature Number: SPRS186L, December 2001 - Revised November 2005, P.69
9. Texas Instruments, TMS320C62X/C67X, Programmers' Guide, Dallas, TX (May 1999)

Calculation of the Minimum Time Complexity Based on Information Entropy

Xue Wu

Department of Microelectronic and Nanoelectronic Engineering,
Room 130A, Zijing1#Building, Tsinghua University, Beijing, P.R. China
wuxiqh@yahoo.cn

Abstract. In order to find out the limiting speed of solving a specific problem using computer, this essay provides a method based on the entropy of information. The relationship between the minimum time complexity and the information entropy change is illustrated. Several examples are served as evidence of such connection. Meanwhile some notices of modeling these problems are proposed. Finally, the nature of solving problems with computer programs is disclosed to support the theory and a redefinition of the information entropy in this field is proposed. This will develop a new field of science.

Keywords: information entropy, time complexity, algorithm, entropy change.

1   Introduction

As new approaches to algorithm optimization become more and more popular in researches, it is a matter of greater urgency to determine whether an algorithm of handling a specific problem reaches the limiting speed or not instead of trying to improve an algorithm continuously. Such demand arouses a technique to discover the boundary of the velocity, the minimum time complexity of a program, which is based on two assumptions. These assumptions consequently give birth to the relevance between information entropy change and the so-called minimum time complexity.

Information is an abstract conception. There was not a widely acceptable measurement of information quantification until the father of information theory C. E. Shannon provided a novel conception of information entropy in 1948 [1], [2]. Shannon first associated probability with information redundance in mathematic language [1]. His discovery made a great contribution to the field of communication, meanwhile it also left clues to the consistency between information entropy change and the nature of figuring out an issue using computer [3], [4], [5]. This directly led to the establishment of the first assumption.

Since computers were invented, the amount of information which is generated by an operation in a computer program has remained unknown to most people. The significance of operations' productivity has even been ignored. However it is necessary to concentrate on the efficiency of an operation with the purpose of building the bridge between information entropy change and the minimum time complexity. Therefore the second assumption arises.

N. Meghanathan et al. (Eds.): CCSIT 2012, Part II, LNICST 85, pp. 376–385, 2012.

After the proposition of these two fundamental assumptions, there comes the great need of evidence to support this theory. Just then two examples appear and become the pillars of the theory. Looking for the maximum value and sorting a group of numbers are the names of these two problems. The results of the calculation based on information entropy for these two issues in some special models are the same with the time complexities of the known fastest programs. This fact motivates a demand for notices of modeling these problems. With the help of the notices, the nature of solving problems using computer programs is discovered to testify the theory and a redefinition of the information entropy is proposed. This event heralds a new field of science to be developed [5].

2   Two Basic Assumptions

During the information transmission and storage process, there is a part of code that does not express the substance of the information. The amount of such code is called information redundance. Moreover making people realize some unaquainted knowledge is able to be regarded as giving people some substantial information [6]. Therefore the procedure is exactly the change of information redundance. According to the relationship between information redundance and information entropy, the first assumption that the nature of figuring out a problem is the same as a change of information entropy is set up.

No matter how complex an operation is, it is composed of some simple ones. Operations like equation, being greater than and being smaller than are typical instances of these basic operations. In consideration of them, each elementary operation is able to figure out a question like whether a statement is true or false. The amount of information that consists in such questions is regarded as 1 bit. Therefore the fact that every basic operation generates 1 bit information is presented as the second assumption.

3   Theory Description and Modeling of Two Examples

The fundamental role of information is to eliminate people's uncertainties of matters around them. The information entropy is used to measuring the degree of these uncertainties [6]. Shannon's conception of the entropy is based on the following equation:

$$H(x) = -\sum_{i=1}^{n} P(x_i) \log_2 (P(x_i))$$ (1)

In the equation, $H(x)$ is the information entropy, $P(x_i)$ is the probability of the incident that x equals to x_i [7]. In line with the two assumptions a theory that the minimum time complexity is the same with the change of information entropy is brought out. It can be expressed in the following form:

$$\text{Time complexity} = \Delta H(x) = H(x) - H_0(x)$$ (2)

$H(x)$ is the initial entropy. $H_0(x)$ is the final entropy [8]. With regard to a specific question, the initial entropy is fetched through modeling of this problem [1]. The modeling criterion has not been clearly clarified, however an imprecise standard that the sequence which expresses the final relationships among data or belongs to the same sort of sequence with the final result should be regarded as the state x_i is proposed. This rule will be interpreted by two examples in detail later on. When a problem is figured out, the information which people want to know is determined. In other words, the sequence is eventually decided. Therefore the probability of the situation that this sequence appears is 1 [9]. According to (1), the final entropy of an issue is obtained.

$$H_0(x) = \log_2(1)$$
$$= 0 \tag{3}$$

Backed by the modeling standard and the value of the ultimate information entropy, the minimum time complexities of looking for the maximum value and sorting a group of numbers are easy to discuss.

3.1   Modeling of Seeking the Maximum Value

In order to make a model of looking for the maximum value, the form of the sequence that is able to expresses the characteristics of the final result should be decided first. We can abstract this problem into the following structure:

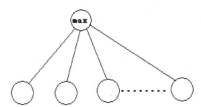

Fig. 1. Abstract structure of seeking the maximum

The top element in Fig. 1 represents the maximum value and the other elements below it are the rest of the numbers. The lines between them are called keys. They denote the size relationships between the maximum value and the others. Each size relationship has two possible conditions: "Greater" or "Not greater". If each key's condition is determined as "Greater", then the top element turns out to be the maximum. This fact indicates that these keys convey the final result. Therefore the serial of keys can be regarded as the sequence that we want.

There are n-1 keys in this sequence. According to the statement that each key has two possible situations, there are 2^{n-1} different sequences in all. Every sequence has a probability of $(0.5)^{n-1}$ to be the final sequence. Use (1), we can obtain the initial information entropy.

$$H(x) = -\sum_{i=1}^{2^{n-1}} 0.5^{n-1} \log_2(0.5^{n-1})$$
$$= n - 1 \tag{4}$$

As $H_0(x)$ equals to 0, with the help of (2) the minimum time complexity is got from the result of the calculation.

$$\text{Time complexity} = \Delta H(x) = n - 1 \tag{5}$$

Therefore the calculated minimum time complexity is O(n). According to the survey of various algorithms, the time complexity of the fastest program which is able to solve the problem is also O(n). These two time complexities are the same in such model. This indicates that the theory of the consistency between the information entropy change and the minimum time complexity of the computer program is proved in this issue.

3.2   Modeling of Sorting a Group of Numbers

Being similar to the circumstances of seeking the maximum value, another type of sequence needs to be decided before we calculate the minimum time complexity of sorting a group of numbers. Inspired by the idea of seeking the maximum value, keys between every two elements should be established in order to express the final relationships among data. Just as the circumstances in solving the problem, looking for the maximum, each key has two possible situations. If we decide the value of every key, the correct sequence will be presented. With the thinking as before, the sequence of these keys is considered what we want. Meanwhile, the number of the sequences is considered to be $2^{0.5n(n-1)}$ with the help of the permutation and combination theory. According to this method to do so, we will get a result like this:

$$H(x) = 0.5n(n-1) \tag{6}$$

Therefore, the minimum time complexity is O(n^2). This time complexity is the same with that of Bubble sort and insertion sort [10]. These methods are fast enough, however, just as we know, the fastest algorithm is merge sort the time complexity of which is able to reach O($n\log_2(n)$) [10]. O($n\log_2(n)$) is much smaller than O(n^2), this fact indicates that O(n^2) is not the minimum time complexity and O($n\log_2(n)$) takes place of it. As a result, there may be a contradiction in this theory. Nevertheless, if we consider this issue more carefully, we will discover that we have ignored some important point, the independence of the keys. For example, if there are only three numbers, all situations which are based on the theory of permutation and combination are shown in the following figures:

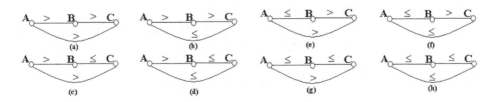

Fig. 2. Situations of three elements

In reality, not all of the eight situations are able to occur. Fig. 2(b) and Fig. 2(g) are two examples of these circumstances. Taking account of the size relationships among them, there are contradictions in the two figures cited above. Thinking about Fig. 2(b) in details, we'll get the following information: A is greater than B; B is greater than C; A is not greater than C. According to the first two points, A should be greater than C, however Fig. 2(b) provides an opposite relation. Therefore the situation in Fig. 2(b) does not exist. The same conclusion is drawn from Fig. 2(g).

As the total number of data grows, more and more situations appear and we directly regarded them as legal ones, but in fact they should not be included in the collection of the sequences. If we exclude them, the total number of the situations will correspondingly reduce to $n!$. It is easier to think in another way in order to explain why the number equals to $n!$ after reduction. When the serial of keys are decided, one sequence of the numbers is determined. Meanwhile one sequence of the numbers indicates one sequence of "Greater" or "Not greater". This is true, because the sequence that we choose is able to express the characteristic of the final result and the sequence of the numbers is exactly the result in the problem of sorting a group of numbers. Therefore, the sequence of the numbers is capable of being the state x_i. Based on the permutation and combination theory again, the number of the states is $n!$. For the reason that every state has the same probability to be the ultimate one, (1) and (2) provide us the following information:

$$\text{Time complexity} = \log_2(n!) \tag{7}$$

Time complexity is an approximation of a program's speed. Moreover, the number of the elements should be large enough in order to make the approximation meanful. In the case that n is a large number, there is a classical approximaiton.

$$\ln(n!) = n\ln(n) - n \tag{8}$$

Based on (7), we can get the following result:

$$\begin{aligned}\log_2(n!) &\approx n\log_2(n) - n\log_2(e) \\ &\approx n\log_2(n)\end{aligned} \tag{9}$$

Therefore, the minimum time complexity is $O(n\log_2(n))$. The result is the same with that of the merge sort [10]. This fact confirms the correctness of the theory again.

4   Notices of Modeling Problems

Even though there is not a precise criterion of modeling problems, several notices should be clarified in order to get the correct result.

4.1   Relationship between Final Result and the Sequence

In the problem of sorting a group of numbers, we are able to choose the permutation of the numbers as the sequence because the final result is one of the permutations.

This fact proposes a new decription of the criterion that the state and the final result belong to the same type of sequence. Meanwhile the characteristic that the sequence should express the final relationships among data is eliminated. However, such modification of the rule is not correct.

Considering the problem of seeking the maximum value, if we regard the final result as the sequence, then an element is considered as the sequence and the number of the states will be n. According to (1), we are easy to find out that the minimum time complexity is $\log_2(n)$ in this model. As we know, the time complexity of solving this problem is not able to decline to this amount. Therefore the final result can not serve as the state in all problems.

However being aware of which problem's final result is capacable of being the sequence is not enough, we need to discover the reason why some of them are able to be the sequence and the others are not.

In the problems of sorting a group of numbers, the final result is a serial of numbers in order. We regard this type of sequence as the state and we are able to calculate the minimum time complexity which conforms to that of the fastest program. The reason why this consistency is established can be explained in the following way. The result of sorting a group of numbers is a serial of numbers in order. The only feature of the result is the order. Therefore the final result itself is able to express its characteristic. We call this trait information independence. When the problem is solved, the information entropy reduces to 0. This means that the sequence we choose is decided. Fortunately, the sequence we determine is the final result and because of its information independence the final result contains all the final relationships among data. Thus, in this problem we can regard the final result as the sequence.

Nevertheless, the circumstances of seeking the maximum value are different from those of sorting a group of numbers. The final result of seeking the maximum value is the maximum number. Even though the maximum number shows us its magnitude, it is not able to convey its characteristic, being the maximum. Therefore, the consequence of this problem is not information independent and this fact leads to the invalidity of regarding the final result as the sequence.

In a nutshell, the sequence which is considered to be the state should express the final relationships among data. Only if the final result is information independent, is it possible to substitude the final result for the sequence in order to simplify the state calculation.

4.2   Final Information Entropy and the Sequence

In order to determine which sequence is able to be taken as the state, the imprecise criterion is not enough, because there are various sequences which are capable of representing the final relationships among data. For instance, in the problem of looking for the maximum value, besides the sequence we choose, a sequence that contains the relationships between each two numbers accords with the criterion too. Therefore, another factor should be taken into account for the purpose of excluding the extra sequences.

Recalling the discussion in Section 3, when a problem is solved, the information entropy declines to 0. This means that the sequence is determined. However this fact will not happen, if we regard the sequence which expresses the relationships between each two numbers in the problem of seeking the maximum value. When the maximum value is located, there are only n-1 keys determined in the sequence and the rest of the keys remains unknown. Therefore, the entropy of information is not 0 in this case and the magnitude of the information entropy should be calculated again. This will bring in more work. Not only do we need to calculate both initial and final information entropies, we also need to determine the locations of the n-1 keys in the sequence.

Whereas, thing is not that easy as it looks like. The locations of the n-1 keys are able to provide several different states. Meanwhile, the sequence itself has several states too. It seems right to take these two types of states into account in order to find out the initial and final number of the states. But these two types of states are not totally different, there does exist an overlap between them. Therefore, if we consider in this way, modeling this problem will be more complex and a great amount of extra work should be done.

As a result, it is a good way to model problems with the sequence that makes the final information entropy decline to zero. We call this type of sequence 0-type sequence. Choosing the 0-type sequence as the state is a routine way to model problems. However in some problems, the 0-type sequence is not easy to find. This arouses another sequence to replace it. The ideas above remind us that we are able to regard some sequences that are in accord with the imprecise criterion as the state. If we are easier to handle the complex relationship between those two types of states than to establish the 0-type sequence, it will be a better way to select this sequence instead of the 0-type sequence.

4.3   Equation Simplification in Specific Circumstances

While calculating the time complexity of the two problems in Section 3, we can find out that the equation is able to be simplified. Because the possibilities of all states are the same and the final information entropy is zero, the equation can be expressed in the following form (n is the number of the states):

$$\text{Time complexity} = \log_2(n) \tag{10}$$

This simplified equation discloses another characteristic of the states in the models of problems. That is the equality of the states' possibilities. This feature is a factor that we need to consider when we are going to select the sequence and it is also an inevitable result because the sequence satifies the imprecise criterion. The necessity can be proved by the following evidence.

If some states' probabilities of being the final sequence are different from others, this will indicates that these states have different numbers of sub-states. Since each state is able to be the final sequence, meanwhile the sequence and the result is one to one, therefore if a state with one sub-state can be the final sequence and a state with two sub-states is also capable of being the final sequence, the two results which they provide belong to different types. This means that the format of the final result is not determined. However in a specific problem the format of the final result is settled. Thus, it is not possible to make a state with different probability.

5   Nature of Solving Issues with Computer Programs

In Section 4, the equation to calculate the time complexity is simplified. According to (10), there is a logarithmic relationship between the minimum time complexity and the number of the states.

As everyone knows, the time complexity of the fastest program for searching, bisearch also has a logarithmic relationship with the number of the elements. However this coincidence does not happen occasionally, a connection does exist between searching and solving a problem with computer program.

Think about it theoretically. In Section 3, solving problems using computer programs is interpreted as determining which state is able to be the final state. As the theory says, at the beginning of solving problems, there are a number of states and we don't know which state is capable of being the final one. These states act as a list and our target is to find out which state is in accord with the characteristics of the final result. The list is named as lookup table of problems and the final result is called searching target. Therefore, solving a problem with computer programs is transformed into a problem of searching. The nature of resolving issues turns out to be raveling out a problem of searching.

Since the minimum time complexity of searching is $\log_2(n)$ (n is the number of the elements), so the minimum time complexity of any problem is able to reach $\log_2(n)$ (n is the number of the states).

6   Redefinition of Information Entropy

In Section 5, no matter what the problem is like, it is able to be considered as a searching problem when we want to solve it by computer programs. Hence the minimum time complexity is related to the number of comparisons which are required to find the searching target. Based on the theory, if the connection between the minimum time complexity and the information entropy is valid, there will be a relationship between information entropy and the corresponding searching problem. Considering the fact that the information entropy has a similar logarithmic relationship to that of the searching problem, a redefinition of the information entropy is proposed in the field of settling issues.

In the redefinition of the information entropy, it is defined as the minimum number of comparisons, which computers need to execute in order to find the searching target in the lookup table of the problem in the worst case. This definition focuses on using computer programs to solve problems. Meanwhile it is also in accord with the original definition proposed by Shannon based on the calculation in Section 4. Therefore the new definition is a special case of Shannon's definition.

Computer is a discrete binary system. It is able to resolve problems with definite results. According to the discussion in Section 4, the states of the problem are equiprobable. Thus, the equation of the information entropy can be reduced to the simple logarithmic form while considering such problems. This is the reason why we replace the original definition by the new one in this field. Moreover, this definition helps us to think about this type of issues more directly and conveniently.

7   Conclusion

As the result of the assumption that the process of solving a problem is the same as making a change in the information entropy and the postulation that an operation in computer program is able to generate 1 bit information, the theory that the minimum time complexity of settling a specific issue with computer programs equals to the information entropy change in the model of the problem with special characteristics is established.

Seeking the maximum value and sorting a group of numbers are served as evidence to support this theory. The coincidence that these two time complexities equal to the results of the calculation backs the validity of the principle. Meanwhile, (2) is proposed to calculate the minimum time complexity.

While we are calculating the minimum time complexity based on the information entropy, a pivotal problem of how to modeling issues arises. Thus, several notices are put forward in order to make the process of modeling problems more complete.

The first notice is about the imprecise criterion. This notice remind us that not all the problems are able to regard their final results as the sequences. If and only if the final result of the problem is information independent, is it correct to choose the final result as the sequence. In other words, the only criterion of selecting the sequence is that the sequence must be able to convey all the final relationships among data and taking the final result as the sequence is only a simplification of a special case.

Secondly, while selecting the sequence, there are a lot of sequences that are in accord with the imprecise criterion. This notice acts as a guide for us to choose the most befitting sequence among them. In the notice, the sequences are separated into two types. One is the sequence with zero final information entropy, which is called 0-type sequence; the other is the sequence with non-zero final information entropy. While calculating the number of the states, the circumstances of the sequence with non-zero final information entropy are very complex, but the cases of the 0-type sequence are easily figured out. However, the 0-type sequence is not usually established easily. If we can consider the complex circumstances of the sequence with non-zero final information entropy clearly, we will be able to take such sequence instead of the 0-type sequence. Therefore, the notice indicates that we should choose the 0-type sequence to make the calculation easier in general cases and we can select the sequence with non-zero final information entropy in some special cases, if we are able to think about the circumstances clearly.

An important characteristic of the states in the models of the problems is clarified in the final notice. This characteristic is described as the equiprobability of the states. In the analysis, the characteristic is proved to be necessary, because the result of the problem has a certain format. Meanwhile the equiprobability also leads to a simplification of the equation to calculate the minimum time complexity.

After the simplification of the equation is made, the similarity between the calculated result and the minimum time complexity of the searching problem is discovered. Such similarity arouses a further consideration of the relationship between the searching problem and the nature of solving problems with computer programs. Since the minimum time complexity of searching has the same form with that of the simplified information entropy and there are lookup table and the searching target in the model of the problem, so the nature of solving problems with computer programs is regarded as resolving searching problems.

With the help of the discovery that the nature of solving issues with computer programs is no more than raveling out searching problems, the information entropy is redefined as the minimum number of comparisons, which computers need to execute in order to find the searching target in the lookup table of the problem in the worst case. This redefinition is in accord with the original definition made by Shannon.

In summary, all the conclusions above herald a new field of science to be developed.

References

1. Gang, C.: Shannon Information Model in E-commerce Information Analysis. In: International Joint Conference on Artificial Intelligence, pp. 580–583 (2009)
2. Verdú, S.: Fifty Years of Shannon Theory. IEEE Transactions on Information Theory 44(6), 2057–2078 (1998)
3. Wang, Y.: Analyses on Limitations of Information Theory. In: International Conference on Artificial Intelligence and Computational Intelligence, pp. 85–88 (2009)
4. Shannon, C.E.: A Mathematical Theory of Communication. Bell System Technical Journal 27, 379–429, 623–656 (1948)
5. Shannon, C.E.: The Bandwagon. IEEE Transactions on Information Theory 2, 3 (1956)
6. Hatfield, A.J., Hipel, K.W.: Understanding and Managing Uncertainty and Information. In: IEEE International Conference on System, Man and Cybernetics, pp. 1007–1012 (1999)
7. Zhao, M., Ye, X., Han, K., Li, Y.: Research on Digital Image Edge Detection with Local Entropy and Fuzzy Entropy Algorithms. In: IEEE International Conference on Information and Automation (ICIA), pp. 2477–2482 (2010)
8. Xie, X., Zang, X.-Y., Guan, Z.-L.: Analytic Demonstration on the Irrationality of Negative Entropy Principle. In: International Conference on Management Science and Engineering, pp. 109–115 (2008)
9. Wang, X., Ge, Y., Wang, X.: Research on Manthematical Theory of Information Acquisition. In: Proceedings of International Conference on Information Acquisition, pp. 59–70 (2004)
10. Iqbal, S.Z., Gull, H., Muzaffar, A.W.: A New Friends Sort Algorithm. In: 2nd IEEE International Conference on Computer Science and Information Technology, pp. 326–329 (2009)

Enhancing E-Learning through Cognitive Structures for Learning Sports

S. MuthuLakshmi[*], S. Nagasundari, S.P. Surender Nath, and G.V. Uma

Dept. of Information Science & Technology,
Anna University, Chennai -600025, India
{muthusubramanian2185,nagasundarisuresh,spsuren78}@gmail.com,
gvuma@annauniv.edu

Abstract. Enhancing e-Learning through understanding and taking into account the cognitive structures of learner and trainer in learning sports is a new avenue of research. E-Learning has made its steps into all disciplines, while sports domain remains a discipline that involves physiological variables in learning. Learning sport is incomplete until a learner is trained physically and is ready to actually play the sport. The curiosity to know how e-Learning methods can be utilized for learning sports has led the work to look into the learning theories. The behaviorist approach can be efficient at the initial level. The cognitive approach has been identified as an efficient approach in advanced level learning. Cognitive theory of learning also proposes feedback mechanism, contiguity, repetition, and reinforcement. This research is to explore the possibility of enhancing e-learning using cognitive theoretical approach in learning sports.

Keywords: e-Learning, cognitive structure, physiological variables, Contiguity and Repetition Mechanism.

1 Introduction

In current scenario, there are many forums to learn sports. Due to the advancement in various technologies, learning sports is facilitated through e-learning system. *E-learning* refers to the use of Internet technologies to deliver a broad array of solutions that enhance knowledge and performance [1]. E-*learning* is commonly referred to the intentional use of networked information and communications technology in teaching and learning. It is otherwise termed as online learning, virtual learning, distributed learning, network and web based learning. Fundamentally, they all refer to educational processes that utilize information and communications technology to mediate asynchronous as well as synchronous learning and teaching activities [5]. *E-Learning* is the use of technology to enable people to learn anytime and anywhere. E-Learning can include training, the delivery of just-in-time information and guidance from experts [4].

---

[*] Corresponding author.

N. Meghanathan et al. (Eds.): CCSIT 2012, Part II, LNICST 85, pp. 386–392, 2012.

Cognitive structures are defined as the mental processes through which any information could be understood [3].The following section discusses the various cognitive structures in learning.

1.1   Cognitive Structures in Learning

Cognitivism is a learning theory which deals with the internal mental processes of the mind and how these processes could be used to endorse effective learning [6].

1. **Analysis Phase:** The tasks are first analyzed and then broken down into steps [6][7].
2. **Design Phase:** These bits of information are then used to enlarge learning in instructional design curriculum [6].
3. **Acquiring Phase:** This information is then taught from the most simple to the most complex depending on the learner's prior schema [6][7].
4. **Process Phase:** The mind contains such mental representations as logical propositions, rules, concepts, images, and analogies, and it uses mental procedures such as deduction, search, matching, rotating, and retrieval [8][9][10][11].

According to Cognitive theorists, learning is a process achieved through contiguity and repetition. It is also inferred that acquisition or reorganization of the cognitive structures is a part of learning process [2].

E-learning introduced many learner centered approaches to experience a real time learning of school sports. But when e-learning is implemented, it lacks the interactions between the learner and the trainer compared to the traditional training process. It's very hard to determine the learner's knowledge level and hence the learning process is not too effective. So the cognitive structures of the learner and trainer are employed to enhance the learning effectiveness of the E-learning sports training.

2   Proposed Work

This paper proposes a methodology based on cognitive structures of learners and trainers to enhance learning sports through e-learning. The overall system is viewed as three sub-systems: learner sub-system, e-learning sub-system, trainer sub-system. The following fig.1 depicts the architecture of Cognitive Structures in e-learning.

2.1   Learner Sub-system

The learner has mental schema, inadequate knowledge, and logical processes. Fig. 2 illustrates the components of the learner .These components are taken into account by the trainer before suggesting any concrete steps in learning. The cognitive structure of

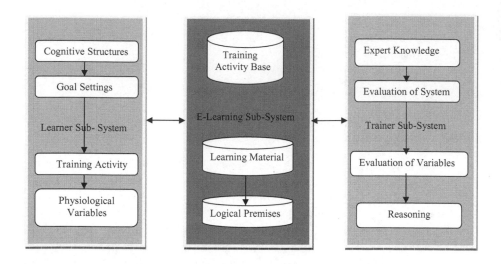

Fig. 1. Architecture of Cognitive Structures in e-learning

the learner presupposes that the learner has a mental schema which can be updated, modified or extended depending on the particular inadequate knowledge the learner holds in his intellectual repository. The learner presents his abilities and prior knowledge of the domain to the trainer. The learner is assessed by the trainer on his/her ability to take up a particular sport learning activity. The learner's ability is evaluated using his cognitive structures that are one's ability to perceive, inculcate, and to execute. If the learner's abilities are adequate enough to take up the lessons on the particular area of sport that the learner is willing to take, the trainer sub-system would proceed further in providing e-learning material. The assessment of the learner is done with the mental schema and mental ability (intellectual), the spirit of the learner and motivation for learning (psychological), and physical ability (physical) of the learner. The presupposition is that the learner has a little prior knowledge of what he/she is intending to learn. If the learner is not well equipped with the details of the sport, a basic knowledge through limited active participation in a sport or through literature or through visuals is taken into consideration.

The learner sub-system

- Communicates his/her prior knowledge on sport
- Communicates his/her motivational factors
- Communicates his/her physical variables
- Communicates his/her results of training activity
- Follows the feedback and suggestion from the trainer
- Takes lessons
- Goes through repetitions
- Reaches the goal

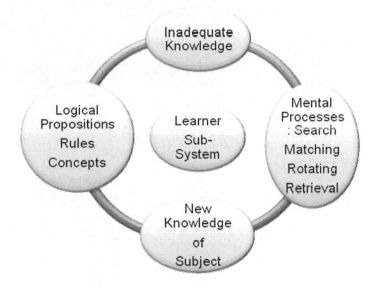

Fig. 2. Learner Sub-System

2.2   Trainer Sub-system

Trainer receives the data from the learner on learner's abilities, mental schema, cognitive ability, choice of sport, and the prior knowledge on sport. The data is processed by the trainer with the available tools for assessing the learner's mental and physical abilities. Appropriate sport activities are suggested by the trainer. The trainer checks the compatibility and the validity of the prior knowledge of the learner on the particular sport that the learner is intending to learn. The trainer plans the lessons based on the nature and the validity of the prior knowledge of the learner. The trainer suggests modules, lessons, trainings and tricks and evaluates the physiological variables collected from the learner. After having evaluated the progress of the learner in learning, gives feedback and motivators.

The trainer sub- system is depicted pictorially in the following fig.3
The trainer sub-system

- Assesses the learner's abilities
- Evaluates and proposes the right sport
- Gets data of efficiency and effectiveness of the learner
- Compares the learner data with the ideal values
- Suggests training modules
- Gives feedback and motivations.

Fig. 3. Trainer Sub-System

2.3   E-Learning Sub-system

The e-Learning sub-system contains modules for training the learner on various sports. The trainer calls the particular module of the sport the learner has decided to learn. The e-Learning sub-system contains training activity repository, e-material base, the standard logical premises on physiological variables and fitness. The e-Learning sub-system provides the facility for the learner-trainer interactions. The interactions between the learner and the trainer are multiple and can be repetitive.

The following fig. 4 depicts the e-Learning Sub-System which

- Contains modules on various sports
- Contains logical premises
- Contains training activities storage.

2.4   Feedback Mechanism

A prior knowledge of the sport might mean learning or unlearning. The good methods and tricks are to be confirmed and strengthened and bad methods and tricks are to be eliminated. For example, if someone has learnt to throw the ball wrongly, then it has to be modified or corrected or totally given up. From the constant feedback from the trainer sub-system, the learner is able to categorically judge his prior knowledge on the particular sport to be under the category of learning or to be under unlearning. Learner receives a positive feedback to reinforce learning a particular aspect of the domain under learning or a negative feedback to reinforce unlearning a particular aspect of the domain that has been part of the prior knowledge.

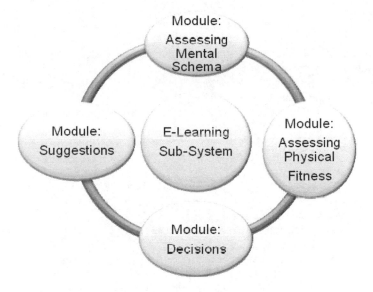

Fig. 4. E-Learning Sub-System

2.5   Contiguity and Repetition Mechanism

The model of cognitive frame in learning, contiguity and repetition are the vital methods of reinforcement in learning. The interactive system between the learner and the trainer has a feedback loop. Every time the learner wants to know his/her status and appropriateness of his/her training activity, he/she gets regular and constant feedback from the trainer. The trainer may decide to suggest the same type of lesson until the learner satisfactorily performs. Repetition of a particular lesson or training module is done until there is a significant growth in the learning process or until the stipulated time expires. The trainer might have a scale for each learner uniquely assessed from the abilities of the learner from their mental schema communication.

3   Conclusion

The knowledge level of the sports person about the sports activity and the learner's abilities are evaluated using cognitive structures. The data of efficiency and effectiveness of the learner is the knowledge gained by the trainer in the proposed system. The learner interacts with the trainer, wherein training modules are suggested, and finally feedback and motivations are given to the learner according to the knowledge base. Thus the learning effectiveness of the E-learning system is enhanced through the usage of learner knowledge cognitive structures in the e-learning architecture.

References

1. Rosenberg, M.: e-Learning: Strategies for Delivering Knowledge in the Digital Age, p. 28. McGraw-Hill, New York (2001)
2. Good, T.L., Brophy, J.E.: Educational psychology: A realistic approach, 4th edn. Longman, White Plains (1990)
3. Garner, B.K.: Getting to Got It!: Association for Supervision and Curriculum Development (2007)
4. e-Learning Consulting (2011),
   `http://www.e-learningconsulting.com/consulting/what/e-learning.html`
5. Naidu, S.: E-learning A Guidebook of Principles, Procedures and Practices, 2nd Revised edn., CEMCA (2006)
6. Learning Theories and Instructional Design,
   `http://www.outsource2india.com/learningsolutions/articles/learning-theories.asp`
7. Online Learning theories | Cognitivism | Constructivism | Behaviorism, http://www.about-elearning.com/learning-theories.html
8. Cognitive Science (Stanford Encyclopedia of Philosophy),
   `http://plato.stanford.edu/entries/cognitive-science/`
9. Chandrakant: Life Stress and Social Support Among HIV positive (August 2011),
   `http://jessy-chandrakant.blogspot.com/`
10. Shay: The Complex Mind: Ideas on Emergent Consciousness | Total Eclipse, May 5 (2006),
    `http://total.eclipse.co.il/2006/05/05/the-complex-mind-ideas-on-emergent-consciousness/`
11. Introduction to Cognitive Science: From Stanford Encyclopedia of Philosophy, Cognitive Science, First published September 23 (1996); substantive revision April 30 (2007),
    `http://douban.com/group/topic/2212422/`

Speaker Independent Connected Digit Recognition Using VQ and HMM in Additive Noise Environment

A. Revathi[*] and Y. Venkataramani[**]

Saranathan College of Engineering, Trichy
revathidhanabal@rediffmail.com, principal@saranathan.ac.in

Abstract. The main objective of this paper is to discuss the effectiveness of concatenated perceptual features and the noise reduction technique based on wavelet transform and Recursive least square filtering in getting the good recognition rate for the peculiar combination of connected digits in additive noise environment. The proposed concatenated perceptual features are captured and code book indices are extracted. Expectation maximization algorithm is used to generate discrete HMM models for the connected digits. Speech recognition system is evaluated on clean and noisy test speeches and the selection is based on which model gives maximum log likelihood value. Speeches for this work are randomly chosen from "TI Digits_1", "TI Digits_2" databases. This concatenated perceptual feature yields the accuracy of 81.4% and 73% for the combination of connected digits (10 – 19) and (12-19,21,31,41,51,61,71,81,91). Pink noise, white noise, babble noise and factory noise are considered in this work.

Keywords: Hidden markov model (HMM), Frequency response, Speech recognition, Vector quantization (VQ), Perceptual linear predictive cepstrum (PLP), Noise, Wavelet transform, Recursive least square (RLS) filtering.

1 Introduction

Speech recognition involves the decoding of speech signal in sequential manner based on the observed acoustic features of the signal and exploitation of known relations between acoustic features and phonetic symbols. Evaluation of speech recognition system on clean training and test speeches normally provides good accuracy. Nowadays, it becomes a challenging task to provide a robust speech recognition system in the presence of stationary and non-stationary noise. Our goal is to maximize the speech recognition rate in a noisy environment. Possible applications of this work are recognition of telephone numbers or bank account numbers from a noisy recorded speech by intelligence and police surveillance, investigation of disputed credit card number provided over phone in a noisy environment. Yuval Cohen et.al [1] discussed

---

[*] Professor, Dept.of ECE.
[**] Director.

N. Meghanathan et al. (Eds.): CCSIT 2012, Part II, LNICST 85, pp. 393–402, 2012.
© Institute for Computer Sciences, Social Informatics and Telecommunications Engineering 2012

the application of speech enhancement algorithm to evaluate the connected word recognition in a noisy environment. Mosakiyo Fujimoto et.al [2] used GMM based speech estimation method and EM based noise estimation method are used for evaluating the noisy speech recognition systems. Carlos Lima et.al has done spectral normalization [3] to improve the accuracy of isolated word recognition. Synaptic adaptation and two tone suppression techniques are implemented by Serajul Haque et.al [4] to enhance speech recognition accuracy. Multi band approach using wavelet transform is used by Wesam Alkhaldi et.al [5] in speech recognition system. Throat microphone for accurate voicing detection is used by Tomas Tebem et.al [6] to improve the performance of the speech recognition system. MFCC and wavelet packets are used by Phani Kumar et.al [7] for speech recognition in a noisy environment. Pitch detection approach is used by Rashmi Makhaijani et.al [8] to enhance speech in speech recognition. Akshiyo K.Swain et.al [9] extracted unbiased LPC parameters by using orthogonal least squares method to improve the speech recognition rate. LMS adaptive filters are used by Jose Louis Oropezo Radriguez et.al [10] to improve the speech recognition rate in noisy environments. LMS adaptive filters and wavelets are used by Jose Louis Oropezo Radriguez et.al [11] to improve the speech recognition rate in noisy environments. A.Revathi et.al [12] anaysed the use of perceptual features and iterative clustering approach for performing isolated digits/continuous speech recognition. Combination of vector quantization and HMM is used by A.Revathi et.al [13] to evaluate the speech recognition system. Voice activity detection algorithm is used by Xiaokun Li et.al [14] to improve the recognition performance in noisy environments. Statistical model based voice activity detection and noise suppression is used as front end tool by Mosakiyo Fujimoto et.al [15] for automatic speech recognition in noisy environments. Syllables are used as acoustic units by Azmi M.M. et.al [16] to perform Arabic speech recognition in noisy environment. In this work, stationary and non-stationary noises such as white noise, factory noise, pink noise and babble noise are considered to evaluate the noisy speech recognition system. Better results are due to the implementation of additional preprocessing techniques such as wavelets and adaptive RLS filters prior to conventional preprocessing stages. Results obtained are comparable to the case of clean speech recognition.

2   Feature Based on Cepstrum

The short-time speech spectrum for voiced speech sound has two components: 1) harmonic peaks due to the periodicity of voiced speech 2) glottal pulse shape. The excitation source decides the periodicity of voiced speech. It reflects the characteristics of speaker. The spectral envelope is shaped by formants which reflect the resonances of vocal tract. The variations among speakers are indicated by formant locations and bandwidth.

2.1   PLP Extraction

PLP (perceptual linear predictive cepstrum) speech analysis method [17-19] models the speech auditory spectrum by the spectrum of low order all pole model. The detailed procedure for PLP (perceptual linear predictive cepstrum) extraction is given below. This perceptual feature mainly emphasizes the need for critical band analysis which integrates energy spectral density in the frequency range (0-8) kHz for obtaining the speech auditory spectrum. Loudness equalization is a pre emphasis block used to emphasize the upper and middle part of the spectrum and cube root compression is done to reduce the dynamics of the speech spectrum. Block diagram for perceptual features extraction is shown in Fig.1.The relationship between frequency in Bark and frequency in Hz is specified as in (1)

$$f(bark) = 6 * arcsinh(f(Hz)/600) \qquad (1)$$

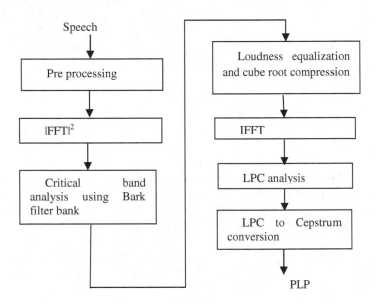

Fig. 1. PLP Extraction Model

3   Speech Recognition Based on VQ and HMM

Speech database considered in this work contains speeches of 8 female speakers and 8 male speakers. 8 speeches of 4 female and 4 male speakers are used for training. 10 speeches of other 4 female and 4 male speakers are used for testing. Connected digit recognition system is evaluated for 800 test speeches for connected digits (10-19) and 1280 test speeches for connected digits (12-19,21,31,41,51,61,71,81,91). Connected digits are formed by concatenating the respective isolated digits from TI digits_1 and TI digits_2 database. For creating a training model, speech signal is first pre-emphasized using a difference operator. Hamming window is applied on differenced speech frames of 16 msecs duration with overlapping of 8 msecs. Then the PLP feature is extracted and it is concatenated with its differential feature. For each training model corresponding to connected digits, training set of K utterances are used (spoken by many speakers) where each utterance constitutes an observation sequence of some appropriate spectral or temporal representation. For each digit or speech, HMM models are developed with state transition probability distribution, observation symbol probability distribution and initial probability distribution that optimize the likelihood of the training set observation vectors. For discrete HMM, models are initialized with 256 observation sequences and 8 states. Code book indices are used as input to train the models. Clustering algorithm is used to obtain cluster centers and code book indices for training vectors of the connected digits considered for training.To evaluate the performance of the noisy speech recognition system, noises such as babble noise, white noise, factory noise and pink noise are taken from "Noise data" database. Noises are added to the test speeches at various levels so that SNR values of different ranges are obtained. Speech recognition is done by using the combination of VQ and discrete HMM techniques [20,21]. For discrete HMM, models are initialized with 256 observation sequences and 8 states and code book indices are used as input to train the models. In some cases, noise is added to the test speech in such a way that SNR is found to be negative (i.e.) noise energy is dominating the speech energy. In this work, noise suppression technique based on wavelets and adaptive RLS filtering as additional preprocessing technique is implemented along with conventional preprocessing stages such as pre emphasis, frame blocking and widowing to enhance the performance of the system. This noisy test speech undergoes first level of wavelet decomposition using 'Haar' wavelets and the approximation coefficients in the first level are suitably up sampled to generate a signal in which there is no contribution due to high frequency disturbance. Adaptive RLS filtering is subsequently applied and the filter coefficients are adaptively changed to minimize the least square error between the desired output and the actual output. Finally, noise reduced speech similar as that of clean test speech is obtained.

For testing, observation sequences of the feature vectors of the clean or noisy test speeches are applied to all the training HMM models. HMM models for each connected digit are already trained with state probability distribution matrices, observation symbol probability distribution matrices and initial probability distribution vectors. For each model, log likelihood values are calculated. Selection of the speech or digit is done by comparing likelihood values and recognized speech is the one whose model likelihood is the highest.

4   Results and Discussion

The performance of clean connected digits recognition system based on concatenated perceptual features is evaluated by applying test speech vectors to all the HMM training models. Log likelihood values for each model are computed. Selection is based on the comparison of log likelihood values and decision is made with respect to the model which provides the maximum log likelihood value. Speech recognition rate is the number of correct choices over the total number of test speeches. System is evaluated for 80 test speeches for each connected digit. The individual accuracy of peculiar combination of connected digits (12,13,14,15,16,17,18,19,21,31,41,51,61,71,81,91) is shown as a bar chart in Fig.2 and there is a clear indication of obtaining 100% accuracy for one connected digit (31). This connected digit is considered for the evaluation of noisy speech recognition system for some of the low and high frequency noises whose frequency distribution characteristics are depicted in Fig.3.

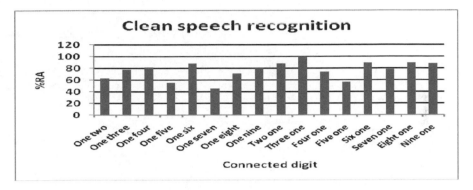

Fig. 2. Comparison chart of individual accuracy of connected digits (12,13,14,15,16,17,18, 19,21,31,41,51,61,71,81,91)

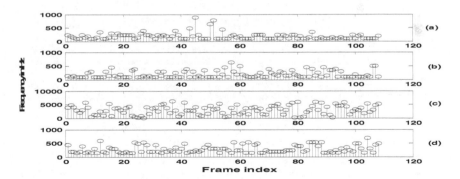

Fig. 3. Illusration of the frequency distribution of noises (a) Factory noise (b) Pink noise (c) White noise (d) Babble noise

From the Fig.3, it is evident that factory noise, pink noise and babble are low frequency noises and white noise is a high frequency noise. Following plots in Fig.4 and Fig.5 indicate the effectiveness of the additional preprocessing technique based on wavelets and adaptive RLS filtering in removing additive low frequency babble noise (SNR = 0db) from noisy speeches.

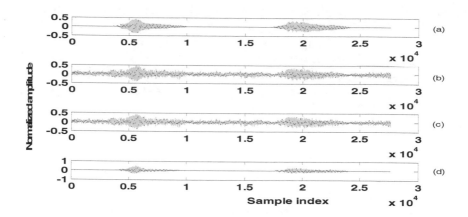

Fig. 4. Illusration of the effect of addional preprocessing for babble noise using signal characteristics. (a) Clean speech (b) Noisy speech (c) reconstructed speech after first level of wavelet decomposition (d) Noise reduced speech after RLS filtering.

Spectrogram plots in Fig.5 depict the importance of the additional preprocessing techniques with respect to the retention of speech frequencies in the noise reduced speech after RLS filtering stage.

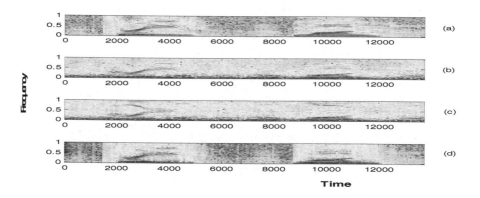

Fig. 5. Illusration of the effect of addional preprocessing for babble noise using spectrogram. (a) Clean speech (b) Noise speech (c) reconstructed speech after first level of wavelet decomposition (d) Noise reduced speech after RLS filtering.

Following plots in Fig.6 and Fig.7 indicate the effectiveness of the additional preprocessing technique based on wavelets and adaptive RLS filtering in removing additive high frequency white noise (SNR = 7db) from noisy speeches.

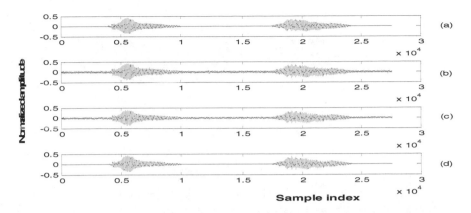

Fig. 6. Illusration of the effect of addional preprocessing for white noise using signal characteristics. (a) Clean speech (b) Noisy speech (c) reconstructed speech after first level of wavelet decomposition (d) Noise reduced speech after RLS filtering.

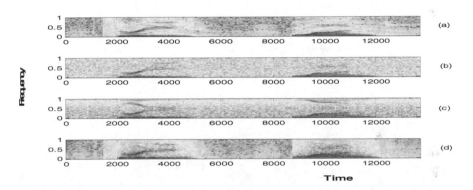

Fig. 7. Illusration of the effect of addional preprocessing for white noise using spectrogram. (a) Clean speech (b) Noisy speech (c) reconstructed speech after first level of wavelet decomposition (d) Noise reduced speech after RLS filtering.

Fig.8 demonstrates the frequency distribution of the clean speech, noisy speech (Addition of pink noise to the test speech at SNR = 1 db), Reconstructed speech after wavelet decomposition and noise reduced speech after RLS filtering stage. From these plots, it is evident that most of the low frequencies present in the clean speech are reproduced in the noise reduced speech. Subjective test is performed on the noise reduced speeches and it is clear that the noise reduced speeches utter in the similar manner as that of the clean test speeches.

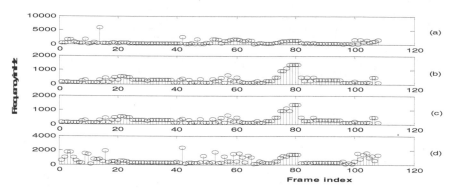

Fig. 8. Illusration of the effect of addional preprocessing for pink noise using frequency distribution characteristics. (a) Clean speech (b) Noisy speech (c) reconstructed speech after first level of wavelet decomposition (d) Noise reduced speech after RLS filtering.

Fig.9 is the comparison chart of the evaluation of the noisy speech recognition system. Pink noise, factory noise, babble noise and white noise are added to the test speeches at various levels and it is understood that there is not too much deterioration in terms of accuracy even if the noise energy is dominating the signal energy for several cases. From the Fig.9, it is understood that the system gives the better accuracy for the addition of pink noise to the test speeches at various levels.

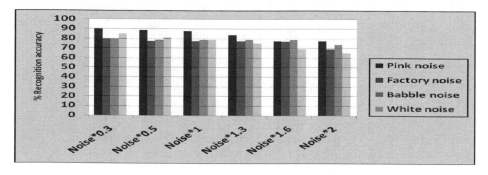

Fig. 9. Illustration of the effect of noises on accuracy

5   Conclusions

This paper proposes the use of additional preprocessing technique and concatenated PLP feature for evaluating VQ+HMM based speaker independent peculiar combination of connected digits recognition schemes and the evaluation is done on clean and noisy test speeches. In HMM based technique, discrete HMM models are developed using code book indices as input and these models developed for connected digits are considered for system evaluation. Perceptual based features normally perform well in developing robust speech recognition system, because they inherently depict the perceptually important characteristics of the speech. Even though the noises considered in this work have frequencies falling in the speech frequency range, accuracy is not very much degraded because the noise reduced speech duplicates all the frequencies present in the clean test speech. Noise reduction is mainly performed by applying the combinational technique based on wavelet transform and adaptive RLS filtering on the noisy test speeches. Better results are obtained for noisy speech recognition even though the significant amount of noise is added to the test speeches. This is actually due to the use of additional preprocessing technique based on wavelets and RLS filtering along with conventional preprocessing. This additional preprocessing works well for both low frequency and high frequency noises.

References

[1] Cohen, Y., Erell, A.: Enhancement of connected words in an extremely noisy environments. IEEE Transactions on speech and Audio Processing 5(2), 141–148 (1997)

[2] Fujimoto, M., Ariki, Y.: Robust speech recognition in additive and channel noise environments using GMM and EM algorithm. In: Proceedings of Int. Conf. on Acoustics, Speech and Signal Processing, pp. 941–944 (2004)

[3] Lima, C., Almeida, L.B., Mohreiro, J.L.: Robust feature extraction for speech recognition in noisy environment. In: Proc. Int. Conf. Signal Processing, vol. (6), Beijing (2002)

[4] Haque, S., Togoui, R., Zakrich, A.: Perceptual features for automatic speech recognition in noisy environments. Int. Journal on Speech Communication 1(51), 58–75 (2009)

[5] Weaam, A., Fakhir, W., Hamdy, N.: Automatic speech Recognition in noisy environments using wavelet transforms. In: Proc. 45th Midwest Symposium on Circuits and Systems, Oklahoma, pp. 463–466 (2002)

[6] Tebem, T., Verhelst, W., Capman, F., Beangenlie, F.: Improved speech recognition in noisy environments by throat microphone for voice activity detection. In: Proceedings of 18th European Signal Processing Conference, pp. 1978–1982 (2010)

[7] Phani Kumar, P., Vardhan, K.S.N., Sriramakrishna, K.: Perfromance evaluation of MLP for speech recognition in noisy environments using MFCC and wavelets. Int. Journal on Computer Science and Communication 1(2), 41–45 (2010)

[8] Makhaijani, R., Shrawardkar, U., Thakre, V.M.: Speech enhancement using pitch detection approach for noisy environment. Int. Journal on Engineering science and Technology 3(2), 1764–1769 (2011)

[9] Swain, A.K., Abdullah, W.: Estimation of LPC parameters of speech signals in noisy environments. In: Proceedings of TENCON, Thailand, pp. 139–142 (2004)

[10] Rodríguez, J.L.O., Guerra, S.S., Fernández, L.P.S.: Using Adaptive Filter to Increase Automatic Speech Recognition Rate in a Digit Corpus. In: Rueda, L., Mery, D., Kittler, J. (eds.) CIARP 2007. LNCS, vol. 4756, pp. 78–87. Springer, Heidelberg (2007)

[11] Rodríguez, J.L.O., Guerra, S.S.: Using Adaptive Filter and Wavelets to Increase Automatic Speech Recognition Rate in Noisy Environment. In: Gelbukh, A., Kuri Morales, Á.F. (eds.) MICAI 2007. LNCS (LNAI), vol. 4827, pp. 1015–1024. Springer, Heidelberg (2007)

[12] Revathi, A., Venkataramani, Y.: Perceptual features based isolated digit and continuous speech recognition using iterative clustering approach. In: Proc. IEEE International Conference on Networking and Communication, Chennai, pp. 155–160 (2009)

[13] Revathi, A., Venkataramani, Y.: Speaker independent continuous speech and isolated digits recognition using VQ and HMM. In: Proc. IEEE Int. Conf. on Communication and Signal Processing, Calicut, pp. 198–202 (2011)

[14] Li, X., Deng, Y.: Combining speech energy and edge information for efficient voice activity detection in noisy environments. In: Proc. 19th Int. Conf. on Pattern Recognition, Tamba, FL, pp. 1–4 (2008)

[15] Fujimoto, M., Ishizuka, K., Nakatani, T.: Study of Integration of Statistical Model-Based Voice Activity Detection and Noise Suppression. In: Proc. Annual Conf. of INTERSPEECH, Brisbane, Australia, pp. 2008–2011 (2008)

[16] Azmi, M.M., Tolba, H.: Syllable based automatic Arabic speech recognition in noisy environment. In: Proc. Int. Conf. on Audio, Language and Image Processing, Sanghai, pp. 1436–1441 (2008)

[17] Hermansky, H., Tsuga, K., Makino, S., Wakita, H.: Perceptually based processing in automatic speech recognition. In: Proc. IEEE Int. Conf. on Acoustics, Speech and Signal Processing, Tokyo, vol. 11, pp. 1971–1974 (1986)

[18] Hermansky, H., Margon, N., Bayya, A., Kohn, P.: The challenge of Inverse E: The RASTA PLP method. In: Proc. Twenty Fifth IEEE Asilomar Conf. on Signals, Systems and Computers, Pacific Grove, CA, USA, vol. 2, pp. 800–804 (1991)

[19] Hermansky, H., Morgan, N.: RASTA processing of speech. IEEE Transactions on Speech and Audio Processing 2(4), 578–589 (1994)

[20] Rabiner, L., Juang, B.H.: Fundamentals of speech recognition. Prentice Hall, NJ (1993)

[21] Rabiner, L., Juang, B.H.: Hidden Markov models for Speech Recognition. Proc. Technometrics 33(3), 251–272 (1991)

Decomposition+: Improving ℓ-Diversity for Multiple Sensitive Attributes

Devayon Das and Dhruba K. Bhattacharyya

Department of Computer Science and Engineering,
Tezpur University-784028, India
devayon@acm.org, dkb@tezu.ernet.in

Abstract. In this paper, we analyse existing privacy-transformation techniques in the field of PPDP that anonymize datasets with Multiple Sensitive Attributes (MSA). Of these, we present an analysis of Decomposition, an algorithm which generates a dataset with distinct ℓ-diversity over MSA using a partitioning approach. We discuss some improvements which can be made over Decomposition: in the realms of its running time, its data utility, and its applicability in the case of Multiple Release Publishing. To this effect, we describe *Decomposition+* an algorithm that implements some of these improvements and is thus more suited for use in real-life scenarios.

Keywords: Privacy Preserving Data Publishing, ℓ-diversity, Decomposition, Multiple Sensitive Attributes, Multiple Release Publishing.

1 Introduction

The rapidly growing fields of *Privacy Preserving Data Mining* (PPDM), and its newer cousin *Privacy Preserving Data Publishing*(PPDP), essentially deal with issues that can be stated in very few terms: private data should be leveraged to infer useful patterns, but not to infer private, sensitive information. However, this simple statement becomes quite difficult to model as a problem. This is because, (i) given a dataset, it is difficult to differentiate data which is sensitive from data which has legitimate purpose of utility, and (ii) as sensitive data is obscured in the dataset, its general utility for non-nefarious purposes also diminishes. Indeed, every privacy preserving data publication method will lose some information; if not, it is equivalent to disclosing the data unprotected[1]. Given the rise of the rate at which personal datasets are being published, the problem gains significance.

PPDP distinguishes itself from PPDM in the context of the usage of anonymized data. While PPDM techniques are tailor-made for the use of an anonymized dataset to a specific data mining purpose, PPDP encompasses those techniques which a data-publisher may use to secure privacy of data against a generic data-mining purpose[2]. There are a large number of approaches and techniques involved in PPDM, such as Synthetic Data Generation, Perturbation, Micro-Aggregation, Suppression and Anatomization. For a more

N. Meghanathan et al. (Eds.): CCSIT 2012, Part II, LNICST 85, pp. 403–412, 2012.

comprehensive survey, the reader is directed to [3,2]. Many privacy models, such as k-anonymity[4] and ℓ-diversity[5] isolate some attributes in the dataset as Sensitive Attributes (SA). These are important from a data utility and mining perspective, and also pose risk if they are linked to a particular individual represented in the dataset. Most implementations of these algorithms (and many more) focus on a Single Sensitive Attribute (SSA) for simplicity and convenience, instead of Multiple Sensitive Attributes (MSA), which are more useful as an anonymization policy and more suitable to real-life datasets. As such, algorithms implementing MSA are of significant interest.

Another important scenario which modern anonymization techniques should take into account, is the case of ever improving datasets and anonymization policies. Over time, datasets are corrected, and published under different anonymization techniques. When datasets are re-published, the releases could be combined to infer sensitive information, unless precautions are built into the anonymization techniques to prevent such attacks. Thus we require a privacy-preserving framework which ensures that (i)the disclosure of sensitive information in published datasets are limited to a small and measurable quantity, (ii)Multiple Sensitive Attributes are protected against disclosure, (iii)the disclosure risk does not escalate when data is published again in the future, and (iv)the utility of the published dataset is maximized (by a measurable quantity) while enforcing these constraints.

2   Background

Celebrated privacy models, such as k-anonymity[4], ℓ-diversity[5] and closeness[6] make a preliminary set of common assumptions for the sake of simplicity: (i)the data to be protected (or anonymized) is considered to be a set of tuples in a table T = $\{t_1, \ldots, t_m\}$, where $t_i, (1 \leq i \leq m)$ is a tuple, (ii)each tuple t_i, having attributes $< c_1, \ldots, c_n >$, describes one individual person, (iii)attributes of the table can be divided into three distinct, disjoint sets of attributes: (a)*Explicit Attributes*, such as {Name, Social Security Number}, which individually can link a record to a person, explicitly. These are usually removed during the process of anonymization; (b)*Quasi Identifiers* (QIDs), such as {date of birth, gender, location}, which although individually do not identify a person, but considered as a composite, can be used to link the record with a person; (c)*Sensitive Attributes* (SA), such as {Salary} or {Medical Condition}, are needed for analysis but have potentially sensitive consequences if linked to an individual with strong certainty; (d)*Non-sensitive Attributes* which don't fall into any of the above categories and can be retained as-is in the anonymized data (called microdata). Importantly, the choice of partitioning the attributes between SA and QID is crucial in determining its privacy risk and well as data-utility. This choice however is a matter of policy[4].

Definition 1: *k-anonymity:*[4] A set of data is said to be k-anonymous iff each unique sequence of QIDs appears in T with at least k occurrences. Greater the value of k (k being a positive integer), greater the protection against of record being linked with certitude to a particular person and greater the ambiguity of the published data.

k-anonymity is usually accomplished through generalization or suppression[7]. In generalization, QIDs of multiple records are replaced with one generalized value, forming groups called *Equivalence Class*. In supression values which do not conform to k-anonymity are not released at all. Newer alternates to generalization based on Partitioning such as Anatomy[1] eliminate the information-loss involved in generalization by generating two projections of the dataset, one containing QIDs and the other the sensitive attributes.

Definition 2: *ℓ-diversity principle*[5]: An equivalence class is said to be ℓ-diverse when there are at least ℓ *well-represented* values for the sensitive attribute. The ℓ-diversity privacy model overcomes a shortcoming of the k-anonymity: while k-anonymity does not specify the selection criteria of SA values in the equivalence class. *Well-represented* could be construed as distinct ℓ-diversity:

Definition 3: *Distinct ℓ-diversity*[6]: An equivalence class is said to have distinct ℓ-diversity if there are at least ℓ distinct values for the sensitive attribute.

2.1   From SSA towards the MSA Case

Real world data-sets, such as the UCI Adult Dataset[8], usually would have a large number of attributes. Since most established algorithms anonymize datasets with only a single sensitive attribute, the data publisher is left with the choice of having to identify which one attribute should be chosen as the sensitive attribute. An alternative to these is to have a model which has multiple SAs. This scenario is known to be that of *Multiple Sensitive Attribute* (MSA). MSA has been widely mentioned in literature[5,9,10] but, as Ye et al.[11] report, there are few algorithms which implement anonymization in the MSA case. This is because when algorithms such as ℓ-diversity Incognito[5] are extended to the MSA case, a large loss of utility[12] occurs. If more work were to be done in the MSA case, this choice would neither be necessary nor needed. The few works found in our survey, dealing with MSA, are outlined here:

In [12], the authors showed the difficulty in achieving ℓ-diversity in the MSA case. At the same time, achieving MSA is trivial for k-anonymity, because k-anonymity does not restrict the distribution of SAs the equivalence class. Experimental results indicate introduction of significant distortion in the resultant data and small relative error for random SQL queries. In [13] the authors describe a privacy model, Multi-Sensitive Bucketization (MSB) and three MSB-based algorithms: maximal-bucket first (MBF), maximal single-dimension-capacity first (MSDCF), and maximal multi-dimension-capacity first (MMDCF). While they achieve good data utility, an analysis of privacy guarantees is absent. Ye et al.[11] apply an existing and well-understood privacy model, ℓ-diversity, in the MSA case and use an interesting vertical partitioning technique to form ℓ-diverse groups. Their algorithm, Decomposition is discussed and analysed in the next section.

3   Decomposition

The algorithm of Decomposition[11] which satisfies ℓ-diversity in the MSA case, is of interest. This is in part because it explores an alternate to generalization: vertical partitioning in achieving ℓ-diversity. Partitioning, which has been implemented in various guises[1,14] can provide better data utility than generalization, in many cases. For a balanced analysis of partitioning, refer to [15].

Partitioning usually implies that a table T with attributes $A_1, \ldots, A_m$ is vertically partitioned into two or more sub-tables $\overline{T}_1, \ldots, \overline{T}_n$ such that any table $\overline{T}_i, 1 > i \geq n$ has attributes $A_j, \ldots, A_k$ where $1 \geq j \geq k \geq n$. The join of two or more sub-tables forms a *lossy view* of the underlying data. Decomposition works by partitioning T vertically into sensitive attributes and non-sensitive attributes. The SA-table (see Table 3) are further partitioned horizontally into *SA-groups* of records such that each group contains at least ℓ distinct sensitive attribute instances for each sensitive attribute. Every tuple in the QID-table is associated with one SA-group (see Table 4). Apart from this, the sensitive attributes are released in a separate table which cannot be linked with the other released table. To reduce information loss, the number of SA-groups created are maximized by Ye et al. through a largest-ℓ group forming procedure, which they prove creates the maximum number of groups possible.[1]:

The largest-ℓ group forming procedure applies to creating SA-groups with respect to only one SA. To extend it to the MSA case, the authors have designated one of the many sensitive attributes as Primary Sensitive Attribute S^{pri} with corresponding diversity requirement of ℓ^{pri}, which is chosen by the publisher as a matter of policy. Once SA-groups are formed by applying the largest-ℓ group forming procedure with respect to S^{pri}, the SA-table may still not satisfy $\ell_1, \ldots, \ell_d$-diversity with respect to all the non-primary sensitive attributes. To rectify this, Ye et al. introduce a noise addition step. To add noise, in every tuple in the SA-table, for every sensitive attribute S^i which does not satisfy ℓ_i-diversity, the value of S^i is replaced from a set defined as the Linkable Sensitive Value[11].

Adding noise causes distortion. However, the use of Diversity Penalty in the partitioning stage ensures that each SA-group conforms to $\ell_1, \ldots, \ell_d$-diversity as much as possible. Thus minimal amount of noise is added in this stage. Thus, Decomposition generates three tables for publishing from the original data. Table 1 shows a dataset, which has not been anonymized. Table 4 (QID-table), 3 (SA- table G) and 2 (Marginals T_S) show the published microdata when Decomposition is applied.

3.1   Discussion

Decomposition ensures distinct ℓ-diversity in the MSA case, which is a well understood privacy model and can thwart attribute-linking and record-linking attacks. It also gives better data utility than generalization. However, Decomposition has certain weaknesses: (i)using partitioning only to form ℓ-diverse data

---

[1] Theorem 2 in [11].

Table 1. The Microdata table

Tuple #	Gender	ZipCode	Birthday	Occupation	Salary
1 (Alice)	F	10078	1988-04-17	Nurse	1
2 (Betty)	F	10077	1984-03-21	Nurse	4
3 (Carl)	M	10076	1985-03-01	Police	8
4 (Diana)	F	10075	1983-02-14	Cook	9
5 (Ella)	F	10085	1962-10-03	Actor	2
6 (Finch)	M	10085	1988-11-04	Actor	7
7 (Gavin)	M	20086	1958-06-06	Clerk	8
8 (Helen)	F	20087	1960-07-11	Clerk	2

Table 2. Marginals

Occupation	Salary
Nurse	1
Nurse	4
Police	8
Cook	9
Actor	2
Actor	7
Clerk	8
Clerk	2

Table 3. Sensitive attributes of Table 1 after Decomposition

Group	Occupation	Salary
1	Police	1
1	Nurse	2
1	Actor	8
1	Clerk	4
2	Nurse	2
2	Actor	4
2	Cook	7
2	Clerk	9

Table 4. QIDs and non-sensitive attributes of Table 1 after Decomposition

Group	Gender	ZipCode	Birthday
1	F	10078	1988/04/17
	F	10085	1962/10/03
	M	20086	1958/06/06
	M	10076	1985/03/01
2	F	10077	1984/03/21
	M	10085	1988/11/04
	F	10075	1983/02/14
	F	20087	1960/07/11

over the primary sensitive attribute, not other SAs, (ii)the choice of noise values could further be improved to reduce information loss, (iii)is not suitable in cases where records could be added later, which is a practical, real-life requirement.

4   Decomposition+

Based on our analysis of Decomposition in the last section, we attempt to improve upon it in the following two broad areas: (i)extending Decomposition to the continuous release scenario, (ii)Optimizing noise value selection.

(i)**Extending Decomposition to the continuous release scenario:** From a practical and long-term view, PPDP would involve the same or related data being anonymized and published multiple times. For example, a hospital may release information on a monthly basis, and may have patients who exist in multiple releases. This extended scenario could occur in the one of these three situations: (i) Multiple Release, (ii)Sequential Release and (iii)Continuous Release, also known as the Incremental Dataset Release.

In Continuous Release scenario, different anonymized releases of the same underlying data are released at different points in time, where records have been added, removed, or updated in the underlying data. The attempt is to include these changes in the published data, while reducing risk of the use of these changes in infering sensitive information. In order to enable continuous release in our proposed algorithm, if the anonymized dataset is published as a release of three tables $\hat{T}_0 = \{\hat{T}_0^M, \hat{T}_0^Q, \hat{T}_0^S\}$ where $\hat{T}_0^M$ is the marginal, $\hat{T}_0^Q$ is the QID-table, and $\hat{T}_0^S$ is the SA-table, our concern would be that p future releases of $\hat{T}_i$ $(0 \le i \le p)$ should not be linked to each other to leak sensitive information. Byun et al.[16] define an Inference Channel which is useful in formalizing this risk. We extend this to the $\ell_1, \ldots, \ell_d$-diversity[2] case:

Definition 4: *Inference Channel for $\ell_1, \ldots, \ell_d$-diversity*: Let $\hat{T}_i$ and $\hat{T}_j$ be two $\ell_1, \ldots, \ell_d$-diverse releases of T. An inference channel exists between $\hat{T}_i$ and $\hat{T}_j$, denoted by $\hat{T}_i \rightleftharpoons \hat{T}_i$ if observing $\hat{T}_i$ and $\hat{T}_j$ together increases the probability of attribute disclosure of an attribute S^k in either $\hat{T}_i$ or $\hat{T}_j$ to a probability greater than $1/\ell_k, (1 \le k \le d)$

Thus every new release $\hat{T}_{n+1}$ must be inference-free from all the previous releases, as defined as:

Definition 5: *Inference-free data release for $\ell_1, \ldots, \ell_d$-diversity:* Let $\hat{T}_0, \ldots, \hat{T}_n$ be a sequence of previously releases of T, each of which is $\ell_1, \ldots, \ell_d$-diverse. A new $\ell_1, \ldots, \ell_d$-diverse release $\hat{T}_{n+1}$ is said to be inference-free iff $\nexists \hat{T}_i, i = 1, \ldots, n$ s.t. $\hat{T}_i \rightleftharpoons \hat{T}_{n+1}$.

Given the above, Byun, et al. proved that addition of a new equivalence class (or a new SA-group) to a release does not cause an inference channel to a previous release[3] as long as each SA-group is $\ell_1, \ldots, \ell_d$-diverse. If a tuple is inserted into an SA-group, the SA group must already be $\ell_1, \ldots, \ell_d$-diverse, and the tuple must remain in the same SA-group across releases.

Thus, we employ the largest-ℓ group forming procedure to the available records and unlike Decomposition we retain residual tuples for future anonymization, and do not add them to existing SA-groups. The rationale for this is to enable creation of new SA-groups when more tuples are added to the dataset. To avoid a situation where some tuples are never published at all, we assign, to each tuple t, a starvation penalty, defined as $P_s(t) = b - a$, where t is introduced into the underlying data table T after $\hat{T}_0, \ldots, \hat{T}_a$ releases have been made, and t first appears in a published release after another $\hat{T}_{a+1} \ldots \hat{T}_b$ releases.

When the number of distinct residual tuples becomes greater than ℓ^{pri}, we attempt to form an SA-group from ℓ^{pri} distinct tuples with tuples with the highest starvation penalty.

(ii)Improving the noise selection procedure: When the largest ℓ-group forming procedure is applied to the dataset, non-primary SAs may not conform to distinct $\ell_1, \ldots, \ell_d$-diversity. Noise is added to remove an offending value, which is a non-primary sensitive attribute value occurring more than once in the SA-group. Offending values can be identified during the d-SA-ℓ-diversity checking

---

[2] $\ell_1, \ldots, \ell_d$-diversity is defined in in [11].
[3] Section 4.3 of [16].

process described in our algorithm. Decomposition accomplishes this by adding a value from the set defined by $LSV(S^i, G) - G.S^i$ where S^i is the non primary SA, T^s is the Sensitive Table, $\bowtie$ is natural join, and S^{pri} is the primary SA. If this set contanins more than one element, Decomposition randomly chooses a value and merges it with the SA-group, assumes that all values in the set are equally distant from the original offending value and therefore any value chosen from the set is equally valid. However this may not be the case. For example, comparing Table 3 and 6, we see that the value '4' has been added as noise because tuple 5 and 8 appear have the same value 2 for salary. Now, $LSV(Salary, G_1) = \{1, 2, 4, 7, 8\}$ and $LSV(Salary, G_1) - G_1.Salary = \{4, 7\}$. Now, the offending value is 2. Clearly 4 and 7 are not equally distant from 2. Therefore it is necessary to devise a method to choose a noise value which is semantically closest to the offending value. To quantify semantic distance between sensitive attributes, we use the Hierarchical Distance[6], considering the fact that in ℓ-diversity essentially treats all attributes in the SA-group as categorical data[5]. Hierarchical Distance is defined as follows: if H be the height of the domain hierarchy tree, the distance between two attribute values v_1 and v_2 is defined to be $level(v_1, v_2)/H$, where $level(v_1, v_2)$ is the height of the lowest common ancestor node of v_1 and v_2. Our algorithm, Decomposition+, accepts as input a hierarchy tree for every non-primary sensitive attribute. In light of the above discussions, our algorithm Decomposition is as follows:

Table 5. Residual tuples in each group for different values of ℓ_{pri}

Table 6. SAs from Table 1 without addition of noise

Attribute No.	Distinct Values	ℓ_{per}
Age (1)	73	n.a
Final-Weight (2)	100	n.a
Marital Status (3)	7	n.a
Race (4)	5	n.a
Gender (5)	2	n.a
Work-class (6)	14	7
Education (7)	16	3
Hours per week (8)	99	2
Relationship (9)	6	3

Group	Occupation	Salary
1	Police	1
1	Nurse	2
1	Actor	8
1	Clerk	
2	Nurse	2
2	Actor	4
2	Cook	7
2	Clerk	9

4.1   Algorithm for Decomposition+

Input: (i)Table T with sensitive attributes $S_1, S_2, S_3 \ldots Sd$, one of them being the primary: S_{pri}, (ii) Diversity parameters $\ell_1, \ell_2, \ell_3 \ldots \ell_d$, (iii) The hierarchical category tree H_i of each S_i where $i \neq pri, 1 \leq i \leq d$, (iv)Penalty Threshold $P_s^{threshold}$

Data: (i)$\mathfrak{B}$, the set of buckets formed by primary sensitive attributes. $\mathfrak{B} = (B_i)$, (ii)$\mathcal{G} = \Phi$, $\mathcal{G}$ is the set of SA-groups.

Output: the decomposed table T^* which satisfies $(\ell_1, \ell_2, \ldots \ell_d)$-diversity

Algorithm:

1. Sort $\mathfrak{B}$ by decreasing size
2. *while* $|\mathfrak{B}| \geq \ell_{pri}$
2.1 Randomly remove one tuple from B_0. 2.2 set $G = \{t_1\}$;
2.3 *for* $i \leftarrow 2$ to ℓ_{pri}
2.3.1 Remove one tuple t_i from B_i, that minimizes $P(t_i, G)$;
2.3.2 $G = G \bigcup t$;
2.3.3 Mark any attribute values which repeat
2.4 $\mathcal{G} = \mathcal{G} \bigcup G$;
3 *foreach* residual tuple t
3.1 *if* $P_s(t) > P_s^{threshold}$ *then*
3.1.1 Find SA group G that minimizes $P(t, G)$;
3.1.2 $G = G \bigcup t$; mark any attribute values which repeat
4 *foreach* non-primary sensitive attribute S^i and each SA-group G
4.1 *if* $G.S^i$ does not satisfy ℓ_i-diversity *then*
4.1.1 $LSV(G, S^i) = \prod_{S^i} T^S \bowtie G.S^{pri} - G.S^i$;
4.1.2 $R_V \leftarrow$ repeated value in S^i;
4.1.3 Select value N from $LSV(G, S^i)$ such that hierarchical distance $H(v_i, R_V)$ is minimized (where v_i is a member of the set $LSV(G, S^i)$)
4.1.4 Merge N into $G.S^i$ *until* $G.S^i$ satisfies ℓ_i-diversity.

4.2 Discussion

Based on the theoretical improvements proposed, and the algorithm presented, we may conclude that (i)our algorithm builds upon Decomposition by allowing tuples to be added to the underlying dataset after it has been anonymized and published. This facilitates greater flexibility in real life scenarios where tuples may be added removed or updated and may appear in multiple releases of the same data, (ii)the addition of new tuples does not dilute the protection offered in previous releases of the data, (iii)the proposed algorithm Decomposition+ also chooses a better noise value compared to Decomposition, which chooses randomly over the allowed values, (iv)Decomposition+ chooses noise value as close to the original value. This provides better utility, especially when the space of allowed noise values are large and when Decomposition chooses a particularly distant noise value. This is done while maintaining ℓ-diversity.

5 Experiments

To experimentally evaluate our proposed algorithm, we implemented Decomposition+ and applied it on the UCI Adult Dataset[8]. Experiments were conducted on a workstation running Ubuntu 11.04 (32-bit) with 3 GB RAM. Decomposition+ and associated preprocessing tools were implemented in Python v2.7. Data was supplied to the programs in Comma Separated Values format. Some analysis was done using Microsoft Excel 2007. The dataset was preprocessed in the same manner as described in [11] for a level playing field: (i)There were

32561 tuples in the dataset and after removing tuples with missing attribute instances, 30162 records were left, (ii) out of 14 attributes of the Adult dataset Nine (9) attributes were retained: *Age, Final-Weight, Martial Status, Race, Gender, Work-class, Education, Hours per Week* and *Relationship*, (iii) *Work-class* was used as Primary Sensitive Attribute, (iv)of these, the first four attributes were deemed as QIDs and the remaining were deemed as MSA, with corresponding ℓ-diversity parameters of 7, 3, 2, 3 respectively.

Occurrence of residual tuples: In the first instance, in order to study the effect of the choice of ℓ_{pri} on the number of tuples, we published only those tuples which are grouped during the largest ℓ group forming procedure for different input values for ℓ_{pri} between 0 and the maximum permissible value, 7. The importance of this analysis is that the higher the value of ℓ_{pri} chosen, the greater will be the protection offered. However, the greater the number of tuples which remain unpublished, the more the published data will differ from the original (See Table 7(a)). In the current scenario $\ell_{pri} = 5$ would be a good tradeoff between privacy and future utility. If the data were to have a more even distribution of primary sensitive attribute instances, a higher value of ℓ_{pri} would be preferable.

Performance: In order to measure how the choice of ℓ_{pri} affects performance, we used the Python module CProfile to measure running times for different values of ℓ_{pri}. Results are given in Figure 7(b). The results we recorded are significantly faster than those reported by Ye et al for Decomposition. However, this could be because of multiple causes such as CPU speed and implementation dependency. What is clear is that a smaller value of ℓ_{pri} causes larger number of buckets to be formed which require exponentially greater CPU seconds to distribute among SA-groups. We also noticed that the calculation of *Diversity Penalty* requires a inordinately large amount of CPU cycles (about 43.7% of total time).

Table 7. Results of our experiments

(a) Residual tuples in each group for different values of ℓ_{pri}

(b) ℓ_{pri} versus performance (in CPU seconds)

7	6	5	4	3	2	1
929	-	-	-	-	-	-
1060	117	-	-	-	-	-
1265	322	0	-	-	-	-
2053	1110	412	0	-	-	-
2485	1542	844	1	0	-	-
22272	21329	20631	19661	18348	14410	0

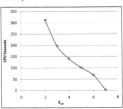

6   Conclusion and Further Work

Decomposition+ is an interesting and practical improvement, albeit one of many possible improvements, of Decomposition. Other improvements could be targeted to improve the efficiency of largest ℓ group forming procedure. Ye et al. do not specify the nature of how the set of all buckets in Decomposition, are formed. In our opinion, because buckets are reduced in size by one, a specific optimized datastructure to represent the collection of buckets can be useful. Further work could be extended to two interesting directions. One would be to apply decomposition over MSA to achieve (n, t)-closeness or other privacy models. The second, and more important work would be to apply Decomposition to very large datasets, which are known to suffer from the Dimensionality Curse[3].

References

1. Xiao, X., Tao, Y.: Anatomy: Simple and effective privacy preservation. In: Proceedings of the 32nd Intl. Conference on Very Large Data Bases, VLDB Endowment, pp. 139–150 (2006)
2. Fung, B.C.M., Wang, K., Chen, R., Yu, P.S.: Privacy-preserving data publishing: A Survey of Recent Developments. ACM Computing Surveys 42, 1–53 (2010)
3. Aggarwal, C.C., Yu, P.S. (eds.): Privacy-Preserving Data Mining. Advances in Database Systems, vol. 34. Springer, US (2008)
4. Sweeney, L.: k-anonymity: A Model for Protecting Privacy. Intl. Journal on Uncertainty, Fuzziness and Knowledge-based Systems 10, 557–570 (2002)
5. Machanavajjhala, A., Kifer, D., Gehrke, J., Venkitasubramaniam, M.: l-diversity: Privacy beyond k-anonymity. ACM Transactions on Knowledge Discovery from Data (TKDD) 1, 3 (2007)
6. Li, N., Li, T., Venkatasubramanian, S.: t-Closeness: Privacy Beyond k-Anonymity and l-Diversity, vol. (2). IEEE (2007)
7. Sweeney, L.: Achieving k-Anonymity Privacy Protection Using Generalization And Suppression. Intl. Journal on Uncertainty, Fuzziness and Knowledge-based Systems 10, 571–588 (2002)
8. Frank, A., Asuncion, A.: UCI Machine Learning Repository (2010)
9. Zhao, V., Wang, J., Luo, Y., Lei, J.: (α, β, k)-anonymity: An effective privacy preserving model for databases. In: 2009 Intl. Conference on Test and Measurement, pp. 412–415. IEEE (2009)
10. Venkatasubramanian, S.: Closeness: A New Privacy Measure for Data Publishing. IEEE Trans. on Knowledge and Data Engineering 22, 943–956 (2010)
11. Ye, Y., Liu, Y., Wang, C., Lv, D., Feng, J.: Decomposition: Privacy Preservation for Multiple Sensitive Attributes. In: Zhou, X., Yokota, H., Deng, K., Liu, Q. (eds.) DASFAA 2009. LNCS, vol. 5463, pp. 486–490. Springer, Heidelberg (2009)
12. Gal, T.S., Chen, Z., Gangopadhyay, A.: A Privacy Protection Model for Patient Data with Multiple Sensitive Attributes. Intl. Journal of Information Security and Privacy 2, 28–44 (2008)
13. Yang, X.C., Wang, Y.Z., Wang, B., Yu, G.: Privacy preserving approaches for multiple sensitive attributes in data publishing. Jisuanji Xuebao/Chinese Journal of Computers 31, 574–587 (2008)
14. Zhang, Q., Koudas, N., Srivastava, D., Yu, T.: Aggregate Query Answering on Anonymized Tables. In: 2007 IEEE 23rd Intl. Conference on Data Engineering, pp. 116–125. IEEE (2007)
15. Xiao, X., Tao, Y.: Anatomy: Privacy and Correlation Preserving Publication. Technical Report i, Chinese University of Hong Kong, Hong Kong (2006)
16. Byun, J., Sohn, Y., Bertino, E., Li, N.: Secure Anonymization for Incremental Datasets. In: Jonker, W., Petković, M. (eds.) SDM 2006. LNCS, vol. 4165, pp. 48–63. Springer, Heidelberg (2006)

Radix-4 Modified Interleaved Modular Multiplier Based on Sign Detection

Mohamed A. Nassar and Layla A.A. El-Sayed

Department of Computer and Systems Engineering,
Alexandria University, Alexandria, Egypt
eng.mohamedatif@gmail.com, labohadid@yahoo.com

Abstract. Data Security is the most important issue nowadays. A lot of cryptosystems are introduced to provide security. Public key cryptosystems are most common cryptosystems used for securing data communication. Modular multiplication is the basic operation of a lot of public key cryptosystems such as RSA, Diffie-Hellman key agreement (DH), ElGamal, and ECC. Abd-el-fatah et al. introduced an enhanced architecture for computing modular multiplication of two large numbers X and Y modulo given M. In this paper, a modification on that architecture is introduced. The proposed design computes modular multiplication by scanning two bits per iteration instead of one bit. The proposed design for 1024-bit precision reduced overall time by 38% compared to the design of Abd-el-fatah et al.

Keywords: efficient architecture, carry-save adder, sign detection, sign estimation technique, modular multiplication, FPGA, RSA.

1 Introduction

As a result of increasing of data communications over different networks, data security is the most important issue nowadays. There are a lot of PK (Public Key) cryptosystems used like RSA [10], Diffie-Hellman key agreement (DH) [7], ElGamal and ECC [1].

PK cryptosystems are implemented on coprocessor [8] for accelerating cipher operation and removing overhead of computing modular multiplication (A * B mod M) from main processor, so a lot of implementations are introduced. The goal of this implementation is to reduce complexity and improve performance. Most of PK cryptosystems is based on modular exponentiation which is based on modular multiplication.

Implementation of modular multiplication can be categorized into classical and interleaved. Classical implementation tries to solve the multiplication problem by computing multiplication and then reducing the result. Interleaved implementation interleaves multiplication with reduction at the same time. Reference [3] has detailed survey about classical and interleaved algorithms. An Example of interleaved algorithm is Montgomery modular algorithm [3, 14, 15].

N. Meghanathan et al. (Eds.): CCSIT 2012, Part II, LNICST 85, pp. 413–423, 2012.

In our proposed architecture, we introduce modification on architecture of interleaved modular multiplication based on improved sign detection [1]. One of benefits of modular multiplication based on sign detection is no need to save any value in a look up table. Another benefit is that the overall time is better than the architecture with look up table proposed by Amanor [2].

The rest of the paper is organized as follows: section 2 presents back ground and related work of interleaved Modular multiplication. Section 3 describes in details our proposed modification based on improved sign detection. It also proves the correctness of the new architecture. Section 4 summarizes results of the implementation compared with the architecture of Abd-el-fatah et al. [1]. A conclusion is given in Section 5.

2   Interleaved Modular Multiplication

The idea of the interleaved modular multiplication is to reduce the intermediate result produced from multiplication at each iteration to the range [0, M-1]. Let X, Y, M and R be the multiplicand, the multiplier, the modulus and the result respectively, and let n be the number of bits in their binary representation. Table 1 shows the standard algorithm [2, 4].

Table 1. Standard interleaved modular multiplication [2,4]

Input: $X = (x_{n-1} .... x_0)$, $Y = (y_{n-1}......y_0)$, $M = (m_{n-1}.....m_0)$
where $0 \leq X, Y < M$
Output: $R = X * Y \bmod M$
0-   R = 0;
1-   **for** i = n-1 downto 0
2-   R = R * 2;
3-   I = y_i * X;
4-   R = R + I;
5-   **if** (R ≥ M) then R = R − M;
6-   **if** (R ≥ M) then R = R − M;
7-   **end for**;

The algorithm scans Y starting from the MSB. At each iteration, R is incremented twice per iteration at worst case, once by R (step (2)) and another conditional increment by X (steps (3) and (4)) which means R after performing step (4) will satisfy the following inequality: $0 \leq R < 3M$. At the end of each iteration, the condition (R ≥ M) has to be checked at most twice (steps (5) and (6)) so that R has to be less than M.

At each iteration, three main operations are performed; shift (step (2)), addition, subtraction (step (4), (5) and (6)) and comparison (steps (5) and (6)). Addition, subtraction and comparison are complex operations. For large numbers addition and subtraction, CSAs are used. Comparison (Steps (5) and (6)) needs a comparator between R and M. Worst case comparison will also results in a large propagation delay, as all bits from both numbers have to be compared [1]. The comparison needs both numbers to be in their final form, which conflicts with the CSA output form. For optimizing steps (5) and (6), two recent proposed algorithms and corresponding architectures [1, 4] were introduced as follows.

2.1 Redundant Interleaved Modular Multiplication

In [4], the authors specified some modifications that can be applied to the standard algorithm mentioned in Table 1 in order to simplify and significantly speed up the operations inside the loop. Table 2 shows the proposed algorithm. The authors showed how to reduce time by further exploiting pre-calculation of values into a lookup table. LookUp(i) function (steps (1), (8)) returns value of ith entry in the look up table.

Table 2. Redundant interleaved modular multiplication algorithm[4]

Input: $X = (x_{n-1} \dots x_0), Y = (y_{n-1} \dots y_0), M = (m_{n-1} \dots m_0)$ where $0 \leq X,Y < M$
Output: $P = X * Y \, Mod \, M$
Precomputing lookup table entries
0- $S = 0; C = 0$
1- $A = LookUp(xn-1)$
2- **for** i=n-1 downto 0
3- $S = S \, mod \, 2n$
4- $C = C \, mod \, 2n$
5- $S = 2*S$
6- $C = 2*C$
7- $(S,C) = CSA(S,C,A)$
8- $A=LookUp(2*(sn + 2*cn+1 + cn)+xi-1)$
9- end **for**
10- $P = (S + C) \, mod \, M$

2.2 Modified Interleaved Modular Multiplication Based on Sign Detection

Modified Interleaved Modular Multiplication based on Sign Detection (MIMM) algorithm replaced comparisons (steps (5), (6)) in standard algorithm mentioned in Table 1 by determining the sign of the quantity (R − M). The Sign determination is performed using the "Sign Detection" technique. This technique is explained in the next sub-section [1, 16].

2.2.1 Sign Detection
Previous work [16] proposed a technique for the sign estimation of a number. This technique uses a window of only two bits taken from a number represented in (sum, carry) pair. The window count starts from the MSB and moving downwards. The technique produces three possible results: positive (+ve), negative (-ve) and

unsure (+/-ve). The unsure (+/-ve) result is reached when the number is either too large or too small [16]. Frequently reaching the unsure (+/-ve) result is the drawback of this technique [1].

AbdelFattah et al. [1] has enhanced the sign estimation technique, so that an exact sign can be determined for any number. A window of length (W) is taken from a number represented in (sum, carry) pair.

The detect-sign technique DS(S, C) can be defined as follows [1]:

Let X be an n-bit number represented in (S, C) pair:

1. Let W(s), W(c) be the windows taken from S, C respectively.
2. Let Temp = W(s) +W(c).
3. If the MSB of Temp is '0' then P is positive.
4. Else if Temp != "11….11" then P is negative.
5. Else(Temp is all ones) request another carry-save addition, update (S, C) and Go to (1).

In case of the unsure (+/-ve) result (step (5)), S and C are fed back again to CSA, and CSA will produce a new permutation of S and C for the same result. The detailed proof of the correctness of detect-sign technique is provided in [1].

2.2.2 Algorithm

The proposed algorithm is shown in Table 3. DS(R - M) function (steps (5) and (6)) applies sign detection technique for the number (R - M).

Table 3. Modified interleaved modular multiplication [1]

Input: $X = (x_{n-1} …. x_0)$, $Y = (y_{n-1}……y_0)$, $M = (m_{n-1}…..m_0)$
$\quad$ *where* $0 \le X,Y < M$
Output: $R = X * Y \bmod M$
0- R = 0
1- **for** i = n-1 downto 0
2-   R = R * 2
3-   I = yi * X
4-   R = R + I;
5-   if **DS**(R - M)=+ve R = R − M
6-   if **DS**(R - M)=+ve R = R − M
7- end **for**

2.2.3 The Architecture

Fig. 1 shows the architecture of MIMM [1]. The main modules of the architectures are:

1. Carry-Save Adder;
2. Detect-Sign Module (DS);
3. Controller;
4. Registers (SavedSum, SavedCarry);
5. Multiplexers (MUX$_1$, MUX$_2$, MUX$_3$).

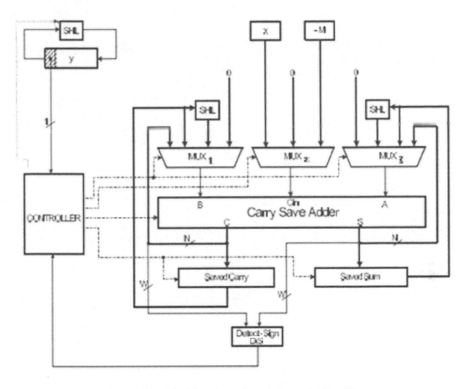

Fig. 1. Modified interleaved modular multiplier [1]

MIMM computes modular multiplication without a pre-computational phase, or predefined sets for moduli [1, 9].

3   Radix-4 Modified Interleaved Modular Multiplier Based on Sign Detection

The idea is to enhance the performance of MIMM by scanning two bits instead of one bit at each iteration. Let X, Y, M and R be the multiplicand, the multiplier, the modulus and the result of modular multiplication respectively (R = X * Y mod M), and let n be an even number of bits in their binary representation as follows.

$$X = \sum_{i=0}^{n-1} x_i\, 2^i,\ Y = \sum_{i=0}^{n-1} y_i\, 2^i, M = \sum_{i=0}^{n-1} m_i\, 2^i$$

The algorithm is shown in Table 4. Steps (5), (6) and (7) are performed at each iteration to ensure that intermediate result R satisfies the following inequality: $0 \le R < M$.

Table 4. Radix-4 modified interleaved modular multiplication based on sign detection algorithm

Input: $X = (x_{n-1} \ldots x_0)$, $Y = (y_{n-1} \ldots y_0)$, $M = (m_{n-1} \ldots m_0)$
where $0 \leq X, Y < M$ and $n \bmod 2 = 0$
Output: $R = X*Y \bmod M$
0- $R = 0$
1- **for** $i = n/2 - 1$ downto 0
2- $R = R * 4$
3- $I = [y_{n-1}\ y_{n-2}] * X$
4- $R = R + I$
5-   **if** $DS(R - 4M) = +ve$ $R = R - 4M$
6-   **if** $DS(R - 2M) = +ve$ $R = R - 2M$
7-   **if** $DS(R - M) = +ve$ $R = R - M$
8- $Y = Y << 2$
9- end **for**

3.1   Proof of Correctness

It is required to prove that the final result R is correct, i.e. $0 \leq R < M$. First we prove that the upper bound of the intermediate result R (step (4) of the algorithm mentioned in Table 4) is less than 7M as follows:

For the first iteration:

- At step (4), $R = [y_{n-1}\ y_{n-2}] * X < 3M$.
- Steps (5), (6) and (7) guarantee that M satisfies the following inequality: $0 \leq R < M$.

For the ith iteration where $i > 0$:

- At step (4), $R = R * 4 + [y_{n-1}\ y_{n-2}] * X < 7M$.
- Steps (5), (6) and (7) guarantee that M satisfies the following inequality: $0 \leq R < M$.

Table 5 shows all possible ranges for intermediate result R (Step (4)) and the corresponding action to reduce it.

Table 5. All possible ranges for R and the corresponding actions

Range	*Step(s) where subtraction(s) is(are) confirmed*
$0 \leq R < M$	No action
$M \leq R < 2M$	Step 7 (R – M)
$2M \leq R < 3M$	Step 6 (R = R –2M)
$3M \leq R < 4M$	Steps 6 and 7 (R = R –3M)
$4M \leq R < 5M$	Step 5 (R = R – 4M)
$5M \leq R < 6M$	Steps 5 and 7 (R = R – 5M)
$6M \leq R < 7M$	Steps 5 and 6 (R = R – 6M)

For example, if the intermediate result R (step (4)) is between 3M and 4M, the procedure will be:

1. $DS(R, 4M) => -ve => 3M \leq R < 4M$;
2. $DS(R, 2M) => +ve => R = R - 2M => M \leq R < 2M$;
3. $DS(R, M) => +ve => R = R - M => 0 \leq R < M$.

3.2   The Architecture

As shown in Fig.2, the main modules found in the proposed architecture are:

1. Carry-Save Adders (CSA_1 and CSA_2);
2. Detect-Sign module (DS);
3. Registers (SavedSum, SavedCarry);
4. Two-bit left shifters for shifting Y, 2*SavedSum, 2*SavedCarry, and computing -4M;
5. One-bit left shifters for computing 2X and -2M;
6. Multiplexers (MUX_1, MUX_2, MUX_3);
7. The Controller.

Our architecture is an adaptation of MIMM architecture [1]. The main differences between our architecture and MIMM architecture shown in Fig. 1 are:

1. Another CSA called CSA_2 was added to compute 3*X;
2. Two-bit left shifters are used to shift the input Y and compute -4*M;
3. MUX_1 and MUX_2 have different number of inputs as shown in Fig 2;
4. The controller module is more complex than that of MIMM.

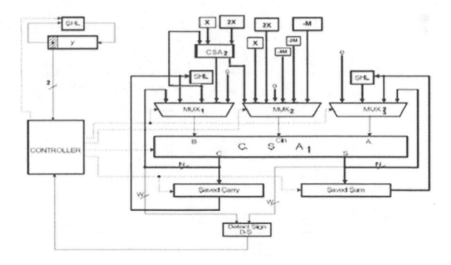

Fig. 2. Architecture of radix-4 modified modular multiplication based on sign detection

4   Implementations and Results

Synthesis using Xilinx Synthesis Tool (XST) was performed on a Xilinx FPGA Vertex XC4VFX12 [6, 11, 12]. The synthesis of the VHDL implementations of the architectures was performed with speed optimization goal [13]. Architectures are verified using software library called MIRACL [5] as follows: using MIRACL, three random numbers are generated (A, B and M where A and B are less than M) and Result R (R = A * B mod M) is computed. A, B and M are loaded on different architectures and R′ (output result from each architectures) is compared with corresponding R.

The synthesis tool (XST) generated the design reports for each of the implemented multipliers. The minimum clock period, and total number of slices used for each implementation are tabulated and graphically analyzed. Number of slices and Maximum frequency used for the different architectures are shown in Table 6 and Table 7 respectively.

Table 6. Number of slices used for the different architectures

Precision	MIMM	Radix-4 MIMM	Radix-4 MIMM area increase
32	222	373	68%
64	415	612	47%
128	803	1163	45%
256	1584	2277	44%
512	3117	4493	44%
1024	6221	8930	44%

Table 7. Maximum frequency for the different architectures

Precision	MIMM(MHZ)	Radix-4 MIMM (MHZ)
32	521.38	371.47
64	490.44	333.67
128	491.64	311.24
256	404.69	263.37
512	344.23	311.72
1024	308.83	325.84

From Table 6, Radix-4 has on average 48% more area than MIMM; this is due to the more logic in controller and adding other CSAs.

For different precisions, average improvements were calculated for txt data type. Table 8 and Fig. 3 summarize average overall operation time for the different architectures. Also Table 8 summarizes average speed up of our architectures for different precision.

Table 8. Average overall operation time consumed by the different architectures for txt data type

Precision	Average overall operation time		
	MIMM(ns)	Radix-4 MIMM (ns)	Relative speed up gain for Radix-4 MIMM
32	196.99	218.74	-10%
64	425.73	489.81	-13%
128	792.41	921.17	-16%
256	2074.79	2491.75	-17%
512	4931.96	4301.25	15%
1024	11138.68	8091.18	38%

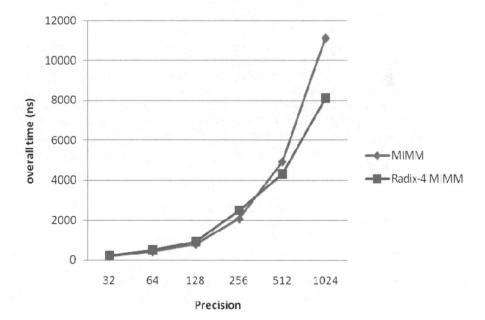

Fig. 3. Average overall operation time consumed by the different architecture for txt data type

5   Conclusion

In this paper, a new proposed interleaved modular multiplication algorithm and the corresponding architectures (Radix-4 MIMM) were introduced. The proposed architecture is based on sign detection technique which is responsible for determining the sign of a number represented in a (Sum, Carry) pair. Radix-4 MIMM architecture improved substantially the time requirement compared with MIMM architecture when the operands size is more than 256 bits. The relative speedup gain of Radix-4 MIMM architecture compared with MIMM is up to 38% for 1024-bit precision. Our architecture has not a pre-computational phase or any restrictions on moduli which make our architectures more efficient and more flexible than existing architectures. The architectures were implemented for different precisions 32, 64, 128, 256, 512 and 1024 bits. VHDL was used to implement different architectures. Simulations were performed on a Xilinx FPGA XC4VFX12.

References

1. Fattah, A., et al.: Efficient Implementation of Modular Multiplication on FPGAs Based on Sign Detection. In: Proc. 4th International Design and Test Workshop (IDT), pp. 1–6 (February 2010),
   http://ieeexplore.ieee.org/search/freesrchabstract.jsp?tp=&a
   rnumber=5404160&openedRefinements%3D*%26filter%3DAND%28NOT%2
   84283010803%29%29%26searchField%3DSearch+All%26queryText%3De
   fficient+implementation+sign+detection
2. Narh Amanor, D.: Efficient Hardware Architectures for Modular Multiplication. M.S. thesis, University of Applied Sciences Offenburg, Germany (February 2005)
3. Nedjah, N.: A Review of Modular Multiplication Methods and Respective Hardware Implementations. Proc. Informatica 30, 111–129 (2006)
4. Narh Amanor, D., Paar, C., Pelzl, J., Bunimov, V., Schimmler, M.: Efficient hardware architectures for modular multiplication on FPGAs. In: Proc. International Conference on Field Programmable Logic and Applications, pp. 539–542 (2005)
5. MIRACL, Multi-precision Integer and Rational Arithmetic C/C++ Library, http://www.shamus.ie/ (last referenced January 20, 2011)
6. Xilinx, Inc. Foundation Series Software, http://www.xilinx.com (last referenced January 20, 2011)
7. Diffie, W., Hellman, M.E.: New Directions in Cryptography. IEEE Transactions on Information Theory IT-22(6), 644–654 (1976)
8. Paniandi, A.: A Hardware Implementation of Rivest-Shamir-Adleman Co-processor or Resource Constrained Embedded Systems. M.S. thesis, University of Technology Malaysia (April 2008)
9. Knezevic, M.: Faster Interleaved Modular Multiplication Based on Barrett and Montgomery Reduction Methods. IEEE Transactions on Computers 59(12), 1715–1721 (2010)
10. Rivest, R.L., Shamir, A., Adleman, L.: A Method for Obtaining Digital Signatures and Public-Key Cryptosystems. Communications of the ACM 21(2) (February 1978)

11. Timing Constraints User Guide,
    http://www.xilinx.com/support/documentation/sw_manuals/xilin
    x12_3/ug612.pdf (last referenced March 20, 2011)
12. Virtex-5 FPGA User Guide,
    http://www.xilinx.com/support/documentation/user_guides/ug19
    0.pdf (last referenced March 20, 2011)
13. VHDL Reference Manual,
    http://www.usna.edu/EE/ee462/manuals/vhdl_ref.pdf
    (last referenced March 20, 2011)
14. Tenca, A.F.: A Scalable Architecture for Modular Multiplication Based on Montgomery's
    Algorithm. IEEE Transactions on Computer 52(9) (September 2003)
15. Pinckney, N.: Parallelized Radix-4 Scalable Montgomery Multipliers. Journal of Integrated
    Circuits and Systems, 28–30 (2008)
16. Kop, Q.K., Hung, C.Y.: Fast algorithm for modular reduction. IEE Proceedings,
    Computers and Digital Techniques 145, 265–271 (1998)

Adapting Temporal Aspects to Static GIS Models

K.C.S. Murti and Viksit Agarwal

Birla Inst. of Technology & Science, Pilani,
Hyderabad Campus
Jawahar nagar, Hyderabad, 500078, India
{chandra.kavuri,viksit.agarwal}@gmail.com

Abstract. Conventional GIS data models emphasize static representation of real world Geographic features. There are several real world problems where this assumption is not valid. For example the boundary of a lake changes with time depending on the inflow due to rains. The feature's geometry, its attributes and the topology with respect to its adjacent features are temporal. Current models used in commercial GIS do not support efficient persistence of the temporal history, provide temporal queries and deal with time variant topological changes. Study of current spatio-temporal models has been done and suitable techniques to enhance current spatial models with temporal aspects without breaking existing functionality has been explored. Moving object data model and its variations have been found to be an appropriate candidate for such enhancement. This paper describes the extension of spatial data model and its schema of a commercial GIS tool for supporting moving object data and creation of typical temporal analysis and query commands.

Keywords: Temporal Geographical Information System (TGIS), Spatio-Temporal data, Topology, Spatio-Temporal Models (STM), Moving Object Model.

1   Introduction

Geographic Information System (GIS) is a computer system capable of assembling, storing, manipulating, and displaying geographically referenced information, i.e. data identified according to their locations. GIS represents graphic reality i.e. location, geometry; links attribute data to the objects and builds spatial relationship among objects. GIS has made significant impacts on the ways we handle spatial data. These impacts are reflected not only by the wide range of GIS applications in various fields but also through the development of new data representation methods and analysis capabilities available to the GIS users. GIS still needs robust models to solve real world problems . These models have to handle geographic complexity, temporal aspects, scale differences, generalization, and accuracy in a robust way.

Most of commercial GIS tools handle the real world geographic features in a static way. In fact, no geographic feature is static. Either they will be fast moving or slow moving. So every feature's geometry, its attributes and the topology with respect to its adjacent features is temporal. The temporal granularity can be discrete or

N. Meghanathan et al. (Eds.): CCSIT 2012, Part II, LNICST 85, pp. 424–434, 2012.
© Institute for Computer Sciences, Social Informatics and Telecommunications Engineering 2012

continuous. The real world objects can be broadly classified as continuously changing objects (Moving vehicles..), objects that are basically static, but they are changed by events that have duration (Lake boundaries..) and objects that are always static and change only by sudden events (land parcels..) Current models used in GIS do not support efficient persistence of the temporal history, provide temporal queries and deal with time variant topological changes. Hence, spatio-temporal models come into play.

An excellent review of Spatio-Temporal database models is presented by Pelekis et all [1] with typical applications in LIS. The paper summarizes the capabilities of different models and considers Moving Object model as a promising candidate for robust implementation. Geographic Markup Language (GML) is published by OGC (Open GIS Consortium) for representation of geographic data and is a standard for exchange of spatial data. The standard has evolved further to represent Spatio Temporal supporting (i.e) Moving Object models in later versions.[6] GML now supports Dynamic Features to support temporal information to some extent. Heavy software base is developed by commercial vendors supporting static GIS models. Rudimentary changes cannot be done for temporal support in commercial packages, except to adapt STM in a loosely coupled way. This paper discusses a possible strategy in this direction.

2   Characteristics Spatio-Temporal Data Models

Spatio-Temporal data models are the core of a Spatio-Temporal Information System (STIS); they define object data types, relationships, operations and rules to maintain database integrity. A rigorous data model must anticipate spatio-temporal queries and analytical methods to be performed in the STIS. Spatio-temporal database models are intended to deal with real world applications, where spatial changes occur over the time line. A serious weakness of existing models is that each of them deals with few common characteristics found across a number of applications. Thus the applicability of the model to different cases fails on spatio-temporal behaviors not anticipated by the application used for the initial model development.

The study of the literature of the domain highlighted a set of precise characteristics of existing models that stand for the requirements of spatio-temporal database community. These requirements fall in four categories.

The first category deals just with the nature of time including the basic features that are used to describe it. The second category handles the pure spatial aspects of the existing approaches. The third deals with the unified spatio-temporal semantics, while the last category considers the query capabilities of the models. If these requirements are followed carefully in the process of designing a spatio-temporal database model, a robust and expandable model can be achieved, capable of dealing with most of the real world spatio-temporal processes (Pelekis et. al. [1]).

2.1   Temporal Semantics

Granularity: Granularity is specified by an anchored point on the time axis and a partitioning length. The anchored point denotes where the partitioning begins while the partitioning length denotes the size of each granule. Different applications require different levels of granularity.

Temporal operations: A series of specific operations describing temporal relationships have been proposed and proved necessary in handing any time-referenced information (e.g. timepoint T "inside" temporal period A which "meets" period B).

Time density: Time density is closely related to the types of changes/events that can occur to the value of a thematic or spatial characteristic. This issue arises whether time should be modeled as discrete or as continuous elements.

Representation of time: Time is represented by timestamps, where representation methods are different for each model. This criterion allows us to compare each modeling technique, by whether maintaining the duration of the status of an object or recording events that imply status change.

Lifespan: This factor shows if a model supports and deals with the duration of an event. This also concerns whether a model keeps track of the history of the real world objects, in terms of storing the lifespan of a discrete phenomenon or the temporal differences for a continuous one.

2.2   Spatial Semantics

Structure of space: This criterion represents the two basic approaches for computer storage of geographic data, which are the raster and vector spatial data models. Raster data are structured as an array of cells, pixels or voxels for 2D or 3D representations respectively. Vector techniques describe each spatial object in terms of start and end points.

Orientation/Direction: This standard demonstrates whether a model supports the orientation and the direction features that real world objects show in space (e.g. on the left side of, to the right).

Measurement: This issue examines whether it is possible to get a value of a spatial object (e.g. length, perimeter, distance etc.) using a particular model or if a model supports comparative operations such as bigger, longer.

Topology: This criteria establishes whether the model supports different topological relationships for the real world spatial objects.

2.3   Spatio-Temporal Semantics

Data types: Examples of spatial data types are the point, line and region whereas temporal point and interval are samples of temporal data types. Moving point and moving region are characteristic cases of unified spatio-temporal data types.

Type of change: This norm compares the models if they are able to deal with changes in shape and size of the objects. Models are also evaluated whether a change in the description of a spatio-temporal object can be combined with a synchronous representation of the change of an object's position. This norm further considers whether a model supports spatio-temporal real world objects that change continuously or just objects that are subject to discrete changes. Another criterion that further categorizes existing approaches that follow the continuous paradigm is whether the latter can deal with the movement of the spatial objects over time.

Evolution in time & space: This factor shows if there are defined functions like evolution, creation, fusion etc. to observe and describe the movement or change of objects in space, independently from their object identification. The norm is also applied to compare models on the existence of operations able to calculate the velocity and/or the acceleration of the movement of spatio-temporal objects.

Space-time Topology: This criterion sets a standard whether models can estimate metrics like values of distance, direction and change in size of a particular object. It further evaluates the ability of the models to represent topological relationships between (in particular continuously) evolving spatial objects for a certain period of time.

Object identities: Another issue that can be employed to evaluate the modeling ability of existing spatio-temporal data models is the manipulation of the identity of an object. In particular, the lifespan of an object is an important application dependant variable. The question is when does "change" affect an object so as not to be called the same object any more? Some times it may be more appropriate to destroy the original instance of an object and re-create a new one, due to an extensive change. Another critical issue is that of splitting or unifying objects.

Dimensionality: With this criterion, models are examined whether they support 2 dimensions to model the spatio-temporal objects, as traditional GIS do. Although two and half dimensional solutions exist (perspectives, stereo views etc.), volumetric 3 dimensional GIS provide advantages in displaying spatio-temporal data. In more recent approaches, relegating the attribute value associated with grid locations to a fourth dimension, time can be introduced as a fifth.

2.4   Query Capabilities

Existing spatio-temporal database models can be characterized based on their query capabilities:

Static spatial Queries : Queries about locations, spatial properties, and spatial relationships. The queries are on stationary spatial objects involving the location, topology and the attributes of the object.

Temporal properties and relationships: The queries are temporal value, time range and temporal relationships. (ex: What is the location of object at time t? What is the region in which the object moved during this period? What are the objects which are within 1 Km range at time *t*? etc.

Spatio-temporal behaviors and relationships: This set of queries involve space and time on discretely or continuously changing objects. (ex: Find the location where the train with this ID is at time *t*. It can be spatio-temporal range queries (ex. Find all the goods trains around the city moving this night?)

3   Moving Object Data Models

When we try integration of space and time, we are dealing with geometries changing over time. In general, geometries cannot only change in discrete steps, but continuously, and then we are talking about moving objects. If only the position in space of an object is relevant, then moving point is a basic abstraction; if the extent is also of interest, then the moving region abstraction captures moving as well growing or shrinking regions.

Researchers Erwig et.al. [2], have tried to model such spatio-temporal databases using this concept of moving object. While there is extensive literature on the evolution of Spatio-temporal models, let us restrict to moving object models, which is the appropriate model planned for implementation. Moving points and moving regions are viewed as three-dimensional (2D + time) or higher dimensional entities whose structure and behavior is captured by modeling them as abstract data types. The objective is to integrate such abstract data types into any extensible DBMS. This approach models the time as integral part of the spatial entities. The time dimension is based on the linear, discrete/continuous, absolute time model and initially only valid time is considered. The model captures both change and movement   ex: The trajectory of a moving point can be described either as a curve, or as a polygonal line in 2D space.

3.1   ADTs for Moving Objects

Base types: The base types are int, real, string, and bool. All base types have the usual interpretation, except that each domain is extended by the value "undefined".

Spatial Types: Basic are point, line, and region. A value of type point represents a point in the Euclidean plane or is undefined.. A line value is a finite set of continuous curves in the plane. A region is a finite set of disjoint parts called faces, each of which may have holes. The point set paradigm expresses that space is composed of infinitely many points.

Time Type: Type "instant" represents a point in time or is undefined. Time is considered to be linear and continuous, i.e., isomorphic to the real numbers.

Moving Types: From the base types and spatial types, we derive corresponding temporal types. The type constructor moving is used for this purpose. For all "moving" types we introduce extra names by prefixing the argument type with an "m", that is, mpoint, mpoints, mline, mregion etc. The temporal types obtained through the moving type constructor are functions, or infinite sets of pairs.

3.2   Temporal Operations

Relevant operations [3] can be defined on temporal objects based on context and application. Such an operation may return a spatial or temporal or moving types.

Some examples are illustrated here with. If a moving point (or point set) changes its position only in discrete steps, then operation_locations returns its projection as a points value. Operation_routes similarly returns the projection of a discretely moving line value. Some practical examples of moving objects is given below

_ Land_Parcel (name: string, owner: string, area: mregion)
_ Lake (name: string, area: mregion)
_ Road (name: string, route: mline)
_ Tree (name: string, centre: mpoint)

Examples Typical Operations of Moving Objects

_Operation (mregion-> mreal) area   applied to a time-varying real number representing the size of the lake at all times
_Operation (mregion x mpoint -> mboolean) inside applied against a land_parcel and a tree computes a time-varying boolean representing when the tree has been moved or planted in a parcel
_ Operation (mpoint X mpoint -> mreal) distance calculates the time-varying distance between two trees at all times.

4   Methodology and Implementation

Review of current methodologies [4] and models was done keeping the suitability and adaptability of the methods for implementation. Moving Object Data model is found to be most suited because: This model is close to reality and abstraction level is much higher and supports representation of continuous changes in geometries. The representation is data-type oriented, with emphasis on generality, closure and consistency. It models the time as integral part of the spatial entities. It can be integrated into any extensible DBMS. There is redundancy in storage of temporal data.

4.1   Overview of GeoMedia® Data Model

GeoMedia® Professional [5] is the next generation Geographic Information System (GIS) product. GeoMedia is an enterprise GIS tool for capturing Geo referenced data, creating an enterprise database as warehouses, providing spatial queries, spatial manipulations and publishing maps. This product has unique feature which enables to view geographic data from different sources, in a unified way irrespective of the source formats. Users can do spatial analysis from heterogenous sources seamlessly in a single environment.

Geographic Data Objects (GDO) are programmable database objects based on the Microsoft Data Access Object (DAO) model (Fig. 1). The Microsoft Component Object Model (COM) design provides the automation for data access and data update. GeoMedia® Professional combines DAO concepts and COM with geographic aspects of geodetic coordinate systems, geometry, and graphics display.

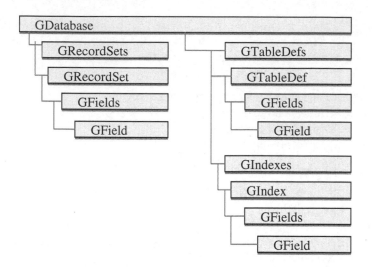

Fig. 1. Geographic data Objects (GDO) of GeoMedia©

Expansions to the DAO model allow database definition, population, and update through the GDO model. These expansions consist of the following.

Geometry fields are defined to store geometric information. Standard Tables are defined to aid in manipulating and updating geographic information. Coordinate Systems Table provides coordinate system information used to project geometry. Metadata is table data about the GDO structure and contents. It is used by automation and built-in GeoMedia® Professional commands to return supplementary information for feature geometry and attributes. For example, it returns the name of the primary geometry field, a list of all feature tables, and so forth.

GeoMedia® Professional talks to the various data sources using GDO. Intermediate components called as GDO data servers read the native data and serve data to GeoMedia® Professional client using GDO. Each data server is specific to a native data type. Information about and manipulation of a GDatabase object is performed through its methods and properties. The GTableDef object is the stored definition of a database table. GTableDef that has specific metadata defined are recognized as feature classes in GeoMedia® Professional. GField represents a column of data similar to DAO but extended to support spatial data types.. Each feature class is designated a primary geometry type (Point, Line, Area, Compound, Text or None). Geometry data is stored in geometry GFields in GTableDef in the form of GDO blobs.

4.2   Temporal Schema Design

The static point feature class resides in GeoMedia® static warehouse. In reality, the temporal information about the moving point will be an input in the form of stream of data samples (t1, x1, y1), (t2, x2, y2), … and so on.

The source of this temporal data can be from GPS. To simulate this behavior in the present work, a linear feature has been used to define the trajectory of moving point that is moving with a uniform speed. The linear feature class that is used to input the trajectory of a moving point resides in a GeoMedia® warehouse static data model. In this table, each moving point feature is uniquely identified by a primary key "ID". A new metadata table is created that stores the temporal table name corresponding to this linear feature class. In the proto-type implementation, since there is no relevance of presence of static point feature class table, the metadata table stores the mapping of input linear feature class table name and the temporal data table. But in reality the metadata table should store the temporal table name against the static feature class table name. In the temporal table, the "ID" field of the linear feature class is made a foreign key that establishes a relationship between the two tables. Once the temporal data is generated it has no relation with the static table. In other words, all temporal analysis will be done using only the temporal data table.

The metadata table is used for book-keeping of all the temporal data tables present in the warehouse. Also, if a temporal table needs to be updated or refreshed, the mapping will be used by the Create Temporal Data command to show the already existing temporal data table name.

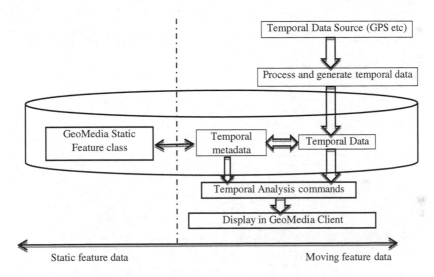

Fig. 2. Data Flow and relation of static and temporal data

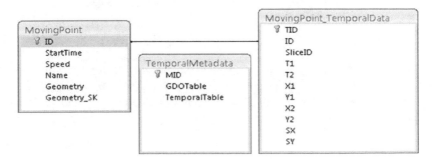

Fig. 3. Relationship among temporal data tables in GDO

4.3   Temporal Data Creation

Data input is done using Insert Feature command of GeoMedia® Professional in the form of linear feature class that represents the trajectory of the moving point. At the time of digitization of the linear feature, the uniform speed and start time of the moving point are also input as the attribute values. A command has been developed to perform the rest of processing and prepare the temporal data for further analysis. The command takes the following input:

- Input linear feature class that represents the trajectory of moving point.
- Read write connection name that contains the linear feature class and will be used to create temporal data and metadata tables.
- Name of the temporal data table to be created for a moving point.

The following flow chart explains the processing and data flow during the data input and preparation step:

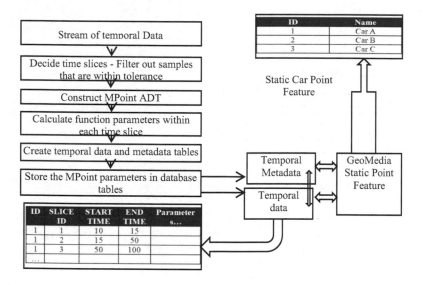

Fig. 4. Create Temporal Data command processing flow

4.4   Results

Two temporal analysis commands – "Display Moving Points" and "Profile Moving Point" have been developed. Display Moving Points command creates the point geometries at a given instant and displays them in map window. The below flow chart explains the processing of the command:

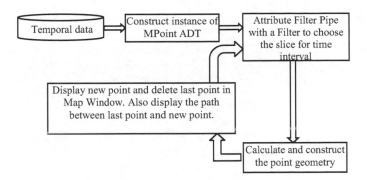

Fig. 5. Profile moving point processing

Profile moving parts command creates point geometries at a given regular interval of time, and displays them in map window at refresh intervals. When it adds the new point, it deletes the old point and draws a path between the two points; this makes the point appear moving in the GeoMedia® Professional map window. The road network considered in this example is a real data of Interstates (highways connecting different states) within Alabama, USA. On each of the interstates, one car is moving at predefined randomly selected speeds forming a trajectory.

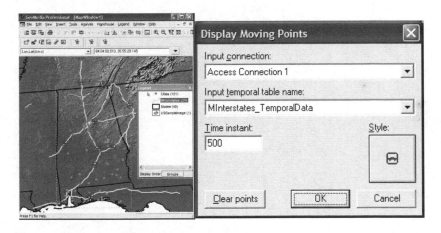

Fig. 6. Display moving points screen and command parameters

5   Conclusions

Moving Object Data model requires very less storage space to store temporal data compared to other models. The model requires only the function parameters to be stored with in each slice that describes the motion of the moving object. The model can be incorporated in commercial GIS products without affecting its existing static data and functionality. Implementations does not have dependency on any specific DBMS. Temporal queries can be handled similar to any spatial queries and persisted.

References

1. Pelekis, N., Theodoulidis, B., Kopanakis, I., Theodoridis, Y.: Literature Review of Spatio-Temporal Database Models. Knowledge Engineering Review 19(3), 235–274 (2004)
2. Erwig, M., Guting, R.H., Schneider, M., Vazirgiannis, M.: Spatio-Temporal Data Types: An Approach to Modeling and Querying Moving Objects in Databases. GeoInformatica 3(3), 265–291 (1999)
3. Guting, R.H., Bohlen, M.H., Erwig, M., Jensen, C.S., Lorentzos, N.A., Schneider, M., Vazirgiannis, M.: A Foundation for Representing and Querying Moving Objects. ACM Transactions on Database Systems 25(1), 1–42 (2000)
4. Langran, G., Chrisman, N.R.: A Framework for Temporal Geographic Information Systems. Cartographica 25(3), 1–14 (1988)
5. GeoMedia® Professional developers' and users' help documents
6. TGML - Extending GML by Temporal Constructs - A Proposal for a Spatiotemporal Framework in XML

A Basic Comparison of Different Memories
for Object Oriented Computer Architecture

Ankit V. Patel and Paresh Mathur

U. V. Patel College of Engineering,
Ganpat University, Mehesana, Gujarat, India
{ankit.themark,paresh.2047}@gmail.com

Abstract. This position paper is focused on the abstract model of Object Oriented Computer Architecture and specifically the memory unit of such a computing system which would be able to handle the type of object oriented computing proposed in the paper. The memory unit plays a very crucial part because it will have to be radically different from what we call a memory unit in the present contexts. This parallel nature of computing in an OOCA allows it to use different memory architectures both as shared memory and distributed memory. Here we compare the pros and cons of using these types of memories in an OOCA.

Keywords: Computer Architecture, Object oriented models, parallel systems, Memory Organization.

1   Motivation

Even though there have been many advances in the computer hardware technology (better memory units, better control units, faster and more reliable processors, etc basically putting more transistors on one chip) there is a large divide between the way we think about hardware and software. We need to think outside of this system if we want to exploit the technological progress in semiconductor technology or VLSI design. Object oriented programming has revolutionized the world of programming from its inception in 1960s in the Simula language. The concepts like encapsulation, extensibility, modularity and abstraction are very powerful tools which may be used in the context of hardware to remove some of the bottle necks. But this would require a revolutionary change in the way we think about computation and processors.

2   Related Research

A remarkable amount of research has been done in the field of alternative computer architectures. By 1980's Myers [1] had correctly identified the need for resolving the semantic gap between the computer architectures and the programming languages. The Object Oriented Languages like Java and Ruby offer platform independent software development and also facilities like readability of code & higher

N. Meghanathan et al. (Eds.): CCSIT 2012, Part II, LNICST 85, pp. 435–443, 2012.

abstractions. The Exokernel research at MIT [2] focuses on increasing the performance of applications without using any commercially available Operating System. They emphasizes on treating the hardware as the operating system, thus eliminating the need of at least one level of the hierarchy. Also the bare PC research at Utah [3] will help developers write applications for application specific PC's again eliminating the need of an operating system.

The Bare Machine Computing research at Towson University, lead by Dr. Ramesh K. Karne [4] focuses on making application specific computing machines which run without any software installed on them. He has implemented applications like webmail, Secure VOIP, TLS protocol on a bare PC [5, 6, and 7].

Our previous position paper [8] tried to describe, in a very abstract way, how the memory model of an OOCA would work.

3   Small Introduction to OOCA Memory Model

The OOCA has to use a special kind of memory which is radically different from our current concepts. The memory unit in OOCA does not just store data but stores whole "objects". An object has two parts, one is the data member and the other is the function member. The data members are the processed results and parameters of the function members. Thus the memory also has some processing power in it to regularly keep updating the data members in accordance with the function members.

An OOCA memory is not just a *data* storage unit, but an *object* storage unit (the difference being the processing power). An abstract model of Object memory is given in the figure 1.

As seen in the figure, the Object Memory consists of three main parts.

Storage Unit: To store data members as well as function members.
Processing Unit: To handle memory management and function processing.
Interfaces: To interact with object processing unit.

3.1   Memory Unit

This is used to store the data as well as the function members. The data memory and function memory need not be separate, and they can be part of a large RAM memory. But it would be more efficient to have the data memory in a rewritable memory like a RAM or hard disk as it is dynamic. While on the other hand as the function memory is static for a given object it could be stored in a ROM. It is also not necessary to have a large data memory separate for each Object.

A much more efficient way would be to have a conventional memory unit like RAM or Hard Disk and a pointer storage unit as the data memory. The data memory can have pointers to the memory location where the data is stored in the hard disk. This will use the resources much more efficiently. Something similar can be done with the function memory. It can hold pointers to the location where the function program is stored in the memory.

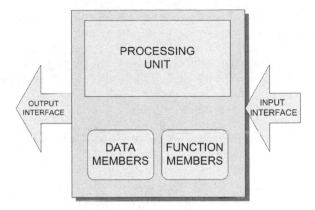

Fig. 1. An Abstract Model of Object Memory

3.2   Processing Unit

The processing unit is essentially an ALU combined with a control unit. The processing unit updates the data members by executing the functions defined inside the object. Apart from processing the function members, it also has to handle the interfaces. The object is accessed through a set of input and output interfaces. The commands passed to the input interface has to be processed to first determine the type of command (is it to pass an argument or to fetch some data or execute a function), then accordingly the control unit of the processing unit will execute the relevant function.

3.3   Interface

The object stored in the object storage unit interacts with the object processing unit or other objects by the means of interfaces. These interfaces are predefined and implemented in hardware. There are two types of interfaces

1)   Input: Used to pass arguments to the object function members.
2)   Output: Used to fetch data from the object.

The input interface is used to give arguments to the function members. Again the arguments are passed as pointers. But unlike the normal computers, these pointers will have two parts.

1)   The object address, to tell the object from which we want to fetch data.
2)   The data member address, to know which data member to fetch from a given object.

The input interface will also handle the queries that are done on the object. To fetch a data member or the executed result of the function member, the object processing unit will have to call the input interface with a predefined command (and pass necessary arguments) and then accept the result from the output interface.

In an object oriented language, there is no evident difference between the syntax of fetching a data member or a function member. In the same way in object oriented computer architecture, the output interface will have no distinction between fetching a data member or a function member. This will encapsulate all the details of the object execution behind that interface. In an object oriented programming language there is a function defined which fetches the data members through an interface, like wise we can have the function members store their results inside the data memory and then a similar interface can be there to fetch a data or the result of the function member.

4   Options for Memories That Can Be Used in OOCA

As stated previously OOCA has a highly parallel architecture. Any real world implementation of OOCA would require more than one object with each object executing its functions in parallel. Thus we have to choose between the different topographies of parallel computing systems. The two most broad and basic categories for parallel memories are

1) **Shared Memory:** In this type of memory all the processors can access the memory as a global address space. In other words, there is one large storage location and all the processors can access any part of that memory at any given instant of time.

2) **Distributed Memory:** In this type of memory all the processors have their local address space and require a communication protocol to transfer data from one processor memory to another.

These two are the broad options that we have for our OOCA memory topology. As is evident there are advantages and disadvantages of each type of memory. Apart from common cons like fetch time or maintaining the state concurrency, there are some other pros and cons which are specific to OOCA memories.

An OOCA memory is supposed to facilitate the implementation of the concepts of an Object at hardware level. Each of the above said topology help in implementation of one or more concepts of Object orientation by their inherent nature. Other concepts can be added with a little modification to the topology.

5   Using Shared Memory in OOCA

In a shared memory, there is a huge storage space which is available as a global address space to all the processors. Thus all the objects will share the same data memory (and also memory to store functions). This type of memory allows all the objects to access the data or function members of every other object in the system. This ease in access and efficient use of memory is a trade off with the protection of data from accidental or intentional misuse by the user. As all the objects can access all the parts of global memory all the time, there may be buffer overflows or other ways of corruption of memory.

5.1   Using Uniform Memory Access Shared Memory

The block diagram of a uniform Memory Access Shared Memory in a 4 object OOCA is given in figure 2 below.

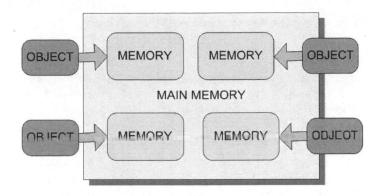

Fig. 2. Four object OOCA system with UMA shared memory

As can be seen in the figure, the main memory is divided into chunks of memories which serve as the data and function storage units for the four objects OOCA system. In this type of systems, each object will not have an actual dedicated memory as there storage unit. But the storage unit will comprise of a memory unit which will store pointers to the location of actual data in the big main memory. This approach allows dynamic memory and facilitates the implementation of a garbage collection unit.

Some characteristics of this type of topology are:

Efficient Use of Memory: As can be seen, with the UMA approach the main memory can be used very efficiently. While adding new objects, the new object can be assigned memory much more efficiently. With a memory control and garbage collection unit, one may as well give only that much memory to a given object that it is actually using.

Standard Interfaces with Memory: As the interface with the memory can be of only one type, all the objects will have to have an implementation of that standard interface in them. As is inherent in the OOCA model, each object will have a very different processing unit. This is because the processing unit has to process different kind of data for different types of objects. Thus the standard interfaces have to be implemented in every object.

Standard Fetch Time for data from other objects: As all the data is stored in a global address space, the fetch time for getting data of one object is exactly same as getting data from other object.

Load sharing of processing power may be done between objects: As all the memory is in the global address space, the value of data members and even the code of function members can be accessed by any processor in the system. Also fetch time of accessing memory of any object is exactly the same. Thus, if urgently required, we may bend the rules and the processing power of one object may be made accessible to another object. This type of arrangement would make judicious use of all the processing power available in the system.

5.2   Using Non Uniform Memory Access Shared Memory

The block diagram of a Non Uniform Memory Access Shared Memory in a 8 object OOCA is given in figure 3 below.

In a NUMA topology, there are two or more UMA shared memories connected with a bus. The given object may access its own memory, or fetch data from any other memory via this standard bus. In this topology the bus protocol has to be standard and implemented on top of all the objects.

It has the following characteristics:

Different types of processors in the same system: In a UMA topology, the most preferable and ideal condition is when all the processing units of all the objects are either exactly the same or very similar to each other. This is required because we have to access the same memory for all the objects. But when you use a NUMA structure, you may have lots of different types of processors which talk with their custom memory. This helps in implementing any optimization techniques one might want for faster memory access. But the only constrain here is that the processors must also be able to communicate over the bus protocol so it can transfer data to and from its memory.

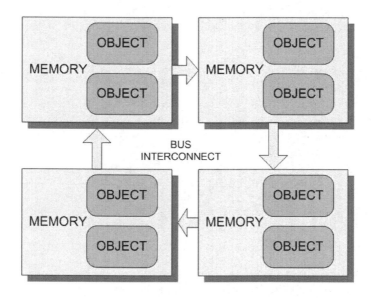

Fig. 3. Eight Object OOCA system with NUMA shared Memory

Higher Fetch Times for Fetching Memories of other Objects: For a UMA all the memories are defined in a globally mapped memory unit. Thus the fetch time to access the data of other objects is exactly the same as that of access data of the same object. But in NUMA the data of other object has to be fetched over the bus protocol which would make it slightly slower than the fetch time of accessing data from the same object.

It facilitates the implementation of Inheritance Principle of OOP: When one object inherits function and data members of another object it has said to have "inherited" from that object. From the block diagram of NUMA we can see how two objects can be grouped to use a single memory. This type of architecture helps in implementing an inheritance mechanism inside the architecture itself. Similar objects can be grouped together and inherit functions from other objects so as to implement the inheritance concept.

New objects can be easily added: One thing that is most exciting about a NUMA is the ease with which you can add new objects. If you want to add a new object to a UMA system, we have to first analyze the memory which is left in the system which poses a certain constrain over expansion of any given system. But with a NUMA, you just have to add it to the bus interconnection (which usually has a ring topology). But care has to be taken to reroute the fetch requests in such a way so as not to disturb the previous system.

6   Using Distributed Memory in OOCA

The block diagram of OOCA with distributed memory is given in figure 4 below.

In a distributed memory, a complete object (processing unit and storage unit) is one entity. These are connected via a bidirectional bus over which the objects can communicate.

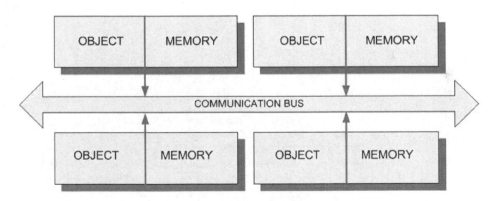

Fig. 4. Four object OOCA system with Distributed memory

Some characteristics of this type of topology are:

Scalability: This type of topology can be scaled infinitely in theory. We can add arbitrarily many objects to the bus. But of course the bus protocol and bus control unit that is used in the system will limit the amount of objects that may be added to the given bus.

High Level Of Abstraction Can Be Achieved: As all the processing and function members of the object are not visible to other objects, it would help in achieving a high level of abstraction. If some object wants to access the data member or function member of any other object, it just has to give out a call on the bus and wait for the reply.

7   Conclusion

As in any other engineering problem, deciding the optimal type of parallel memory for OOCA is a question of tradeoffs. Using any particular type of memory for all the architectures would not be the right way to go about designing an OOCA computer. For deciding which type of memory topology to use, we must first have a clear idea of what the system would comprise of and what would be its future expansions.

Having said that, some rules of thumb may be established for deciding the type of memory that should be used. For example, if the system is small (say less than 10 object of low complexity) one may use UMA shared memory architecture. It is most suitable as it is easy to implement and also easy to manage.

But for a larger system, one has to use a NUMA or go for a distributed memory architecture altogether. These architectures allow for high complexity and high number of objects in a system. Also expanding the system by adding few more objects is a lot easier in these topologies as we have to just connect them to a bus and then the bus communication protocol will facilitate the rest.

References

[1] Myers, G.J.: Advanced Computer Architecture, p. 17. John Wiley & Sons (1982)
[2] Ford, B., Back, G., Benson, G., Lepreau, J., Lin, A., Shivers, O.: The Flux OSKit: A Substrate for OS and Language Research. In: Proc. of the 16nth ACM Symp. on Operating Systems Principles, St. Malo, France, pp. 38–41 (October 1997)
[3] Engler, D.R.: The Exokernel Operating System Architecture, Ph.D. Thesis, MIT (October 1998)
[4] Karne, R.K.: Application-oriented Object Architecture: A Revolutionary Approach. In: 6th International Conference, HPC Asia 2002 (December 2002)
[5] Khaksari, G.H., Wijesinha, A.L., Karne, R.: Secure VoIP using a Bare PC. In: 3rd International Conference on New Technologies, Mobility and Security, NTMS (2009)
[6] Emdadi, A., Karne, R.K., Wijesinha, A.L.: Implementing the TLS Protocol on a Bare PC. In: The 2nd International Conference on Computer Research and Development, ICCRD 2010, Kaula Lumpur, Malaysia (May 2010)
[7] Patrick, A., Wijesinha, A.L., Karne, R.: The Design and Performance of a Bare PC Webmail Server. In: The 12th IEEE International Conference on High Performance Computing and Communications, AHPCC 2010, Melbourne, Australia, September 1-3, pp. 521–526 (2010)
[8] Mathur, P., Patel, A.V.: A memory Model of Object Oriented Computer Architecture. In: The International Conference on Intelligent Systems and Data Processing
[9] Mancl, D., Havanas, W.: A study of the impact of C++ on software maintenance. In: Proceedings Conference on Software Maintenance (1990)

[10] Cockshott, P.: Performance evaluation of the Rekursiv object oriented computer. In: Proceedings of the Twenty-Fifth Hawaii International Conference on System Sciences, vol. i (1992)

[11] Harrison, A., Moulding, M.R.: Data fusion on the Rekursiv object-oriented architecture. In: IEE Colloquium on Principles and Applications of Data Fusion, pp. 3/1–3/3 (1991)

[12] Duncan, R.: A survey of parallel computer architectures. Computer 23(2), 5–16 (1990)

Performance Evaluation of Segmentation of Frog-Eye Spot Lesions on Tobacco Seedling Leaves

P.B. Mallikarjuna and D.S. Guru

Department of Studies in Computer Science, Manasagangothri,
University of Mysore, Mysore-570006, Karnataka, India
pbmalli@yahoo.com, dsg@compsci.uni-mysore.ac.in

Abstract. In this paper, a new algorithm for segmentation of frog-eye spot lesions on tobacco seedling leaves is proposed. Segmentation algorithm consists of mainly two steps. First step is to approximate lesion extraction using contrast stretching transformation and morphological operations such as erosion and dilation. Second step refines the outcome of first step by color segmentation using CIELAB color model. We have also conducted a performance evaluation of segmentation algorithm by measuring the parameters such as Measure of overlapping (MOL), Measure of under-segmentation (MUS), Measure of over-segmentation (MOS), Dice similarity measure (DSM), Error-rate (ER), Precision (P) and Recall (R). In order to corroborate the efficacy of the proposed segmentation algorithm, an experimentation is conducted on our own dataset of 400 segmented areas of tobacco seedling leaves which are captured in uncontrolled lighting conditions. Experimental results show that our proposed segmentation algorithm achieved best average DSM and MOL accuracy as compared to our previous segmentation algorithm.

Keywords: Image enhancement, CIELAB color model, Lesion area segmentation, Performance measures.

1 Introduction

Agriculture plays an important role in economy of any nation. Economy of agricultural industries is directly depends on the quality production of agriculture. A stable agricultural industry ensures a country of food security, source of income, source of employment. Therefore, to improve agriculture production and its quality, farmers should practice precision agriculture.

Precision agriculture focuses on getting maximum quality output with minimum input. The objectives of precision agriculture are profit maximization, agriculture input rationalization and environmental damage reduction, by adjusting the agriculture practices to the site demands. To achieve these objectives some practices which are site specific application of agrochemicals to remove diseases at seedling (nursery) level and plant level, right time harvesting of crops and grading (quality inspection) of crops are to be adopted. Human intervention in these practices raises many disadvantages such as wrong diagnosis of diseases in crops, wrong quality

N. Meghanathan et al. (Eds.): CCSIT 2012, Part II, LNICST 85, pp. 444–453, 2012.
© Institute for Computer Sciences, Social Informatics and Telecommunications Engineering 2012

analysis of crops, man power, labor cost and time consuming. Therefore, we need to automate these practices to increase efficiency and speed using computer vision (CV) algorithmic models.

Diagnosis and detection of diseases at nursery stage is very important in any crop. The emergence and spreading of frog-eye spot lesions have become more common in tobacco at nursery (seedling) phase because of climate and environmental factors. The symptoms of frog-eye spots on a leaf are characterized by small spots of size 2mm with circular central grey or white dead tissue as shown in Fig ?(a). Apart from our work [1] no other attempt can be traced on disease detection on leaf of tobacco seedlings. However few attempts can be traced on other crops. Enhancing color differences in images by means of vectorial normalization was proposed to better separation of diseases [2]. Conversion of a RGB image into H, I3a, and I3b color transformation and segmenting the transformed image by analyzing the distribution of intensities in a histogram was explored to identify plant disease visual symptoms [2]. Color co-occurrence method (CCM) was used in conjunction with statistical classification algorithms to identify diseased and normal leaves under laboratory conditions [4]. An algorithm to classify fall armyworm damaged maize plants and an undamaged maize plant at simplified lighting conditions has also been recommended [5]. A back propagation neural network (BPNN) and a gray level co-occurrence matrix (GLCM) were used to evaluate the texture features of the lesion area in seedling diseases [6]. Fuzzy feature selection techniques are proposed for identifying diseases on cotton leaves [7]. Grading method of leaf spot disease on soya bean leaf using image processing techniques was proposed [8]. A method of recognizing disease in a cucumber leaf based on image processing and support vector machine was developed [9]. Digital image analysis and spectral reflectance data are used to quantify damage by greenbugs in wheat crop [10]. Severity of fungal disease in a spring wheat crop was estimated using hyperspectral crop reflectance data vectors and corresponding disease severity field assessments [11]. Fuzzy feature selection approach was proposed to diagnose and identify diseases in cotton crop. This approach reduces the dimensionality of the feature space so that it leads to a simplified classification scheme [12]. A method of using wavelet transform was developed to detect pests in stored grains [13]. An image processing algorithm was proposed for automatic identification of whiteflies, aphids and thrips in greenhouse. The size and color components were selected as features for automatic identification [14].

In our previous work [1], we segment the lesions on leaf of tobacco seedlings and classify them in to three classes: Anthracnose, Frog-eye spot and Uninfected area. In our current work we improved the accuracy in segmenting the Frog-eye spot lesions. We compared our current segmentation algorithm with previous segmentation algorithm by measuring the performance evaluation measures such as Dice coefficient (DC), Error-rate (ER), Measure of overlapping (MOL), Measure of under-segmentation (MUS), Measure of over-segmentation (MOS), Precision (P) and Recall (R).

2   Proposed Segmentation Algorithm

The proposed segmentation algorithm consists of two steps. The first step involves approximate lesion extraction using contrast stretching transformation and morphological operations such as erosion and dilation. Second step refines the outcome of first step by color segmentation using CIELAB color model.

We propose the following method to segment the lesion area. The RGB image (Fig. 1(a)) of tobacco seedling leaf is transformed into a B-channel gray scale image (Fig. 1(b)). The gray scale image is enhanced using a contrast stretching transformation [15] with an adjustable parameter (m) and is given by

$$G = f(g) = 1/[1+(m/g)^E]$$ (1)

where,

   g represents the intensities of the input image

   m represents threshold

   E controls the slope of the function

The contrast stretching transformation compresses the values greater than m into a narrow range of dark levels in the output image G, similarly it compresses the values less than m into a narrow band of light levels in the output image G. The enhanced gray scale image (Fig. 1(c)) is transformed into binary image using threshold T_1. The erosion and dilation operations using a disk structuring element of radius one is applied on the obtained binary image (Fig. 1(d)) to remove uninfected areas. A suitable threshold T_2 is used to remove small uninfected areas left in Fig 1(e), i.e., the areas which are less than T_2 pixels are removed as shown in Fig. 1(f). However, selecting a suitable threshold is a challenging task. If small threshold values are selected there are chances of retaining uninfected areas of small size and if large threshold values are selected there are chances of eliminating the lesion areas. Hence, fixing up a suitable threshold T_2 such that there are less probability for lesion areas to be missing. Fig 2 shows the extracted lesion areas of Fig. 1(a). While extracting lesion areas we have considered k pixels around the seed point of lesions. However, selecting a suitable k value is a challenging task. If small k value is selected there are chances of losing lesion information and if large k value is selected there are chances of extracting adjacent lesions information.

From Fig 2 it is observed that extracted lesions include lesion area and also healthy area. Therefore CIELAB color model is used to segment the lesion area from the healthy area. CIELAB is an approximately uniform color system. Its values are calculated by non-linear transformations of CIE XYZ. In this system, Y represents the brightness (or luminance) of the color, while X and Z are virtual (or not physically realizable) components of the primary spectra. The CIE XYZ tristimuli are standardized with values corresponding to the D65 white point: $X_0 = 95.047$, $Y_0 = 100$, $Z_0 = 108.883$. It is then transformed into the standardized tristimuli to the CIELAB Cartesian coordinate system using the following metric lightness function.

$$L = \begin{bmatrix} 166\times(Y/Y_0)^{1/3} - 16 & for\,(Y/Y_0)^{1/3} > 0.00856 \\ 903.3\times(Y/Y_0) & otherwiswe \end{bmatrix} \qquad (2)$$

The chromacity coordinates a* and b* are derived using:

$$a^* = 500\times[\,(X/X_0)^{1/3} - (Y/Y_0)^{1/3}\,]$$
$$b^* = 200\times[\,(Y/Y_0)^{1/3} - (Z/Z_0)^{1/3}\,] \qquad (3)$$

The chromacity coordinates represent opponent red-green scales (+ a red, - a greens) and opponent blue-yellow scales (+ b yellows, - b blues). Since color of the healthy area in the extracted lesions varies from light green to dark green, the chromacity coordinate a^* is used to segment lesion from the healthy area. The a^* value is calculated for each extracted lesion image pixel. If the value of a^* is greater than a predefined threshold then the corresponding pixel is considered as a lesion pixel else it is considered as a healthy pixel. Segmented Frog-eye spot lesion areas of Fig 2 using CIELAB color model are shown in Fig 3.

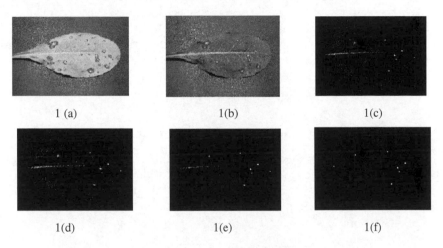

1 (a)   1(b)   1(c)

1(d)   1(e)   1(f)

Fig. 1 (a)-1(f). Segmentation of frog-eye spot lesion areas on a tobacco seedling leaf

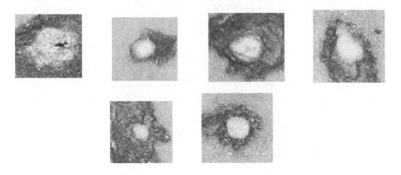

Fig. 2. Extracted Frog-eye spot lesion areas of Fig. 1(a)

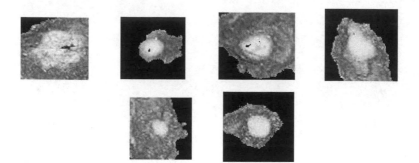

Fig. 3. Segmented Frog-eye spot lesion areas of Fig. 2 using CIELAB color model

3   Evaluation of Proposed Segmentation Algorithm

Measuring the performance of a segmentation algorithm is necessary for two reasons: based on a performance metric, good parameter settings can be found for a segmentation algorithm and the performance of different segmentation approaches can be compared. The region based measures are used when the size and location measurement of the area of the object is essential and is the objective of the segmentation. Therefore, the following region based measures are used to evaluate the proposed segmentation algorithm.

3.1   Measure of Overlap (Jaccard Similarity Measure)

This measure is also known as the area overlap measure (AOM) or the Jaccard similarity measure [16] and is defined as the ratio of the intersection of segmented lesion area S and ground truth lesion area G and the union of segmented lesion area S and ground truth area G. Measure of overlap (MOL) is given in equation 4.

$$MOL = \frac{|S \cap G|}{|S \cup G|} \tag{4}$$

where

$$MOL = Measure\,of\,ovrerlap$$
$$S = Segmented\;area$$
$$G = Ground\,truth\,area$$

3.2   Measure of under Segmentation

This measure is defined as the ratio of the unsegmented lesion area U and the ground truth lesion area G [16]. Measure of under segmentation (MUS) is given in equation 5.

$$MUS = \frac{|U|}{|G|} \tag{5}$$

Where

$U =$ *Unsegmented lesion area*

$G =$ *Ground truth area*

$$U = |G \backslash (S \cap G)|$$

Where

$S =$ *Segmented area*

3.3   Measure of over Segmentation

This measure is defined as the ratio of the segmented non-lesion area V and the ground truth area G [16]. Measure of over segmentation (MOS) is given in equation 6.

$$MOS = \frac{|V|}{|S|} \tag{6}$$

Where

$V =$ *Segmented non – lesion area*

$S =$ *Segmented lesion area*

$$V = |S \backslash (S \cap G)|$$

Where

$G =$ *Ground truth lesion area*

3.4   Dice Similarity Measure (DSM)

Dice similarity measure (DSM) is derived from a reliability measure known as the kappa statistic [17] and computes the ratio of the intersection area divided by the mean sum of each individual area. Let C denote the contour of the segmented area, C_r the reference contour, $A(C)$ the set of pixels enclosed by contour C, $A(C_r)$ the set of pixels enclosed by contour C_r and $|C|$ the cardinality of set C. Then the Dice similarity measure (DSM) is defined as.

$$DSM = \frac{2 \times |A(C) \cap A(C_r)|}{|A(C) + A(C_r)|} \tag{7}$$

3.5   Error Rate (ER)

The error rate ER is defined as the normalized agreement of segmentation results and the ground truth [17]. Let C denote the contour of the segmented area, C_r the reference contour, $A(C)$ the set of pixels enclosed by contour, $|C|$ the cardinality of set C, and $\oplus$ exclusive or logical operation. The error rate ER is given in equation 8.

$$ER = \frac{\left|A(C) \oplus A(C_r)\right|}{\left|A(C) + A(C_r)\right|} \tag{8}$$

3.6 Precision

Precision is the fraction of segmented areas that are relevant to the query. It is given by

$$Precision = \frac{\left|\{Relevant\ areas\}\right| \cap \left|\{Segmented\ areas\}\right|}{\left|\{Segmented\ areas\}\right|} \tag{9}$$

3.7 Recall

Recall is is the fraction of the areas that are relevant to the query that are successfully segmented. It is given by

$$Recall = \frac{\left|\{Relevant\ areas\}\right| \cap \left|\{Segmented\ areas\}\right|}{\left|\{Relevant\ areas\}\right|} \tag{10}$$

4 Experimental Results

4.1 Dataset

Images of tobacco leaves in colour are acquired using a Sony digital colour camera in an uncontrolled real tobacco field. The colour signals from the camera are transferred as a 24 bit RGB colour image data (1632 × 1224) using a personal computer. The leaves used for imaging are randomly selected from the tobacco seedling bed at Central Tobacco Research Institute (CTRI), Hunsur, Karnataka, India and captured at uncontrolled lighting condition. A total of 400 areas are extracted from 50 frog-eye infected leaves of tobacco seedlings using the segmentation algorithm proposed in section 2. To set up the threshold values of parameters m, T_1, T_2 and k, we conducted experimentation by varying the values of parameters. Experimentally it is found that the values of T_1, T_2, m and k are 0.5, 60, 200 and 25 respectively. i.e., for these values proposed segmentation algorithm has achieved best segmentation performance results.

4.2 Results

The segmentation performance is calculated based on the comparison between the manually segmented ground truth G for lesion area and segmentation result S generated by the image segmentation approach. In order to corroborate the efficacy of the proposed segmentation algorithm, six performance measures such as Measure of overlapping (MOL), Measure of under-segmentation (MUS), Measure of over-segmentation (MOS), Dice similarity measure (DSM), Error-rate (ER), Precision (P) and Recall (R) are calculated for 400 segmented areas of 50 frog-eye spot infected tobacco seedling leaves. Segmentation performance results of proposed segmentation algorithm and the existing segmentation algorithm [1] for representative sample shown in figure 1 are tabulated in Table 1 and Table 2 respectively. Precision and recall results of proposed segmentation algorithm for representative samples are tabulated in Table 3. Average segmentation performance results of 400 extracted lesions for both proposed segmentation algorithm and the existing segmentation algorithm [1] are calculated and tabulated in Table 4. A segmentation algorithm is said to be superior when performance parameters MOL, DSM, Precision and Recall are high and MUS, MOS and ER are low. From Table 4 it is understood that the proposed segmentation algorithm has achieved high value for MOL, DSM, Precision and Recall and low value for MUS, MOS and ER when compared to the existing segmentation algorithm [1].

Table 1. Segmentation performance results of proposed segmentation algorithm for representative sample shown in Fig.1

Lesions	MOL	MUS	MOS	DSM	ER
1	0.6682	0.2366	0.0952	0.8011	0.1999
2	0.7792	0.0104	0.2104	0.8759	0.1241
3	0.6925	0.1906	0.1169	0.8183	0.1817
4	0.7052	0.0228	0.2720	0.8271	0.1729
5	0.6849	0.0328	0.2823	0.8130	0.1870
6	0.7861	0.0219	0.1920	0.8803	0.1197

Table 2. Segmentation performance results of the existing segmentation algorithm [1] for representative sample shown in Fig.1

Lesions	MOL	MUS	MOS	DSM	ER
1	0.4285	0.5651	0.0064	0.5999	0.4001
2	0.3804	0.1066	0.5130	0.5511	0.4489
3	0.4847	0.4733	0.0420	0.6529	0.3471
4	0.6412	0.0427	0.3161	0.7814	0.2186
5	0.5871	0.3286	0.0843	0.7398	0.2602
6	0.5237	0.0171	0.4592	0.6874	0.3126

Table 3. Precision and recall results of proposed segmentation algorithm for representative samples

Samples	Precision	Recall
T1	1	1
T2	0.8571	0.5455
T3	0.7143	0.6667
T3	1	0.7500
T4	1	1
T5	1	1
T6	1	1
T7	0.9091	0.7692
T8	0.8333	0.7143
T9	1	0.9167
T10	1	1

Table 4. Performance results of proposed segmentation algorithm and the existing segmentation algorithm [1]

Segmentation performance measures	Proposed segmentation algorithm	Segmentation algorithm [1]
Average MOL	0.7371	0.4915
Average MUS	0.0952	0.1851
Average MOS	0.1677	0.3234
Average DSM	0.8270	0.6496
Average ER	0.1730	0.3504
Average Precision	0.9472	0.9472
Average Recall	0.8122	0.8122

5   Conclusion

In this work a model for segmenting frog-eye spots lesions in tobacco seedlings has been developed. Lesion areas are segmented efficiently using image enhancement, dilation and erosion operations and color segmentation using CIELAB color model. Proposed segmentation algorithm has evaluated by performance measures. Proposed segmentation algorithm is superior when compared to the existing algorithm [1]. In future we will extend this work to other tobacco seedlings diseases.

References

1. Guru, D.S., Mallikarjuna, P.B., Manjunath, S.: Segmentation and Classification of Tobacco Seedling Diseases. In: COMPUTE 2011 Proceedings of the Fourth Annual ACM Bangalore Conference (2011)

2. Vizhanyo, T., Felfoldi, J.: Enhancing colour differences in images of diseased mushrooms. Computers and Electronics in Agriculture 26, 187–198 (2000)
3. Camargo, A., Smith, J.S.: An image-processing based algorithm to automatically identify plant disease visual symptoms. Biosystem Engineeing 102, 9–21 (2009)
4. Pydipati, R., Burks, T.F., Lee, W.S.: Identification of citrus disease using color texture features and discriminant analysis. Computers and Electronics in Agriculture 52, 49–59 (2006)
5. Sena, D.G., Pinto, F.A.C.: Fall Armyworm Damged Maize Plant Identification using digital Images. Biosystem Engineeing 85(4), 449–454 (2003)
6. Huang, K.: Application of artificial neural network for detecting phalaenopsis seedling diseases using color and texture features. Computers and Electronics in Agriculture 57, 3–11 (2007)
7. Zhang, Y., Mao, H., Hu, B., Li, M.: Features selection of cotton disease Leaves Image Based on Fuzzy Feature selection techniques. In: Proceedings of the 2007 International Conference on Wavelet Analysis and Pattern Recognition, pp. 124–129 (2007)
8. Weizheng, S., Yachun, W., Zhanliang, C., Hongda, W.: Grading Mehod of Leaf Spot Disease Based on Image processing. In: 2008 International Conference on Computer Science and Software Engineering, pp. 491–494 (2008)
9. Youwen, T., Tianlai, L., Yan, N.: The recognition of Cucumber Disease Based on Image Processing and Support Vector Machine. In: 2008 Congress on Image and Signal Processing, pp. 262–267 (2008)
10. Mirik, M., Michels Jr., G.J., Kassymzhanova-Mirik, S., Elliott, N.C., Catana, V., Jones, D.B., Bowling, R.: Using digital image analysis and spectral reflectance data to quantify damage by greenbug (Hemitera: Aphididae) in winter wheat. Computers and Electronics in Agriculture 51, 86–98 (2006)
11. Muhammed, H.H.: Hyperspectral Crop Reflectance Data for characterizing and estimating Fungal Disease severity in Wheat. Biosystem Engineeing 95(1), 9–20 (2005)
12. Zhang, Y.C., Mao, H.P., Hu, B., Li, M.X.: Features Selection of Cotton leaves Image based on Fuzzy Feature Selection Techniques. In: International Conference on Wavelet Analysis and Pattern Recognition, pp. 124–129 (2007)
13. Zhou, L., Tong, X. J.: Application of Two-Dimension Wavelet Transform in Image process of Pests in Stored Grain. Seventh International Conference on Machine Learning and Cybernetics, pp. 2790-2793 (2008)
14. Cho, J., Choi, J., Qiao, M., Ji, C., Kim, H., Uhm, K., Chon, T.: Automatic identification of whiteflies, aphids and thrips in greenhouse based on image analysis. International Journal of Mathematics and Computers in Simulation 1(1), 46–53 (2007)
15. Gonzalez, R.C., Woods, R.E., Eddins, S.L.: Digital Image Processing using Matlab. Pearson Education (2007)
16. Elter, M., Held, C., Wittenberg, T.: Contour tracing for segmentation of mammographic masses. Physics in Medicine and Biology 55, 5299–5315 (2010)
17. Yuan, X., Situ, N., Zouridakis, G.: A narrow band graph partitioning method for skin lesion segmentation. Pattern Recognition 42, 1017–1028 (2009)

Password Authentication Using Context-Sensitive Associative Memory Neural Networks: A Novel Approach

P.E.S.N. Krishna Prasad[1], B.D.C.N. Prasad[2],
A.S.N. Chakravarthy[3], and P.S. Avadhani[4]

[1] Department of CSE,
Aditya Engineering College, Kakinadas, India
[2] Dept. of Computer Applications,
P V P Siddhartha Institute of Technology, Vijayawada, India
[3] Department of CSE & IT, Sri Aditya Engineering College, Kakinada, India
[4] Dept. of CS & SE, Andhra University, Visakhapatnam, India
{1surya125,2bdcnprasad}@gmail.com,
{3asnchakravarthy,4psavadhani}@yahoo.com

Abstract. Passwords are the most widely used form of authentication. In many systems the passwords, on the host itself, are not stored as plain text but are encrypted. However, conventional cryptography based encryption methods are having their own limitations, either in terms of complexity or in terms of efficiency. The conventional verification table approach has significant drawbacks and storing passwords in password table is one of the drawbacks.

In the present paper, we propose a cognitive neural model using Context-Sensitive Associative Memory Model(CSAM) for password authentication, which is derived from cognitive domain and vector logic. According to the model, the product of two vectors is an associative memory(context-dependent) that plays critical role in the neural networks domain. In this model the output (encrypted password) is associated with the Kronecker Product of an input (key) and a context (password). The encrypted password is decoded with key and the context-dependent memory (Krnocker product) to get the original password. The proposed system provides better accuracy and quicker response time to authenticate the password but this model requires more space for holding context-dependent associative memory.

Keywords: Password Authentication, Cryptography, Associaitive neural memory, Kronecker Product, context-sensitive memory models.

1 Introduction

Security is a broad topic which covers many issues. Security is essential for data operation today. Information or commerce exchanges need security and reliability. Authentication is a critical part of any network security policy.In fact,

N. Meghanathan et al. (Eds.): CCSIT 2012, Part II, LNICST 85, pp. 454–468, 2012.

Authentication is the act of confirming the truth of an attribute of a datum or entity. This might involve confirming the identity of a person, tracing the origins of an artifact, ensuring that a product is what it's packaging and labeling claims to be, or assuring that the computer program is a trusted one. One familiar use of authentication and authorization is access control. Authentication validates the identity of a user or device. When using a mutual authentication scheme, not only the client is authenticated, but also the network itself. In remotely accessed computer systems the user authenticates/identifies himself to the system by sending a secret password.

Process of authentication can be defined as developing a unique mapping process from given secret password to some other unique information in a defined domain. The guarantee of security doesn't only depend on unique mapping but greatly depend upon difficulties associated with getting back the password from the mapped formation. Password authentication is the foremost mechanism for verifying the identity of computer users, even though it is well known that people frequently choose passwords that are vulnerable to dictionary attacks. The motivation for addressing the security and shortcomings of traditional password-based authentication is that users tend to choose passwords that are easy to remember, which in the case of textual passwords usually implies that they are easy to obtain by searching through a carefully formed dictionary" of candidate passwords[1].

A computer system that is supposed to be used only by those authorized must attempt to detect and exclude the unauthorized. Its access is, therefore, usually controlled by insisting on the authentication procedure to establish, with some degree of confidence, the identity of the user, hence granting those privileges as may be authorized to that identity[2].

Common examples of access control involving authentication include:

1. A captcha is a means of asserting that a user is a human being and not a computer program.
2. A computer program using a blind credential to authenticate another program
3. Entering a country with a passport
4. Logging in to a computer
5. Using a confirmation E-mail to verify ownership of an e-mail address
6. Using an Internet banking system
7. Withdrawing cash from an ATM.

1.1   Password

Use of strong passwords lowers overall risk of a security breach, but strong passwords do not replace the need for other effective security controls. The effectiveness of a password of a given strength is strongly determined by the design and implementation of the authentication system software, particularly how frequently password guesses can be tested by an attacker and how securely information on user passwords is stored and transmitted. Risks are also posed by several means of breaching computer security which are unrelated to password strength.

1.2   Password Authentication

The idea of password assignment is to base the authentication of an identity on something the user knows. In other words, the distinguishing characteristic is knowledge. In a security perspective it should be seen as a user-remembered key. Password should ideally be a random string of letters, numbers and other symbols, which is far from reality in most of the systems. The whole notation of passwords is based on an oxymoron. The idea is to have a random string that is easy to remember.

Drawbacks with traditional password authentication:

1. User password is difficult to memorize.
2. User cannot freely choose the password
3. User cannot change his password
4. It cannot stand with forgery attack.

Our proposed method can stand with Replay and forgery attacks. Many of the deficiencies of password authentication systems arise from the limitations of human memory. If human were not required to remember the password, a maximally secure password would be one with maximum entropy: it would consist a string as long as the system allows, with characters selected from all those allowed by the system. Some passwords are very easy to remember, but also very easy to guess with dictionary searches. In contrast, some passwords are very secure against guessing but difficult to remember[1].

The biggest problem with the above systems is that they are vulnerable to "over the shoulder" attacks where someone can simply observe the combination and ordering of images used to login to the system. This problem is not unique to graphical authentication systems as it is still possible to observe finger movement of a slow typist to discern a password in a traditional password system although the traditional password model avoids the direct over the shoulder attack by hiding the entered password behind asterixes or a similar typographical symbol or glyph which is not possible when the user needs to click on an images. The traditional password model also fails in this respect as key presses can be logged by specialized hardware or software to reconstruct the password.

An additional problem is the small number of combinations available. If you have 4 stages of 16 images each there ares 65536 combinations which are trivial for a computer to brute force if no restriction is placed on maximum number of trails. It is therefore required to protect the system further using either delays between attempts (with a maximum number of attempts) or increasing delays between attempts to discourage automated brute forcing of the combination.

Password strength is a measure of the effectiveness of a password in resisting the guessing and brute-force attacks. In its usual form, it estimates how many trials an attacker who does not have direct access to the password would need, on average, to guess it correctly. The strength of a password is a function of length, complexity, and unpredictability[3].

1.3 Alphanumeric Password (Textual)

Alphanumeric password is derived from a Character Set. There are so many types of Character sets depending upon the application where we need authentication. One of the well known Character Set is the American Standard Code for Information Interchange (ASCII). It is a character-encoding scheme based on the ordering of the English alphabet. ASCII includes definitions for 128 characters: 33 are non-printing control characters (now mostly obsolete) that affect how text and space is processed; 94 are printable characters, and the space is considered as an invisible graphic. A common attack against password authenticated system is the dictionary attack. An attacker can write a program that, imitating a legitimate user, repeatedly tries different passwords, say from a dictionary, until it gets the correct password. We present an alternative defence against dictionary attacks by using Graphical password [2].

1.4 Graphical Password

The most common computer authentication method is to use alphanumerical usernames and passwords. This method has a significant drawbacks. For example, users tend to pick passwords that can be easily guessed. On the other hand, if a password is hard to guess, then it is often hard to remember. To address this problem, we a developed authentication method that use pictures as passwords.

Usage of graphics (images) instead of alphanumerical passwords is based on two neglected facts:

1. A picture is worth a thousand words.
2. Humans remember pictures better than words.

Although, the main argument for graphical passwords is that people are better at memorizing graphical passwords than text-based passwords, the existing user studies are very limited and there is not yet convincing evidence to support this argument. Our preliminary analysis suggests that it is more difficult to break graphical passwords using the traditional attack methods such as brute force search, dictionary attack, or spyware. However, since there is not yet wide deployment of graphical password systems, the vulnerabilities of graphical passwords are still not fully understood [2].

Conversion of image to matrix (or text). By using the following procedure it can be converted any image into a matrix, consisting of a set of numbers representing all the pixels of the image. After converting image[2] into a matrix consisting of set of numbers that gives as input to the neural network and the network train with image matrix servers as a training sample.

One ought to read color of each pixel of the image, and to convert the color into red, green and blue (RGB) parts, as each color can be produced using these colors.

$$\begin{pmatrix} 135 & 206 & 235 & 154 & 85 & 25 & 69 & 158 & \dots\dots\dots 196 \\ 148 & 58 & 157 & 35 & 154 & 129 & 35 & 78 \dots\dots\dots\dots 254 \\ \multicolumn{8}{c}{\dots\dots\dots\dots\dots\dots\dots\dots\dots\dots\dots\dots\dots\dots\dots\dots\dots\dots\dots\dots} .45 \\ \multicolumn{8}{c}{\dots\dots\dots\dots\dots\dots\dots\dots\dots\dots\dots\dots\dots\dots\dots\dots\dots\dots\dots\dots} .255 \\ 148 & 58 & 157 & 35 & 154 & 129 & 35 & 78\dots\dots\dots\dots 148 \end{pmatrix}$$

Fig. 1. Matrix representation of an image

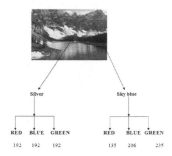

Fig. 2. Reading pixel values

2   Cognitive Domain and Vector Logic

Cognitive functions[10, 13, 14] rely on the extensive use of information stored in the brain, and the searching for the relevant information for solving some problem is a very complex task. Human cognition largely uses biological search engines, and assuming that to study cognitive function need to understand the way these brain search engines work. The approach is to study multi modular network models, able to solve particular problems that involve information searching. The building blocks of these multi modular networks are the context dependent memory models.

These models work by associating an output to the Kronecker product[3, 10] of an input and a context. Input, context and output are vectors that represent cognitive variables[3, 10–12]. The present model constitute a natural extension of the traditional linear associator, showing that coding the information in vectors that are processed through association matrices, allows for a direct contact between these memory models and some procedures that are now classical in the Information Retrieval field. One essential feature of context-dependent models is that they are based on the thematic packing of information, where by each context points to a particular set of related concepts. The thematic packing can be extended to multi modular networks involving input-output contexts, in order to accomplish more complex tasks. Contexts act as passwords that elicit the appropriate memory to deal with a query. We also show toy versions of several "neuromimetic" devices that solve cognitive tasks as diverse as decision making or word sense disambiguation. The functioning of these multi modular networks can be described as dynamical systems at the level of cognitive variables.

Vector logic is a mathematical model of logic in which the truth values are mapped on elements of a vector space. The binary logical functions are performed by rectangular matrices operating on the Kronecker product of their vectorial arguments. The binary operators acting on vectors representing ambiguous (fuzzy) truth values generate many-valued logics. "Eduardo Mijraji[10, 13]" showed that, within the formalism of vector logic, it becomes possible to obtain truth-functional definitions of the modalities "possibility" and "necessity". These definitions are based on the matrix operators that represent disjunction and conjunction respectively, and each modality emerges by means of an iterative process.

The mathematical representations of logic have opened illuminating perspectives for the understanding of the logical constructions created by the humans. These representations have also provided us with powerful technical instruments that present a wide spectrum of applications. Recently, an algebraic representation of the propositional calculus in which the truth values are mapped on the elements of a vector space has been described. In this representation, the logical computations are performed by matrix operators[6]. In particular, binary operations are executed by rectangular matrices that act over the Kronecker product of their vectorial arguments. This algebraic model of logic has been denominated "vector logic", and has been discovered for investigating a neural model.

3   Context-Sensitive Auto-associative Memories

Memory plays a major role in Artificial Neural Networks[10, 13]. Without memory, Neural Network cannot be learned itself. One of the primary concepts of memory in neural networks is Associative neural memories[25]. It accesses the memory by its contents, not by where it is stored in the neural pathways of the brain. This is very powerful; given even a poor photograph of a person we are quite good at reconstructing the persons face quite accurately. This is very different from a traditional computer where specific facts are located in specific places in computer memory. If only partial information is available about this location, the memory cannot be recalled at all.

Traditional measures of associative memory performance are its memory capacity and content-addressability. Memory capacity refers to the maximum number of associated pattern pairs that can be stored and correctly retrieved while content addressability is the ability of the network to retrieve the correct stored pattern. Obviously, the two performance measures are related to each other.

Associative neural memories[7] are concerned with associative learning and retrieval of information (vector patterns) in neural networks. These networks represent one of the most extensively analyzed classes of artificial neural networks. One of the primary functions of the brain is associative memory. It associate the faces with names, letters with sounds, or we can recognize the people even if they have sunglasses or if they are somehow elder now.

Associative memories can be implemented either by using feed forward or recurrent neural networks. Such associative neural networks are used to associate one set of vectors with another set of vectors, say input and output patterns. The aim of an associative memory is, to produce the associated output pattern whenever one of the input patterns is applied to the neural network. The input pattern may be applied to the network either as input or as initial state and the output pattern is observed at the outputs of some neurons constituting the network.

According to the way that the network handles errors at the input pattern, they are classified as interpolative and accretive memory. In the interpolative memory it is allowed to have some deviation from the desired output pattern when added some noise to the related input pattern. However, in accretive memory, it is desired the output to be exactly the same as the associated output pattern, even if the input pattern is noisy. The memory in which the associated input and output patterns differ is called hetero-associative memory, and called auto-associative memory if they are the same - another classification.

Context-sensitive auto-associative memories[5, 8] are models that allow the retrieval of different vectorial responses given the same vectorial stimulus, depending on the context presented to the memory. The contextualization is obtained by the Kronecker product between two vectorial entries to the associative memory: the key stimulus and the context. These memories are able to display a wide variety of behaviors that range from all the basic operations of the logical calculus (including fuzzy logics) to the selective extraction of features from complex vectorial patterns.

In the present contribution, we show that a context-dependent memory matrix stores a large amount of possible virtual associative memories that awaken in the presence of a context. It shows how the vectorial context allows a memory matrix to be representable in terms of its singular-value decomposition. We describe a neural interpretation of the model in which the Kronecker product is performed on the same neurons that sustain the memory.

The present investigation explores, with numerical experiments, the reliability of chains of contextualized associations. In some cases, random disconnection produces the emergence of oscillatory behaviors of the system. The current task results in that associative chains retain their performances for relatively large dimensions. Finally, it analyze the properties of some modules of context-dependent auto associative memories inserted in recursive nets: the perceptual auto organization in the presence of ambiguous inputs (e.g. the disambiguation of the Necker's cube figure), the construction of intersection filters, and the feature extraction capabilities.

A system of networks consisting of first net which constructs the Kronecker product between two vectors and then sends it to the second net that sustains a correlation memory, defines a context-sensitive associative memory. In the real nervous system of higher mammals, the anatomy of the neural connections surely exhibits a considerable amount of local imprecision superimposed on a regular global layout. In order to evaluate the potentialities of the multiplicative devices to constitute plausible biological models, we analyze the performances of a context-sensitive memory when the multiplicative net, responsible for the construction of the Kronecker product, presents an incomplete connectivity. The investigation shows that a large dimensional system is able to support a considerable amount of incompleteness in the connectivity without a great deterioration of the memory. It establishs a scaling relationship between the degree of incompleteness, the capacity of the memory, and the tolerance threshold to imperfections in the output. And then it analyzes some performances that show the versatility of this kind of network to represent a variety of functions. These functions include a context-modulated novelty filter, a network that computes logical modalities and an adaptive searching device.

3.1 Kronecker Product and the Vector Operator

Let A be an $m \times n$ matrix and B an $p \times q$ matrix. The $m.n \times p.q$ matrix is called the Kronecker product[30] of A and B.

The resultant matrix is represented as

$$A \otimes B = \begin{pmatrix} a_{1,1}B & a_{1,2}B & \dots & a_{1,n}B \\ a_{2,1}B & a_{1,2}B & \dots & a_{1,n}B \\ \cdot & \cdot & \dots & \cdot \\ \cdot & \cdot & \dots & \cdot \\ \cdot & \cdot & \dots & a_{n,p}B \\ a_{m,1}B & a_{m,2}B & \dots & a_{m,n}B \end{pmatrix}$$

Some Properties of Kronecker Product: It is also called the tensor product. Some properties of the Kronecker product[30] as:

- for a scalar a, $a \otimes A = A \otimes a = a.A$,
- for scalars a and b, $aA \otimes bB = abA \otimes B$,
- for conforming matrices, $(A \otimes B)(C \otimes D) = AC \otimes BD$,
- $(A \otimes B)^T = A^T \otimes B^T$, $(A \otimes B)^H = A^H \otimes B^H$,
- for vectors a and b, $a^T \otimes b = ba^T = b \otimes a^T$,
  (Note: $a.a^T = a \otimes a^T$),
- for square nonsingular matrices A and B:
  $(A \otimes B)^{-1} = A^{-1} \otimes B^{-1}$
- $tr(A \otimes B) = tr(A).tr(B)$,
- $rank(A \otimes B) = rank(A).rank(B)$.

In addition to these properties, some more properties can be attributed to kronecker product, the present task needs these properties which are included in the list mentioned.

3.2 Numerical Example for Encoding and Decoding

A simple example is illustrated with a mathematical model, how the encoding and decoding mechanism applied on textual and graphical password for encoding and decoding approaches.

Let A and B be the two matrices of sizes 3×3 and 2×2, given as

$$A = \begin{pmatrix} 1 & 1 & 0 \\ 0 & 1 & 1 \\ 1 & 0 & 1 \end{pmatrix}_{3\times 3} \quad \& \quad B = \begin{pmatrix} 1 & 0 \\ 1 & 1 \end{pmatrix}_{2\times 2}$$

Encoding Matrix as Memory matrix. The resultant of matrix is represented as a memory matrix M, as encoded matrix of $A \otimes B$:

$$E(M) = A \otimes B = \begin{pmatrix} 1 & 0 & 1 & 0 & 0 & 0 \\ 1 & 1 & 1 & 1 & 0 & 0 \\ 0 & 0 & 1 & 0 & 1 & 0 \\ 0 & 0 & 1 & 1 & 1 & 1 \\ 1 & 0 & 0 & 0 & 1 & 0 \\ 1 & 1 & 0 & 0 & 1 & 1 \end{pmatrix}$$

Decoding Matrix as original input A. Let the matrix B is supplied as one of the input to decoding matrix and the second one as the encoded matrix M and then to get the resultant matrix as original matrix A, on needs yo follow as:

$$M_1 = E(M).B_1 \text{ where } B_1 \text{ is } 1^{st} \text{ column vector}$$

$$M_1 = \begin{pmatrix} 1 & 0 & 1 & 0 & 0 & 0 \\ 1 & 1 & 1 & 1 & 0 & 0 \\ 0 & 0 & 1 & 0 & 1 & 0 \\ 0 & 0 & 1 & 1 & 1 & 1 \\ 1 & 0 & 0 & 0 & 1 & 0 \\ 1 & 1 & 0 & 0 & 1 & 1 \end{pmatrix} \cdot \begin{pmatrix} 1 \\ 1 \end{pmatrix}$$

$$M_1 = \begin{pmatrix} 1 & 1 & 0 \\ 2 & 2 & 0 \\ 0 & 1 & 1 \\ 0 & 2 & 2 \\ 1 & 0 & 1 \\ 2 & 0 & 2 \end{pmatrix}$$

$$M_1^T = \begin{pmatrix} 1 & 2 & 0 & 0 & 1 & 2 \\ 1 & 2 & 1 & 2 & 0 & 0 \\ 0 & 0 & 1 & 2 & 1 & 2 \end{pmatrix}$$

$$M_2 = M_1^T.B_2$$

(Note: 2 denotes second column vector of B)

$$M_2 = M_1^T . \begin{pmatrix} 0 \\ 1 \end{pmatrix}$$

$$M_2 = \begin{pmatrix} 2\ 0\ 2 \\ 2\ 2\ 0 \\ 0\ 2\ 2 \end{pmatrix}$$

Finally, $A = \lambda.M_2^T = \begin{pmatrix} 1\ 1\ 0 \\ 0\ 1\ 1 \\ 1\ 0\ 1 \end{pmatrix}$

where $\lambda = 0.5$, here A is a Password matrix and B is a Key matrix.

4   Algorithm for Encoding and Decoding the Password

4.1   Password Encoding

The procedure for encoding a password P with the given key K is as follows:

A context-dependent associative memory M acting as encoding model is a matrix

$$M = \sum_{i=1}^{m} P_i[P_i \bigotimes \sum_{j(i)} K_j]^T \tag{1}$$

where P_i are column vectors password (the set P is chosen orthonormal), and $K_{j(i)}$ are column vectors mapping to Key accompanying the ith password (also an orthonormal set).

By feeding the context-sensitive associative module M with Key K, the system retrieves the possible password associated with the key.

At resting conditions the system is grounded in an indifferent state g. The mathematics of the model implies the priming of the memory with a linear combination which has an equal weight

$$M(g \bigotimes I_{m \times n}) = \sum_{i} < P_i, g > P_i(\sum_{j(i)} K_j^T) = \sum_{i} P_i(\sum_{j(i)} K_j)^T \tag{2}$$

where $g = \sum_i P_i$ and I is the $n \times n$ identity matrix. From (2) it is evident that, after the priming, the context-dependent memory becomes a classical memory associated password with the specified key.

4.2   Password Decoding

The procedure for decoding matrix is as follows:

Step 1: Initial Memory matrix:

$$M_0 = E(M) \tag{3}$$

Step 2: For each column vector of K_j, where j^{th} column
do

$$M_j = M_{j-1}^T.K_i \tag{4}$$

Step 3:

$$M_j = M_j^T \tag{5}$$

repeat the steps 2 and 3 until for all j columns of K.

Step 4: if $P == \lambda.M_j^T$ then

    the decoded matrix is the original matrix P

      else

    the decoded matrix is not an original matrix P

    where λ is a learning constant.

The structural representation of Context-sensitive associative memory model (CSAM) for password authentication is represented in Figure 3, Figure 3(a) represents encoding process and Figure 3(b) represents decoding process

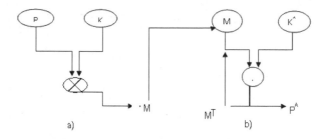

Fig. 3. Password authentication using CSAM

5   Result Analysis

Authentication process can be done through both normal text as one input and image as another input. Using both input the chosen model encoding into memory model and then decoding the memory model through either normal text password as one input to get the image or chosen image as another input to get the normal password. The process is presented below:

1. Text password is given by the user. Any password using a particular character set can be used. Suppose to enhance the security then the given text password can be normalized using any available normalization process. The input of textual password is shown in Figure 4
2. Now an image can be given as input by choosing any image from the available source or from data repository. Then the result process is shown in Figure 5
3. When the text and image are given as input to the system, then system immediately encodes these two passwords by applying encoding technique of the chosen model and then the result is stored onto the database in the form of encoded representation. The process is shown in Figure 6

Fig. 4. Text as one input

Fig. 5. Image as another input

Fig. 6. Encryption

4. In the decoding process, choose text as one input and the encoded data as another input. By applying decoding mechanism of the associative memory model to get the chosen image as output to the environment. The result status is shown in Figure 7

5. In the decoding process choose image as one input and the encoded data as another input. By applying decoding mechanism of the associative memory model to get the original text password as output to the environment. The result status is shown in Figure 8

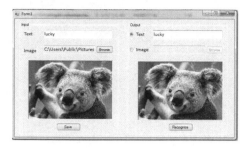

Fig. 7. Decryption through text

Fig. 8. Decryption through image

6   Conclusion

Memory is not just a passive store for holding ideas without changing them; it may transform those ideas when they are being retrieved. There are many examples showing that what is retrieved is different from what was initially stored. Simple Associative memories are static and contain very low memory so that they cannot be applied in the applications where high memory is required. A simple model describing context-dependent associative memories generates a good vectorial representation of basic logical calculus. One of the powers of this vectorial representation is the very natural way in which binary matrix operators are capable to compute ambiguous situations. This fact presents a biological interest because of the very natural way in which the human mind is able to take decisions in the presence of uncertainties. Also these memories could be used to develop expert agents to the recent problem domain.

Converting text password to binary form and converting image to binary form is a big issue here in this method. If we choose images which are having more pixel density the encoding and decoding processes will take more time. To overcome this problem less density images can be used or changing image from one format to other format will also reduce the image density value.

Context-sensitive associative neural memory model is more powerful and more secure model for authentication both textual passwords and image passwords.

For normal case of textual passwords,either private key, public key using some available mechanisms or any user defined key is used as another input to this model to encrypt and decrypt into original one.

Using the present model,some applications like banking, email, mobile based devices, to provide better and better security than the currently available mechanisms like DES and AES algorithms.

References

1. Doja, M.N., Kumar, N.: User Authentication Schemes For Mobile And Handheld Devices. INFOCOMP - Journal of Computer Science 7(4) (December 2008)
2. Krishna Prasad, P.E.S.N., Chakravarthy, A.S.N., Avadhani, P.S.: A Probabilistic Approach For Authenticating Text Or Graphical Passwords Using Back Propagation. IJCSNS International Journal of Computer Science and Network Security 11(5) (May 2011)
3. Mizraji, E., Pomi, A., Valle-Lisboa, J.C.: Dynamic searching in the brain. Cogn. Neurodyn. 3, 401–414 (2009)
4. Cyber Security Tip ST04-002. Choosing and Protecting Passwords. US CERT (retrieved June 20, 2009)
5. Pomi, A., Olivera, F., Mizraji, E.: Context-sensitive auto-associative memories as expert systems in medical diagnosis. BMC Medical Informatics & Decision Making (2006)
6. Hugues, G.E., Cresswell, M.J.: An Introduction to Modal Logic. Methuen, London (1972)
7. Prasad, B.D.C.N., Krishna Prasad, P.E.S.N.: A Study on Associative Neural Memories. (IJACSA) International Journal of Advanced Computer Science and Applications 1(6) (December 2010)
8. Prasad, B.D.C.N., Krishna Prasad, P.E.S.N., Sagar, Y.: A Comparative Study of Machine Learning Algorithms as Expert Systems in Medical Diagnosis (Asthma). In: Meghanathan, N., Kaushik, B.K., Nagamalai, D. (eds.) CCSIT 2011, Part I. CCIS, vol. 131, pp. 570–576. Springer, Heidelberg (2011)
9. Horng, G.: Password authentication without using password table. Inform. Processing Lett. 55, 247–250 (1995)
10. Mizraji, E.: Modalities in Vector Logic. Notre Dame Journal of Formal Logic 35(2) (Spring 1994)
11. Mizraji, E.: Reasoning with associative memories. Biological Complexity (1997)
12. Udi, M.: A simple scheme to make passwords based on one-way function much harder to crack. Computer Security 15(2), 171–176 (1996)
13. Pomi, A., Eduardo, M.: Semantic Graphs & Associative memories. Physical Review (2004)
14. Pomi, A., Eduardo, M., Alvarez, F.: Multiplicative contexts in associative memories. Biosystems 32, 145–161 (1994)
15. Eduardo, M.: Context-dependent associations in Linear distributed Memories. Bulletin Math., Biol., 195–205 (1989)
16. Pomi, A., Eduardo, M., Valle-Lishoa, C.J.: Dynamic searching in the Brain. Cognitive Neurodynamics, 401–414 (2009)
17. Mello, S.D., Franklin, S., Ramamurthy, U., Buars, B.: A cognitive Science based Machine Learning Architecture. AAAI (2006)

18. Mizraji, E.: Neural Memories and Search Engines. International Journal of General Systems 37(6), 715–732 (2008)
19. Mizraji, E., Lin, J.: A dynamical approach to logical decisions. Complexity 2, 56–63 (1997)
20. Mizraji, E., Lin, J.: Fuzzy decisions in modular neural networks. Int. J. Bifurcation and Chaos 11, 155–167 (2001)
21. Pomi, A., Mizraji, E.: A cognitive architecture that solves a problem stated by Minsky. IEEE on Systems, Man and Cybernetics B (Cybernetics) 31, 729–734 (2001)
22. Biddle, R., Chiasson, S., van Oorschot, P.C.: Graphical Passwords: Learning from the First Twelve Years. Technical Report TR-11-01, School of Computer Science, Carleton University (January 4, 2011)
23. Ku, W.-C.: Weaknesses and Drawbacks of a Password Authentication Scheme Using Neural Networks for Multiserver Architecture. IEEE Transactions on Neural Networks 16(4) (July 2005)
24. Obaidat, M.S., Macchiarolo, D.T.: An on-line neural-network system for computer access security. IEEE Trans. Ind. Electron. 40, 235–242 (1993)
25. A multilayer neural-network system for computer access security. IEEE Trans. Syst., Man, Cybern. 24, 806–813 (1994)
26. Schmidt, T., Rahnama, H., Sadeghian, A.: A Review of Applications of Artificial Neural Networks in Cryptosystems. In: Seventh International Symposium on Neural Networks, Shanghai, China, June 6-9 (2010)
27. Agarwal, G., Shukla, R.S.: Security Analysis of Graphical Passwords over the Alphanumeric Passwords. Int. J. Pure Appl. Sci. Technol. (2010)
28. Suo, X., Zhu, Y., Scott Owen, G.: Graphical Passwords: A Survey. In: Proceedings of 21st Annual Computer Security Applications Conference, Tucson, Arizona, December 5-9 (2005)
29. Pomi-Brea, A., Mizraji, E.: Memories in context. BioSystems 50, 173–188 (1999)
30. van Loan, C.F.: The ubiquitous Kronecker Product. JCAM (Elsevier), 85–100 (1999)

A Heuristic Approach for Community Detection in Protein Networks

Sminu Izudheen[1] and Sheena Mathew[2]

[1] Department of Computer Science,
Rajagiri School of Engineering & Technology
sminu_i@rajagirtech.ac.in
[2] Division of Computer Science, School of Engineering,
Cochin University of Science & Technology
sheenamathew@cusat.ac.in

Abstract. Protein-protein interactions play a vital role in identifying the outcome of a vast majority of cellular mechanisms. But analyzing these complex data to identify community structures which can explain the activities of protein networks were always been a challenge. This paper reports the use of triangular modularity of protein network as an effective method to identify these community structures.

Keywords: Community Detection, Protein-Protein Interaction, Protein Networks, Spectral Optimization.

1   Introduction

Proteins involved in the same cellular processes often interact with each other, and these protein-protein interactions are fundamental to almost all biological processes [1]. The protein systems undergoing interactions with other polypeptides are particularly rich of natively unfolded tracts and these unfolded patches were discovered to be involved in both protein-protein interactions and aggregation in many different systems [2], [3]. Several efforts have been made to identify these interactions, so that biological systems can be understood better. With the emergence of a variety of techniques like yeast-two-hybrid, mass spectrometry and protein chip technologies, enormous amount of protein-protein interaction data are available [4]. However, due to the limitations in the techniques to handle such data, analysis of data in terms of biological function has not kept pace with data acquisition.

Protein complexes performing a specific biological function often contain highly connected protein modules [4]. These connected modules can be considered as community structures of protein networks. Even though community structures can better explain the activities of protein networks, this area is not well explored. But as identifying these community structures could be able to produce some useful findings, there exists some scope in investigating more on this. This motivated us to carry out

N. Meghanathan et al. (Eds.): CCSIT 2012, Part II, LNICST 85, pp. 469–475, 2012.
© Institute for Computer Sciences, Social Informatics and Telecommunications Engineering 2012

the present investigations on community structures and the results obtained prove that it is a promising method to detect community structures in protein networks.

A number of methods are proposed to detect community structures in complex networks. These include hierarchical clustering, graph partitioning based on network modularity, k-clique percolation, and many others [5]. Nevertheless, we preferred to make use of the decomposition algorithm (GN algorithm) proposed by Newman and Girvan due to its ability not only to divide networks effectively, but also to refuse to divide them when no good division exists.

2   Methods

2.1   Triangular Modularity Detection

The concept of community structure in complex networks was first pointed out in the by Girvan and Newman [6], and it refers to the fact that nodes in many real networks appear to group in subgraphs in which the density of internal connections is larger than the connections with the rest of nodes in the network. One of the most successful approaches to identify the community structure of complex networks is through the quality function called *modularity* [6], [7], which will define modules as well as provide a quantitative measure to find them. Here, we use motifs in the network to detect sub structures in a network. The modularity for weighted directed networks [8] is calculated as:

$$Q(C) = \frac{1}{2w} \sum_{i=1}^{N} \sum_{j=1}^{N} \left(w_{ij} - \frac{w_i^{out} w_j^{in}}{2w} \right) \delta(C_i, C_j), \tag{1}$$

where w_{ij} is the weight of the connection from the ith to the jth node, $w_i^{out} = \sum_j w_{ij}$ represents the output strength and $w_j^{in} = \sum_i w_{ij}$ the input strength, $2w = \sum_{ij} w_{ij}$ gives the total strength of the network, C_i is the index of the community to which the node i belongs, and the Kronecker δ is 1 if nodes i and j are in the same community, and 0 otherwise. For undirected networks, $w_i^{out} = w_i^{in} \equiv w_i$.

Given a partition C of an unweighted network, motif modularity can be represented as the fraction of motifs inside the communities minus the fraction in a random network [9], given by

$$Q_M(C) = \frac{\sum\limits_{i1i2...iM} \prod\limits_{(a,b) \in EM} W_{iaib}(C)}{\sum\limits_{i1i2...iM} \prod\limits_{(a,b) \in EM} W_{iaib}} - \frac{\sum\limits_{i1i2...iM} \prod\limits_{(a,b) \in EM} n_{iaib}(C)}{\sum\limits_{i1i2...iM} \prod\limits_{(a,b) \in EM} n_{iaib}}. \tag{2}$$

where

$$n^{ij} = w_i^{out} w_j^{in},$$
$$w_{ij}(C) = w_{ij}\delta(C_i, C_j)$$
$$n_{ij}(C) = n_{ij}\delta(C_i, C_j)$$

This can be extended to find the community of triangles in a network. Applying equation (2), triangle motif can be expressed as

$$Q_\Delta(C) = \frac{\sum\limits_{ijk} w_{ij}(C)w_{jk}(C)w_{ki}(C)}{\sum\limits_{ijk} w_{ij}w_{jk}w_{ki}} - \frac{\sum\limits_{ijk} n_{ij}(C)n_{jk}(C)n_{ki}(C)}{\sum\limits_{ijk} n_{ij}n_{jk}n_{ki}}. \tag{3}$$

2.2   Triangular Modularity in Protein Networks

Protein interactions can be compared with an undirected graph with proteins as vertices and interactions as edges. We represented this interaction as an adjacency matrix. To detect the community structure in the protein network, we identified the triangular motifs in the network. Since we are considering an undirected graph, the triangle modularity [10] can be represented as

$$Q_\Delta(C) = \sum_i \sum_j \sum_k B_{ijk}\delta(C_i, C_j)\delta(C_j, C_k)\delta(C_k, C_i). \tag{4}$$

where

$$B_{ijk} = \frac{w_{ij}w_{jk}w_{ki}}{\sum\limits_i \sum\limits_j \sum\limits_k w_{ij}w_{jk}w_{ki}} - \frac{(w_iw_j)(w_jw_k)(w_kw_i)}{\sum\limits_i \sum\limits_j \sum\limits_k (w_iw_j)(w_jw_k)(w_kw_i)}.$$

2.3   Spectral Optimization of Triangular Modularity in Protein Networks

Once we have the triangular modularity, next task is to define some optimization algorithm to calculate the modularity value. This is important since large number of traids can be formed. Here we propose spectral optimization [10] to perform this task. To detect the community structure in a network, eigen spectrum of the modularity matrix is used. We compute the leading eigenvector of the modularity matrix and divide the vertices into two groups according to the signs of the elements in this vector, with vertices whose corresponding elements are positive moves to one group and the rest moves to the other group. This process is repeated recursively, giving two partitions in each step until no new splits are possible.

One of the advantages of this algorithm over conventional partitioning methods is that, there is no need to constrain the group sizes or artificially forbid the trivial solution with all vertices in a single group. If there is no positive eigenvalues of the modularity matrix, then the leading eigenvector is the vector (1,1,1, ...) corresponding to all vertices in a single group. In this case, the algorithm is telling us that there is no division of the network that results in positive modularity. Hence the algorithm has the ability not only to divide networks effectively, but also to refuse to divide them when no good division possible.

To perform spectral optimization on the modularity value calculated in equ.(4), we need to perform some transformations. In Belkacem Serrour et al [11], triangular modularity is reduced to standard spectral form as:

$$Q_\triangle(S) = \frac{3}{4} \sum_i \sum_j s_i M_{ij} s_j .$$ (5)

where

$$M_{ij} = \sum_k B_{ijk} .$$

2.4   Kernighan-Lin Optimization on Protein Networks

During each iteration of the algorithm, before dividing the network into two communities, the groups created by the spectral optimization is further improved by applying Kernighan-Lin optimization [12]. KL algorithm moves the vertices among the two groups to increase the modularity. For an arbitrary two-way partition S, the algorithm partition S into two sets A and B such that external cost is minimized. Suppose A^* and B^* represents a minimum cost two-way partition, then algorithm identifies $X \subset A$ and $Y \subset B$ with $|X| = |Y| \leq n/2$, such that interchanging X and Y produces A* and B*. In order to find X and Y from A and B without finding all possible choices, maximize the gain value,

$$g = D_a + D_b - 2c_{a,b} .$$ (6)

where, $c_{a,b}$ is the cost between vertices a and b, and D_a and D_b are the difference between external and internal cost given by

$$D_a = \sum_{y \in B} C_{ay} - \sum_{x \in A} C_{ax} .$$ (7)

$$D_b = \sum_{y \in A} C_{by} - \sum_{x \in B} C_{bx} .$$ (8)

We have applied KL optimization on sub groups created from Spectral optimization. Following steps are performed to identify X from A. First, D values for all elements in the group are calculated and the one with maximum value is selected as a_1. Second, set aside a_1 and recalculate D for the set $A-\{a_1\}$. Continue the same until all nodes are exhausted, identifying $a_1, a_2, .. a_n$. Repeat the same on B to identify $b_1, b_2, .. b_n$.

Calculate the corresponding gain g_1, g_2, .. g_n. Choose k to maximize the gain $G = \sum_{i=1}^{k} g_i$ and select X as $a_1, a_2, .. a_k$ and Y as $b_1, b_2, .. b_k$. If $G>0$, reduction in cost of G can be achieved, which means we can interchange X and Y between A and B. If $G=0$, we have arrived at a local minimum and we have to repeat the steps by taking a_2 and b_2 as pivot elements. Results obtained shows that we will be able to reach a global optimum maximum in three iterations.

2.5   Dataset

For the present study protein interaction data is downloaded from MIPS [13] and MINT [14] databases.

3   Results

In this section we presents the results of the spectral optimization of triangular modularity applied to real protein interaction data from individually performed experiments. The results are then simulated using NS2. Fig.1 shows the simulated result for data downloaded from MIPS database. It represents the interaction between 193 different proteins represented as a protein interaction network. Here, shown as groups are the communities detected when we optimize the triangular modularity of the network.

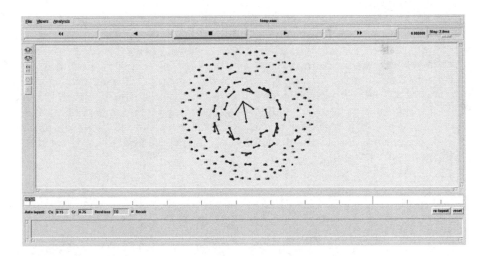

Fig. 1. Communities detected by optimizing triangular modularity of protein interaction data downloaded from MIPS

Fig.2 represents the protein interaction network of 205 different human proteins downloaded from MINT. From the figure it is clear that the algorithm is able to detect communities from this network also.

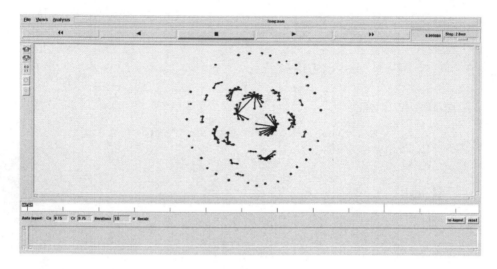

Fig. 2. Communities detected by optimizing triangular modularity of protein interaction data downloaded from MINT

4   Conclusion

In this paper, we have demonstrated the use of triangular modularity as a promising method to analyze protein interactions. The method proved to be powerful in extracting community structures from protein networks. To show this, we have used Newman-Girvan algorithm to calculate triangular modularity. The modified algorithm have been tested on protein interaction data retrieved from databases like MIPS and MINT and are able to recover community patterns in protein networks.   Hence community structure prediction proposed here can be applied to complex disease network to explore the relationship between human genetic disorders and the corresponding disease genes.

References

1. Hakes, L., Lovell, S.C., Oliver, S.G., et al.: Specificity in protein interactions and its relationship with sequence diversity and coevolution. PNAS 104(19), 7999–8004 (2007)
2. Uversky, V.N., Segel, D.J., Doniach, S., Fink, A.L.: Association-induced folding of globular proteins. Proc. Natl. Acad. Sci. USA, 5480–5483 (1998,95)
3. Zbilut, J.P., Colosimo, A., Conti, F., Colafranceschi, M., Manetti, C., Valerio, M., Webber Jr., C.L., Giuliani, A.: Protein aggregation/folding: the role of deterministic singularities of sequence hydrophobicity as determined by nonlinear signal analysis of acylphosphatase and Abeta (1-40). Biophys. J. 85, 3544–3557 (2003)

4. Harwell, L.H., Hopfield, J.J., Leibler, S., Murray, A.W.: From molecular to modular cell biology. Nature 402, c47–c52 (1999)
5. Bader, D., et al.: Approximating betweenness centrality. Georgia Institute of Technology (2007)
6. Girvan, M., Newman, M.E.: Community structure in social and biological networks. Proc. Natl. Acad. Sci. USA 99, 7821–7826 (2002)
7. Newman, M.E.J., Girvan, M.: Finding and evaluating community structure in networks. Phys. Rev. E 69, 026113 (2004)
8. Arenas, A., Duch, J., Fernández, A., Gómez, S.: Size reduction of complex networks preserving modularity. New J. Phys. 9, 176 (2007)
9. Arenas, A., Fernández, A., Fortunato, S., Gómez, S.: Motif-based communities in complex networks. Journal of Physics A: Mathematical and Theoretical 41, 224001 (2008)
10. Newman, M.E.J.: Modularity and community structure in networks. Proceedings of the National Academy of Sciences USA (103), 8577 (2006)
11. Serrour, B., Arenas, A., Gómez, S.: Detecting communities of triangles in complex networks using spectral optimization. Computer Communications (May 11, 2010)
12. Kernighan, B.W., Lin, S.: An efficient heuristic algorithm for partitioning graphs. The Bell System Technical Journal (February 1970)
13. Munich Information Center for Protein Sequences, http://www.helmholtz-muenchen.de/en/mips/home/index.html
14. MINT: the Molecular INTeraction database, http://mint.bio.uniroma2.it/mint/Welcome.do

Single Reduct Generation by Attribute Similarity Measurement Based on Relative Indiscernibility

Shampa Sengupta[1] and Kr. Das[2]

[1] M.C.K.V. Institute of Engineering - 243, G.T. Road (North),
Liluah, Howrah 711204, West Bengal
[2] Bengal Engineering and Science University,
Shibpur, Howrah 711103, West Bengal
shampa2512@yahoo.co.in, akdas@cs.becs.ac.in

Abstract. In real world everything is an object which represents particular classes. Every object can be fully described by its attributes. Any real world dataset contains large number of attributes and objects. Classifiers give poor performance when these huge datasets are given as input to it for proper classification. So from these huge dataset most useful attributes need to be extracted that contribute the maximum to the decision. In the paper, attribute set is reduced by generating reducts using the indiscernibility relation of Rough Set Theory (RST). The method measures similarity among the attributes using relative indiscernibility relation and computes attribute similarity set. Then the set is minimized and an attribute similarity table is constructed from which attribute similar to maximum number of attributes is selected so that the resultant minimum set of selected attributes (called reduct) cover all attributes of the attribute similarity table. The method has been applied on glass dataset collected from the UCI repository and the classification accuracy is calculated by various classifiers. The result shows the efficiency of the proposed method.

Keywords: Rough Set Theory, Attribute Similarity, Relative Indiscernibility Relation, Reduct.

1 Introduction

In general, considering all attributes highest accuracy of a classifier should be achieved. But for real-world problems, there is huge number of attributes, which degrades the efficiency of the Classification algorithms. So, some attributes need to be neglected, which again decrease the accuracy of the system. Therefore, a trade-off is required for which strong dimensionality reduction or feature selection techniques are needed. The attributes contribute the most to the decision must be retained. Rough Set Theory (RST) [1, 2], new mathematical approach to imperfect knowledge, is popularly used to evaluate significance of attribute and helps to find minimal set of attribute called reduct. Thus a reduct is a set of attributes that preserves partition. It means that a reduct is the minimal subset of attributes that enables the same classification of elements of the universe as the whole set of attributes. In other words, attributes that do not belong to a reduct are superfluous with regard to classification of elements of the universe. Hu et al. [3] developed two new algorithms

N. Meghanathan et al. (Eds.): CCSIT 2012, Part II, LNICST 85, pp. 476–487, 2012.
© Institute for Computer Sciences, Social Informatics and Telecommunications Engineering 2012

to calculate core attributes and reducts for feature selection. These algorithms can be extensively applied to a wide range of real-life applications with very large data sets. Jensen et al. [4] developed the Quickreduct algorithm to compute a minimal reduct without exhaustively generating all possible subsets and also they developed Fuzzy-Rough attribute reduction with application to web categorization. Zhong et al. [5] applies Rough Sets with Heuristics (RSH) and Rough Sets with Boolean Reasoning (RSBR) are used for attribute selection and discretization of real-valued attributes. Komorowsk et al. [6] studies an application of rough sets to modelling prognostic power of cardiac tests. Bazan [7] compares rough set-based methods, in particular dynamic reducts, with statistical methods, neural networks, decision trees and decision rules. Carlin et al. [8] presents an application of rough sets to diagnosing suspected acute appendicitis.

The main advantage of rough set theory in data analysis is that it does not need any preliminary or additional information about data like probability in statistics [9], or basic probability assignment in Dempster-Shafer theory [10], grade of membership or the value of possibility in fuzzy set theory [11] and so on. But finding reduct for classification is an NP-Complete problem and so some heuristic approach should be applied.

In the paper, a novel reduct generation method is proposed based on the indiscernibility relation of rough set theory. In the method, a new kind of indiscernibility, called relative indiscernibility of an attribute with respect to other attribute is introduced. This relative indiscernibility relation induces the partitions of attributes, based on which similarity between conditional attributes is measured and an attribute similarity set (ASS) is obtained. Then, the similarity set is minimized by removing the attribute similarities having similarity measure less than the average similarity. Lastly, an attribute similarity table is constructed for ASS each row of which describes the similarity of an attribute with some other attributes. Then traverse each row and select the attribute of that row which has maximum similar attributes. Next, all the rows associated with the selected attribute and its similar attributes are deleted from the table and similarly select another attribute from the modified table. The process continued until all the rows are deleted from the table and finally, selected attributes, covering all the attributes are considered as reduct, a minimum set of attributes.

The rest of the paper is organized as follows: Similarity measurement of attributes by relative indiscernibility and single reduct generation are described in section 2 and section 3 respectively. Section 4 explains the experimental analysis of the proposed method and finally conclusion of the paper is stated in section 5.

2   Relative Indiscernibility and Dependency of Attributes

Formally, a decision system DS can be seen as a system $DS = (U, A)$ where U is the universe (a finite set of objects, $U = <x_1, x_2,...x_m>$) and A is the set of attributes such that $A = C \cup D$ and $C \cap D = \emptyset$ where C and D are the set of condition attributes and the set of decision attributes, respectively.

2.1   Indiscernibility

A per the discussion in section 2, each attribute $a \in A$ defines an information function: $f_a : U \rightarrow V_a$, where V_a is the set of values of a, called the domain of attribute. Every subset of attributes P determines an indiscernibility relation over U, and is denoted as $IND(P)$, which can be defined as, $IND(P) = \{(x, y) \in U \times U \mid \forall\ a \in P,\ f_a(x) = f_a(y)\}$. For each set of attributes P, an indiscernibility relation IND(P) partitions the set of objects into a m-number of equivalence classes [ ] defined as partition U/IND(P) or U/P is equal to $\{[x]_p\}$ where $|U/P| = m$. Elements belonging to the same equivalence class are indiscernible; otherwise elements are discernible with respect to P. If one considers a non-empty attributes subset, $R \subset P$ and $IND(R) = IND(P)$, then $P - R$ is dispensable. Any minimal R such that $IND(R) = IND(P)$, is a minimal set of attributes that preserves the indiscernibility relation computed on the set of attributes P. R is called reduct of P and denoted as R = RED(P). The core of P is the intersection of these reductions, defined as $CORE(P) = \cap RED(P)$. Naturally, the core contains all the attributes from P which are considered of greatest importance for classification, i.e., the most relevant for a correct classification of the objects of U. On the other hand, none of the attributes belonging to the core may be neglected without deteriorating the quality of the classification considered, that is, if any attribute in the core is eliminated from the given data, it will be impossible to obtain the highest quality of approximation with the remaining attributes.

2.2   Relative Indiscernibility

Here, the relation is defined based on the same information function: $f_a : U \rightarrow V_a$ where V_a is the set of values of a, called the domain of attribute. Every conditional attribute Ai of C determines an relative (relative to decision attribute) indiscernibility relation (RIR) over U, and is denoted as RIRD(A$_i$), which can be defined by equation (1).

$$RIR_D(A_i) = \{(x, y) \in \Pi_{A_i}[x]_D \times \Pi_{A_i}[x]_D \mid f_{A_i}(x) = f_{A_i}(y) \forall\ [x]_D \in U/D\} \qquad (1)$$

For each conditional attribute A_i, a relative indiscernibility relation RIR$_D(A_i)$ partitions the set of objects into a n-number of equivalence classes [ ] defined as partition U/ $RIR_D(A_i)$ or U$_D$/A$_i$ is equal to $\{[x]_{A_{i/D}}\}$ where $|\ U_D/A_i\ | = n$. Obviously, each equivalence class $\{[x]_{A_{i/D}}\}$ contains objects with same decision value which are indiscernible by attribute A$_i$.

To illustrate the method, a sample dataset represented by Table 1 is considered with eight objects, four conditional and one decision attributes.

Table 1. Sample Dataset

	Diploma(i)	Experience(e)	French(f)	Reference(r)	Decision
x_1	MBA	Medium	Yes	Excellent	Accept
x_2	MBA	Low	Yes	Neutral	Reject
x_3	MCE	Low	Yes	Good	Reject
x_4	MSc	High	Yes	Neutral	Accept
x_5	MSc	Medium	Yes	Neutral	Reject
x_6	MSc	High	Yes	Excellent	Reject
x_7	MBA	High	No	Good	Accept
x_8	MCE	Low	No	Excellent	Reject

Table 2. Equivalence classes induces by indiscernibility and relative indiscernibility relations

Equivalence classes for each attribute by relation IND(P)	Equivalence classes for each conditional attribute by relative indiscernibility relation RIRD(A_i)
$U/_D = (\{x_1, x_4, x_7\}, \{x_2, x_3, x_5, x_6, x_8\})$	$UD/_i = (\{x_1, x_7\}, \{x_2\}, \{x_3, x_8\}, \{x_4\}, \{x_5, x_6\})$
$U/_i = (\{x_1, x_2, x_7\}, \{x_3, x_8\}, \{x_4, x_5, x_6\})$	$UD/_e = (\{x_1\}, \{x_5\}, \{x_2, x_3, x_8\}, \{x_4, x_7\}, \{x_6\})$
$U/_e = (\{x_1, x_5\}, \{x_2, x_3, x_8\}, \{x_4, x_6, x_7\})$	$UD/_f = (\{x_1, x_4\}, \{x_2, x_3, x_5, x_6\}, \{x_7\}, \{x_8\})$
$U/_f = (\{x_1, x_2, x_3, x_4, x_5, x_6\}, \{x_7, x_8\})$	$UD/_r = (\{x_1\}, \{x_6, x_8\}, \{x_2, x_5\}, \{x_4\}, \{x_3, x_7\})$
$U/_r = (\{x_1, x_6, x_8\}, \{x_2, x_4, x_5\}, \{x_3, x_7\})$	

2.3 Attribute Similarity

An attribute A_i is similar to another attribute A_j in context of classification power if they induce the same equivalence classes of objects under their respective relative indiscernible relations. But in real situation, it rarely occurs and so similarity of attributes is measured by introducing the similarity measurement factor which indicates the degree of similarity of one attribute to another attribute. Here, an attribute Ai is said to be similar to an attribute A_j with degree of similarity (or similarity factor) $\delta_f^{i,j}$ and is denoted by $A_i \rightarrow A_j$ if the probability of inducing the same equivalence classes of objects under their respective relative indiscernible relations is $(\delta_f^{i,j} \times 100)\%$, where $\delta_f^{i,j}$ is computed by equation (2). The details for computation of similarity measurement for the attribute similarity Ai $\rightarrow$ Aj (Ai $\neq$ Aj) is described in algorithm "SIM_FAC" below.

$$\delta_f^{i,j} = \frac{1}{|U_D/A_i|} \sum_{[x]_{A_{i/D}} \in U_D/A_i} \frac{1}{|[x]_{A_{i/D}}|} \max_{[x]_{A_{j/D}} \in U_D/A_j} ([x]_{A_{i/D}} \cap [x]_{A_{j/D}}) \qquad (2)$$

Algorithm: SIM_FAC(A_i , A_j)/* Similarity factor computation for attribute similarity Ai $\rightarrow$ Aj */
Input: Partitions $U_D/A_i = \{[x]_{A_{i/D}}\}$ and $U_D/A_j = \{[x]_{A_{j/D}}\}$

         obtained by applying relative indiscernibility relation
         RIR_D on A_i and A_j respectively.
Output: Similarity factor $\delta_f^{i,j}$

Begin
    For each conditional attribute A_i {
        /* compute relative indiscernibility RIRD (A_i) using (1)*/

$$RIR_D(A_i) = \{(x,y) \in \Pi_{A_i}[x]_D \times \Pi_{A_i}[x]_D \mid f_{A_i}(x) = f_{A_i}(y) \forall [x]_D \in U/D\}$$

```
        RIR_D (A_i) induces equivalence classes U_D/A_i = {[x]_{A_{i/D}}}
} /*end of for*/
/* similarity measurement of A_i to A_j */
```
$$\delta_f^{i,j} = 0$$
```
For each [x]_{i/D} ∈ U_D/A_i
{    max_overlap = 0
    For each [x]_{j/D} ∈ U_D/A_j
    {    overlap = |[x]_{i/D} ∩ [x]_{j/D}|
        if (overlap > max_overlap) then
                max_overlap = overlap
    }
```
$$\delta_f^{i,j} = \delta_f^{i,j} + \frac{max\_overlap}{|[x]_{i/D}|}$$
```
}
```
$$\delta_f^{i,j} = \frac{\delta_f^{i,j}}{|U_D/A_i|}$$
```
End.
```

To illustrate the attribute similarity computation process, attribute similarity and its similarity factor are listed in Table 2 for all attributes of Table 1.

Table 3. Describe the degree of similarity of all pair of attributes

Attribute Similarity $(A_i \rightarrow A_j)$	Equivalence Classes by $RIR_D(A_i)$ (U_D/A_i)	Equivalence Classes by $RIR_D(A_j)$ (U_D/A_j)	Similarity factor of A_i to A_j $(\delta_f^{i,j})$
i → e	$\{x_1, x_7\}$, $\{x_2\}$, $\{x_3, x_8\}$, $\{x_4\}$, $\{x_5, x_6\}$	$\{x_1\}$, $\{x_5\}$, $\{x_2, x_3, x_8\}$, $\{x_4, x_7\}$, $\{x_6\}$	$\delta_f^{i,e} = 0.8$
i → f	$\{x_1, x_7\}$, $\{x_2\}$, $\{x_3, x_8\}$, $\{x_4\}$, $\{x_5, x_6\}$	$\{x_1, x_4\}$, $\{x_2, x_3, x_5, x_6\}$, $\{x_7\}$, $\{x_8\}$	$\delta_f^{i,f} = 0.8$
i → r	$\{x_1, x_7\}$, $\{x_2\}$, $\{x_3, x_8\}$, $\{x_4\}$, $\{x_5, x_6\}$	$\{x_1\}$, $\{x_6, x_8\}$, $\{x_2, x_5\}$, $\{x_4\}$, $\{x_3, x_7\}$	$\delta_f^{i,r} = 0.7$
e → i	$\{x_1\}$, $\{x_5\}$, $\{x_2, x_3, x_8\}$, $\{x_4, x_7\}$, $\{x_6\}$	$\{x_1, x_7\}$, $\{x_2\}$, $\{x_3, x_8\}$, $\{x_4\}$, $\{x_5, x_6\}$	$\delta_f^{e,i} = 0.83$
e → f	$\{x_1\}$, $\{x_5\}$, $\{x_2, x_3, x_8\}$, $\{x_4, x_7\}$, $\{x_6\}$	$\{x_1, x_4\}$, $\{x_2, x_3, x_5, x_6\}$, $\{x_7\}$, $\{x_8\}$	$\delta_f^{e,f} = 0.83$
e → r	$\{x_1\}$, $\{x_5\}$, $\{x_2, x_3, x_8\}$, $\{x_4, x_7\}$, $\{x_6\}$	$\{x_1\}$, $\{x_6, x_8\}$, $\{x_2, x_5\}$, $\{x_4\}$, $\{x_3, x_7\}$	$\delta_f^{e,r} = 0.76$

Table 3. (*Continued*)

$f \rightarrow i$	$\{x_1, x_4\}, \{x_2, x_3, x_5, x_6\},$ $\{x_7\}, \{x_8\}$	$\{x_1, x_7\}, \{x_2\}, \{x_3, x_8\},$ $\{x_4\}, \{x_5, x_6\}$	$\delta_f^{f,i} = 0.75$
$f \rightarrow e$	$\{x_1, x_4\}, \{x_2, x_3, x_5, x_6\},$ $\{x_7\}, \{x_8\}$	$\{x_1\}, \{x_5\}, \{x_2, x_3, x_8\},$ $\{x_4, x_7\}, \{x_6\}$	$\delta_f^{f,e} = 0.75$
$f \rightarrow r$	$\{x_1, x_4\}, \{x_2, x_3, x_5, x_6\},$ $\{x_7\}, \{x_8\}$	$\{x_1\}, \{x_6, x_8\}, \{x_2, x_5\},$ $\{x_4\}, \{x_3, x_7\}$	$\delta_f^{f,r} = 0.75$
$r \rightarrow i$	$\{x_1\}, \{x_6, x_8\}, \{x_2, x_5\},$ $\{x_4\}, \{x_3, x_7\}$	$\{x_1, x_7\}, \{x_2\}, \{x_3, x_8\},$ $\{x_4\}, \{x_5, x_6\}$	$\delta_f^{r,i} = 0.7$
$r \rightarrow e$	$\{x_1\}, \{x_6, x_8\}, \{x_2, x_5\},$ $\{x_4\}, \{x_3, x_7\}$	$\{x_1\}, \{x_5\}, \{x_2, x_3, x_8\},$ $\{x_4, x_7\}, \{x_6\}$	$\delta_f^{r,i} = 0.7$
$r \rightarrow f$	$\{x_1\}, \{x_6, x_8\}, \{x_2, x_5\},$ $\{x_4\}, \{x_3, x_7\}$	$\{x_1, x_4\}, \{x_2, x_3, x_5, x_6\},$ $\{x_7\}, \{x_8\}$	$\delta_f^{r,f} = 0.8$

The computation of $\delta_f^{i,j}$ of each attribute similarity using equation (2) in Table 2 can be understood by Table 3, in which similarity i → e in first row of Table 3 is considered, where, $U_D/i = \{x1, x7\}, \{x2\}, \{x3, x8\}, \{x4\}, \{x5, x6\})$ and $U_D/e = \{x1\}, \{x5\}, \{x2, x3, x8\}, \{x4, x7\}, \{x6\}).$

Table 4. Illustrates the similarity factor computation for i → e

$[x]_{i/D}$ of U_D/i	Overlapping $[x]_{e/D}$ of U_D/e with $[x]_{i/D}$ of U_D/i	$[x]_{i/D} \cap [x]_{e/D}$	$T = \dfrac{1}{\lvert[x]_{i/D}\rvert} \displaystyle\max_{[x]_{e/D} \in U_D/e}([x]_{i/D}$ $\cap [x]_{e/D})$
$\{x_1, x_7\}$	$\{x_1\}$ $\{x_4, x_7\}$	$\{x_1, x_7\} \cap \{x_1\}$ $\{x_1, x_7\} \cap \{x_4, x_7\}$	$\dfrac{1}{2}$
$\{x_2\}$	$\{x_2, x_3, x_8\}$	$\{x_2\} \cap \{x_2, x_3, x_8\}$	$\dfrac{1}{1}$
$\{x_3, x_8\}$	$\{x_2, x_3, x_8\}$	$\{x_3, x_8\} \cap \{x_2, x_3, x_8\}$	$\dfrac{2}{2}$
$\{x_4\}$	$\{x_4, x_7\}$	$\{x_4\} \cap \{x_4, x_7\}$	$\dfrac{1}{1}$
$\{x_5, x_6\}$	$\{x_5\}$ $\{x_6\})$	$\{x_5, x_6\} \cap \{x_5\}$ $\{x_5, x_6\} \cap \{x_6\}$	$\dfrac{1}{2}$
$\delta_f^{ie} = \dfrac{1}{\lvert[x]_{i/D}\rvert} \sum_{[x]_{i/D} \in U_D/i} T = \dfrac{1}{5}\left(\dfrac{1}{2}+\dfrac{1}{1}+\dfrac{2}{2}+\dfrac{1}{1}+\dfrac{1}{2}\right) = \dfrac{4}{5} = 0.8$			

2.4   Attribute Similarity Set

For each pair of conditional attributes (Ai, Aj), similarity factor is computed by "SIM_FAC" algorithm, described in section 2.3. The similarity factor of $A_i \rightarrow A_j$ is higher means that the relative indiscernibility relations RIRD(Ai) and RIRD(Aj) produce highly similar equivalence classes. This implies that both the attributes Ai and Aj have almost similar classification power and so $A_i \rightarrow A_j$ is considered as strong similarity of Ai to Aj. Since, for any two attributes Ai and Aj, two similarities $A_i \rightarrow A_j$ and $A_j \rightarrow A_i$ are computed, only one with higher similarity factor is selected in the list of attribute similarity set ASS. Thus, for n conditional attributes, n(n-1)/2 similarities are selected, out of which some are strong and some are not. Out of these similarities, the similarity with $\delta_f^{i,j}$ value less than the average δ_f value are discarded from ASS and rest is considered as the set of attribute similarity. So, each element x in ASS is of the form x: Ai→Aj such that Left(x) = Ai and Right(x) = Aj. The algorithm "ASS_GEN" described below, computes the attribute similarity set ASS.

Algorithm: ASS_GEN(C, δ_f)

```
/* Computes attribute similarity set {Ai→Aj} */
  Input: C = set of conditional attributes and δf =2-D
         contains    similarity factors between each pair
         of conditional attributes.
Output: Attribute Similarity Set ASS
Begin
     ASS = {}, sum_δf = 0
     /* compute only n(n - 1)/2 elements in ASS */
     for i = 1 to |C| - 1
     {  for j = i+1 to |C|
        {  if (δf^{i,j} > δf^{j,i}) then
           {    sum_δf = sum_δf + δf^{i,j}
                ASS = ASS ∪ {Ai → Aj}
           }
           else
           {    sum_δf = sum_δf + δf^{j,i}
                ASS = ASS ∪ {Aj → Ai}
           }
        }
     }
/* modify ASS by only elements Ai → Aj for which δf^{i,j} >avg_δf */
```

$ASS_{mod} = \{\}$

$avg\_\delta_f = (2\times sum\_\delta_f) / |C|(|C|-1)$

```
for each {Ai → Aj}∈ ASS
{    if (δf^{i,j} >avg_δ_f) then
        {    ASSmod = ASSmod ∪ {Ai → Aj}
             ASS = ASS - { Ai → Aj}
        }
}
     ASS = ASSmod
End
```

Algorithm "ASS_GEN" is applied and Table 4 is constructed from Table 2, where only six out of twelve attribute similarities in Table 2 are considered. Thus, initially, ASS = {i → f, i → r, e → i, e → f, e → r, r → f} and $avg\_\delta_f = 0.786$. As the similarity factor for attribute similarities i → f, e → i, e → f and r → f are greater than avg_δ_f, they are considered in the final attribute similarity set ASS. So, finally, ASS = {i → f, e → i, e → f, r → f }.

Table 5. Illustrates the selection of attribute similarities

Attribute Similarity ($A_i{\rightarrow}A_j$; i $\neq$ j and $\delta_f^{i,j} > \delta_f^{j,i}$)	Similarity factor of A_i to A_j ($\delta_f^{i,j}$)	$\delta_f^{i,j} > \delta_f$
i→f	$\delta_f^{i,f} = 0.8$	Yes
i→r	$\delta_f^{i,r} = 0.7$	
e→i	$\delta_f^{e,i} = 0.83$	Yes
e→f	$\delta_f^{e,f} = 0.83$	Yes
e→r	$\delta_f^{e,r} = 0.76$	
r→f	$\delta_f^{r,f} = 0.8$	Yes
Average δ_f	0.786	

3   Single Reduct Generation

The attribute similarity obtained so far is known as simple similarity of an attribute to other attribute. But, for simplifying the reduct generation process, the elements in

ASS are minimized by combining some simple similarity. The new similarity obtained by the combination of some of the simple similarity is called compound similarity. Here, all x from ASS with same Left(x) are considered and obtained compound similarity is Left(x) → ∪ Right(x) ∀x. Thus, introducing compound similarity, the set ASS is refined to a set with minimum elements so that for each attribute, there is at most one element in ASS representing either simple or compound similarity of the attribute. The detail algorithm for determining compound attribute similarity set is given below:

```
Algorithm:   COMP_SIM(ASS)

    /* Compute the compound attribute similarity of attributes*/
    Input: Simple attribute similarity set ASS
    Output: Compound attribute similarity set ASS
    Begin
          for each x ∈ ASS
          {    for each y (•x) ∈ ASS
               {    if(Left(x) = = Left(y)) then
                    {    Right(x) = Right(x) ∪ Right(y)
                         ASS = ASS - {y}
                    }
               }
          }
End
```

Finally, from the compound attribute similarity set ASS, reduct is generated. First of all, select an element, say, x from ASS for which length of Right(x) i.e., |Right(x)| is maximum. This selection guaranteed that the attribute Left(x) is similar to maximum number of attributes and so Left(x) is an element of reduct RED. Then, all elements z of ASS for which Left(z) ⊆ Right(x) are deleted and also x is deleted from ASS. This process is repeated until the set ASS becomes empty which provides the reduct RED. The proposed single reduct generation algorithm is discussed below:

Algorithm: SIN_RED_GEN(ASS, RED)

```
Input: Compound attribute similarity set ASS
Output: Single reduct RED
Begin
        RED = φ
```

```
While (ASS • φ)
{     max = 0
      for each x ∈ ASS
      {  if(|Right(x)| > max) then
         {  max = |Right(x)|
            L = Left(x)
         }
      }
    for each x ∈ ASS
      {     if (Left(x) = = L) then
            {   RED = RED ∪ Left(x)
                R = Right(x)
                ASS = ASS - {x}
                for each z ∈ ASS
                    if(Left(z) ⊆ R) then
                        ASS = ASS - {z}
                break
            }
      }
} /*end-while*/
Return (RED)
End
```

Applying "COMP_SIM" algorithm the set ASS = {i → f, e → i, e → f, r → f} is refined to compound similarity set ASS = {i → f, e → {i, f}, r → f}. So, the selected element from ASS is e → {i, f}, and thus e ∈ RED and ASS is modified as ASS = {r → f}. And, in the next iteration, r ∈ RED and ASS =φ. Thus, RED = {e, r}.

4   Results and Discussions

The proposed method computes a single reduct for glass dataset selected from UCI machine learning repository [12]. At first, all the numeric attributes are discretized by ChiMerge [13] discretization algorithm. To measure the efficiency of the method, k-fold cross-validations, where k ranges from 1 to 10 are carried out on the reduced dataset and classified using "Weka" tool [14]. The proposed method and well known dimensionality reduction methods such as 'Cfs Subset Eval' (CFS) method [15], 'Consistensy Subset Evaluator' (CON) method [16] are applied on the dataset and observed that the proposed method, CFS and CON reduce the number of attributes into six, six and seven whereas the actual number of attributes is nine. Then the reduced dataset is applied on various classifiers and accuracies are measured, listed in Table 5. Average accuracy by proposed method is much higher than that by CFS and CON.

Table 6. Accuracy comparison by proposed, CFS and CON reduction proces

Classifier	Proposed Method	CFS	CON
Naïve Bayes	65.73	43.92	47.20
SMO	62.44	57.94	57.48
KSTAR	83.57	79.91	78.50
AdaBoost	44.60	44.86	44.86
Bagging	76.53	73.83	71.50
Multi Class Classifier	64.32	66.36	64.49
J48	72.30	68.69	64.02
PART	77.00	70.94	68.69
Average accuracy (%)	**68.31**	**63.31**	**62.09**

5   Conclusion

The relative indiscernibility relation introduces in the paper is an equivalence relation which induces a partition of equivalence classes for each attribute. Then, the degree of similarity is measured between two attributes based on their equivalence classes. Since, the target of the paper is to compute reduced attribute set for decision making, so application of equivalence classes for similarity measurement is the appropriate choice.

References

1. Pawlak, Z.: Rough sets. International Journal of Information and Computer Sciences 11, 341–356 (1982)
2. Pawlak, Z.: Rough set theory and its applications to data analysis. Cybernetics and Systems 29, 661–688 (1998)
3. Hu, X., Lin, T.Y., Jianchao, J.: A New Rough Sets Model Based on Database Systems. Fundamental Informaticae, 1–18 (2004)
4. Jensen, R., Shen, Q.: Fuzzy-Rough Attribute Reduction with Application to Web Categorization. Fuzzy Sets and Systems 141(3), 469–485 (2004)
5. Zhong, N., Skowron, A.: A Rough Set-Based Knowledge Discovery Process. Int. Journal of Applied Mathematics and Computer Science 11(3), 603–619 (2005); BIME Journal 05(1) (2005)
6. Komorowski, J., Ohrn, A.: Modelling Prognostic Power of Cardiac tests using rough sets. Artificial Intelligence in Medicine 15, 167–191 (1999)
7. Bazan, J.: A Comparison of dynamic and nondynamic rough set methods for extracting laws from decision tables. In: Rough Sets in Knowledge Discovery. Physica Verlag (1998)
8. Carlin, U., Komorowski, J., Ohrn, A.: Rough Set Analysis of Patients with Suspected Acute Appendicitis. In: Proc., IPMU (1998)

9. Devroye, L., Gyorfi, L., Lugosi, G.: A Probabilistic Theory of Pattern Recognition. Springer, New York (1996)
10. Gupta, S.C., Kapoor, V.K.: Fundamental of Mathematical Statistics. Sultan Chand & Sons, A.S. Printing Press, India (1994)
11. Pal, S.K., Mitra, S.: Neuro-Fuzzy pattern Recognition: Methods in Soft Computing. Willey, New York (1999)
12. Murphy, P., Aha, W.: UCI repository of machine learning databases (1996), http://www.ics.uci.edu/mlearn/MLRepository.html
13. Kerber, R.: ChiMerge: Discretization of Numeric Attributes. In: Proceedings of AAAI 1992, Ninth Int'l Conf. Artificial Intelligence, pp. 123–128. AAAI-Press (1992)
14. WEKA: Machine Learning Software, http://www.cs.waikato.ac.nz/~ml/
15. Hall, M.A.: Correlation-Based Feature Selection for Machine Learning PhD thesis, Dept. ofComputer Science, Univ. of Waikato, Hamilton, New Zealand (1998)
16. Liu, H., Setiono, R.: A Probabilistic Approach to Feature Selection: A Filter Solution. In: Proc.13th Int'l Conf. Machine Learning, pp. 319–327 (1996)

Adaptive QoS-Aware Web Service Composition

Deivamani Mallayya and Baskaran Ramachandran

Anna University, Chennai, 600 025, India
{deivamani,baaski}@cs.annauniv.edu

Abstract. Service oriented architecture is a challenging area to fervently focus on. In that web service composition plays a vital role. The main crux behind composition lies on the effective selection of available web services in order to provide the value added services on the fly. Quality of Service (QoS) is one of the non functional properties of the web services, which is used to evaluate the degree to which the service can satisfy the service request. In the proposed approach, the composition is handled based on the QoS the web service has provided in its previous attempts towards composition. A separate process of updating the beliefs and reputation is been identified which stores the appropriate belief factor against the candidate web service in the process registry. Instead of having the QoS as a constant provider specified value, our approach assigns the value based on the end users feedback. The paper discusses the approach used in identifying the quality of the web service composition and the efficiency of composing relevant services for the service request.

Keywords: Service Composition, Quality-of-Service(QoS), Belief, Graph Construction, Service Oriented Architecture.

1   Introduction

Web services are software application intended to do a particular functionality and thereby obeys all the open standards of service oriented architecture namely WSDL (Web Service Description language) for description of the web service, UDDI (Universal Description, Discovery and Integration) to register the web service to the registry and SOAP (Simple Object Access Protocol) to enquire and access the web services. The service provider creates and registers the web service with the registry. When there is a request for a service, the registry is searched to find the appropriate web service and the same is been delivered back to the requester [1].

Composition was innovated as a single web service could not assure the entire need of the requester. Composition is a service designed from a set of selected web services. Initially, composition was introduced to please the novice's but now it has been welcomed by people of all knowledge level. The main crux of the composition lies behind the effective selection of the web services. Once the services have been identified, the flow between those services has to be judged. This flow of information from one web service to the other should happen synchronously.

N. Meghanathan et al. (Eds.): CCSIT 2012, Part II, LNICST 85, pp. 488–497, 2012.
© Institute for Computer Sciences, Social Informatics and Telecommunications Engineering 2012

Based on the time and methodology by which the candidate web services are transferred as composition, they are named as manual, semi-automatic, automatic or dynamic. The proposed approach concentrates on dynamic composition. Some of the requirements for dynamic web service composition includes: automation, dynamicity, semantic capabilities, QoS awareness, partial observing ability, correctness, scalability, domain independence, and so on. The degree to which these requirements are incorporated determines the efficiency of composition.

Automation is innovated with the intention to minimize the user intervention and thereby minimize the time spent, eliminate the human errors which in turn reduces the overall cost of the system. Dynamicity is the ability of the system to provide a composite service at run time. Compared to static composition, dynamic service composition overcomes the issues like binding the web service which is no longer available at run time (which were available at design time), the services being replaced by the new ones (once they are published by the providers).

Several approaches have been analyzed to provide composition. Semantic capabilities with web services are the much targeted area in SOA [2]. Compared to syntactic similarity, composition based on the semantic similarity gives much meaningful composition. Various tools have been devised to construct ontology, from which the semantics of the service request is been analyzed and selection of candidate web services is been done from the registry. Apart from the core functionality of the web services, the non functional properties like Quality of service (QoS) are also taken into account. The importance of having QoS properties at the constraint in selecting a candidate web service occurs, when the functional requirement stated by the service request is satisfied by more than one service. So if QoS properties are used to compose the web services, we could ensure the composition not only guarantee the service been requested, but also promises quality in the same.

2   Related Work

The QoS parameters of the web service are used in service composition in many ways. The candidate web services are composed to form a composition by plug and play technology. J.L. Pastrana et al has presented a tool for composition which connects the other candidate web services with connectors to which the web services are plugged in at the time of composition [3]. The adaption of the web services to the connectors was done by using OWL ontology.

Ping Wang et al proposed a new method for composition by selecting the correct set of candidate service based on QoS done based on fuzzy linear programming which helps in identifying dissimilarity of service alternatives, selecting the correct candidate service with respect to the users preference and acceptance level [4][5].

Once the services are identified, ranking among them is the most vital task. Ranking among the web services are handled with QoS, a measure of requester's satisfaction or experience with the service [6][11]. Ranking of web service has to be done in the view point of users and system brokers. The relation between the different QoS properties also has to be taken to account. LIU Feng has proposed his research on user aware QoS based web service composition by using quantum based genetic algorithm[9]. Yuan-sheng Luo et al demands that QoS properties which are been locally used for selecting the web service alone would not be sufficient for an efficient web service [15].

3   Service Composition Architecture

A sole web service by itself could not guarantee the intend expectation of the user. And hence the innovation of Web service composition came to picture. **Composition** is a service coined from several candidate web service, served to the requester as a response to the service request. This composition could be carried out in many ways, by using semantics, context, aspects and many more. The main intension behind providing the service composition is to serve the services to the requester in a more efficient manner, and thereby promote the trust and reputation of the service provider with respect to each candidate web service. The driving wheel behind composition is on timing and synchronization of web services.

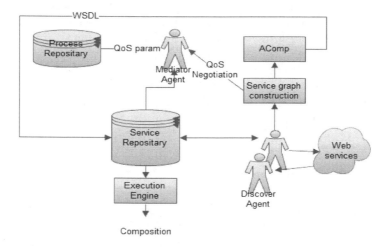

Fig. 1. Architecture of Adaptive QoS- aware Web Service Composition

Our approach to web service composition is based on the non functional property, the QoS. Fig 1 sketches the overall architecture of Adaptive QoS- Aware Web Service Composition. The system consists of five subcomponents: the process repository, the service repository, Service Graph Construction, A-Comp and Execution Engine.

Quality of service properties are used to select the candidate web services from the registry. Based on the type of application, the system is going to function in; the selection of QoS might get changed. In common some of the QoS properties to mention include: availability, importance, cost, runtime, success ratio, trustworthiness, security and so on.

3.1   Construction of QoS-Domain Ontology

The selection of candidate web service and the composition is done with the help of ontology. Ontology is a representation of concepts, their properties and relationship among the concepts. The proposed approach uses extended domain ontology with QoS properties included. A sample rdf format is been shown below [8][14].

```
<webService rdf:id="trainAvailability">
  <functional rdf:id="class">
     ............ .
  </functional>
  <NonFunctional rdf:id="QoS">
    <QoSParam rdf:id="Availability"/>
      <hasImpact>
        <QoSImpact rdf:id ="VeryHigh" />
      </hasImpact>
      <hasRelationship>
        <relationship rdf:id="performance/>
      </hasRelationship>
      <hasMetric>
        <metric rdf:id="successRate"/>
      </hasMetric>
    </QoSParam>
  </NonFunctional>
</webService>
```

3.2   Composition of Web Services

The composition of web services is performed by three steps namely: Selection of web services, Graph Construction and Best path Identification.

Selection of Web Services. A web service composition WS_c, is a service coined from a subset of web services registered in the registry which satisfies the QoS requirements stated by the user. The requirements are specified in terms of availability, cost, success rate, trust, security and performance. The selection of QoS parameters favors both the provider and the beneficent [7]. The level of QoS parameter that is being expected by the requester has to be determined from the user request. The selection of web services is handled by the selection agent with the level of QoS needed as the input. In our proposed approach of service selection, all the services which satisfy the determined QoS level are been selected.

We define a Web Service Composition problem A-Comp as

- Let $N = \{WS_1, WS_2, WS_3,.....WSn\}$ be the set of web services registered in the registry.
- Web service WS = (WS_functional_params, WS_Non_functional_params)
- DeterminedQoS = $(Service_{Req}, Expected_{Res})$
- WS_{Select} = select(WS_Non_functional_params, DeterminedQoS)

Based on the service request Service$_{Req}$ and the expected response Expected$_{Res}$ from the requester, the DeterminedQoS is been identified. Considering a web service as a set of functional and non functional parameters, web services, which has a value of non functional parameter greater than the DeterminedQoS are selected.

Graph Construction

As shown in the Fig 2, graph is been generated. The web services WS$_1$ to WS$_7$ are the subset of available number of web services which satisfied the value of DeterminedQoS. From the set of available web services various paths are been analyzed which satisfies the service request, Service$_{Req}$ and the expected result, Expected$_{Res}$. In the below example, we could identify various paths, from which the best possible path would be selected in the next step of the theorem.

From the set of available web services, treating each web service as a node, various paths are identified based on the flow of information. Each path in the graph defines one composition for the service request. The graph and the path determination is done using existing AI algorithms. The paths of the graph are then represented in the form of linked list. Each entry in the list represents the composition of the service request.

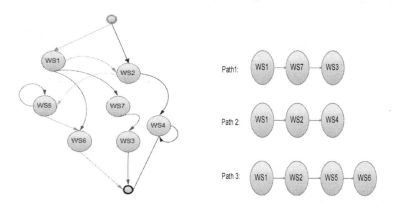

Fig. 2. A Sample graph of web service with the possible paths

Best Path Identification – Selecting the best composition for the service request

From the linked list representation arrived from task 2, the final task would be the identifying the best path and presenting the same to the requester. In identifying the

$$WS_c = \frac{\sum_{i=0}^{m}(AvailWS_i + CostWS_i + SucessRate\,WS_i + SecurityWS_i + TrustWS_i + Performanc\,eWS_i)}{m}$$

best, again the non functional parameter, the QoS, comes to picture. The QoS parameters are selected in par with the provider and the beneficent. The selection is based on the below given formula. if 'n' be the available set of web services which satisfy the 'DeterminedQoS', each web service composition would be comprised of a subset of web services say m.

3.3   Methodology

The selection of best composition from a set of paths identified from the graph is lies the effectiveness of composition. Initially the composition lies solely on the weight-age given by the provider to the web service during registering in UDDI via WSDL file. Once the web service is consumed by the requester, based on their usage or through their explicit feedback on that candidate web service, the ranking among the other peers gets differed [13]. Upon using the web services, the requester registers a belief factor with respect to each candidate web service of the composition in the process registry. The belief factor is a numerical value. Higher belief value depicts the level of trust and reputation towards the web service. A feedback mechanism could be a questionnaire, likes etc [12][13].

In our proposed approach, an adaptive composition of web service based on the expected QoS is been analyzed. In the composition, the user might not be satisfied in a single web service. Say in our previous example from Fig 2, if WS_5 of path 3 alone is not reputed with respect to the user, a different composition just by changing that service alone would be devised, provided there is a similar kind of request in the near future. With minimal change in the WSDL file, a more qualified composition could be given in a minimal time.

The algorithm (algorithm 1) is designed to rank the various possible combinations of web service composition. CandidateWSList is the list of all web services those have been shortlisted, which satisfies the expected QoS requirements of the requester. DeterminedQoS is the expected QoS, which is been identified by from the preprocessing stage of composition. Weighted average of all the QoS properties of the candidate web service is been compared with its peers to identify the best composition. The first 'if' statement satisfies if there is a composition with a highest significance. In such a scenario, the composition with the highest QoS is declared as the best and been presented to the user.

Algorithm 1. QoS-Aware WSC (CandidateWSList, DeterminedQoS)

Initialize
      CompRank =0,
      CompToBePresented = 0.
      For each 'i' in CandidateWSList
      CompRank$_i$ = Compute the weighted sum of QoS w.r.t the CandidateWSList$_i$
            If (CompRank$_i$ > CompRank)
                  CompRank = CompRank$_i$;
                  CompositionToBePresented = i;
            End if
            If(CompRank$_i$ = CompRank)
                  Beleif$_i$ = checkBeleif(i)
                  Beleif$_{current}$ = checkBeleif(CompToBePresented);
                        If(Beleif$_i$ > Beleif$_{current}$)
                              CompositionToBePresented = i;
                        EndIf
            EndIf
            If(Beleif$_i$ = Beleif$_{current}$) //Select arbitrarily
            EndIf
      End for

The second if statement would satisfy when two or more services are equal in terms both functional and non functional properties. The adaptive capacity of our system plays a major role. The belief of the corresponding web services with respect to the users is been analyzed and the option with the better belief is been offered. Lastly, if there is a scenario where we could not find a difference in any means from the functionality to the belief factor, we state that they both are equal and the best composition is been selected arbitrarily.

4   Experimental Results and Discussions

Our proposed QoS aware composition is analyzed for tourism domain. A sample ontology of tourism domain is been created. As discussed, the ontology also contains the QoS information of the candidate web services. The proposed approach is also verified against composition which has not considered QoS as a measure.

Considering a query related to tourism domain, the preprocessing phases of composition have identified, train, hotel, travels and restaurant as the candidate web service. The preprocessing step also includes the computation of 'DeterminedQoS' based on the request and the expected result. Those services that satisfy DeterminedQoS are selected. The various paths are been identified. Our scenario resulted in 5 compositions. Evaluation of the best composition both with and without QoS is been discussed below.

Without QoS Measure in determining composition
Each web service with respect to the functionality is been rated based on its functionality. This rating does not differ among the users. They stay constant and it's up to the provider or the registry to update the value.

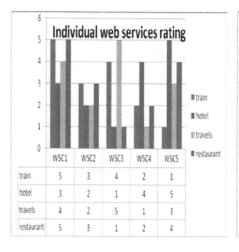 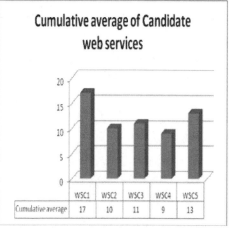

Fig. 3. Experimental result of composition without QoS paramaters

With QoS Measure in determining composition

In this approach, each web service is attached with QoS properties. The QoS properties are selected in concern with both the service provider and service requester. The QoS parameters considered with respect to provider are availability, cost, time and security. Trust and reputation are the factors been considered for requester. As there is a change in QoS properties between the design and run time, a change in composition is noticed.

From the Fig 4, it's noted that composition 3 is much better than composition 1 which has been analyzed at compile time. In the run time, based on the expected QoS based result, the WSDL file is been changed accordingly and composition is been provided in a short time span.

Comparative Study

There are various approaches defined for composition in literature. Table 1 summarizes the comparative study of those approaches with the proposed approach. The comparison is based on the features like service connectivity, the strategy used for composition, inclusion of QoS, the evaluation mechanism and graph representation. Our approach is to compose the web service based on both the semantic and QoS aspects of the web services and has all the features and so the approach is considered efficient when compared.

Table 1. Comparison of proposed framework with existing frameworks

Composition	Connectivity	Composition Strategy	QoS Modeling	Graph Support
Syntactic	Yes	Workflow	No	No
Semantic	Yes	Workflow + AI	No	Yes
QoS driven	Yes	Workflow	Yes	No
Semantic+ QoS driven	Yes	Workflow + AI	Yes	Yes

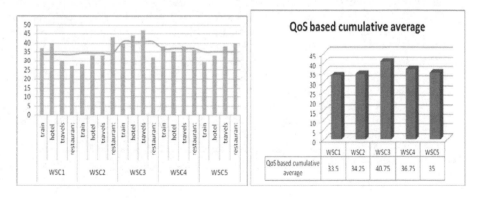

Fig. 4. Experimental result of composition with QoS paramaters

5   Concluding Remarks

With the existence of various attempts to web service composition, QoS aware web service paves way for the dynamic composition. The selection of services from the registry is would happen only if it satisfies the minimum expectation value stated by the customer. The degree to which the composition is efficient depends on the 'DetermineQoS' computation and the number of services in the registry which satisfies the computed 'DetermineQoS'. The use of a measure in the selection of web services makes a prominent selection and also minimizes the selection space. A separate module form monitoring the user's expectations namely the QoSMonitoring helps in identifying the expectation of the user at run time. Thus the paper discusses the importance and dynamic revision of QoS in the selection and composition of web services. The attempt to update the belief factor based on the feedback in the process registry and subsequently in the extended QoS-Domain ontology plays the major role in the adaptation of the web service composition at run time. As a future work, the addition of aspects in composing the web services is been proposed to get even finer result.

References

1. Huang, A.F.M., Lan, C.-W., Yang, S.J.H.: An optimal QoS-based Web service selection scheme. Information Sciences, 3309–3322 (2009)
2. Liu, M., Shen, W., Hao, Q., Yan, J.: An weighted ontology-based semantic similarity algorithm for web service. Expert Systems with Applications (2009)
3. Pastrana, J.L., Pimentel, E., Katrib, M.: QoS-enabled and self-adaptive connectors for WebServices composition and coordination. Computer Languages, Systems & Structures 37(1) (April 2011)
4. Wang, P., Chao, K.-M., Lo, C.-C., Huang, C.-L., Li, Y.: A Fuzzy Model for Selection of QoS-Aware Web Services. In: Proceedings of the IEEE International Conference on e-Business Engineering (ICEBE 2006), pp. 585–593 (2006)
5. Wang, P.: An Entropy Decision Model for Selection of QoS-Aware Services Provisioning. Department of MIS, Kun Shan University, Taiwan (2006)
6. Tran, V.X., Tsuji, H., Masuda, R.: A new QoS ontology and its QoSbased ranking algorithm for Web services. Journal on Simulation Modeling Practice and Theory, Science Direct 17(8), 1378–1398 (2009)
7. Toma, I., Foxvog, D., Jaeger, M.C.: Modeling QoS characteristics in WSMO. In: Proceedings of the First Workshop on Middleware for Service Oriented Computing, pp. 42–47 (2006)
8. Yu, T., Lin, K.-J.: Service Selection Algorithms for Web Services with End-to-End QoS Constraints. In: Proceedings of the 2005 IEEE International Conference on e-Technology, e-Commerce and e-Service, Hong Kong, China, pp. 129–136 (March 2005)
9. Liu, F., Lei, Z.-M.: Research on user-aware QoS based Web services composition. The Journal of China Universities of Posts and Telecommunications, Science Direct 16(5), 125–130 (2009)

10. Lv, C., Dou, W., Chen, J.: QoS-Aware Service Selection Using QDG for B2B Collaboration. In: Proceedings of the Fourteenth IEEE International Conference on Parallel and Distributed Systems, pp. 336–343 (2008)
11. Rong, W., Liu, K., Liang, L.: Personalized Web Service Ranking via User Group combining Association Rule. In: Proceedings of the IEEE International Conference on Web services, pp. 445–452 (2009)
12. Choi, S.W., Her, J.S., Kim, S.D.: QoS metrics for evaluating services from the perspective of service providers. In: Proc. IEEE Intl. Conf. on e-Business Engineering, pp. 622–625 (2007)
13. Papaioannou, I.V., et al.: A QoS ontology language for web services. In: Proceedings of 20th International Conference on Advanced Information Networking and Applications, pp. 18–25. IEEE Computer Society (2006)
14. Protégé, Ontology Editor (2007), http://protege.stanford.edu/
15. Luo, Y.-S., Qi, Y., Hou, D., Shen, L.-F., Chen, Y., Zhong, X.: A novel heuristic algorithm for QoS-aware end-to-end service composition. Science Direct (2010)

Key Dependent Feature Point
Based Image Watermaking Scheme

Ramesh Kumar Surapathi[1], Kamalika Datta[1], and I. Sengupta[2]

[1] School of Computer Engineering,
KIIT University,
Bhubaneswar PIN- 751024
[2] Dept. of Computer Science & Engineering,
Indian Institute of Technology Kharagpur,
Kharagpur PIN-721302

Abstract. An approach to a blind discrete Wavelet Transformation (DWT) domain feature point based image watermarking technique is proposed in this paper. The embedding of the watermark is performed into the image feature points defined by the Harris detector and the additional feature points are generated from the existing feature points using a key dependent algorithm. The proposed method is simple and secure. It is also experimentally found to be robust against various geometric and noise attacks.

Keywords: Image watermarking, DWT, Feature point extraction, Harris detector.

1   Introduction

With the rapid growth of Information Technology in particular, communication technology had pave the way for the usage of many multimedia data. These multimedia data includes images, audios and videos. As these data are very easily available, illegal copying and distribution are the two major issues of concern. To overcome from such issues, different copyright protection techniques are proposed in literature. One of the major forces to protect the multimedia data from illegal copying is Digital Watermarking. In this paper, we focus on Image Watermarking.

Digital Image Watermarking is a technique in which some additional information is embedded into the image file, which later helps to trace the authenticity of the particular image. Broadly, Image Watermarking techniques are divided into visible and invisible image watermarking. Visible image watermarking is a technique in which a logo is placed in the original image which identifies the owner of the image. On the other hand, invisible watermarking can again be divided into temporal domain and spatial domain techniques. Temporal domain techniques are those where the watermarks are directly embedded by changing the pixel values of the image, whereas in spatial domain techniques, the original image passes through some transformations before the watermark embedding. Spatial domain image watermarking techniques performs better as compared to simple temporal domain techniques. Again spatial

N. Meghanathan et al. (Eds.): CCSIT 2012, Part II, LNICST 85, pp. 498–507, 2012.
© Institute for Computer Sciences, Social Informatics and Telecommunications Engineering 2012

domain techniques can further be divided into DCT based image watermarking, FFT based image watermarking and DWT based image watermarking.

The following section two gives a brief survey of review works. In section three, the proposed technique is discussed, Section four discusses the experimental observations and finally Section five provides a brief conclusion.

2   Review Works

Spectral domain watermarking is heavily preferred over the spatial domain because of the robustness of the embedded watermark. The spectral domain image watermarking branches into DCT, DFT and DWT.

In [1] and [2], the combination of DCT and DWT has been joined together to give rise to a better and robust embedding scheme. In [5], the original image is transformed by DWT into four bands of frequencies (LL, LH, HL, and HH) using haar wavelet and then, DCT is performed in each of the four bands where the watermark image is embedded directly into the four bands. The coefficient of embedding in the LL band is 0.1 and the coefficient of embedding in the higher frequency bands is 0.2.

In [2], DCT or DWT is carried out on the original image to decompose the original image into various frequency components and then additive or multiplicative embedding of the one level DCT or DWT decomposed watermark is done in the mid frequency components of the decomposed original image. The linear relation between the transform coefficients of the watermark and a security key makes the watermark visually imperceptible. This is a semi blind watermarking scheme.

In [3], a DCT-SVD non blind based image watermarking scheme has been proposed .DCT is carried out on the original image which is haphazardly arranged into four different frequency bands on which SVD (Singular Value Decomposition) is carried out .The watermark undergoes Discrete Cosine Transform and SVD to form singular watermark values. The singular values of the original image are modified using the singular values of the watermark. This embeds the watermark into the image. The extraction of the watermark needs the original image.

In [5], a semi-blind DWT based image watermarking scheme has been illustrated. The original image is first decomposed using the 'haar' wavelet into three hierarchical levels using Discrete Wavelet Transform. The watermark is scrambled through a PN sequence and is embedded in the selected coefficients of the transformed image in HL, LH and HH bands at all levels and in the LL band of the third level. The watermark detection requires the original image.

In [6] Hu et al proposed a method of DWT domain feature point based image watermarking technique where he generated four image feature points using an intersection based feature point detector. Further using these feature points, some additional points are generated and then triangulation is performed in a key dependent manner, thereafter embedding is performed in the resulting triangles. In [7] Priya et al proposed a DWT domain image watermarking scheme which is geometric invariant. This scheme is found to be robust against some of the geometric attacks.

A feature point based image watermarking [8], [9] is a method of recovering the image from the distortions using the feature points as a content descriptor. Feature points are often the corners or edges of the image. The identification of feature points robust to distortions are detected is the key landmark. Using these feature points, this paper enhances the embedding technique. Harris detector [10] is the required algorithm for the detection of the feature point within an image. Harries detector relies on both the Harris measure and the Gaussian scale representation. Therefore, a combination of both follows in the extraction of the feature points.

In this paper, we propose an feature point based image watermarking technique in DWT domain which is found to be robust against various geometric and other noise attacks. Our technique is found to be secure and imperceptible. Experiments have been carried out, which shows that the watermark image retains its quality.

3   Proposed Approach

The approach used here is a blind watermarking scheme of embedding the watermark in the wavelet domain. In our proposed approach, we perform a 3 level decomposition on the blue component of an original image in DWT domain using Haar wavelet. From the level 3 diagonal coefficient of image, the feature points are generated by Harris detector. Using the key dependent property, additional numbers of feature points are generated from the existing feature points and the watermark is finally embedded into the extracted feature points. The key used in the extraction of additional feature points acts as a secret key for security.

3.1   Embedding Technique

The embedding technique is a feature point based image watermarking scheme wherein watermark is embedded in the feature points of the third level diagonal coefficients. The Major postulates of the embedding technique are underlined herein:

1) Perform a 3 level DWT decomposition.
2) Extraction of feature points using a Harris Detector.
3) Generation of new feature points using a Key Dependent Algorithm.
4) Watermark Embedding.

3.1.1 Third Level DWT Decomposition
The blue component of an original image is first decomposed using the Haar wavelet into three hierarchical levels using DWT. Experiments have shown that the embedding of watermark on the diagonal coefficient of the blue component of an image results in high PSNR value. So, in our proposed technique the feature point's extraction is performed on the level 3 diagonal coefficient using a Harris detector.

3.1.2 Extraction of the Feature Points
Extraction of the feature points from the diagonal coefficient using a Harris detector algorithm involves the following steps: 1) Compute x and y derivatives of original image I using a convolution kernel dx and dy. Let the derivatives be Ix and Iy.

2) Compute products of derivatives at each pixel.

$$I_x^2 = I_x * I_x;$$
$$I_y^2 = I_y * I_y;$$
$$I_{xy} = I_x * I_y;$$

3) compute the sum of products of derivatives at each pixel using a Gaussian filter.

$$S_x^2 = G * I_x^2;$$
$$S_y^2 = G * I_y^2;$$
$$S_{xy} = G * I_{xy};$$

4) Compute the response of the detector at each pixel.

$$R = (S_x^2 . * S_y^2 - S_{xy}^2) - k * (S_x^2 + S_y^2)^2;$$

5) Find out the points with large corner response function R (R> threshold).
6) Take the points of local maxima of R.
The points generated are the required feature points. The feature points generated from the diagonal coefficient are shown in fig. 1(a).

Fig. 1 (a).

3.1.3 Key Dependent Algorithm
From the existing feature points, the remaining numbers of required feature points are extracted depending upon the number of bits of the watermark. For the extraction of new feature points, we use a Key Dependent algorithm. This involves the generation of pseudo random numbers depending on a secret key, which is stored for the watermark extraction.

The steps involved in the key dependent algorithm are as follows:

1) Compute the bounding box of the existing feature points as follows.
X1 = Minimum x coordinate of the existing feature points
X2 = Maximum x coordinate of the existing feature points
Y1 = Minimum y coordinate of the existing feature points
Y2 = Maximum y coordinate of the existing feature points.

The Bounding Box is defined by {(X1, Y1), (X2, Y1), (X2, Y2), (X1, Y2)}.

2) Generate two uniform deviates h1 and h2 from the secret key. Then a new point is generated as

$$X = \lfloor (X1*(h1/200) + X2*(1-(h1/200))) \rfloor \, ;$$
$$Y = \lfloor (Y1*(h2/200) + Y2*(1-(h2/200))) \rfloor \, ;$$

3) Repeat step2, until the total number of feature points are equal to the number of bits of the watermark. All the feature points are shown in fig. 1(b).

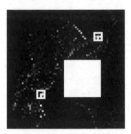

Fig. 1 (b).

3.1.4 Watermark Embedding

The watermark bits are embedded into the feature points by the formula,

$$D3(x, y) = D3(x, y) + 0.15*w(x1, y1);$$

x, y are the coordinates of the feature points
X1, y1 are the coordinates of the watermark
D3 is the level 3 diagonal coefficient
W is the watermark.

The original and the watermarked image is shown in fig 1(c) and fig 1(d) respectively.

Fig. 1 (c).   Fig. 1 (d).

3.2   Extraction Technique

The extraction of the watermark from the watermarked image requires the presence of the original image and the secret key.

1) Perform a 3 level DWT decomposition on original image and watermarked image.
2) Extraction of feature points using a Harris detector.
3) Generate new feature points using a Key Dependent Algorithm.
4) Watermark extraction is done.

Perform 3-level decomposition on the blue components of original image and watermarked image. Generate again all the feature points of the original image by repeating steps 3.1.2 and 3.1.3 using the secret key. Then the watermark is extracted from the feature points of original image and the watermarked image by using the formula,

$$W(x1, y1) = (Dw3(x, y) - D3(x, y))/0.15;$$

x, y are the coordinates of the feature points
Dw3 is the level 3 diagonal coefficient of watermarked image
D3 is the level 3 diagonal coefficient of watermarked image
W is the watermark.

The original and extracted watermark is shown in fig 1(e) and fig 1(f) respectively.

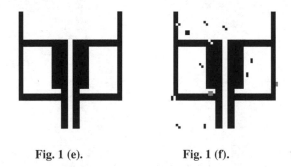

Fig. 1 (e).   **Fig. 1 (f).**

4   Experimental Results

This section discusses the experimental results of our proposed watermarking scheme. The algorithm has been implemented using Matlab7. Rest of the section is characterized into:

1) Performance Evaluation without attacks
2) Watermark Extraction from various attacks
3) Performance Evaluation with attacks.

4.1   Performance Evaluation without Attacks

For this evaluation, we have taken the images Lena, Baboon, Airfield, and Peppers as shown below. On every image, the proposed watermarking technique is performed and then the respective PSNR value of the image is calculated by comparing the watermarked image with its original image. The results of the evaluation are shown in the table 1.

Lena   Baboon

Airfield   Peppers

Table 1. PSNR calculation of various watermarked images

Images	PSNR Values
Lena	38.9119
Baboon	36.8103
Airfield	38.3127
Peppers	38.1698

4.2   Watermark Extraction from Various Attacks

We have taken the Lena image to present the results of the watermark extraction. To evaluate the robustness of the proposed watermarking scheme, various attacks are tested.

Fig. 2 (a).   Fig. 2 (b).

All these attacks are simulated using Matlab7. After each attack, the watermark is extracted by the proposed technique. The original Lena image of size 512*512 and the original watermark are shown in fig 2(a) and fig 2(b). The various attacks tested and their respective attacked images and the watermark retained are shown below.

Various Attacks Tested

Scaling at 2:1

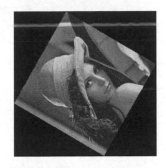

Rotation by 60°

Combination of scaling at 2:1
And rotation by 90°

Transform

JPEG Compression by 1:19

Gaussian noise of mean and
Variance 0.5

Salt & Pepper Noise of noise   Extracted Watermark
Density 0.2

4.3   Performance Evaluation with Attacks

To evaluate the imperceptibility of the proposed technique, few common attacks are tested on the watermarked Lena image and their respective PSNR values are shown in Table 2. All these attacks are performed using Adobe Photoshop CS3.

Table 2. Attacks on Images and the PSNR values

Lena Attacks	PSNR Values
JPEG Compression 1:19	32.4393
Gaussian Noise (2%)	32.9937
Sharpen Edges	35.1832
Uniform Noise (2%)	35.5392
Salt & Pepper Noise (0.001)	33.5771
Poisson Noise	28.0450
Speckle Noise(0.001)	35.0616

5   Conclusion

A feature point based image watermarking scheme in DWT domain is proposed in this paper. DWT is performed on the blue component of the image up to third level and the diagonal coefficients of the third level are chosen for embedding the watermark. Use of the secret key in embedding entails the presence of the secret key at the receiving side for watermark extraction, which is the feature which protects the watermark from being tampered by attackers. All the experimental results are found to be resistant against various signal processing attacks, geometrical and noise attacks.

References

1. Fotopoulos, V., Skodras, A.N.: A Subband DCT Approach to Image Watermarking. Electronics Laboratory Computer Technology Institute (CTI) University of Patras (July 1999)
2. Tripathi, S., Jain, R.C.: Novel DCT and DWT based Watermarking Techniques for Digital Images. Birla Institute of Technology & Science, Pilani. V. Gayatri, HP LABS
3. Sverdlov, A., Dexter, S., Eskicioglu, A.M.: Robust DCT-SVD Domain Image Watermarking for Copyright Protection: Embedding Data in All Frequencies. Department of CIS, Brooklyn College, the Graduate Center the City University of New York (2004)
4. Huang, X., Chen, Z.: A Wavelet Based Scene Image Fusion Algorithm. School of Automation Science and Electrical Engineering, Beijing Institute of Aeronautics and Astronautics. In: Proceedings of IEEE Tencon 2002 (2002)
5. Safabaksh, R., Zaboli, S., Tabibiazar, A.: Digital Watermarking on Still Images Using Wavelet Transform. Computer Engineering Department, Amirkabir University of Technology (2002)
6. Hu, S.: Key-dependant decomposition based image watermarking Published by ACM 2004 Article. In: Proceeding MULTIMEDIA 2004 Proceedings of the 12th Annual ACM International Conference on Multimedia ©2004 table of contents (2004) ISBN: 1-58113-893-8
7. Nantha Priya, N.R., Lenty Stuwart, S.: Robust Feature Based Image Watermarking Process. International Journal of Computer Applications © 2010 by IJCA Journal (5) - Article 3 (2010)
8. Tang, C.W., Hang, H.M.: A feature-based robust digital image watermarking scheme. IEEE Transaction. Signal Process. 51(4), 950–959 (2003)
9. Alghoniemy, M., Tewfik, A.H.: Geometric invariance in image watermarking. IEEE Transaction. Image Process. 13(2), 145–153 (2004)
10. Harris, C., Stephens, M.: A combined corner and edge detector. In: Proceedings of 4th Alvey Vision Conference, pp. 147–151 (1988)

A Survey on ATTACK – Anti Terrorism Technique for ADHOC Using Clustering and Knowledge Extraction

K. Sudharson[1] and V. Parthipan[2]

[1] Department of Information Technology, S.A. Engineering College, Chennai, India
mail@sudharson.in
[2] Department of Computer Science, Thirumalai Engineering College, Kanchipuram, India
parthipansp@gmail.com

Abstract. Analyzing and predicting behavior of node can lead to more secure and more appropriate defense mechanism for attackers in the Mobile Adhoc Network. In this work, models for dynamic recommendation based on fuzzy clustering techniques, applicable to nodes that are currently participate in the transmission of Adhoc Network. The approach focuses on both aspects of MANET mining and behavioral mining. Applying fuzzy clustering and mining techniques, the model infers the node's preferences from transmission logs. The fuzzy clustering approach, in this study, provides the possibility of capturing the uncertainty among node's behaviors. The results shown are promising and proved that integrating fuzzy approach provide us with more interesting and useful patterns which consequently making the recommender system more functional and robust.

Keywords: MANET Mining, Fuzzy Clustering, Knowledge Discovery.

1 Introduction

A mobile ad hoc network (MANET), is a self-configuring infra structure less network of mobile devices connected by wireless links. Nodes in mobile ad-hoc network are free to move and organize themselves in an arbitrary fashion. Each user is free to roam about while communication with others. The path between each pair of the users may have multiple links and the radio between them can be heterogeneous. Web personalization is a process in which Web information space adapts with user's interests [7]. Same way in MANET the nodes are continuously participating in the routing is recorded in transmission log file with node's interest rate. Web usage mining techniques are widely employed for extracting knowledge about user interests [6]. Likewise, MANET mining Techniques are widely employed for extracting knowledge about the node interest. However, as the vagueness and imprecision in node interests are key features of MANET systems, traditional models which use hard computing techniques are inadequate. Since, the navigational behavior of nodes on the MANET is uncertain, using fuzzy clustering algorithms are more suitable for behavioral mining.

The rapid growth of communication networks such as the Internet and wireless mesh networks has spurred the development of numerous collaborative applications.

N. Meghanathan et al. (Eds.): CCSIT 2012, Part II, LNICST 85, pp. 508–514, 2012.

Reputation and trust play a pivotal role in such applications by enabling multiple parties to establish relationships that achieve mutual benefit. In general, reputation is the opinion of the public towards a person, a group of people, an organization, or a resource. In the context of collaborative applications such as peer-to-peer systems, reputation represents the opinions nodes in the system have about their peers and peer-provided resources. Reputation allows parties to build trust, or the degree to which one party has confidence in another within the context of a given purpose or decision. By harnessing the community knowledge in the form of feedback, reputation based trust systems help participants decide who to trust, encourage trustworthy behavior, and deters dishonest participation by providing a means through which reputation and ultimately trust can be quantified and disseminated. Without such mechanisms, opportunism can erode the foundations of these collaborative applications and lead to peer mistrust and eventual system failure. A rich variety of environments and applications has motivated research in reputation systems. The success of a reputation system is measured by how accurately the calculated reputations predict the quality of future interactions. This is difficult to achieve in an environment where any party can attempt to exploit the system to its own benefit. Some attacks have a narrow focus and only affect the reputation of the misbehaving identity or a few selected targets. This paper concerned with distributed association rule mining algorithm in finding frequent malicious behaviour of the node. The work is different from many existing algorithms where most of existing algorithms focusing only on the reputation-based mechanisms that improve security in MANETS. Our distributed algorithm focuses on association between the nodes in order to reduce the malicious nodes in Adhoc Network. Also we propose Clustering Techniques to identify the good nodes and grouping them accordingly and this allows us to recognize crucial spots in changing node behaviour time to time. This paper is the first survey focusing on the characterization of reputation systems based on mining techniques and threats facing them from a computer science perspective. Our work contributes to understanding which reputation system design components are vulnerable, what are the most appropriate defense mechanisms, and how these defense mechanisms can be integrated into existing or future reputation systems to make them resilient to attacks.

This paper is organized as follows .In section2; we discuss the background study the related works. In section 3 we discuss the proposed work explained to find the Node Behavior and finally clustering techniques also described in detail. Section 4 Discussion, Section 5 is Conclusion and future work.

2   Background Study

In the recent years many researches tries to predict the node behavior. Castellano et al. have presented an approach for expressing similarity between Web users according to their access patterns. They considered the access time to a web page as a parameter in the model [4]. Castellano et al. have also used a neuro-fuzzy model to develop a Website personalization framework for dynamic suggestion of URLs to users [5]. Likewise, in this model it supposes to find the similarity between the nodes according to their accessing path. This approach considered the node access time on particular path as parameters to find the misbehaving node which are deviating from the normal routing time and mechanism. A different approach is purposed in the work of Kraft et al. in which they extracted fuzzy rules from user profiles and used them for information retrieval. Web user profiles usually reflect only access behavior of users and not keywords on a website. In this work, they rated web pages for building user interest profiles [3]. In Our approach the knowledge is extracted from the node profiles and used them for finding node behavior. A bi clustering approach to correlate web users and pages are purpose in the work of [9], their purposed approach is a three step process which concentrates on the principles of spectral clustering analysis and provides a fuzzy relational scheme for both user and page clusters but they didn't consider to active users for providing dynamic recommendation. Another approach for combination of content mining and web usage mining in order to predicting user navigational behavior is represented by [8]. The frequent word sequences are used for capturing textual content of web pages. Log files data are combined with content clusters for extracting rules about user's behavior. In our approach we concentrate on clustering analysis and provide fuzzy relation scheme for node and transmission path usage mining, Another approach for combination of path mining and path usage mining in order to predicting user navigational behavior. Log files data are combined with node clusters for extracting rules about node's behavior .Their work is improved in this work by employing fuzzy techniques for node clustering and predicting rated recommendations for active node. In this paper we propose a model applying both node and path clustering using fuzzy techniques for better dynamic recommendation process.

3   Proposed Model

(I) Our Model

The ADOHC personalization model is to provide the paths transparently provides node with the personalized environment. When node requests a path, the neighbor node retrieves and replies the requested path followed by a list of paths which may be interested to the node.

Two major steps of a ADOHC personalization system are knowledge discovery and recommendation. In first step, node preferences are identified using log data called path usage data (PUD).In the next step, the achieved knowledge is used to identify the possibly interested paths to the nodes. This recommendation can be done in different ways such as adding related hyperlinks to the last web page requested by the user [2]. In this paper, Represented method dynamically recommends the highest match score paths to active node. Represented method steps are described in the following sections:

3.1   Knowledge Discovery Process

In this step, using the previous behavior of each node, knowledge that represents node's preferences is extracted. For extracting knowledge from path usage data, 6 steps will be performed as described in the following:

3.1.1 Preprocessing

Log files have useful information about access of all nodes to specific routes. Extracting these information, reformatted log file which contains useful information such as "time, date, accessed path and IP address" is formed and useless requests such as accesses to different paths are removed from log file in data cleaning process.

3.1.2 Path Clustering

In this work, we used mining approach for path clustering. Assume $P = \{p1, p2, ... pk\}$ is the set of k routes. Applying 3 following steps, paths were grouped in path based clusters.

Stepl. Assign each path to a single node.

Step2. Merge primary clusters based on the Jaccard coefficient similarity measure. Defined as:

$$sim(p_x, p_y) = \frac{|p_x \cap p_y|}{|p_x \cup p_y|}$$

$|px \cap py|$ represents the number of common path and $|px \cup py|$ represents total number of paths between two basic nodes.

Step3. The second step repeated until all paths being clustered into a pre defined number of path clusters. $\mathbf{DC} = \{\mathbf{DC_1}, \mathbf{DC_2}, ... \mathbf{DC_n}\}$ is the result set. Each $\mathbf{DC}|$ represents a set of paths with similar distance.

3.1.3 Integration

In this step, the previously obtained path clusters are merged with reformatted log file and according to the result, access table can be produced. Then, nodes are clustered based on their behavior in access to path clusters. Assume U= {UI, U2 , ... , Um} as a set of nodes where each node is identified by distinct IP address and A= { A1, A2, ... , Am } is a set of node's accesses to path clusters. For example A_k indicates the access list of node, k, to a subset of path clusters $(A_k \varepsilon DC$, for K=1 to n). Access table is represented as a matrix with **m** rows and **n** columns where each entry represents the interest degree of $i\text{-}th$ node to $j\text{-}th$ path cluster. We use the interest degree which proposed by Castellano et aI., They defined it as the ratio of the number of accesses to each path cluster to the total number of accesses to all path clusters for each node [6].

$$Val(DC_i, U_i) = \frac{|\{DC_j | DC_j \in A_i\}|}{|A_i|}$$

Calculated matrix will be the input data for clustering algorithm.

3.1.4 Node Clustering

According to access matrix, nodes with similar interests can be clustered together. In this work, we used fuzzy c-means (FCM) method for clustering nodes. UC= {UC$_1$, UC$_2$,...,UCn} is result set where each UCj represents a set of nodes with similar interesting patterns.

3.1.5 Final Preparation

In reformatted log file, for each log entry, accessed path were substituted by most related path cluster and similarly, IP address will be replaced by the most relevant node cluster. The result of this step is input data for rule mining step.

3.1.6 Rule Mining

Varity number of algorithms such as Apriori, Eclat and FP-Growth are proposed by researchers for generating association rules [1]. Extracted rules show that which group of nodes and when are interested to what kinds of path clusters. We used apriori algorithm for mining our frequent item set.

3.2 Recommendation Process

Using results obtained from previous step, some related information can be recommended to a group of nodes. For example, {Node Cluster=UC7} => {path Cluster=DCl} means that paths in path cluster 1 can be recommended to nodes in node cluster 7.

3.2.1 Support Identification

If a new node starts a transaction, our model matches the new node with the most similar node clusters and provides suitable recommendations to him. Thakur et al. represented a criterion called support value which was calculated through following steps: [2]

Step 1: Assign active node to a new cluster. UC$_{new}$ = {Unew}.

Step2. Complete access matrix for active node according to the equation 2.

Step3. Calculate support value of UCnew to existing node clusters UC$_i$ using Equation 3.

$$support(UC_{new}, UC_i) = \frac{\sum |user(val(DC, UC_{new}) - val(DC, UC_i))|}{UC_i \cup UC_{new}}$$

val(DC, UQ) shows the interesting value of nodes in UC$_i$ to the documents in selected DC.

3.2.2 Match Score Identification

The match score calculation defines highest match node cluster for active node. Match score criterion is represented by Thakur et al. This parameter between UC_{new} and UQ is defined as following [2].

$$match(UC_{new}, UC_i) = 1 - support(UC_{new}, UC_i)$$

This give us a list of corresponding node clusters from the highest match score down to lowest match score.

4   Discussion

The work of taherizadeh et al. has improved in this paper by employing fuzzy clustering and supporting active node by a range of rated relevant recommendations. The results of this path based recommender system have been successfully modeled in this paper. Suggested recommendation model combines path and node clustering using fuzzy approach. Applying model on the access log file of nodes, a set of rated path was derived from node preferences for dynamic recommendation.

The advantages of the proposed model are summarized as following. Firstly, this model acts effectively in identifying node preferences. Uncertainty among node interests is an important issue which is clearly considered in this approach. Our model captures the uncertainty in node navigational patterns and establishes an effective recommendation strategy. Additionally, this approach provides dynamic user clustering for active nodes and supports them with personalized environment. Moreover, any changes in path can be simply informed to all group nodes which are highly interested on that particular path. While the advantages of the model are clear, there are some limitations in this research area that we consider them as future research directions. Path clustering and node clustering in this approach are considered in separate processes which is time consuming. In order to solve this problem a Two-way clustering method may be used. This strategy in the same time not only clusters the objects but also the features of the objects will be clustered. Next common limitation in clustering algorithms is defining a suitable number of clusters which can be surmounted by employing QT clustering algorithm which does not require specifying the number of clusters and when running several times, always returned result is as the same.

5   Conclusion and Future Work

In this paper, a model for dynamic recommendation based on fuzzy clustering techniques, applicable to nodes that are in highly mobile and sparse environment was proposed. In this work, node mining was integrated to path usage mining for finding nodes interesting rules. In this way, we investigated fuzzy clustering techniques for node clustering based on the knowledge obtained from node's previous behaviors. Then a fuzzy technique was used for grouping a new node in an existing node cluster. Finally based on extracted rules the Suggested paths was added to requested node and represented to current node dynamically. Our work will be extended by employing other clustering strategy.

Acknowledgment. This research is funded by Director, Thiru P.Venkatesh Raja S.A.Engineering College, Chennai. Motivated and supported by Mr.N.Partheeban Asst Prof. Department of Computer Science and Engineering, Mr.Ahmed Mudasar Ali Asst Prof., Mrs.S.Veena Asst Prof., Department of Information Technology, S.A.Engineering College, Chennai, and Mr.D.Dhanasekaran Asst.prof., Loyola-ICAM College of Engineering And Technology, Chennai.

References

1. Goethals, B.: Survey on Frequent Pattern Mining. P.O. box 26, FIN-00014 Helsinki, Finland (2003)
2. Thakur, B.K., Abbas, S.Q., Trivedi, A.K.: A Recommender System to Personalize the Environment of Web User. In: IEEE International Advance Computing Conference, Patiala, India (2009)
3. Kraft, D.H., Chen, J., Martin Bautista, M.J., Vila, M.A.: Textual Information Retrieval with User Profiles Using Fuzzy Clustering and Inferencing. In: Intelligent Exploration of the Web. Physica-Verlag, Heidelberg (2002)
4. Castellano, G., Fanelli, A.M., Mencar, C., Alessandra Torsello, M.: Similarity-based Fuzzy clustering for user profiling. In: IEEE/WIC/ACM International Conferences on Web Intelligence and Intelligent Agent Technology -Workshops (2007)
5. Castellano, G., Fanelli, A.M., Plantamura, P., Torsello, M.A.: A Neuro-Fuzzy Strategy for Web Personalization. In: Proceedings of the Twenty-Third AAAI Conference on Artificial Intelligence (2008)
6. Singh, M.P.: Practical Handbook of Internet Computing. In: Singh, M.P. (ed.) Web Usage Mining and Personalization. CRC Press (2005)
7. Nasraoui, O.: World Wide Web Personalization. In: Wang, J. (ed.) Encyclopedia of Data Mining and Data Warehousing, Idea Group (2005)
8. Taherizadeh, S., Moghadam, N.: Integrating web content mining into web usage mining for finding patterns and predicting users behaviors. International Journal of Information Science and Management 7(1), 51–66 (2009)
9. Koutsonikola, V.A., Akali, A.I.: A fuzzy bi clustering approach to correlate web users nad web pages. Int. J. Knowledge and Web Intelligence 1(1/2), 3–23 (2009)

SecureWear: A Framework for Securing Mobile Social Networks

Baishakhi Ray and Richard Han

University of Colorado, Boulder,
Department of Computer Science
baishakhi.ray@gmail.com, rhan@cs.colorado.edu
http://www.cs.colorado.edu/

Abstract. With the rising popularity of social networks, people have started accessing social networking sites from anywhere, any time, and from a variety of devices. Exploiting this ubiquity, the social networking data of an individual can be coupled with her geographical location to build different context aware applications. However, the existing infrastructure to share this personalized data forces users to compromise their privacy. In this paper, we present a secure framework, which allows interaction of social network information with location-based services, without compromising user privacy and security. Through exchanging an encrypted nonce ID (EID) associated with a verified user location, our framework allows location-based services to query its vicinity for relevant information without disclosing user identity. We further argue that, this kind of framework should be adopted as a common security framework for mobile-social interaction to meet privacy requirements.

Keywords: mobile computing, social network, security, privacy, wearable device.

1 Introduction

With the advent of mobile social networks [12,6], an exciting new paradigm emerges, in which, local environments with numerous electronic and mobile/wireless devices are bathed with social networking information. Context-related information and services are increasingly used for spontaneous socializing and collaboration. However, when users participate in such communication, they unconsciously leave private information traces that can undermine their privacy.

In this work, we explore one such simple application that notifies the user whenever her Facebook friend is nearby. The application is deployed on smart phones as well as on a electronic shirt. When running on a cellphone, it notifies the user, which friends are located nearby. In case of wearable shirt, the application indicates if someone is around by lighting an embedded LED (green for a friend, red for foe).

This application represent a larger class of context-aware applications in which both the current location of the user as well as their social networking information are extracted to provide context. In this way, the user leaves trace of his identity which can be misused. In particular, mobile social networks introduce security and privacy challenges. A user may not always want to reveal their identity, location, or preference

N. Meghanathan et al. (Eds.): CCSIT 2012, Part II, LNICST 85, pp. 515–524, 2012.

information. Moreover, a user may wish to reveal different part of their preference depending on their location, time, mood, presence/status of other users, etc. Wearable MoSoNets are even more challenging from a security and privacy point of view due to extreme resource and user interface constraints associated with embedded wearable items.

The contribution of this work is to introduce a common security framework for resource-challenged mobile social networks. We demonstrate an implementation of the framework on smart-phones and wearable shirts. The framework provides a general architecture that can be extended to any mobile device capable of communicating over wireless media.

2   System Architecture

Let us first introduce a sample application area to motivate the assumed system architecture. Consider Maya is an undergraduate student who wants to find a classmate from her algorithm class to share some thoughts on a homework problem . She can set an alarm on her mobile device, where if a classmate is around, she will be notified. Now, let's assume the algorithm class buddies have a Facebook group for their class discussion. Hence, Maya's mobile alarm application has to retrieve the Facebook IDs of all students registered in the group and search locally to find a match. Such an application would need a system that could announce wirelessly the local presence of each user, and link that user identity with their social network profile in order to facilitate communication among matched users.

The basic system thus consists of three components: mobile devices/wearables, an access point(optional), and a social network. Our particular implementation uses electronic shirts as the wearables, a laptop as the local access point, and Facebook as the social network. We chose wearables over mobile devices to show that our framework is suitable for resource constrained devices as well.

The shirts and laptop communicate with each other wirelessly via Bluetooth and the laptop communicates with Facebook via an internet connection. In the case of smartphones, we can omit the requirements of access points, as the smartphones can use their own wifi or cellular services. The overall system model is shown in Figure 1.

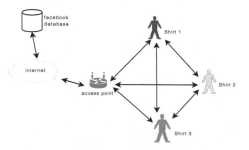

Fig. 1. Basic System Model

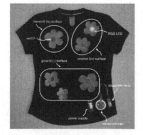

Fig. 2. Wearable Shirt

2.1   System Model

The eShirts. Each wearable shirt contains an embedded micro-controller, a Bluetooth radio, and an RGB-LED. Commercially available LilyPad Arduino modules [8] were stitched to each shirt using conductive threads. Such a shirt is shown in Figure 2. Each electronic shirt (e-shirt) broadcasts its Facebook ID periodically using the embedded Bluetooth device. Bluetooth was chosen due to its limited range and low power usage.

The Access point. The access point relays data between the e-shirt and Facebook.com. It must be able to send and receive data to and from the e-shirts and run code that accesses the Facebook APIs [1].

We have implemented the access point functionality on a laptop as well as on phones (Nokia N80). Cellphone-based access points allow users to move from place to place, without disrupting ongoing communications. in addition to e-shirts, cellphones can also serve as the end client communication devices. We have used the Java 2ME Wireless Toolkit to program the cellphone and J2SE for the laptop.

Social Network Information. We have selected the Facebook database as our backend data server. We retrieved social networking information through java library of Facebook API [1].

In this application, one e-shirt listens for Facebook IDs announced wirelessly by nearby e-shirts and checks Facebook's database to see whether this user is on its friend list. If yes, the embedded LED glows green, else red.

2.2   Threat Model

The basic system architecture described in Section 2.1 models a typical context-sensitive mobile social networking infrastructure. However, existing implementations of such systems compromise users' privacy. For example, a person wearing e-shirt can easily be tracked by listening to its broadcast ID. More over, a malicious user A, can spoof B's ID to falsely register B's presence.

We have identified some of the major threats that existing mobile social systems impose. These are explained by a running example as presented in Figure 1.

1. **Spoofing:** e-shirt1 can spoof e-shirt2's Facebook ID. In that case, if e-shirt1 disguises e-shirt2's ID to e-shirt3, then e-shirt2 will falsely appear to be in e-shirt3's vicinity.
2. **Eavesdropping:** e-shirt2 can steal e-shirt1's password. In the above simplified model, to retrieve data from Facebook, at least once in every session, shirts have to login to the Facebook. During login they have to send Facebook login ID and password information to the access point. If this is not protected by any cryptographic method, anybody eavesdropping on wireless communications by other shirts can steal their login ID and password.
3. **Replay :** Say e-shirt3 eavesdrops on e-shirt1's Facebook ID. As e-shirt1 is broadcasting its ID, this will reach e-shirt3 and e-shirt3 can simply forward the packet to any remote location to make it appear as if e-shirt1 is in that location.
4. **Compromised shirt:** An e-shirt itself can be compromised to the extent that the advertised embedded Facebook ID is a fake one.

5. **Energy exhaustion:** e-shirt1 can continuously broadcast its own Facebook ID. Listening that every time e-shirt2 will query the Facebook database through access point, thus losing considerable amounts of energy. Alternatively, e-shirt1 can continuously spoofing several other Facebook ID and send them to e-shirt2. Thus e-shirt2 will query Facebook to resolve each received Facebook ID every time. Thus all its energy will be consumed and ultimately it will shut itself down.

To handle the above discussed threats, we propose a security framework in section 3.

3   Security Architecture and Solutions

As identified in Section 2.2, security and privacy vulnerabilities are great challenges for context-sensitive mobile social networks. To provide security, the simplest approach would be to use some standard cryptographic techniques, where each wireless mobile social device, say an e-shirt or cellphone, will encrypt its Facebook identity before broadcasting it. The other nearby devices, if legitimate users, will decrypt the received packet and retrieve the ID. The major problems with this approach are:

1. How do you know who is a legitimate user? If a person buy an e-shirt, registers its Facebook ID through some means and starts using it, how will it become a valid user? Here the concept of a trusted third party authentication comes into the picture, which can endorse the validity of an electronic shirt.
2. Secondly, running all the standard cryptographic algorithms on embedded systems like e-shirts requires a significant amount of processing power and energy consumption. As the computational power of the wearable chip is quite constrained, and it runs on a small battery, this limits the use of standard security algorithms.
3. Broadcasting authenticated data to all the wearable shirts in the vicinity is even more challenging. Established authentication policies rely on either asymmetric digital signatures method or on purely symmetric solutions [20]. The asymmetric method is impractical in wearable domain; one of the main reasons are that long signatures with high communication overhead requires 50-1000 bytes per packet, very high overhead to create and verify the signature. The symmetric method is also infeasible: Gennaro and Rohatgis initial work required over 1 Kbyte of authentication information per packet [14], and Rohatgis improved k-time signature scheme requires over 300 bytes per packet [22].

In this paper we have proposed a new security framework, particularly suitable for the mobile social network domain. We have introduced a proxy server **eShirt.com**, whose role is to authenticate each of the local wireless devices. In our example, eShirt.com will validate each e-shirt. If e-shirts pass the validity check, then eShirt.com contacts Facebook to retrieve the requested information and sends that back to the concerned e-shirts.

In Section 3.1 the new security model is discussed and 3.2 analyses how this model takes care of all the threats identified previously.

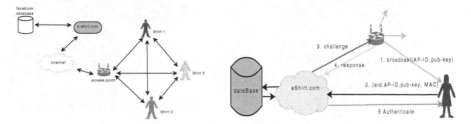

Fig. 3. System Model introducing eshirt   **Fig. 4.** AP Authentication Message Flow

3.1   Security Model

As shown in Figure 3, we have introduced an authentication server **eShirt.com** in between the access point and the social-network database, which is Facebook in this case.
The whole communication can be categorized into six phases:

1. Registering an e-shirt to eShirt.com
2. Registering Access point to eShirt.com
3. Communication between local access point and eShirt.com
4. Communication between two e-shirts.
5. Communication between an e-shirt and local access point.
6. Communication between eShirt.com and Facebook.

Registering to eShirt.com. The user has to register and activate a new e-shirt, to the
trusted 3rd party proxy server eShirt.com, before he starts using it. The registration process requires the user to login to Facebook, so that their Facebook-ID can be retrieved
and it needs the username, password to register to eShirt.com. See Figure 5. We believe
that users wishing to exploit the unique power of mobile social networks will be willing
to divulge this information to the mobile social network provider. For example, kids
desiring the fun of being able to use the e-shirt to identify friend/foe would be willing
to let an eShirt provider know who are their friends on Facebook. This is of course a
simplified example, and we imagine much more sophisticated applications that exploit
the power of mobile + social interactions. Once registered, each user will get a unique
eShirt.com ID. From now on, we will term this eShirt.com ID as EID. corresponding
to each EID, an unique MAC-Key is generated using CBC-MAC[20]. The user has to
download both EID and MAC-Key in order to activate the e-shirt and it will be embedded in the shirt unless reloaded again. The user can login to eShirt.com as shown in
Figure 6 and retrieve all its relevant information later.

Corresponding to each user, the eShirt.com will maintain a database which is shown
in table 1.

Access point authentication: Each AP has to register itself with eShirt.com and eS-
hirt.com will give it an unique identifier (AP-ID), a digitally signed public key and a
private key as shown in Table 2.

Fig. 5. Registration Page to eShirt.com   **Fig. 6.** Login Page to eShirt.com

Table 1. eShirt.com database for e-shirt   **Table 2.** eShirt.com database for AP

user	password	Facebook-ID	eid	MAC-key

login	Password	AP-ID	Pub-key	Priv-key

When an e-shirt wants to establish a connection with the AP, the e-shirt will select a random AP based on the availability. The AP broadcasts a signed public key along with its AP-ID to the e-shirt. The e-shirt will tag its own EID with the received message and do a MAC operation to received message i.e,public key and AP-ID and EID, with the stored MAC-key and send it to eShirt.com along with EID. The table 3 and 4 show the corresponding packet formats.

Table 3. AP Authentication Packet   **Table 4.** packet from AP to e-shirt

EID	AP-ID	Pub-key	MAC

AP-ID	signed-public-key

When eShirt.com gets the digitally signed public key and AP-ID, it verifies it with the received MAC message to avoid tampering. It will then validate the (AP-ID: public-key) pair against its own AP database 2. If matches, it sends a random secret to the AP by sending a message encrypted by the public key of the AP. The AP should decrypt the message with its private key and send it to the eShirt.com encrypting through its private key. If the eShirt.com can decipher it, it'll send a signal to the related e-shirt (encrypted message) authenticating the AP. Figure 4 shows the entire communication that takes place to select an authenticated AP.

e-shirt to e-shirt talk. Once the e-shirt selects an authenticated AP, it can start to communicate with its neighboring e-shirts. Our security model ensures the following basic two security features:

- Even if the attacker can see the packet, it cannot derive any useful information.
- It has to be endorsed that the packet is coming from the proper user, so nobody can even eavesdrop on the packet.

An e-shirt will synchronize its time and location with the selected AP. An e-shirt will then keep a track of time through some internal counter increment and synchronize itself with the AP periodically. If the e-shirt changes its location, it has to select another

AP through the same authentication procedure and has to be synchronized with the new AP. In the new security scheme, instead of broadcasting Facebook-ID, each eshirt broadcasts its EID along with a unique monotonically increasing number called nonce, time-stamp and location data (as available from AP). These four fields constitute our basic data communication unit.

$$D_{org} = (EID, NONCE, TIMESTAMP, LOCATION); \qquad (1)$$

$$E = D_{(K_{encr}, nonce)}, \; where \; D = (nonce, timestamp, location); \qquad (2)$$

$$M = MAC(K_{mac}, nonce|D) \qquad (3)$$

The last three fields are encrypted as they can be retrieved easily by the eShirt.com if the EID is known. To maintain data integrity, a MAC operation will be performed on the whole data, i.e., EID and the encrypted data, by the MAC key stored in the e-shirt. To attain the security constrains as discussed above, we propose a packet structure shown in Figure 7. The K_{mac} and K_{encr} are derived from the original key embedded in the e-shirt, as per the method described in Section 4.

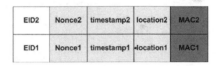

Fig. 7. eShirt-eShirt talk : Packet Structure   **Fig. 8.** packet received at eshirt.com

Thus the complete message that is sent from e-shirt1 to e-shirt2 is as follows:

$$Shirt1-> Shirt2 : D, MAC(K_{mac}, nonce|D) \qquad (4)$$

verification at e-shirt.com. Once an e-shirt, say e-shirt2 receives the broadcast data from e-shirt1, it tags its own packet of same format as 2 and sends it to the eShirt.com through local access point. The eShirt.com receives the packet shown in figure 8 from e-shirt2.

In Figure 8 , 1 corresponds to e-shirt1 (the broadcaster), and the 2 corresponds to the receiver e-shirt2. Once eShirt.com receives this packet, it'll first check the credentials of e-shirt1, i.e., EID1. eShirt.com knows the K_{mac} corresponding to EID1, and thus it can check the received MAC. If correct, then it knows that the content contained within the packet is from e-shirt1 and has not been tampered with. It then checks the fields corresponding to e-shirt2, and if incorrect discards the packet as not coming from e-shirt2. If the credentials of e-shirt2 also match, eShirt.com now knows that the packet came from e-shirt2 and has not been tampered with. It then checks from the Facebook database whether these two shirt owners are friends or foes. If friends, eShirt.com sends a secure encrypted message to e-shirt2 to glow its green light, else glow its red light.

Along with identity verification, eShirt.com checks the corresponding time-stamp and locations between the two shirts. If the timestamps do not match within certain error limit, then eShirt.com discards the packet. This is based on the assumption that e-shirt2 can receive a pretty old packet from e-shirt1 and by then e-shirt can move out of the environment. Similarly, if the geographic location doesn't match within certain error limit, eShirt.com simply discards the packet.

3.2   Threat Prevention

In this section we will discuss how our proposed security model takes care of the threats discussed in section 2.2.

1. **Spoofing:** As the Facebook ID is not embedded in any shirt, the Facebook ID cannot be spoofed. Even if some attacker spoofs EID (eshirt id), that will not help as every time the credential is checked by eShirt.com against the MAC key and unique nonce. As the MAC key is secret and is known only by the eShirt.com server and corresponding e-shirt, no outsider can retrieve that. So spoofing is not possible.
2. **Eavesdropping:** This is taken care by the fact that there is no login to Facebook in every session. In fact in this scheme the direct interaction between e-shirt and Facebook is not required anymore. As mentioned, only in the registration process a user has to give his/her Facebook ID to to the eShirt.com server.
3. **Replay:** If e-shirt3 is an eavesdropper and it's forwarding e-shirt1's packet to e-shirt2, which is in different environment, then the eShirt.com can detect the theft. First the server will check the time-stamp value of both and then the location. If e-shirt1 and e-shirt2 are in different location, then this will be caught. If the eavesdropper forwards an old packet, that can also be caught from the time-stamp value. In the case of a replay attack, eShirt.com will inform the two shirts in concern. Then they can backoff their transmission for a certain time.
4. **Compromised shirt:** If the shirt itself is compromised and the user can suspect that, it can nullify its eShirt.com ID and re-register again.
5. **Energy exhaustion:** As discussed, if a shirt is attacked by some malicious user, eShirt.com can detect that and it'll let the shirt know about the attack. The shirt can switch itself off for a certain time and then again check its environment through normal operation. This can help mitigate an energy exhaustion attack.

4   Implementation and Results

One of the major issues we need to keep in mind while implementing our security protocol in eshirt is the limited computing power and memory in the eshirt. To save memory we use a single block cipher for encryption, decryption and MAC computation as suggested by [20]. We have selected RC5 as the block cipher due to low computational and memory requirement of the cipher [20]. We use our own implementation of RC5 algorithm instead of using the standard openssl one as the overheads of the openssl implementation is too large for our purposes. For encryption and decryption, we use RC5 in CTR mode and for computing MAC we use CBC-MAC as suggested by Perrig et al. [20]. In our experiment we found, the average round-about time for detecting a new e-shirt and glowing the LED based on friend and foe information is around 1.5 sec.

5   Background and Related Work

Social Networks. According to Facebook.com's statistics page, the site has over 750 million active users [2], making it the 5th most trafficked website in the world. Existing social networks already allow users to share a rich set of contextual data online. The amount of data and the type of data stored on these sites is growing daily. Remarkably, Facebook alone gets over 14 million new photos uploaded to it every day. Also, the way in which user access that data is expanding. Facebook applications allow developers to provide users with new ways of accessing data. More than 95% of Facebook users have at least one Facebook application installed [2]. The existence of such data and access to it through the Facebook API allow for a simple touch sensor and LED to become a gateway to an entire world of applications and information. In effect, the wearable and its use become a part of a users digital identity.

Wearable Sensing and Actuation. A large body of work has explored wearable sensing platforms that detect information about a wearer's movements, physiological state and location, primarily to support context aware applications [13,18,19]. Another class of projects have investigated how communicating wearable devices can augment real-world interactions and experiences. For example, Borovoy et al. developed communicating name tags that tracked wearer's face to face interactions and allowed wearers to easily exchange virtual business cards [5]. A final class of relevant devices has employed wearable and textile-based actuators for a variety of purposes. Several designers have used LEDs in wearables displays [9,3,11,4]. Our system differs from previous ones in its integration of wearable, socially relevant sensing and actuation with a social networking system.

MoSoNets & TechoSharking. Some existing work in "MoSoNets" has merged social networks with mobile devices. Dating application on mobile phones [17] and a Bluetooth-based presence sharing system called Serendipity [12] have combined local and social information, but the outcomes are fairly closed systems which are cut off from the wider online social networking phenomenon. Research in context-aware smart spaces [15] and context-aware UIs [16,10,21] hint at some of the possibilities of MoSoNets, but are largely disconnected from the phenomenon of online social networks. However this approach does not manage to exploit the richness of information existing both in the social network and integrate this with the physical actions of the user.

However, our previous work [6,7] tried to bridge this gap by accessing social networking information from smart phone and wearable devices. But they have not investigated the security and privacy threats inherent in such application.

6   Conclusion

Research on the intersection of mobile computing and social networks is still rather immature. The integration of wearables into a MoSoNet demonstrates the extent to which these new technologies may be integrated in users' physical interactions. While MoSoNets offer the promise of bringing people closer together, they also pose a threat to security and privacy by bringing malicious users closer to people.

The MoSoNet application presented in this paper shows a sample scenario to demonstrate potential privacy threats in cyber-physical interaction and builds a proof-of-concept framework that mitigates such threats.

References

1. Facebook developer resource,
   `http://developers.facebook.com/resources.php`
2. Facebook statistics,
   `http://www.facebook.com/press/info.php?statistics`
3. Nyx illuminated clothing, `http://www.nyxit.com/`
4. Berzowska, J., Coelho, M.: Kukkia and vilkas: Kinetic electronic garments. In: Proceedings of the IEEE International Symposium on Wearable Computers (2005)
5. Borovoy, R., McDonald, M., Martin, F., Resnick, M.: Things that blink: computationally augmented name tags. IBM Systems Journal 35(3-4) (1996)
6. Beach, A., Gartrell, M., Akkala, S., Elston, J., Kelley, J., Nishimoto, K., Ray, B., Razgulin, S., Sundaresan, K., Surendar, B., Terada, M., Han, R.: Whozthat? evolving an ecosystem for context-aware mobile social networks. IEEE Network 22(4), 50–55 (2008)
7. Beach, A., Ray, B., Buechley, L.: Touch Me wE@r: Getting Physical with Social Networks. In: IEEE International Conference on Computational Science and Engineering, vol. 4, pp. 960–965 (2009)
8. Buechley, L., Eisenberg, M., Catchen, J., Crockett, A.: The lilypad arduino: Using computational textile to investigate engagement, aesthetics and diversity in computer science education. In: CHI, pp. 423–432 (2008)
9. Buechley, L., Eisenberg, M.: Fabric pcbs, electronic sequins, and socket buttons: Techniques for e-textile craft. Personal and Ubiquitous Computing (2007)
10. Cheverst, K., Davies, N., Mitchell, K., Friday, A.: Experiences of developing and deploying a context-aware tourist guide: The guide project. In: ACM MobiCom, pp. 20–31 (2000)
11. Dunne, L.E., Toney, A., Ashdown, S., Thomas, B.: Subtle garment integration of technology: A case study of the business suit. In: IFAWC (2004)
12. Eagle, N., Pentland, A.: Social serendipity: Mobilizing social software. IEEE Pervasive Computing 4(2) (April-June 2005)
13. Choudhury, T., et al.: The mobile sensing platform: An embedded activity recognition system. IEEE Pervasive Computing 7(2), 32–41 (2008)
14. Gennaro, R., Rohatgi, P.: How to sign digital streams, pp. 180–197. Springer, Heidelberg (1997)
15. Microsoft Vision Group; Microsoft easyliving,
    `http://research.microsoft.com/easyliving/`
16. Harter, A., Hopper, T., Steggles, P., Ward, A., Webster, P.: The anatomy of a context-aware application. In: Mobicom 1999, pp. 59–68 (August 1999)
17. Iwatani, Y.: Love: Japanese style. In: WIRED (1998)
18. Madan, A., Pentland, A.: Vibefones: Socially aware mobile phones. In: ISWC, pp. 109–112 (2006)
19. Pentland, A.: Socially aware computation and communication. IEEE Computer 38(3), 33–40 (2005)
20. Perrig, A., Szewczyk, R., Wen, V., Culler, D., Tygar, J.D.: Spins: Security protocols for sensor networks. Wireless Networks, 189–199 (2001)
21. Priyantha, N., Miu, A., Balakrishnan, H., Teller, S.: The cricket compass for context-aware mobile applications. In: ACM MobiCom, pp. 1–14 (2001)
22. Rohatgi, P.: A compact and fast hybrid signature scheme for multicast packet authentication. In: CCS 1999, pp. 93–100. ACM, New York (1999)

Throughput Analysis of Next-Hop Forwarding Method for Non-linear Vehicular Ad Hoc Networks

Ram Shringar Raw and D.K. Lobiyal

School of Computer and Systems Sciences,
Jawaharlal Nehru University,
New Delhi, India
rsrao08@yahoo.in, lobiyal@gmail.com

Abstract. Position based routing plays a significant role in multi-hop Vehicular Ad hoc Networks (VANETs), due to high mobility of nodes. Selection of next-hop node is crucial to improve the performance of routing. In this paper, we have proposed a method for selecting next-hop forwarding node based on the distance between the source and next-hop node and link quality. Next-hop node is selected based on Expected Progress Distance (EPD) criteria. The EPD is estimated in terms of expected distance between the source and next-hop node. The expected delay (E_D) and throughput (T_h) are also estimated for the proposed method. The mathematical model derived for calculating EPD, delay, and throughput are simulated in MATLAB and evaluated the performance of the proposed method.

Keywords: VANET, MANET, Next-Hop Forwarding, Position Based Routing, Greedy Forwarding, EPD, Delay, Throughput.

1   Introduction

Current advances in wireless communication systems are enabling a new vehicular communication system to improve and protect road transportation. Vehicular Ad Hoc Network (VANET) [1] is the budding and challenging subclass of Mobile Ad Hoc Networks (MANETs) [2]. VANET is composed of a large number of vehicles providing connectivity to each other. We assume that vehicles move in any direction with high mobility. Neighboring vehicles that are within a transmission range directly communicate over a wireless links. End-to-end connectivity between source and destination vehicle in VANET requires multi-hop packet forwarding by intermediate vehicles. VANET supports vehicles that are equipped with computing device, short range wireless interface and GPS receiver [3].

Position based routing can be defined as a next-hop forwarding method in which a node uses the position information of both itself and the destination node to determine a route. Therefore, position based routing protocols does not require any information about the global topology of the network. Unlike traditional routing protocols, position based routing protocols can address the challenges present by interesting properties of VANETs [4].

N. Meghanathan et al. (Eds.): CCSIT 2012, Part II, LNICST 85, pp. 525–534, 2012.

The dynamic topology of VANET reduces the throughput and efficiency of the routing protocols. Therefore, various approaches have been recommended to improve the throughput and the efficiency of position based next-hop forwarding [5], [6], [7] for linear and non-linear topology network. In this paper, we propose a forwarding method for non-linear network to select the next-hop node using next-hop forwarding method. We also use a link metric that is Expected Progress Distance (EPD) to evaluate the performance of forwarding method.

The rest of this paper is organized as follows. We discuss the related work in section 2. In section 3, the design of proposed method is introduced. Section 4 presents the mathematical analysis of the proposed method. Results and performance evaluation is presented in section 5. Finally, we conclude this paper in section 6.

2   Related Work

Takagi and Kleinrock [8] proposed the first position based routing protocol that is MFR routing protocol which is based on the notion of progress. MFR is a well-known loop-free method for finding a route in a network by utilizing position information of nodes [9]. The neighbor with the greatest progress on the straight line joining the source and destination is chosen as next-hop node for sending packets further. Therefore MFR forwards the packet to the node that is closest to the destination node in an attempt to minimize the number of hops [10].

Kranakis [11] proposed the DIR (referred as the Compass Routing) is based on the greedy forwarding method in which the source node uses the position information of the destination node to calculate its direction. Then the message is forwarded to the nearest neighbor having direction closest to the line drawn between source and destination. Therefore, a message is forwarded to the neighboring node minimizing the angle between itself, the previous node, and the destination. A GEDIR [9] is a loop free location based routing algorithm. It is the variant of greedy routing. In GEDIR, a source node forwards packets to its neighbor nodes that are closest to the destination node.

Hiraku, Akira, and Kenichi [12] proposed the next-hop forwarding method by limiting the forwarding distance for linear vehicular ad hoc networks. This is position based routing method based on the greedy forwarding method. In some cases, performance (packet delivery ratio and throughput) of the network may degrade due to longer forwarding distance because longer forwarding distance can cause transmission errors in the wireless network. When the maximum forwarding distance increases, the propagation loss increases and the transmission quality of the wireless link, such as packet delivery ratio degrades. To stop degradation in the network, next-hop forwarding by limiting the forwarding distance method is useful. In this method the author calculated the Expected Progress Distance (EPD) to select the next-hop node by choosing among neighbor nodes that are within a predefined maximum forwarding distance (see Fig. 1). This method improves both the forwarding distance and the transmission quality of the wireless link.

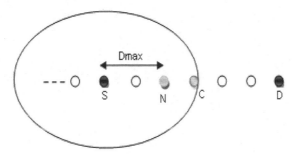

Fig. 1. Greedy forwarding by limiting the forwarding distance method (linear case)

3   Proposed Work

In this section, we propose a next-hop forwarding method by limiting the forwarding distance for non-linear network. In a dense non-linear network such as city traffic network, nodes are distributed randomly and move in any direction. In such traffic network, numbers of moving and stopped vehicles are very large, spacing between vehicles is small, and fixed road side infrastructure is available. However position-based routing in city scenarios faces a lot of challenges due to potentially more irregular distribution of vehicle nodes, forced mobility, and difficult signal reception. City vehicular ad-hoc network defined as dense and large network where source nodes have many alternative paths to destination nodes. The shortest-path position-based routing protocols frequently select paths that have the minimum number of hops rather than the maximum expected capacity.

3.1   Next-Hop Forwarding Method by Limiting the Forwarding Distance for Non-linear Network

This method considers both forwarding distance and transmission quality to selects a next-hop node. In this method, forwarding node selects a neighbor node as the next-hop node by choosing among neighboring nodes that are within a predefined maximum forwarding distance. The next-hop node is selected using the EPD link metric. This method gives better performance in terms of transmission quality considering Expected Transmission Time (ETT).

In Fig.2, S and D are source and destination nodes. N is the next-hop node and C is the closest to destination node. D_{max} is the maximum forwarding distance between forwarding node (source node) and next-hop node. As greedy forwarding method decides the next-hop node by exchanging Hello packets and selects the neighbor node that is closest to the destination node as the next-hop node. In this method, a neighbor node with good reception environment and the closest to the destination is selected as next-hop node. As shown in the Fig.2, source node S selects node N (not node C) as the next-hop node for further transmission.

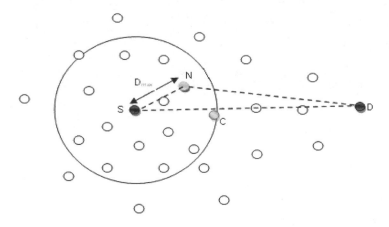

Fig. 2. Greedy forwarding by limiting the forwarding distance method (non-linear case)

3.2   Next-Hop Node Selection

The progress distance is obtained through position information of forwarding node, neighbor nodes, and destination node. Using the neighbor information table, forwarding node find the next-hop node whose *EPD* is maximum among all neighboring nodes. As shown in the Fig.2, neighbor node *N* is selected as the next-hop node. In the greedy forwarding method, neighbor node *C* is selected as the next-hop node because it is the closest neighbor to the destination node within the transmission range. When we consider *ETT*, the node nearest to the forwarding node (source node) is selected as the next-hop node because smallest *ETT* gives the best transmission quality of the wireless link in the ad hoc networks.

4   Mathematical Analysis

In this work, we consider the non-linear network where vehicles move on the road in every direction. The distance between nodes is assumed to be a random variable with Poisson distribution. The path loss depends on the forwarding distance between forwarding node and next-hop node. To select next-hop node with good transmission quality, limiting the maximum forwarding distance is more effective. In this section, we study the expected distance to next-hop node $E(D_{max})$, *ETT*, and *EPD* to select a next-hop node with good transmission quality.

4.1   Expected Distance to Next-Hop Node

One of the metrics used in any vehicular network is end-to-to-end delay that depends on the criteria used to select the next-hop node for forwarding the packets. Selecting next-hop node at the maximum distance from the source or close to the destination is to reduce the number of hops occurring in a route. Here it is assumed that the minimum number of hops in a route results in minimum end-to-end delay. Since we have considered a non-linear network of randomly distributed nodes, it is difficult to determine the exact value of maximum distance between a source and next-hop node. Therefore, this distance can be considered as a random variable and its expected value can be determined. Let assumed that a source node S has n neighbors in the direction of destination node. Let N is the next-hop node of source node S (see Fig. 2). Let d_1, d_2, d_3..., d_n denotes the distances between source node S and its neighbors [13]. D_{max} is the maximum distance between the source node S and its one-hop nodes, i.e.

$$D_{max} = Max_{i=1}^{n} d_i \tag{1}$$

We can calculate the expected value of distance D_{max} between the source node and its neighbors as follows:

Let $F(D_{max})$ and $f(D_{max})$ be the *CDF* and *PDF* of D_{max}. Then,

$$F(D_{max}) = P[d_1 \leq D_{max}, d_2 \leq D_{max}, , ..., d_n \leq D_{max}]$$

$$= \prod_{i=1}^{n} P[d_i \leq D_{max}] = \left(\frac{D_{max}}{R}\right)^n \tag{2}$$

Similarly,

$$f(D_{max}) = \frac{d}{d_{D_{max}}} F(D_{max}) = \frac{n}{R}\left(\frac{D_{max}}{R}\right)^{n-1} \tag{3}$$

The expected value of D_{max} is,

$$E(D_{max}) = \int_0^R D_{max} \cdot f(D_{max}) \, dD_{max}$$

$$= \int_0^R D_{max} \cdot \frac{n}{R}\left(\frac{D_{max}}{R}\right)^{n-1} \, dD_{max}$$

$$= \frac{n}{R^n}\left[\frac{D_{max}^{n+1}}{n+1}\right]_0^R = \frac{nR}{n+1} \tag{4}$$

4.2   Expected Progress Distance (EPD)

The expected maximum distance between a source and its next-hop node computed in (4) can be used in determining the shortest path between an original source and final destination. Number of hops (hop counts) can be calculated to divide the distance between original source and final destination by the maximum distance obtained by (4). Hop counts is one of the most common routing metric used in most MANET protocols such as AODV, DSR, DSDV, GSR, OLSR and GPSR. But, this is a simple metric to find shortest route between a source and destination.

Hop counts are one equal unit and independent from the quality or other characteristics of the links. Therefore, hop counts though, minimizes the number of hops in the multi-hop network, but it may not minimize end-to-end delay. To take quality of link into account we have also considered transmission time along with the maximum distance between source and next-hop node. Transmission time varies from link to link and thus its exact value cannot be determined. Therefore, we have considered it as a random variable and determined its expected value.

The *ETT* (Expected Transmission Time) routing metric [14] is an isotonic metric and it is used to maximize the throughput of the path by measuring the link capacities and would increase the overall performance of the network. *ETT* may be defined in two ways. Firstly, it is defined in terms of Expected number of Transmission (*ETX*) as follows:

$$ETT = ETX \cdot \frac{S}{L} \tag{5}$$

Where S is the size of a packet and L is the bandwidth of the link. *ETX* [15] is a path metric that is used to maximize the network throughput by measuring loop-free paths and link quality in the wireless network. It is simply the sum of the *ETX* value of each link along the path. When the *ETX* metric is lesser for a link, the wireless link is better. In position based greedy forwarding method, *ETX* is measured by using periodically broadcast control messages which are sent very frequently. Let p is the probability to deliver a packet successfully and $q = 1-p$ is the probability of failure to deliver a packet. *ETX* to successfully deliver a packet to the next-hop [16] can be estimated as:

$$ETX = \sum_{n=1}^{\infty} x \cdot p^x (1-p)^{x-1}$$

$$= \frac{1}{(1-p)} \tag{6}$$

The relationship between the *ETT* of a link and *ETX* can be defined as:

$$ETT = ETX \cdot \frac{S}{L} = \frac{S}{L \cdot (1-p)} \tag{7}$$

To improve the performance network expected distance $E\ (D_{max})$ calculated in (4) is combined with *ETT* to compute a new *EPD* metric for a link. This new metric is used to select a next-hop node to transmit a packet from source to destination. Therefore, link metric, *EPD* is calculated as expected distance to next-hop node $E\ (D_{max})$ divided by the expected one-hop transmission time *ETT* [12] as follows:

$$EPD = \frac{Expected\ Distance\ to\ Next\ Hop\ Node}{Expected\ one\ hop\ Transmission\ Time} = \frac{E(D_{max})}{ETT}$$

$$= \frac{nR}{ETT \cdot (n+1)} \tag{8}$$

4.3   Expected Delay and Throughput

It is common in VANETs that the nodes move within a certain transmission range. Therefore, network performance directly depends on the number of hops with average delay in a VANET. Delay is one of the key parameter to be considered for vehicular network traffic [17]. It is defined as the time taken for a packet to be transmitted across a network from source to destination. Throughput of the network is universally proportional to the average delay between source and destination [18]. Throughput of the network can be estimated as follows:

$$Delay\ (E_D) = \frac{Expected\ Progress\ Distance\ (EPD)}{Bandwidth\ of\ the\ Link\ (L)} = \frac{n\ R}{ETT\cdot(n+1)} \cdot \frac{1}{L} \tag{9}$$

$$Throughput(T_h) = \frac{ETT\cdot(n+1)\cdot L}{nR} \tag{10}$$

5   Results and Performance Analysis

The mathematical model proposed here has been simulated using MATLAB. In the simulation, we have deployed the nodes randomly. The transmission range of nodes has been fixed at 250m. The network area is a squared region of 2000m. This model has been used to calculate the *EPD*. We have evaluated the impact of network size (i.e., number of nodes in the network) and *ETT* on Expected Progress Distance. In the simulations, results have been computed in terms of expected progress distance between source and next-hop node.

5.1   Expected Progress Distance (EPD)

Fig. 3 shows the corresponding result for expected progress distance. From the Fig. 3 we can observe that as the number of nodes increases, the expected progress distance between forwarding node and next-hop node is also increases. We have computed the results of *EPD* for varying network size for different transmission range since it impacts the *EPD*. The results have been computed by fixing transmission range at different values of *R, i.e.* 250m, 265m and 280m respectively. As shown in the figure, *EPD* is better for R = 280m than R = 265m since higher transmission range provides better value of *EPD*. Further, *EPD* increases as the node density increases because nodes fall closer and link quality is better between closer nodes.

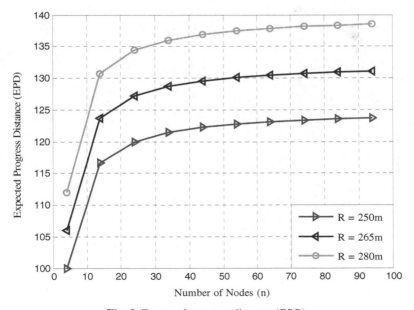

Fig. 3. Expected progress distance (*EPD*)

5.2   Delay (E_D) and Throughput (T_h)

Delay and throughput are most important parameter to be considered for vehicular traffic. Fig. 4 shows the variation in average delay as the number of nodes increases. We can observe that as the number of nodes increases, the average delay between forwarding node and next-hop node is decreases. Delay is always higher for higher *ETT* (*ETT* = 14) compared to lower *ETT* (*ETT* = 10).

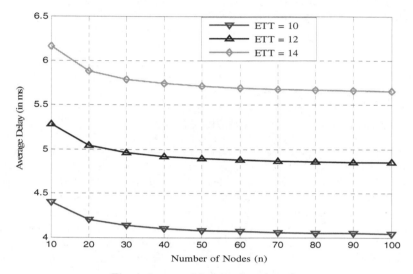

Fig. 4. Average delay as a function of *n*

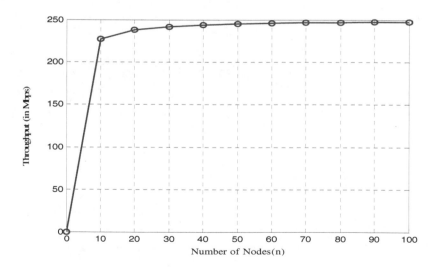

Fig. 5. Throughput (T_h, in Mbps)

Fig. 5 shows that number of nodes directly affects the throughput of VANETs communications. From the numerical analysis, we can see that initially throughput increases faster as number of nodes increases and network becomes saturated at 85 nodes and get maximum throughput for the maximum number of nodes for a fixed transmission range.

6   Conclusion

In this paper, we have proposed a method for selecting next-hop forwarding node based on the distance between the source and next-hop node and link quality. In this method, the neighbor node that has the maximum *EPD* is selected as the next-hop node among neighboring nodes. Nodes in the network have higher *EPD* when the network size is large and small *ETT*. Delay and throughput are estimated for selected next-hop node. Network performance in terms of throughput will be maximized for the maximum number of nodes for a fixed transmission range. Therefore, this method by limiting the forwarding distance is an effective position-based routing method to forward packets from source to destination with good transmission quality of wireless link.

References

1. Moustafa, H., Zhang, Y.: Vehicular networks: Techniques, Standards, and Applications. CRC Press (2009)
2. Murthy, C.S.R., Manoj, B.S.: Ad Hoc Wireless Networks: Architectures and Protocols. Pearson (2008) ISBN 81-317-0688-5
3. Manvi, S.S., Kakkasageri, M.S.: Issue in Mobile Ad hoc Networks for Vehicular Communication. IETE Technical Review 25(2) (2008)
4. Raw, R.S., Das, S., Agarwal, A.: Thoughts on Vehicular Ad Hoc Networks (VANETs) in the Real World Traffic Scenarios. International Journal Computer Science Management System (IJCSMS) 3(1), 19–26 (2011)
5. Raw, R.S., Lobiyal, D.K.: VANET: Position-Based Routing in Urban Environment - A Technical Review. In: TRANSTEC 2010, New Delhi (2010)
6. Takano, A., Okada, H., Mase, K.: Performance Comparison of a Position-Based Routing Protocol for VANET. IEEE (2007)
7. Mauve, M., Widmer, J.: A Survey on Position-Based Routing in Mobile Ad Hoc Networks. IEEE Network (November/December 2001)
8. Takagi, H., Kleinrock, L.: Optimal transmission ranges for randomly distributed packet radio terminals. IEEE Transactions on Communications 32(3), 246–257 (1984)
9. Stojmenovic, I., Ruhil, A.P., Lobiyal, D.K.: Voronoi diagram and convex hull based Geocasting and routing in wireless networks. In: Wireless Communications and Mobile Computing. John Wiley & Sons Ltd. (2006)
10. Raw, R.S., Lobiyal, D.K.: E-DIR: A Directional Routing Protocol for VANETs in a City Traffic Environment. International Journal of Information and Communication Technology (IJICT) 3(2), 242–257 (2011) ISSN: 1466-6642
11. Kranakis, E., Singh, H., Urrutia, J.: Compass routing on geometric networks. In: Proc. 11th Canadian Conference on Computational Geometry, Vancouver (August 1999)

12. Okada, H., Takano, A., Mase, K.: A Proposal of Link Metric for Next-Hop Forwarding Methods in Vehicular Ad Hoc Networks. IEEE (2009)
13. Yi, C., Chuang, Y., Yeh, H., Tseng, Y., Liu, P.: Streetcast: An Urban Broadcast Protocol for Vehicular Ad-Hoc Networks (2009)
14. Guerin, J., Portman, M., Pirzada, A.: Routing Metrics for Multi-Radio Wireless Mess Networks (2008)
15. Yang, Y., Wang, J., Kravets, R.: Desiging Routing Metrics for Mesh Networks (2006)
16. Addagada, B.K., Kisara, V., Desai, K.: A Survey: Routing Metrics for Wireless Mess Networks (May 5, 2009)
17. Asif, H.M., Sheltami, T., Shakshuki, E.: Power Conumption Optimization and Delay minimization in MANET. In: Proceedings of MoMM (2008)
18. Hongfei, L., Zhongiun, Y., Tao, W., Lijun, L., Fu, Z.: Throughput and Reliability Analysis of Information Broadcasting Protocol in VANETs. IEEE (2010)

A Novel Algorithm for Prediction of Protein Coding DNA from Non-coding DNA in Microbial Genomes Using Genomic Composition and Dinucleotide Compositional Skew

Baharak Goli, B.L. Aswathi, and Achuthsankar S. Nair

State Inter-University Centre for Bioinformatics,
University of Kerala,
Trivandrum 695581, India
baharak_goli@yahoo.com

Abstract. Accurate identification of genes encoding proteins in genome remains an open problem in computational biology that has been receiving increasing consideration with explosion in sequence data. This has inspired us to relook at this problem. In this study, we propose a novel gene finding algorithm which relies on the use of genomic composition and dinucleotide compositional skew information. In order to identify the most prominent features, two feature selection techniques widely used in data preprocessing for machine learning problems: CFS and ReliefF algorithm applied. The performance of two types of neural network such as multilayer perceptron and RBF network was evaluated with these filter approaches. Our proposed model led to successful prediction of protein coding from non-coding with 96.47% and 94.18 % accuracy for MLP and RBF Network respectively in case of CFS and 94.94 % and 92.46 % accuracy for MLP and RBF Network respectively in case of ReliefF algorithm.

Keywords: Identification of protein coding DNA, genomic composition, dinucleotide compositional skew, feature selection methods, machine learning.

1 Introduction

With the speedy development of genome sequencing technologies and databases the amount of genomic data has been increasing almost exponentially. Till date, 1646 microbial genomes have been sequenced successfully, while sequencing of more than 4900 microbial genomes are currently in progress. The most important biologically functional parts of DNA sequence of any organism are its genes. Genes control all major biological processes of an organism through the complex expression of their cognate gene products. Therefore, gene identification from genome sequences and

N. Meghanathan et al. (Eds.): CCSIT 2012, Part II, LNICST 85, pp. 535–542, 2012.

their biological importance in most of living organisms is a challenging issue in bioinformatics and computational biology [1]. A Large number of computational algorithms have been proposed to predict protein-coding DNAs over the last two decades [2], [3], [4], [5], [6]. These algorithms can be divided into two categories. The approaches in the first category, the ab initio programs, are based on various statistics of DNA sequences, which usually use training datasets from already known coding and non-coding sequences to find the discriminant function [7], [8]. The second category known as homology-based programs, includes algorithms that are based on similarity search in large databases of genomic information [9], [10], [11], [12], however these algorithms are not perfect due to lack of experimentally verified proteins in databases. Recently another type of gene prediction tools have developed which combine the result from two or more gene finding tool and have a higher performance[13]. In this study we have developed a statistics-based approach to discriminate protein coding DNA from non-coding DNA based on the use of genomic composition and dinucleotide compositional skew information.

2   Materials and Methods

2.1   The Dataset

We selected Escherichia coli k12 MG1655 for our development available in the Integrated Microbial Genomes (IMG) database [14]. Protein coding sequences and non-coding sequences shorter than 100 were excluded. The final number of protein coding DNA was 4334 and non-coding was 1823.

2.2   Feature Transformation

The quantitative characteristics of DNA that we took into our consideration included nucleotide composition and nucleotide compositional skews. The nucleotide composition comprised of the frequencies of base (4 features), dimer (16 features), trimer (64 features), AG content, GC content, GT content and atomic composition (5 features). Nucleotide compositional skews included GC skew, AT skew, AG skew, TC skew, GT skew, Purine skew and Kito skew. The dinucleotide compositional skew indices are calculated as differences between single strand frequencies of certain nucleotides divided by the total of the frequencies. For example, the GT skew is computed as the value of ([G]-[T])/([G]+[T]) where brackets indicate the absolute values of correspondent nucleotides. The skew method plays an important role in studying the base composition bias related to both DNA replication [15] and transcription processes [16]. Graphical representation of AT skew for a protein coding DNA and non-coding of same size (500 nt) shows remarkable discriminative pattern (Figure 1).

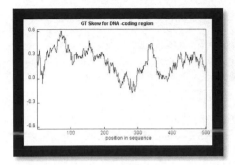

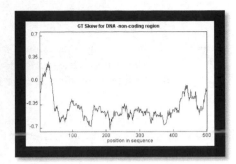

GT skew for coding region
id |6463119031 |
for Ecoli K-12 MG1655
Maximum value:0.792
Minimum value:-0.172

GT skew for non-coding region
id |NC_000913_4266331_4266831|
for Ecoli K-12 MG1655
Maximum value:0.32
Minimum value:-0.743

Fig. 1. Graphical representations of AT skew for a coding and non-coding DNA sequence

2.3   Feature Subset Selection Techniques

The performance of a classifier totally depends on the relations between a number of features, training set size and classifier complexity. Hence large number of features comprises an obstacle to efficiency of classification algorithms by increasing computation time and   [17] over-fitting the training data set [18] a smallest subset of important and prominent features that attains maximal classification performance, faster classification models and smaller data bases should be retained. Feature selection is one of the important techniques in data preprocessing for machine learning and data mining problems. It trashes out irrelevant, noisy and redundant features, speeds up the data mining algorithm and improves prediction accuracy [19]. For this purpose we adopted two well-known feature selection techniques such as CFS (correlation-based feature selection) [20] and ReliefF feature selection algorithm [21] to select the appropriate discriminatory set of features. We briefly describe these feature selection algorithms below. In this study 96 features generated from the transformation step explained above and after feature selection a total of 19 features remained.

2.3.1   Correlation-Based Feature Selection Algorithm (CFS)

The correlation-based feature selection algorithm has been proved as a powerful technique in removing both unrelated and redundant features. It assesses the significance of subsets of features and uses a best first-search heuristic. This heuristic algorithm considers the relevance of individual features for predicting the class along with the level of correlation among them. The main logic in CFS is that good feature subsets include those features that are highly correlated with the target class and uncorrelated with each other. The CFS function is defined as follows:

$$M_s = k \, \bar{r}_{cf} / \sqrt{(k + k(k-1) \, \bar{r}_{ff})} \qquad (1)$$

where M_s is the heuristic subsets evaluator function when the subset (s) containing k features, $\bar{r}_{cf}$ is the feature-classification correlative average value where (f∈S) and $\bar{r}_{ff}$ is the feature-feature correlation average value.

2.3.2   Relief Feature Selection Algorithm (ReliefF)

ReliefF is a simple and powerful feature selection technique. It is an extension of Relief algorithm [22] developed to use in classification problems. It evaluates the relevance of features with strong dependencies between them. At each step of an iterative process, an instance k is selected randomly from the dataset and the weight for each feature is updated based on the distance of k to its NearHit (nearest neighbors from the same class) and NearMiss (nearest neighbors from each of the different classes). This process is iterated n times, where n is a predefined parameter. Generally n is equal to the number of samples in dataset. Finally the best subset includes those features with relevance above a chosen threshold t.

2.4   Building of Neural Networks

Artificial neural network is a supervised learning algorithm used commonly to solve classification problems. In this study, two types of neural networks configurations, multilayer perceptron trained by the back propagation algorithm and RBF network, were chosen. The weka suite, machine learning workbench developed in java programming language was used for implementation [23].

Back-propagation networks are apparently the most common and widely used algorithm for training supervised neural networks [24], [25], [26]. It has less memory requirements than most techniques and usually reaches an adequate error level significantly fast. It can be adopted on most types of networks, however it is most suitable for training multilayer perceptrons. RBF networks are supervised neural networks which are popular alternative to the MLPs which employ reasonably lesser number of locally tuned units and are adaptive in nature. They are widely used for pattern recognition and classification problems. RBF networks are suitable for modeling nonlinear data and can be trained in one phase instead of using an iterative process as in MLPs [27], [28].In this study, the training set consisting of 4334 coding and 1823 non-coding elements was given to the each network in the 10-fold cross-validation scheme. The accuracy of classification using each network was measured. For the comparison of the networks, the time taken by each network to build the model was also noted.

3   Results

3.1   Evaluation of Performance

The performance of our proposed models were estimated using standard 10-fold cross-validation in which the whole dataset is randomly partitioned into ten evenly-sized subsets. During each test, a neural network is trained on nine subsets and then tested on the tenth one. This method is repeated ten times so that each subset is used for both training and testing on each fold. Performance is measured for each test set, and the mean is reported as overall accuracy. Several measures were used to evaluate the performance of the neural networks (TP, TN, FP and FN representing true positive, true negative, false positive and false negative respectively).

Specificity=TN/ (TN+FP)*100
Sensitivity=TP/ (TP+FN)*100
Precision=TP/ (TP+FP)*100
Matthews correlation coefficient = $(((TP*TN)-(FP*FN)))/(\sqrt{(TP+FP)*(TP+FN)*(TN+FP)*(TN+FN)})$
Accuracy= TP+TN/ (TP+TN+FP+TN)

Table 1. Performance of gene finding tools

Method	Sn (%)	Sp (%)	Pc (%)	MCC	Acc (%)
Multilayer perceptron + cfs	97.09	95.00	97.88	0.91	96.47
RBF Network + cfs	91.99	99.39	99.72	0.87	94.18
Multilayer perceptron + relief-f	95.29	94.13	97.47	0.88	94.94
RBF Network+relief-f	90.23	97.75	98.96	0.8378	92.46

The comparison of performances of different neural networks is shown in Table 1.Multilayer Perceptronin conjunction with correlation-based feature selection algorithm produced highest classification result. Time taken to build the models were 81.56 seconds for multilayer perceptron and 5.03 seconds for RBF network in case of correlation-based feature selection and 83.86 seconds for multilayer perceptron and 7.19 seconds for RBF network in case of relief feature selection algorithm in the same work station.

Self-consistency test and independent test (shown in Table 2) were also performed to evaluate the prediction model. Self-consistency test reflects the consistency of the developed model. It is an evaluation method to estimate the level of fitness of data in a developed method. In self-consistency test, observations of training datasets are predicted with decision rules acquired from the same dataset.The accuracy of self-consistency reveals the fitting ability of the rules obtained from the features of training sets. Since the prediction system parameters obtained by the self-consistency

Table 2. Accuracy of each classifier for self-consistency and independent data test

Method	Self-consistency test (%)	Independent data test(%)
Multilayer perceptron+cfs	97.09	95.61
RBF Network+cfs	94.15	93.83
Multilayer perceptron + relief-f	94.90	94.48
RBF Network+ relief-f	92.65	92.08

test are from the training dataset, the success rate is high. However poor result of self-consistency test reflects the inefficiency of classification method.In independent dataset the training set composed of two-thirds of protein coding DNA, and two-thirds of the non-coding sequences. The remaining sequences were used as the testing set.

4   Discussion

Existing gene finding tools employ different biological information for identification of protein coding regions. In this study, a novel gene finding algorithm which relies on the use of genomic composition and dinucleotide compositional skew information was proposed. Our results indicate that genomic composition and dinucleotide compositional skew in conjunction with two feature selection methods: Correlation-based feature selection and the Relief-F algorithm followed by two classification algorithms, multilayer perceptron and RBF Networks are significantly useful features in classification of protein coding DNA from non-coding. The ability of these discriminant features is evident from the above mentioned performance evaluation techniques.

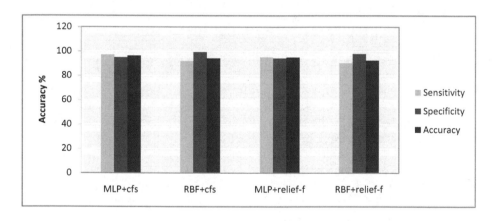

Fig. 2. Average Specificity, Sensitivity and Accuracy for the various methods

References

1. Baldi, P., Brunak, S.: Bioinformatics: The Machine Learning Approach. The MIT Press, Cambridge (1998)
2. Fickett, J.W.: The gene identification problem: an overview for developers. Comput. Che. 20, 103–118 (1996)
3. Mathé, C., Schiex, M.-F., Rouzé, P.: Current methods of gene prediction, their strength and weaknesses. Nucleic Acids Res. 30, 4103–4117 (2002)

4. Wang, Z., Chen, Y.Z., Li, Y.X.: A brief review of computational gene prediction methods. Geno. Prot. Bioinfo. 2, 216–221 (2004)

5. Do, J.H., Choi, D.K.: Computational approaches to gene prediction. Journal of Microbiology 44(2), 137–144 (2006)

6. Bandyopadhyay, S., Maulik, U., Roy, D.: Gene Identification: Classical and Computational Intelligence Approaches. IEEE Transactions on Systems, Man and Cybernetics, Part C 38(1), 55–68 (2008)

7. Delcher, A.L., Harmon, D., Kasif, S., White, O., Salzberg, S.L.: Improved microbial gene identification with GLIMMER. Nucleic Acids Res. 27, 4636–4641 (1999)

8. Besemer, J., Lomsadze, A., Borodovsky, M.: GeneMarkS.:A self-training method for prediction of gene starts in microbial genomes. Implications for finding sequence motifs in regulatory regions. Nucleic Acids Res. 29, 2607–2618 (2001)

9. Gish, W., States, D.: Identification of protein encoding regions by database similarity search. Nature Genet. 3, 266–272 (1993)

10. Robison, K., Gilbert, W., Church, G.: Large-scale bacterial gene discovery by similaritysearch. Nat. Genet. 7, 205–214 (1994)

11. Frishman, D., Mironov, A., Mewes, H.W., Gelfand, M.: Combining diverse evidence for gene recognition in completely sequenced bacterial genomes. Nucleic Acids Res. 26, 2941–2947 (1998)

12. Badger, J.H., Olsen, G.J.: CRITICA.:Coding region identification tool invoking comparative analysis. Mol. Biol. Evol. 16, 512–524 (1999)

13. Tech, M., Merkl, R.: YACOP: enhanced gene prediction obtained by a combination of existing methods. Silico Biol. 3, 441–451 (2004)

14. Markowitz, V.M., Korzeniewski, F., Palaniappan, K., Szeto, E., Werner, G., Padki, A., Zhao, X., Dubchak, I., Hugenholtz, P., Anderson, I., Mavromatis, K., Ivanova, N., Kyrpides, N.C.: The Integrated Microbial Genomes (IMG) system. Nucleic Acids Research 34, D344–D348 (2006)

15. Touchon, M., Nicolay, S., Audit, B., Brodie, B., Arneodo, A., d'Aubenton, C.Y., Thermes, C.: Replicationassociated strand asymmetries in mammalian genomes Toward detection of replication origins. PNAS 102(28), 9836–9841 (2005)

16. Fujimori, S.: GC–compositional strand bias around transcription start sites in plants and fungi. BMC Genomics 6(26), 1471, 2164/6/26 (2005)

17. Hall, M., Holmes, G.: Benchmarking Attribute Selection Techniques for Discrete Class Data Mining. IEEE Trans. Knowl. Data Eng. 15, 1–16 (2003)

18. Wang, C., Ding, C., Meraz, R.F., Holbrook, S.R.: PSoL.: A positive sample only learning algorithm for finding non-coding RNA genes. Bioinformatics 22, 2590–2596 (2006)

19. Liu, H., Yu, L.: Towards integrating feature selection algorithms for classification and clustering. IEEE Transactions on Knowledge and Data Engineering 17(3), 1–12 (2005)

20. Hall, M.A.: Correlation based feature selection for machine learning. Doctoral dissertation, The University of Waikato, Dept of Comp. Sci. (1999)

21. Marko, R.S., Igor, K.: Theoretical and empirical analysis of relief and rreliefF. Machine Learning Journal 53, 23–69 (2003)

22. Kira, K., Rendell, L.A.: A practical approach to feature selection. In: Proceedings of the Ninth International Workshop on Machine Learning, pp. 249–256. Morgan Kaufmann Publishers Inc. (1992)

23. Hall, M., Frank, E., Holmes, G., Pfahringer, B., Reutemann, P., Witten, I.H.: The WEKA Data Mining Software: An Update. SIGKDD Explorations 11(1) (2009)

24. Werbos, P.J.: Beyond Regression: New Tools for Prediction and Analysis in the Behavioral Sciences. PhD thesis, Harvard University (1974)

25. Parker, D.B.: Learning-logic. Technical report, TR-47, Sloan School of Management, MIT, Cambridge, Mass (1985)
26. Rumelhart, D.E., Hinton, G.E., Williams, R.J.: Learning internal representations by error propagation in Parallel distributed processing. Explorations in the Microstructure of Cognition, vol. I. Bradford Books, Cambridge (1986)
27. Moody, J., Darken, C.J.: Fast learning in networks of locallytuned processing units. Neural Computing 1, 281–294 (1989)
28. Broomhead, D.S., Lowe, D.: Multivariate functional interpolation and adaptive networks. Complex Syst. 2, 321–355 (1988)

User-Centric Situation Awareness in Ubiquitous Computing Environments

Gautham Pallapa[1] and Sajal K. Das[2]

[1] West Corporation, Omaha NE 68154, USA
gpallapa@west.com
[2] University of Texas at Arlington, Arlington TX 76019, USA

Abstract. The rising popularity of ubiquitous computing has resulted in a paradigm shift from generic to user-centric solutions, requiring seamless integration of heterogeneous devices and sensors in the environment to constantly monitor and perform tasks traditionally performed by the user. There is a considerable push, therefore, to develop systems capable of perceiving user behavior, and adapting to their idiosyncrasies. In this paper, we discuss limitations of the interpretations of context, and extend them for improved context awareness. We discuss a user-centric approach to perception of activity in the environment, and use the obtained knowledge in understanding user activities. We present a system for perceiving situations, and discuss an approach to empower the user to develop complex, yet intuitive, rules. We evaluate the performance of the system in a dynamic ubiquitous environment.

Keywords: Ubiquitous Computing, Situation, Context, User-centric.

1 Introduction

Ubiquitous computing represents the concept of seamless *"everywhere"* computing and aims at embedding technology unobtrusively within everyday devices [1], by providing appropriate services and information to users based on their current position (location), current applications running on user devices (state), or activities performed in the environment (situation awareness). A ubiquitous system should perceive appropriate user context, and develop dynamic rules and policies customized to user behavior, while reducing user interaction. Behavior can be described by a finite number of activities, characterized by entities playing particular roles and being in relation within the environment. Indeed, it is imperative to understand the potential relationship between computation and context, resulting in the need for effective situation perception.

In this paper, we present a user-centric system for capturing user behavior and activity in a ubiquitous computing environment. A new definition of context, focused on activity is proposed, and a new structure called a Situation Tree is developed to represent context, devices, and actions. Our system dynamically adapts to user behavior, and empowers users to customize the system according to their requirements, intuitively, yet efficiently. The performance of the system is analyzed with two complex user activities.

N. Meghanathan et al. (Eds.): CCSIT 2012, Part II, LNICST 85, pp. 543–552, 2012.

2   Motivation and Related Work

Human behavior is defined by a finite number of states called situations, characterized by entities playing particular roles within the environment. Perceptual information from different environmental sensors is associated to situations, roles, and relations, connected within a network, where a path describes behavior. Human behavior and needs evolve over time, requiring an adaptive context model.

Consider the following scenario: *John is a patient in an assisted environment, and his physician uploads the regimen to the system and monitors his progress remotely, with system alerts to remind John to take his medicine when needed. Based on his recovery, John's physician changes his regimen or medication, and the system now alerts John accordingly. The system also registers usage of medication, and informs John to fill his prescription in advance.* This scenario incorporates concepts of remote and local patient monitoring, handling sensitive information, and pro-active predictive actions performed by the system.

Consider another scenario: *Mary wants to try a recipe and accesses the ingredients from the refrigerator and pantry. Some of the items required are depleted during preparation and Mary makes a note to add them to the grocery list. After cooking, she finds that she wants to store the recipe for future reference.* Normally, Mary would file the recipe for future reference, and add the depleted items to her grocery list. At a future date, she would need to manually search for the recipe and check if necessary ingredients are available for preparation. It would benefit the user if the system could accomplish all these tasks with a minimal amount of intervention.

The system should perceive user situations, and perform most of the tasks, reducing user interaction. Recognizing daily activities is challenging, especially in a home or assisted environment [2, 3], since users can perform these activities in several ways. Underlying sensors must report features robustly across various sensing contexts [4]. Human activity recognition in the context of assisted environments using RFID tags has been investigated in [5,6]. Though this approach involves extensive tagging of objects and users, it demonstrates that hierarchical organization of probabilistic grammars provides sufficient inference power for recognizing human activity patterns from low level sensor measurements. A sensing toolkit for activity detection and recognition has been discussed in [7]. Systems deployed in ubiquitous environments are characterized by multiple smart cooperating entities and perform high-level inferencing from low-level sensor data reporting [8, 9]. Presence of such heterogeneous sensors and devices drives the need for appropriate perception of situations.

3   Context

Context is defined as *"any information relevant to an interaction that can be used to characterize the situation of an entity. An entity is a person, place, or object that is considered relevant to the interaction between a user and an application, including the user and application themselves"* [10]. This implies that context only exists if there is an interaction between the user and the application, limiting context to an occurrence of an event. If the user is sleeping and not interacting with any application, we would lose valuable information of the context (sleeping). In a pressure sensitive floor, when no one walks or sits, absence of a user is still information. Context therefore, should not be just an interaction between the user and application, but any information obtained from the user actions (or inactions) with respect to an application.

Context is more than just data or information - it is knowledge. We define these three terms in the following way: *Data* is just an informal piece of information without explicit structure or format. *Information* is interpretation of informal pieces of data which are associated with a particular context. When contextual information is interpreted and understood, we then have *knowledge*.

We define Context of an entity as *"a collection of measured and inferred information of a state or environment in which the entity interacts, either passive or active, to enable perception of the current state of the entity from the obtained knowledge, which influences inference of the future states"*. Our definition stresses upon information collected from various sensors, and inherent information obtained from reasoning about the state or environment, which form knowledge. We use this knowledge to perceive the state of the entity and consider decision making as a function of prior context about an entity, allowing us to predict future states.

4   Perceiving Situation

Consider the environment shown in Figure 1(a). Let $S = \{s_1, s_2, \ldots, s_m\}$ sensors be distributed in this environment. Each sensor monitors a zone around it, calculated in the following manner: Draw a straight line connecting a sensor and its neighbor. The perpendicular bisector of this line forms the edge demarcating the zones of these adjacent sensors. If a wall is encountered within the zone, then that wall forms the edge of the zone for the sensor.

Definition 1. *Context Element*

A context element c_i contains the information from sensor s_i. Therefore, $C = \{c_1, c_2, \ldots, c_m\}$ contains the data from m sensors distributed in the environment.

Let $D = \{d_1, d_2, \ldots, d_k\}$ be k devices present in the environment. We define a device as an object in the environment which the user accesses or interacts with. Sensors and devices are collectively called nodes, and assume n nodes in the environment, where $n = m + k$.

In the initial discovery phase, location of all nodes is obtained and a Minimum Spanning Tree (MST) is calculated, to enable tracking of user activity (Figure 1(b)). We represent a user entering and leaving a zone as an edge in the MST. If an edge is not found, then we log the activity, and upon repeated usage of that path, we append it to the MST and remove the existing path between the two nodes. When a user enters a node's zone, we assume that the node generates a context element and transmits it to the system.

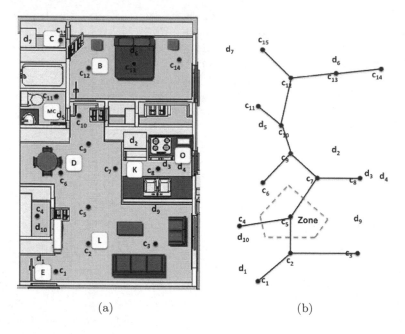

(a)   (b)

Fig. 1. Ubiquitous computing environment of our system showing (a) Floor plan and distribution of nodes, (b) Minimum Spanning Tree and calculation of a zone

Definition 2. *Situation*

A situation $\gamma(t)$ *is a sequence of context elements* $c_1, c_2, \ldots$, *terminated by a device at time* t. *In other words,*
$\gamma(t) = c_1 c_2 \ldots, c_i d_j$, *where* $i \in \{1, \ldots, n\}$, $j \in \{1, \ldots, k\}$ *represents a situation at time* $t, \gamma(t) \in \Gamma$.

Context elements correspond to non-terminal, and devices correspond to terminal symbols respectively. As the user moves in the environment, context elements corresponding to zones in which the user traverses are obtained, with elements processed in an online manner.

4.1   Capturing Action

In order to capture user activity, we associate action words or "*verbs*" to each node. Let v_i be a verb associated with node i. Each type of node is assigned verbs according to their capability. For instance, a sensor capturing user motion would be assigned verbs "walk", "stand", and "sit". If we assume that a normal person walks 1 m/s, and average house size is 200 m^2, the user would enter an exit a zone once per second on an average. The nodes, therefore, would need to report with a very low frequency (about 1 Hz). When the user is within the zone of node i, we assign v_i to it, where the verb would correspond to "walk". If the user is still in the same zone after 2 reporting cycle, we upgrade the verb as $v_i' = $ "*stand*". Some verbs associated with devices are "switch on", "switch off", "access", "replace", etc. In order to differentiate between verbs of the context element and verbs of the device, let $V = \{v_1, v_2, \ldots, v_p\}, p \le m$ correspond to verbs associated with context elements and $A = \{a_1, a_2, \ldots, a_p\}, q \le k$ correspond to the set of verbs associated with devices. A situation in our approach is interpreted as an activity in the environment, and can be represented as $user\ (subject) \to verb\ (action) \to environment\ (devices,\ context\ elements)$.

4.2   Initial Configuration

Initially, the system has to be trained to perceive user activity. Consider an arbitrary user activity pattern where the system informs the user to take medication. The user, currently in the living room, gets up and moves to the bathroom, via the bedroom, and accesses the medicine cabinet (d_5). This activity is represented by sequence $c_2 v_1 c_5 v_1 c_9 v_1 c_{10} v_1 c_{11} v_1 d_5 v_2$, with the user's initial position as a location in zone of c_2. The system obtains the first (context, verb) pair and compares it with the next (context, verb) pair in the sequence. Since verbs in both the pairs are similar, it uses the following rule:

Rule 1 Simple Contraction: *Sequence $xvyv, x, y \in N$ can be represented as $(x, y)v$. This rule is commutative, i.e., $vxvy, x, y \in N$ is represented as $v(x, y)$.*

The system contracts the first two (context, verb) pairs and compares this with the next (context, value) pair observed, Rule 2 is then used.

Rule 2 Compound Contraction: *Sequence $(c_1, c_2)vc_3 v, \{c_1, c_2, c_3 \in C\}$ is contracted to $(c_1, c_3)v$. This rule is commutative, contracting the sequence to $v(c_1, c_3)$, eliminating redundant context when identical action is performed over multiple context elements.*

Rule 3 Device Listing: *Sequence $v(d_1, d_2)vd_3, \{d_1, d_2, d_3 \in D\}$ contracts to $v(d_1, d_2, d_3)$. This rule captures devices that the user has interacted with.*

The system continues contracting the sequence till we obtain $(c_2, c_{11})v$. The Situation Tree is constructed upon encountering terminal symbol d_5.

Definition 3. *An activity is considered complete when any situation s_i, terminating at device d_i with verb v is immediately followed by a situation s_{i+1} terminating at the same device, but with verb v'.*

Rule 4 Complement Rule: *Sequence terminating with $v(d_1, d_2, \ldots, d_i), \{d_i \in D\}$, is constructed until complement $v'(d_1, d_2, \ldots, d_i), \{d_i \in D\}$ is encountered. This rule ensures that any device accessed/switched-on is replaced/switched-off.*

Rule 5 Activity: *An activity is defined as usage of a device d_i if situation γ_i, terminating at device d_i with verb $v = $ "access/switch on" is immediately followed by a situation γ_{i+1} terminating at d_i with verb $v' = $ "replace/switch off".*

For situations with activities between accessing and replacing a device (for e.g., talking on a phone while cooking), the sequence is decomposed into: activity performed up to device access, intermediate activity, and device release.

Rule 6 *Decomposition:* *If a sequence terminates with a device or a set of devices, with the subsequent verb not a complement of the prior verb, construct a new sequence for the current activity, until the complement is encountered.*

Using these rules, sequences are represented using a structure called a *Situation Tree*. The Situation Tree $(S-Tree)$ is a binary tree constructed bottom-up, from the sequence of context elements, verbs and devices, and possesses the following properties:

Property 1. *The root of any subtree of a S-Tree is always a verb.*

Property 2. *The left child of any verb is non-terminal(context element or verb).*

Property 3. *The right child of the root is either terminal (device) or a subtree of terminals.*

Property 4. *The right child of any intermediate verb, whose parent is not its complement, is a context element.*

Property 5. *The right child of any intermediate verb, whose parent is its complement, is a terminal or a subtree of terminals.*

Property 6. *The left subtree of any intermediate verb represents prior activity.*

4.3   Designing Complex Rules

In order to resolve perceiving current state of user activity, many systems incorporate a form of *"Event − Condition − Action"* (ECA) rules to perform actions based on event triggers. An example of an ECA rule is given below:

```
rule: "Cooking_Rule":
Event: (location == "Kitchen")
Condition
    (device == "Oven") &&
    (status == "On")
Action:
  assign activity == "Cooking"
```

ECA rules, however, tend to become complex and require manual decomposition and chaining of logical operations to encompass multiple events, reducing their user-friendliness. Additionally, since events trigger an action, conditions might not consider prior user activity (history). For instance, in the activity discussed in Section 4.2, developers might choose to discard user movement from c_2 to c_{10}, and focus on context information obtained from c_{11} onwards, resulting in loss of information, essential in understanding user behavior for situation prediction.

Our system improves user interaction and allows the user to specify custom rules naturally. Assume that the user needs to create a rule to turn the television on when she walks from the bedroom to the living room. Using ECA rules would involve initial location as "Bedroom", final location as "Living room", and a series of operations to include the activity of walking. Our system handles this in a graceful manner. The user enters the rule without decomposition as "If user walks from Bedroom to Living room, turn on the television". The system identifies the subject is the user and the rest of the rule, "walks from Bedroom to Living Room, turn on the television" is the activity. It then parses the rule sequentially. The first word is a verb "walk" v_1 followed by keyword "from". From Rule 2, it obtains the next two elements c_{12}, and c_3, and constructs the sequence $(c_{12}, c_3)v_1$. It then looks up the MST (Figure 1(b)) and expands the sequence to $c_{12}c_{10}c_9c_7c_5c_2c_3v_1$. The segment "turn on ($v_2$) the television" is then translated to v_2d_9 and appended to the initial sequence. After parsing the rule, therefore, we obtain the situation $\gamma(t) = c_{12}c_{10}c_9c_7c_5c_2c_3v_1v_2d_9$.

Suppose the user now moves from the bedroom to the living room along a different path $c_{12}c_{10}c_9c_5c_3$. The sequence obtained would be $c_{12}v_1c_{10}v_1c_9v_1c_5v_1c_3v_1$. Using Rules 1 and 2, the sequence still reduces to $(c_{12}, c_3)v_1$, and the system turns the television on. It also registers the new path taken by the user, and upon frequent usage, the system perceives that this is a preferred path, and updates its spanning tree. The system also observes user behavior, and develops dynamic rules based on user history. The advantages of this approach are two-fold: (1) The system allows the user to create user-friendly rules (2) The system can be dynamically customized to user behavior and idiosyncrasies.

5   Analysis

In this section, we analyze our system's performance using the cooking scenario described in Section 2. Mary has customized a rule in the system as "Store a new recipe". Our system is made to understand the meaning of "recipe" by defining a recipe with the following steps:

1. **Access** ingredients from the refrigerator and/or pantry.
2. **Spend** time at the kitchen counter preparing the ingredients for cooking
3. **Cook** the ingredients by **spend**ing time at the stove with the stove on
4. **Switch** off the stove and **move** dish to the dining table.

We assume that all users are honest. A honest user is one who accesses any device or item with the intent of using the device or item. A single usage is equal to one unit of the item consumed or one instance of the device being used. We have also limited recipe generation to entering the sequence of steps observed by the system, and additional nuances such as *stirring*, *sautéing*, *etc.*, along with quantities of the ingredients are additional user input.

Let us assume that Mary was initially in the zone of c_6 (Figure 1(a)), moves to the kitchen, and accesses ingredients in the refrigerator and pantry. Let d_2 and d_3 correspond to the refrigerator and pantry respectively, Let $\{d_{2-1}, d_{2-2}, d_{2-3}, d_{2-4}\}$

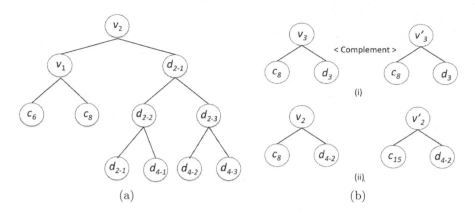

Fig. 2. Structure of S-Trees (a) After accessing ingredients, (b)(i) After switching off the stove, (b)(ii) When d_{4-2} is misplaced

and $\{d_{4-1}, d_{4-2}, d_{4-3}\}$ be the ingredients accessed, and verbs $v_1 = $ "$walk$", $v_2 = $ "$access$". Initially, the system monitors Mary's activity and observes her movement from c_6 to c_8, and terminates the situation when she accesses d_{2-1}. The initial sequence is therefore, represented as

$$\gamma_1 = c_6 v_1 c_7 v_1 c_8 v_1 c_8 v_2 d_{2-1} \tag{1}$$

Since the situation terminated with a device, the system, now observes the next (context, verb) pair, to satisfy the Complement Rule (Rule 4). Instead, when it encounters another device (d_{2-2}), it perceives that multiple devices are being accessed, and therefore, follows Rule 3. It simultaneously continues monitoring for a (context, verb) pair satisfying Rule 4, until:

$$\gamma_2 = c_8 v_2 d_{2-1} c_8 v_2 d_{2-2} c_8 v_2 d_{2-3} c_8 v_2 d_{2-4} c_8 v_2 d_{4-1} c_8 v_2 d_{4-2} c_8 v_2 d_{4-3} c_8 v_3 d_3 \tag{2}$$

The situation at this stage is given by $\gamma(t) = \gamma_1 + \gamma_2$. When the system encounters $c_8 v_3 d_3$, it perceives that the user has started a different activity. Therefore, from Rule 6, it creates a new S-Tree, and continues monitoring. The S-Tree for $\gamma(t)$ is constructed after applying Rules 1, 2, 3 is represented in Figure 2(a).

When Mary finishes cooking and switches off the oven, the sequence $c_8 v'_3 d_3$ is encountered. The system then uses Rules 4, and 5 to ascertain that the activity of cooking has been completed (Figure 2(b)(i)). When Mary places the dish on the dining table, the sequence $c_8 v_1 c_7 v_1 c_6 d_8$ signals the system that the recipe is complete and can be filed in the system. When Mary starts replacing the ingredients, the system deletes the corresponding node in the S-Tree until no right child exists, and the S-Tree is cleared, as the system perceived that all tasks are completed.

Occasionally, the user might misplace an ingredient, and the system informs the user accordingly. Let us assume that Mary misplaced ingredient d_{4-2} in the closet(c_{15}) instead of the pantry. The system now has a situation where "access" of d_{4-2} was at c_8 but "replace" was at c_{15}, as depicted in Figure 2(b)(ii). The system would then generate the complement of the expected replace as $c_8 v_2 d_{4-2}$, and prompts Mary to "replace d_{4-2} in d_4". Mary then accesses d_{4-2}, thereby deleting $c_{15} v_2 d_{4-2}$ (using Rule 4), and when the ingredient is replaced in the pantry, all S-Trees related to the activity are cleared.

6 Evaluation

We simulated the environment shown in Figure 1(a) with up to 100 sensors and 200 devices. We initially trained the system with 10 scenarios representing average daily user activity. We considered a total of 25 verbs, over 10 types of sensors to describe possible actions. We then simulated user movement, randomizing the path to introduce perturbations in generated sequences. Additionally, we altered user path after every 500 runs, to observe our system's adaptation to new user behavior. We conducted 10000 simulated runs and present an average of the results obtained.

The effect of the number of verbs on false positives/negatives is shown in Figure 3. We observed that our system is not affected by false positives, though a significant increase in false negatives was observed with increase in the number of verbs. This could be attributed to the number of verbs assigned to the types of sensors. For instance, it is difficult for our system to differentiate between a user standing, or sitting in a location. Resolution of ambiguity required additional input from surrounding sensors.

We then varied the number of context elements with a fixed set of 10 verbs. Figure 4 depicts the average of 10000 test runs. While occurrence of false positives and negatives were comparable, increasing the verbs to 25 resulted in a significant increase in false negatives. Supplementing context information from surrounding sensors resolved ambiguity and improved situation perception.

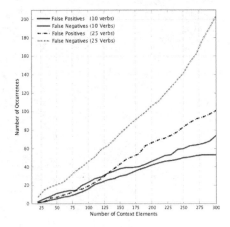

Number of verbs	Runs = 5000		Runs = 10000	
	False Positives	False Negatives	False Positives	False Negatives
5	1	2	1	1
10	1	4	2	9
15	2	11	3	28
20	4	26	7	68
25	7	47	11	122

Fig. 3. Effect of verbs on False Positives and Negatives

Fig. 4. Effect of context elements and verbs over false positives and negatives

7   Conclusion

In this paper, we presented a user-centric system for capturing user behavior and activity in a ubiquitous computing environment. We discussed limitations of current definitions of context, and proposed a definition of context focused on activity. Situation Trees were developed to represent context, devices, and actions. We investigated rules required for perceiving situations and evaluated our system with two complex user activities. We showed how our system dynamically adapts to user behavior, and empowers users to customize the system according to their requirements, intuitively, yet efficiently. Situation Trees are envisioned to construct dynamic situation grammar customized to user behavior and history of user activity, and facilitate developers and users to create complex context-aware rules effortlessly to handle diverse scenarios in a ubiquitous computing environment.

References

1. Weiser, M.: The future of ubiquitous computing on campus. Comm. of the ACM 41(1), 41–42 (1998)
2. Bell, G., Dourish, P.: Yesterdays tomorrows: notes on ubiquitous computings dominant vision. Personal Ubiquitous Computing 11(2), 133–143 (2007)
3. Wang, S., Pentney, W., Popescu, A., Choudhury, T., Philipose, M.: Commonsense-based Joint Training of Human Activity Recognizers. In: Proc. 21st Intl. Joint Conf. on AI (2007)
4. Ermes, M., Parkka, J., Mantyjarvi, J., Korhonen, I.: Detection of Daily Activities and Sports With Wearable Sensors in Controlled and Uncontrolled Conditions. IEEE Trans. on Information Technology in Biomedicine 12(1), 20–26 (2008)
5. Philipose, M., Fishkin, K.P., Perkowitz, M., Patterson, D.J., Fox, D., Kautz, H., Hahnel, D.: Inferring activities from interactions with objects. IEEE Pervasive Computing 3(4), 50–57 (2004)
6. Tapia, E.M., Intille, S.S., Larson, K.: Activity Recognition in the Home Using Simple and Ubiquitous Sensors. In: Ferscha, A., Mattern, F. (eds.) PERVASIVE 2004. LNCS, vol. 3001, pp. 158–175. Springer, Heidelberg (2004)
7. Wimmer, R., Kranz, M., Boring, S., Schmidt, A.: A Capacitive Sensing Toolkit for Pervasive Activity Detection and Recognition. In: Fifth Annual IEEE Intl. Conf. on Pervasive Computing and Communications, pp. 171–180 (2007)
8. Naeem, U., Bigham, J.: Activity recognition using a hierarchical framework. In: Second Intl. Conf. on Pervasive Computing Technologies for Healthcare, Pervasive Health 2008, pp. 24–27 (2008)
9. Osmani, V., Balasubramaniam, S., Botvich, D.: Human activity recognition in pervasive healthcare: Supporting efficient remote collaboration. J. Netw. Comput. Appl. 31(4), 628–655 (2008)
10. Dey, A.K.: Understanding and using context. Personal Ubiquitous Computing 5(1), 4–7 (2001)

A Review of QoS Driven Optimal Selection of Web Services for Compositions

Demian Antony D'Mello[1] and V.S. Ananthanarayana[2]

[1] Department of Computer Science and Engineering,
St. Joseph Engineering College, Mangalore - 575 025, India
demian.antony@gmail.com
[2] Department of Information Technology, National Institute of Technology
Karnataka, Srinivas Nagar, Mangalore - 575 025, India
anvs@nitk.ac.in

Abstract. Web services technology promises to enable rich, flexible and dynamic interoperation of highly distributed and heterogeneous applications using Web standards. The providers of composite Web services involving composition plan with different flow patterns need to discover and select suitable candidate Web services for each task of the composition plan at runtime. The dynamic nature of Web services prompts a need for the mechanism to enable the frequent editing of QoS offers of composite Web services by the Composite Service Providers (CSP). In this paper, the authors present a detailed survey of literature in QoS based selection for Web service compositions. The paper also presents different architectures for QoS aware Web service compositions and evaluates various QoS aware selection techniques. The authors classify QoS aware selection techniques for composition based on the nature of composition plan, complexity of QoS requirements and nature of techniques/methodology used in the selection and QoS aggregation.

Keywords: Web Services, Compositions, Aggregation, Quality of Service, Service Selection, Broker Architecture.

1 Introduction

A Web service is defined as an interface which implements the business logic through a set of operations that are accessible through standard Internet protocols. The eXtensible Markup Language (XML) based protocols namely Universal Description, Discovery and Integration (UDDI), Web Service Description Language (WSDL) and Simple Object Access Protocol (SOAP) are the *three* major building blocks of Web services. The conceptual Web services architecture facilitates both atomic (elementary) and composite Web services to be published into the service registry for discovery without any implementation distinctions. The composite Web services involving composition plan normally select Web services for the individual tasks at runtime which satisfy local (task level) or global (end-to-end) QoS constraints. The QoS offers of such composite Web services are dependent on individual Web services selected for each task of the

N. Meghanathan et al. (Eds.): CCSIT 2012, Part II, LNICST 85, pp. 553–562, 2012.

composition plan. The dynamic nature of Web services enforces the providers of composite Web services to estimate and update (publish) the QoS offers regularly. The frequent editing of QoS offers of composite Web services is necessary since the provider of composite Web service has to compete with other Web services offering same set of functions/operations.

In order to update the QoS and service offers of composite Web services regularly, the provider requires a tool to estimate QoS of composite Web service and to advertise a competitive service offer based on his requirements. In literature, the QoS of composition is evaluated based on the requirements involving single QoS property [2] or combinations of multiple QoS properties [3]. While evaluating QoS of composition, the Web services are selected for the tasks based on either local [2] or global [3] QoS constraints. As the service offers play a role in selection of business Web services, the composite business Web service has to be created by selecting good quality and profitable services for all the tasks which satisfy both QoS and service offer requirements of the composite service provider. Publishing of composite Web services involve publishing of its functional, QoS and service offer specific information into the repository (registry) [4]. Therefore, QoS and service offer for the composite Web service need to be estimated prior to the publishing activity. To obtain estimation on QoS and service offers, QoS and service offer aggregation schemes are required for the composite Web services involving different composition patterns. A selection mechanism has to be defined to select the most suitable Web service for the tasks of composition plan based on the provider's requirements and preferences.

2   QoS Driven Selection for Compositions

The selection of most suitable (best in terms of quality, compatibility and service offers) Web service for the various tasks is a crucial issue in Web service composition. In order to update the QoS and service offers of composite Web services regularly, the provider requires a mechanism to estimate the QoS of composite Web service and to advertise a competitive service offer based on his requirements and preferences. As a motivating example, consider the conference (or symposium) arrangement scenario. Assume that, there exists a single service, which caters to the requirements of conference arrangement involving various tasks. The different tasks are: booking of hall or hotel for presentations (or discussions), catering service for food on conference days, vehicle for local travel, a service provider to decorate the venue, city tour (night or day) arrangement service, conference bag and conference kit providers. Fig.1 represents the composition plan involving composition patterns of the conference arrangement service. The rectangles represent individual task nodes and ovals represent composition pattern nodes.

Over the Internet, many service providers are available for the atomic activities like hotel booking, vehicle hiring etc. The provider of the conference arrangement service tries to arrange the conference with low costs, expects good response from the reputed service providers for atomic activities and would like

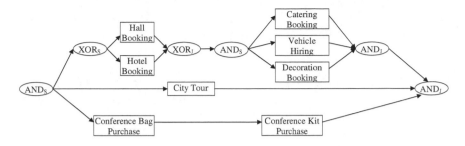

Fig. 1. Motivating Example: A Conference Arrangement Service

to offer discounts on the service charge. As an example, consider the composite service provider's requirements as follows. "The service should be delivered at a faster rate with the lowest cost or popular (reputed) service provider who offers service discounts". The conference arrangement service should satisfy the provider's requirements defined on the multiple QoS properties and service offers by assigning suitable (or best) Web services to the tasks of the composition plan. Thus, a need arises to estimate QoS and net profit from service offers, to update (frequently) QoS and service offers of the composite Web services based on the provider's requirements and preferences.

A QoS driven selection problem for compositions can be defined as follows. "Given a flow pattern (composition pattern) based composition plan of composite Web service involving activities (tasks) and candidate Web services (their QoS and service offers) for each task of the composition plan, estimate the QoS and competitive service offers for the composite Web service, by selecting suitable Web services to each task based on the provider's QoS properties and service offers with varied preferences". The QoS and competitive service offers for the composite Web service can be estimated by selecting suitable Web services for each task of the composition. The Web services need to be selected based on the provider's QoS and service offer requirements and preferences. The estimated QoS and profit from various service offers help the provider to frequently update or publish the QoS and competitive service offers for a composite Web service.

3   Architectures for QoS Driven Compositions

Dynamic composition of Web services requires the discovery of different service providers that satisfy given functional and nonfunctional requirements of consumers [5]. The QoS optimal composite Web service is today's need as the requesters are keen on the delivery of QoS by service providers. In literature, a model driven methodology has been proposed for building new Web service compositions that are QoS optimized [6]. Various architectures have been proposed towards the management and monitoring of QoS aware dynamic composition [7] and composite Web services involving composition patterns [8]. Different composition patterns have been defined to represent composite Web services involving multiple execution paths [9]. In literature, different QoS models have been defined to describe QoS of compositions at the level of part names i.e. operations [10] and compositions involving transactions [11]. In order to estimate QoS properties of composition at runtime, researchers have defined QoS aggregation schemes for different composition patterns [9].

The QoS based composition of Web services is facilitated by defining either *Broker based* or *Agent based* architectures. In broker based architecture, the broker plays a major role in managing and building Web service composition rather than execution of composition [4]. The other functionalities of the broker include composition schema search, composition plan optimization and QoS optimal selection of Web services to the tasks of composition plan [12]. In literature, agent technology is used to compose Web services based on QoS constraints, where the agents are responsible for the discovery, selection and execution of composite process [13]. The authors of [4] propose broker based architecture for the selection of QoS optimal and profitable Web services for compositions. Fig.2 presents the broker based architecture which facilitates the composite Web service provider to select an optimal Web service for each task in order to publish QoS and attractive service offers into QoS registry and Service Offer (SO) registry respectively. The broker architecture consists of *three* registries which include *service registry*, *QoS registry* and *SO registry*. The *register* operation is defined between the Web service providers and broker which facilitates QoS and service offer aware Web service publishing.

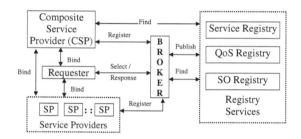

Fig. 2. The Broker Based Architecture for Compositions

4   Review of QoS Based Web Service Compositions

The QoS based Web service composition involves discovery and optimal selection of candidate Web services for each task of the composition plan which is either sequential or parallel (composition pattern based) in nature. In literature, various techniques have been defined towards optimal (local or global) selection and assignment of Web services to the tasks of composition plan. Fig.3 depicts the classification of selection techniques for QoS based Web service composition. The selection techniques for compositions can be broadly classified based on the nature of composition plan as *selection for sequential plan* and *selection for parallel plan*.

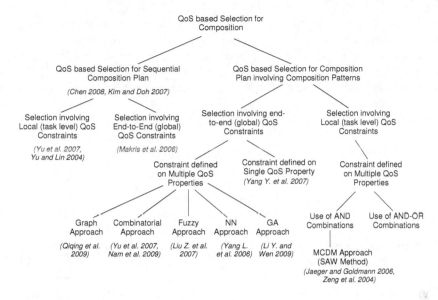

Fig. 3. Taxonomy of Web Service Selection Techniques for QoS Composition

4.1 Selection Techniques for Sequential Plan

The selection mechanisms for the sequential composition plan assign QoS optimal Web services to the tasks which satisfy the requirements defined on the
multiple QoS properties [14]. In literature, a number of mechanisms have been
proposed towards the selection of QoS optimal Web services for sequential composition plan based on either local (task level) or global QoS requirements. The
authors [3][15] map the service selection problem for sequential composition to 0-
1 Multi-dimension Multi-choice Knapsack Problem (MMKP or MCKP) which is
NP complete. In literature, an exhaustive search [3], heuristic approach [17] and
dynamic programming algorithms [15] are proposed to solve MMKP problem.
The authors of [3] propose Multi Constraint Shortest Path (MCSP) problem for
the graph model (service candidate graph) of a composition plan. A single QoS
property is also used to find the global (end-to-end) optimal solution for the
sequence of tasks [3]. The authors of [2] perform the selection based on single
QoS property for the graph model with a solution to Single Source Shortest
Path Problem (SSSP). The main problem associated with QoS based sequential
composition is that, all discovered services for the tasks need to be executed
sequentially. This kind of execution increases the cost of composition in terms
of QoS, especially execution duration of composite service.

4.2 Selection Techniques for Parallel Plan

Suitable candidate Web services for each task of the parallel (workflow pattern) composition plan are assigned based on the task level QoS requirements

defined on the multiple QoS properties with varied preferences. In literature, the suboptimal solution to the QoS based composition is obtained through Simple Additive Weighting (SAW) method of Multiple Criteria Decision Making (MCDM or MADM) technique [9][16] and k-armed bandit theory [14]. The selection techniques for QoS based composition involving end-to-end requirements are defined on the multiple QoS properties with varied preferences. A number of mechanisms (approaches) have been proposed by researchers to find an optimal or suboptimal Web service assignment for the composition plan involving composition patterns.

A. Selection Based on Global QoS Requirements

In literature, an optimal Web service assignment is performed through optimization of an objective function using global planning. Some of the solutions for global planning problem are: *Graph approach, Combinatorial approach, Genetic algorithm approach, Neural network approach* and *Fuzzy logic approach*. In literature, various solutions have been proposed towards the Directed Acyclic Graph (DAG) modeling of the the multi-objective optimization problem [18]. A *Service Candidate Graph* to model the general flow structure of composition plan is proposed in [3], which explains the use of MCSP algorithm (e.g. Bellman-Ford) to solve the problem. The main idea of service selection is to maximize an application specific utility function under the end-to-end QoS constraints. A dynamic programming based solution is proposed [19] to solve multi-stage decision making problem which is modeled as a *service graph*. The service graph contains various candidate Web services with calculated QoS as a weight on the edges. The major problem of graph approach is that, the high computational complexity for the composition plans involving large number of patterns. The inclusion of separate nodes and edges for each discovered Web service increases the computational efficiency of the approach as the efficiency is dependent on the size of the graph model.

The combinatorial approach for the optimal assignment of Web services to the tasks of composition involves optimization of objective function subjected to a set of QoS requirements. The popular approaches are: *Linear programming Approach, Greedy (Heuristic) Approach* and *Bottom-up Approach*. In linear programming approach, the QoS aware composition problem is modeled as *Integer Programming problem (0-1 IP problem)* [3] [16] or *Mixed Integer Linear Programming (MILP) problem* [20]. The paper [16] proposes a middleware platform for QoS composition which maximizes the user satisfaction expressed as utility functions over QoS attributes, while satisfying the constraint set by the user and the structure of the composite service. The selection of an execution plan relies on the application of a Multiple Criteria Decision Making (MCDM) technique on the quality matrix of the execution path. The Integer Programming method selects an optimal execution plan without generating all possible execution paths. The computation cost of global planning by exhaustive searching is very high even in very small scale in aspect of the number of the tasks with few candidate Web services.

Greedy approach represents the simple heuristic rules which are applied to find locally optimal solutions and later used to obtain globally optimal solution to the composition plan [9]. The backtracking based discarding subsets algorithm [9] uses a search tree which consists of nodes, each representing a possible pair of a candidate Web service and the task. The algorithm establishes a sub-tree cutting rule based on the QoS threshold estimation. The advantage of this algorithm compared to a straight global selection lies in the idea to cut sub-trees representing unfavorable combinations to save computational efforts. This approach normally identifies an optimal solution still meeting the QoS constraints, but the authors establish a cutting rule based on threshold estimation efficient execution.

In literature, heuristic approach has been proposed [21] for composition based on either single or multiple global QoS requirements. The heuristic algorithm finds an optimal solution to problems of moderate size without exploring the entire solution space [5]. The bottom-up approach has been used towards an optimal assignment of services for the tasks of composition plan. The bottom-up approximation mechanism which has been proposed [9] works on heuristic rules to obtain an optimal or suboptimal solution. The proposed combinatorial approaches are computation intensive in nature as the finding of an optimal solution for global QoS requirements is NP hard.

Genetic Algorithms (GA) are designed with the idea of applying the biological principle of evolution to artificial systems. GA iterates the search for the best solution and a finite string of symbols named genome is created to present the solution [22]. The evolution is made by means of *two* operators: the crossover operator and the mutation operator [23]. In literature, genetic algorithms have been proposed for an optimal selection based on global QoS requirements [23][24]. The structure of genetic algorithm is characterized by the special relation matrix coding scheme of chromosomes and the population diversity is handled with simulated annealing. The concept of fuzzy logic and matching defined on fuzzy rules is adopted to find an optimal assignment for QoS aware composition based on global QoS requirements [25]. The preferences of Web service requesters are modeled as fuzzy rules [26] which are used for comparison and ranking of Web service combinations. Neural Network (NN) is another powerful tool used for describing and deposing nonlinear relations [19]. The NN and its variant structures are proposed in literature to model and solve QoS aware composition: a multistage decision making problem. The major problem associated with GA, fuzzy logic and NN based techniques is the nature of iterative processing and redundant operations which increases the time complexity of optimal Web service selection and assignment mechanism.

B. Selection Based on Local (Task level) QoS Requirements

The mechanisms proposed in literature towards Web service composition for end-to-end QoS constraints provide an optimal solution. Such mechanisms require more computational time to find an optimal service assignment due to the complex nature of the problem involving global QoS requirements with multiple QoS properties and preferences. In order to obtain suboptimal (sometimes optimal) solution towards the assignment of Web services to tasks, the service selection should be defined based on the task level QoS requirements.

The authors of [9] proposes a pattern based selection algorithm which explores a combinatorial problem of selection of candidates for Web service compositions. The algorithm determines the best assignment, considering each composition in isolation and takes advantage of an existing representation of the composition by using the composition pattern. The algorithm performs *four* steps: (a) The algorithm walks recursively into the structure and identifies pattern elements that do not contain any sub-patterns (b) For all tasks within such an element, all sets of candidate assignments are evaluated. The combination that delivers the best score is chosen (c) An optimal solution for a particular pattern is determined, by moving one level upwards to evaluate assignment within the new pattern (d) The above steps are repeated until the whole composition is covered and one aggregated QoS is returned. The algorithm shows the best resulting QoS as compared to other heuristic approaches. The problems with this algorithm are: (i) The algorithm seems to depend strongly on composition structure, because it shows the largest deviation of execution time (ii) The algorithm cannot meet global QoS constraints.

In order to advertise the QoS of composite Web service, QoS of composition plan need to be estimated at runtime. Towards this need, SAW method may be applied to find locally optimal and globally suboptimal solution to QoS aware composition. In literature, the authors of [16] have used SAW method towards an optimal assignment of Web services to the tasks of composition plan involving different composition patterns. The advantage of such a mechanism, is that the assignment of Web services to tasks is always suboptimal solution and sometimes they may yield optimal solution. The suboptimal solution for QoS of composition is suitable for advertisement of QoS as, the QoS properties represent maximum tolerable value.

5   Conclusion

The QoS based optimal selection of Web services for composition is an important research issue in the field of Web services. This paper makes a complete survey of the literature and evaluates QoS based Web service composition architectures and selection mechanisms. In literature, the Web services are composed based on multiple QoS properties involving only AND combinations. From the selection for QoS composition review tree (Figure 3), it is observed that, the Web services are not composed based on the QoS requirements (local or global) involving both AND and OR combinations of multiple QoS properties and their preferences (weights).

References

1. Kreger, H.: Web Services Conceptual Architecture (WSCA 1.0) (2001),
   http://www.ibm.com/software/solutions/webservices/pdf/wsca.pdf
2. Makris, C., Panagis, Y., Sakkopoulos, E., Tsakalidis, A.: Efficient and adaptive discovery techniques of Web Services handling large data sets. Journal of Systems and Software, 480–495 (2006)

3. Yu, T., Zhang, Y., Lin, K.: Efficient Algorithms for Web Services Selection with End-to-End QoS Constraints. ACM Transactions on the Web 1(1), Article 6, 1–26 (2007)

4. D'Mello, D.A., Ananthanarayana, V.S.: Quality and Business Offer Driven Selection of Web Services for Compositions. In: Prasad, S.K., Routray, S., Khurana, R., Sahni, S. (eds.) ICISTM 2009. CCIS, vol. 31, pp. 76–87. Springer, Heidelberg (2009)

5. Menasce, D.A.: Composing Web Services: A QoS View. IEEE Internet Computing, 88–90 (November-December 2004)

6. Grønmo, R., Jaeger, M.C.: Model-Driven Methodology for Building QoS-Optimised Web Service Compositions. In: Kutvonen, L., Alonistioti, N. (eds.) DAIS 2005. LNCS, vol. 3543, pp. 68–82. Springer, Heidelberg (2005)

7. Momotko, M., Gajewski, M., Ludwig, A., Kowalczyk, R., Kowalkiewicz, M., Zhang, J.-Y.: Towards Adaptive Management of QoS-Aware Service Compositions – Functional Architecture. In: Dan, A., Lamersdorf, W. (eds.) ICSOC 2006. LNCS, vol. 4294, pp. 637–649. Springer, Heidelberg (2006)

8. Patel, C., Supekar, K., Lee, Y.: A QoS Oriented Framework for Adaptive Management of Web Service Based Workflows. In: Mařík, V., Štěpánková, O., Retschitzegger, W. (eds.) DEXA 2003. LNCS, vol. 2736, pp. 826–835. Springer, Heidelberg (2003)

9. Jaeger, M.C., Rojec-Goldmann, G.: SENECA – Simulation of Algorithms for the Selection of Web Services for Compositions. In: Bussler, C.J., Shan, M.-C. (eds.) TES 2005. LNCS, vol. 3811, pp. 84–97. Springer, Heidelberg (2006)

10. Aiello, M., Rosenberg, F., Platzer, C., Ciabattoni, A., Dustdar, S.: Service QoS Composition at the Level of Part Names. In: Bravetti, M., Núñez, M., Tennenholtz, M. (eds.) WS-FM 2006. LNCS, vol. 4184, pp. 24–37. Springer, Heidelberg (2006)

11. Liu, A., Huang, L., Li, Q.: QoS-Aware Web Services Composition Using Transactional Composition Operator. In: Yu, J.X., Kitsuregawa, M., Leong, H.-V. (eds.) WAIM 2006. LNCS, vol. 4016, pp. 217–228. Springer, Heidelberg (2006)

12. Kim, Y., Doh, K.: A Trust Type Based Model for Managing QoS in Web Services Composition. In: 2007 International Conference on Convergence Information Technology. IEEE (2007)

13. Rong, W., Liu, K., Liang, L.: Association Rule based Context Modeling for Web Service Discovery. In: 10th IEEE Conference on E-Commerce Technology and the Fifth IEEE Conference on Enterprise Computing, E-Commerce and E-Services, pp. 229–304. IEEE (2008)

14. Chen, Y.: Web Services Composition with Incomplete QoS Information. In: IEEE 8th International Conference on Computer and Information Technology Workshops. IEEE (2008)

15. Yu, T., Lin, K.: Service selection Algorithms for Web Services with End-to-end QoS Constraints. In: IEEE International Conference on E-Commerce Technology. IEEE (2004)

16. Zeng, L., Benatallah, B., Ngu, A.H.H., Dumas, M., Kalagnanam, J., Chang, H.: QoS-Aware Middleware for Web Services Composition. IEEE Transactions on Software Engineering 30(5), 311–327 (2004)

17. Berbner, R., et al.: Heuristics for QoS-aware Web Service Composition. In: IEEE International Conference on Web Services (ICWS 2006). IEEE (2006)

18. Qiqing, F., Xiaoming, P., Qinghua, L., Yahui, H.: A Global QoS Optimizing Web Services Selection Algorithm based on MOACO for Dynamic Web Service Composition. In: 2009 International Forum on Information Technology and Applications. IEEE (2009)

19. Yang, L., Dai, Y., Zhang, B., Gao, Y.: A Dynamic Web Service Composite Platform Based on QoS of Services. In: Shen, H.T., Li, J., Li, M., Ni, J., Wang, W. (eds.) APWeb Workshops 2006. LNCS, vol. 3842, pp. 709–716. Springer, Heidelberg (2006)
20. Ardagna, D., Pernici, B.: Global and Local QoS Constraints Guarantee in Web Service Selection. In: IEEE International Conference on Web Services (ICWS 2005). IEEE (2005)
21. Yang, Y., Tang, S., Xu, Y., Zhang, W., Fang, L.: An Approach to QoS-aware Service Selection in Dynamic Web Service Composition. In: Third International Conference on Networking and Services (ICNS 2007). IEEE (2007)
22. Li, Y., Wen, T.: Quality and Relation Driven Service Selection for Web Services Composition. In: 2009 International Conference on New Trends in Information and Service Science. IEEE (2009)
23. Ma, C., He, Y., Xiong, N., Yang, L.T.: VFT: An Ontology-based Tool for Visualization and Formalization of Web Service Composition. In: 2009 International Conference on Computational Science and Engineering. IEEE (2009)
24. Liu, S., Liu, Y., Jing, N., Tang, G., Tang, Y.: A Dynamic Web Service Selection Strategy with QoS Global Optimization Based on Multi-objective Genetic Algorithm. In: Zhuge, H., Fox, G.C. (eds.) GCC 2005. LNCS, vol. 3795, pp. 84–89. Springer, Heidelberg (2005)
25. Liu, Z., Huang, Y., Jian, W., Zhou, J., Guo, H.: Solving Fuzzy QoS Constraint Satisfaction technique for Web Service Selection. In: International Conference on Computational Intelligence and Security Workshops 2007. IEEE (2007)
26. Agarwal, S., Lamparter, S.: User preference Based Automated Selection of Web Service Compositions. In: ICSOC Workshop on Dynamic Web Processes, Seiten, pp. 1–12. IBM, Erscheinungsort, Amsterdam, Netherlands, Referierte Verffentlichung (2005)

Location Service Management Protocol for Vehicular Ad Hoc Network Urban Environment

Salim M. Zaki, M.A. Ngadi, Shukor Abd Razak,
Maznah Kamat, and Johan Mohamad Shariff

Department of Computer Systems and Communications,
Faculty of Computer Science and Information Systems,
Universiti Teknologi Malaysia
salimzki@gmail.com,
{dr.asri,shukorar,kmaznah,johan}@utm.my

Abstract. Location based service is used in vehicular ad hoc networks (VANET) to locate a node's position before the start of any communica- tion. The existing location services proposed for Mobile Ad hoc Networks (MANET) suffer from low scalability in VANET environments. Protocols proposed for VANET do not consider load balance on location servers, and do not consider realistic information for selecting location servers which affect the protocols efficiency. This paper proposes a Quorum- Based Location Service Management Protocol (QLSP) which is designed for urban area topology utilizing specific node information such as the distance to intersection centre point, and speed in selecting main loca- tion server. Formation of quorum location servers is achieved by the main location server through the nomination of other nodes located at the in- tersection based on their direction of movement. QLSP shows excellent performance in reducing overhead of control packets, provides a high de- livery ratio of packets to destination, and reduces the end-to-end delay of routing packets. The performance of the protocol is then compared to other existing location service protocols.

Keywords: vehicular ad hoc networks, location service protocol, load balance.

1 Introduction

Vehicular Ad Hoc Networks (VANETs) integrate the capabilities of wireless net- works to transportation systems. This may offer blanket connectivity to mobile users and provides the exchange of useful information between them.

VANETs applications are wide and promise useful services such as cooperative intersection safety and map localization [1]. VANET's applications need positions of nodes in order to route messages between source and destinations. Position-based routing protocols are suitable routing protocols for VANET environments compared to reactive and proactive protocols. This class of protocols needs, as a prerequisite, a location service that could determine the location of a given destination ID in order to enable the position-based protocol to communicate with the destination.

N. Meghanathan et al. (Eds.): CCSIT 2012, Part II, LNICST 85, pp. 563–574, 2012.
© Institute for Computer Sciences, Social Informatics and Telecommunications Engineering 2012

Many location service protocols have been proposed. However, they all employ different strategies when selecting nodes to act as location servers as well as different update schemes used to pinpoint the location of related nodes in relation to their corresponding location servers. The majority of these protocols are designed for MANET [2] and sensor networks environments. Location service protocols suffer from limitations and challenges, especially when they are applied in VANET urban environments. The nature of urban areas, such as intersections and obstacles represented by buildings and the restricted movement of vehicles on roads affect the performance of the protocol in determining the location of various destinations.

This paper considers a location service protocol designed especially for urban environments, avoiding some of the limitations faced by current location services when applied to the VANET environment. The Quorum-Based Location Service Protocol (QLSP) utilizes the quorum group of location servers in order to distribute the load on multi servers. QLSP uses two parameters: vehicle distance to the centre point of an intersection and the speed of the node in selecting the main location server. The node which demonstrates the best distance values to the centre point of intersections, combined with low speed, is nominated as a main location server (MLS). In addition to MLS, a group of nodes is selected by the MLS to form the members of a quorum group called Passing Location Servers (PLSs). The functions of PLSs are to distribute the load onto intersec- tions within the vicinity and to minimize packet transmission delays.

The rest of the paper is organized as follows. Section 2 reviews some location service protocols and discusses the problems faced by these protocols when applied in the VANET environment. Section 3 describes the proposed location service protocol. Section 4 discusses the simulated result, while section 5 concludes the paper.

2   Related Work

This section gives a review of some of current location service protocols for MANET and VANET. In addition, discussion concerning the urban environment and the main challenges faced by location services in VANET urban environment are also included.

Mainly, the location service protocols are divided into two branches: Flooding-based, and Rendezvous-based. Rendezvous based protocols were classified into two categories: hashed-based and quorum-based [3].

One of the early location services is Distance Routing Effect Algorithm for Mobility (DREAM) [4] which floods node location information in the network. The main problem with these flooding based location services is network overhead, especially when the network is dense as in VANET urban area which can cause packet collisions and delays.

A flat hashing-based location service algorithm called Intersection Location Service (ILS), was proposed in [2]. ILS utilizes the characteristics of street inter-sections. For fault tolerance, a distributed hash function called Chord algorithm, which is also used for query process, is used. ILS chooses a location server for every intersection and hashes this location server to selected intersection using intersection ID. This is a limitation because it does not ensure the stability of the selected location server because the lowest node ID could be a fast moving which will only be assigned for a short period of time. Map Based Location Service (MBLS) [5] uses specified points to select location servers. MBLS selects location servers based on waypoint, which cannot guarantee a good location in selecting a location server.

In ad hoc networks, quorum systems were used in different ways for different purposes such as location service, disseminating information, and location tracking [6] [7]. Quorum systems show good performance in terms of load balance and fault tolerance. The mobile nature of nodes in ad hoc networks increase the possibility of node failure due to nodes moving outside the range of other nodes or out of a specified region, in addition to failure of battery in sensor network and MANET. In XYLS protocol [8] [9] a node starts sending its location and ID information in a north-south direction. Any nodes receiving these messages broadcast it either south or north, and so forth. Consequently, nodes on this line will form location servers, thus they can reply to any received query. The problem facing this protocol is that if any node along the north-south line moves away, the connection to other nodes is lost and delivery updates cannot be achieved. Some solutions were proposed for this problem, but it assumes immobile nodes or movement in the same direction, however, it might not be a realistic solution in real world environments.

The existing location services have been designed the first time for use in MANET applications [10]. These location services perform well in MANET environments, but not when applied to VANET, as the environment is dramatically different. The differences are due to the high speed nodes of VANET, where the high speed of mobile nodes in ad hoc environments causes a high frequency of link breakage [11]. Losing a connection with a destination pushes the source to locate the destination location again by querying the location server nodes about the location of this destination. This process generates another problem represented in control packet overhead generated by query requests and reply packets in dense networks. Second, the restricted mobility in VANETs environment such as in urban and highway roads makes it different than MANET where the mobility of nodes is considered random.

From the previous observations on the current problems facing location services, it is clear that the main problem is updating location of nodes efficiently and getting high ratios of packet delivered to destinations with low overhead. Thus, this paper addressed the problems faced by current location services in VANET environment and handled this solution efficiently by proposing QLSP protocol enhancing packet delivery packets and reducing overhead and distributing the load on multi servers.

3   Proposed Location Service Protocol

This section explains the design of Quorum-Based Location Service Protocol (QLSP), which consider urban environment topology where selecting location servers is done near the road intersections. Centre point is defined as the intersection of roads. The intersection coordinates (Xc, Yc) are provided to nodes, thus each node can compare its position relative to the intersection centre point. A node can be nominated as a location server if its position is inside the intersection vicinity, moving at low speed, and closest to centre point. Main location server is selected among nodes at the intersection because it is here where nodes usually stop, providing the high probability of a stable node. The trade-off between a nodes' distance to intersection centre point and slow speed values is practical for selecting the most stable node. A stable node is the node that has the chance to stay for a longer time within an intersection area and close to the centre, making it within range of most of nodes in that vicinity. This stability is designed to reduce control packets overhead, leading to increased performance of end-to-end communications. It is assumed that each node is provided with 802.11 communication abilities in order for them to communicate with each other. Additionally, each node knows its position through global positioning system (GPS) and knows its neighbours location through beacons, which include ID, position, speed, and direction of node. Each node receives information of its speed and direction from the mobility model and propagates through beacons to inform neighbour nodes.

3.1   Location Server Selection

A node always checks the beacon it receives from neighbouring nodes to see if there are any location servers in range. Beacon packets include useful information about each node as shown below, which enables the location server to distinguish it from other nodes. The ID of a node is used to distinguish a node among other nodes, while the position is required to enable position based routing protocol to forward message to destination. Speed is one of the criteria used in determining the best candidate for a location server. Direction will be used to select other members of the quorum group for each direction. The LS field indicates the role of a node. The field is set to 1 if a node is a location server; a 0 indicates it is a normal node. The Flag field determines the quorum group of location servers a node belongs to. With the beacon information, nodes are able to know each other's information and the information is used during the nomination of the best node as a main location server which is based on shortest distance and lowest speed.

BEACON = (ID, Position (X, Y), Direction,Speed, LS, Flag)

QLSP uses two parameters in selecting a location server: velocity of a node's movement, and its distance from the centre point. A node periodically checks its position to determine whether it is inside the intersection vicinity or not as depicted in Fig. 1. It also checks beacons it receives from neighbours. If a node finds itself close to the centre of the intersection and it stops or moves at a lower speed compared to its neighbours, it will be nominated as a location server. Once it is nominated, it will change its status in the beacon to declare itself as a location server. Nodes close to this location server one or two-hops away need to send their updates to this LS. The location server located at intersection vicinity is called Main Location Server (MLS), and this MLS will construct quorum group by selecting some nodes to hold the location information of nodes called Passing Location Server (PLS). If MLS moves away from the intersection centre point, it has to send its location table to the newly nominated MLS in order to avoid reconstruction of locations table.

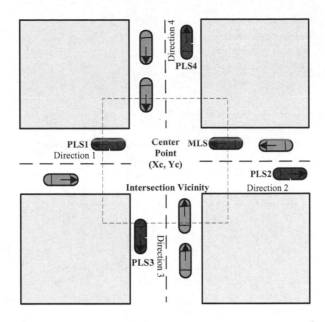

Fig. 1. Selecting Location Server inside Intersection

A criterion for selecting these PLSs is basically based on their direction of movement. MLS will select n number of PLSs which is equal to the number of roads which branch out of the intersection. Both MLS and PLSs form one quorum of location servers for an intersection. MLS selects PLSs based on their direction of movement. The main LS periodically checks the number of PLSs within its range; if the number is below a threshold it then selects other nodes to be the new PLS. Selecting new PLSs is based on a hybrid method combining unicast and multicast sending. If the number of available PLSs in range of MLS is, for example, 1, and there are still 3 more PLSs to fulfil the four road segments going out of that particular intersection, a multicast sending is invoked by MLS. But if the needed number of PLSs is only 1, then MLS only unicasts the location information table to that particular node. QLSP avoids broadcasting packets inside intersection vicinity to avoid packet collisions which usually leads to degradation in network performance.

PLS has two main functions. Firstly, it functions as a backup in case of MLS failure, and secondly, it acts as a location server answering queries sent to MLS at intersection vicinity. This reduces overhead on MLS and reduces the hop count a query packet may take to reach an MLS that has the location destination node. MLS updates PLSs of new nodes joining the intersection and hash their nodes to MLS. Algorithm 1 shows the sequence of steps to select the location server and construct the quorum.

Algorithm 1. Location Server Selection Algorithm

1: Node arrives at intersection vicinity

2: **do while** node inside intersection

3:    **if** it is first node inside intersection

4:        **then** nominate self as an MLS

5:        Change Beacon's LS status to 1 and indicate quorum group in flag field
        Start locations table construct

6:        Check neighbors in location table for selecting PLSs

7:    **else if** it is not first node or it is MLS and moves away of intersection's vicinity

8:        Input to bestNode method node's speed and distance

9:        Input to bestNode method neighbors' speed and distance

10:        **if** distance < neighbors' distance and speed < neighbors' speed

11:            **then** nominate self as an MLS

12:            Change Beacon's LS status to 1 and indicate quorum group in flag field

13:            Check neighbors in location table for selecting PLSs

14:        **else**

15:            Nominate closest neighbor with slowest speed as MLS
            Transfer locations table to new MLS

16:            Change Beacon's LS status to 1 and indicate quorum group in flag field

17:            Check neighbors in location table for selecting PLSs

18:        **endif**

19:    **endif**

20: **enddo**

3.2   Location Update

The update packet contains a node's ID, position, speed, direction, quorum group ID, and MLSs position. Intermediate nodes forward the packet through a geographical forwarding scheme based on closest neighbour to destination. Once the update packet is received by any PLS, it does not directly send this update packet to MLS; instead, it collects the received update packets and invokes the sending of update messages to the MLS after a period of time. This process ensures less frequent sending of packets towards MLS and intersection vicinity. The node stops sending updates to its MLS once it becomes closer to another quorum group of location servers. It then hashes itself to the newly discovered MLS and starts to update its location to the new location server.

3.3   Location Query

Source nodes send a location query message to acquire the location of the destination node. Initially, the source node is assumed to know the destinations ID, and then it includes this ID in the query packet along with source ID, source position, and source quorum of location servers information in addition to times- tamps. The query message is sent to MLS at intersections that it is hashed to, if it is one hop away as shown in Fig. 2. Otherwise, the forwarder that receives the query will check its

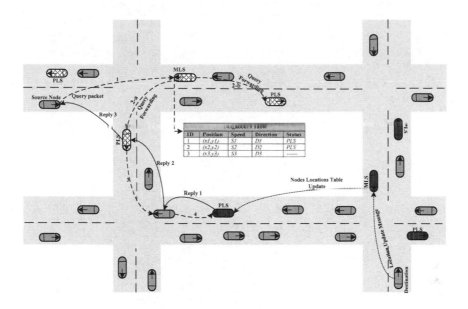

Fig. 2. Querying a destination's location

database about any cached up-to-date information entry of the destination. If there is an up-to-date location for destination, then a reply message is generated and sent it to the query originator to stop forwarding towards MLS. Otherwise, intermediate nodes keep forwarding query packets to MLS or any near PLS. Once MLS or PLS receives this query it looks up its own location table which includes all nodes information hashed their locations to it. If there is an entry to the queried node then the destination node resides on the same intersection. MLS or PLS reply with the latest received location of destination to source, and then the source uses this location to communicate with the destination. In the case that MLS and PLS have no location information about destination, the query packet will be forwarded as shown in Fig. 2 (messages 2-a and 2-b) to surrounded location servers quorums on surround intersections.

The query packet has a TTL field which expires after a given period of time to avoid looping over the network. The query originator has the right to originate another query after a period of time equal to TTL. If there is no reply about a query after a period of time equal to TTL, the originator will resend the query.

4   Results and Discussion

The performance measures of QLSP protocol are evaluated using Jist/SWANS simulator [12]. Simulated road scenarios for an urban area are extracted from TIGER/Lines map files [13] representing down-town Chicago, with a dimension of an area of around 800 square meters. The distance between adjacent intersections is 200 meters horizontally. Benchmarking QLSP is done against three location service protocols; Self Organizing Location Servers (SOLS) [14], ILS [2], and Terminode [15]. SOLS is a location service protocol designed for MANET, while ILS is a hash-based VANET location service, while Terminode is a home region location service protocol. Simulation parameters for the simulation are summarized in Table 1 below:

Table 1. Simulation Parameters

Parameter	Value
Simulation area	800m * 800m
Number of vehicles	200
Transmission range	100m
MAC protocol	IEEE 802.11 DCF
Simulation time	300s
Beacon Interval	1 beacon/second
Maximum Vehicles velocity	14 meter per second

The metrics used to evaluate the performance of the proposed protocol are control packet overhead, ratio of packet delivery, and end-to-end delay against vehicle speed.

Fig. 3 shows the load distribution around the intersections as represented by the number of queries answered by MLS and its PLSs quorum members of QLSP. Each

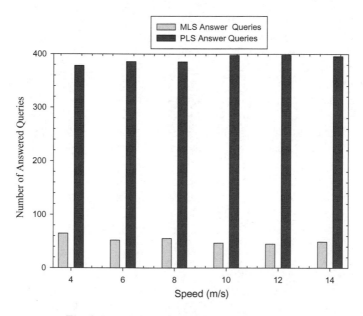

Fig. 3. Load balance around intersection vicinity

PLS is assigned a different direction and then all PLSs surround MLS from almost all directions. PLSs are thus enabled to answer any query sent to MLS. Other protocols such as SOLS do not select slave location servers based on directions; instead it selects them based on the number of nodes inside the wireless range of the master node, such that the majority of the queries are answered by the master node. As ILS assigns each intersection a location server, it answers all the queries, leading to degradation in overhead as discussed the in sections below. Thus, balancing the loads on MLS's located at dense areas (i.e., intersection) is successfully handled by QLSP. The higher the load on MLS, the higher the contention on the transmission medium among nodes located in the vicinity of intersections. Consequently, a high load on the main location server degrades the overall performance of the protocol. However, QLSP avoids this issue and distributes the load onto multi servers.

QLSP in Fig. 4 shows superior packet delivery compared to other protocols over all different speeds as the urban area topology is followed, and location based servers are assigned to intersections in addition to the distribution of PLSs on road segments surrounding the intersections. In ILS, for instance, delivery is lower than QLSP as all queries are sent directly to the intersection location server and the area is already dense. This may lead to a high rate of packet collisions, which degrades the delivery of packets to their destinations. QLSP avoids this by distributing the load on multi-servers. The Terminode protocol broadcasts every received packet inside home region, as a result, low packets delivery.

Fig. 5 shows that QLSP overhead is lower than other protocols, as expected, from the load balance results. This is because with the vicinity of intersections, the number of control packets such as beacons, update locations, and queries with their replies is high. Thus, selecting PLSs for different directions to work as location servers reduces

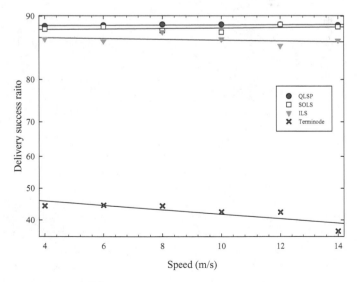

Fig. 4. Average packets delivery ratio

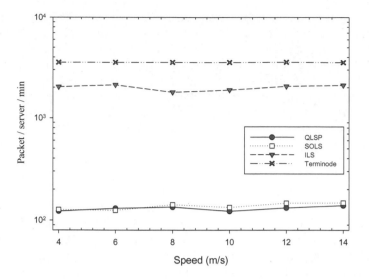

Fig. 5. Overhead per server

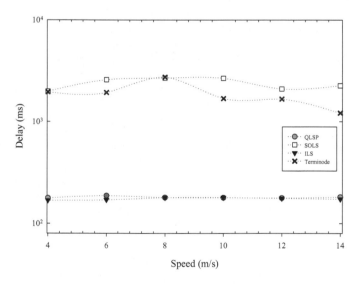

Fig. 6. Average end-to-end delay

the load in the vicinity of intersections ILS manages too many control packets because all packets, such as query and updates, are sent directly to the location server located at the intersection which is increasing the overhead on this server. SOLS broadcasts duplicate nodes locations to slaves, leading to additional overhead, but here the additional overhead is minor as SOLS does not select location servers based on intersection. Thus, location servers could be located at places with a low number of nodes, and low overhead, but at the cost of high packet routing delays. Terminode has very high overhead, mainly due to the broadcast of each received packet by Terminodes inside the home region.

Fig. 6 shows that the end-to-end delay of QLSP is lower than SOLS and Terminode and this is because PLSs in QLSP minimizes the number of hops a packet should usually take. The selection of location servers, based on intersection, efficiently directs the forwarding of queries and update packets over well connected nodes until they reach a PLS or MLS of the specified quorum group. Terminode and SOLS show higher end-to-end delays as they use specified regions within the network area and assign a number of nodes to work as location servers. As a consequence, packet routing suffers as a high number of hops are required to reach the specified location server.

5   Conclusion

In this paper, a location service protocol is proposed for urban area topology that exploits intersections to select the best node to act as a main location server based on two parameters: nodes distance to center point of intersection and speed. QLSP protocol efficiently designates the nodes located at the intersection to be location servers. Having MLS as the main location server and PLSs as backups provides not only a fault tolerance system but also provides load balance at dense intersections leading to reduced communication overhead and end-to-end delay.

Acknowledgement. This research has been supported by Universiti Teknologi Malaysia (UTM), Research Management Centre (RMC), project vote No. 77271.

References

1. US Census Bureau Tiger/Line (2009),
   http://www.census.gov/geo/www/tiger/
2. Bai, X.-Y., Ye, X.-M., Li, J., Jiang, H.: Vls: A map-based vehicle location service for city environments. In: The IEEE ICC 2009 Proceedings (2009), doi:978-1-4244-3435-0/09
3. Barr, R.: Swans scalable wireless ad hoc network simulator - user guide. Online at: Cornell Research Foundation (2004), http://jist.ece.cornell.edu/swans-user
4. Basagni, S., Chlamtac, I., Syrotiuk, V.R., Woodward, B.A.: A distance routing effect algorithm for mobility (dream). In: Proceedings of the 4th Annual ACM/IEEE International Conference on Mobile Computing and Networking, pp. 76–84 (1998)
5. Blazevic, L., Buttyan, L., Capkun, S., Giordano, S., Hubaux, J.P., Le Boudec, J.Y.: Self organization in mobile ad hoc networks: the approach of terminodes. IEEE Communications Magazine 39(6), 166–174 (2001)
6. Boukerche, A., Oliveira, H., Nakamura, E., Loureiro, A.: Vehicular ad hoc networks: A new challenge for localization-based systems. Computer Communications 31(12), 2838–2849 (2008)
7. Boussedjra, M., Mouzna, J., Bangera, P., Pai, M.: Map-based location service for vanet. In: International Conference on Ultra-Modern Telecommunications Workshops, pp. 1–6 (2009)

8. Chang, Y.-J., Wu, S.-Y.: Intersection Location Service for Vehicular Ad Hoc Networks with Cars in Manhattan Style Movement Patterns. In: Sandnes, F.E., Zhang, Y., Rong, C., Yang, L.T., Ma, J. (eds.) UIC 2008. LNCS, vol. 5061, pp. 284–296. Springer, Heidelberg (2008)

9. Das, S.M., Pucha, H., Hu, Y.C.: On the scalability of rendezvous-based location services for geographic wireless ad hoc routing. Computer Networks 51, 3693–3714 (2007)

10. Lee, H., Welch, J.L., Vaidya, N.H.: Location tracking using quorums in mobile ad hoc networks. Ad Hoc Networks, 371–381 (2003)

11. Liu, D., Stojmenovic, I., Jia, X.: A scalable quorum based location service in ad hoc and sensor networks. In: IEEE International Conference on Mobile Adhoc and Sensor Systems (MASS), pp. 489–492 (2006)

12. Liu, D.D., Jia, X.H.: Location service, information dissemination and object tracking in wireless sensor networks by using quorum methods. In: Wireless Sensor Networks and Applications, pp. 235–258. Springer, US (2008)

13. Owen, G., Adda, M.: Sols: Self organising distributed location server for wireless ad hoc networks. International Journal of Computer Networks & Communications (IJCNC) 1(1), 18–31 (2009)

14. Sharma, S., Alatzeth, V., Grewal, G., Pradhan, S., Helmy, A.: A comparative study of mobility prediction schemes for gls location service. In: IEEE 60th Proceedings of the Vehicular Technology Conference, pp. 25–31 (2004)

15. Stojmenovic, I., Vukojevic, B.: A routing strategy and quorum based location update scheme for ad hoc wireless networks (1999)

CNT Based Channel Interconnect for CMOS Devices

Ginto Johnson and Vinod Pangracious

Department of Electronics and Communication Engineering, Rajagiri School of Engineering
and Technology, Kerala, India
gintojohnson1988@gmail.com, vinod.pangracious@rajagiritech.ac.in

Abstract. MOSFET device dimensions and dimensions of interconnects have
been scaled down to increase density, functionality and performance of a chip.
Recently, scaling down of dimensions, that has now reached to the nano regime,
have led to various issues like electromigration as in the case of interconnects
and hot carrier effects, drain induced barrier lowering and so on in case of
MOSFET's. Researchers are thus trying to find other options for interconnects
and also new architectures to replace the conventional MOSFET's. This paper
is a study of Carbon Nanotube which is gaining interest of researchers both as
device interconnect and channel-interconnect. The behavior of CNT with length
and diameter is considered. A study of various parameters like mobility,
conductance etc. of the CNT is done. This paper focuses on CNT based FET's,
that are gaining interest as replacements for conventional CMOS, in many
modern circuits and also new devices.

Keywords: CNT, CNFET, HSPICE, simulation.

1   Introduction: Carbon Nanotubes

Carbon is known to form two stable allotropes- diamond and graphite. Sumio Iijima
discovered fullerene-related carbon nanotubes in 1991. Carbon nanotubes (CNTs) are
cylindrical carbon molecules with outstanding mechanical, electrical, thermal, and
chemical properties. The chemical bonding of carbon nanotubes is composed entirely
of sp2 bonds, similar to those of graphite. These bonds, which are stronger than the
sp3 bonds found in alkanes, provide nanotubes with their unique strength and they
naturally align themselves into ropes held together by Van der Waals forces.

The structure of a CNT can be conceptualized by wrapping a one-atom-thick layer of
graphite (or graphene) into a seamless cylinder. CNTs are of two types, namely, single-
walled carbon nanotubes (SWCNTs) and multi-walled carbon nanotubes (MWCNTs).
Depending on the direction in which they are rolled (called chirality), a CNT can be
semiconducting with a distinct band gap or it can be metallic with no band gap. The
relationship between n and m (i.e. direction in which they are rolled) defines three
categories of CNTs- metallic, semiconductive and chiral. The bending of C-C bond will
introduce stress and thereby affecting the electrical properties. Metallic CNT's are being
used in interconnects, both local and global and could also be used in 3D integrated
circuits. Semiconductive CNT's are gaining application as channel interconnects. CNT

N. Meghanathan et al. (Eds.): CCSIT 2012, Part II, LNICST 85, pp. 575–585, 2012.
© Institute for Computer Sciences, Social Informatics and Telecommunications Engineering 2012

based FET's i.e. CNFET's make use of the ballistic transport mechanism that is confined to the CNT channel and thereby reduce many of the short channel effects.

1.1   Ballistic Transport and Phonon Scattering in CNT

Ballistic transport is the transport of electrons in a medium with negligible electrical resistivity that occurs due to scattering. In general, the resistivity exists because an electron, while moving inside a medium, is scattered by defects, or by the atoms/molecules composing the medium that simply oscillate around their equilibrium position. The electron within its mean free path exhibits ballistic transport. Ballistic transport is observed when the mean free path of the electron is (much) bigger than the size of the medium that contains/delimits the medium through which the electron travels, such that the electron alters its motion only by hitting against the walls.

The term phonon refers to a special type of vibrational motion in which lattice uniformly oscillates at some frequency. In case of solids having different elements or bond strength between atoms, the phonon vibrations are of two types- optical phonons and acoustic phonons. Thus there are two types of scattering based on phonon i.e. acoustic phonon scattering (near-elastic) and optical phonon scattering (inelastic). The mean free path in case of optical phonon scattering is around 15nm and that for acoustic phonon scattering is around 150nm. The effective phonon scattering will be combination of both optical and acoustic phonon scattering. The scattering, both elastic scattering and phonon scattering contributes towards the resistivity in case of CNT.

2   Interconnects: Issues in Nano-Regime

The interconnect in an integrated circuit distributes clock and other signals as well as provides power or ground to various circuits on a chip. The International Technology Roadmap for Semiconductors (ITRS) emphasizes the high speed transmission needs of the chip as the driver for future interconnects development. The challenges in interconnect technology arise from both material requirements and difficulties in processing. The susceptibility of common interconnect metals to electromigration at high current densities (10^6 A/cm^2) is a problem. The electrical resistivity of Cu increases with a decrease in dimensions due to electron surface scattering and grain-boundary scattering. Such size effects arise from interface roughness and small grain size, which are hard to overcome.

Along with lower thermal conductivity and increasing current density demands from small dimension interconnects, the rising Cu resistivity also poses a reliability concern due to Joule heating that induces significant metal temperature rise. The large metal temperature rise exponentially degrades interconnect electro migration (EM) lifetime and severely limits the maximum current carrying capacity of future Cu interconnects. Also copper interconnects require lots of drivers for satisfactory performance. As an effect of grain boundary scattering, surface scattering and background scattering, the total resistivity of Cu wire will increase. This increase in resistivity will create issues with the current conductivity and also delay.

Table 1. [13]: Minimum density of SWCNT required for exceeding the minimum Cu wire conductivity (ITRS 2010)

Technology year	2009	2010	2011	2012	2013	2014
MPU/ASIC metal 1 $^1/_2$ pitch(nm)	54	45	38	32	27	24
Cu effective resistivity($\mu\Omega$-cm)	3.8	4.08	4.3	4.53	4.83	5.2
Minimum density(nm^{-2}) for SWCNT	0.188	0.175	0.166	0.158	0.148	0.138

On the processing side, creating high aspect ratio contacts with straight walls is an extremely difficult task. Plasma damage and cleaning of high aspect ratio features also pose concerns. Void-free filling of high aspect ratio features is an equally difficult task.

3   CNT as Interconnects

CNT's are considered to be possible replacements for Cu wires as interconnects. CNTs which are a few nanometer long have better conductivity than Cu wire. The electronic transport in metallic SWCNTs and MWCNTs occurs ballistically over long lengths owing to their nearly one dimensional electronic structure. This enables nanotubes to carry high currents with negligible heating.

Although the current-carrying capacity of an isolated CNT is much greater than that of Cu, it has a high resistance (theoretical minimum of 6.45 kΩ [7], [8]). In practice, the observed resistance of an individual CNT can be much higher [8], [9], due to the presence of imperfect metal–nanotube contacts. The high resistance of an individual CNT necessitates the use of a bundle (rope) of CNTs conducting current in parallel to form a low-resistance interconnect. While MWCNT bundles are easier to fabricate, dense metallic SWCNT bundles have greater advantages in terms of interconnect performance.

Effect Of CNT Length. For lengths greater than mean free path of electron in CNT (1µm) scattering will be more. This causes decrease in electrical conductance (Fig 1 (a)) and drift velocity (Fig 1(d)). Thermal conductance (Fig 1(b)) decreases with length while propagation delay (Fig 1(c)) will increase.

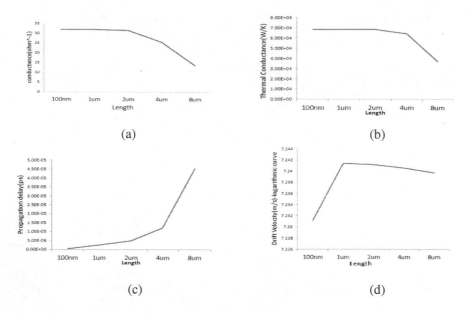

(a)

(b)

(c)

(d)

Fig. 1. [14]: (a) Electric conductance (b) Thermal conductance (c) Propagation delay and (d) Drift Velocity for Bundled CNT's as a function of length

Field Effect Mobility. The field effect mobility will increase with the length of the CNT and beyond 1μm it attains saturation. The saturation mobility is dependent on the charge density of the CNT. Lower the charge density higher will be the saturation mobility. The field effect mobility of CNT's will increase with diameter of the CNT. For higher charge densities the mobility will decrease for same diameter of CNT.

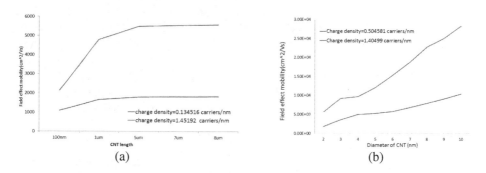

(a)

(b)

Fig. 2. [14]:(a)Field effect mobility with CNT length and (b) FE mobility with CNT diameter

Conductance. Conductance will increase with charge density of the CNT but will reach saturation at higher charge densities. This can be extended by increasing the diameter of the CNT. As seen from Fig 3(b) for same charge density the conductance will be higher for larger diameter CNT's.

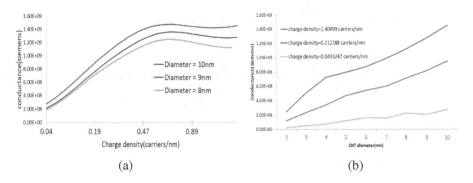

(a)   (b)

Fig. 3. [14]: (a)Conductance Vs. charge density for different CNT diameter and (b) variation of conductance with CNT diameter

4   Carbon Nanotubes as Channel Interconnect

Carbon nanotubes (CNTs) and carbon nanotube field effect transistors (CNFETs) have demonstrated extraordinary properties and are widely accepted as the building blocks of next generation VLSI circuits. Various structures making use of CNT's are under study or development, such as Cylindrical CNFET, Schottky barrier CNFET, Single gated CNFET, Double gated CNFET, etc.

Carbon-nanotube field-effect transistor (CNFET) avoids most of the fundamental limitations for traditional silicon MOSFETs. With ultra-long (~1 μm) mean free path (MFP) for elastic scattering, a ballistic or near-ballistic transport can be obtained with an intrinsic carbon nanotube (CNT) under low voltage bias.

In planar CNFET, parallel semiconducting CNTs are grown on or transferred to a substrate. The regions of CNTs under the gate are undoped. The conductivity of these undoped regions is controlled by the gate. The source and drain regions of the CNTs are heavily doped. The gate, source and drain contacts, and interconnects are defined by conventional lithography.

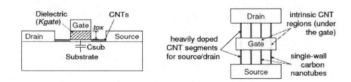

Fig. 4. [3]: Carbon –Nanotube Field Effect Transistor (CNFET)

The CNFET consists of contacts, p+ doped source and drain regions of semiconducting CNTs for PFET or n+ doped source and drain regions of semiconducting CNTs for NFET and undoped or intrinsic regions of CNTs under the gates. The distances between gates and contacts are limited by the lithographic feature size. Since CNTs are grown on the substrate, the inter-CNT distance is not limited by lithography. Multiple carbon nanotubes are allowed under the same gate (i.e. multiple tubes per device). The CNTs at the ends observe less charge screening effects than those in the middle.

4.1   Study Based on HSPICE Model of CNFET

A general study based on HSPICE model of CNFET [3][4] is done. The drain characteristics are similar to that of MOSFETs. From the obtained gate characteristics we can see that the current becomes saturated at high gate voltages. Applying higher gate voltage will not further increase the current through the CNFET channel i.e. the CNT. The point of saturation can be extended by applying higher drain to source voltage.

Applying gate voltage will cause more electrons to accumulate in the CNT channel. By applying more gate voltage more number of electrons will be pumped into the CNT. High drain to source voltage can pull these electrons and cause more current to flow. In case of lower Vds, the flow of electrons is slow and the current will be saturated at lower gate voltages itself.

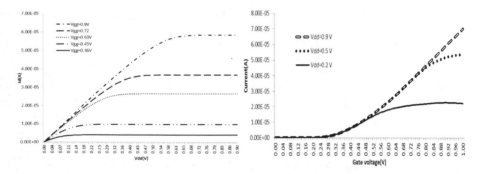

Fig. 5. Drain current Vs Drain Voltage and Drain current Vs Gate voltage

Effect of Temperature. When the temperature increases there is a decrease in the current through the CNFET. This can be considered due to the increase in the resistance. From the slope of the Drain current Vs drain voltage(Idd Vs Vdd) curve, the resistance for CNFET is found to increase with temperature.

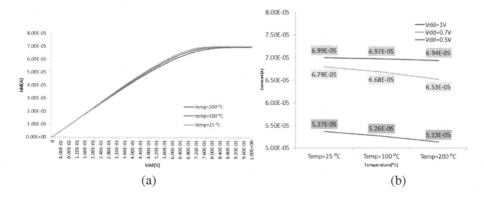

(a)   (b)

Fig. 6. Drain current for different temperature

Table 2. Increase in resistance of CNFET with increase in temperature

Temperature(°C)	25 °C	100 °C	200 °C
Resistance(Ω)	9.572K Ω	9.77K Ω	10.045K Ω

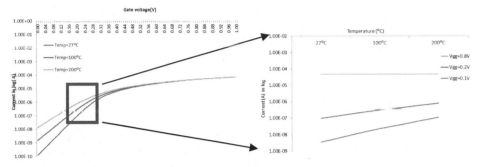

Fig. 7. Current observed when varying the gate voltage for different temperatures

The effect of increase in temperature (Fig 7), is more for low gate voltages(Vgg=0.1V) than higher gate voltages(Vgs=0.8V). Increase in temperature increases the subthreshold current through the CNFET.

Table 3. Increase in subthreshold current with temperature

Temperature(°C)	25 °C	100 °C	200 °C
Subthreshold current(A)	2.87E-08	1.938E-07	9.5E-07

The current through the CNFET increases with increase in temperature for same gate voltage. Threshold voltage shows a decrease as the temperature increases(Fig 8).

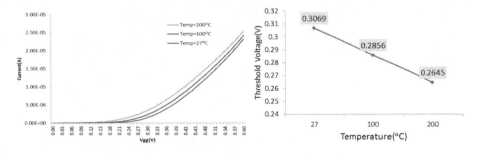

Fig. 8. Effect of temperature on threshold

Effect of Channel Length. The current though CNFET will increase as we go on increasing the length of CNT channel, as long as the scattering effects are negligible. For same voltage the current through the given CNFET is higher for longer channel CNFET (Fig 9).

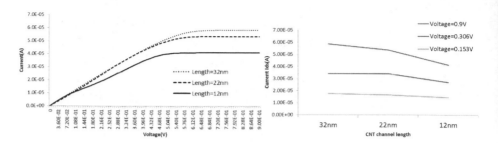

Fig. 9. Effect of channel length of CNFET on current

Gate Oxide Thickness. The thickness of gate oxide is an important parameter. In nanoscale devices, a high k dielectric is used that has high breakdown electric field and also prevents injection of electrons into the gate region. The current increases as we decrease the gate oxide thickness (Fig 10). As the gate oxide thickness is reduced, voltage drop across oxide is less and more voltage is available over the CNT channel, thereby increasing the effect of gate voltage control and more electrons are pumped into the CNT channel.

As in the case of MOSFET's, when the thickness of gate oxide is reduced ,low gate voltage is required to turn on the device and thus for lower gate oxide thickness we have lower threshold device (Fig 11). Threshold voltage for CNFET with 10nm gate oxide thickness is around 0.4V while for the oxide thickness of 1nm the threshold voltage reduces to 0.35V.

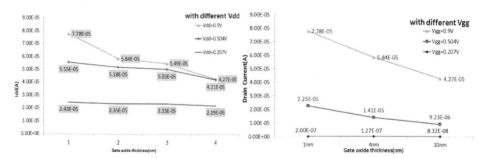

Fig. 10. Variation of current with the gate oxide thickness

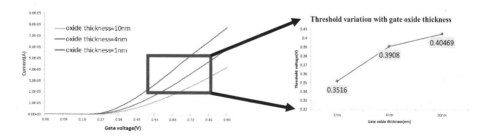

Fig. 11. Threshold variation with the gate oxide thickness

Subthreshold Current. Beyond the threshold, the current increases linearly with the applied gate voltage (Fig. 12). In the subthreshold region, which is less than 0.2V here, the current increases exponentially. CNT based FET's have got significant subthreshold current as per the given CNFET model. Calculated subthreshold current from Fig 12. is 3.82E-08A. This shows that even in subthreshold region the CNFET has high current. So they can be also used in devices operating in subthreshold region.

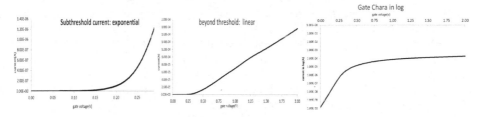

Fig. 12. The current in subthreshold, beyond threshold region and in log scale

Number of CNT's and Type of CNT used in Channel. There is not much change in current when the width of the gate region is increased (Fig. 13(a))as most of the current flows through the CNT itself. So if we increase the number of CNT channels, an increase in current is observed (Fig.13(b)). As for MOSFET, gate width also plays a major role in the amount of current through the channel. Metallic CNT have higher current than the chiral type CNT, while semiconductive type CNT has lowest current (Fig.13(d)).

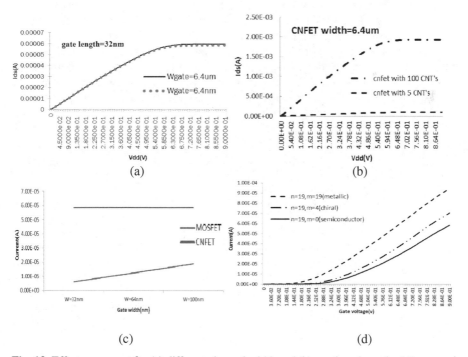

Fig. 13. Effect on current for (a) different channel width and (b) number channels (c) comparison of MOSFET AND CNFET current with gate width and (d) for different types of CNT channels

5   Conclusion

Depending upon the chirality, there are metallic and semiconducting CNT's. Metallic CNT's find application as interconnect materials. Semiconducting CNT's are used as channel interconnects in MOSFETs. The conduction process through the CNT is ballistic transport mechanism under the condition that the channel length is kept comparable to the mean free path (~1um). CNT's have got inherent resistance against electromigration and have high thermal conductivity and electrical current density.

Electrical conductance of CNT's decreases and propagation delay increases with increase in CNT length. It is also observed that drift velocity will increase till the mean free path of electron in CNT. Beyond the mean free path length, the drift velocity decrease due to scattering. Single walled and multi walled CNT and their bundles are used for interconnect applications.

CNT's are used as channel interconnects in FET's. The CNT can be placed between two doped regions that act as source and drain or can be made to have Schottky contact (metal–semiconductor contact). A study based on HSPICE model for CNFET was done. As per the model, the drain characteristics where found similar to the MOSFET while current reaches saturation for higher gate voltages while keeping the drain to source voltage constant. This current saturation at higher gate voltages can be extended by increasing Vdd. The current in subthreshold region is found to be exponentially increasing while the current beyond subthreshold is increasing linearly. There is variation of threshold with temperature and also with gate oxide thickness. These properties are similar to the MOSFETs. It was observed that the current through CNTFET remains same when the gate width is reduced keeping the channel length constant, while in the case of MOSFET the gate width also have significant contribution in current. To increase the current through the CNFET the number of CNT channels are to be increased. Significant amount of subthreshold current is present in CNFET. CNFET's can be used in low voltage applications. The amount of current and also the subthreshold current can be reduced by reducing the number of CNT's in the channel.

Reference

1. Srivastava, N., Li, H., Kreupl, F., Banerjee, K.: On the Applicability of Single-Walled Carbon Nanotubes as VLSI Interconnects. IEEE Transactions on Nanotechnology 8(4) (July 2009)
2. Dresselhaus, M.S., et al.: Carbon nanotubes: Synthesis, structure, properties and applications. Springer, Heidelberg (2001)
3. Deng, J., Philip Wong, H.-S.: Modeling and Analysis of Planar-Gate Electrostatic Capacitance of 1-D FET with Multiple Cylindrical Conducting Channels. IEEE Transactions on Electron Devices 54(9) (September 2007)
4. Deng, J., Philip Wong, H.-S.: A Compact SPICE Model for Carbon-Nanotube Field-Effect Transistors Including Nonidealities and Its Application—Part I: Model of the Intrinsic Channel Region. IEEE Transactions on Electron Devices 54(12) (December 2007)

5. Patil, N., Lin, A., Myers, E.R., Ryu, K., Badmaev, A., Zhou, C., Philip Wong, H.-S., Mitra, S.: Wafer-Scale Growth and Transfer of Aligned Single-Walled Carbon Nanotubes. IEEE Transactions on Nanotechnology 8(4) (July 2009)
6. Zhao, Y., Liao, A., Pop, E.: Multiband Mobility in Semiconducting Carbon Nanotubes. IEE Elec. Device Lett. 30, 1078 (2009)
7. McEuen, P.L., Fuhrer, M.S., Park, H.: Single-walled carbon nanotube electronics. IEEE Trans. Nanotechnol. 1(1), 78–85 (2002)
8. Liang, W., Bockrath, M., Bozovic, D., Hafner, J.H., Tinkham, M., Park, H.: Fabry-perot interference in a nanotube electron waveguide. Nature 411, 665–669 (2001)
9. Hunger, T., Lengeler, B., Appenzeller, J.: Transport in ropes of carbon nanotubes: Contact barriers and Luttinger liquid theory. Phys. Rev. B 69, 195406-1–195406-4 (2004)
10. Banerjee, K., Srivastava, N.: Are Carbon Nanotubes the Future of VLSI Interconnections? Electrical and Computer Engineering, University of California, Santa Barbara, CA 93106
11. Srivastava, N., Banerjee, K.: Performance Analysis of Carbon Nanotube Interconnects for VLSI Applications. Department of Electrical and Computer Engineering, University of California, Santa Barbara, CA 93106
12. Cho, H., Koo, K.-H., Kapur, P., Saraswat, K.C.: Performance Comparisons Between Cu/Low-κ, Carbon-Nanotube, and Optics for Future On-Chip Interconnects. IEEE Electron Device Letters 29(1) (January 2008)
13. International technology roadmap for semiconductor (2005)/(2003)/(2010)
14. Nanohub, http://nanohub.org/

Conviction Scheme for Classifying Misbehaving Nodes in Mobile Ad Hoc Networks

S. Sridhar[1] and R. Baskaran[2]

[1] Dept. of Computer Applications, Easwari Engineering College, Chennai
ssridharmca@yahoo.co.in
[2] Dept. of Computer Science and Engineering, CEG, Anna University, Chennai
dr.baskaran10@gmail.com

Abstract. A Mobile ad-hoc network (MANET) is a wireless network, self-configuring, capable of self-directed operation, hastily deployable and operates without infrastructure. Nodes cooperate to provide connectivity, operates without centralized administration. Nodes are itinerant, topology can be very dynamic and nodes must be able to relay traffic since communicating nodes might be out of range. The dynamic nature of MANET makes network open to attacks and unreliability. A node may be unsuccessful to cooperate during routing, sometimes may even disturb the routing transaction. The Qos parameters like PDR, throughput and delay are affected directly due to such behavior of nodes and it is termed as misbehaving nodes. A trust-based system can be used to track this misbehaving of nodes, spot them and isolate them from routing and provide reliability. In this paper a trust based reliable AODV protocol is presented which implements a trust value for each node. Every node is defined as reliable node if its trust value is greater than threshold value, if not it's a misbehaving node. This enhances reliability in AODV routing and results in increase of PDR, decrease in delay and throughput is maintained. This work is implemented and simulated on NS-2. Based on simulation results, the proposed protocol provides more consistent and reliable data transfer compared with normal AODV, if there are misbehaving nodes in the MANET.

Keywords: Ad-hoc, AODV, MANET, Trust, Misbehaving node, Qos.

1 Introduction

Mobile ad-hoc network is an extraordinarily testing vibrant network. They don't rely on existing infrastructure to support communication. Each mobile node acts as an end node when it is the source or destination of a communication and forwards packets for other nodes when it is an intermediate node of the route. Mobile Ad-Hoc network [1] is a system of wireless mobile nodes that self-organizes itself in dynamic and temporary network topologies. Mobile ad hoc networks are suitable for dynamic environment where no infrastructure or temporarily established mobile applications are used, which are cost effective. Ad hoc networks are easier to deploy than wired networks and are found many applications, such as in rescue, battlefields, meeting

N. Meghanathan et al. (Eds.): CCSIT 2012, Part II, LNICST 85, pp. 586–593, 2012.

rooms etc., where either a wired network is unavailable or deploying a wired network is inconvenient. Distributed state in unreliable environment, dynamic topology, limited network capacity, variable link quality, interference and collisions, energy-constrained nodes, flat addressing, scaling issues, heterogeneity are few challenges faced by MANET. Mobile ad hoc network routing protocols face some challenges like node mobility that causes frequent topology changes , the changeable and erratic ability of wireless links and packet losses. Mobile nodes also face troubles like limited power, computing and bandwidth resources.

There have been many ad-hoc routing protocols, which fall into several categories: proactive routing protocols such as dynamic Destination-Sequenced Distance-Vector routing (DSDV), Optimized Link State Routing (OLSR), Topology Broadcast based on Reverse Path Forwarding (TBRPF), on-demand routing protocols such as Dynamic Source Routing (DSR), AODV, Signal Stability-based Adaptive routing (SSA). Proactive routing protocols have little delay for route discovery and are robust enough to link breaks and obtain a global optimal route for each destination. However, their routing overhead is also high. On-demand routing protocols are easy to realize and their overhead is low. But routes in on-demand routing protocols are easy to break in the case of topology variations. In AODV [2] node doesn't have any information about other nodes until a communication is needed. By broadcasting HELLO packets in a regular interval, local connectivity information is maintained by each node. Local connectivity maintains information about all the neighbors.

Recent Qos solutions are planned to operate on trusted environments and totally assume the participating nodes to be cooperative and well behaved [3,4]. Such assumptions are not valid in dynamic environments like MANETs. Providing different quality of service levels in a persistently changing environment is a challenge because: Unrestricted mobility causes QoS sessions to suffer due to recurrent path breaks, thereby requiring such sessions to be reestablished over new paths. The link-specific and state-specific information in the nodes is inherently imprecise due to the dynamically changing topology and channel characteristics. Hence, incorrect routing decisions may chop down Qos parameters performance. Inadequate bandwidth, storage space and battery life also drastically influence the performance of the QoS parameters.

This traditional AODV is to perform its job based on the trust values calculated for each node and to decide whether to take part or to be isolated from routing. The trust value is calculated for each node and based on this trust value AODV decides whether the corresponding node is still reliable or not. If nodes trust value is less than the threshold then the node is declared to be misbehaving node and an alternate path is selected. This trust based routing mechanism helps to identify and eliminate misbehaving nodes in MANET and performs an efficient and effective routing, which results in improving Qos parameters like PDR, throughput and delay.

2   Literature Survey

Mobile ad hoc networks are apt for mobile applications either in antagonistic environments where no infrastructure is available, or temporarily established mobile applications, which are cost decisive. In recent years, application domains of mobile ad hoc networks gain more and more significance in non-military public organizations and in commercial and industrial areas. Medium access control, routing, resource management, quality of service and security are the research areas for mobile ad hoc network. The importance of routing protocols in dynamic networks has directed a lot of mobile efficient ad hoc routing protocols.

A security-enhanced AODV routing protocol called R-AODV (Reliant Ad hoc On-demand Distance Vector Routing) [5] uses a modified trust mechanism known as direct and recommendations trust model and then incorporating it inside AODV. This enhances security by ensuring that data does not go through malicious nodes that have been known to misbehave. Each node is given a trust value and this value is associated with the possibility of the node to perform a packet drop. With the inclusion of trust mechanism, it is expected that using R-AODV would result in a higher percentage of successful data delivery as compared to AODV. It is also expected that the normalized routing load and end-to-end delay would increase.

A framework for estimating the trust between nodes in an ad hoc network based on quality of service parameters using probabilities of transit time variation, deleted, multiplied and inserted packets, processing delays to estimate and update trust [6]. This paper clearly shows that only two end nodes need to be concerned and attain reduced overhead. The framework proposed in this paper is applicable and useful to estimate trust in covert unobservable and anonymous communications. This results in detecting regular packets drops and delay detection.

A schema is formed via direct and indirect approach to compute trust value among anonymous nodes [7]. To evaluate trust values the parameters like reputation, knowledge, observation and context were used. The trust schema that is build is used to allow resource to be shared among trusted nodes. The result obtained is then mapped with the access privileges to take appropriate actions.

A routing protocol, which adds a field in request packet and also stores trust value indicating node trust on neighbor based on level of trust factor [8]. The routing information will be transmitted depending upon highest trust value among all. This not only saves the node's power by avoiding unnecessary transmitting control information but also in terms of bandwidth (channel utilization), which is very important in case of MANET. The malicious node can attack on the control packet and misbehave in the network. A trusted path is used irrespective of shortest or longest path, which can be used for communication in the network. It calculates route trust value on the complete reply path, which can be utilized by source node for next forthcoming communication in the network. Thus security level is improved and also malicious node attacks are prevented in the network.

A trust model introduced in the network layer leads to a secure route between source and destination without any intruders or malicious nodes in the network [9]. This trust based routing protocol concentrates both in route and node trust. Node Trust Calculation Process is done by introducing a new data structure neighbor table in each node of the MANET. Node trust is calculated by the collective opinion of node's neighbors. The resultant trust value is placed in trust value field of neighbor table. Node trust calculated based upon the information that one node could collect about the other nodes. Route Trust Calculation Process is done using a modified extended route table. With this minimum overhead, eliminates the malicious node as well as establish a best-trusted route between source and destination.

TAODV [10], an enhanced AODV protocol was proposed with a concept of trust values for calculating trust values of nodes. The changes made to the existing protocol are, two new control packets TREQ (Trust request) & TREP (Trust Reply) and a modified extended routing table with four new fields; positive events, negative events, route status, opinion. This provided a reliable routing.

3   Proposed Work

Routing in mobile ad hoc networks is pretentious due to the dynamic nature of nodes, which are not stable and keep moving. But still nodes communicate with each other and exchange data within the available nodes on the network. The architecture of the proposed work is presented in Fig. 1.The node trust plays a very crucial role in MANET routing. Trust factor here focuses on identifying the misbehaving nodes and helps nodes to select an alternate path to carry on routing successfully. The proposed work concentrates on identifying misbehaving nodes using the trust level values. For every node a trust level value is calculated and if this value decreases below the threshold value then the node is declared as misbehaving node and an alternate path is selected.

The trust level value calculation is based on two main parameters qrs and qrf, where qrs is defined as rate of success which is calculated based on number of neighboring nodes who have successfully received (rreq) from the source node and qrs defined as rate of failure which is calculated based on number of successful replies (rrep) received by the source node which has sent rreq.

$$Qrreq_i = \frac{qrs - qrf}{qrs + qrf} \cdots Qrreq \neq 0 \tag{1}$$

$$Qrrep_i = \frac{qrs - qrf}{qrs + qrf} \cdots Qrrep \neq 0 \tag{2}$$

$$TL = T_i(rreq) * Qrreq_i + T_i(rrep) * Qrrep_i \tag{3}$$

Where, TL is the trust level value and T_i(rreq) & T_i (rrep) are time factorial at which rreq and rrep are sent by the nodes respectively and it is calculated as 1 plus hop counts and i varies from 1 to number of nodes taking part in routing and Qrrep and Qrreq are intermediate values. Using the above-mentioned formula the trust level value is calculated for each node during routing and is checked against the threshold value (assumed to be as 5). If lesser than threshold then node is a misbehaving node and will not be suitable for further routing and an alternate path is selected for further routing. This checks every node with its trust value to make itself robust and trustworthy for effective and efficient routing.

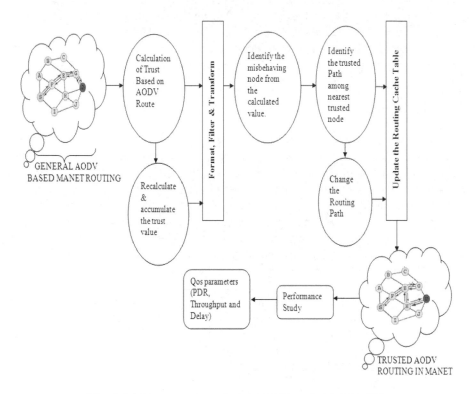

Fig. 1. Architecture of trust based AODV routing in MANET

4   Evaluation Results

The recital of proposed trust based AODV protocol is analyzed using NS-2 simulator. The network is designed using network simulator with maximum of 50 nodes. Other parameters based on which the network is created are given in Table1. Results are obtained from this simulation applying both general AODV and proposed AODV protocols. The proposed AODV protocol has shown good improvement over the QoS parameters like PDR & Delay. PDR is increased and delay is reduced compared to the general AODV. Throughput is maintained. Graphs are used to compare the results of the existing AODV and proposed AODV protocol and clearly indicate the improvement of the proposed protocol.

Table 1. Simulation Parameter Values

Parameter	Value
Network size	1600 x 1600
Number of nodes	50
Transmission range	250 meters.
Movement speed	100 kbps
Traffic type	CBR
Packet size	5000
Simulation time	30 minutes.
Maximum speed	100 kbps
Time interval	0.01 sec.
MAC layer protocol	IEEE 802.11
Protocol	AODV
NS2 version	2.34

Simulation results were obtained and compared. The results show a good improvement than the exiting approach. The proposed protocol has performed well than the existing AODV protocol which lacks in Qos parameters like PDR and delay when compared with the proposed AODV protocol. The results obtained are shown in Table 2, which shows the values obtained using general AODV and proposed AODV at different node sizes. The traditional AODV is affected due to the existence of misbehaving nodes, which results in low packet delivery ratio and also causes the delay to increase. The proposed protocol has shown improved Qos parameters values where trust values are used to identify the misbehaving nodes in the route and immediately take an alternate path to successfully complete the routing. This approach of the proposed AODV protocol has resulted in an increased packet delivery ratio and a decreased delay involved in routing.

Table 2. Comparison of Result with node size

Node Size	General AODV			Proposed Trust based AODV		
	PDR	Delay	Throughput	PDR	Delay	Throughput
25	82.98	0.24615	75771.43	92.20	0.22153	75771.43
50	70.05	0.84972	114559.89	91.06	0.64979	114559.89
100	64.43	1.44347	148339.67	90.03	0.92683	148339.67
200	62.36	1.65589	150748.56	84.32	0.93536	150748.56
300	60.65	1.78687	150836.74	81.26	0.94825	150836.74

Graph 1 indicates how the proposed protocol has shown a good decrease in Delay when compared to the general AODV. Graph 2 shows the increase in PDR when compared with the general AODV.

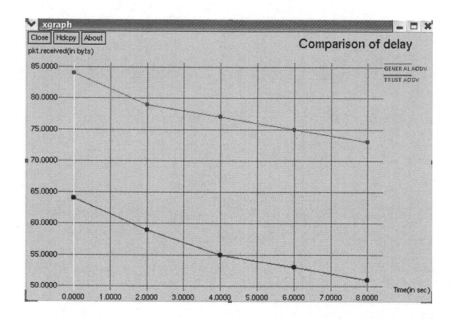

Graph 1. Comparison of general AODV Delay and Trust based AODV Delay

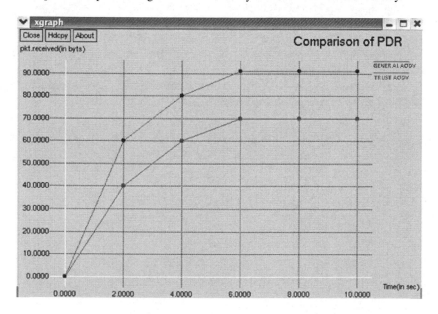

Graph 2. Comparison of general AODV PDR and Trust based AODV PDR

5 Conclusion and Future Enhancements

In this paper, a trust based AODV protocol is proposed. Trust level values for each node are calculated to identify the misbehaving nodes during routing. A node is declared as misbehaving nodes if their trust level value is less than the threshold value and this leads to an alternate path selection for further routing. This trust based routing mechanism has proved to be increasing the performance of the proposed protocol and also shows good improvement of Qos parameters like PDR and delay The same scheme can also be implemented on other MANET routing protocols and also implement some techniques for authenticating the packet and the node which take part in routing.

References

1. Kortuem, G., Schneider, J., Preuitt, D., Thompson, T.G.C., F'ickas, S., Segall, Z.: When Peer to-Peer comes Face-to-Face: Collaborative Peer-to-Peer Computing in Mobile Ad hoc Networks. In: 1st International Conference on Peer-to-Peer Computing, Linkoping, Sweden, pp. 75–91 (August 2001)
2. Perkins, C., Royer, E., Das, S.: Ad hoc on-demand Distance Vector Routing, RFC-3651
3. Hu, Y.: Enabling Secure High-Performance Wireless Ad Hoc Networking, PhD Thesis, Carnegie Mellon University, CMU (2003)
4. IIyas, M.: The Handbook of Wireless Ad Hoc Network, CRC (2003)
5. Jassim, H.S., Yussof, S.: A Routing Protocol based on Trusted and shortest Path selection for Mobile Ad hoc Network. In: IEEE 9th Malaysia International Conference on Communications (2009)
6. Umuhoza, D., Agbinya, J.I.: Estimation of Trust Metrics for MANET Using QoS Parameter and Source Routing Algorithms. In: The 2nd International Conference on Wireless Broadband and Ultra Wideband Communications (2007)
7. Abu Bakar, A., Ismail, R., Jais, J.: Forming Trust in Mobile Ad -Hoc Network. In: 2009 International Conference on Communications and Mobile Computing (2009)
8. Mangrulkar, R.S., Atique, M.: Trust Based Secured Adhoc on Demand Distance Vector Routing Protocol for Mobile Adhoc Network (2010)
9. Menaka, A., Pushpa, M.E.: Trust Based Secure Routing in AODV Routing Protocol (2009)
10. TAODV: A Trusted AODV Routing protocol for Mobile ad hoc networks (2009)

Virtual Interactive Prototyping

Kurien Zacharia, Eldo P. Elias, and Surekha Mariam Varghese

Mar Athanasius College of Engineering, Kothamangalam, India
{kurienzach,eldope}@gmail.com, surekha@mace.ac.in

Abstract. In this paper, we introduce a new method of technology enhanced prototyping called Virtual Interactive Prototyping (VIP). Prototype is a model that mimics the static or working behavior of an actual product before manufacturing the product. Prototyping is implemented by displaying the individual components over a physical model constructed using Cardboard or Thermocole in the actual size and shape of the original product. The components of the equipment or product such as screen, buttons etc. are then projected using a projector connected to the computer into the physical model. Users can interact with the prototype like the original working equipment. Computer Vision techniques as well as sound processing techniques are used to detect and recognize the user gestures captured using a web camera and microphone. VIP is a fast, flexible and interactive prototyping method and has many advantages over existing immersive video prototyping methods.

Keywords: Prototyping, Augmented Reality, Image Processing, Sixth Sense.

1 Introduction

Virtual Interactive Prototyping is an interactive prototyping method that allows to create and test prototypes easily by using computer simulated objects displayed on to an actual physical model using a projector. This means user can create a model on the computer and test it out using a real physical model without actually assembling any component using the concept of augmented reality. Interaction with the physical model is achieved through use of computer vision technologies for tracking the user movements.

Prototype is a model (working or static) that allows the product to be visualized or simulated before an actual product is put to manufacturing line. Currently there are different prototyping methods available depending upon the kind of product that we want to manufacture. Physical mockups (Hardware Prototyping) have always played an important role in the early conceptual stages of design. It involves creating a static model of the product from cheap and readily available materials such as paper, cardboard, Thermocol etc. They are commonly used in the design and development electronic equipments such as mobile phones, physical mockups are used in early stages of design to get a feel of the size, shape and appearance of the equipment.

Another kind of prototyping that is particularly used for design of electronic equipment's is the software simulation. The software required for the equipment is

N. Meghanathan et al. (Eds.): CCSIT 2012, Part II, LNICST 85, pp. 594–603, 2012.

written and then run in simulator software inside the computer. This method allows testing the software of the product and the user interactions with it.

The disadvantage of the above methods is that the user experience remains disjoint. In Hardware prototyping the user gets the touch and feel of the product but does not include the working or interactions with the product. In software based simulations the user gets to know how the product with interact but he has no touch and feel of the actual product.

Other methods of prototyping like using a prototyping workbench allows to create hardware interface with relative ease, but the cost factor makes them beyond the reach of most small and medium scale industries. VIP is a fast, flexible and interactive prototyping method's and has many advantages over existing prototyping methods.

Virtual Interactive Prototyping (VIP) is a virtual reality prototyping method based on Sixth Sense[1] and an existing prototyping method called Display Objects[2]. A physical model in the shape and size of the actual product is constructed using Paper, Cardboard or Thermocol . The components of the equipment such as (viz. screen, buttons etc.) are then projected from a projector connected to the computer into the physical model. A web camera tracks the user's gestures as well as the physical model and reacts appropriately. The accuracy of touch detection using computer vision alone is not sufficient for sensing. Therefore a microphone is attached to the surface, and the change in input level from the touch of the finger is detected. By combining the input from the microphone and camera a usable interactive system is developed. VIP uses Computer Vision techniques as well as Sound processing techniques to detect user interactions so that the user can touch and interact with the prototype like actual working equipment. The system model used in VIP is shown in Figure 1.

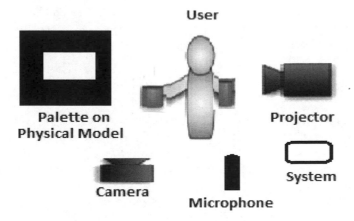

Fig. 1. The Model

2   Related Work

Display objects [2] introduced the concept of virtual models that can be designed on a Macintosh system and then projected to real physical models called display objects.

The disadvantage of the system is that user interactions in this system is based on expensive high end infrared based camera which require calibration each time the system is put to work.

Sixth Sense is an innovative computing method that uses user gestures to perform day to day activities. Sixth Sense uses a camera, a mini projector, microphone, and color markers to track fingers. Sixth Sense suggests a new method of interaction . It is used for a variety of interesting applications such as checking flight delays with flight ticket and automatically getting the reviews of books just by showing its Cover etc. In Sixth sense, markers with distinct color are placed in each of the fingers. Positions of the fingers are identified by locating the positions of the color markers.

The concept of interactive techniques for product design has been used elsewhere. Avrahami, D. and Hudson used interactive techniques for product design [3]. Use of static virtual artefacts has been proposed for the analysis of team collaboration in virtual environments [4]. The display methods uses projections to render a realistic model of the object according to the users viewing position. Also [5] (Maldovan, K., Messner, J.I. and Faddoul, M., (2006)) used a virtual mockup process for reviewing designs of physical structures such court rooms, restaurants etc. Pushpendra et. al. proposed an approach using immersive video with surround sound and a simulated infrastructure to create a realistic simulation of a ubiquitous environment in the software design and development office[6].

This paper proposes a system combining the technology used in the sixth sense system to implement the prototyping method as proposed in the display objects method. The result is a very low cost system with minimal setup or calibration time without compromising on the usability and performance of the system.

Similar technologies are being employed to create gadgets like Optimus Maximus Keyboard [7] in which each key can be programmed to display and be used for any user configurable purpose. Digital paper systems[8] employs sensors placed in papers to create an interactive paper.

3   Implementation

Common Image and sound processing techniques are extensively used in implementing the concept. EmguCV, which is a C# wrapper for the OpenCV image processing library developed by Intel is used for image processing. The Open Source Computer Vision Library (OpenCV)[9] is a comprehensive computer vision library and machine learning written in C++ and C with additional Python and Java interfaces. It officially supports Linux, Mac OS, Windows, Android etc.

The programming language used is C#.net as it facilitates fast development. For audio capturing and processing BASS audio processing library is used. All the core libraries that are used for implementing VIP are open source and platform independent. However VIP is implemented in Windows platform.

The major processing modules are

3.1   Image Processing

User interacts with the model using hand gestures. Color markers are placed on the user's fingers for distinguishing the commands. For tracking the interactions of the user, the position and colour of the fingers are sensed using standard image processing algorithms for edge detection and segmentation.

An HSV Color space based Color segmentation algorithm is used to isolate the color of the color marker. The center point of the segmented region is roughly taken as the position of the user's finger. For tracking the motion of the display object, first corners of the physical prototype are located. A grayscale based edge detection algorithm is used for this purpose. The image of the product is then fitted into this rectangle using image transforms.

Segmentation

For tracking the user actions, the image of the color marker should be separated from the picture captured by the live camera. The segmentation algorithm removes all other color from the input image other than the color of the color marker. Output of the segmentation algorithm is a black and white image with all areas black except the portions having the color of the color marker. The features extracted from this are the edges. They are extracted by looking for the difference b/w pixel values. Where there is an abrupt change in the pixel value (like b/w black and white) we define it as an edge.

Color values are represented in 8 bit format in the system. An HSV based color segmentation algorithm is used for better efficiency. Images are represented in 8 bit bitmapped format, which used a 3 dimensional matrix for storing pixel values. The threshold values for Hue, Satuation and Value are represented as HueThreshL, HueThreshH, SatThreshL, SatThreshH, ValThreshL, ValThreshH. Algorithm 2 describes the steps in the segmentation.

Algorithm 1. Segmentation Algorithm

```
for i=0 to imgmat->width
for j=0 to imagmat->height
color<-imgmat[x,y];
if(color.hue < HueThreshH && color.hue >HueThreshL &&
color.sat>SatThreshL && color.sat <SatThreshH &&
color.Value > ValThreshL && color.Value < ValThreshH)
imgmat[x,y] = 255;
else imgmat[x,y] = 0;
```

Tracking

The tracking algorithm includes a convex hull based algorithm to find construct a convex hull based feature extraction system. The extracted features are stored in a feature list. These features are then tracked for different kinds of interactions. The input to the tracking algorithm is the Binary mask produced by the segmentation algorithm. Tracking algorithm is described in Algorithm 2.

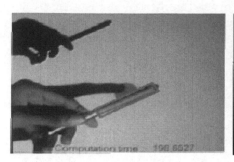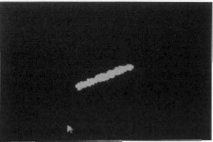

Fig. 2. Result of segmentation (left) and tracking (right)

Algorithm 2. Tracking Algorithm

```
for i=0 to imgmask.width
for j=0 to imgmask.height
for k=0 to 8
if (color[imgmask[x,y]-imgmask[x,k%3]]>colorthreshold)
if(x>maxx && y > maxy)
    point3 = point(x,y);
else if(x>maxx && y < miny)
    point2 = point(x,y);
else If(x<minx && y> maxy)
    point4 = point(x,y);
  else if(x<minx &y<miny)
    point1 = point(x,y)
```

3.2   Sound Processing

Image processing techniques have limitations in detecting whether the user has touched the virtual prototype or not. Therefore we use a microphone attached to the Virtual Prototype to detect whether the user has touched it or not. The input from the microphone is first passed through a Band Pass Filter to reduce background noise and then the amplitude of the resultant signal is compared with a threshold value to detect taps.

4   Constructing the Prototype

To construct a prototype the user will have to first drag and drop all the necessary components from a virtual palette into the virtual prototype using hand gestures. The components can be then rearranged, moved and resized inside the Virtual Prototype. After all the required components are set up, the user can then start the software simulation of the product. This means he can use it like real equipment, in the way the programmer has programmed it. The user can have both the touch and feel of a real hardware prototype as well as all the interactions.

5   Interaction Techniques

The workbench incorporates both one-handed and two handed techniques so that the user can interact with the model with one hand while browsing interaction elements with the other. The non-dominant hand is typically used to hold the physical model, while the dominant hand picks up interaction elements from the Palette. The Palette can be held or placed on a surface if hands are occupied with a physical model. Interaction elements are then pasted and placed onto the physical model using simple tapping and dragging techniques. To allow recognition of finger action by the system, fingers need to be augmented with a Vicon marker. Typically, only one or two fingers need to be enhanced in this way. Gestures allow fine-grained actions on the physical model and Palette.

5.1   Pointing

Pointing simply consists of moving the finger over the surface of a physical model or Palette. This does not result in an action until the surface is touched.

Fig. 3. User using color marker for pointing clicking etc.

5.2   Tapping

Users can select elements on the surface of the Palette by tapping them once. This causes the element to be copied to a virtual clipboard on the tip of the finger. If a physical model is subsequently tapped, the clipboard element is placed where that tap has occurred.

5.3   Clicking

Users can lock interaction elements on the panel by tapping the "Play" button on the Palette. This provides for functional interaction with elements on the surface of the panel, allowing users, for example, to press buttons that trigger some visual action. After devices are locked, any tap is interpreted by the Quartz Composer engine as a click on the element that executes its associated functionality.

5.4   Dragging

Users can select elements on the surface of the Palette by tapping them once. This causes the element to be copied to a virtual clipboard on the tip of the finger. If a physical model is subsequently tapped, the clipboard element is placed where that tap has occurred.

5.5   Pinch/Release

The Pinch gesture is initiated by bringing a thumb and index finger into contact with the extremities of a target element, and then drawing the thumb and index finger together. The Release gesture is performed by reversing this action. This acts to resize the interaction element upon which it is performed. In addition to these refined interaction techniques, the workbench supports a number of more coarse-grained (two handed) gesture-based interaction techniques.

5.6   Wiping

Users can move through layers of content on the surface of the panel by performing a wipe gesture, from the bottom left corner of the physical model upward. When editing objects, this is used to reveal the Quartz Composer patch that underlies the functionality of the panel. Layers can be closed by an inverse wipe.

5.7   Drag and Drop

Users can pick up an element through a tap on one of the items, for example, the Palette, then touching an empty area of another, causing the element to be copied to the empty area at the location of the tap.

5.8   Two-Handed Pinch/Release

The effect of this gesture is the same as the regular Pinch/Release, but performed by two-handed operation using the index fingers. This allows for a greater range of the gesture, and is very suitable for interactions on larger surfaces.

6   Programming Interaction Elements

After display elements are placed on the physical model, a script generates a Quartz file for the panel that can be edited in one of three ways: on a computer, on the Palette, or on the physical model itself. The physical model is placed in edit mode by pressing a button on the Palette, or by providing a wipe gesture on its surface. To connect input elements with output elements, users drag connectors from the outlets of the former onto the inlets of the latter in Quartz Composer on a laptop. A screen element, in turn, is scripted through the contents of a movie file connected to one of its inlets. Simple interactive behaviors are limited to simple actions, such as starting, stopping or scrolling through the movie file displayed on the screen element. More complicated behaviors are made possible by dragging Quartz Composer subpatches from the palette onto the physical model, and connecting inlets and outlets. These subpatches are programmed on the computer, rather than on the display panel. Because subpatches are a regular part of Quartz Composer, they may contain Objective-C code to further extend behaviors ranging from video feeds, to screen captures, Flash content, live webpages, etc. Since display panel is made out of real materials, it is easy to extend its behavior with real world artifacts as well, mixing properties of bits with those of atoms. For example, paper sketches or physical buttons can be easily affixed on the physical prototype, and linked with interactive content. This not only allows quick iterative revisions of the physical model, but also allows for physical elements to be mixed with digital elements, for example, to provide feedback for an on-screen input element. One example of this is the use of physical pushpins to simulate surface effects of buttons displayed on the surface. This allows for feedback when interacting with the physical prototype.

Fig. 4. Contruction of a prototype

7   Features of the System

The main advantage of the system that we propose is the combination of both hardware and software prototyping. Apart from that this systems needs only $1/8^{th}$ of the cost of creating a real prototype from scratch. This method also allows for real time modifications of the prototype, which is not possible on a real prototype. Also we plan to implement this software as Open Source software so that it will reduce any software costs, and the cost of the system would be purely hardware costs. Since all the libraries that we use are open source, we can make this system also Open Source.

7.1   Limitations

The system is sensitive to lighting conditions, since it mainly rely on image capturing and processing. Too bright or too low light can hamper the system performance. Color segmentation cannot be accurately done when the background is fast moving.

8   Conclusion

A key issue in the new electronic era is the effort required for rapid prototyping and evaluation of user interfaces and applications. Existing technologies for these tasks are either slumpy (e.g. paper prototypes, mental walkthroughs) or require a near full-scale deployment. VIP, a rapid prototyping workbench for designing new devices which projects functional interfaces over 3D physical objects is discussed in this paper. It provides a low-cost and rapid means to prototype user interfaces and applications. VIP targets a much earlier stage of physical design with functional prototyping than normally possible. It helps in creating physical prototypes with functional content fast, and with little effort.

VIP can be of great help for small and medium scale industries, since they cannot afford to build a prototype using a prototyping workbench. Such industries include the flourishing small scale mobile phone manufactures, which are based on relatively small capital and does the job of assembling pre made parts rather than building own components.

VIP, saves the electronic equipments used in prototyping and reduces electronic waste contributing to environment preservation and overall sustainable development. VIP can be termed as Green Technology.

References

1. Mistry, P.: Sixth Sense, http://www.pranavmistry.com/sixthsense
2. Akaoka, E., Ginn, T., Vertegaal, R.: Display Objects: Prototyping Functional Physical Interfaces on 3D Styrofoam, Paper or Cardboard Models. Proceedings of ACM (2010)
3. Avrahami, D., Hudson, S.E.: Forming Interactivity: A Tool for Rapid Prototyping of Physical Interactive Products. In: The Proceedings of the ACM Symposium on Designing Interactive Systems, DIS 2002, pp. 141–146 (2002)

4. Gopinath, R.: Immersive Virtual Facility Prototyping for Design and Construction Process Visualization, M.S. Thesis, The Pennsylvania State University, University Park, PA (2004)
5. Maldovan, K., Messner, J.I., Faddoul, M.: Framework for Reviewing Mockups in an Immersive Environment. In: 6th International Conference on Construction Applications of Virtual Reality, Orlando, FL, August 3-4, 6 pages (2006)
6. Singh, P., Ha, H.N., Olivier, P., Kray, C., Blythe, P., James, P.: Rapid Prototyping and Evaluation of Intelligent Environments using Immersive Video. In: Proceedings of the MODIE 2006 Workshop, MobileHCI 2006, Espoo, Finland, pp. 36–41 (2006)
7. Optimus. Optimus Maximus Keyboard (2008),
   http://www.artlebedev.com/everything/optimus/
8. Holman, D., Vertegaal, R., Altosaar, M.: PaperWindows: Interaction Techniques for Digital Paper. In: The Proceedings of CHI 2005, pp. 591–599. ACM Press (2005)
9. OpenCV Libray, http://www.sourceforge.com/opencv

Chaotic Masking of Voice Bitstream Using Mixed Sequences for Authorized Listening

Musheer Ahmad[1], Bashir Alam[1], and Omar Farooq[2]

[1] Department of Computer Engineering, Faculty of Engineering and Technology,
Jamia Millia Islamia, New Delhi-110025, India
[2] Department of Electronics Engineering, ZH College of Engineering and Technology,
AMU, Aligarh-202002, India

Abstract. The voice-based communication becomes extensively vital in the application areas of military, voice over IP, voice-conferencing, phone banking, news telecasting etc. It greatly demands to preserve sensitive voice signals from the unauthorized listening and illegal usage over shared/open networks. To address the need, we propose a chaos-based symmetric encryption technique to protect voice bitstreams over insecure transmission channel. The technique utilizes the features of high dimensional chaos like Lorenz and Chen systems to generate highly unpredictable and random-like sequences. The encryption keys are dynamically extracted from the pretreated chaotic mixed sequences, which are then used to mask the voice bitstream for integrity protection of voice data. The experimental analyses like auto-correlation, signal distribution, parameter-residual deviation, key space and key-sensitivity demonstrate the effectiveness of the proposed technique for secure voice communication.

Keywords: Voice communication, security, chaotic systems, voice encryption.

1 Introduction

With the advancement of modern wireless telecommunication and multimedia technologies, a huge amount of sensitive voice data travels over the open and shared networks. Voice-based communication becomes prominent in the application areas of military, voice over IP, e-learning, voice-conferencing, phone banking, phone stock market services, news telecasting etc. These applications are critical with respect to integrity protection of voice data and privacy protection of authorized users. The probable security threats in a voice-based communication system as highlighted by voice over IP security alliance [1] are: social threats, interception and modification threats, denial of service threats, service abuse threats, physical access threats and interruption of service threats. Hence, the need of high level security system is pre-requisite of any secure voice communication system to forestall these attacks. The cryptographic techniques are to be developed and deployed which can address and fulfill the increasing security demands of secure voice-based communication. The conventional cryptographic techniques are efficient for the text data. But they computationally fail in providing ample security due to the bulk data capacity and

N. Meghanathan et al. (Eds.): CCSIT 2012, Part II, LNICST 85, pp. 604–611, 2012.

high redundancy of voice data. Therefore, the design of efficient voice security methods demands new challenges which can provide high security to the voice data. To achieve this, a number of voice encryption techniques have been suggested [2-10]. Among them, the chaos-based techniques are considered efficient for dealing with bulky, redundant voice data. They provide fast and highly secure encryption methods. This is because of the reason that the chaotic systems are characterized with high sensitivity to its initial conditions, ergodicity, random behavior, and long periodicity. The cryptographic properties such as diffusion, confusion and disorder can be achieved by applying iteration operations to these systems.

In this paper, a symmetric voice encryption technique is proposed, to meet the demands of high security, privacy and reliability of secure voice communication system. The features of high dimensional chaotic systems are exploited in the design. The sequences generated by chaotic systems are pre-processed, quantized and mixed to produce cryptographically and statistically better encryption keys, which masked the voice bitstream. The results support the effectiveness and suitability of the proposed technique for voice data encryption.

2   Proposed Voice Encryption

The one dimensional chaotic systems have some inherent weaknesses such as: (1) they provide low key space, (2) their iteration operations generate single sequence and (3) they are weak against adaptive parameter synchronous attack [11]. Therefore, the 3D Lorenz and Chen chaotic systems are employed in the design. Each of these systems generates three distinct stochastic chaotic sequences on iteration operations, which makes encryption faster. Moreover, the Lorenz and Chen systems are more complex and generate more unpredictable sequences than 1D systems. The differential equations given below describe the Lorenz and Chen systems.

Lorenz Chaotic System

$$\dot{x}_1 = \sigma(x_2 - x_1)$$
$$\dot{x}_2 = rx_1 - x_1x_3 - x_2 \qquad (1)$$
$$\dot{x}_3 = x_1x_2 - \rho x_3$$

Chen Chaotic System

$$\dot{y}_1 = a(y_2 - y_1)$$
$$\dot{y}_2 = (c - a)y_1 - y_1y_3 + cy_2 \qquad (2)$$
$$\dot{y}_3 = y_1y_2 - by_3$$

Where $x_1(0)$, $x_2(0)$, $x_3(0)$ are initial conditions, while σ, r, ρ are positive constants of Lorenz system. Let $\sigma=10$ and $\rho=8/3$, the research shows that the Lorenz system exhibits chaotic behaviour when $r > 24.74$. Where as, $y_1(0)$, $y_2(0)$, $y_3(0)$ are initial conditions and a, b, c are parameters of Chen system. The Chen system is chaotic for $a=35$, $b=3$, $20 \leq c \leq 28.4$. The equations of Lorenz and Chen systems are quite similar, but topologically they are very different due to parameters r of Lorenz and c of Chen system. These 3D differential equations are solved using RungeKutta-4 method with step size of 0.001. The ideal cryptographic sequence should have good statistical properties. The pre-processing done in Eq. 3 and 4 enhances the statistical properties of the chaotic sequences generated by the Lorenz and Chen systems [11,12].

$$\hat{x}_k(i) = x_k(i) \times 10^5 - floor(x_k(i) \times 10^5) \tag{3}$$

$$\hat{y}_k(i) = y_k(i) \times 10^6 - floor(y_k(i) \times 10^6) \tag{4}$$

Where $k=1$, 2, 3 and $i > 0$ is iteration count. Now, the pre-processed chaotic sequences $0 < x_k(i)$, $y_k(i) < 1$ are quantized and converted into binary bitstreams $\omega_k(i)$ and $\varphi_k(i)$. The quantization is governed by the following transformation:

$$\omega_k(i) = \begin{cases} 0 & if \quad \hat{x}_k(i) < 0.5 \\ 1 & if \quad \hat{x}_k(i) \geq 0.5 \end{cases} \tag{5}$$

$$\varphi_k(i) = \begin{cases} 0 & if \quad \hat{y}_k(i) > 0.5 \\ 1 & if \quad \hat{y}_k(i) \leq 0.5 \end{cases} \tag{6}$$

The six bitstreams $\omega_k(i)$ and $\varphi_k(i)$ are combined and mixed using XOR operations according to the rules described in Eq. 7 to generate cryptographically better chaotic mixed bitstreams Φ_1, Φ_2, Φ_3 and Φ_4. On mixing, the bitstreams become highly random and uncorrelated. After mixing operation, the mixed bitstreams are fed to a 4×1 multiplexer which dynamically selects one of randomly generated bits $\Phi_1(i)$, $\Phi_2(i)$, $\Phi_3(i)$, $\Phi_4(i)$ to produce the next member of output keystream. The multiplexer require two select lines S_1S_0, the select lines should not be static for dynamic operation of MUX. The select lines are made dependent to the random bits $\omega_k(i)$ and $\varphi_k(i)$ for its dynamic operation. The select lines for iteration i are evaluated as $S_0=\omega_1(i)\oplus\omega_2(i)\oplus\omega_3(i)$ and $S_1=\varphi_1(i)\oplus\varphi_2(i)\oplus\varphi_3(i)$. The diagram of proposed voice encryption system is shown in Fig. 1.

$$
\left.
\begin{aligned}
\phi_1(i) &= \omega_1(i) \oplus \varphi_2(i) \oplus \omega_3(i) \\
\phi_2(i) &= \varphi_3(i) \oplus \omega_1(i) \oplus \varphi_1(i) \\
\phi_3(i) &= \omega_2(i) \oplus \varphi_1(i) \oplus \varphi_2(i) \\
\phi_4(i) &= \omega_3(i) \oplus \omega_2(i) \oplus \varphi_3(i)
\end{aligned}
\right\}
\tag{7}
$$

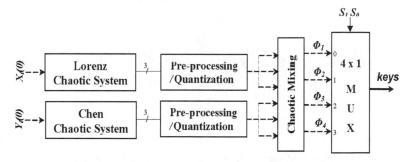

Fig. 1. Block diagram of proposed chaos-based voice encryption system

3 Results and Discussions

In this section, the experimental analyses are presented to demonstrate the effectiveness of the proposed system. The initial values taken for experimentation are as follows: $X(0)=(x_1(0)=13.3604, x_2(0)=7.2052, x_3(0)=21.5026, \sigma=10, \rho=8/3, r=28)$, $Y(0)= (y_1(0) = -10.058, y_2(0)=0.368, y_3(0)=37.368, a=35\ b=3, c=28)$ and $t=4000$. The two chaotic systems are first iterated t times and these $6{\times}t$ values are discarded to remove the transient effect. The auto-correlation function of the output keytream is shown in Fig. 2. It is clear from the figure that keystream has good delta-function form thereby meeting the requirement of cryptographic random sequence. The function has a maximum value of 0.0056984 for non-zero shift.

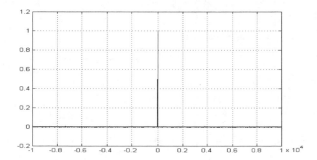

Fig. 2. Auto-correlation function of output keystream

A voice signal having 59114 samples, sampled at rate of 16 KHz is encrypted using the proposed system. The original voice signal is pre-processed and quantized to get the corresponding voice bitstream. The voice bitstream is then XORed with the keystream. The simulation of voice encryption is shown in Fig. 3. As it can be seen that the encrypted voice signal shown in Fig. 3(b) is totally distinct from the original voice signal shown in Fig. 3(a) and it is randomly distributed like a noise signal. The signal distribution in Fig. 3(b) is completely flat/uniform at two extreme ends. This shows the effectiveness and suitability of the proposed scheme for voice encryption.

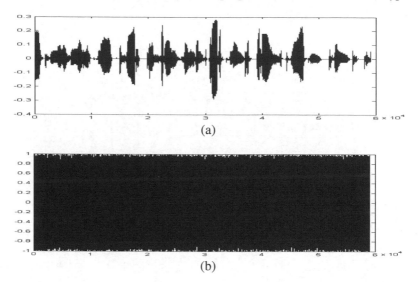

Fig. 3. Voice encryption: (a) Original voice signal (b) Encrypted voice signal

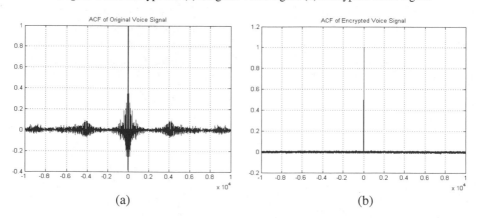

Fig. 4. Auto-correlation function of (a) Original and (b) Encrypted Voice Signals

The auto-correlation function depicts the random distribution of signal. According to the Golomb's randomness postulate, the sequence should have equality/uniformity in signal distribution and auto-correlation is delta-function. The auto-correlation of the original and encrypted signals are sketched and shown in Fig. 4. It is evident from the plot shown in Fig. 4(b) that the encrypted voice signal has delta-function form. The auto-correlation functions of original and encrypted voice signals have a maximum value of 0.8707092 and 0.0152536 for non-zero shift, respectively. Hence, the encrypted signal is exhibiting random signal like behaviour. In order to determine the extent to which the encrypted signal is deviated from the original signal, Sufi *et al.* [13] uses percent residual deviation (PRD) parameter described in Eq. 8. The parameter provides the measure of dissimilarity between original and encrypted signals. The percent residual deviation (ψ) for original $O(i)$ and encrypted $E(i)$ voice signals comes out as 1695.196, where as it is found to be 0.0 for original and decrypted signals. This shows that the encrypted signal is deviated up to a large extent from its original signal.

$$\psi = 100 \times \sqrt{\frac{\sum_{i=1}^{n} [O(i) - E(i)]^2}{\sum_{i=1}^{n} O^2(i)}} \tag{8}$$

To demonstrate the key sensitivity, only one parameter of key is changed at a time by a tiny amount of $\Delta = 10^{-10}$, keeping all other parameters of key unchanged and the scheme is applied to recover the voice signal. The results of demonstration are shown in Fig. 5. To quantify the sensitivity, the percentage difference between original and recovered voice signals is calculated and listed in the Table 1. It is clear from the Fig. 5 and Table 1 that voice recovered with tiny changed key has random behaviour and is totally different from the original voice.

Table 1. Percentage difference between original voice and voice recovered with incorrect key

#	Test	% difference	#	Test	% difference
1	$x_1(0) + \Delta$	99.664	8	$y_1(0) + \Delta$	99.657
2	$x_2(0) + \Delta$	99.617	9	$y_2(0) + \Delta$	99.648
3	$x_3(0) + \Delta$	99.629	10	$y_3(0) + \Delta$	99.639
4	$\sigma + \Delta$	99.599	11	$a + \Delta$	99.582
5	$\rho + \Delta$	99.583	12	$b + \Delta$	99.641
6	$r + \Delta$	99.630	13	$c + \Delta$	99.576
7	$t + 1$	99.572	14	$\Delta = 0$	0.0

   The key space of the encryption system should be large enough to resist the brute-force attack. In the proposed scheme, all initial conditions and parameters constitute the secret key of encryption system. For a 10^{-10} floating point precision, all key parameters can take 10^{10} possible values. Therefore, the key space comes out as $t \times (10^{10})^{12} \approx 2^{408}$, which is large enough to resist the exhaustive attack. The proposed voice encryption system is highly sensitive to a tiny change in secret keys.

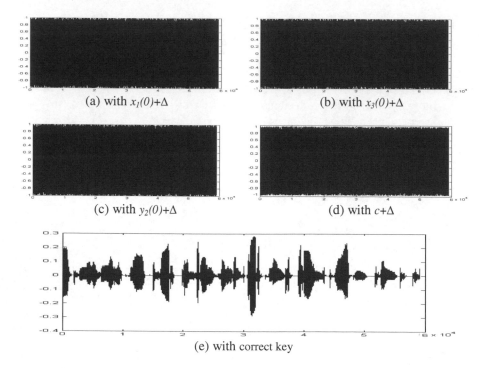

(a) with $x_1(0)+\Delta$ (b) with $x_3(0)+\Delta$

(c) with $y_2(0)+\Delta$ (d) with $c+\Delta$

(e) with correct key

Fig. 5. Recovered voice signals with (a) $x_1(0)+\Delta$, (b) $x_3(0)+\Delta$, (c) $y_2(0)+\Delta$, (d) $c+\Delta$ and (b) $\Delta=0$ i.e. correct key

4   Conclusion

In this paper, a chaos based voice encryption scheme is proposed. The voice bitstream is masked using randomly generated chaotic mixed binary sequences. High dimensional chaotic systems like Lorenz and Chen are employed to generate more complex and unpredictable six chaotic sequences. After quantization and mixing operations, the method generates statistically and cryptographically better encryption keys. Experimental analysis demonstrates the effectiveness of the scheme for voice encryption. The results of statistical analyses like auto-correlation function, signals distribution, percent-residual deviation, key space and key sensitivity indicate high security and suitability of the proposed scheme for practical voice encryption.

References

1. VoIP Security Alliance. VoIP Security and Privacy Threat Taxonomy, version 1.0, http://www.voipsa.org/Activities/taxonomy.php (last accessed in July 2011)
2. Orceyre, M.J., Heller, R.M.: An Approach to Secure Voice Communication Based on the Data Encryption Standard. IEEE Communications Society Magazine, 41–50 (1978)

3. Lin, Q.H., Yin, F.L., Mei, T.M., Liang, H.: A Blind Source Separation Based Method for Speech Encryption. IEEE Transaction on Circuits and Systems-I 53(6), 1320–1328 (2006)
4. Su, Z., Jiang, J., Lian, S., Hu, D., Liang, C., Zhang, G.: Selective Encryption for G.729 Speech using Chaotic Maps. In: Multimedia Information Networking and Security, pp. 488–492 (2009)
5. Guo, J.I., Yen, J.C., Pai, H.F.: New Voice over Internet Protocol technique with Hierarchical Data Security Protection. IEE Proceedings Vision, Image & Signal Processing 149(4), 237–243 (2002)
6. Wong, K.W., Man, K.P., Li, S., Liao, X..: A more Secure Chaotic Cryptographic scheme based on Dynamic Look-up table. Circuits, Systems and Signal Processing 24(5), 571–584 (2005)
7. Tang, K.W., Tang, W.K.S.: A Chaos-based Secure Voice Communication System. Industrial Technology, 571–576 (2005)
8. Man, K.P., Wong, K.W., Man, K.F.: Security Enhancement on VoIP using Chaotic Cryptography. Industrial Electronics, 3703–3708 (2006)
9. Qi, H.F., Yang, X.H., Jiang, R., Liang, B., Zhou, S.J.: Novel End-to-End Voice Encryption Method in GSM System. Networking, Sensing and Control, 217–220 (2008)
10. Palmieri, F., Fiore, U.: Providing true end-to-end security in converged voice over IP infrastructures. Computers & Security 28(6), 433–449 (2009)
11. Fu, C., Zhang, Z., Cao, Y.: An Improved Image Encryption Algorithm Based on Chaotic Maps. Natural Computation, 189–193 (2007)
12. Ahmad, M., Farooq, O.: A Multi-level Blocks Scrambling based Chaotic Image Cipher. In: Ranka, S., Banerjee, A., Biswas, K.K., Dua, S., Mishra, P., Moona, R., Poon, S.-H., Wang, C.-L. (eds.) IC3 2010. CCIS, vol. 94, pp. 171–182. Springer, Heidelberg (2010)
13. Sufi, F., Han, F., Khalil, I., Hu, J.: A Chaos-based Encryption Technique to Protect ECG Packets for Time Critical Telecardiology Applications. Security and Communication Networks 4(5), 515–524 (2011)

A Framework for Transparency in SHGs

A.B. Sagar

Department of Computers and Information Sciences
Hyderabad Central University, Hyderabad
India
bablusagar@gmail.com
www.uohyd.ernet.in

Abstract. A Self Help Group [SHG] is a small homogeneous gathering of persons who join on a voluntary basis in order to undertake some common activity through mutual trust and mutual help. SHG system is conceptualized basically to address the problem of rural unemployment, and empowering people to make them economically self-dependent. But, there is a possibility of it being turned into a commercial unit negating the very thesis it espouses.In the last decade we have seen an increased use of the term "transparency" in different contexts such as business, political affairs, education, administration and government. Transparency is considered an indispensable ingredient in social accountability and necessary for preserving and guaranteeing ethical and fair processes. Transparency is related to visibility of information. Lack of transparency leaves the organization and stakeholders in blind states. The growing importance to the requirement of transparency in businesses was the motivation to study Transparency in SHGs. This paper persents a framework for transparency and also outlines the implementation of transparency through Member Behavioral Model (MBM) and Task Execution Cycle (TEC).

Keywords: SHG, Transparency, Self Help Groups, social values.

1   Introduction

Transparency implies visibility of information related to fi nancial and non-financial matters of the organization and its stakeholders. It should be noted that transparency does not mean opening up the intellectual property files or company's classified documents. Transparency has been, for long, a general requirement for good governance. The right to be informed and to have access to the information has been an important issue in modern societies. Transparency — which can be defined as the accessibility of information to stakeholders of a business, regarding matters that affect their interests[1] — can shape and revolutionize business practice in the present modern society.

Recent observations revealed that there is an increase in societal attention to the issue of transparency. It was also predicted that transparency will become the required

---

[1] Tapscott and Ticoll 2003, p. 22.

N. Meghanathan et al. (Eds.): CCSIT 2012, Part II, LNICST 85, pp. 612–626, 2012.

premise for gaining and maintaining customer trust and good relationships with all stakeholders. The same is true for SHGs also. Transparency in SHGs can lead to trust of all stakeholders.

2   Transparency

Operational functionality of SHG cheifly consists task execution. Every SHG divides the tasks among the members. Tasks execution happens at member level. And these tasks constitute the tasks of the SHG.

Transparency in SHG is related to financial and non-financial reporting. Financial reporting includes tracking of monetary data Non-financial reporting is reporting on task execution.

SHGs' businesses involve several interdependencies. Mutual trust between interdependencies is pivotal. For mutual trust, the interdependencies viz. customers, suppliers and funding agencies connected with SHG, want the SHG information to be open and visible. Also, transparency in a SHGs business builds Trust(between stakeholders and SHG), mutual faith (between SHGs), and confidence (in the involved members of the SHG).

2.1   Degree of Transparency

We can classify transparency into three degrees : opaqueness, translucency and clarity. Two more degrees can be described namely "black hole" and "dazzle". They are used to describe the two extreme situations where no information is released by a SHG or too much information is disclosed, respectively.

Opaqueness is when a SHG does not disclose any information to its stakeholders and hence there is no transparency, So a transparent SHG should not have opaque degree in its Transparency.

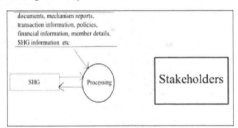

$$\therefore T_{SHG} \nRightarrow opaque$$

Fig. 1. Opaque SHG

Translucency is when a SHG discloses its information partially. Therefore a translucent SHG is not a transparent SHG. A SHG cannot be tranparent until it discloses all of its information.

$$\therefore T_{SHG} \nRightarrow translucent$$

Clarity is when a SHG discloses all of its information. A SHG having clear disclosure of information is a transparent SHG.

$$\therefore T_{SHG} \nRightarrow clear$$

2.2   Dimensions in Transparency

Klotz et al. (2008) suggests nine dimensions of transparency. They stratify their nine dimensions into three distinctive groups – recognition, facilitation and enabling. We adopt only six of Klotz et al's nine dimensions, stratifying these by the dimension of time (pre, per, and post). Thus each of the task will have three phases viz. pre-activity, per-activity and post-activity. Pre-activity transparency within and between two SHGs involves actors recognition of responsibilities and interdependencies. Per-activity transparency within and between two SHGs involves actors recognition of status and problems. Post-activity transparency within and between two SHGs involves the facilitation of performance understanding and feedback.

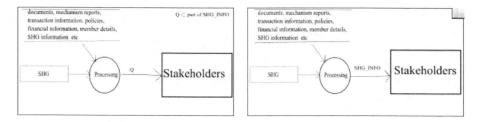

Fig. 2. Translucent & Clear Transparencies

Let 'w' be the activity to be done by the SHG. Let w_i , w_j , w_k be the pre-activity, per-activity and post-activity phases of the work w. Each phase requires communication with stakeholders. Suppose a SHG's activity (w) is to irrigate and supply five tonnes of corn, then this activity can be divided into three phases: pre-activity (w_i), per-activity (w_j) and post-activity (w_k). Each activity involves communication with entities like governing bodies, subordinates, members, peers or competitors. In w_i, communication with supervisor/governing bodies involves describing how much land they are going to use, expenditure estimates, how many members are going to work in it, skills and experience possessed by the members, what fertilizers and chemicals are being used, what techniques are being employed, how waste is disposed, how much each member earns, delivery dates, other responsibilities undertaken by the SHG, etc. And communication with the subordinates involves describing terms and conditions laid down by the supervising/governing bodies, number of hours each member should work, wages for the members, responsibilities of each member, skills and experience required in the members, etc. Communication with the peers and competitors include enquiring regarding problems that are faced in their experience, enquiring how they solved specific issues, seeking suggestions, viewing their data, reports, bills, etc.

The transparency of activity 'w' is T_w . T_w is sum of transparencies of the three phases i.e. transparency of pre-activity (T_{wi}), transparency of per-activity (T_{wj}) and transparency of post-activity (T_{wk}).

$$T_w = T_{wi} + T_{wj} + T_{wk}$$

Interestingly, there is a direct relationship between the degree of transparency and the phases of activity. Degree of transparency is progressive. It progresses with the progressing phases of the activity. Thus, prior to pre-activity the degree of transparency is null (or *opaque*). If the transparency conditions are met in the pre-activity phase, the degree becomes *translucent*. If the transparency conditions are satisfied at per-activity phase and post-activity phase, then degree of transparency becomes *clear*.

Table 1. Degree of Transparency & Activity Phases

Degree	Activity Phases
Opaque	Before Pre-activity
Translucent	After Pre-activity
	After Per-activity
Clear	After Post-activity

The below figure shows the progressing transparency degree with progressing activity phases.

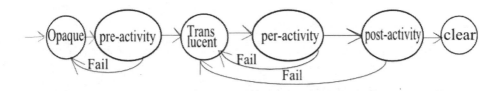

Fig. 3. Progressing Transparency Degree With Progressing Activity Phases

It is observed that after each activity phase, the degree of transparency is increasing. So it is of interest to us to define the cheif constituent of each activity phase which affect the degree of transparency. At each activity phases we define mandatory transparency dimensions. Though transparency dimensions are task- and situation-dependent, some dimensions are mandatory. Klotz et. al. (2008) suggested nine dimensions of transparency. We are adopting six of Klotz et al's nine dimensions, stratifying them into the these three activity phases (pre, per, and post)[2]. Recognition of responsibilities and interdependencies are primarily of concern before the realization of a given activity (pre-activity). Recognition of status and problems are primarily related to transparency into an ongoing activity (per-activity). Similarly, understanding of performance and feed-back are related to post-activity transparency.

---

[2] A Framework for Transparency. Økland Andreas , Lillebo Børge , Amdahl Eva , Seim Andreas.

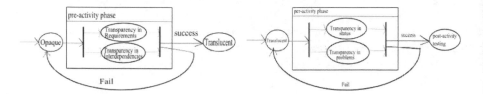

Fig. 4. Transparency dimensions in Pre-activity Phase & Per-activity Phases

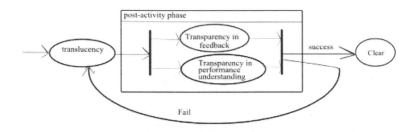

Fig. 5. Transparency dimensions in Post-activity Phase

2.3   Perspectives in Transparency

There are three main perspectives in Transparency: static transparency, dynamic transparency and radical transparency.

(1) Static Transparency: In Static Transparency reporting information is standardized and is done in official formats — such as the financial statements required by various government agencies, comprehensible format for customers, etc. However this is not a very efficient type of transparency because in this type, disclosure is "telling" rather than "sharing", and the flow of information is mainly unidirectional i.e. from the SHG to stakeholders. Since there is no on demand display of information, it does not fully portray the meaning of transparency.

$_{static}T_{SHG}$ means unidirectional flow of information from SHG to Stakeholders.

$$_{static}T_{SHG} \implies \forall info \in SHG, S \in Stakeholders,$$
$$flow(info, SHG, S) \land \neg flow(info, S, SHG)$$

flow(info,SHG,S) indicates that the information ('info') flows from SHG to Stakeholders ('S'). Since this is Static Transparency, the info flow is only unidirectional i.e. SHG to S. But the converse, i.e. flow(info,S,SHG) does not hold true. That is, info could not flow from Stakeholders (S) to SHG. There is no possibility for the stakeholders to request and obtain information of their choice. They only get what the SHG chooses to reveal. This kind of transparency is also called selective transparency. Thus static transparency gives liberty to the SHGs but not to the stakeholders.

A SHG adopts static transparency when its rules for reporting are all predefined (by the governing bodies), and it need not respond to stakeholder's queries.

(2) Dynamic Transparency is where the organization and its stakeholders can exchange, share and compare information and adapt its online behavior and electronic requests and queries to the answers and reactions of respective counterparts.

$$_{\text{dynamic}}T_{\text{SHG}} \implies \forall info \in SHG, S \in Stakeholders,$$
$$flow(info, SHG, S) \wedge flow(info, S, SHG)$$

(3) Radical Transparency refers to the capability of a firm's top management to employ internet-based technologies, such as rss, blogs and collaborative websites, in order to create a direct and continuous dialogue with customers and other stakeholders. Radical transparency may be represented by:

$$_{\text{radical}}T_{\text{SHG}} \implies \forall info \in SHG, S \in Stakeholders,$$
$$stream(info, SHG, S) \wedge stream(info, S, SHG)$$

stream(info,SHG,S) is similar to the flow function but the difference being that the flow is continuous.

3   Implementating Transparency

The implementation of transparency can be made through member behavior model and task execution cycle. The member behavioral model outlines the behavior of every member and SHG. The Member Behavioral Model (MBM) provides an imprint of generic behavior of each member or SHG with respect to different types of items i.e. tasks, requests, reports, acks, etc.

3.1   Member Behavioral Model (MBM)

The primitives of the MBM are explained below:

TMonitor: The TMonitor is a continuously running process which keeps monitoring for items like tasks, acks, requests, reports, etc. When it receives an item it immediately forwards it to Rpt.

Rpt: Rpt has varied functionalities depending on the item it receives. If item is a task, it will notify the task sender about the receipt of the task. And it will forward the task to ExTsk for execution of the task. If the item is an ack, it will store the ack in the Repst against the corresponding task it has dispatched. If the item is a request, it will query the Repst and generate a report and dispatch it to the requester. If the item is a report, it will store the report in the Repst against the corresponding task.

ExTsk: The functionality of ExTsk is to log the stages a task passes through when a SHG/member executes the task. If the received task is feasible to that member (or SHG), execution is started. Else, if the task is partially feasible, then task is split into three portions (feasible part, assign part, remainder part). The assign part is assigned to a different member/SHG. Soon after the report is received that the assign part is executed, the remainder part is executed. After completing the exection of the whole task, it sends the task completed notification to Rpt to be forwarded to the notification recipients. While executing the task, it will write the intermediate task status to the store Repst through Rpt. So that the status of task is available at every executing phase of the task.

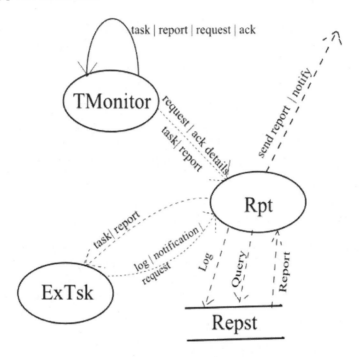

Fig. 6. Member Behavioral Model (MBM)

3.2   Task Execution Cycle (TEC)

The Task Execution Cycle (TEC) gives the different states that a task undergoes during task execution. The different states are described below:

Recv: The task is in Recvd state if it is just received. It will wait there until the member/SHG is ready to take it up and start initiation and execution.

Initiate: The task moves to Initiated state if the member/SHG has considered execution.

Execute: The task moves to Executing state when the member/SHG has started execution or is continuing exectuion after waking up from sleep.

Assign: The task moves to assigned state if the task was assigned to a different member/SHG.

Sleep: The task moves to sleep state once the task was assigned.

Abort: If the task was found to be infeasible or if the assignment fails, then the task moves to aborted state.

End: The final state of every task is the End state.

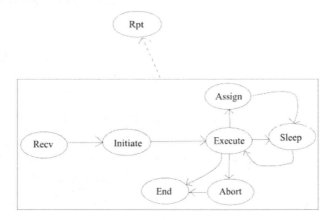

Fig. 7. Task Execution Cycle

Now implementation of transparency in task execution can be done by transparency messages defined on the TEC. Every task passes through the states given in Task Execution Cycle. For each state, transparency messages provide financial and non-financial information. When the task reaches a state, a transparency message is sent to the notification recipient. The transparency messages carry both predefined information and also dynamic information.

3.2.1 Task Properties
Executing a task is the basic operation of member and SHG. So we start by defining tasks. A task has all required information about the financial and non-financial details. Every task, besides other attributes, must have the following attributes:

Task Id: Identification token of the task

Parent Task: If the task is subtask of a bigger task, then this is the id of the parent task.

IsPartitionable: Yes, if the task can be split and distributed; No, if it has to be executed at only one place.

Risks: Risks involved with the task.

Task Type: Whether the given task is technical or non-technical.

Creation Date: Date when the task was created.

Excluded Executors: Restricted executors list.

Task Stakeholders: All the stakeholders who are related to the task.

Task Status: Status of the task, indicating how far the task was completed.

Skills Needed: List of skills needed to execute the task.

Skills Levels Needed: Level of skills needed for executing the task; excellent, fair, medium, poor skill levels.

Task Infrastructure: Infrastructure that would be required for the execution of the task.

Task Priority: Priority of the task; Low, medium, high.

Start By Date: The date by which one has to start the execution of the task.

Interdependencies: Interdependencies of the task.

Task Supervisor: The member / SHG in-charge of the task.

Complete By Date: The date by which one has to complete the execution of the task.

Notification Recipients: Stakeholders that are to be notified about the status of the task.

Responsibilites: Responsibilites that are to be undertaken by the task executor.

Task Initiator: Identity of the one who initiated the task.

Potential Executors: Executors for whom the task is meant.

Cost of Task: Cost of the task estimated using variables like the resources and skills it involves and its significance (priority)

Other operations related to tasks are sending reports, ack, requests, notifications,etc. When a request is received, it has to be processed and response (report) must be sent to the requester. When a task is received, an acknowledgment must be sent to the sender. During the execution of the task, task status is to be notified to the notification recipients and requeters. And when a log or report is received, it is stored in the repository.

In MBM, each module has different functionalities.

3.2.2   Actions Performed by Modules of MBM

Table 2.

Module	Actions	Item
TMonitor	Receives Task	\<Task \>
	Receives Report	\<Report \>
	Receives Ack	\<Ack \>
	Receives Request	\<Request \>
Rpt	Receives Task	\<Task \>
	Receives Report	\<Report \>
	Receives Ack	\<Ack \>
	Receives Request	\<Request \>
	Receives Log	\<Log \>
	Receives Notification	\<Notification \>
	Sends Report	\<Report \>
	Sends Notification	\<Notification \>
	Sends Query	\<Query \>
ExTsk	Receives Task	\<Task \>
	Receives Report	\<Report \>
	Sends Log	\<Log \>
	Sends Notification	\<Noitification \>
	Sends Request	\<Request \>

3.2.3 Messages

As discussed earlier, transparency is implemented using transparency messages. These transparency messages are application specific. However, some of the transparency messages are mandatory and they are given below.

Ack	RecvdTask
RecvdReport	InitiatedTask
ExecutingTask	AssignedTask
AbortedTask	EndedTask
RecvdRequest	RecvdReport

3.2.4 Messages Descirption

<Ack >-   Ack to be sent to the Repository for logging about receipt of task, request, or report.

<RecvdTask > - Message to be sent to the task sender. This is the acknowledgment to the sender that the task was received.

<RecvdReport> - Message to be sent to the report sender. This is the acknowledgment to the sender that the report was received.

<InitiatedTask> - Message to be sent to the task notification recipients that the given task execution is initiated.

<ExecutingTask> - Message to be sent to the task notification recipients that the given task execution is being executed.

<AssignedTask> Message to be sent to the task notification recipients that the given task execution was assigned to another member/SHG

<AbortedTask> Message to be sent to the task notification recipients that the given task execution is Aborted.

<EndedTask> Message to be sent to the task notification recipients that the given task execution has ended.

<RecvdRequest> Message to be sent to the requester that the request was received

<RecvdReport> Ack sent to the report sender that the report was received successfully.

3.2.5 Message Formats

<RecvdTask>- <RecvdTask> <task Id> from <task assigner Id> on <date> <time> <RecvdTask >

<InitiatedTask> - <InitiatedTask>   <task Id>   on <date>   <time>   with <responsibilities> and <interdependencies> <Initiated-Task>

<ExecutingTask> - <ExecutingTask >   <task Id>   <date>   <time>   <status> <problems> <ExecutingTask>

<AssignedTask> -<AssignedTask> <task Id> <assigned to>   on <date> <time> <AssignedTask>

<SleepTask> - <SleepTask> <task ID> <wake up upon> <event> <SleepTask>

<AbortedTask> - <AbortedTask> <task Id> aborted due to <reason> on <date> <time> <AbortedTask>

<EndedTask > - <EndedTask><task Id> on <date> <time> <ended with success/failure/abort> <feedback> <performance understanding> <EndedTask>

<Ack> <Ack> <ack Id> on <date> <time> for <task Id/request Id/report Id> from <member Id> <shg Id><Ack>

<RecvdRequest> - <RecvdRequest> from <member Id> <shg Id> regarding <task Id> on <date> <time> <to be responded by date & time > <RecvdRequest >

<RecvdReport> <RecvdReport> <Report Id> on <date> <time> from <member Id> <shg Id> for <task Id > and <request Id > sent on <date > <time > <RecvdReport >

<Log> - <Log> <task Id> <task status> <problems> <other info> <date> <time> by <member ID> <shg Id> <Log>

3.2.6 Databases

During the implementation of transparency using MBM and TEC, we will be needed to maintain the following databases.

TASKS_DB,
ASSIGNED_TASKS_DB,
ABORTED_TASKS_DB,
INITIATED_TASKS_DB,
REQUESTS_DB,
TMONITOR_DB,
RPT_DB,

RECVD_TASKS_DB,
SLEEPING_TASKS_DB,
ENDED_TASKS_DB,
ACK_DB,
REPORTS_DB,
EXTSK_DB,
LOG_DB

TASKS_ DB : contains table which has information about every task.
TASKS_ DB (Task Id , Task Type , Task Status , Task Priority , Task Supervisor , Task Initiator , Parent Task , Creation Date&Time , Activation Date&Time , Start By Date&Time , Complete By Date&Time , Potential Executors , IsPartitionable , Excluded Executors , Skills Needed , Skills Levels Needed , Notification Recipients , Cost of Task , Risks , Task Stakeholders , Task Infrastructure , Interdependencies , Responsibilites , Notification Recipients)

RECVD_TASKS_DB : Contains information about all received tasks.
RECVD_TASKS_DB(Task Id , Received From , On Date&Time , Start Date&Time , Completion Date&Time , Notification Recipients , Potential Executors , Infrastructure Requirements , Skill Requirements , Responsibilities , Interdependencies , Risks , Priority , Parent Task)

INITIATED_TASKS_DB : Contains information about all initiated tasks.
INITIATED_TASKS_ DB(Task   Id , Initiation   Time , Initiation   Date , Noti cation Recipients , Initiating   Member   Id , Proposed   Executors , Proposed   Completion Date&Time , Skills Available For Task , Infrastructure Available , Priority Given)

EXECUTING_TASKS_DB: Contains information about all executing tasks.
EXECUTING_TASKS_DB(Task   Id , Status , Problems , Noti cation   Recipients , Members Involved , Skills Involved)

ASSIGNED_TASKS_DB: Contains info about assigned Tasks
ASSIGNED_TASKS_DB(Task   Id , Assigned   To , On   Date&Time , Start Date&Time , Completion   Date&Time , Noti cation   Recipients , Infrastructure Requirements , Skill   Requirements , Responsibilities , Interdependencies , Risks , Priority , Parent Task)

SLEEPING_TASKS_DB: Contains info about sleeping Tasks
SLEEPING TASKS DB (Task Id , Slept On Date&Time , Waking Up Event , Woke Up Date&Time, Noti cation Recipients)

ABORTED TASKS DB: Contains info about aborted Tasks
ABORTED TASKS DB (Task Id , Aborted On Date&Time , Reason , Noti cation Recipients , Aborted By Member Id)

ENDED_TASKS_DB: Contains info about ended Tasks
ENDED TASKS DB (Task Id , Noti cation Recipients , Ended On Date&Time , Feedback , Performance Understanding)

ACK_DB: Contains info about acknowledgments
ACK_DB (Ack Id , Noti cation Recipients , Sent On Date&Time , Corresponding Id of Task/Request/Report , Success / Failure , RecvdSenderDetails , PreparingAck , SendingAck , AbortingAck , EndedAckSend)

REQUESTS_DB: Contains info about requests.
REQUESTS_DB (Request Id , Noti cation Recipients , Sent On Date&Time , Corresponding Task , Success / Failure , PreparingRequest , SendingRequest , AbortedRequest EndedRquesting)

REPORTS_DB : Contains info about reports..
REPORTS_DB (Report Id , Noti cation Recipients , Sent On Date&Time , Corresponding Task , Success / Failure , QueryingRepst GeneratingReport SendingRequest Abort/Fail EndReporting)

LOG_DB: Contains info about logs.
LOG_ DB (Log Id , Made By , Date&Time , Log Data , Noti cation Recipients)

TMONITOR_DB: Contains info about reports..
TMONITOR_DB(Received Item , Sender's Id , Date&Time)

EXTSK_DB : Contains info about ExTsk
EXTSK_DB(Received Item , Senders Id , Date&Time , Sending Log/ Noti cation/ Request Id , Date&Time)

RPT_DB: Contains info about Rpt.
RPT_DB (Received Item , Senders Id , Date&Time , Sending Report / Task / Query / Log /Noti cation Id Date&Time)

3.2.7 Rules of the Model

1. $\forall$ Task t $\in$ ASSIGNED_TASKS_DB $\exists$ t $\in$ RECVD_TASKS_DB $\cap$ t $\in$ INITIATED_TASKS_DB $\cap$ t $\in$ SLEEPING_TASKS_DB
2. If t $\in$ ENDED_TASKS_DB, then t $\in$ RECVD_TASKS_DB $\cap$ t $\in$ INITIATED_TASKS_DB $\cap$ t $\in$ EXECUTING_TASKS_DB
3. The different possible paths and corresponding states of Task's lifecycle are:
   - Recvd $\rightarrow$ Initiate $\rightarrow$ Execute $\rightarrow$ End
   - Recvd $\rightarrow$ Initiate $\rightarrow$ Execute $\rightarrow$ Assign $\rightarrow$ Sleep $\rightarrow$ Execute $\rightarrow$ End
   - Recvd $\rightarrow$ Initiate $\rightarrow$ Execute $\rightarrow$ Abort $\rightarrow$ End
   - Recvd $\rightarrow$ Initiate $\rightarrow$ Execute $\rightarrow$ Assign $\rightarrow$ Sleep $\rightarrow$ Execute $\rightarrow$ Abort $-\rightarrow$ End
4. If t $\in$ ABOTRED_TASKS_DB, then t $\in$ RECVD_TASKS_DB $\cap$ t $\in$ INITIATED_TASKS_DB $\cap$ t $\in$ EXECUTING_TASKS_DB $\cap$ t $\in$ ASSIGNED_TASKS_DB $\cap$ t $\in$ SLEEPING_TASKS_DB
5. If t $\in$ SLEEPING_TASKS_DB, then t $\in$ RECVD_TASKS_DB $\cap$ t $\in$ INITIATED_TASKS_DB $\cap$ t $\in$ EXECUTING_TASKS_DB $\cap$ t $\in$ ASSIGNED_TASKS_DB
6. Every state has an associated transparency message.

3.2.8 Transparency Metric

Transparency metric quantifies the level of transparency that is maintained by the SHG or a member. Transparency metric can be computed using TEC from the number of transparency messages transmitted by the task executor. Since each transparency messages is attributed with a value, depending on the number of messages sent and the value associated with the sent messages, transparency can be computed.

4   Conclusion

The proposed model successfully implements Transparency as defined in this paper. Degree of Transparency can be assessed using the number of transparency messages corresponding to a task. For e.g., if a task has hundred transparency messages associated with its execution, the task initiator can define custom thresholds for opaqueness, translucency and clarity. During execution of the task, as the task executor sends the transparency messages, the count of the messages gives the degree of transparency. The dimensions of transparency are realized by defining various transparency messages in the phases of the task i.e. pre-activity, per-activity and post-activity phases. In the pre-activity phase, transparency messages related to requirements and interdependencies are defined. In the post-activity phase, transparency messages related to status and problems are defined. And in the post-activity phase, transparency messages related to feedback and performance understanding are defined. Thus the dimensions of Transparency are implemented. The perspectives of transparency are assessed based on the operational behavior of the task executor. If the task executor operates on simplex mode of communication, i.e. only sends messages but does not receive any queries from the stakeholders, then the transparency is Static transparency. And, if the task executor maintains duplex mode i.e. not only sends messages but also receives queries and responds to them, then the transparency is Dynamic transparency. Radical transparency is when the task executor streams the messages and maintains duplex mode of communication. Radical transparency is a form of static transparency with the interval between the transmission of messages being very small. Thus perspectives of transparency are implemented. Thus the proposed model successfully implements the degree, dimension and perspective of transparency as defined in this paper.

Acknowledgments. I would like to thank Prof. Hrushikesha Mohanty whose guidance and thoughts have become the source for my research work and life. This work is funded by Rajiv Gandhi National Fellowship.

References

1. Andreas, Ø., Børge, L., Eva, A., Andreas, S.: A Framework for Transparency. In: 21st Annual Conference of the Production and Operation Management Society, USAID, CARE, GTZ/NABARD, Vancouver, Canada, May 07- May 10 (2010)
2. Vaccaro, A., Madsen, Æ.: Corporate dynamic transparency: the new ICT-driven ethics? Ethics Inf. Technol. 11, 113–122 (2009)
3. Tapscott, D., Ticoll, D.: The naked corporation. Free Press, New York (2003)
4. Transaction Model, Network and Information Systems Management, University of Paisley (2000)
5. Madsen, P.: Dynamic Transparency, Prudential Justice and Corporate Transformation: Becoming Socially Responsible in the Internet Age. Journal of Business Ethics 90, 639–648 (2009)
6. Vaccaro, A., Madsen, P.: Transparency in business and society: introduction to the special issue. Ethics Inf. Technol. 11, 101–103 (2009)
7. Parikh, T.: Rural Microfinance Service Delivery: Gaps. Inefficiencies and Emerging Solutions (2007)
8. Sa-Dhan: The Association of Community Development Finance Institutions, A Study Report On SHG Federation In India: Emerging Structures and Practices (July 2004)
9. Bhawan, V.: National Workshop on SHG Federations, New Delhi (May 2008)
10. Kuo, H.-C., Tsai, T.-H., Huang, J.-P.: Building a Concept Hierarchy by Hierarchical Clustering with Join/Merge Decision (2008)

11. APMAS, Optimizing SHGs (October 2005)
12. APMAS, SHG Federations in India: A Status Report (2007)
13. EDA Rural Systems and APMAS, Self-help groups in India: A Study of Lights and Shades, A joint initiative of CARE, CRS, USAID and GTZ, New Delhi (2006)
14. MYRADA, Impact of Self Help Groups (Group Processes) on the Social/Empowerment Status of Women Member In Southern India. Paper presented at the Seminar on SHG-bank Linkage Programme, New Delhi (November 2002)

Classification of Text Documents Using B-Tree

B.S. Harish[*], D.S. Guru, and S. Manjunath

Department of Information Science and Engineering, SJCE, Mysore
Department of Studies in Computer Science, University of Mysore,
Manasagangothri, Mysore, Karnataka, India
bsharish@ymail.com, dsg@compsci.uni-mysore.ac.in,
manju_uom@yahoo.co.in

Abstract. In this paper, we propose an unconventional method of representing and classifying text documents, which preserves the sequence of term occurrence in a test document. The term sequence is effectively preserved with the help of a novel datastructure called 'Status Matrix'. In addition, in order to avoid sequential matching during classification, we propose to index the terms in B-tree, an efficient index scheme. Each term in B-tree is associated with a list of class labels of those documents which contain the term. Further the corresponding classification technique has been proposed. To corroborate the efficacy of the proposed representation and status matrix based classification, we have conducted extensive experiments on various datasets.

Keywords: Text documents, Term sequence, B-Tree, Classification.

1   Introduction

Bag of Word (BoW) is one of the basic methods of representing a document. The BoW is used to form a vector representing a document using the frequency count of each term in the document. This method of document representation is called as a Vector Space Model (VSM) [1]. The major limitation of VSM is that the correlation and context of each term is lost which is very important in understanding a document. Jain and Li [2] used binary representation for given document. The major drawback of this model is that it results in a huge sparse matrix, which raises a problem of high dimensionality. Hotho et al., [3] proposed an ontology representation for a document to keep the semantic relationship between the terms in a document. This ontology model preserves the domain knowledge of a term present in a document. However, automatic ontology construction is a difficult task due to the lack of structured knowledge base. Cavanar., (1994) [4] used a sequence of symbols (byte, a character or a word) called N-Grams, that are extracted from a long string in a document. In a N-Gram scheme, it is very difficult to decide the number of grams to be considered for effective document representation. Another approach [5] uses multi-word terms as vector components to represent a document. But this method requires a sophisticated automatic term extraction algorithms to extract the terms automatically from a

---

[*] Corresponding author.

N. Meghanathan et al. (Eds.): CCSIT 2012, Part II, LNICST 85, pp. 627–636, 2012.
© Institute for Computer Sciences, Social Informatics and Telecommunications Engineering 2012

document. Wei et al., (2008) proposed an approach called Latent Semantic Indexing (LSI) [6] which preserves the representative features for a document. The LSI preserves the most representative features rather than discriminating features. Thus to overcome this problem, Locality Preserving Indexing (LPI) [7] was proposed for document representation. The LPI discovers the local semantic structure of a document. Unfortunately LPI is not efficient in time and memory [8]. Choudhary and Bhattacharyya (2002) [9] used Universal Networking Language (UNL) to represent a document. The UNL represents the document in the form of a graph with words as nodes and relation between them as links. This method requires the construction of a graph for every document and hence it is unwieldy to use for an application where large numbers of documents are present.

After giving an effective representation for a document, the task of text classification is to classify the documents to the predefined categories. In order to do so, many statistical and computational models have been developed based on Naïve Bayes classifier, K-NN classifier, Centroid Classifier, Decision Trees, Rocchio classifier, Neural Networks, Support Vector Machines [10].

Although many text document representation models are available in literature, frequency-based BoW model gives effective results in text classification task. Indeed, till date the best multi-class, multi-labeled categorization results for well known datasets are based on BoW representation [11]. Unfortunately, BoW representation scheme has its own limitations. Some of them are: high dimensionality of the representation, loss of correlation with adjacent words and loss of semantic relationship that exist among the terms in a document [12]. Also the main problem with the frequency based approach is that given a term, with lesser frequency of occurrence may be appropriate in describing a document, whereas, a term with the higher frequency may have a less importance. Unfortunately, frequency-based BoW methods do not take this into account [9]. Hence there is a need for developing a new scheme for document representation preserving the correlation among adjacent words. This motivated us to use a new datastrcuture called "Status Matrix" [13] which effectively represents a text document and thereby giving a better classification results.

The paper is organized as follows. The working principle of the proposed method is presented in section 2. Details of experimental settings and results are presented in section 3. The paper is concluded in section 4.

2   Proposed Method

In this section, we propose a new method of representing documents based on preserving the sequence of term occurrence in a document. Subsequently, we present the corresponding classification model.

2.1   Representation Stage

Let there be k number of classes each containing n number of documents. A simple text processing algorithm is employed to extract the terms (words) present in each document. From the extracted set of words, stop words are removed. For each class say C_j, $j = 1, 2, ..., k$, set of all words present in the documents of that class is formed. From these set of words an inverted list structure is formed for each of the word by associating the labels of the class of the documents that contain that particular word. The list of class labels associated with a word may contain many class labels as it is not uncommon that the documents of different classes contain the same word. The words and their associated lists of class indices are recommended to be stored in the knowledge base to support classification of an unknown test document.

However, this representation requires a linear time searching, which is not acceptable in real pragmatic scenario. Thus in order to speed up classification and to make the representation scheme dynamic supporting addition and deletion of documents, we recommend to index the documents using an existing indexing data structure. To do this task, one may think of many indexing structures like multidimensional binary trees [14], G-Tree [15], KDB Tree [16] and BD Tree [17]. However, each structure has got its own limitations [18] with respect to handling the data and storage methods. Thus, in our work we make use of B-Tree structure as it is simple and less complex. Moreover, B-Tree is used because of its availability, its simplicity and less complexity in addition to its balanced nature.

The proposed B-tree based system can be easily extended towards dynamic databases, as it is very easy to include new documents. In addition, insertion of new documents is as simple as just the insertion of set of words into the existing set and updating the associated term lists. With respect to the proposed representation scheme, insertion of a document into the database is simply a process of inserting the terms present in the document into the B-tree. In order to insert a term T corresponding to the document to be inserted, the B-tree is accessed through to find out the location of T in the B-tree. If T is already present in the database, the insertion problem is reduced to the problem of getting the list of documents updated by appending the index of the document to be inserted. On the other hand, if a term T is not present in the database then no doubt we are at the node U where T is expected to be present. If U contains fewer than $(r-1)$ terms (r is the order of the B-tree), T is simply inserted into U in a sorted order. Otherwise, unlike conventional B-tree insertion procedure where the node is eventually split into two nodes, in our work, we recommend to look at the siblings of the node to find if any a free location, so that by data movements we can get the T term accommodated at the node U itself without splitting it up. Indeed this modification suggested to the conventional B-tree insertion process significantly enhances the efficacy of the insertion procedure particularly on a very large B-tree. The complexity of using the B-tree is of $O(\log_r t)$, where t is the number terms stored in the B-tree and r is the order of the B-tree.

For an illustrative purpose, we consider four different classes of documents. For each class we have created a knowledge base as follows. Given a set of training documents of an individual class, stopwords from each training documents are eliminated and the terms are pooled to form a knowledge base. The knowledge base obtained for four different classes are given below:

K1: categorization,documents,implement,metric,similarity,text

K2: algorithms,categorization,mining,similarity,video

K3: algorithms,efficient,enhancements,filter,image

K4: algorithms,congestion,networks,protocols,routing.

The terms present in the knowledge base along with their class labels are stored in a B-tree for the purpose of fast retrieval.

A B-tree of order $r=3$ is constructed (Figure 1) to store the distinct terms and each term in the B-tree is attached with its respective list of class indices. The index table containing all terms for each of the documents to be stored is created as shown in Table 1.

2.2   Classification

Sequence of occurrence of words in any text plays a major role in understanding the text document. However, most of the existing methods do not preserve the sequence of occurrence of words as they assume that the word occurrence is independent of text representation.

Simple method to check the sequence of occurrence of words is same as common longest substring matching. Thus, one can think that the problem of classifying a test document is reduced to the problem of finding out a common longest subsequence of terms in the database. In practice, this is not acceptable as the process of substring matching has non-deterministic polynomial time complexity.

Hence, in this section we propose an alternative method of matching and classification of text documents. For the purpose of preserving the sequence of occurrences of words in a test document we recommend to use the concept of status matrix. Status matrix representation was proposed for the purpose of recognition of partially occluded object recognition, where status matrix representation is a binary matrix preserving the order in which the information occurs.

2.3   Computational Complexity of Classification

As there are k classes and a query document contains t_q terms, we require $O(t_q \log_r t)$ computations to create a status matrix of size M.

A status matrix is a binary matrix where the entries are either 0 or 1. The status matrix is of dimension $k \times t_q$ where, k is the number of classes, and t_q is the number of terms in the query text document after preprocessing.

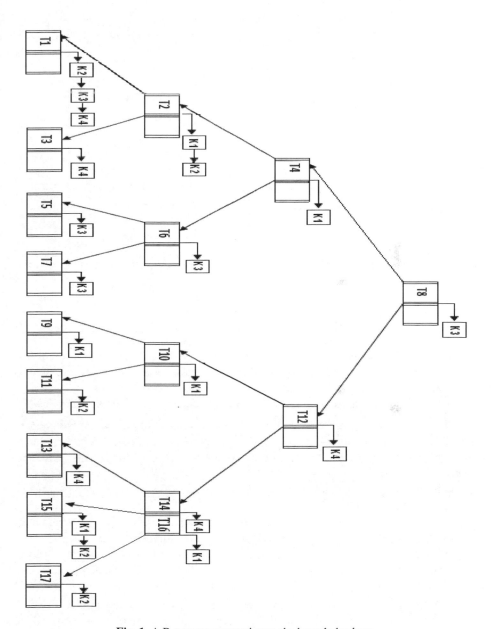

Fig. 1. A B-tree representation to the knowledge base

Table 1. The index table for the illustrated example

Index	Terms	Index	Terms
T1	Algorithms	T 10	Metric
T2	Categorization	T 11	Mining
T3	Congestion	T 12	Networks
T 4	Documents	T 13	Protocols
T 5	Efficient	T 14	Routing
T 6	Enhancements	T 15	Similarity
T 7	Filter	T 16	Text
T 8	Image	T 17	Video
T 9	Implement		

The B-tree is accessed through in search of each term and the lists of document indices corresponding to that term are retrieved from the database. If the ith term T_i of the query document is present in the knowledge base of the class C_j, then the entry corresponding to the row of C_j and the column T_i in the status matrix is set to 1, otherwise it is set to 0. That is, if M is a status matrix, then, M is given by

$$M_{ij} = \begin{cases} 1 & \text{if } T_i \in C_j \\ 0 & \text{otherwise} \end{cases} \qquad (1)$$

Assuming each row of the status matrix as a binary string, we then look for a row with a longest substring containing only 1s. The class corresponding to that row is declared to be the class of the test document.

As an illustration, let us consider the following paragraph as a query document d_q.

"Text categorization is not a trivial problem. The complexity of the problem lies in how to define a similarity metric between the documents, and then how to implement a computationally efficient algorithm to solve the problem given this similarity metric".

In order to classify this document we first eliminate stopwords present in it, which results with the following set of terms.

{text, categorization, trivial, problem, complexity, similarity, metric, documents, implement, computationally, efficient, algorithms, similarity, metric}.

This query document totally contains 14 terms. Now it is understood that as there are 4 classes and the query document has 14 terms, we have the status matrix of size 4×14 as shown in Table 2.

Once the status matrix is constructed we search through the status matrix in search of longest matched sequence. Now, the test document is assigned to the class which has longest matched sequence of terms present in the query document. Here in this example the query document is given the class label 1.

Table 2. Status matrix obtained for query document d_q

	T_1	T_2	T_3	T_4	T_5	T_6	T_7	T_8	T_9	T_{10}	T_{11}	T_{12}	T_{13}	T_{14}
k_1	1	1	0	0	0	1	1	1	1	0	0	0	1	1
k_2	0	1	0	0	0	1	0	0	0	0	0	1	1	0
k_3	0	0	0	0	0	0	0	0	0	0	1	1	0	0
k_4	0	0	0	0	0	0	0	0	0	0	0	1	0	0

3   Experimental Setup

3.1   Dataset

To test the efficacy of the proposed model, we have used the following five datasets. The first dataset is standard 20 Newsgroup Large [19]. It contains 20000 documents categorized into 20 classes. The second dataset consists of vehicle characteristics extracted from wikipedia pages (vehicles- wikipedia) [20]. The dataset contains 4 categories that have low degrees of similarity. The dataset contains four categories of vehicles: Aircraft, Boats, Cars and Trains. All the four categories are easily differentiated and every category has a set of unique key words. The third dataset is a standard 20 mini newsgroup dataset which contains about 2000 documents evenly divided among 20 Usenet discussion groups. This dataset is a subset of 20 newsgroups which contains 20,000 documents. In 20 MiniNewsgroup, each class contains 100 documents in 20 classes which are randomly picked from original dataset. The fourth dataset is constructed by a text corpus of 1000 documents that are downloaded from Google-Newsgroup. Each class contains 100 documents belonging to 10 different classes (Business, Cricket, Music, Electronics, Biofuels, Biometrics, Astronomy, Health, Video Processing and Text Mining). The fifth dataset is a collection of research article abstracts. All these research articles are downloaded from the scientific web portals. We have collected 1000 documents from 10 different classes. Each class contains 100 documents.

3.2   Experimentation

In this section, we present the results of the experiments conducted to demonstrate the effectiveness of the proposed status matrix based method on all the five datasets viz., 20 newsgroup large, vehicles wikipedia, 20 mini newsgroup, google newsgroup and research article abstracts. During experimentation, we conducted two different sets of experiments. In the first set of experiments, we used, 50% of the documents of each class of a dataset to create training set and the remaining 50% of the documents for testing purpose. On the other hand, in the second set of experiments, the numbers of training and testing documents are in the ratio 60:40. Both experiments are repeated 5 times by choosing the training samples randomly. The minimum, maximum and the average value of the classification accuracy of all the 5 trials are presented in Table 3.

Table 4 shows the comparative analysis of the results on five datasets mentioned above. It is clear from the Table 4, that the proposed model achieved good classification accuracy on three benchmark datasets and also on our own dataset (Google Newsgroup and Research article abstracts), when compared with other well known classifiers viz. Naïve Bayes, KNN and SVM classifier. This is because of the proposed model has a capability of classifying the documents at two stages (one is at voting stage and the other is at term sequence stage). It is also worth mentioning that the incorporation of status matrix improves the performance of a voting classifier.

Table 3. Classification accuracy of the proposed method on different data sets

Dataset	Training Vs Testing	Minimum Accuracy (5 Trials)	Maximum Accuracy (5 Trials)	Average Accuracy (5 Trials)
20 Newsgroup Large	50 vs 50	79.65	84.20	82.64
	60 vs 40	84.35	87.85	86.35
Vehicles Wikipedia	50 vs 50	70.65	72.85	71.60
	60 vs 40	74.95	76.00	75.45
20 Mini Newsgroup	50 vs 50	64.65	68.95	66.91
	60 vs 40	71.00	76.85	73.95
Google Newsgroup	50 vs 50	86.70	89.70	88.74
	60 vs 40	89.85	96.00	93.33
Research Article Abstracts	50 vs 50	86.25	90.25	88.52
	60 vs 40	89.00	91.25	90.13

Table 4. Comparative analysis of the proposed method with other classifiers

Dataset Used	Voting Classifier	Voting + Status Matrix Classifier (Proposed Method)	Naïve Bayes Classifier	KNN Classifier	SVM Classifier
20 Newsgroup Large	82.55	87.85	86.50	70.00	85.65
Google Newsgroup	93.50	96.00	80.00	46.25	48.25
Vehicle-Wiki	67.50	76.00	74.00	64.50	63.00
20 Mini Newsgroup	66.25	71.12	66.22	38.73	51.02
Research Article Abstracts	86.75	91.25	-	-	-

4   Conclusion

In this paper, we have proposed the classification of text documents using B-Tree. Further, we have presented a new datastructure called status matrix through which, we make an attempt to preserve the sequence of term occurrence in the query document. In addition, in order to avoid sequential matching during classification, we propose to index the terms in B-tree, an efficient index scheme. In order to investigate the effectiveness and robustness of the proposed method, experimentation is conducted on five different datasets. The experimental results tabulated in Table 4, indicate that the proposed method offers better performance results than other three well-known classifiers. In the proposed method we have pooled the terms of training documents of each class to create a knowledge base. For a given query document we create the status matrix to preserve the sequence of the term appearance in the query document. As we have pooled the terms in the knowledge base we are not preserving the term sequence during training stage. Along with this the presence of continuous 1's in status matrix do not ensure that the database contains any document having same sequence of terms present in the test document. Hence in our future work we try to study the sequence of the term appearance using the concept of status matrix even on training documents and there by preserving the topological sequence of term occurrence in a document useful for semantic retrieval.

References

1. Salton, G., Wang, A., Yang, C.S.: A Vector Space Model for Automatic Indexing. Communications of the ACM 18, 613–620 (1975)
2. Li, Y.H., Jain, A.K.: Classification of Text Documents. The Computer Journal 41, 537–546 (1998)
3. Hotho, A., Maedche, A., Staab, S.: Ontology-based text clustering. In: International Joint Conference on Artificial Intelligence, USA, pp. 30–37 (2001)
4. Cavnar, W.B.: Using an N-Gram based document representation with a vector processing retrieval model. In: The Third Text Retrieval Conference (TREC-3), pp. 269–278 (1994)
5. Milios, E., Zhang, Y., He, B., Dong, L.: Automatic term extraction and document similarity in special text corpora. In: Sixth Conference of the Pacific Association for Computational Linguistics (PACLing 2003), Canada, pp. 275–284 (2003)
6. Wei, C.P., Yang, C.C., Lin, C.M.: A Latent Semantic Indexing-based approach to multilingual document clustering. Journal of Decision Support System 45, 606–620 (2008)
7. He, X., Cai, D., Liu, H., Ma, W.Y.: Locality Preserving Indexing for document representation. In: SIGIR, pp. 96–103 (2004)
8. Cai, D., He, X., Zhang, W.V., Han, J.: Regularized Locality Preserving Indexing via Spectral Regression. In: ACM International Conference on Information and Knowledge Management (CIKM 2007), Portugal, pp. 741–750 (2007)
9. Choudhary, B., Bhattacharyya, P.: Text clustering using Universal Networking Language representation. In: Eleventh International World Wide Web Conference (2002)
10. Seabastiani, F.: Machine Learning in Automated Text Categorization. ACM Computing Surveys 34, 1–47 (2002)

11. Bekkerman, R., Allan, J.: Using Bigrams in Text Categorization. CIIR Technical Report, IR – 408 (2004)
12. Bernotas, M., Karklius, K., Laurutis, R., Slotkiene, A.: The peculiarities of the text document representation, using ontology and tagging-based clustering technique. Journal of Information Technology and Control 36, 217–220 (2007)
13. Dinesh, R.: POOR: Partially Occluded Object Recognizers – Some Novel Techniques. Ph.D. Thesis, University of Mysore (2006)
14. Bentley, J.L.: Multidimensional binary search trees used for associative searching. Communications of ACM 18(9), 509–517 (1975)
15. Kumar, A.: G – tree: A new datastructure for organizing multidimensional data. IEEE Transactions on Knowledge and Data Engineering 6(2), 341–347 (1994)
16. Robinson, J.T.: The KDB tree: A search structure for large multidimensional dynamic indexes. In: Proceedings of ACM SIGMOD Conference, Ann Arbor, MI, pp. 10–18
17. Dandamudi, S.P., Sorenson, P.G.: An empirical performance comparison of some variations of the k-d tree and bd tree. Computer and Information Sciences 14(3), 134–158 (1985)
18. Punitha, P.: IARS: Image Archival and Retrieval Systems. Ph.D. Thesis, University of Mysore (2005)
19. http://kdd.ics.uci.edu/databases/20newsgroups/20newsgroups.html
20. Isa, D., Lee, L.H., Kallimani, V.P., Rajkumar, R.: Text document preprocessing with the Bayes formula for classification using the support vector machine. IEEE Transactions on Knowledge and Data Engineering 20, 23–31 (2008)

Comparison between Different Feature Extraction Techniques to Identify the Emotion 'Anger' in Speech

Bageshree V. Pathak[1] and Ashish R. Panat[2]

[1] Cummins College of Engg for Women, Pune, India
bvpathak100@yahoo.com
[2] Priyadarshani Indira College of Engg., Nagpur, India
ashishpanat@gmail.com

Abstract. In this paper, three different techniques of feature extraction for identification of emotion in speech have been compared. Traditional feature like LPCC (Linear Predictive Cepstral Coefficient) and MFCC (Mel Frequency Cepstral Coefficient) have been described. Linear features like LFPC which is FFT based have been explained. Finally TEO (Teager Energy Operator) based nonlinear LFPC features in both time and freqnency domain have been proposed and the performance of the proposed system is compared with the traditional features. The comparison of each approach is performed using SUSAS (Speech Under Simulated and Acid Stress) and ESMBS (Emotional Speech of Mandarin and Burmese Speakers) databases. It is observed that proposed system outperforms the traditional systems. Analysis will be carried for identification mainly of the emotion 'Anger' in this paper.

Keywords: feature vector, VQ, MFCC, cepstrum, HMM, TEO, LPCC, LFPC.

1 Introduction

Speech is the vocalized form of human communication. Each spoken word is created out of the phonetic combination of a vowel and consonant speech units [9]. In order to obtain good representation of speaker characteristics, speech data needs to be analysed using suitable analysis technique. In the analysis technique proper frame size is selected and extracting the relevant features is carried out in the feature extraction stage.

A number of studies have been conducted to investigate acoustic indicators to detect emotion in speech. The characteristics most often considered include Fundamental frequency F0, duration [2], [17],intensity [l], spectral variation [2], [5] and wavelet based subband features [6]. In these researches, features used are mostly derived from linear speech models. However, in recent years, non-linear features derived from Teager Energy Operators (TEO) [7], [8] are explored.

Human auditory system is assumed to have a filtering system in which the entire audible frequency range is partitioned into frequency bands [9]. According to Fletcher [10], speech sounds are pre-processed by the peripheral auditory system through a bank of bandpass filters. These auditory filters perform the process of frequency weighing for frequency selectivity of ear.

N. Meghanathan et al. (Eds.): CCSIT 2012, Part II, LNICST 85, pp. 637–643, 2012.

2   Pre Processing

Initially, the acoustic wave is transformed into a digital signal, which is suitable for voice processing. A microphone or telephone handset converts the acoustic wave into an analog signal [12]. This analog signal is conditioned with antialiasing filtering to compensate for any channel impairments. Before sampling, the antialiasing filter limits the bandwidth of the signal to approximately the Nyquist rate. [12]. The conditioned analog signal is then sampled to form a digital signal by an analog-to-digital (A/D) converter [17]. Today's A/D converters for speech applications typically sample with 12–16 bits of resolution at 8000–20000 samples per second. The speech is further subjected to windowing by passing it through a Hamming window and a frame size of 10 to 30 m sec is chosen for analysis .

3   Feature Extraction

The speech signal can be represented by a sequence of feature vectors. In this section, the selection of appropriate features is discussed. This is known as feature selection. There are a number of feature extraction techniques based on speaker dependent parameters like Pitch, Formants, Energy, Intensity, LPC etc.

3.1   Traditional Features

MFCC [15] and LPCC are the most widely used feature extraction techniques. In sound processing, the Mel-Frequency Cepstrum (MFC) in sound signal processing is basically a representation of the short-term power spectrum of the sound signal. By taking linear cosine transform of a log power spectrum on a nonlinear scale i.e. mel scale frequency we get MFCC [3]. Mel-frequency cepstral coefficients (MFCCs) are derived from a type of cepstral representation of the audio clip. This frequency warping can allow for better representation of sound and act a distinctive feature for every speaker. The following equation is used to compute the Mel for given frequency f in HZ:

$$F (Mel) = [2595 * \log 10[1+ f /700]$$

LPCC yield better results than MFCC while discriminating different languages. It also shows that language identification performance may be increased by encompassing temporal information by including acceleration features. Gaussian Mixture Model (GMM) is normally used along with these techniques for modeling of the speech signal [15].

3.2   Linear Features

The Linear parameters that are generally considered in evaluating changes in speech signal characteristics are intensity, duration, pitch, spectrum of vocal tract, glottal source effect and vocal tract articulator profiles. The last two parameters cannot be derived directly from the speech signal but require measurements directly related to the speaker which restricts the flexibility [8].

Intensity: In general the average intensity observed increases with emotions like anger or some type of high workload. It was also found that mainly vowels and semivowels show a significant increase in intensity while consonants do not.

Pitch: Pitch is the most widely considered parameter of emotion evaluation. Pitch contours, variance and distributions show variations when speech is subjected to emotions as shown in figure 1.

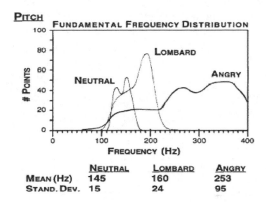

Fig. 1. Variation of Pitch, for Neutral and Angry emotions

FFT based Log-Frequency Power Coefficients (LFPC) are designed to simulate logarithmic filtering characteristics of human auditory system by measuring spectral energies [13]. First, the signal is segmented into short-time windows which are 16ms for emotion speech samples. The reason for using short frame length for emotion database is that it includes female speech utterances which have shorter pitch period than male speech and frame size needs to cover two pitch period of fundamental frequency. The window is moved with the frame rate 9ms for emotion speech samples. The frequency content is calculated in each frame using Fast Fourier Transform (FFT) method. This power spectrum is accumulated into a bank of log-frequency filters. The filter bank splits input speech signal into multiple outputs by passing through the parallel set of band pass filters. Energy in the filter bank output is calculated. For each speech frame 12 LFPCs are obtained.

3.3 Non-linear Features

An alternative way to characterize speech production is to model the airflow pattern in the vocal tract. The underlying concept here is that while the vocal tract articulators do move to configure the vocal tract shape, it is the resulting airflow properties which serve to excite those models which a listener will perceive as a particular phoneme. Studies by Teager emphasized this approach with further investigations by Kaiser to support those concepts [7]. In an effort to reflect the instantaneous energy of nonlinear vortex-flow interactions, Teager developed an energy operator. TEO (Teager Energy Operator) is a non-linear differential operator which detects modulations in the speech signal and further decomposes the signal into AM and FM components. Using the shape of a pitch normalized TEO profile, good performance can be obtained for speech produced under angry, loud, clear, and Lombard effect speaking conditions. The features relating to spectral shape should be incorporated into Teager Energy Operation as well. For this reason, TEO based nonlinear properties in combination with the LFPC are investigated, which is commonly applied in the time domain [7],[8]. In this paper, TEO in both time and frequency domain are considered [13]. In Time Domain LFPC (NTDLFPC) the speech signal is windowed and passed through TEO and then FFT and LFPC are applied to the signal. In and Nonlinear Frequency Domain LFPC (NFDLFPC), the speech signal is windowed and converted to frequency domain by using FFT and then applied to TEO and finally LFPC are extracted as shown in figure2 below.[13]

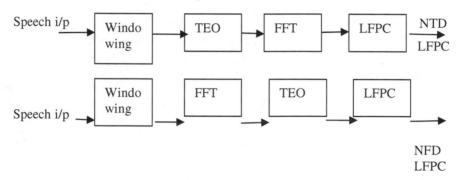

Fig. 2. TEO in time and frequency domain

4   Emotion Database

For emotion classification, a database ESMBS which is specifically designed and set up for text-independent emotion classification is used [14]. The database includes short utterances covering the six emotions, namely Anger, Disgust, Fear, Joy, Sadness and Surprise. A total of six native Burmese language speakers (3 males and 3 females), six native Mandarin speakers (3males and 3females) are employed to generate 720 utterances. Sixty different utterances, ten each for each emotional mode, are recorded for each speaker. The recording is done in a quiet environment using a mouthpiece microphone.

SUSAS (Speech Under Simulated & Actual Stress Database) [13], [14] was established in order to conduct research into the analysis and recognition of speech produced in noise and under stress. SUSAS consists of a wide variety of stresses and emotions of 32 speakers (13 female, 19 male) to generate in excess of 16,000 isolated-word utterances. The stress domains included were: i) talking styles (slow, fast, soft, loud, angry, clear, question), ii) single tracking computer response task or speech produced in noise (Lombard effect), iii) dual tracking computer response task, iv) subject motion-fear tasks (G-force, Lombard effect, noise, fear), and v) psychiatric analysis data (speech under depression, fear, anxiety). A common highly confusable vocabulary set of 35 aircraft communication words also make up the database.

5   Result

It is seen that different types of stress and emotion may affect different frequency bands differently and an improved stress classification features should be obtained by analyzing energy in different frequency bands [13].

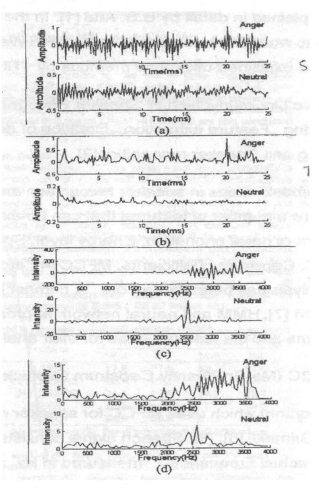

Fig. 3. a) Time domain representation of Anger and Neutral condition of the word 'destination'. b) TEO in Time Domain. c) TEO in Frequency Domain d) Frequency domain version of the word 'destination' using SUSAS database.

The time domain and frequency domain representations together with the results after the TEO operation for the emotion Anger and Neutral speaking styles are shown in Figure3. Anger has the higher frequency content than Neutral. Furthermore, as can be seen from Figure 3(c) for Anger, TEO operation suppresses certain intensity values in the frequency range 3 to 3.2k Hz down to near zero because of nonlinear property analysis. This results in loss of important information for high frequency range, which is an essential feature of Anger [6]. Between NFD-LFPC (Figure 3(c)) and NTD-LFPC (Figure 3(b)), it can also be observed that nonlinear energy variations in frequency domain, present more significant discrimination among different speaking conditions. Anger has high intensity in higher frequency regions [14]. Neutral has higher intensity values in lower frequency scales. This emphasizes that Teager Energy Operation in frequency domain is more capable than in time domain to detect stress. The same trend has been observed between Anger (high arousal) and Sadness (low arousal) emotions. However, the graphical representations using emotion samples are not included and can be found in [14].

6   Conclusion

In this paper, comparison between novel systems for emotion classification is carried out. Traditional features like MFCC and LPCC are compared along with linear acoustic feature LFPC and nonlinear acoustic features NTD-LFPC which is in time domain and NFD-LFPC which is in frequency domain [14]. It is found that linear LFPC and nonlinear acoustic feature in frequency domain are important in representing speaking styles. After comparing the two approaches for TEO operation, it is observed that nonlinear variation of energy distribution using frequency domain analysis gives a better representation than in the time domain analysis. When comparing LFPC based features and two traditional features MFCC and LPCC, it is found that features LFPC, NFD-LFPC and NTD-LFPC perform well over the two traditional features. This has already been shown in fig3 above.

Refrences

1. Rabiner, L.R., Schafer, R.W.: Digital Processing of Speech Signals. Pearson Education Publication
2. Bou-Gbde, S., Hansen, J.H.L.: A novel training approach for improving speech recognition under adverse stressful environments. In: EUROSPEECH 1997, Rhodes, Greece, vol. 5, pp. 2387–2390 (September 1997)
3. Emerich, S., Lupu, E., Apatean, A.: Emotion Recognition from speech and Facial Expressions Analysis. In: 17th European Signal Processing Conference, EUSIPCO 2009 (2009)
4. Tarng, W., Chen, Y.-Y., Li, C.-L., Hsie, K.-R., Chen, M.: Applications of Support Vector Machines on Smart Phone Systems for Emotional Speech Recognition. World Academy of Science, Engineering and Technology (2010)
5. Bou-Ghazale, S.E., Hame, J.H.L.: Stress perturbation of neutral speech for synthesis based on hidden Markov models. IEEE Transactions on Speech & Audio Processing 6(3), 201–216 (1998)
6. Sarikaya, R., Gowdy, J.N.: Subband based classification of speech under stress. Proceedings of the IEEE on Acoustics, Speech, and Signal Processing 1, 569–572 (1998)
7. Non, G., Hansen, J.H.L., Kaiser, J.F.: Nonlinear feature based classification of speech under stress. IEEE Transactions on Speech & Audio Processing 9(3), 201–216 (2001)

8. Cairns, D., Hansen, J.H.L.: Nonlinear analysis and detection of speech under stressed conditions. J. Acoust. Soc. Am. 96(6), 3392–3400 (1994)
9. Rabiner, L.R., Jug, B.H.: Fundamentals of Speech Recognition. Prentice Hall, Englewood Cliffs (2010)
10. Fletcher, H.: Auditory Patterns. Review of Modern Physics 12, 4745 (1940)
11. Nadeu, D.M., Hemando, J.: Time and frequency filtering of filter-bank energies for robust HMM speech recognition. Speech Communication 34(1-2), 93–114 (2001)
12. Campbell Jr., J.P.: Department of Defense Fort Meade, MD. Speaker Recognition
13. Nwe, T.L., Foo, S.W.: Detection of Stress and Emotion in Speech Using Traditional and FFT based Log Energy Features. In: ICICS-PCM 2003, Singapore (2003)
14. Nwe, T.L.: Analysis and Detection of Human Stress and Emotion from Speech Signals. Ph. D. Thesis, National University of Singapore (2003)
15. Kandali, A., Routray, A., Basu, T.K.: Emotion recognition from Assamese speeches using MFCC features and GMM Classifier. In: Proceedings of IEEE Region 10 Conference 2008, Hyderabad, India (2008)
16. Recognition of emotions in speech by a hierarchical approach. In: 3rd International Conference on Affective Computing and Intelligent Interaction and Workshops, ACII 2009, Amsterdam, September 10-12, pp. 1–8 (2009)
17. Kotti, M., Patterno, F., Kotropoulos, C.: Speaker-independent negative emotion recognition. In: Proc. 2nd Int. Workshop Cognitive Information Processing, Elba Island, Italy, pp. 417–422 (June 2010)
18. Mower, E.: A Framework for Automatic Human Emotion Classification Using Emotion Profiles. IEEE Transactions on Audio, Speech and Language Processing 19(5) (July 2011)

Feature Image Generation Using Energy Distribution for Face Recognition in Transform Domain

Vikas Maheshkar[1], Sushila Kamble[1], Suneeta Agarwal[1], and Vinay Kumar Srivastava[2]

[1] Computer Science & Engg. Department,
[2] Electronics & Communication Engg. Department,
Motilal Nehru National Institute of Technology,
Allahabad, 211004, India
`v_maheshkar@yahoo.com, {sushila,suneeta,vinay}@mnnit.ac.in`

Abstract. In this paper, we propose a feature image generation method for face recognition. Feature extraction is done using three transforms viz. Discrete Cosine Transform, Slant Transform and Walsh Transform. Energy distribution defined as magnitude of effective information is used to create a feature image in transform domain by retaining high energy distribution coefficients. The proposed method consists of three steps. First, the face images are transformed into the frequency domain. Second, transformed coefficient matrix and energy distribution matrix is divided into three equal regions. Thresholds are selected in each region to retain the most significant features. Finally feature image is generated from these coefficients. Recognition is performed on generated feature images using Mahalanobis distance. Experimental results shows that the proposed method improve the face recognition rate as compared to previously proposed methods.

Keywords: Face Recognition, Discrete Cosine Transform (DCT), Slant Transform (ST), Walsh Transform (WT), Energy Distribution (ED), Mahalanobis distance.

1 Introduction

In Biometrics inherent characteristics of human beings are used for verification and validation. Face recognition use biometric features for Identifying or verifying one or more persons in the scene using a stored database of faces if a still or video image of a scene is given. There is an increasing need for face recognition technology due to concerns in security such as in identification for authentication, Law enforcement and surveillance, smart cards, access control, for perceptual user interfaces. However, the general problem of face recognition remains to be solved, since most of the systems to date can only successfully recognize faces when images are obtained under prescribed conditions. The problem added due to effects of illumination could cause the system to degrade the performance and are larger than the difference between individuals. The most common issues are expression, aging, distractions such as glasses or changes in hairstyle, illumination problem and the pose problem as proposed by Ramanathan N, et al., [13]. To cope with the issues and to construct a computational model is quite difficult. While designing a system certain issues are needs to be challenged since faces are complex, multidimensional, and subject to change over

N. Meghanathan et al. (Eds.): CCSIT 2012, Part II, LNICST 85, pp. 644–653, 2012.
© Institute for Computer Sciences, Social Informatics and Telecommunications Engineering 2012

time. Thus, face recognition is an unsolved problem under the conditions of pose and illumination variation, but still attracts significant research efforts.

In face recognition, feature extraction is most important, and it involves the reduction of high dimensional image data into low dimensional feature vector. Principal Components Analysis (PCA) technique resolve high dimensional problem giving dimension reduction, and is one of the most frequently used technique. Mathematical transforms such as Discrete Fourier Transform (DFT), Discrete Wavelet Transform (DWT), Discrete Cosine Transform (DCT) has been widely used to generate feature vectors. Weilong Chen, Meng Joo Er, and Shiqian Wu, [15] use DCT to generate feature image by using PCA and Linear Discriminant Analysis. In particular, many data compression techniques employ the DCT, which has been found to be asymptotically equivalent to the optimal Karhunen-Loeve Transform (KLT) for signal decorrelation. In DCT, coefficients with large magnitude are mainly located in the upper-left corner of the DCT matrix. They are the low spatial frequency DCT components in the image. M. J. Er, W. Chen, and S. Wu.[11] states that the DC or the first three low frequency coefficients have been truncated in order to decrease the effects of the illumination variation. C. Sanderson and K. K. Paliwal [2] shows that the polynomial coefficients are derived from the 2D-DCT coefficients obtained from the spatially neighboring blocks. Jiang and Feng [10] showed that removal of DC element enables the reconstructed facial image to be robust to lighting changes and removal of high-frequency DCT coefficients to be robust to scaling variations. X.Y. Jing and D. Zhang [16] proposed an approach to find discriminant bands (a group of coefficients) in the transformed space. Their approach searches the discriminant coefficients in the transformed space group by group. In this case, it is possible to lose a discriminant coefficient placing beside the non- discriminant coefficients in a group as shown by Dabbaghchian, S., Aghagolzadeh, A., and Moin M.S.[3]. DCT obtains the optimal performance of PCA in facial information compression and the performance of DCT is superior to conventional transforms. Jean Choi et al. [7] proposed face recognition using energy probability to generate a frequency mask without attention to the class.

Slant and Walsh transforms are also popular transforms used in the face recognition techniques. In Slant transform the coefficient selection affects the performance of the face recognition scheme significantly. The high frequency components are relatively vulnerable to compression operations, while the low frequency components must be retained for visual quality of the face image. The middle frequency band retains the overall information as stated by Anthony T. S. Ho, et al. [1]. The Slant transform has more useful middle and high frequency bands. The concept of an orthogonal transformation containing Slant basis vector was introduced by Enomoto and Shibata [4]. The Slant vector is a discrete saw tooth waveform decreasing in uniform steps over its length. Slant vectors are suitable for efficiently representing gradual brightness change in a face image. Walsh kernel is separable and symmetric and its function holds unique sequency value. Jia, Xiaoguang and Nixon, Mark S. [9] has used the Walsh Transform to extract the facial profile from a frontal view to provide a measure for automatic face recognition. The Walsh power spectrum is used to derive profile from the intensity projection of the face image. The work proposed by H B Kekre, et al. [6] used transform based technique and compares the performance with vector quantization (VQ) technique. Transform based face recognition technique considers full and partial feature vector of an image. Jia, X. and

Nixon, M. S. [8] describes a measure of the facial profile feature from a frontal view of the face for automatic face recognition.

In this paper, we propose a new feature image generation method to enhance the image classification and improve the recognition. We consider different transform (DCT, Walsh, or Slant), and information of different frequency bands is retained separately. Energy distribution is used to set the parameters for the selection of different frequency bands to construct feature image. Using this we retain the important coefficients of each band generating the feature image suitable for recognition. The recognition achieves better recognition results compared to traditional approaches of face recognition.

The rest of the paper is organized as follows. In Section 2, the methodologies used are briefly introduced. This includes the different transforms used (DCT, Slant Transform, Walsh Transform). Also the energy distribution and Mahalanobis distance are defined. Section 3 describes the proposed technique and experimental results are described in Section 4. At end in Section 5 conclusions are mentioned.

2   Methodology

2.1   Energy Distribution (ED)

Energy is one of the important characteristic of image defined by following equation

$$Energy_C = \sum_{u=1}^{N} \sum_{v=1}^{N} |F(u,v)|^2$$

Where, $F(u,v)$ represents image in transform domain.

Energy Distribution $ED(u, v)$ represents the energy contribution of each transformed coefficient and is given by following equation:

$$ED(u,v) = \frac{|F(u,v)|^2}{Energy_C}$$

The magnitude of $ED(u, v)$ gives Energy Distribution matrix.

3   Proposed Technique

In the proposed technique we consider two datasets viz. training datasets containing set of face images for extracting the relevant information and test dataset for the face image to be recognized. The face images in the training dataset are converted to transform domain (DCT, Slant or Walsh). The transformed coefficients after zigzag scan are divided equally into three bands, namely low frequency, middle frequency and high frequency and are represented by *TCvector*. This is shown diagrammatically in Figure 1.Low frequency coefficients are related to illumination variation and smooth regions (like forehead, cheeks etc) of face. High frequency coefficients represent noise and detailed information of edge. The middle frequency coefficients represents the basic structure of the of face image. It shows that each band contains important information. Hence we cannot ignore the low frequency components to compensate illumination variations if the image is not so much affected by lighting conditions. Similarly we cannot truncate the high frequency coefficients to remove noise as they are responsible for details and edge information of the image.

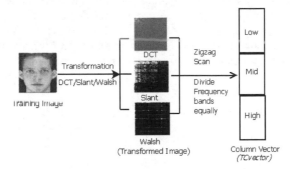

Fig. 1. Formation of Column Vector (*TCvector*)

Energy is used to describe a measure of "information" in an image. *Energy Distribution* represented by *ED(u, v)* as described in section 2.1 gives the contribution of individual transformed coefficients. Let M be the total number of facial images of training dataset and N as width and height of all images. The *ED*, of size NxN, is converted into the column vector by performing Zigzag scan of length N*N represented by *EDvector*. The *EDvector* is divided into three equal regions similar to the *TCvector*.

The high value of *ED(u, v)* means more valid information. To achieves reduction in data while retaining the important features we set different thresholds in three regions of *EDvector*. Energy distributions below the different thresholds in different regions of *EDvector* are set to zero.

$$Featureimage(u,v) = \begin{cases} 0 & , & if\ ED(u,v) < threshold \\ F(u,v) & , & otherwise \end{cases}$$

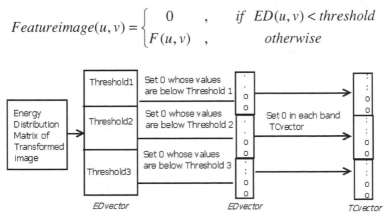

Fig. 2. Feature Image Generation

Finally we generate Feature image represented as *Featureimage(u,v)* by retaining corresponding coefficients of *TCvector* that we retained in the *EDvector*. This is shown diagrammatically in Figure 2.

Figure 3 depicts the whole procedure of face recognition by Feature Image Generation. Face images in the training set are converted into Transform domain. The Energy distribution is defined as criterion of selecting effective facial features. Energy distribution is calculated for the dimension reduction of data and optimization of valid information. Similar procedure is carried out for test image to form *TFeatureimage(u,v)*. Mahalanobis distance between set of *Featureimage(u,v)* and the test image formed as *TFeatureimage(u,v)* is calculated. The *Featureimage(u,v)* which gives minimum distance from the set of training images and test image will give recognized face.

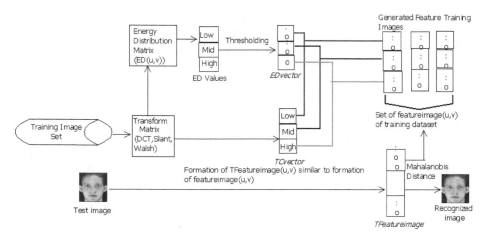

Fig. 3. Proposed Technique for face Recognition

4   Experimental Results

To validate the results we implement the proposed technique in MATLAB 2010. The experimentation is carried out on ORL dataset and Yale dataset. To prove the robustness of the technique, we considered only two poses of each individual (out of 10 poses of each individual in the training dataset) i.e., 80 images of 40 individuals are considered in case of ORL training dataset [5]. Similarly in case of Yale dataset 30 images (two poses of each individual) of 15 people in the training dataset are considered. Test dataset contains poses that are different than the training dataset.

4.1   Experimental Result Analysis Based on ORL Face Dataset

We implement our technique by using DCT, Slant and Walsh Transform. Figure 4 shows test image and its correctly recognized image. All the input test images correctly recognizes the face from the training dataset even if there is change in emotions like- neutral, smile, laughter, sad/disgust and poses like looking front, looking left, looking right, looking up, looking up towards left, looking up towards right, and looking down.

Fig. 4. Test image and corresponding recognized faces of ORL dataset

Table 1 shows the recognition rate using DCT transform with different thresholds in low, mid and high frequency bands. The experimentation is carried out on different threshold combinations to decide the correct threshold for the better recognition rate. But due to space limitations we had shown only two set of thresholds with threshold1 30 in low frequency band, threshold2 7 in mid frequency band and threshold3 0.4 in high frequency band for the first set. The second set of different thresholds is prepared with threshold1 as 35, threshold2 as 10 and threshold3 as 0.7. The second set thresholds show the improvement in the recognition rate. The proposed technique is also compared with standard PCA as introduced by M. Turk and A. Pentland [12] and DCT normalization technique as used by Štruc, V. and Pavešić, N [14]. Table shows that the proposed technique has high recognition rate as compared to other techniques.

Table 1. Recognition rate of ORL Face dataset using DCT

ORL Dataset Recognition				
	No. of correctly recognized faces			
Test Images	Proposed DCT[30,7,0.4]	Proposed DCT[35,10,0.7]	PCA (Mahalanobis)	DCT Normalization
Images(1-10)	9	9	8	8
Images(11-20)	9	9	8	8
Images(21-30)	7	8	5	5
Images(31-40)	10	10	8	8

Table 2 shows the face recognition rate using Slant and Walsh transform with different thresholds. Here a set of threshold with values [35, 7 and 0.4] are considered and tested on Slant transform and the Walsh transform. The result is also compared with PCA and DCT normalization techniques. From the table it is clear that the proposed technique gives approximately same results on DCT, Slant as well as Walsh transforms. This shows that the technique is robust to any kind of transform used.

The comparative study of different transforms with different set of thresholds is done by plotting the No. of training images tested against the corresponding recognition rate. Figure 5 shows the plot for DCT transform with Thresholds [30, 7, 0.4] and Figure 6 with Thresholds [35, 10, 0.7] respectively. Figure 7 shows the plot for Slant and Walsh Transform with Thresholds [35, 10, and 0.7].

Table 2. Recognition rate of ORL Face dataset using Slant and Walsh transform

ORL Dataset Recognition				
Test Images	No. of correctly recognized faces			
	Proposed Slant[35,7,0.4]	Proposed Walsh[35,7,0.4]	PCA Mahalanobis	DCT Normalization
Images(1-10)	9	9	8	8
Images(11-20)	9	9	8	8
Images(21-30)	7	7	5	5
Images(31-40)	10	10	8	8

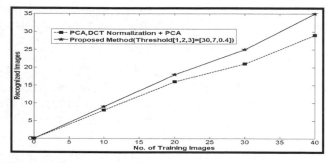

Fig. 5. Plot of No. of training images tested Vs. recognition rate [DCT (30, 7, 0.4)]

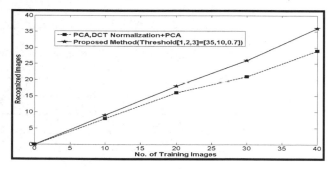

Fig. 6. Plot of No. of training images tested Vs. recognition rate [DCT (35, 10, 0.7)]

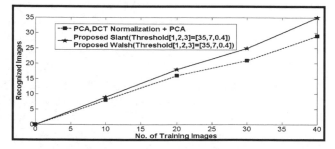

Fig. 7. Plot of No. of training images tested Vs. recognition rate (Slant & Walsh transform)

4.2   Experimental Result Analysis Based on YALE Face Database

Yale face dataset comprises eleven frontal images of each of fifteen people, wherein the images have different face expressions, with or without glasses, and these images are taken under different illumination conditions [17]. Figure 8 shows test image and its correctly recognized image. The test image and the recognized images vary in facial expressions with or without glasses, etc.

Fig. 8. Test image & corresponding recognized images of YALE dataset

The proposed technique is tested on YALE dataset using DCT, Slant and Walsh transform. Table.3 shows the experimental results using DCT transform with set of different thresholds [30, 7, and 0.4] and [35, 7, 0.4]. As seen from the Table 3 the proposed technique using DCT on YALE dataset gives maximum recognition rate with threshold set of [30, 7, and 0.4].

Table 3. Recognition Table of YALE Face Dataset

Recognition Table of YALE Face Dataset				
Range of Images	Proposed DCT [30,7,0.4]	Proposed DCT [35,7,0.4]	PCA (Mahalanobis)	DCT Normalization
Images(1-15)	10	9	7	7

Table.4 shows recognition rate on Slant and Walsh transform with thresholds [35, 7, and 0.4]. From the table 3 and 4 it is evident that the face recognition rate on thresholds [35, 7, and 0.4] for Slant and Walsh transform and on thresholds [30,7,0.4] for DCT transform is same.

Table 4. Recognition Table of YALE Face Dataset

Recognition Table of YALE Face Dataset				
Range of Images	Proposed Slant [35,7,0.4]	Proposed Walsh [35,7,0.4]	PCA (Mahalanobis)	DCT Normalization
Images(1-15)	10	10	7	7

The comparative study of different transforms with different set of thresholds is done by plotting the No. of training images tested. Figure.9 shows the plot for DCT with Thresholds [35, 7, and 0.4] and [30, 7, and 0.4]. Similarly Figure 10 shows the plot for Slant and Walsh transform with Thresholds [35, 10, and 0.7].

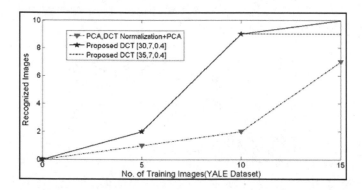

Fig. 9. Recognition Graph of proposed work using DCT transform on YALE Face Dataset

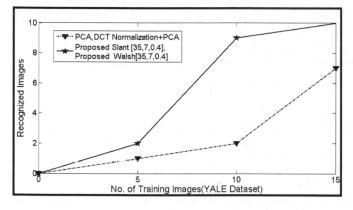

Fig. 10. Recognition Graph of proposed work using Slant and Walsh transform on YALE Face Dataset

5   Conclusion

Transform based feature image is generated for face recognition. Our method consists of three steps. First, face images are transformed into Transform domain. Second, Transform coefficients acquired from face image is applied on energy distribution for the selection of different thresholds. Third, in order to obtain the most expressive features only higher value energy distribution coefficients are kept, this facilitates the selection of useful Transform coefficients for face recognition. For the purpose of retaining most distinctive features of individual we optimize information by different thresholds. At last, distance measure is done directly on generated feature image by

Mahalanobis distance without using PCA. As PCA is not used, efficiency also get increased. The experimental results with ORL face database shows that the proposed method has shown better recognition performance than existing methods.

References

1. Ho, A.T.S., Zhu, X., Guan, Y.L., Marziliano, P.: Slant transform watermarking for textured images, Circuits and Systems In: Proceedings of the 2004 International Symposium, ISCAS 2004, V-700–V-703, vol. 5, pp. 23–26 (2004)
2. Sanderson, C., Paliwal, K.K.: Features for Robust Face-Based Identity Verification. Journal of Signal Processing 83, 931–940 (2003)
3. Dabbaghchian, S., Aghagolzadeh, A., Moin, M.S.: Reducing the effects of small sample size in DCT domain for face recognition. In: International Symposium on Telecommunications, IST 2008, pp. 634–638 (2008)
4. Enomoto, Shibata, K.: Orthogonal Transform Coding System for Television Signals. IEEE Transaction on Electromagnetic Compatibility 13(3), 11–17 (1971)
5. Samaria, F., Harter, A.: Parameterisation of a Stochastic Model for Human Face Identification. In: Proceedings of 2nd IEEE Workshop on Applications of Computer Vision, Sarasota FL (1994)
6. Kekre, H.B., Sarode, T.K., Natu, P.J., Natu, S.J.: Performance Comparison of Face Recognition using DCT and Walsh Transform with Full and Partial Feature Vector Against KFCG VQ Algorithm. In: IJCA Proceedings on International Conference and Workshop on Emerging Trends in Technology (ICWET), vol. (5), pp. 22–29 (2011)
7. Choi, J., Chung, Y.-S., Kim, K.-H., Yoo, J.-H.: Face Recognition using Energy Probability in DCT Domain. In: 2006 IEEE International Conference on Multimedia and Expo., pp. 1549–1552 (2006)
8. Jia, X., Nixon, M.S.: Profile Feature Extraction via the Walsh Transform for Face Recognition. In: Proc. Int. Conf. on Intelligent Robots and Visual Communications, pp. 46–52 (1992)
9. Jia, X., Nixon, M.S.: Analysing front view face profiles for face recognition via the Walsh transform. Pattern Recognition Letters 15(6), 551–558 (1994)
10. Jiang, J., Feng, G.: Robustness analysis on facial image description in DCT domain. Electronics Letters 43(24), 1354–1356 (2007)
11. Er, M.J., Chen, W., Wu, S.: High Speed Face Recognition Based on Discrete Cosine Transform and RBF Neural Networks. IEEE Transactions on Neural Networks 16(3), 679–691 (2005)
12. Turk, M., Pentland, A.: Eigenfaces for Recognition. Journal of Cognitive Neurosicence 3(1), 71–86 (1991)
13. Ramanathan, N., Chellappa, R., Roy Chowdhury, A.K.: Facial similarity across age, disguise, illumination and pose. In: Proceedings of the International Conference on Image Processing, ICIP 2004, pp. 1999–2002 (2004)
14. Štruc, V., Pavešić, N.: Illumination Invariant Face Recognition by Non-Local Smoothing. In: Fierrez, J., Ortega-Garcia, J., Esposito, A., Drygajlo, A., Faundez-Zanuy, M. (eds.) BioID MultiComm 2009. LNCS, vol. 5707, pp. 1–8. Springer, Heidelberg (2009)
15. Chen, W., Er, M.J., Wu, S.: PCA and LDA in DCT domain. Pattern Recognition Letters 26, 2474–2482 (2005)
16. Jing, X.Y., Zhang, D.: A face and palmprint recognition approach based on discriminant DCT feature extraction. IEEE Transactions on Systems, Man and Cybernetics 34(6), 2405–2415 (2004)
17. Yale University, Department of Computer Science, Center for Computational Vision and Control, cvc.yale.edu (1997)

A Comparative Study of Placement of Processor on Silicon and Thermal Analysis

Ramya Menon C. and Vinod Pangracious

Department of ECE, Rajagiri School of Engineering and Technology,
Kochi, Kerala
ramyamenonc@gmail.com, pangracious@googlemail.com

Abstract. Today when we have stepped into the second decade of this century, the integrated circuits are getting more and more complex with multicore processors. With technology scaling, more devices are being integrated into a small area. As a result, heat dissipation in integrated circuits (ICs) has increased. The processor is one of the highest heat generating components in an IC. The temperature generated in an integrated circuit varies with factors like number of processors, processor modes, their dimensions and arrangement on Silicon. In this paper we are presenting two simulation results. First one was obtained by analyzing how the area occupied by processor affects the temperature distribution. This study is extremely important as the area occupied by processors scales down with technology. The second study was to find out how the processor location and modes can affect temperature distribution in multicore processors. The processors at 2.4GHz frequency were analyzed in both active and idle modes. The highest and lowest temperatures and the location of hotspot in each case were analyzed.

Keywords: Floorplan, Hotspot, Peak Temperature, Simulation, Through Silicon Via.

1 Introduction

The processor architects spend considerable time in analysing the thermal behavior of various circuits. The temperature developed in an integrated circuit mainly depends on floorplan and power consumed by individual devices or units. A floorplan is the way in which the devices are arranged on the Silicon surface. Hotspot is the simulator that gives the temperature developed in each of the individual units by taking floorplan and power values as input. Its advantages are ease of use and computational efficiency. In this paper we present the results of our experiments in two phases to find the location and the value of the maximum temperature developed. The location of maximum temperature is called hotspot. In the first phase, we carried out two sets of experiments considering only a single processor to analyze how the temperature is affected by varying the area occupied by the processor on Silicon surface. The first set of experiments were carried out by considering the processor in active mode and the second set of experiments were carried out by considering the processor in idle mode. In the second phase, we did experiments with varying number of processors each with

N. Meghanathan et al. (Eds.): CCSIT 2012, Part II, LNICST 85, pp. 654–662, 2012.

equal dimensions. The experiments were carried out with different processor modes and position on Silicon surface and temperature was analyzed.

2   Experimental Phase 1

In the first phase, ten experiments were carried out with a single processor to study the affect of area of processor in different modes on temperature values. The processor in the active mode consumed 50.9W power and that in the idle mode consumed a power of 13.7W.

2.1   Silicon Area versus Temperature Simulations Experimental Setup

A square shaped Silicon substrate with width 0.016m was taken. In the first experiment, a processor in active mode occupied the entire Silicon surface. A processor in the idle mode occupied the entire Silicon area in the second experiment. In the third and fourth experiments, the entire area of Silicon was divided into two equal sized units, each with width 0.016m and height 0.008m. The processor occupied one of these units and the other unit was vacant. Here the area occupied by processor was reduced to half of that in the first and second experiments. The processor in the third experiment was in active mode and the one in the fourth experiment was in idle mode. The entire Silicon area was divided into four identical units each with width and height 0.008m in the fifth and sixth experiments. The processor occupied one of these units and all the other three units were vacant. All the odd numbered experiments were carried out with active processor and even numbered experiments were carried out with the processor in idle mode. In the seventh and eighth experiments, the entire Silicon area was divided into eight equal sized units. The processor occupied only one by eighth of the total Silicon area. The remaining seven units were vacant. Each unit had a height of 0.008m and a width of 0.004m. In the last two experiments, the entire Silicon area was divided into sixteen equal sized units, each with a width of 0.004m and height of 0.004m. Among these units, fifteen were vacant and the processor occupied only a single unit. The details of first phase experiment are given in table 1.

Table 1. Details of the first phase experiments

Experiment No:	Total Si area (m^2)	Area occupied by processor (m^2)	Processor mode	Lowest temperature (K)	Highest temperature (K)
1	.000256	.000256	Active	326.23	327.66
2	.000256	.000256	Idle	320.32	320.71
3	.000256	.000128	Active	323.94	330.05
4	.000256	.000128	Idle	319.71	321.35
5	.000256	.000064	Active	323.52	334.36
6	.000256	.000064	Idle	319.6	322.51
7	.000256	.000032	Active	323.33	341.45

Table 1. (*Continued*)

8	.000256	.000032	Idle	319.54	324.42
9	.000256	.000016	Active	323.19	354.96
10	.000256	.000016	Idle	319.51	328.06

2.2   Temperature Profile

The temperature profile obtained in the first phase is shown in the Fig. 1. The deep red color represents the hotspot and the dark blue region represents the coolest region. As the temperature increases the color gradually changes in the order dark blue, light blue, green, yellow, orange and finally red. In all the ten experiments, the hotspot was developed in the unit in which the processor was present.

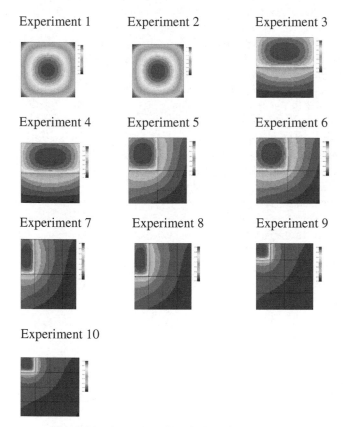

Experiment 1   Experiment 2   Experiment 3

Experiment 4   Experiment 5   Experiment 6

Experiment 7   Experiment 8   Experiment 9

Experiment 10

Fig. 1. The thermal profile of phase 1 experiments

2.3   Result Analysis

The temperatures obtained in the first phase have been plotted in the following four graphs. The x-axis shows the processor area in square meters and the y-axis shows the temperature in degree Kelvin. Fig.2 shows the comparison of active and idle mode temperatures and fig. 3 shows the comparison of the highest and the lowest temperatures.

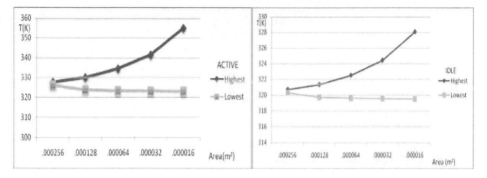

Fig. 2. The comparison of active and idle mode temperatures

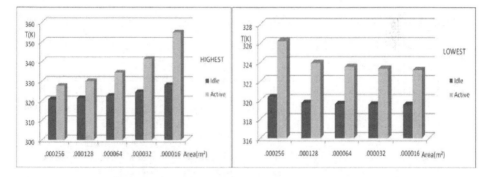

Fig. 3. The comparison of highest and lowest temperatures

3   Experiment Phase 2 Setup

The phase two was an extension of the experiments5 and 6 of phase 1. Here also a square shaped Silicon substrate with width 0.016m was taken. The entire silicon area was divided into four identical units in the floorplan with width 0.008m and height 0.008m. The number of processors, their location and modes varied in each experiment. The processor in the active mode consumed 50.9W power and that in the idle mode consumed a power of 13.7W.

3.1   Processor Placement Simulations

In the second phase, sixteen experiments were carried out. The first six experiments were carried out using two processors. The next four experiments were carried out using three processors and the final six experiments had four processors. The floorplans for each of the sixteen experiments is as shown in fig.4. The arrangements of the processors can be better understood from the table 2.

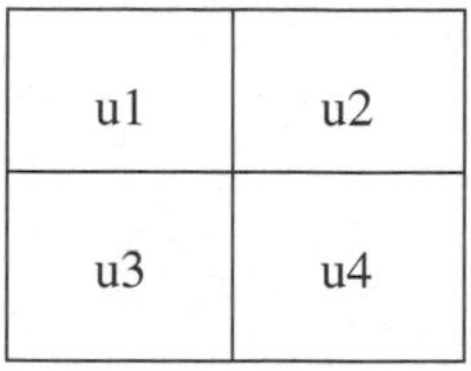

u1	u2
u3	u4

Fig. 4. The floorplan in the second phase experiments

Table 2. The arrangement of processors in second phase

Experiment No:	Total number of processors	u1	u2	u3	u4
1	2	1 idle processor	1 idle processor	vacant	vacant
2	2	1 idle processor	1 active processor	vacant	vacant
3	2	1 active processor	1 active processor	vacant	vacant
4	2	1 idle processor	vacant	vacant	1 idle processor
5	2	1 idle processor	vacant	vacant	1 active processor
6	2	1 active processor	vacant	vacant	1 active processor
7	3	1 idle processor	1 idle processor	1 idle processor	vacant
8	3	1 idle processor	1 idle processor	1 active processor	vacant
9	3	1 active processor	1 active processor	1 idle processor	vacant
10	3	1 active processor	1 active processor	1 active processor	vacant
11	4	1 idle processor	1 idle processor	1 idle processor	1 idle processor
12	4	1 idle processor	1 idle processor	1 idle processor	1 active processor
13	4	1 idle processor	1 active processor	1 idle processor	1 active processor
14	4	1 idle processor	1 active processor	1 active processor	1 idle processor
15	4	1 idle processor	1 active processor	1 active processor	1 active processor
16	4	1 active processor	1 active processor	1 active processor	1 active processor

3.2   Temperature Profile and Result Analysis

The temperature profile of all the 16 experiments in second phase is shown in fig. 5. Here also the deep red color represents the hotspot and the dark blue region represents the coolest region. As the temperature increases a gradual change in the color of the profile from blue to red can be noted.

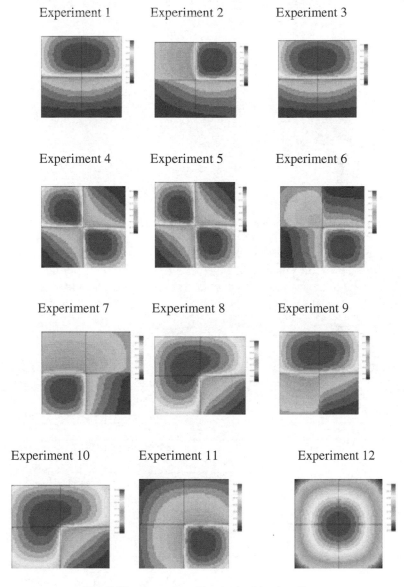

Fig. 5. The thermal profile obtained in phase2

Experiment 13   Experiment 14   Experiment 15

Experiment 16

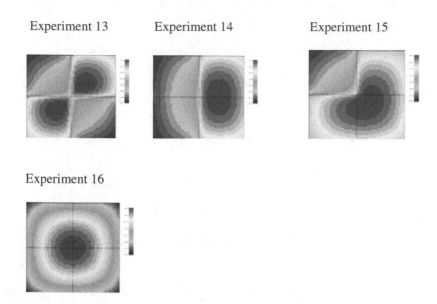

Fig. 5. (*Continued*)

The experiments with similar thermal profile are experiments 1 & 3, experiments 4 & 6, experiments 7 & 10 and experiments 11 & 16. The lowest and highest temperature values obtained in each of the sixteen experiments is given in table 3. The peak temperature value obtained in experiment6 was slightly lesser than experiment3. Similarly, the peak temperature value obtained in experiment4 was slightly lesser than experiment1 and that in experiment14 was slightly lesser than experiment13.

Table 3. Analysis of the second phase experiments

Experiment No:	Lowest Temperature (K)	Highest Temperature (K)	Hotspot Location
1	321.26	324.56	Equally distributed in u1 and u2
2	325.21	336.27	u2
3	329.72	341.96	Equally distributed in u1 and u2
4	321.53	324.19	u1 and u4
5	326.04	336.01	u4
6	330.70	340.60	u1 and u4
7	322.97	326.44	u1, u2 and u3. Major portion in u1
8	327.52	337.94	u3
9	331.47	343.76	u1and u2 with majority in u1

Table 3. (*Continued*)

10	336.07	348.95	u1, u2 and u3. Major portion in u1
11	326.84	328.39	At the centre of the entire Silicon area
12	330.77	339.86	u4
13	335.35	345.56	Equally distributed in u2 and u4
14	336.01	344.60	Equally distributed in u2 and u3
15	339.94	350.80	u1,u2 and u3. Major portion in u4
16	350.45	356.19	At the centre of the entire Silicon area

4   Conclusion

In all the ten experiments of phase1 hotspot was located in the centre of the processor. The lowest temperature value obtained remained almost constant both in idle and active modes when the area of the processor was reduced after the initial change. But in both the modes the highest temperature value continued to increase with decrease in area. When the area of the idle processor was reduced to one by sixteenth of the initial value the peak temperature increased by 7.35 degree Kelvin. For the processor in active mode, the peak temperature increased by 27.3 degree Kelvin when the area was reduced to one by sixteenth.This is about 3.7 times the peak temperature rise in idle mode. In phase 2 experiments, the lowest temperature was noticed in the first case that is two idle processors lying adjacent to each other. By arranging the processors diagonally opposite to each other the hotspot temperature is reduced. In all the experiments involving active processors, the entire region or a portion of hotspot was associated with active processor. The experiments with same processor number and location but different modes had similar thermal profile. But those which were conducted using active processors generated more heat.

5   Future Work

We will extend our experiments to three dimensional (3D) ICs. The temperature analysis will become more complex in three dimensional circuits. We will be concentrating more on a thermal aware floorplan for 3D structures. A thermal aware floorplan will reduce the peak temperature values in the different layers of such circuits. Then we will work on Through Silicon Via (TSV) modeling and thermal management solutions for 3D integrated circuits.

References

1. Stan, M.R., et al.: HotSpot: a Dynamic Compact Thermal Model at the Processor-Architecture Level. Dept. of Electrical and Computer Engineering; University of Virginia; Charlottesville, VA 22904 (accepted for the Special issue on Therminic 2002 as paper T02MEJ14)
2. Multicore Processors – A Necessity by Bryan Schauer; ProQuest (September 2008)
3. Das, S., Chandrakasan, A., Reif, R.: Design tools for 3-D integrated circuits. In: Proc. of ASP-DAC, pp. 53–56 (2003)
4. Banerjee, K., et al.: 3-D ICs: a novel chip design for improving deep-submicrometer interconnect performance and systems-on-chip integration. Proceedings of the IEEE (5), 602–633 (2001)
5. Topol, A.W., et al.: Three-dimensional integrated circuits. IBM Journal of Research and Development (4-5), 494–506 (2006)
6. Cong, J., et al.: Thermal via planning for 3-D ics. In: Proc. of ICCAD, pp. 745–752 (2005)
7. Goplen, B., et al.: Placement of thermal vias in 3-d ics using various thermal objectives. IEEE T-CAD 25(4), 692–709 (2006)
8. Jain, A., et al.: Thermal modeling and design of 3D integrated circuits. In: Proc. of Int. Conf. on TTPES (2008)
9. Natarajan, V., et al.: Thermal and power challenges in high performance computing systems. In: Proc. ISTD-TPE (2008)
10. Shi, S., Zhang, X., Luo, R.: The thermal-aware floorplanning for 3D ICs using Carbon Nanotube. In: 2010 IEEE Asia Pacific Conference on Circuits and Systems (APCCAS), December 6-9. Dept. of Electron. Eng., Tsinghua Univ. Beijing, Beijing, China (2010)
11. Heo, S., et al.: Reducing power density through activity migration. In: Proc. of ISPD (2003)
12. Skadron, K., et al.: Temperature-aware microarchitecture: modeling and implementation. In: TACO, pp. 94–125 (2004)
13. Su, H., et al.: Full chip leakage estimation considering power supply and temperature variations. In: Proc. of ISPD, pp. 78–83 (2003)
14. Vlach, J., et al.: Computer methods for circuit analysis and design. Springer, Heidelberg (1983)
15. Incropera, F.P., et al.: Fundamentals of heat and mass transfer. John Wiley and Sons (2007)

Author Index